THE
Forrestal
DIARIES

THE
Forrestal
DIARIES

Edited by Walter Millis

WITH THE COLLABORATION OF
E. S. DUFFIELD

NEW YORK · THE VIKING PRESS · MCMLI

SET IN BASKERVILLE, CALEDONIA, AND PERPETUA TYPES
AND PRINTED IN THE UNITED STATES OF AMERICA

Part of this book was serialized in
the *New York Herald Tribune* and
other newspapers and an excerpt
from it appeared in *Life*.

PUBLISHED ON THE SAME DAY IN THE DOMINION OF CANADA
BY THE MACMILLAN COMPANY OF CANADA LIMITED

MANUFACTURED BY THE H. WOLFF BOOK MFG. CO.

Contents

Contents

The three Forrestal boys, Henry, James, and William, 1894.

Forrestal's Princeton senior-class picture from the 1915 *Nassau Herald*.

St. Anselm School baseball team, 1905; James Forrestal seated lower left.

General Dwight D. Eisenhower and Secretary of the Navy Forrestal, following a conference at the Allied Commander's advance headquarters in
Normandy, August 1944.

Fleet Admiral Chester W. Nimitz (left) and Rear Admiral Forrest P. Sherman (right) talking with Secretary Forrestal (center) during an official inspection of the Pacific fleet in February 1945.

The Secretary of the Navy on his visit to Berlin, late July 1945.

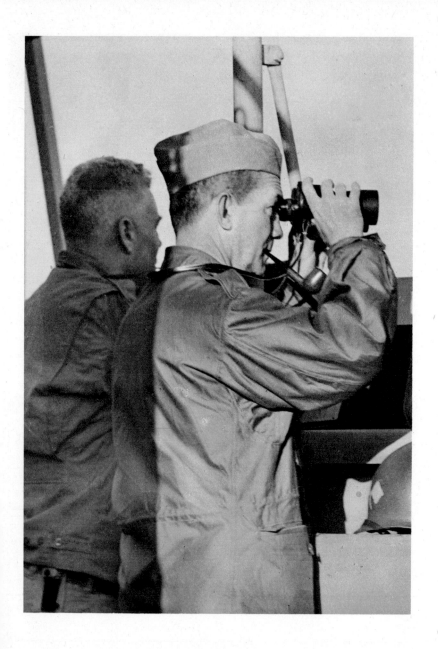

Secretary Forrestal at the invasion of Iwo Jima, on the bridge of the flagship of the amphibious force, February 1945.

James Forrestal, first Secretary of Defense, taking the oath of office, administered by Chief Justice Fred M. Vinson, September 17, 1947

The Secretary of Defense congratulating Dr. Vannevar Bush, after the latter was sworn in as chairman of the Research and Development Board, September 30, 1947. Thomas Hargrave, chairman of the Munitions Board, at the back.

Secretary Forrestal during one of his rare moments of relaxation, at the Royal Ottawa Golf and Country Club, August 1948.

The Secretary of Defense with the Joint Chiefs of Staff, late 1948. Left to right: Rear Admiral Louis E. Denfeld, Chief of Naval Operations; General Hoyt S. Vandenberg, Chief of Staff, U.S. Air Force; Secretary Forrestal; General Omar N. Bradley, Chief of Staff, U.S. Army.

Secretary Forrestal at the dedication of the National Press Room, September 1948, with Mrs. Raymond Clapper and Mrs. Frederick C. Painton, widows of World War II correspondents who gave their lives covering the war.

The Secretary of Defense conferring with General of the Army Eisenhower upon the latter's return to the Pentagon as a consultant to the National Military Establishment, February 1949.

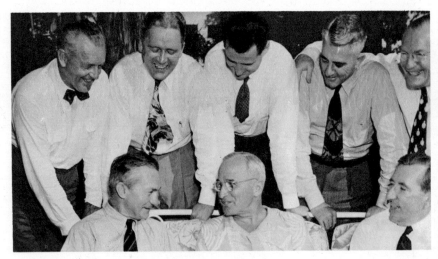

President Truman and his guests at Key West, November 1948. Front row, left to right: James Forrestal, the President, Senator Claude Pepper; back row, left to right: Mr. Paul E. Fitzpatrick, Governor Fuller Warren, Representative George A. Smathers, Mr. C. V. Griffin, Mr. Leonard Hicks.

Secretary Forrestal with the President on the lawn of the Little White House, Key West, November 1948.

James Forrestal

Foreword

When James Forrestal resigned as Secretary of Defense in March 1949, he left in his office a large accumulation of personal files and papers. Most of these were stored in some half a dozen steel filing cases and sundry other boxes and crates, and after his death were turned over to the executors of his estate. There was in addition, however, a more private record. This was the "diary," as he called it, which he had kept in one form or another since the middle of 1944, shortly after his appointment as Secretary of the Navy.

On leaving office Forrestal, already seriously ill, went for recuperation to Hobe Sound, Florida. From there he sent instructions that the diary, together with a few detached documents, should be deposited at the White House. This was an unusual request. One can only infer that it reflected Forrestal's awareness of the confidential nature of much of this material and his desire to insure it, under any eventualities, against irresponsible publication.

Even casual examination of the diary notes makes it evident that they were not dictated with textual publication in mind. They were probably set down, among other reasons, as material for the book which Forrestal at one time or another thought of writing, in which he could have exercised his own judgment as to inclusions, omissions or explanations. He was not to enjoy this opportunity. By sending the papers to the White House he left them safeguarded in responsible hands; he had scrupulously discharged his own obligation to prevent improper or careless disclosure, and he cannot be held accountable for the appearance of anything in this book—prepared after his death from material which he had no chance to edit or to review.

That responsibility fell to others—and they have felt that, once the wisdom of publication was agreed upon, it was not for them to exercise any censorship except for unarguable reasons. The circumstances were as follows:

After Forrestal's death the papers remained under seal in the White House until January of 1950, when they were examined by representatives of the White House, of the estate and of the Department of Defense. The diary was found to consist of fifteen loose-leaf binders, containing something less than three thousand typewritten pages in all. Their contents were of several kinds. Many of the pages were simply the daily calendars of appointments, with no further notation. Some, especially in the earlier portions of the diary, bore only pasted-in newspaper clippings or similar memorabilia. Many carried copies of important secret documents, originating in Forrestal's own or in other Departments, obviously retained for reference. The larger part of the material, however, was made up of the diary notes proper—tersely dictated memoranda of significant meetings, conversations, luncheon and dinner interviews, with occasional reflective comments on men or events.

The whole was arranged in strictly chronological order; otherwise there was no particular plan or pattern in the material. The dictated notes were in no sense a daily record of the usual diary kind. Often days or weeks would go by without an entry; although, conversely, on his trips abroad Forrestal generally kept a daily itinerary and a fairly full account of events. It was his habit, on returning from stated meetings of the Cabinet, the State-War-Navy Committee and (later) the National Security Council, to dictate a brief summary of what had been said; sometimes he had assistants take these notes and entered them rather than reports of his own. He included notes of many more casual conversations that happened to interest him, but often omitted any reference whatever to matters which must have been of first concern to him at the time. Frequently a diary note appears on some special aspect of a current problem, with nothing in the prior material to indicate the background and nothing later to show the outcome. The diary proper comes virtually to an end with Forrestal's return from his flying trip to Europe, made just after the election in November 1948; thereafter, the daily appointment calendars were regularly entered up to the time of his departure from office at the end of March 1949, but other entries appear with increasing rarity.

This material as a whole presented many problems, both of public and of editorial policy. On re-examining it in the spring of 1950 the representatives of the government removed nine documents, of a technical nature, as plainly prejudicial to military security. The representatives of the estate were then given the option of leaving the remainder for security review—an obviously lengthy and uncertain process—or of accepting it with a view to publication, under an engagement that nothing would actually be published until it had been cleared for security by the Department of Defense. The estate chose the latter course; and the diary and accompanying papers were transferred to its possession with this undertaking.

The primary responsibility for analyzing and organizing the material fell upon Eugene S. Duffield, as agent for the estate. Mr. Duffield, presently (1951) assistant publisher of the *Cincinnati Enquirer*, served as special assistant to Forrestal from 1942 to 1945; he was an important member of the original team which Forrestal, as Under Secretary of the Navy, enlisted to help with the colossal problems of wartime procurement and expansion that fell to him. When publication rights were acquired by the *New York Herald Tribune*, the latter assigned me, its assistant chief editorial writer, as editor of the projected volume. We have worked in close collaboration. Mr. Duffield has done much of the research and correlation of the documents; he supplied rough drafts for some of the sections and has contributed very considerably to the result. I must accept sole responsibility for the final arrangement and for the content and phrasing of the editorial comment. I must at the same time acknowledge the further assistance of The Viking Press, which acquired the book rights.

From the first, the editorial task was not easy. On the one

hand, there was little or no thematic continuity in the material; on the other hand, it lacked the temporal continuity of a running day-by-day record. There obviously had to be a certain amount of rearrangement and considerable editorial interpolation to relate the various entries to one another and to the events to which they referred. This necessity, moreover, aggravated the already serious problem of bulk. The total mass of notes, documents, quotations, clippings in the diary volumes alone (quite aside from the often valuable additional material in the correspondence files) runs, probably, to well over half a million words. It was obvious that ordinary publishing requirements must at best enforce a large amount of omission and selection.

In endeavoring to meet the editorial issues involved several general principles were adopted. One was to present the material more or less in the chronological sequence in which it was entered, with no more than minor regrouping here and there to bring out more clearly one or another theme which may have been predominant at a given period. Even here it seemed advisable to proceed with care. Forrestal's problems did not come to him in neatly organized array, but helter-skelter, each intricately confused with all the others; and his attitude on one subject was often closely and necessarily influenced by developments occurring in some other field at the same time. Chronology has not been slavishly observed; but it has been recognized that every departure from it for the sake of topical clarity involved a certain risk of distortion, and such departures have been kept to a minimum.

A second principle was that Forrestal's words must be left to speak for themselves, with only such editorial comment as seemed necessary for continuity and understanding. This raised certain hazards. Forrestal customarily recorded the views of those with whom he talked without indicating whether or not he agreed; at times he set down some item of rumor or gossip without any assessment of its accuracy; he often quoted what someone told him had been said by a third person. The diary recorded, as diaries usually do, many confidential statements given in haste or without thought of the possible public effect. Forrestal may himself occasionally have misunderstood or inaccurately summarized what was said. Had he lived, he would have supplied his own checks on all such matters; for others to attempt to do so for him would be to risk entanglement in a perilous morass of censorship and conjecture, leading probably to confusions worse than those it was sought to avoid. It would have placed editor and publishers in an impossible position, had they assumed, without authority, the responsibility for altering or suppressing the record as it had been released to them. It seemed far preferable to let the entries stand for what they were—data reports, not necessarily final or authentic in themselves, but authentically reflecting the world in which Forrestal moved as it impinged upon him. It was so that they had originally been dictated, and it seemed reasonable to ask the reader to accept and evaluate them as such.

A third principle was to present, as far as possible, everything in the record of significance or public interest. As has been said, omission and selection on a large scale were unavoidable; and here it was necessary to establish certain criteria. In general, the omitted material falls into the following categories:

1. The merely routine, ephemeral or repetitious.

2. Words, phrases, often whole sentences or more, eliminated in order to tighten up the dictated text or clarify the significant ideas.

3. More extended references to subjects which have since been thoroughly publicized, and on which the Forrestal notes add no new light. A good example is the Pearl Harbor investigation. The earlier pages of the diary include numerous entries on this subject, but as they contain little or nothing not already public property all have been excluded.

4. References to subjects with which Forrestal was not primarily concerned and which receive only passing and fragmentary mention in the diary. In his summaries of Cabinet discussions, for example, Forrestal often recorded remarks on topics outside the range of his immediate responsibility; some of

these, no doubt, might be useful to specialists in the relevant fields, but where they were too casual to be of interest to the general reader they have as a rule been omitted.

5. A certain number of references to persons, by name, which might raise questions of fairness, if not of libel. Occasionally—though very rarely—Forrestal recorded some rumor or comment reflecting on the honesty or loyalty of an individual, not as his own judgment but simply as something he had heard from others. He would certainly never have published such things himself without a careful check on the accuracy of the allegation, and it would be clearly inappropriate for others to do so.

There is a final category of omissions. After the diary had been edited in accordance with the foregoing principles, the completed typescript was submitted to the Department of Defense, under the original agreement with the estate, for security review. As a result of this review a few passages—representing in all only a very small fraction of the whole and not, for the most part, of any great public interest—were eliminated as directly violative of military security. A rather larger portion was condensed, paraphrased or in some instances omitted entirely on the ground that it might materially embarrass the current conduct of international relations, and that its publication would therefore not be in the national interest. Here there was no sinister suppression. What was most often involved were confidential remarks attributed to foreign statesmen which, while innocent enough in themselves, were not made for publication and could be distorted for propaganda effect. While paraphrase has at times been used to conceal the source of some idea or to avoid direct quotation from which questionable inferences might be drawn, it is believed that the essentials of the record have in all respects been preserved.

It must be emphasized that in making this review the Department of Defense assumed no responsibility for either the factual accuracy of the published material or the views and policies it might express. While the present volume has been "screened" for security, it is in no sense an official document and carries no stamp, even by inference, of official approval.

There were, in addition, certain technical difficulties to be considered. In several instances the diary notes were obviously garbled in dictation. One example is a case in which the words "a tax" appear in a context that makes it plain that "attacks" was what Forrestal had dictated. Where changes of any possible consequence have been made on such grounds between the original typescript and the printed text, they have been indicated; but many minor instances of misspellings, dropped plurals, omitted articles and the similar little slips to which dictation is vulnerable have been corrected without notice to the reader. A uniform style in capitalization, punctuation and so on has been adopted. All this, perhaps impermissible in dealing with a manuscript, seems justifiable in the case of dictated material. Occasionally paragraph breaks have been introduced where they do not appear in the original.

The diary proper has frequently been supplemented by recourse to Forrestal's letters and recorded telephone calls. These were taken from the files originally transferred to the estate, which did not fall under the undertaking to submit for security clearance. It was often necessary to resort to this material in order to fill the many gaps in the diary itself; but in general it has been used in this way only. There has been no attempt to make this volume in any sense a "life and letters," or to study and exhaust all the available correspondence. The single aim has been to publish the Forrestal diary, with only enough editorial interference and supplementation to bring it together into a coherent and readable whole. The editor has tried to be helpful without being officious—for this has from the beginning been conceived as James Forrestal's book rather than as a book about him written by others.

The line has not, however, been an easy one to draw. If the editorial comment has strayed to one side or the other, it is possible only to ask the reader's forbearance.

WALTER MILLIS

Biographical Introduction

In many ways James Forrestal was an exceptional figure
among the high officers of government during the war and
immediate postwar years. He coupled outstanding administrative abilities with an unusually reflective and philosophic bent
of mind; he combined a tireless and aggressive energy with a
complex, sensitive and often introspective personality; he
cloaked an essential shyness under an air of pugnacity, and a
method that relied heavily on patience and persuasion under a
manner that could at times seem brusque to the point of grim-
ness. Even in outward appearance he was unusual among the
general run of Washington administrators and political leaders.
In almost any group photograph that includes him, his rather
small, athletic figure—with the neat, iron-gray hair, the thin
and tightly compressed lips, the intent, gray-blue eyes set in a
combative Irish face, made even more combative by the
broken and flattened nose—presents a striking contrast to the
more conventional features of his colleagues.

His public career was no less unusual. It was one of the few
on the higher levels that bridged the war years under Franklin
Roosevelt, the postwar demobilization under Truman and the
critical opening phases of the "cold war" which followed. For
some time before his resignation in March 1949, he was the
sole survivor of the Roosevelt Cabinet still serving in that of
Mr. Truman. He was a Roosevelt appointee who was not and
never had been a New Dealer; he was one of the wartime
"businessmen in government," who had come into it well before the war and was to remain long after most of the other

businessmen had returned to more lucrative fields; he was among the ablest of Truman's lieutenants, but he was never in the intimate inner circle of the new administration. Always resistant to any kind of personal publicity, he was at the same time keenly aware of the press and public opinion and was skillful as well as frank in dealing with them. He had a fund of charm which he knew how to use when it served him, and was adept in those political and personal relationships which are so important in successful Washington administration; but these skills were grounded on a singularly solid moral base—a deep sense of duty and of dedication which permitted no compromise, for the sake of political maneuver or personal prestige, with what he felt as an overriding obligation to the interests of the United States. He was not a man of many friendships, but there was nothing of the recluse about him, and those friends he made were devotedly attached to him. His inmost life was in more than ordinary degree his own. Clearly capable of strong emotions, he kept them under an iron control—a control so rigid that its breakdown at the end contributed to his tragic death.

Forrestal was born on February 15, 1892, in what was then Matteawan and is now a part of Beacon, New York—an east bank Hudson River town in the bottom corner of Dutchess County, twenty miles below the Roosevelt estate at Hyde Park. His father, James Forrestal, had come from Ireland as a boy in the 1850s, crossing the ocean alone, although he was only nine years old, to join his mother, who had emigrated some time before and was living near Matteawan. The elder Forrestal learned the carpenter's trade; in 1875 he established what was to grow into a substantial contracting and construction business at Matteawan, and five years later he married Mary A. Toohey, the daughter of a neighboring farmer and landholder. The future Cabinet officer, the youngest of the three sons born to them, was christened James Vincent; he seldom used the middle name in later life though he did not definitely drop it until he became Secretary of the Navy.

"Vince" Forrestal, as he was then called, passed through the local schools, demonstrating the quickness of his mind by gradu-

ating from the Matteawan High School in 1908, at the age of
sixteen. His first ambition (and it was one, his friends believe,
which he harbored throughout his life) was for a newspaper
career, and he got a job as a reporter on the *Matteawan Evening Journal*. He later transferred to the *Mount Vernon Argus,*
and in 1910 went to the *Poughkeepsie News Press.* That was
the year of political upheaval, when Woodrow Wilson was
elected Governor of New Jersey and the young Franklin D.
Roosevelt was sent to the New York State Senate. Forrestal's
father had long been active in local politics—as a Cleveland
Democrat he had been postmaster of Matteawan during Cleveland's second administration—while the editor of the *News
Press,* Richard E. Connell, was running for Congress on the
Democratic ticket. Roosevelt cultivated the elder Forrestal, visiting the home at Matteawan several times in the course of the
campaign; and the son, left virtually in charge of the Poughkeepsie paper, was obviously in the thick of the battle. Roosevelt kept up his friendship with the Forrestals after he went to
Washington as Assistant Secretary of the Navy; while years
later, when the younger Forrestal, by that time himself Secretary of the Navy under Roosevelt, accompanied the latter on a
campaign tour, he was vividly to recall "the torchlight parades
and political meetings in the village of Matteawan." But he
was never attracted by party politics. At Princeton he was, as a
Northern Democrat, something of a *rara avis* to his friends;
but in his senior year he declared himself as without political
affiliation.

Three years of local journalism were enough to convince him
that he would need a college education if he was to advance
his career, and in the fall of 1911 he entered Dartmouth. In
the following year he transferred to Princeton, perhaps feeling that it offered him better opportunities and wider contacts.
There he promptly went out for the *Daily Princetonian.* Its
chairman that year was Ferdinand Eberstadt; the senior was
at once struck by the sophomore's character and abilities, and
Eberstadt was to become perhaps his closest friend and associate
throughout Forrestal's later career. In college Forrestal was universally known as "Runt," but the nickname was no reflection

on his capacities. In the class of 1915 he is remembered as a hard worker who never became a "grind"; by some he is remembered also for a generous readiness to lend unpublicized help in time of need—a readiness that characterized him, to an extent of which few are aware, throughout his life. He became a member of Cottage; by his senior year he was on the student council and was himself chairman of the *Princetonian*. His class discerningly voted him "most likely to succeed" by a wide margin, and he ran fourth, incidentally, both as "biggest bluffer" and as having "done most for Princeton."

Forrestal did not, however, wait to take a degree. He seems to have had an idea of returning in the fall to make up the necessary credits; if so, it was never realized. Instead he took a job with the Tobacco Products Corporation, selling cigarettes. But the prospects this offered seemed unappealing. In 1916 he entered the investment banking house of William A. Read & Co. (shortly to become Dillon, Read & Co.), and with that firm he was to make his business career.

On the outbreak of war in 1917 Forrestal enlisted as a seaman in the Navy. He soon transferred to the aviation branch; and as both naval aviation and its training facilities were still in a rudimentary state, he was sent to train in Canada with the Royal Flying Corps. After some three hours of instruction (including one bad crack-up) he was passed as Naval Aviator No. 154, and returned to the United States to receive his ensign's commission. He was not to see combat service, however, as his war duty was in the Office of Naval Operations in Washington. From this he emerged at the Armistice as lieutenant, junior grade, and returned to the bond department of Dillon, Read. There he put all his capacities for initiative, hard work and thorough study into the business of selling bonds; he soon established himself as one of the abler young men in Wall Street and his rise was rapid. He was made partner in 1923 and by 1926 was vice president.

In October of the latter year he married Mrs. Josephine Ogden of Huntington, West Virginia, who was at the time a member of the staff of *Vogue*. Two sons were born to them, Michael and Peter. By his associates of Dillon, Read days Forrestal is remembered not only for his energy and his success but also for his scrupulous fairness, his refusal to take credit that belonged to his subordinates or to press claims for preferment over others he thought more entitled to it. He is remembered for his charm, his sense of humor and for his continuing private generosities. While he had not been obliged to work his own way through college (his family had given him substantial assistance), he was interested in those who needed a hand in the educational struggle; and he arranged in these years to help a number of young men through college in such a way that the beneficiaries themselves were unaware of the source of the aid. Forrestal gave away a great deal of money in the course of his life, but never with fanfare, and there is little record of such matters in his available papers.

Forrestal was always a wide and serious reader; he was at the same time always careful to keep himself in athletic physical trim. He had boxed at Princeton, and he continued that particularly strenuous form of exercise thereafter until, in the middle thirties, his nose was crushed and flattened in a sparring match at the Racquet Club. The accident rather markedly altered his appearance, but the suggestion of a tough fistfighter which it left on him probably did him no disservice in the rough-and-tumble of wartime Washington.

In 1938—he was then forty-six—he succeeded Clarence Dillon as president of Dillon, Read. A quietly driving ambition had brought him early to the top. He had wealth, power and position; the career to which he had set his hand had culminated in a fine success. Perhaps it was partly for that very reason that two years later he was to abandon it and, as it turned out, to abandon it for good. In June of 1940 it was announced, to the surprise of many in and out of Wall Street, that the president of Dillon, Read had resigned to enter the New Deal administration as one of Franklin Roosevelt's special administrative assistants.

There was initiative on both sides. Having made his own fortune, Forrestal was undoubtedly urged by his strong sense of obligation toward service to the country. War had come in Europe in September 1939. Forrestal was not deceived by the "phony war" period which followed; he was aware of the perils before the nation and of the efforts and sacrifices they were likely to demand, and before the year was out he was at least considering going into government. President Roosevelt, on the other hand, had long been shifting the emphasis of his administration from the domestic issues of the New Deal era to the growing menaces of international affairs. When full crisis broke with Hitler's attack upon the West in May 1940, the President called immediately for a major effort of rearmament and war production—and it was obvious that the effort could not succeed without the wholehearted cooperation of the large industrial and financial interests with which the New Deal had so often been in conflict. Roosevelt had many reasons for trying to broaden the base of his administration. Forrestal had never taken any part in politics, but he came from a Democratic background; he had taken a more liberal view than had others in the financial community of the reforms which the New Deal had imposed on Wall Street, and the administration was anxious to enlist his services.

In the exciting days of May 1940 there was much talk and rumor of a "coalition" government. The President scouted this; but on June 20 he announced the appointment of two eminent Republicans, Henry L. Stimson and Frank Knox as, respectively, Secretary of War and Secretary of the Navy. Three days later it was confirmed that Forrestal would become the fourth of the recently created administrative assistants in the White House—the so-called "secret six" who were to serve, as the President had put it, with complete loyalty and a "passion for anonymity." Initially Forrestal was asked to work, as liaison officer with the agencies concerned, on certain plans dealing with Latin-American economic relations. He was not happy in the assignment, and it was to last only six weeks.

By an act signed on June 20, the day the Stimson and Knox appointments were announced, Congress had created the post of Under Secretary of the Navy. On August 5 the President nominated Forrestal for the position, and he was sworn in on the 22nd. As a completely new office, it was without either staff, tradition or even general acceptance by the Navy. Congress had left the definition of its duties to the Secretary. On the day after he was sworn in, Secretary Knox assigned Forrestal an assortment of responsibilities covering contract, tax and legal matters and liaison with certain civilian agencies. "There was little indication," as Robert H. Connery observes, "in the not too clear directive assigning this odd lot of unrelated duties to the Under Secretary, that this office was to develop as the chief material coordinating agency of the Navy Department." [1] Nor would the directive alone have been enough to achieve such a result. It was a combination of Forrestal's own very great abilities on the one hand, with the swiftly rising pressure of events on the other, which step by step transformed the Under Secretary's office into the controlling center of the whole industrial and procurement side of the Navy's vast wartime effort.

Obviously no one man came anywhere near to "building" the wartime Navy. That was a gigantic cooperative achievement. But Forrestal was the one man more responsible than any other for "buying" it. He was, that is to say, the major link connecting the military demand to the civilian productive system and, in turn, connecting the civilian economy to the military uses of its products. He was to find on taking office that the established provisions for maintaining this vital nexus between civilian and military, while sufficient and smooth-working under peacetime conditions, were quite inadequate to meet the colossal loads which war was about to impose. He had to solve for himself, with one improvisation after another, the constantly enlarging problems which this situation entailed. He had to bring the existing naval material bureaus and procurement agencies into a coordinated structure capable of meeting the enormous new demands upon them. He had to create adequate legal agencies for overseeing the drawing of contracts, and adequate statistical agencies for controlling production, program and inventory.

---

[1] Robert H. Connery, *The Navy and the Industrial Mobilization in World War II*, p. 56. This valuable study, undertaken at Forrestal's suggestion but not published until 1951, includes a judicious but illuminating exposition of Forrestal's work as Under Secretary, 1940 to 1944.

He had to consider the impact of the Navy's demand upon the general price structure, and do his part in gearing the Navy's claims over materials and factory capacity to those of the Army and the civil population. He had to meet novel problems in financing industry's expansion, in utilizing small producers, in the renegotiation of contracts as war needs changed or slacked off. And from first to last he had to find the capable men who could be enlisted from the top ranks of industry, finance and the law to carry all the multitudinous burdens which naval mobilization and wartime naval administration imposed.

Vast as the administrative task came to be, he did not permit it to nail him to his desk or isolate him from the fighting fronts which were the one end toward which the whole effort was directed. In the spring of 1941 he flew to London to establish contact with the British and deal with matters raised by the newly authorized Lend-Lease system. In 1942, after the opening of the first "shoe-string" offensive at Guadalcanal, he visited the Southwest Pacific; early in 1944 he was at Kwajalein atoll, watching the central Pacific offensive gathering momentum, while a year later, at Iwo Jima, he was to be the first Secretary of the Navy to land under fire in the midst of a still undecided amphibious operation. In all the tangles of naval administration, he never lost sight of its ultimate purpose or of the fighting men whom the administrators existed to support and serve. It was at Iwo that Forrestal voiced his "tremendous admiration and reverence for the guy who walks up beaches and takes enemy positions with a rifle and grenades or his bare hands."

On April 28, 1944, Secretary Knox died suddenly of a heart attack. Forrestal, highly competent, a devoted public officer and now thoroughly familiar with the huge naval organization, was —at any rate under wartime conditions—the only possible successor. He was sworn in as Secretary of the Navy on May 19, 1944. He was never to admit, then or later, that he was anything but an investment banker, and until the end he was to list his Washington home address as "temporary." But high office and, what was more important to Forrestal, its high and heavy responsibilities to the American people, had claimed him. The "temporary" residence was to last for nearly nine years in all. It was shortly after taking office as Secretary that he began the diary record which forms the bulk of the book that follows. In it one may read the continuation and the completion of the story of one of America's outstanding public servants through some of the most difficult and critical years of American history.

THE
Forrestal
DIARIES

CHAPTER I

The End of the Roosevelt Administration

I

4 July 1944   *Reconversion*

Under Secretary Bard, Admiral Robinson and I lunched today
with Senator Harry Truman. We endeavored to persuade him
of the unwisdom of permitting resumption of civilian production, which at the moment is the big issue between Charles Wilson and Donald Nelson, Wilson reflecting the views of the Services as against any broad-scale resumption, whereas Nelson is
pressing for it. I told Senator Truman I thought it was extremely
dangerous, not merely from the standpoint of the effect on production itself, but from the indirect psychological results
that would flow—namely, the assumption that the war was in
the bag. He did not disagree violently but said he could not go
along with our view because he was confronted almost daily
with evidences of closing down of plants because of contract
cancellations or cutbacks. He mentioned specifically some ordnance plants in Missouri, particularly in St. Louis, where ten to
twelve thousand people had been released from their jobs, which
he said would mean they would migrate elsewhere. Our rejoinder was that while this was undesirable, as between that
danger and the danger of creation of an attitude of complacency about the war, there could be no question in our minds
about which was the greater. When he left I had the impression
that we had not made any great headway with our argument.

[It is curious how much is foreshadowed in this, James Forrestal's initial entry in the voluminous collection of notes, memo-

3

[randa, copies of important documents, reports of Cabinet and other high-level meetings, which he was to accumulate from this time onward as his private "diary." This first entry happens to record a meeting with the man under whom, as neither could then know, Forrestal was to serve throughout most of the rest of his career; the relationships between them were to form one of the major themes of the record thus begun. Beneath the specific topic raised at that luncheon discussion there lay issues—greater and reaching far deeper than either could have fully appreciated at the time—which in one form or another were to consume the thoughts and energies of both through all the difficult years ahead. And the attitudes which each brought to this discussion were strikingly prophetic of the attitudes which each would tend to maintain through many future problems and crises, as the basic issues themselves grew only wider and plainer, more complex and more urgent.

There is even a touch of symbolism in the date—July 4, 1944, the national holiday—suggesting, as it were, the fundamental quality of Forrestal's patriotism, the intensity with which he identified himself with the nation he served, the passionate earnestness with which he sensed the vast problems confronting it or sought, with an intellectual restlessness rare among hard-driven practical administrators, to find valid answers for them.

In July 1944 the end of the Second World War was at least in sight. Eisenhower had landed in Normandy the month before and made good his lodgment; the Russians were rolling strongly westward; the Pacific offensives, started on a shoe-string two years earlier on Guadalcanal and in Papua, were accumulating a massive power; at Dumbarton Oaks in Washington, the new world capital, the delegates were about to sit down to design a new world order to be established upon the victory which now seemed ultimately certain. A vast amount of blood was yet to be shed; a vast amount of effort was yet to be expended. But one era of colossal peril, suffering and exertion was drawing toward its close; another era, with its own problems and possibly its own perils as well, was glimmering upon the horizon.

Latent in the argument between Wilson and Nelson, and equally in the fate of Senator Truman's twelve thousand St. Louis

[munitions workers, was the whole basic issue of "balance" between the nation's military commitments and its civil resources
and economy, the issue which in many guises was to dominate the
postwar years. What are the requirements of defense, the limits of
the military obligation? What are the legitimate claims of "normal" social and economic life? Forrestal that day took the simple
and direct view. The war was yet to be won and the winning of it
was paramount to every other consideration. There was no
greater danger than "complacency." Truman, with the politician's
training, was noncommittal and left Forrestal feeling that he had
made "no great headway."

Forrestal was to battle on many later occasions against "complacency"; and in some far more critical differences than this he
was to find in the end that he had made "no great headway" against the Truman position. Much of the subsequent story
revolves around this conflict in the emphasis with which the two
men were to approach their common problems. But this is not to
imply that there was any basic antipathy between them. After
Truman's accession to the presidency Forrestal was to remain consistent in his attitude of loyal respect for the Chief Executive,
while as Democrats of the more conservative persuasion the two
actually had much in common. There is a second entry on this
same meeting:

4 July 1944   *Vice Presidency*
    . . . [Truman] said to me that he was being urged to accept
the nomination for vice president but that he proposed to resist.
I told him that it was his duty to take it in view of the fact that
the alternative would be Henry Wallace. This alternative he
regarded with the same misgivings as myself but still felt he did
not want to take the nomination, saying that he was happy in the
Senate and felt that he was able to exercise as much influence
in government as he wished.

[Actually Forrestal himself was already acutely aware that the
simple answer would not always be adequate. In war the military
commitment is total, and to strike the "balance" against civil life
and resources presents no great difficulty. But peace was ap-

[proaching; and peace, whatever its shape, would still require the maintenance of sufficient defenses. He was worried, as his letters repeatedly show, over "the dangerous assumptions that because we have finished one war we shan't have another." [1] But what would be sufficient? What would have to be defended, and why and how? Such questions inevitably, in an intelligent mind, give rise to others. Even to speak of defense is to raise the problem of power, of world-power relationships and of the uses which other nations and one's own may be expected to make of their military strength.

Earlier in the year, while he was still Under Secretary of the Navy, Forrestal had initiated a project that clearly suggests the bent of his mind and the depth of his interests. This was a course on "The Foundations of National Power" to be introduced into the Navy's V-12 educational program, resting on "the proposition that, in order to understand the world position and responsibilities of our own country, it is necessary to know as much as possible concerning the strengths, aims and policies of other countries. . . . The nature and distribution of political power among nations are matters of basic importance in any discussion of international relations or American foreign policy." [2] The course had been undertaken experimentally at Princeton, and Forrestal was to participate in a conference discussion of the subject to be held there in September. One of his notes for his talk runs: "Our problem—to achieve accommodation between the power we now possess, our reluctance to use it positively, the realistic necessity for such use, and our national ideals."

In one shape or another this was to Forrestal the fundamental problem, and it was never far from his mind throughout the rest of his career. But many other questions inevitably flowed from it. How is power to be made effective? How big and what kind of military establishment was required, and how could it best be organized so that it would in fact meet the complex responsibilities entrusted to it? To raise these questions, moreover, was only to find still others underneath. Forrestal was keenly aware that

---

[1] To Admiral Richard L. Conolly, 7 September 1944.
[2] *Foundations of National Power*, Revised Outline, July 1947, p. 1.

[the military establishment was but one arm of policy and of government, merely a specialized aspect of the national life and economy as a whole.

On the one hand, its responsibilities in the postwar world would be largely determined by the kind of peace that was made, and Forrestal took a serious and on one or two occasions perhaps decisive interest in the activities of the diplomatists and peacemakers. On the other hand, the success with which the military fulfilled their missions must depend in the long run upon the adequacy and competence of the civil government, to which they were subordinate, and upon the workings of politics and public opinion. Forrestal was keenly sensitive to public opinion—at times perhaps oversensitive. He followed it closely, was always in touch with newspapermen and commentators, filled his files with articles and clippings that seemed significant to him and paid considerable attention to the Navy's and later to the Defense Department's public relations. He was much interested in the structure of civil government (of which, of course, as a civilian officer he was himself an important part), in the inefficiencies of many of its organizational arrangements and in the abilities and idiosyncrasies of the administrators and politicians who staffed it. And since he was ultimately dependent for every activity of the military departments upon Congress he could never be unaware of the legislative branch, of the personalities through whom he there had to work or of the tides of political change and economic interest which they reflected.

As Secretary of the Navy in mid-1944, Forrestal stood close to the crossing point at which all these questions of national policy and diplomacy, military organization, political and economic tendencies, came together. Three years later, as Secretary of Defense, he was to find himself at the very center. He never found final answers for all the issues which his position and his responsibilities forced upon his sensitive mind; neither, however, has anyone else. What makes Forrestal a unique figure in the high levels of war and postwar government was his restless sense that answers were needed, and his constant efforts, while carrying tremendous burdens of intensely practical administrative work, to reach closer to them. It may be that he was destroyed

[in the end by this division between the practical and the reflective man, by a sense of responsibility so large and so imperious that no amount of concrete achievement could satisfy it. However that may be, no one can properly understand the papers he left behind him without realizing that this complexity of attitude and purpose runs deeply through them or without a general grasp of what it was that he was about.

The earliest entries in the diary, together with his letters at the time, well illustrate the range and variety of his interests. Under the heading "Mandated Islands: State Department paper of 22 June 1944," he made an entry on July 7: "I talked with Mr. Stettinius [Edward R. Stettinius, Jr., then Under Secretary of State] today and asked him if this was a serious document and if he understood that the President was committed to it (I added that it seems to me a *sine qua non* of any postwar arrangements that there should be no debate as to who ran the Mandated Islands —that is, the islands formerly owned by Japan in the Central Pacific)." The Navy's immediate interest in the islands lay, of course, in their vital importance as future strategic bases, and Forrestal was to wage a persistent campaign throughout the next year to insure that American control over these base sites should not be incontinently surrendered.

But this specific issue only focused his attention upon the larger importance of the peacemaking in general. An office memorandum asked: "What is the general purpose of the agenda of the Conference at Dumbarton Oaks? Who are the Navy representatives and how thoroughly are we prepared?"[3] It is only an example of many similar memoranda showing his alertness to the significance of what the designers of the new world were doing. Issues of postwar internal reorganization were at the same time becoming very active. Forrestal himself was impressed with the necessity for a permanent system of compulsory military service; he hoped, he wrote to Haydn S. Pearson on August 27, that the latter would continue his "efforts in the direction of a compulsory service bill. The memory of the people of this country is very

---

[3] To Captain O. S. Colclough, 20 July 1944.

[short." He was at the same time skeptical of the rapidly rising agitation for a single unified military department. Admittedly he approached this matter originally from a strongly Navy viewpoint; it was never, however, a narrowly Navy viewpoint. He was to modify his own attitudes more than once; but because he always tried to get to the bottom of the issues before him, the later shifts in his position (if they can really be called so) reflected an underlying consistency of principle which he was formulating as early as mid-1944. The strongest pressures for a single military service came from the Army Air Force and from those who believed with it that "air power" had become the major decisive element in warfare. "I agree," he wrote to H. Calvin Cook on July 14, "that we would be unprepared indeed if we did not possess a land-based force of strategic bombers. The Navy does not oppose this sort of strategic air force"—although it did insist on keeping its own tactical air arm—but "I believe, for some time to come, control of the land, sea and air will be interdependent, and that no one instrument will suffice for all these purposes." And on August 30 he was writing to Representative Carl Vinson, Democrat, of Georgia, then chairman of the House Committee on Naval Affairs, on both subjects.

To Carl Vinson, 30 August 1944

. . . The question of a single Department of Defense. I do not think for a moment we can take this lightly, and I have so told Admiral King [Ernest J. King, Chief of Naval Operations]. . . . Publicity is as much a part of war today as logistics or training and we must so recognize it. I am happy to say that Admiral King shares these views. . . . Compulsory military service is another question which I think we have to give much attention to, and quickly. Unless we get it while the war is still in progress I for one am very skeptical whether it will ever become law. . . .

[The first few diary entries expand the picture of the Secretary of the Navy's preoccupations and responsibilities as this record began, in the final months of Franklin Roosevelt's presidency.

The Secretary of the Treasury [Henry Morgenthau, Jr.] came in with the President, with whom he had had lunch. The President said he had been talking with the Secretary of the Treasury on the general question of the control of Germany after the end of the war. He said that he had just heard about a paper prepared by the Army and that he was not at all satisfied with the severity of the measures proposed. He said that the Germans should have simply a subsistence level of food—as he put it, soup kitchens would be ample to sustain life—that otherwise they should be stripped clean and should not have a level of subsistence above the lowest level of the people they had conquered.

The Secretary of War [Henry L. Stimson] demurred from this view but the President continued in the expression of his attitude and finally said he would name a committee comprising State, War and Treasury which would consider the problem of how to handle Germany along the lines that he had outlined, that this committee would consult the Navy whenever naval questions were involved.

[There follows a parenthesis, added to the same page two years later:

(The paper referred to was one that was prepared by the War Department and was sent to Eisenhower for his information and comments. A Colonel Bernstein apparently secured a copy of it and without going through Army channels showed it to Mr. Morgenthau with the above results. This was the beginning of the so-called Morgenthau Plan of pastoralizing Germany.)

The Secretary of War pointed out that among other things Germany was a highly industrialized nation, that it would be a practical impossibility to shift large segments of the population who depended for their existence on industrial economy back to the land; furthermore, he pointed out that the products of German industry and business were needed for the rebuilding of Europe, particularly the iron and steel from the Ruhr.

[The diary contains still another reference to this matter. In May 1947 Forrestal lunched with Robert P. Patterson, Under Secretary of War, and James F. Byrnes, the Director of War Mobilization. "Among the highlights" of that gathering he noted the following:

The so-called Morgenthau Plan for an agrarian Germany was worked out by Morgenthau and submitted to the Cabinet at a meeting in the summer of 1944 after Morgenthau's return from Europe. . . .
Byrnes recalled that the President proposed his program for Germany at the Cabinet meeting in question after having lunch with Morgenthau. It came as a shock to Hull [Cordell Hull, Secretary of State] and Stimson when he named Morgenthau head of a committee to deal with German matters. At this same lunch he read a number of excerpts from the proposed Army directive indicating his disapproval and scorn of the "soft" policy toward Germany. Byrnes recalled that Hull did not go to the subsequent Quebec Conference and that Morgenthau did, and at that meeting he got Roosevelt's and Churchill's signature to his conception of the treatment of Germany. Byrnes said that Hull was so angry when he got this message that he expressed a desire to resign.

18 September 1944

The Assistant Secretary of War, Mr. [John J.] McCloy, told me tonight that the Secretary of the Treasury, Mr. Morgenthau, had formulated a program of the most severe character in dealing with Germany after its collapse. He said that the Secretary of War was in violent disagreement, that the President had decided to go along with Morgenthau. In general the program, according to Mr. McCloy, called for the conscious destruction of the economy in Germany and the encouragement of a state of impoverishment and disorder. He said he

felt the Army's role in any program would be most difficult because the Army, by training and instinct, would naturally turn
to the re-creation of order as soon as possible, whereas under
this program they apparently were to encourage the opposite.

5 October 1944   *China*

The situation in China is becoming more and more tense.
The last word is that Chiang Kai-shek has turned down the
proposal to have Stilwell [Lieutenant General Joseph W. Stilwell, commanding China-Burma-India theater and Chief of
Staff to Generalissimo Chiang] given command of all Chinese
forces. . . . General Marshall [George C. Marshall, Chief of
Staff] wrote a message for the President to send to Chiang,
taking sharp issue with him on the question of firing Stilwell
and pointing out the serious situation in which China now
finds itself. The President decided not to send this message but
instead to send one of a milder tone and suggesting that General Chennault [Major General Claire Chennault, USAAF]
remain as head of the 14th Air Force; that General Stilwell
remain as Chief of Staff but not Commander in Chief of the
Chinese Forces. . . .

18 October 1944   *Russia*

I saw this morning dispatches from Harriman [W. Averell
Harriman, then Ambassador to Russia] on the future position of Russia in the war against Japan. General Deane [Major
General John R. Deane, chief of the U. S. Military Mission in
Moscow] reported Stalin's willingness to consider now planning
for full Russian participation against the Japanese subject to
Stalin's condition that he would require a build-up of certain
air complements and two months' stockpile for thirty additional divisions in Manchuria. He said that if the Japanese got
any preliminary warning of Russian action they would move
immediately against Vladivostok. At the moment he doubted
that Russia would be able to hold it against their attack but
indicated that with the addition of thirty divisions and the logistic and air support to go with them the Russians could han-

dle such an attack at that time. He thought the secondary objective of the Japanese would be Kamchatka, and their third,
Sakhalin.

4 November 1944

I flew up to Boston today to join the President's train before
the final speech of the campaign at Fenway Park.

I remarked to my aide, Captain Roper, when I went down
to the siding where the Boston & Albany train came in at around
5:30, that "public life is certainly no place for an introvert."
This was prompted by the fact that the railroad yard was full
of political characters from Boston, policemen, Secret Service
agents, photographers and reporters. All the political characters
were in soft gray hats and turned-up overcoat collars. They
were enveloped in conversation and cigar smoke, and there
was a general confidential atmosphere about all hands. The
scene carried me back to the torchlight parades and political
meetings in the village of Matteawan.

Most of the conversation was centered around whether or
not Bob Hannegan, the Democratic National Chairman, and
Majority Leader of the House John McCormack were going to
be able to persuade that leader of the Massachusetts Celts, the
Honorable David I. Walsh, to introduce the President from
the platform in Fenway Park. The Senator said he would go
as far as Framingham but no farther—in other words, that he
would smoke his cigar but wouldn't go upstairs. The intransigence was dealt with by the simple device of not stopping the
train at Framingham. Even so, the Senator sat tight and did
not appear on the platform that evening.

[Thus on the eve of the "fourth-term" election most of the
major themes that were to run through the remainder of the diary had already been announced. It is useful to distinguish them
at the beginning. First there was the problem of winning the war
and writing the peace terms; both issues came more and more to
revolve around Soviet policy. In September he was writing to a
friend:

To Palmer Hoyt, 2 September 1944

I find that whenever any American suggests that we act in accordance with the needs of our own security he is apt to be called a god-damned fascist or imperialist, while if Uncle Joe suggests that he needs the Baltic Provinces, half of Poland, all of Bessarabia and access to the Mediterranean, all hands agree that he is a fine, frank, candid and generally delightful fellow who is very easy to deal with because he is so explicit in what he wants.

Hoping you are the same, I am . . .

[It was from such an approach that Forrestal was led into his long and serious preoccupation with Russian power and purpose and the basic issues of power relations that lay beneath the problem. A second major theme began with the planning of postwar military policy. The primary preoccupation here was with the plan for universal military training; this was soon overshadowed by the long controversy over unification, which was in turn to lead into (and frequently to confuse) the arguments over the military budget. A third major theme lay in the adequacy or inadequacy of our political and administrative system and the workings of our domestic politics. Each of these complex subjects affected and was intimately affected by the development of the others. Forrestal himself, of course, could not consider them serially or in detachment; they were thrust upon his attention or claimed his energies without system or arrangement, but they run through the whole diary, and it can properly be read only by bearing them in mind.

I I

[Franklin Roosevelt was elected to a fourth presidential term on November 7. Whatever Forrestal's inmost reaction may have been, this meant at any rate that matters would continue substantially as before. Forrestal had a markedly double attitude toward public service; along with a clearly passionate interest in his job and a devotion to the responsibilities it entailed, there went a constant and as it were instinctive desire to be rid of it. In the summer he had written to a friend who had congratulated

[him on one of his speeches: "There isn't the slightest chance of my becoming a permanent public ham—I am going to be out of this joint as soon as my conscience lets me."[4] With the election, it was obvious that it would be a long time still before conscience gave the authorization.

Through the succeeding winter his diary entries continued to carry fragmentary notes on a variety of topics that were later to assume first importance. Universal military training was one of them, and on the Friday after the election there was a conference in Secretary Stimson's office with half a dozen of the principal labor leaders—William Green of the AFL, Philip Murray of the CIO, Thomas C. Cashen, Harry W. Fraser, Alexander F. Whitney and William D. Johnston of the rail unions—together with the Secretaries of War and the Navy, General Marshall, Admiral King, Representatives Clifton A. Woodrum and James W. Wadsworth and others.

10 November 1944   *Universal Training*
    . . . Marshall, Stimson and I outlined our views about the need for universal military training legislation. The reaction of the labor people present was sympathetic and cooperative. It was general agreement that the primary need was for education to dissipate the view that this was laid as the foundation for any broad militarily dominated system of control. Suggestion was made and adopted that the Army and Navy collaborate in preparation of a brief statement of objectives, that this be forwarded to the labor people present, and that at a future date the Secretary of War call another meeting. . . .

[Forrestal went on to the Cabinet meeting that day:

10 November 1944   *Cabinet Meeting*
    . . . The Federal Housing Administrator, Mr. Blandford [John B. Blandford, Jr.], reported on plans for postwar housing. The President asked him to submit a memorandum on the possible use of Army and Navy housing, beds, etc., in our war establishments. . . . He asked whether some of these

---
[4] To William S. Charnley, 12 September 1944.

buildings could be dismantled and shipped rather than having
them sold for their break-up value as lumber. Justice Byrnes
raised the question of keeping many of these camps for any
possible military training program after the war. There was
considerable discussion of this subject, and the Secretary of
War and I reported on this morning's meeting with the labor
people. The President said he had been under the impression
that labor would resist the attempt to have a straight-out military training program, but we advised him that our impression
was quite the contrary, that they were sympathetic, cooperative
and quite willing to examine any program that the Army and
Navy would put before them.

[The war still in progress, and in particular the manner of its
    ending, was, however, a more urgent subject, and the Cabinet a
    week later was closer to events.

17 November 1944   *Cabinet Meeting*
   1. The President said he had lunched with Averell Harriman and expressed a little more optimism about possibilities
of cooperation between Russia and China.
   2. He said the meeting between the P. M. [Winston Church-
ill], Stalin and himself would not occur until after inauguration.
   3. He expressed concern about food and other conditions in
Poland; said he felt this would turn out to be the most stricken
region in Europe.
   4. *General policies as regards the rest of Europe*:
        (a) Avoid use of our troops for intracountry disturb-
ances.
        (b) See that people do not starve but not be greatly
concerned about shipment of materials, machinery, etc., particularly to Italy. Leo Crowley [Foreign Economic Admin-
istrator] interjected that the Italians *did* have need for spare
parts and other modernizing of obsolescent and depreciated
machinery.
   5. Mr. [Abe] Fortas, Under Secretary of the Interior, reported that he saw no prospect for liberalization of the rationing of oil.

[Here the shadow of Russia was visible upon the horizon—a shadow that was to grow only greater and more ominous through all the postwar years. Here is also an early, and still wholly confident, mention of what became the Yalta Conference, in which Roosevelt was to make his major attempt to deal with that shadow. And here is an intimation of the easy way in which at that time (it was before the heavy Western reverse in the Battle of the Bulge and while MacArthur still had only a partial hold in the Philippines) the problems of postwar reorganization were being addressed.

Douglas MacArthur himself was perhaps a bit of a problem— particularly to the Navy—and under date of November 22 Forrestal entered in his diary a long memorandum, "MacArthur-Leyte, by Bert Andrews," which had been supplied to him by the Washington correspondent of the *New York Herald Tribune* after the latter's return from a trip to the Philippines. Andrews was frank, and so, apparently, MacArthur had been. In the words of the Andrews report, "[MacArthur] said that every mistake that supposedly intelligent men could make has been made in this war. The North African operation was absolutely useless, yet all the available strength of Great Britain and the United States was thrown into the task."

The general, as he is depicted in the report, was full of two ideas: that the Pacific war had been "starved" in the interests of Europe, and that whereas the MacArthur-Nimitz strategy in the Pacific was skillfully to hit the enemy "where he ain't," the European strategy was to hammer stupidly against the enemy's strongest points. "Patton's army," Andrews paraphrased the general, "which is trying to batter its way through the Vosges in the Lunéville-Baccarat sector, can't do it. He repeated—they can't do it. No army could do it. . . . The Chinese situation is disastrous. It is the bitter fruit of our decision to concentrate our full strength against Germany. . . . He said that if he had been given just a portion of the force which invaded North Africa he could have retaken the Philippines in three months because at that time the Japanese were not ready."

The report goes on to expand the MacArthur views: "He lashed out in a general indictment of Washington, asserting that

['they' are fighting this war as they fought the last war. He said
that most of them have never been in the front lines and that
they aren't rotating field officers back into Washington. (He's not
entirely accurate on this.) Nimitz is his friend and good pal and
closest supporter, and he has a high regard for the Navy. But he
suspects that that regard is not reciprocated. . . .

"In continuing his criticism of Washington he said that the history of the world will be written in the Pacific for the next ten
thousand years. He said we made the same old mistake of inter-
vening in European quarrels which we can't hope to solve because they are insoluble. He said that Europe is a dying system.
It is worn out and run down, and will become an economic and
industrial hegemony of Soviet Russia. . . . The lands touching
the Pacific with their billions of inhabitants will determine the
course of history (repeating) for the next ten thousand years. . . .
Stalin, he believes, also knows the Pacific picture and while fighting in Europe is actually looking over his shoulder toward Asia."
The Russian, MacArthur told his hearers, was determined to reverse the Russo-Japanese war and reacquire Port Arthur as a
warm-water outlet on the Pacific. "If Chiang Kai-shek is over-
thrown, China will be thrown into utter confusion. He said: 'There
was no more reason for replacing Stilwell than there would be for
replacing me.'" The report continues:

"He repeated that the Pacific will become and remain an industrial and economic sphere of world development and, in his
strongest blast against Washington, said 'they' were guilty of
'treason and sabotage' in not adequately supporting the Pacific
while hammering Germany. . . . Throughout all this he never
once referred to 'the Americans' and 'the Japanese,' or to 'our
forces' and 'their forces.' Always it was 'the enemy and I' or 'he
and I,' so much so that it left listeners with the impression of being in the presence of a tremendous ego. Once or twice listeners
tried to ask a question. He doesn't like questions and didn't even
listen. . . ."

Forrestal had the complete report copied into his diary but
added no comment of his own. Within three months he was to
have an opportunity of listening to the general's strategic and
political ideas himself. The diary turns to other subjects.

23 November 1944

I talked with Harry Hopkins tonight about the necessity for creating something similar to the Joint Chiefs of Staff on the civilian side of the American government. I said I felt that if we did not create something similar to the British system for coordinated and focused government action we should not be able to deal with the problems and relationships arising during the postwar period. I said that I thought the function he had discharged while in the White House during the early years of the war should be continued on a partially formalized basis.

I pointed out as an example of what I meant the fact that while Berle's [Adolf A. Berle, then Assistant Secretary of State] Air Conference was going on in Chicago he was meeting resistance from the British, that Morgenthau was conducting negotiations here to give the British many billions of dollars under Lend-Lease, and that I didn't see that we would be doing anything more than acting in the national interest if we used the one negotiation to facilitate the progress of the other. I told him that I considered there is nothing more important in the coming four years than creation of some such machinery.

[Here in rudimentary form was one of the ideas that were to be written into the National Security Act of 1947—an act that, largely as a result of Forrestal's inspiration, sought to go much deeper into the structure of governmental action and policy formation than its primary subject, which was military reorganization and unification, might suggest. Meanwhile, however, the war was paramount, and Forrestal entered an analysis of the two great naval actions of the Philippine Sea and Leyte Gulf which will be of interest to naval historians.

3 December 1944   *Philippines*

The observation has been made . . . that if [Admiral William F.] Halsey had been in command of the covering forces of the U. S. Navy at Saipan we would have inflicted much greater damage on the Japanese fleet at that time, and that, conversely, if [Admiral Raymond A.] Spruance had been in

command of the Third Fleet in . . . the Battle for Leyte Gulf
we would probably have annihilated the central force; that is,
the force that came through San Bernardino Strait. The reason
is this: Spruance did not permit [Admiral Marc A.] Mitscher
to continue in pursuit of the Japanese carrier forces which he
caught up with at dusk on the night of June 18 because he considered his main task as being to provide complete coverage
for our forces conducting the Saipan operations. He was also
conscious that the Japanese might try to lure the bulk of his
forces . . . away from the island and then put in a flank attack which would catch the transports relatively unprotected.

To some extent this is precisely what happened in the Second
Battle of the Eastern Philippines [Leyte Gulf]. Halsey went off
in pursuit of the northern force, the one coming down from
Formosa, and in so doing left the entrance to San Bernardino
Strait uncovered. The Japanese central force came through
these Straits without opposition . . . and moved down unop-
posed to attack the escort carriers. That these carriers were not
completely annihilated was, as Rear Admiral [Ralph A.] Ofstie
said in his report on the engagement, due to an "act of Provi-
dence" rather than to our tactical dispositions.

[With a succeeding entry there came an early hint of Japanese
surrender.

7 December 1944   *Russia-Japan*

Dispatches today from Japan indicate their awareness of increasing difficulty in their situation. Indications that they count
on possible differences between Russia and Anglo-American interests to facilitate their position should they ask for a negotiated peace. Indications also they are fully aware of possibility
of Russia joining the war against them at the proper time.

[Five days later, however, the German counterattack burst into
the Ardennes, and the hopes of the Western Allies were rocked
back by the winter Battle of the Bulge. But with the turn of the
year that danger was under control; and Forrestal's summary of
the Cabinet meeting on January 5 is worth quoting at length,
both as showing the improvement in the atmosphere and as an

[example of Cabinet procedures in the latter days of the Roosevelt administration.

5 January 1945   *Cabinet*

1. The Secretary of State [Mr. Stettinius had now succeeded Cordell Hull] reported that Russia had recognized the Lublin Committee as the Polish government.

2. The Secretary of War [Stimson] reported on the situation on the Western Front—he said that it was our plan to continue exerting pressure on the bases of the German salient and not permit any diversion from this primary pressure. He said the Germans were still making probing attacks but that even if we had to readjust our lines we would endeavor to avoid commitment in any major engagement.

3. The Secretary of the Interior [Harold L. Ickes] reported a developing critical situation in coal. He said John Lewis' attitude would be openly truculent and non-cooperative. He adverted to the broad and unrestricted use of electric power in terms of hotel heating, lighting, night clubs, electric signs, etc., and the suggestion was made that a public campaign along this line might be undertaken by the Army and Navy. He said employment in the mines had been diminishing—thought that a national service act would be helpful both in this and in the event of a strike.

The Secretary also reported on the introduction of Congressman Cole's bill pertaining to the government of Pacific islands. The Secretary of the Navy [Forrestal] was asked about this and he responded that the Navy's suggestion was that Mr. Ickes be made King of Polynesia, Micronesia and the Pacific Ocean Area.

4. The Secretary of the Navy stated that Mr. Kaiser [Henry J. Kaiser, the industrialist and wartime shipbuilder] was in town and would be in due course calling on all hands to try to prevent the chopping off of merchant shipbuilding on the Pacific Coast. Figures were cited as to the requirements for battle-damage repair and general overhaul. Mr. Krug [Julius A. Krug, then chairman, War Production Board] and Mr. Byrnes were in support of this position.

5. The Director of War Mobilization [Byrnes] made the point on shipping that unloading, turn around time were the controlling factors of the shipping problem not the number of ships. . . .

6. The Secretary of Commerce [Jesse Jones] reported that exports in 1944 were $3 billion, imports $4 billion. These figures are exclusive of Lend-Lease, which ran to about $11 billion.

7. He also stated he was sending to the President a report by the Patent Committee which had been named by him. On this point, the Secretary of the Navy made the observation that there was need for establishment of a general government policy on treatment of patents which had evolved out of war work. . . .

["More about the so-called 'public life,' " runs the head of an entry of about this time. "When I was asked to make a short film for the Sixth War Loan Campaign Captain Markey [Gene Markey, then director of Navy Photographic Services] suggested that a certain amount of make-up was desirable. . . . I protested and said I would rather let nature take its course. He said that after I saw the picture in the raw and the heavy black beard which would be revealed thereby I would probably change my mind. I agreed but made the observation that the only real basic change it would have in my mind would be the conclusion to be out and stay out of public life when this present duty is over. In passing he remarked that it was a common practice with all our leaders, from the Prime Minister down to Mr. Willkie and Mr. Dewey." Forrestal's distaste for personal publicity or the meretricious gesture was as acute as his sense of the importance of public relations; his dislike of "public life" was as continuous as the devotion he gave to it.

III

["The nearer we come to vanquishing our enemies," President Roosevelt declared in his annual message on January 6, 1945, "the more we inevitably become conscious of differences

[among victors." The differences were by this time threatening to assume formidable proportions; the Russian armies were now deep in Poland, and the Soviet Union was making no secret of its purpose to seize effective control of all the former border states. Plans for the forthcoming "Big Three" conference, which was to grapple with this and other developing issues, were being publicly discussed; but American policy had not clearly gone much beyond the "unconditional surrender" demand that had been casually announced at the Casablanca press conference two years before. On January 10, Senator Arthur H. Vandenberg of Michigan, the most influential Republican voice on the Foreign Relations Committee, made a decisive speech.

Senator Vandenberg declared that he saw no reason why the United States should not "today" sign a "hard and fast treaty" among the major powers to keep Germany and Japan permanently disarmed—this was to remove Russia's only legitimate reason for appropriating the border states. He advocated a prompt adoption of the system of international order that had been outlined at the Dumbarton Oaks Conference in the preceding fall and called for firm statements to the Axis peoples that "the quicker they unconditionally surrender the cheaper will be unconditional surrender." Senator Vandenberg was largely seconded by his junior colleague, Senator Homer Ferguson. The administration's reaction—as soon as it had recovered from its surprise over this commitment to the new international structure from Republican leaders who in the past had been identified with isolationist views—was to invite a multi-partisan group of senators, including Vandenberg and eight others, to the White House next morning. Forrestal went later that day to the Cabinet meeting.

11 January 1945   *Cabinet*

1. *Foreign Affairs—Senate*: The President reported on what he considered to be a very favorable meeting with nine senators this morning on foreign affairs. He said that he took the occasion to point out that there could not be a sharp division between military and political matters and used our negotiations and relations with the British on *Overlord* [the Normandy

landing] and the Balkans as an example. Justice Byrnes and the Secretary of War [Stimson] took the occasion to say that they felt that Vandenberg's speech in the Senate yesterday was a highly statesmanlike speech and a very hopeful sign of intelligent Republican cooperation on foreign affairs. The Secretary of War pointed out that Senator Vandenberg's proposal for an interim organization to deal with political matters pending the final arrangement of peace was in line with some of Secretary Hull's proposals. The President added that he was considering calling a preliminary meeting of the United Nations sometime after "the Big Three" meeting, possibly in March. The Secretary of State [Stettinius] had suggested that this might be held somewhere in Midwest United States, possibly at French Lick. [A first intimation of San Francisco.] The President said he thought he might encounter some opposition to this from the British on the ground that all recent conferences of this character had been held in the United States and that it was now about London's turn. . . .

[A succession of ensuing entries shows the extent to which the problem of peace—which was more and more becoming a problem of peace with Russia—began to preoccupy the American leaders. Forrestal's most direct interest in the subject, as Secretary of the Navy, was to preserve the strategically vital Pacific island bases in the peace settlements as fulcra of American defensive strength. But his view was larger than that. Already thinking closely on world-power relationships—the subject of the V-12 course he had initiated and which he described in a letter[5] as "our course on politico-military-geographic pragmatism"—he was aware that a policy of "unconditional surrender" which would lead merely to the destruction of Germany and Japan would seriously unbalance the international system in the face of Soviet power. The subject arose in mid-January at the end of a meeting of the "State-War-Navy" Committee, the more or less regular gatherings of the three Secretaries of those Departments or their representatives.

---

[5] To Isaiah Bowman, 17 September 1944.

16 January 1944   *State-War-Navy Meeting*

1.   Principal discussion centered around our negotiations with Switzerland [over the continuing Swiss traffic with Germany]. . . . The Under Secretary of State, [Joseph C. Grew, former Ambassador to Japan] speaking for Mr. Stettinius who was absent, said that the State Department proposed to send negotiators who would trade on a *quid pro quo* basis. I interjected that the military were in accord with that with the qualification that we would like to be sure of getting the *quid* before we gave the *quo*. I said it came down to who did the negotiating, and Mr. Stimson supported me in this, saying that the State Department did not normally produce the type of negotiator who dealt in the vulgar language of being sure of what he got before he signed a document. I suggested that either Stanton Griffis, who did the negotiating with the Swedes on machine tools, or Harvey Gibson be sent over to do the job. Another possibility is Clarence Dillon, if he is physically able to do it. . . .

4.   There was some discussion of the Psychological Warfare Division of SHAEF with the suggestion that a sharp differentiation be made between the German government, the High Command and the Nazi Party in one bloc and the German people. I said it seemed to me clear that the American people would not support (a) mass murder of the Germans; (b) their enslavement; or (c) industrial devastation of the country. The Secretary of War concurred. I further said that in view of that it seemed to me it did not make sense to pay a penalty in terms of the lives of our soldiers on assumptions such as these that we knew would not prevail in the long run. The Secretary of War concurred; but it was agreed that the definition of the phrase "unconditional surrender" and the policy of trying to convey our view to the German people was necessarily a matter of high policy which would have to be developed at a forthcoming meeting.

5.   The Assistant Secretary of War [McCloy] raised the question of infiltration and sabotage in the N. E. I. [the Netherlands East Indies]—cf., into Indo-China—and the Under Secretary of State was asked by the Army to endeavor to secure a determination of policy from the President on this point.

19 January 1945   *Strategy*

Impression: The Army conception of strategy is conditioned mainly by the operations on land. They think in terms of maps, by terrain, contour, land distances. The impression I have is that they do not view the world from the same global standpoint as the Navy and therefore are not aware of the importance of distance, flanking positions, naval capabilities— and necessarily so, because that is not their profession—or of long communications lines by sea and the capabilities of the enemy to cut them. This was pointed up most sharply perhaps by the decision to attack Guadalcanal . . . a position which, both in terms of sea and air, lay athwart our lines to Australia and New Zealand. Through the insistence of the Navy we beat the Japs to it by a margin of about one week, and that decision, in my opinion, was one of the most decisive of the war. . . .

Unity of command: This phrase is an easy bromide, and its implementation has many and difficult aspects. For example: As of today Vice Admiral [Thomas C.] Kinkaid has in his forces under MacArthur six old battleships. Two of these need to be sent back for overhaul and repair. Nimitz made this suggestion but had to get MacArthur's agreement. Mac-Arthur desires to hold them and has so stated. In exercising his prerogatives of command if he insists on this order, he will in a sense be overstepping into the broad authority of Fleet Admiral Nimitz. The units MacArthur needs to accomplish his objectives . . . are obviously a thing of vital interest to him, but the determination of when ships need overhaul or may be necessary for other operations is obviously the interest of . . . Admiral Nimitz.

19 January 1945   *Cabinet*

7. *Postwar*: . . . The President asked what progress was being made on the over-all study of war plants—what should be kept in active use, what should be put under grease, and what disposition should be made of those that could not be used. . . . I told him that the Navy had initiated the study of its industrial plant over a year and a half ago and that we had

our inventory in good order and also a fairly good determination of what plants we wanted to retain and in what degree of operation. . . .

19 January 1945   *Cabinet*

Meetings During Absence of the President: As a sidelight on the Cabinet today was the President's observation that during his absence [he was soon to leave for the Yalta Conference] he was quite willing to have the Cabinet meet under the leadership of whoever was the ranking member at the time. In this connection he recalled that when President Wilson became ill in 1919, with the result that there was no Cabinet meeting for a period of a number of weeks, he became exceedingly angry when Robert Lansing, then Secretary of State, finally called a meeting because of his expressed doubt as to Mr. Wilson's competency to tend to business. The President said that he did not share that point of view and would be quite willing to have the Cabinet convene whenever anyone thought there was business to be dealt with.

20 January 1945   *Meeting with President Roosevelt*

I saw President Roosevelt today on general Navy Department business and talked, among other things, about his vacancy in the Assistant Secretaryship. He suggested the name of Edwin W. Pauley. I said that I knew Mr. Pauley only slightly and asked if Mr. Roosevelt knew him well enough to say to me that he was the proper man for the post. He did not answer directly but made the comment that Mr. Pauley had been the most energetic and successful fund-raiser of the Party. . . .

[Meanwhile, the preparations for the Yalta Conference were going forward. A day or two later Forrestal inserted in his diary a copy of a secret dispatch from General Deane in Moscow. It referred to a paper on Russian participation in the Japanese war, a paper which contained the recommendation that the President should press the Russians for an "agreement in principle" to the basing of American air forces in Siberia. The general reacted emphatically: "It has been my experience that an 'agreement in

[principle' means exactly nothing to the Russians. They are therefore generous in giving such agreements." The general wished
to urge that the President get an absolutely firm commitment admitting our bombers to Siberia on the Russian declaration of war.
Forrestal kept this bit of advice—advice that in much larger matters the Yalta conferees (Forrestal was not one of them) might
well have borne more clearly in mind.

Another document entered at this time was a long and
thoughtful memorandum which the Secretary of War, Mr. Stimson, prepared for the Secretary of State against the latter's departure for Yalta. Mr. Stimson had three main points to make.
He believed it essential first to set up a peace, understood and
firmly guaranteed by the four great powers, before launching the
general peace system; he thought it a mistake to attempt "to formulate the Dumbarton organization before we have discussed
and ironed out the realities which may exist to enable the four
powers to carry out their mission. . . . Any attempt to finally organize a Dumbarton organization will necessarily take place in
an atmosphere of unreality until these preliminary foundations
are established." Secondly, he thought that the Pacific island
bases could not properly be regarded as colonies; they were
rather "defense posts" necessary to the big power responsible for
the security of the area, and their disposition, along with that of
other strategic frontiers and territorial acquisitions, should be settled by the big powers in advance instead of through the proposed trusteeship mechanism of Dumbarton Oaks. "You will get
into needless mazes if you try to set up a form of trusteeship
which will include them before the necessity of their acquisition
by the United States is established and recognized." In the third
place, he foresaw that Russia would be difficult; she would claim,
on the grounds of her own security and her responsibilities as
guarantor of the peace, a control over such buffer states as Poland, Bulgaria and Rumania quite incompatible with their independence. Mr. Stimson thought that these underlying issues
should be threshed out and if possible settled before proceeding
with the world organization.

"For all these reasons," he wrote, "I think we should not put
the cart before the horse. We should by thorough discussion be-

[tween the three or four great powers endeavor to settle, so far as we can, an accord upon the general area of these fundamental problems. . . . If there is a general understanding reached among the larger powers I do not fear any lack of enthusiasm on the part of the lesser fry." Mr. Stimson, however, in a way weakened his own suggestion by emphasizing at the end that questions of Pacific trusteeships or "any territorial questions at all" had best not be raised until the Russians had "clearly committed them-selves" to the war against Japan. No doubt there was at Yalta an earnest effort to follow the lines of his advice. Yet in the result the cart came out ahead of the horse after all.

It is characteristic of Forrestal that this entry is followed by a long unsigned memorandum on the Dumbarton Oaks trusteeship proposals and by an even longer study, also unsigned, of "Russia's Postwar Foreign Policy," analyzing in great detail the lines it could be expected to follow throughout the world. The whole in-terrelated problem of peace and the Soviet Union was growing serious; and the jocose proposal to solve one aspect of it by mak-ing Mr. Ickes King of Polynesia [6] was no more than a passing pleasantry on an increasingly ominous stage.

Franklin Roosevelt was inaugurated for the fourth time on January 20, the day Forrestal had talked with him about the Pauley appointment. Next day the first contingents for Yalta be-gan to take off; the conference met on February 3 and lasted un-til the 12th. Early on the morning of February 12, Pacific time, Forrestal was landing at John Rodgers Field, Pearl Harbor, on an inspection trip through the Pacific. The Marines were to storm the ashy beaches of Iwo Jima a week later, and Forrestal wanted to be there when they did so. He flew by way of Eni-wetok and Saipan; there he boarded Vice Admiral Richmond Kelly Turner's command ship, U. S. S. *Eldorado*, and so arrived off Iwo at 0600, East Longitude Time, on the fateful Monday morning, February 19.

Forrestal was not a vivid descriptive writer, and his diary notes on this, the first appearance of a civilian Secretary of the Navy on the front line of overseas battle action, hardly do justice to the occasion. It was not until the ensuing Friday, February 23, that

[6] See p. 21.

[he managed to get ashore; his account is terse, but it is at least strikingly typical of the man.

Friday, 23 February 1945 (K-time)

Went aboard PCS 1403 (Lt. Cherry in command); closed the shoreline of Iwo Jima and went ashore in a Higgins boat about 1030. On the way in we saw the American Flag being raised by the Marines who had scaled the heights of the Suribachi volcano. Went ashore at Red Beach. Saw the Marine engineers at work and looked into a number of Japanese pillboxes and dugouts, from some of which they were still extracting Japanese snipers. This beach received some shelling during the morning but it was not considerable, although one burst did inflict casualties an hour before we were there.

The strongest impressions were:

1. The difficulty of getting traction in the very loose volcanic ash. . . .

2. The concealment of the Japanese gun positions, their snipers and their command posts. . . .

3. The speed with which transit over the beach had been organized in spite of difficult landing conditions. . . .

[There were no heroics, in spite of the shelling that had caused casualties an hour before. The mentions were for others —Lieutenant Cherry, the Marine engineers, the men on Suribachi. The "impressions" were severely technical. The whole tone recalls a letter he had written the year before:[7] "One reason I don't like honors is that even if they haven't been earned one has to work harder in order to justify the award; and also—and I think there is no hypocrisy in this—I honestly feel that the only ones who really deserve honors in this war are the boys whose only honor will be a quiet grave a long way from home."

Forrestal left the scene the same day in a destroyer, going by way of Guam—where he talked with Fleet Admiral Chester A. Nimitz and other high commanders and tried to improve the press coverage for the Navy's activities—and then flew on to Tacloban Field on Leyte in the Philippines. After visiting naval instal-

[7] To Dean E. S. Wells Kerr, Phillips Exeter Academy, 26 June 1944.

[lations and talking with commanders in that area he went on to MacArthur's headquarters in Manila, where Japanese resistance had ended only five days before.

Wednesday, 28 February 1945

. . . On the . . . question of the war against Japan and our objectives vis-à-vis Japan afterward, he [MacArthur] expressed the view that the help of the Chinese would be negligible. He felt that we should secure the commitment of the Russians to active and vigorous prosecution of a campaign against the Japanese in Manchukuo of such proportions as to pin down a very large part of the Japanese army; that once this campaign was engaged we should then launch an attack on the home islands, giving, as he expressed it, the *coup de main* from the rear while substantial portions of the military power of Japan were engaged on the mainland of Asia.

. . . He said he felt that our strength should be reserved for use in the Japanese mainland, on the plain of Tokyo, and that this could not be done without the assurance that the Japanese would be heavily engaged by the Russians in Manchuria. He expressed doubt that the use of anything less than sixty divisions by the Russians would be sufficient. He saw little chance that the Russians could get an additional thirty divisions activated in Manchuria in less than six months' time. He said he had seen the lists of materials asked for by the Russians and that they did not comprise what would be required for an army of the size indicated. . . .

His conversation indicated a fear that the Russian plan would be to try to persuade us into a campaign on the mainland of China which would be more costly than on the home islands, and at the end of which Stalin could increase his prestige in Asia by pointing out that he had to come in and assure the victory. . . .

[Forrestal added no comment of his own to this, but he brought away certain impressions bearing on the now urgent question of command for the next stage of Pacific operations. In Washington ten days later he made another entry.

In a conversation I had today with Admiral [William D.] Leahy we talked about the future of the Pacific command. He asked me my view about MacArthur. I told him that I thought MacArthur had a high degree of professional ability, mortgaged, however, to his sensitivity and his vanity. I said I thought if it were possible for him [MacArthur] to have a conversation with Nimitz in the same manner in which Admiral Leahy and I were now talking these two men could evolve the framework for command on the basis of Nimitz's thought, namely: The Navy to run the fleet, the Army to conduct the operations when land masses are reached. I said I was reluctant to make any positive recommendation because I was aware of all the many considerations entering into the decision—the quasi-political factors that enter into the decision, the desirability of continuing to utilize MacArthur's services and, balanced against these considerations, the great desirability of having somebody who would cooperate with his heart as well as his head with all other elements necessary to the final assault on Japan.

I said it seemed to me that the matter of the 21st Bomber Command [these were the long-range B-29 strategic bombers, operating against Japan from the Mariana bases under the independent control of the Army Air Force] should be clearly settled, that they were now operating almost entirely on their own without reference to any other military efforts in the Pacific, and it seemed obvious to me that they should be brought into the pattern if full advantage was to be taken of their capabilities. . . .

[Forrestal returned to Washington on the morning of March 4. In the diary under that date there stands a somewhat cryptic memorandum:

Specifications for a Presidential Candidate
1. Looks.
2. Height.
3. Legal or political background.

4. Desire for the job.
5. Political experience.

Of whom or of what he was thinking he did not explain.

IV

[At Forrestal's first Cabinet after his return the atmosphere of confident optimism in which Mr. Roosevelt and his entourage had winged their way back from Yalta had evidently not yet been dissipated. The President enlarged upon his ideas concerning the trusteeship matter, over which the Secretary of the Navy was growing increasingly dubious.

9 March 1945   Cabinet

2. The President made some observations about his conception of the trusteeship idea as applied to territory taken from the enemy, with particular reference to the Pacific Ocean Areas. He said that his idea, which he advanced to Stalin and Churchill, was based on the concept of what he called multiple sovereignty—that is, sovereignty would be vested in all of the United Nations, for example, of the Pacific islands, but that we would be requested by them to exercise complete trusteeship for the purpose of world security. He further said that the Australians had advanced the thesis that they would take by direct acquisition everything south of the equator, leaving to us those islands north of that line. This he said was unacceptable. I said there were a number of places that we ought to have for our naval security—Kwajalein, the Marianas, Truk, etc. He also included Manus in this category and said that he would even be inclined to have military rights on Nouméa while leaving to the French the economic accruals from New Caledonia. The Secretary of War expressed the hope that if the trusteeship idea was adopted the basis of our exercise of powers under it would be very clearly stated so that there could be no misunderstandings in the future. . . .

6. The Secretary of Labor [Frances Perkins] reported on the International Trade Union Conference in London. She said this had evolved into more or less of a clash between the Eng-

lish and Russian delegates. The Russians, she said, comprised members of the intelligentsia who had had training in technical industries (some of them having lived five or six years in the United States) and that they seemed to speak with the sanction of their government. The Russians, according to the American delegates, Mr. [James B.] Carey and Mr. R. J. Thomas, were extremely cordial in their relations with the Americans. She said that one principal theme of discussion in the meeting was the enunciation of a principle that labor in every country had in its hands the power to make war and peace, and that it proposed to use this power in the future. The means of such use were not specified. . . .

7. The head of the War Production Board [Krug] wished to warn the President and the Cabinet that we were fairly close to the limit of production, that we had reached the point where additions to the military programs were beginning to impinge upon and hurt broad segments of our economy which were directly contributory to the war effort. He mentioned specifically matters of work gloves, overalls, shoes and some other matters. . . . He said the problem would become worse as we went into the full peak of the war against Japan, because of the lengthening of the pipeline. For example, in Burma he said there was a six months' supply in the area, there was about one year's supply of various items in the pipeline, and about a three months' stockpile back here. . . . We were faced with the possibility of an almost disastrous situation at the end of the war in handling tremendous amounts of surplus materials of which we would be long—in the theaters of war themselves, in the pipeline, and in the reserves back home—when the war ended. . . .

[Forrestal discussed the matter of bases next day with Admiral King, the Chief of Naval Operations, getting a more precise statement of what the Navy believed would have to be retained. To his entry on this conversation he added a note: "Question to Admiral King: At Cabinet on Friday Paul McNutt [Federal Security Administrator] and Mr. Wallace [then Secretary of Commerce] raised the question of Borneo, Malaya, N. E. I. in general, McNutt saying that if we didn't make some provision for them

[we would have to face the crop of dragon's teeth which he thought were in process of being sown there now."

Dragon's teeth were being sown in many places. But at the next meeting of the three Secretaries, Mr. Stettinius was still cheerfully confident of the results attained at Yalta, as well as at the Inter-American Conference on Problems of War and Peace at Mexico City, which he had attended on his way home.

13 March 1945 *State-War-Navy*

The Secretary of State: A most successful meeting at Yalta, particularly in his opinion as regards Russian-American relationship. Every evidence, he said, of the Russian desire to cooperate along all lines with U. S. . . .

Russians not particularly interested in having the French occupy a part of Germany. Expressed general lack of interest in De Gaulle, and, for that matter, in the Generalissmo [Chiang Kai-shek].

Stalin-Molotov stated unequivocally arrangements should be made by England, Russia and the United States so long as the war is on.

The Prime Minister [Churchill] seems to be going through some sort of a menopause; he talked with great eloquence in meetings but did not follow up in subsequent sessions where substantive matters were dealt with with the same vigor. . . .

At Mexico City he felt there was a satisfactory outcome, particularly as regards the Argentine. Peru, Colombia, Uruguay and Chile made a *démarche* shortly after the session opened, in behalf of the Argentine. He responded by saying the United States would have to withdraw from the meetings if they insisted. He said that he was willing to admit them [the Argentines] provided they would immediately declare war against Japan and Germany. That was transmitted to Perón, who rejected it categorically. As a result of this the powers who were acting in behalf of the Argentine changed their view completely and expressed the greatest indignation at the truculent and uncompromising character of Perón's reply. [Perón declared war before March was out.]

The Secretary of War: He raised the question as to the reparations in kind [from Germany] in the form of labor. He said he understood that it was the Russian desire to have these people in a P. O. W. status and he pointed out that this would mean the burden of feeding them would fall on us and that they would have to be fed in accordance with the terms of the Geneva Convention.

He repeated his concern about the trusteeships concept and told the Secretary of State he thought he would in due course have to get rid of the gentleman in his Department who was the sponsor of this idea. The Secretary of State agreed, said he had discussed this matter last night with Mr. Hull.

[In spite of Mr. Stettinius's glowing report, Forrestal would seem to have had his doubts, for on the following day he entered in his diary an "example of the increasing difficulty of keeping unity of action and thought among the Allies as the victory comes in sight." This referred to an apparent feeler looking toward surrender put out by the German army in Italy, which the Western Allies had left to the Anglo-American command on the ground. When the Russians heard about it they reacted in a high state of indignation over the fact that they had not been fully consulted beforehand. Forrestal thought they were raising "a complete tempest in a teapot," but he noted Averell Harriman's warning that the issue should be met "straightly" now, as otherwise the West would be faced with a repetition of such episodes, predicated on the Russian belief that "we needed them so much that they could get by with anything."

It seems that the British may have been having their doubts as well. Forrestal was not present at the next Cabinet, but he preserved the notes which H. Struve Hensel, Assistant Secretary of the Navy, took for him. The first ran:

16 March 1945   *Cabinet*
Memorandum for Mr. Forrestal
1. *British Relations*: The President indicated considerable difficulty with British relations. In a semi-jocular manner of speaking, he stated that the British were perfectly willing for the United States to have a war with Russia at any time and

that, in his opinion, to follow the British program would be to proceed toward that end.

[Mr. Hensel's notes do not make clear what the President meant by the "British program," though the jocularity indicates that the President was yet to be undeceived as to his success with the masters of the Kremlin. Forrestal's interests for the moment were closer at home. There is a note of March 18 showing that the Navy was seriously concerned over "the possibility of a Japanese carrier strike at San Francisco on the occasion of the United Nations Conference." There was no concrete evidence of such an attempt, but some of the planners thought it so likely that Admirals King, Nimitz and Ingersoll (commander of the Western Seas Frontier) set up elaborate plans for interception, to be executed only if some positive intelligence should come.

29 March 1945   *Combined Intelligence*

Admiral King made the remark today, when I asked him what he thought about a single agency of the government for the collection of intelligence, both internal and external, that he thought this, while it sounded logical, had elements of danger. He pointed out that over a long period of time such an agency might acquire power beyond anything which had been intended for it; that that power, once acquired, might be hard to take away. He questioned whether such an agency could be considered consistent with our ideas of government.

30 March 1945   *Trusteeships*

I met with the Secretary of War and the Assistant Secretary, Mr. McCloy, in the former's office. Mr. Stimson expressed great concern over the trend of thinking as regards the trusteeship discussion at San Francisco. He said he was fearful . . . that we might be tempted into making quixotic gestures the net result of which might be that we would surrender the hardly won islands which we had taken in the Pacific to the principle of trusteeship, whereas the British, Dutch and French would not.

He proposed that he and myself write a letter to the State
Department which would recite the fact that:

(a) These islands were of primary importance not merely to
the security of the United States but of the world, and essential to the success of any world security organization.

(b) That we propose not only to keep them but to exercise
our ownership as a trust on behalf of world security, not for
any national advantage. . . .

[The question was raised at the next meeting of the three Secretaries on April 2. Mr. Stimson read drafts of letters he had prepared for the three of them to send to the President. "The net result of the considerable time of discussion" was that they should
try to get postponement of the whole subject of trusteeships at
the San Francisco Conference and that they should also draft a
public statement, to be made either by the President or the
Secretary of State, to the effect that the United States intended
to keep the islands but "only for the continued insurance of
peace and equity and liberty for all nations and peoples" adjacent
to the Pacific. State was now wholly in agreement with this
course, for which the Army and Navy had been pressing. But
when they met again a week later Mr. Stettinius balked. "He
said," according to a diary note of April 9, "that he did not propose to associate himself with the document which . . . it had
been proposed the three Secretaries should sign. He said . . .
that he proposed to let the document go as a statement by War
and Navy, informing the President that he reserved judgment. I
asked him why he didn't want to go with us on this recommendation and he said that while his private views accorded with ours,
he was under orders to the contrary."

But the April 2 meeting had opened with an item more important than the trusteeship question. It was here that Forrestal
learned that the Yalta honeymoon was over.

2 April 1945   *State-War-Navy Meeting*

. . . The Secretary of State advised of serious deterioration
in our relations with Russia. The President has sent a strong
message to Stalin deploring this condition which he points out

is brought to a focus by the request to have the Lublin Poles invited to San Francisco. He recites the fact that the ties between Russia and this country, knit together by the necessities of war, are in grave danger of dissolution and asks the most serious consideration by the Marshal of the questions involved. . . .

[It is apparent that Forrestal was put at once upon the alert. The next thirty-odd pages of his diary are mainly occupied by copies of the telegrams in which Averell Harriman, from the Moscow Embassy, analyzed Russian policy—with what today seems a rather striking prescience—for the State Department. On April 4 Harriman was cabling that "we now have ample proof that the Soviet government views all matters from the standpoint of their own selfish interests. They have publicized to their own political advantage the difficult food situation in areas liberated by our troops, such as in France, Belgium and Italy, comparing it with the allegedly satisfactory conditions in areas which the Red Army has liberated. . . . The Communist Party or its associates everywhere are using economic difficulties in areas under our responsibilities to promote Soviet concepts and policies and to undermine the influence of the Western Allies. . . . Unless we and the British now adopt an independent line the people under the areas of our responsibility will suffer and the chances of Soviet domination in Europe will be enhanced. I thus regretfully come to the conclusion that we should be guided . . . by the policy of taking care of our Western Allies and other areas under our responsibility first, allocating to Russia what may be left." Harriman already had a prevision of the Marshall Plan when he went on to suggest that "we should, through such economic aid as we can give to our Western Allies, including Greece as well as Italy, re-establish a reasonable life for the people of these countries who have the same general outlook as we have on life and the development of the world. The Soviet Union and the minority governments that the Soviets are forcing on the people of Eastern Europe have an entirely different objective. We must clearly realize that the Soviet program is the establishment of totalitarianism, ending personal liberty and democracy as we know and

[respect it." Since, he went on, the United States could not med-
dle by such methods in the internal affairs of other countries,
"our only hope of supporting" the anti-totalitarian peoples "is to
assist them to attain economic stability as soon as possible."
Harriman stressed the immense economic resources, not a few derived from Lend-Lease and from other aid which they might get
from us, with which the Soviet Union would be left at the end of
the war. "The only hope," he wrote, "of stopping Soviet penetration is the development of sound economic conditions" in the
threatened countries. "I therefore recommend that we face the
realities of the situation and orient our foreign economic policies
accordingly." He urged friendship toward the Soviet Union, but
"always on a *quid pro quo* basis."

On April 6 Harriman was cabling again, in general advocating
a "tough" policy with Russia as the one possible way of maintaining a soundly friendly relationship with her. He included a
shrewd comment on the high hopes of Yalta (scarcely more than
six weeks old): "It may be difficult for us to believe, but it still
may be true that Stalin and Molotov considered at Yalta that by
our willingness to accept a general wording of the declaration on
Poland and liberated Europe, by our recognition of the need of
the Red Army for security behind its lines, and of the predominant interest of Russia in Poland as a friendly neighbor and as a
corridor to Germany, we understood and were ready to accept
Soviet policies already known to us." He had, he said, evidence
that the continued "generous and considerate attitude" adopted
by the United States was regarded in Russia only as a sign of
weakness. "In the compass of this message," he added, "I cannot
list the almost daily affronts and total disregard which the Soviets evince in matters of interest to us." Harriman urged effective reprisals, selecting "one or two cases where their actions are
intolerable and make them realize that they cannot continue
their present attitude except at great cost to themselves." He
recognized the dangers in such a course but thought that the
Russians would ultimately come around.

Again on April 6 Harriman cabled about the problem of
Russian reparations claims on Germany. At this time the German
surrender was still a month away, but Harriman declared that "we

[have no reason to doubt that the Russians are already busily removing from Germany without compunction anything (repeat anything) which they find it to their advantage to remove." This he thought not particularly reprehensible but a sign that it would be a long time before the achievement of any firm agreement with the Russians on reparations and restitutions.

Forrestal entered another Harriman telegram discussing Russian infiltration in Brazil, and still another, dated April 11, on the question of dollar credits for the Kremlin. Harriman described the "enormous plans" for Russian industrial expansion, intended to triple steel production capacity and to run apparently for fifteen or twenty years. Harriman estimated that the Russians probably wanted about $6 billion in credit from the United States to make a start on these vast projects, but he dropped the question as to whether "our basic interest might better be served by increasing our trade with other parts of the world rather than giving preference to the Soviet Union as a source of supply." He thought also that we should consider the conservation of our own natural resources. At all events, "our experience has incontrovertibly proved that it is not possible to bank general good will in Moscow and I agree with the Department that we should retain current control of these credits in order to be in a position to protect American vital interests in the formulative period immediately following the war."

The skies were darkening. And a luncheon gathering on April 9 seems to have been less than optimistic.

9 April 1945   *World Peace*
I had lunch today with Admiral King, Vice Admiral [Russell] Willson and John Foster Dulles.

Dulles indicated great misgivings as to whether the hopes of the nation for an international peace organization flowing out of Dumbarton Oaks and San Francisco might not be raised to too great heights. He said that these questions of a viable machinery for world peace are questions that have been perplexing the minds of statesmen for centuries and that it was unwise, he thought, to assume they would be settled now over night. He said that his own preference was to start for the ideal but

to have a foundation of hard reality; in other words, that the
holding of meetings between the three nations that now exercise power—Russia, Britain and America—was highly desirable; that these three could, so to speak, provide the umbrella
under which the other nations of the world could come in and
between all hands try to work out a lasting peace.

Admiral King also was dubious about the speed with which
we were reaching assumptions that permanent peace could be
arrived at speedily.

Mr. Dulles expressed doubt that it was wise to permit all of
the small nations to express their opinions on all matters of international relationships. I asked, for example, whether we
should be required to consult Honduras or Nicaragua on a
question which concerned our own security. He said the obvious
results of such an arrangement were to invite politics playing
between such small nations and possibly one of the large nations
that did not see eye to eye with its associates. . . .

[None on the higher levels in Washington could have looked
    into the future in those April days without uneasiness. And then,
    three days after this luncheon, there came a memorable Cabinet.

12 April 1945   Cabinet

I was with the Secretary of State, Stettinius, and the Attorney General at 5:45 p.m. when a message came for Mr.
Stettinius to go immediately to the White House. At 5:50 p.m.
I received a message on the telephone asking Attorney General Biddle and myself to go to the White House.

The Secretary of State returned at ten minutes to six and
said that the President had just died.

We went to the Cabinet room of the White House where
there were gathered the Vice President, Secretary Wallace, Secretary Stimson, Secretary Morgenthau, Secretary Perkins, Secretary Wickard, Secretary Ickes, Leo Crowley and "Cap" Krug.

At 6:10 p.m. the Vice President called the Cabinet to order
and said: "It is my sad duty to report that the President died
[at] 5:48. Mrs. Roosevelt gave me this news, and in saying so
she remarked that 'he died like a soldier.' I shall only say that

I will try to carry on as I know he would have wanted me and all of us to do. I should like all of you to remain in your Cabinet posts and I shall count on you for all the help I can get. In this action I am sure I am following out what the President would have wished. . . ."

The Vice President had said he would like to have the Chief Justice swear him in. Mrs. Truman and Truman's daughter arrived about 6:30. The Chief Justice [Harlan F. Stone] came in a few minutes afterward.

At 6:45 the Chief Justice administered the oath of office to the Vice President, and he became the President of the United States.

Mr. Truman responded to the oath firmly and clearly. His only active omission was a failure to raise his right hand when he was repeating the oath with his left hand on the Bible. The Chief Justice had to indicate to him that he should raise his hand—under the circumstances it gave dignity and firmness.

CHAPTER II

The Final Months of War

I

[The issue over the Pacific islands had to be thrashed out, and
Forrestal had a talk about it with Stimson on the 14th, the day
the late President's funeral cortège arrived in Washington. While
Forrestal was at Hyde Park next day for the final ceremonies
there was a conference of State, War and Navy representatives;
the three Secretaries were themselves present at another conference on the 16th and at a final conference next morning with the
American Delegation which had been appointed to San Francisco
and with a long list of State, War and Navy advisers. It seems unnecessary to rehearse the details of what was actually more an
issue of method than of substance. No one wished to give away
the Pacific bases. Stimson and Forrestal wanted to postpone any
discussion of the trusteeship question at San Francisco and secure an authoritative public statement that the United States intended to retain full control of all points necessary for the preservation of future peace in the Pacific. The State Department rejected both ideas as untimely, but agreed to a directive which
made it clear that while the general question of a trusteeship system might be raised at San Francisco there was to be no discussion of trusteeing any particular areas, and that any general system should include provisions permitting the maintenance of full
American military and strategic rights at appropriate points.
So it was settled, and so, in effect, the policy was carried out at
San Francisco and later. But the discussions evoked a character-

[istic expression of Forrestal's underlying philosophy. When he was asked to state the Navy position, he made several points:

17 April 1945   *Trusteeships*

1. Both the Army and Navy are aware that they are not makers of policy but they have a responsibility to define to the makers of policy what they believe are the military necessities of the United States, both for its own defense and for the implementation of its responsibility for maintenance of world peace. . . .

2. I take it as a premise about all discussions of world peace that the United States is to have the major responsibility for the Pacific Ocean security, and if this premise is accepted there flows from it the acceptance of the fact that the United States must have the means with which to implement its responsibilities. . . .

5. I closed by re-emphasizing the fact that retention of power by the United States was not inconsistent with the work on and the hopes for a world peace organization—that those that hate war must have the power to prevent it.

[The last was a postulate Forrestal never abandoned. In the meanwhile, however, there were two wars still to be won. The problem of command for the final campaign in the Pacific—a problem the difficulties of which Forrestal had sensed on his trip in February—was acute. In mid-April there was a formal conference at Guam, almost on the level of international diplomacy, between delegates from the Southwest Pacific Area (MacArthur) and representatives of Pacific Ocean Areas (Nimitz), in which MacArthur's people sought to secure command over all land and air forces in the Pacific, relegating to the Navy the minor role of purely naval support. "Since these ideas," Nimitz tartly reported to King, "were consuming valuable time and delaying constructive planning," he finally authorized his representative to lay down the law on what the admiral would and would not surrender to the general. The Southwest Pacific delegation appears to have retired in discomfiture; "very little useful discussion," Nimitz reported, "has taken place concerning invasion

[plans and preparations, and the SWPA party was apparently not prepared for such discussion." As an "interesting sidelight" he added that General Richard K. Sutherland, MacArthur's Chief of Staff, "says MacArthur will land in Kyushu about D + 3, stay a short time and then return to Manila until time for the Honshu landing." It was a method of command which MacArthur was in fact to adopt years later in the Korean War. At the time, Forrestal had Nimitz's reports copied into his diary; and in the end neither the Kyushu nor the Honshu landing was to prove necessary.

There were other pressing issues before him, and at a meeting with the new President on the afternoon of April 18 he was able to take up several of the broader problems of policy which he knew were lying ahead.

18 April 1945   *President Truman*

At three o'clock Admiral King and I again visited with the President. I made the following recommendations:

1.   That he permit us to proceed with the *reorganization of the Navy* on a staff basis with particular attention to the management and handling of the Navy's industrial establishment— Navy Yards, Ordnance Plants, etc. Approved.

2.   *President's Yacht*: I suggested that he have one of the yachts fitted up for his own use. Admiral King offered the *Dauntless* and it was so agreed.

3.   *Universal Military Training*: The President expressed his approval but said he wanted to give the matter some further study before deciding on the form of his endorsement.

4.   *Postwar Navy*: I said that whenever he had the opportunity we had available about a twenty-five-minute presentation of a preliminary plan for the size of the postwar Navy. He expressed interest and said he would like to see it.

5.   *Pearl Harbor*: I told him that I had got Admiral [H. Kent] Hewitt back to pursue the investigation into the Pearl Harbor disaster. . . . I felt I had an obligation to Congress to continue the investigation because I was not completely satisfied with the report my own Court had made. . . .

6.   *Single Department of Defense*: I made the suggestion

that he reread the Morrow Board Report with the thought that this form might be followed in the study of the desirability of consolidating the two Services.

[This conversation on April 18 was the beginning, as it were, of much subsequent history. But in the spring and summer of 1945 it was the underlying issues of world peace and world power, of the terms used toward our collapsing enemies and of the relations with our difficult Soviet Ally, which occupied the major space in Forrestal's diary.

17 April 1945   *Anglo-American Relations*

Dinner with Lord Halifax [the British Ambassador], General Marshall, Anthony Eden [the British Foreign Minister], Will Clayton [Assistant Secretary of State for Economic Affairs], Mr. Llewellyn and Anthony Eden's Secretaries, Mr. Millard and Mr. Dixon.

Eden expressed some satisfaction that Molotov was coming to San Francisco, although thought it would be a lot better if Stalin himself would come. He said there was a strong possibility of a general election in England before midsummer, but seemed to feel if there were there would be a return of the Conservative Party or a Conservative-Labour Coalition again. [Mr. Eden was wrong in that.] He said Mr. Churchill was in good form but felt very badly about not coming to our President's funeral, but had refrained from doing so because of the feeling it might have embarrassed President Truman.

20 April 1945   *Russia*

I saw Averell Harriman, the American Ambassador to Russia, last night. He stated his strong apprehensions as to the future of our relations with Russia unless our entire attitude toward them became characterized by much greater firmness. He said that, using the fear of Germany as a stalking horse, they would continue on their program of setting up states around their borders which would follow the same ideology as the Russians. He said the outward thrust of Communism was not dead and that we might well have to face an ideological warfare just as vigorous and dangerous as Fascism or Nazism.

20 April 1945   *Cabinet*

. . . The Secretary of War reported that Mr. McCloy had just returned from Europe where he found conditions of chaos and in some cases of near anarchy in Germany; that we would be faced with most intensive and complicated problems after the termination of hostilities. . . .

21 April 1945   *Russia*

Anthony Eden dined with Admiral Leahy and me tonight. He was quite gloomy about the Russians. He ascribed most of the difficulty to Molotov's intransigence. He believed that Molotov did not completely inform Stalin and that when he did talk to him he talked with prejudice toward the British and the United States. He expressed the belief that the chief pivot of Russian policy today was an effort to drive a wedge between England and the United States. . . .

Speaking of the general European situation and the American attitude toward it, responding to an observation that I made about the accomplishments of Metternich after the defeat of Napoleon (I said I had come of late years to have a much clearer appreciation of what Metternich had been able to accomplish), he said that he thought there was an analogy between the position of England and Austria after 1815 and the position of England and the United States now; the United States has taken the place of England and England has taken the place of Austria. After the Napoleonic explosions Metternich was always trying to persuade England that [she] was necessarily involved in European politics, whereas England and English statesmen, very much like our own in the past twenty-five years, wanted to stay out of continental politics but found it impossible to do so.

[Two days later there was a critical meeting.

23 April 1945   *Russia*

The President called a meeting at the White House at two o'clock.

Present: Secretary of State, Secretary of War, Secretary of the Navy, Admiral King, General Marshall, Admiral Leahy, Ambassador Harriman; Major General Deane, Military Observer for the Joint Chiefs of Staff; C. E. Bohlen and Assistant Secretary of State [James C.] Dunn.

The Secretary of State made the announcement that discussions with Molotov which had begun favorably yesterday had developed today most unsatisfactorily. He said that the Russians had receded from their agreement at Yalta with President Roosevelt on the Polish question. He [Molotov] continued to insist on a seat for the Lublin government, which they have recognized as the government of Poland, at San Francisco. In his [Stettinius's] view this was directly contrary to the Yalta understanding that Russia would join Great Britain and the United States in sponsoring and encouraging an entirely free and democratic election in Poland. He said that completely reliable State Department information was to the effect that the Lublin government *did not in any way represent the Polish people*—that any free election would be certain to compel inclusion in the government of people like Premier Mikolajczyk and others of the Polish government in exile.

The President asked the opinion and advice of those present. The Secretary of War said that it was such a newly posed question so far as he was concerned he found great difficulty in making positive recommendations but he did feel that we had to remember that the Russian conception of freedom, democracy and independent voting was quite different from ours or the British and that he hoped we would go slowly and avoid any open break. He said that the Russians had carried out their military engagements quite faithfully and was sorry to see this one incident project a breach between the two countries.

I gave it as my view that this was not an isolated incident but was one of a pattern of unilateral action on the part of Russia, that they had taken similar positions vis-à-vis Bulgaria, Rumania, Turkey and Greece, and that I thought we might as well meet the issue now as later on.

Ambassador Harriman expressed somewhat the same views. Admiral Leahy took the view, on the other hand, more or less the same as that of the Secretary of War, saying he hoped the matter could be put to the Russians in such a way as not to close the door to subsequent accommodation.

The President said that he was seeing Molotov within the hour and that he proposed to put it to him quite bluntly that . . . the San Francisco Conference would go on whether the Russians attended or not and that he would like Molotov to transmit to Stalin his (the President's) question as to whether or not this meant that Russia did not propose to depart from their expressions of cooperation at Yalta. He said that if one part of the agreements which they had entered with President Roosevelt at Yalta were breached he (the President) would consider that the entire Yalta agreement was no longer binding on any of the parties interested.

[In this first serious crisis of policy the new President was reacting with a striking firmness and vigor, which he was to show on more than one subsequent occasion. Mr. Bohlen, then a Special Assistant to the Secretary of State, took more extended notes of the discussion (Forrestal later entered a copy in his diary), which put the President's attitude even more strongly: "The President said . . . that he felt our agreements with the Soviet Union so far had been a one-way street and that he could not continue; it was now or never. He intended to go on with the plans for San Francisco and if the Russians did not wish to join us they could go to hell. . . ."

Some of the other views, as Mr. Bohlen noted them, are interesting. "Mr. Forrestal said . . . he had felt that for some time the Russians had considered that we would not object if they took over all of Eastern Europe into their power. He said it was his profound conviction that if the Russians were to be rigid in their attitude we had better have a showdown with them now than later. . . . Mr. Stimson observed that we would like to know how far the Russian reaction to a strong position on Poland would go. He said he thought that the Russians perhaps were being more realistic than we were in regard to their own security." The comment of Admiral Leahy, who had taken part in the Crimean Conference, comes a little unexpectedly against the general optimism with which the other American participants

[regarded their work: "Admiral Leahy said that he had left Yalta
with the impression that the Soviet government had no intention
of permitting a free government to operate in Poland, and that
he would have been surprised had the Soviet government be-
haved any differently than it had." He thought the agreements
were susceptible to "two interpretations"—Mr. Stettinius, reading
the text, denied this—and that a break would be serious, but that
"we should tell them that we stood for a free and independent
Poland."

General Marshall was even more cautious and brought up
what was undoubtedly in all their minds. He said he "hoped for
Soviet participation in the war against Japan at a time when it
would be useful to us. The Russians had it within their power to
delay their entry into the Far Eastern war until we had done all
the dirty work," and he was inclined to agree that it would be a
serious matter to risk a break. In the end, the President accepted
that risk; he called for a draft of a statement to Stalin which he
could hand to Molotov that evening. The strong view prevailed,
and momentarily at least it worked, as it kept the question of Poland's future open and brought the Russians to San Francisco
without the Lublin Poles. Forrestal's advice had lain closer to the
actualities than the caution of Stimson or the military officers;
but it must be recognized that in the spring of 1945 the importance of bringing Russia into Manchuria in massive force loomed
far larger than it was to do in much later retrospect.

Two days later the end had come in Europe.

25 April 1945   German Surrender

Admiral King came in at 3:45. He said that he had been at
the Pentagon since two o'clock. The President had been talking
over the telephone with the Prime Minister.

Hitler has had a cerebral hemorrhage and Himmler, speaking for the German nation, has offered to the Allies the surrender of all German armies on the Western Front. . . .

[The Nazi world was going down in utter ruin and suicide. But
even in those days of crashing victory in Europe, Forrestal's mind
was turning to the remaining problem. He had not liked the

[Morgenthau Plan for Germany, and he liked even less the prospect of the application of its principles to Japan.

1 May 1945   *State-War-Navy*

. . . There was some talk about Europe and the question of food. I asked the Secretary of War whether he thought Mr. Hoover could be useful. He said he had the same thing in mind. . . . My only reservation was whether Mr. Hoover would be a man that one could work with easily and flexibly— in other words, whether we might not find his *amour-propre* creating difficulties rather than resolving them. Mr. Stimson agreed there was this possibility, and I suggested that he canvass it in his mind before we make a proposal to the President about his employment. Everyone agreed that there was no question that his general knowledge and clearness of thought ought to be available in the present situation.

Political Objectives in the Far East: I raised the question as to whether or not it was time to make a thorough study of our political objectives in the Far East and asked these questions:

1.   How far and how thoroughly do we want to beat Japan? In other words, do we want to morgenthau those islands—do we want to destroy the whole industrial potential?

2.   Do we want to contemplate their readmission to the society of nations after demilitarization?

3.   What is our policy on Russian influence in the Far East? Do we desire a counterweight to that influence? And should it be China or should it be Japan?

4.   Have we given careful thought to the question of how far this country will go toward the complete defeat of Japan— the quick, costly assault versus a long, drawn-out siege? I said that it was conceivable to me that the people that desired a quick victory might turn out to be the appeasers in the case of Japan.

Japanese Emperor: Under Secretary Grew expanded somewhat on his impressions on the idea of the Japanese Emperor. He said his ideas had been misunderstood and misconstrued. He said he was in favor merely of deferring the decision on the question of the Japanese Emperor until we had effected a

military occupation, at which time we could determine whether
he was an asset or a liability. He said he was concerned only
with what could save the maximum of American lives.

[There are several seminal ideas in this last discussion. The
dramatic White House meeting over the Polish question, together
with the ominous developments in Europe, could have left no
thoughtful person too happy with the results of "unconditional
surrender" as it was being applied to Germany. Our "diplomatic
planning of the peace," Forrestal was to say at a high-level
luncheon gathering two years later, "was far below the quality of
planning that went into the conduct of the war. We regarded
the war, broadly speaking, as a ball game which we had to finish
as quickly as possible, but in doing so there was comparatively
little thought as to the relationships between nations which
would exist after Germany and Japan were destroyed." [1] In May
1945 Forrestal himself was already thinking in terms of those
power relationships—terms that most of his countrymen would
not fully grasp for a long time to come. At the moment we were
destroying the principal counterweight to Russia in Europe. Did
we really wish to "morgenthau" the corresponding counterweight
in Asia? If the four questions Forrestal propounded at that gathering of May 1 had been subjected to really searching analysis—
if, indeed, there had been any agency of government equipped
for that kind of analysis—much in later history might have gone
differently. For the moment, Grew's idea about the retention of
the Emperor opened an avenue toward a possible peace in the
Pacific that would mean something less than "morgenthauing"
Japan as well as Germany. Forrestal was to follow that lead with
pertinacity and with effect.

    But consistency of policy in any direction is at best never too
easy in a democratic free society. That same evening Forrestal
dined with Harry Luce, publisher of *Time* and *Life*.

1 May 1945   *San Francisco Conference—Free Press*
    . . . I told him I was struck by the fact that the freedom of
our press gave all the nations with which we do business a tre-

[1] Diary, 25 April 1947.

mendous weapon which they freely employed against our interests. When Molotov wishes to oppose Stettinius at San
Francisco he has access to a free and in fact what sometimes
seems to be a pro-Russian press in this country. The converse
situation obviously could not be imagined in Russia. . . . This
of course is one of the prices we pay for our free institutions,
but at times it is a high and costly price. . . .

I also remarked that in England whenever the government
took a course in foreign affairs it had the solid support of the
British press. I had particularly in mind in my observation the
Washington Post's (Mr. Eugene Meyer's) savage attack on
Mr. Stettinius and his associates as "bush league diplomats."

It seemed to me, I said, that at the moment Mr. Stettinius
was the pitcher for our team and that he was entitled to support
and cheers rather than brickbats and pop bottles from the
American grandstand. I remarked it was clear that Mr.
Stettinius was not a Disraeli, a Metternich or a Machiavelli,
but I remarked that neither had I seen anyone else on the
horizon who had such abilities. I said that if his acts were designed to develop the fact of whether or not the Russians wished
to cooperate in world affairs his policy suited me; that the
sooner we found out the answer to that question the better.

[The final formalities in Europe took another week; but on the
8th of May the Cabinet assembled at eight-fifteen in the morning
at the White House to listen to the President's proclamation and
broadcast on the victory. "At the conclusion of the President's address," says the diary, "we tuned in on Prime Minister Churchill's
speech. We then dispersed." Later in the day he was at the State-
War-Navy meeting. "After the main meeting Stimson told Grew
and myself that he was forming a committee on manhattan to be
headed by Jimmy Byrnes and including [James B.] Conant, [Karl
T.] Compton and [Vannevar] Bush. He asked me whether [Ralph
A.] Bard would be satisfactory as a Navy representative and Grew
whether Clayton could serve for State. . . ." The first successful
explosion of an atomic bomb (in New Mexico on July 16) was
now only two and a half months away. Forrestal must have
been party to the discussions over it, but this cryptic note is

[the only direct reference to the subject that he confided even to his secret diary until after the announcement of the Hiroshima detonation.

11 May 1945   *Russo-Japanese War*

I had a meeting in my office this morning with Ambassador Harriman, Admiral Edwards [Vice Admiral Richard S. Edwards, Deputy Chief of Naval Operations], Vice Admiral Cooke [Charles M. Cooke, Jr., Chief of Staff to Admiral King].

Harriman said he thought it was time to come to a conclusion about the necessity for the early entrance of Russia into the Japanese war. He said he was satisfied they were determined to come in it because of their requirements in the Far East. [He described the territorial concessions made at Yalta.] He said the Russians, he believed, much more greatly feared a separate peace by ourselves with Japan than any fear of ourselves about their concluding such an arrangement. He said he thought it was important that we determine our policy as to a strong or weak China, that if China continued weak Russian influence would move in quickly and toward ultimate domination. He said that there could be no illusion about anything such as a "free China" once the Russians got in, that the two or three hundred millions in that country would march when the Kremlin ordered.

Vice Admiral Cooke said he thought the necessity for Russia's early participation was very much lessened as a result of recent events, although the Army he didn't think shared that view.

Admiral Edwards: The best thing for us would be if the Japanese would agree to a basis of unconditional surrender which still left them in their own minds some face and honor.

[Admiral Cooke was here expressing a view which the Navy, confident of the deadly effect which the attrition by its submarines and carrier strikes had been wreaking on Japanese war potential, came increasingly to hold thereafter. Harriman, about to return to his Moscow post, was for his part urgent to get fresh guidance through the complex considerations which were open-

[ing up. Forrestal attended a meeting at the State Department next day in which the Ambassador put an interesting series of questions.

12 May 1945   *Russia*

. . . Harriman said he should have a clear outline of American policy. . . .

1. The Yalta Agreement: Should it be re-examined in the light of the fact that Russia has not observed its part of that contract, and also in the light of the cessation of hostilities in Europe, which have changed the pattern of fact on which that agreement was drawn?

2. How urgent is the necessity for quick Russian participation in the war against Japan? . . .

4. The occupation of Japan: Should Russia participate or not? He believes that Russia will expect participation . . . although the question was not raised at Yalta.

5. *Korea*: Mr. Roosevelt proposed trusteeship for Korea and Stalin's response at Yalta was, why was there any need of trusteeship if the Koreans could produce a satisfactory government—which in Harriman's view would unquestionably be a Bolshevik or Soviet government.

6. *Hong Kong*: Should we try to get the British out, or try to persuade the Chinese to come to some arrangement by which they would retain some rights there?

7. *Indo-China*: Do we want any military rights in Indo-China? Do we want to let the French have a free hand and drop the proposals for trusteeship? . . .

8. What is our objective as regards the future of Japan? Destruction? Retention as a power? . . .

[These were as searching as the questions Forrestal himself had been asking on May 1; and again history might have been different if all their implications had been faced in 1945 while the war was not yet over. But the best that was done at this meeting was to agree to formulate them "for discussion with the President."

Forrestal was uneasily aware that they needed answer. On May 14 he was writing a note to Senator Ferguson of Michigan,

[enclosing some articles from *The Economist*, which Ferdinand Eberstadt had brought to his attention.

To Homer Ferguson, 14 May 1945

. . . As *The Economist* writer points out, the Bolsheviks have the advantage over us of having a clear-cut line of economic philosophy, amounting almost to a religion, in which they believe is the only solution to the government of men. It is the Marxian dialectic; it is as incompatible with democracy as was Nazism or Fascism because it rests upon the willingness to apply force to gain the end, whether that force is applied externally or by internal commotion.

There is no use fooling ourselves about the depth and extent of this problem. I have no answers—I have been concentrating on something else, just as you have. But we had better try to get an answer, and in doing so we shall need some of the cold and objective thinking which *The Economist* writer has applied.

Needless to say, I shall appreciate your not giving this letter or these thoughts wide circulation or I shall be accused of being an appeaser, a Fascist and various other forms of dangerous thought. I am quite the opposite; I believe Germany has got to be denied the means of making war and I believe this can be done only by supervision over a sufficiently long period. . . . But to ignore the existence of seventy-five or eighty millions of vigorous and industrious people or to assume that they will not join with Russia if no other outlet is afforded them I think is closing our eyes to reality.

[Harriman was evidently putting the case as strongly as he could. In a note of May 14 Forrestal summarized his talks during these days: "He said that their [the Russians'] conduct would be based upon the principle of power politics in its crudest and most primitive form. He said we must face our diplomatic decisions from here on with the consciousness that half and maybe all of Europe might be communistic by the end of next winter, and that if we support Communist armies in China against Chiang Kai-shek we should have to face ultimately the fact that two or three hundred

[millions of people in China would 'march when the Kremlin ordered.' "

Forrestal would doubtless not have given such attention to Harriman's views if he had not been impressed by them; and other evidence was at the same time pouring in. It was also on the 14th that Naval Intelligence came in with a document "to the effect that the Russians have established an elaborate system of espionage in South America with its headquarters in Mexico City." On May 20 there was a long telegram from the naval attaché in Moscow dilating on all the difficulties, irritations, deceptions and delays involved in any attempt to negotiate with Russians. But the country was not yet in the mood to face up to the basic issues of Soviet relations already apparent to Forrestal and Harriman.

President Truman did make one effort to do so. He dispatched Harry Hopkins, already seriously ill and not far from his death, to see what could be done with Moscow. The newspapers inferred at the time that it was primarily to settle the Polish issue, which was continuing to threaten the wreck of the San Francisco Conference. But Hopkins' mandate was somewhat wider.

20 May 1945   *Russia*

I met with Averell Harriman and Charles E. Bohlen of the State Department at Harry Hopkins' house. The latter told me he was going to Russia on behalf of the President to try to get some evaluation of the Russian attitude, and to develop their attitude on many questions which at this time it seems difficult to understand, and on which at the present time there seems a danger of a sharp and substantial division between the United States and Russia. Harry said that he was skeptical about Churchill, at least in the particular of Anglo-American-Russian relationship; that he thought it was of vital importance that we not be maneuvered into a position where Great Britain had us lined up with them as a bloc against Russia to implement England's European policy.

[In retrospect the mission would hardly have seemed well omened either in preparation or in purpose.

II

[In the midst of these critical transition days between the Roosevelt and the Truman administrations, Forrestal was of course
concerned with many other pressing issues aside from those of
high national policy. There was the problem of command in the
Pacific, the mounting of the projected final offensive against the
Japanese home islands, the heavy fighting and severe naval losses
off Okinawa. But only casual traces of all this are found in the
diary. It must always be remembered that the diary was not a
complete record, but essentially an *aide-mémoire*, of matters
great and small, which Forrestal might want for later reference.

One subject that did occupy increasing space in the diary,
doubtless because Forrestal knew that it would be of continuing future importance, was that of military reorganization and
unification. It had two heads, the plans for a postwar universal
military service system, which Forrestal believed to be necessary, and the proposal for a single Department of Defense,
which he seriously questioned. He knew the first would not be
easy to attain.

30 April 1945   *Ex-Secretary Daniels*

I had dinner tonight with the three ex-Secretaries of the
Navy: Josephus Daniels, Charles Francis Adams and Charles
Edison.

Mr. Daniels was in particularly good form and recited a
number of anecdotes of his term as Secretary of the Navy in
World War I. I offered him a glass of sherry before dinner but
he said that as far as he was concerned General Order No. 99
[Mr. Daniels' famous order of June 1, 1914, banning alcoholic
liquor from naval ships and shore stations] was still in effect.
However, at the end of the dinner he did drink a toast to the
memory of President Roosevelt.

He was as intransigent as ever on the question of universal
military training, stating his belief that it was contrary to the
basic philosophy of the Republic and could have, he thought, a
dangerous result in that it would condition the country to

reliance on the concept of universal training rather than the
maintenance of a large and effective Navy.

[Forrestal was pessimistic over the success of the Army's pressure for unification. In a letter of the preceding fall[2] he had observed that as to the single department "I have been telling King,
Nimitz and Company it is my judgment that as of today the
Navy has lost its case, and that either in Congress or in a public poll the Army's point of view would prevail." If that were so,
it was obvious that a merely negative attitude would not be
enough. On May 9 there was a luncheon meeting, recorded in a
diary note which Forrestal set down one year later.

9 May 1946   *Hopkins-King-Marshall Lunch—May 9, 1945*
It was a year ago today that I had Admiral King, General
Marshall and Harry Hopkins at lunch at my house. The purpose of that lunch was to explore with King and Marshall the
possibility of the Army and Navy reaching an agreement as to
the form of our postwar national defense.

I said I thought it was not a very wise use of our time to be
conducting a debate between the Army and Navy on this question. Marshall agreed, but said that he was unshakably committed to the thesis of a single civilian Secretary with a single
military Chief of Staff. At considerable length he described
the condition which prevailed at the end of the last war when
Pershing returned from France with very definite views as to
the creation of a staff for the Army and otherwise reflecting the
lessons learned in World War I. He said that the Secretary of
War, Mr. Weeks, had only a very moderate interest in the
Army; that he would not follow Pershing's advice and, furthermore, would not permit Pershing to see President Harding to
express his views. Marshall continued to express his fear of the
starvation of the Army in another period of peace.

I said that the Navy could not concur in the conception of a
single department but would go a long ways to meet the Army's
view on any reasonable system of cooperation and coordination.

[2] To Palmer Hoyt, 2 September 1944.

[That the problem was actually wider than the mere drawing of a new military organization chart Forrestal was already well aware. On May 15 Senator Walsh, chairman of the Senate Naval Affairs Committee, wrote to him, suggesting that while a single department might be effective in coordinating some defense activities and eliminating some overlapping and expense, "it would not coordinate the efforts and plans of our military establishment with other departments of the government concerned. . . . It would not mobilize . . . the scientific data which has been accumulated in the past few years and the scientific achievements which will undoubtedly be made in the future. It would not set up a competent intelligence organization. . . . If we discard an 'either/or' logic, we may find it is not necessary or desirable to either consolidate the War and Navy Departments . . . or let them remain entirely separate." The Senator doubted whether mere objection to the unification plan would serve any useful purpose and went on to suggest that the Navy Department might make a "thorough study" looking toward a much higher organization of the whole field, under which the two service departments would be integrated under a "Council of National Defense" with organs capable of meeting the various broader problems of coordination which he had mentioned.

Forrestal promptly replied (on May 27) that all this "corresponds substantially to what is taking shape in my own mind." He felt in particular that "the Navy Department cannot be in the position of merely taking the negative in this discussion, but must come up with positive and constructive recommendations." The breadth of his outlook is indicated by a diary note of the following month, in which he spoke of a policy mix-up over a momentarily tense situation that had developed between the French and the Anglo-American forces on the Italian frontier.

6 June 1945   *Haute-Savoie*
    . . . I am more impressed than ever as things develop in the world today that policy may be frequently shaped by events unless someone has strong and clear mental grasp of events; strong enough and clear enough so that he is able to shape policy rather than letting it be developed by accidents.

I quote from a letter sent by Admiral Halsey to Congressman Clifton A. Woodrum, chairman of the Committee on Postwar Military Policy:

"I have one more point to offer: the need for wise, trained men to minister the *National* Policy. We need men who understand the causes of war and conflict, who understand the fundamentals of our aims and ideals, who understand the interrelation of international policies, internal politics, trade and finance and the true significance of military power. . . .

"We must find and train such men—outstanding civilians who have served their country under arms, and outstanding military men who have studied to understand the civil aspects of government and international relations. If we *don't* find and train and employ such men in the service of the United States, we will lose our shirts as we have in the past—and then what avails the sacrifice of life, blood and treasure that we have made?"

[Halsey's was a large order; yet a sound military system could scarcely do less than try to meet it. A week later Forrestal was again discussing the subject with President Truman.

13 June 1945   Aide-Mémoire of Conversation with the President

In my conversation with the President this morning I asked the President to express his wishes on the question of consolidation of the Army and Navy Departments. I said that I didn't want to go against his policy, neither did I want to let ourselves be rushed into something through the organization of public opinion by the War Department to the end of such a consolidation, which might end up by forcing his hand as well as ours. His reply was that he had definite views on a plan for national security which would capitalize the experience of this war, but he did not contemplate the abolition of the War and Navy Departments as separate entities.

I observed that in any such scheme the State Department should be an integral part and he agreed completely, with the observation, however, that there wasn't much material in the State Department to work with. He said that when he was able to get free of his present conversations on international affairs he proposed to take up the whole question of government organization on a staff basis with a view to getting a closely knit, cooperating and effective machinery which would function, I gather, more or less along the lines of the British War Cabinet. I said that I was personally heartily in favor of such a move and I thought it was essential if this government was going to be able to deal effectively with the complex problems that would be coming up in the next two years. . . .

[Here was powerful support for the general system of ideas already crystallizing in Forrestal's mind. He was working at this time on the reorganization of his own Department along clearer and more businesslike lines of responsibility (the diary contains a copy of an "8th Draft" of a proposed executive order to this end); and with his hand thus strengthened by the President's favorable attitude he could now proceed with the larger plan. He enlisted Ferdinand Eberstadt, a close friend and former business associate, who had acquired an intimate knowledge of the industrial side of modern warfare from his work in the War Production Board and other high-level civil agencies, to make the "thorough study" suggested in Senator Walsh's letter. The formal directive was dated June 19:

To F. Eberstadt, 19 June 1945
. . . 1. Would unification of the War and Navy Departments under a single head improve our national security?
2. If not, what changes in the present relationships of the military services and departments has our war experience indicated as desirable to improve our national security?
3. What form of postwar organization should be established and maintained to enable the military services and other government departments and agencies most effectively to provide for and protect our national security?

[At luncheon a couple of weeks later he was talking over the matter with Eberstadt, Harold E. Stassen, "Cap" Krug and Representative W. Sterling Cole of New York, a member of the Postwar Military Policy Committee. Forrestal recalled two vivid

[examples of the danger of leaving one service wholly dependent upon another:

5 July 1945   *Single Department of Defense*
 . . . 1. The Army forgot to include the Navy's require-ments for TNT in the fiscal year 1937–38. The result was that as the war approached the Navy found itself seriously deficient in this explosive. The procedure was that the Navy would get the money in its appropriations and let the Army procure. The Army had no excuse except the simple statement that it forgot.
        2. . . . I remember in the summer of 1940 when Rear Admiral [Herbert F.] Leary, then commander of the Training Section of the Office of the Chief of Naval Operations, was complaining bitterly about the lack of .50 caliber ammuni-tion for his ships to train with, that they were limited to a nominal number of rounds per gun. The reason of course was that the Navy was relying on the Army for the procurement of both guns and ammunition in the case of the .50 caliber weapon.

[The next day, on the other hand, brought a reminder of the dangers of Service disunity.

6 July 1945   *Harry Hopkins*
 I talked with Harry Hopkins this afternoon who said that he was leaving the government to go with the International Gar-ment Workers Union for one day a week on arbitration mat-ters, the rest of the time being free to write. He planned to make a movie if he could get the proper adjustment with the Internal Revenue people. . . . He said he had lunch with the Joint Chiefs of Staff on Tuesday, and it became clear to him that there was complete and solid disagreement as to future command in the Pacific.

[There were many facets to this complex shield. The Eberstadt Report was to run to some two hundred and fifty close-packed pages. It was, however, to be completed by September 25—less than a month after the final surrender in Tokyo Bay—and its

[analysis and recommendations became in fact the principal basis for the unification act finally adopted two years later.

III

[Meanwhile the urgent present could not wait upon the theoretical future. The pressing issue was how to end the war with Japan, behind which there loomed the vaguer, more formidable problem of American relations with the Soviet Union. Harry Hopkins had left Washington on May 23 on his mission to secure an "evaluation of the Russian attitude." It was three days later that Forrestal entered his only diary reference to the subsequently famous case of the magazine *Amerasia*—around which in 1949 and 1950 there were to revolve so many of the charges of Communist infiltration into the State Department.

28 May 1945   *Lieutenant Andrew Roth*

Major Correa [Mathias F. Correa, at the time a special assistant to the Secretary of the Navy] reported to me that the Department of Justice has evidence to the effect that Lieutenant Andrew Roth has been furnishing confidential and secret documents to a man named Jaffe, head of a publication named *Amerasia* in New York City. Jaffe has had intimate relationship with the Russian Consul in New York.

Other Departments of government involved are the Office of Strategic Services, the Department of State, and the Foreign Economic Administration.

Major Correa reported that it was proposed that Lieutenant Roth should be taken into surveillance Wednesday. He said that the FBI thought that unless speedy action were taken important evidence would be dissipated, lost and destroyed. I pointed out that the inevitable consequence of such action now would be to greatly embarrass the President in his current conversations with Stalin, because of the anti-Russian play-up the incident would receive out of proportion to its importance. . . .

I asked Captain Vardaman [Naval Aide to the President] to see to it that the President was informed in this matter and I then called Mr. Edgar Hoover and suggested that he advise

Mr. Tom Clark [then an Assistant Attorney General] and have
him also see that the President is in full information of all the
facts in the matter as well as their implications.

[At the moment this seemed a side issue. At the meeting of the
    three Secretaries next day (State was represented by the Acting
    Secretary, Mr. Grew) they were confronted by major policy de-
    terminations.

29 May 1945   *State-War-Navy Meeting*

The meeting was called at Mr. Grew's suggestion, acting on
instructions from the President who wanted to get from the
military people their view as to what he should say in his
message to Congress on the conduct of the war. It had been
proposed that he say something to indicate that our objectives toward Japan did not include necessarily the destruction
of their political concepts, of their religion, and particularly of
the Emperor as the symbol of their religion. It was agreed that
the time was not appropriate for him to make such a
pronouncement.

I asked whether it would not suffice to say that our view of
unconditional surrender meant that it was the unconditional
surrender of the Japanese military power, that we did not
propose to destroy Japan as a nation. Mr. Dooman [Eugene H.
Dooman, then a special assistant in the State Department, who
had been counselor in the Tokyo Embassy under Grew before
the war and had an intimate knowledge of Japan] said this
would not cover, that he believed that if the Japanese became
imbued with the idea that the United States was set on the
destruction of their philosophy of government and of their
religion we would be faced with a truly national suicidal defense. He said assurances on our lack of desire to destroy them
physically and industrially would not suffice.

30 May 1945   *Hopkins*

I inquired this morning of Mr. McCloy [Assistant Secretary
of War] if he had seen dispatches from Hopkins from Moscow.
He said he had not, and he understood that the orders had

been that these dispatches were not to be seen by King or Marshall. He said he assumed that included others, including the Secretaries of War and Navy. I said I did not like that procedure, that it was reverting to the old business of individual and personal operation and that I didn't think government should be run that way. I said I suspected that it was at Harry's own instigation that this restraint was made. He agreed and expressed the same regret as myself. I said . . . I would certainly not favor his use in such situations unless information he obtained was to be available through the usual channels of government.

8 June 1945   *Cabinet*

The Acting Secretary of State [Grew] reported great progress on the international crises that had been active during the past ten days. . . . The Russians have withdrawn their representations with reference to the veto [in the projected United Nations Security Council] in regard to discussions of breaches of international good conduct in a manner which is completely satisfactory to us. . . .

[This, as Robert Sherwood puts it,[3] "was the real news that the San Francisco Conference had been saved"; and was the major fruit of Harry Hopkins' last mission. If Forrestal had not been allowed to see Hopkins' reports himself, he was given a long memorandum by McCloy, dated June 10, summarizing their contents. It indicated that the mission had gone with what was afterward to seem a deceptive ease. Stalin had been most accommodating. The Soviet armies would be deployed on the Manchurian frontier "on August 8." The Russian dictator insisted that in China he had "no territorial claims"; he would support the Generalissimo, Chiang Kai-shek—"he says there is no other leader strong enough to unify China and he indicates that he will back Chiang in spite of some reservations. . . . Manchuria must be part of a unified China, and Stalin emphasized that he wanted a strong unified China. . . . Stalin said that the U. S. was the only one with

---

[3] Robert E. Sherwood, *Roosevelt and Hopkins* (New York: Harper & Bros., 1948), p. 912.

[resources capable of rebuilding China; the Soviet will have all it
can do to keep itself alive economically and can offer little help."
The two men discussed the composition of the new Polish government in terms which Hopkins evidently considered satisfactory.

Forrestal must have been particularly interested in the discussions on Japan. Stalin indicated that he was "disposed to favor" going through with the unconditional surrender demand, though he
realized the danger that the Japanese would be driven to a finish
fight and made a suggestion which today seems curiously characteristic of Soviet diplomatic methods: "Perhaps we can get a surrender without using the words 'unconditional surrender,' but
give them 'the works' once we get to Japan." (This phrase,
McCloy added, was "an interpretation that Hopkins put upon
Stalin's remarks.") Stalin also intimated that he wanted a zone of
occupation in Japan jointly with the United States.[4] Harriman,
McCloy concluded, "followed with a report of the general effect of Hopkins' visit, which was about what was contained in
Harry's own report. . . . He said that Harry's visit had largely
dispelled the growing suspicion of [that is, felt by] Stalin and
Molotov."

Whatever Forrestal (or Hopkins himself, for that matter) may
have thought about Hopkins' success, he was clearly not satisfied
that the right answer had been found for the Japanese question.

12 June 1945   *State-War-Navy Meeting*

Stimson, Grew, McCloy and I had a general discussion about
the question of "unconditional surrender" of Japan. I said, and
Secretary Stimson concurred, that this was one of the most
serious questions before the country, Stimson saying that it
was in everybody's mind to inqure what was meant by "unconditional surrender," and while there was universal agreement . . . that our national objective was to secure the
demilitarization of Japan it was equally true that no one desired the permanent subjugation of Japan, the enslavement of

---

[4] Only the highlights of the McCloy memorandum are here given, since Sherwood
has published the full texts of Hopkins' own reports.

her people or any attempt to dictate what kind of government.
the country should have. Mr. Grew said that his Department
was now in the process of giving intense and continuous study
to this question with a view to arriving at a precise definition
of our war aims, coupled with an examination of methods by
which the Japanese could escape from the dilemma in which
they got themselves through the deification of the Emperor and
surrounding him with all the mystic symbolism that goes
with a religious deity.

[At Forrestal's meeting with the President next day "we talked
a little about the war with Japan. The President said that before
he left for Europe [to attend the Potsdam Conference] he
wanted to have a meeting of State, War and Navy, plus the Joint
Chiefs of Staff, to secure a clear outline of our national objectives
in Asia." Since the conference was to convene within a month, it
may seem a rather belated attack upon so vast a subject. But to
the men who were responsible for concluding the war, the surrender terms, at least, had to be decided.

19 June 1945   *State-War-Navy Meeting*
   1. *Surrender Terms*: Grew's proposal, in which Stimson
most vigorously agrees, that something be done in the very
near future to indicate to the Japanese what kind of surrender
terms would be imposed upon them and particularly to indicate to them that they would be allowed to retain their own
form of government and religious institutions while at the
same time making it clear that we propose to eradicate completely all traces of Japanese militarism. Both Stimson and
Grew most emphatically asserted that this move ought to be
done, and that if it were to be effective at all it must be done
before any attack was made upon the homeland of Japan. . . .
   Mr. Grew was of the impression that the President had indicated that he was not in accord with this point of view. Mr.
Stimson said that that was not his understanding but rather he
felt that the President did not want to proceed with such a plan
at this moment and in particular did not want the Depart-

ments to abate in any way their preparations for the ultimate
attack because of the existence of such a plan. With this
latter point he indicated he was heartily in accord. . . .

Stimson and Grew further pointed out that Leahy, King and
Nimitz were all in favor of some such approach being made
to the Japanese. . . .

[Nearly two years later, in a reminiscent evening with McCloy,
    Forrestal was to receive further light on the events of this pe-
    riod; and his diary note of the conversation may well be inserted
    here.

8 March 1947   *Meeting with McCloy*

. . . McCloy recalled the meeting with President Truman at
the White House at which the decision was taken to proceed
with the invasion of Kyushu. He said this for him illustrated
most vividly the necessity for the civilian voice in military decisions even in time of war. He said what he had to say was
pertinent not merely to the question of the invasion of the
Japanese mainland but also to the question of whether we
needed to get Russia in to help us defeat Japan. At this particular meeting, which occurred in the summer of 1945, before
the President went to Potsdam, where, under the pressure of
Secretary Byrnes, he stated his principal mission would be to
get the Russians into the war against the Japs, the President
made the rounds of his military advisers and asked them to
tell him whether the Japanese mainland invasion was necessary. They all agreed it was. He finally left it that they would
proceed with the plannings for the invasion of Kyushu but
that they were to raise the question with him again before its
execution and he would reserve decision on whether or not the
attack should be carried into the Tokyo plan [plain?].

As the meeting broke up, McCloy said he had not been asked
but wanted to state his views. (Neither Stimson nor I was at
this meeting.) He said that he thought before the final decision
to invade Japan was taken or it was decided to use the atomic
bomb political measures should be taken; the Japanese should
be told of what had happened to Germany, particularly in

view of the fact that some of their people who had been in Germany were back in Japan and would be able to report on the destruction and devastation which they had witnessed; that the Japs should be told, furthermore, that we had another and terrifyingly destructive weapon which we would have to use if they did not surrender; that they would be permitted to retain the Emperor and a form of government of their own choosing. He said the military leaders were somewhat annoyed at his interference but that the President welcomed it and at the conclusion of McCloy's observations ordered such a political offensive to be set in motion.

[There were other peace problems besides those of Japan:

24 June 1945   *Russia-Turkey*

The Russians last week renewed their pressure on Turkey for a revision of the agreements of Montreux [these were the international conventions controlling the status of the Bosporus and the Dardanelles] with an indication that they would like to detach Turkey from the orbit of British influence. . . . The Turks rejected flatly the suggestion that there could be unilateral adjustment of frontiers between Russia and Turkey. . . . The American Ambassador at Ankara [Edwin C. Wilson] on 20 June said he felt that we should express an interest in this matter at Moscow for the reason that the Russian proposals to Turkey are wholly incompatible with the spirit and principles on which we are seeking with the participation of the Soviet Union to set up a new world organization. . . .

26 June 1945   *State-War-Navy Meeting*

. . . The question of a public statement to the Japanese people outlining the terms of surrender was discussed. Mr. Stimson read a memorandum which he proposed to send to the President. It was agreed by all present that such a statement should be made before the actual invasion of the homeland of Japan was begun. . . . Suggestion was made that Berlin [the Potsdam Conference] might be an appropriate platform. . . . McCloy stated that Stalin would definitely raise the question at the Berlin meeting. He stated that Stalin had no strong views on the subject either way but was prepared to follow our leadership in the matter. It was proposed that drafting should begin upon the form of statement to be put out. . . . [At the bottom of this page in the diary there stands a penciled notation in unusually bold strokes: "OK. F"]

30 June 1945   *Halifax Dinner*

I had dinner at the British Embassy last night with Harry Hopkins and his wife, Lord and Lady Halifax. Halifax asked Hopkins his impressions of Stalin and his desire to cooperate with Britain and the U. S. Hopkins was not very specific in his replies and gave the impression that he had some misgivings on Stalin's willingness to work with his wartime allies in trust and confidence. I expressed it as my view that it would not be difficult to work with Russia provided we were dealing with her only as a national entity; that the real problem was whether or not Russian policy called for a continuation of the Third International's objectives, namely, world revolution and the application of the political principles of the dialectical materialists for the entire world. Hopkins said he doubted if anyone could answer this question, and I added that I doubted if even the Russians themselves could answer it.

We talked some about the British elections. Halifax expressed the view that Churchill would win by a reduced majority. I said that if one were not cynical about the world one could wish for a triumph of the Left in England, France and the rest of Europe, because if the conservatives or middle-of-the-road people remain in power they will be charged with responsibility for all of the inevitable difficulties which must arise when the war is over and in the process of getting Europe back to anything like normal conditions. Hopkins said that he thought the world was now definitely swinging toward the Left, that we were in the middle of the revolution and that it would be unwise to try to oppose it. I replied that it was not inconceivable that the real reactionaries in world politics would be those who now call themselves revolutionaries, because the dynamics of their philosophy all tended toward the concentration of power in the state, with the inevitable result of exploitation of the common man by the masses, or rather, by those who in such a system apply power over the masses—such as Hitler, Mussolini, Stalin and Hirohito.

Hopkins said that England must inevitably go socialist and that Churchill did not want the things for England that the Labour people wanted—federal housing, slum elimination, ownership of industries, etc. I asked Hopkins how any country such as England could go communistic—I said England had been able to exist and subsist because she was a trading nation and that a capitalistic system was essential to the existence of England. . . . I said that such a nation could only become communistic if we, the United States, underwrote the transaction. I pointed out that either Russia or the United States could become communistic because both of us have the raw materials, population, the agricultural production, necessary to the creation of a real socialist state; that England did not have these things—that actually she could subsist only about fifteen million people on the products of her own agriculture and the rest had to be paid for by the services and the processing industries referred to above.

Harry obviously did not want to pursue this conversation too far, because, I suspect, he did not want to be driven to the position that he was advocating either revolution or Communism for this country. And he turned the talk with discussion of universal military service.

[But opportunities for this kind of broad and philosophical review of the world history they were making were comparatively rare. The immediate issues of high policy were urgent.

6 July 1945   *"Unconditional Surrender"*

I talked this evening after the President's Band Concert to Joe Grew. He expressed satisfaction that we had finally whipped into shape the draft of the proposed message to the Japanese by the President, the aim of which is to make more specific what we mean by the phrase "unconditional surrender." He said, however, he was afraid it would be ditched on the way over [to the Potsdam Conference] by people who accompany the President—Bohlen among others—who reflect the view that we cannot afford to hold out any clarification of terms to Japan which could be construed as a desire to get the Japanese war over with before Russia has an opportunity to enter.

[This last was something of a new note. Up to that time the anxiety had all been lest Russia should fail to enter, leaving us "committed and frozen," as Admiral Leahy had put it at a White House meeting, "to the concept of unconditional surrender, maintenance of which might prove extremely costly to us." The idea that it would probably be far harder to keep the Russians out of the Pacific war than to bring them in had been broached by Harriman in May,[5] but was not yet widely accepted. Already, however, the first hints were coming that the Japanese collapse might be more imminent than had been supposed.

13 July 1945   *Japanese Peace Feeler*

The first real evidence of a Japanese desire to get out of the war came today through intercepted messages from Togo, Foreign Minister, to Sato, Jap Ambassador in Moscow, instructing the latter to see Molotov if possible before his departure for the Big Three meeting [the Potsdam Conference], and if not then, immediately afterward, to lay before him the Emperor's strong desire to secure a termination of the war. This he said arose not only out of the Emperor's interest in the welfare of his own subjects but out of his interest toward mankind in general. He was anxious, he said, to see cessation of bloodshed on both sides. Togo said to convey to the Russians the fact that they wanted to remain at peace with Russia, that the Japanese did not desire permanent annexation of any of the territories they had conquered in Manchuria. Togo said further that the unconditional surrender terms of the Allies was about the only thing in the way of termination of the war and he said that if this were insisted upon, of course the Japanese would have to continue the fight.

Sato's response . . . was to protest that the proposals were quite unrealistic; looked at objectively it was clear that there was no chance now of dividing Russia from the other Allies, that the agreement on Poland, on Chapultepec and the Conference at San Francisco showed that England, Russia and the United States were determined to act in concert. Togo's response was that, regardless of Sato's views, he still desired him to carry out his instructions.

[It was a difficult and delicate situation. We were already on the eve of the Potsdam Conference, which convened on July 17, just four days later. The American ability to read the Japanese codes, which had played a decisive part in several critical passages of the war, was now revealing the inmost struggles of Japanese policy as it faced inevitable defeat. How best to deal with this situation, which involved Soviet and American aims as well as the confusions of the Japanese and the possibility that if pressed too hard they would still choose to go down in a suicidal defense, was not an easy question.

15 July 1945   *Japanese Peace Feeler*
    Messages today on Japanese-Russian conversations. Togo, Foreign Minister, insisted that Sato present to Molotov the request of the Emperor himself. Sato's replies insistently pointed out the lack of reality in Togo's apparent belief that there is a chance of persuading Russia to take independent action on the Eastern war. He stated very bluntly and without any coating how fantastic is the hope that Russia would be impressed by Japanese willingness to give up territory which she had already lost. . . . Throughout Sato's message ran a note of cold and realistic evaluation of Japan's position; and he said that the situation was rapidly passing beyond the point of Japan's and Russia's cooperating in the security of Asia but [that the question was] rather whether there would be any Manchukuo or even Japan itself left as entities. The gist of his final message was that it was clear that Japan was thoroughly and completely defeated and that the only course open was quick and definite action recognizing such fact. . . .
    It is significant that these conversations began before there

could have been much effect from the thousand-plane raids of the Third Fleet and several days before the naval bombardment of Kamaishi.

[Forrestal's reference here was to the naval operations, beginning on July 10, in which Japan's communications, industries, coastal installations and the remnants of her fleet were hit with air bombing and naval artillery, delivered, in the words of the official report, by "the greatest mass of sea power ever assembled." These conversations also took place nearly a month before the dropping of the atomic bombs on Hiroshima and Nagasaki.
     On the 24th Forrestal dictated further notes on these Japanese messages:

24 July 1945   *Japanese Peace Feeler*
. . . Finally, on the first of July, Sato sent a long message outlining what he conceived to be Japan's position, which was in brief that she was now entirely alone and friendless and could look for succor from no one. . . . He strongly advised accepting any terms, including unconditional surrender, on the basis that this was the only way of preserving the entity of the Emperor and the state itself. . . .
The response to his message was that the Cabinet in council had weighed all the considerations which he had raised and that their final judgment and decision was that the war must be fought with all the vigor and bitterness of which the nation was capable so long as the only alternative was the unconditional surrender.

[Three days later Forrestal was in Paris on his way—uninvited —to the Potsdam Conference. These intercepted telegrams can only have convinced him that he and Grew were right in their belief that a willingness to preserve the Emperor would open the way to a Japanese surrender which in most other respects would be in effect "unconditional." Curiously enough, Forrestal did not enter in his diary the text of the draft statement which it had been decided at the State-War-Navy meeting on June 26 to have prepared; even more curiously, in his extensive notes on the

[Potsdam trip there is only one mention of the subject. But the definition of peace terms issued at Potsdam on July 26 (just as Forrestal was leaving the United States) clearly shows the influence of the moderate view. It was an invitation to Japan to yield *before* she should be destroyed; it disclaimed any intention that the Japanese should be "enslaved" or deprived of other than their armament industries, while the words "unconditional surrender" occurred only once, in the final paragraph, and restricted even there to "unconditional surrender of all Japanese armed forces." The Emperor was not mentioned; but the proclamation left latitude enough for accepting the "condition"—the retention of the Emperor—on which Japan in fact surrendered some three weeks later.

I V

[Forrestal dined in Paris on the evening of July 27 with Jefferson Caffery, the American Ambassador to France, and others. From Caffery he heard that "the only people in France with a positive line of attack are the Communists under Thorez and Duclos. He said the Russian Ambassador, Bogomolov, is quite candid in admitting the direction of the French Communists by Moscow." Caffery said he had told the President that unless France got some coal from the United States for the coming winter "there would inevitably be Communism and possibly anarchy." Next morning Forrestal "saw Dean Jay at Morgan's," who told him "there was no leadership left among the top industrial people in France; they were all under constant attack and all very discouraged. . . . There is a great inertia still over the people. They are not taking hold with either vigor or firmness." With these gloomy introductions to a shattered Europe, he flew on the same afternoon.

Meanwhile the British electorate had defied the predictions (rather as the American electorate was to do three years later) and retired the Churchill government from office while Mr. Churchill was sitting as head of the British delegation at Potsdam. Forrestal's plane was delayed in landing at Gatow Airport near Berlin by the simultaneous arrival of the planes bearing the new Prime Minister, Mr. Clement Attlee, and the new For-

[eign Minister, Mr. Ernest Bevin, to take over the work. But he was still in time to dine that evening with the President at the temporary "White House" in Babelsberg.

28 July 1945   *European Trip*

. . . He [Mr. Truman] said he was being very realistic with the Russians and found Stalin not difficult to do business with. I asked who he thought would be Stalin's successor, but he said that he doubted if anyone knew. He felt that when that time came there would be revolution in Russia and a struggle for power. Stalin regards all dictatorships except his own as dangerous, particularly Franco's. He referred to an effort on Russia's part to draw the distinction between good and bad dictators. "This, however, is a distinction without a difference."

The President referred to the British elections and expressed surprise that no one seemed to have any idea in advance of what the outcome might be. In our own country the Republicans have no leader capable of crystallizing opinion behind him and certainly cannot steal the liberal lead from the Democrats. The time is not yet ripe for the conservative reaction which can presumably be expected to set in. . . .

Talked with Byrnes [now at Potsdam as American Secretary of State, having succeeded Mr. Stettinius on the conclusion of the San Francisco Conference]. . . . Byrnes said he was most anxious to get the Japanese affair over with before the Russians got in, with particular reference to Dairen and Port Arthur. Once in there, he felt, it would not be easy to get them out. . . .

[Evidently on the question of Russian entry into the Pacific war the wheel was now coming full circle. Forrestal was to get a further sidelight on this two years later at a reminiscent luncheon gathering at which General Dwight D. Eisenhower was present. "When President Truman came to Potsdam in the summer of 1945," Forrestal noted, "he told Eisenhower he had as one of his primary objectives that of getting Russia into the Japanese war. Eisenhower begged him at that time not to assume that he had to give anything away to do this, that the Russians were desper-

[ately anxious to get into the Eastern war and that in Eisenhower's opinion there was no question but that Japan was already thoroughly beaten. When the President told him at the end of the Conference that he had achieved his objectives and was going home, Eisenhower again remarked that he earnestly hoped the President had not had to make any concessions to get them in."

Still later Forrestal recorded his own conclusion. In a note of June 23, 1947, he observed that the Russians would have to come into the Marshall Plan; "they could no more afford to be out of it than they could have afforded not to join in the war against Japan (fifty divisions could not have kept them *out* of this war)." While Forrestal was mistaken about Soviet participation in the Marshall Plan, it does not follow that his estimate as to the Pacific war was wrong.

Next day, a Sunday, Forrestal wandered through the ruins of Berlin and was as deeply impressed by that staggering scene of destruction as are all who have seen it. He also found that others did not share what would seem to have been the President's rather optimistic mood about the Russians.

29 July 1945   *European Trip*

. . . Lunched at General Clay's visitors' house [Lucius D. Clay, at the beginning of his long service as American military governor in Germany], our temporary headquarters, and brought Averell Harriman back with us. Averell was very gloomy about the influx of Russia into Europe. He said Russia was a vacuum into which all movable goods would be sucked. He said the greatest crime of Hitler was that his actions had resulted in opening the gates of Eastern Europe to Asia. . . . [After finding the scheduled Big Three meeting canceled because of Stalin's illness we] went back to Averell's house where I met Ed Pauley, American Ambassador for Reparations, and Chip Bohlen. All hands disturbed by Russian negotiations on reparations. They are stripping every area they are in of all movable goods, and at the same time asking reparations and designating the goods they take as war booty. They are shooting and impressing Germans out of the American district. They shot two, according to Commodore Schade [Henry A. Schade,

head of a naval technical mission], near our house the other
night, one woman for refusing to give up her jewelry and attempting to run away. Averell said this did not represent per-
secutions particularly, but rather reflected the Russians' indifference to life. . . .

Went to see Ernest Bevin and found Bevin in very good
form. He said . . . the only industries they proposed to nationalize were power, railroads, mines and textiles up to the
spinning mills. He indicated he had no use for Laski. . . .[6]

I asked him a question about the Emperor in Japan, whether
he thought we ought to insist on destruction of the Emperor
concept along with the surrender. He hesitated and said this
question would require a bit of thinking, but he was inclined
to feel there was no sense in destroying the instrument through
which one might have to deal in order to effectively control
Japan. He then made a rather surprising statement—for a liberal and a labor leader: "It might have been far.better for all
of us not to have destroyed the institution of the Kaiser after
the last war; we might not have had this one if we hadn't done
so. It might have been far better to have guided the Germans
to a constitutional monarchy rather than leaving them without
a symbol and therefore opening the psychological doors to a
man like Hitler. . . ."

He said he was determined to get going what he called the
three historic axes of European trade—the Baltic axis . . . the
Antwerp axis and the Genoa axis. He said these three were the
classic foci of European trade for hundreds of years back. . . .

I asked him how he was going to deal with Southeastern
Europe, that is, the Balkans, which would be under the control of Russia, and he said he didn't think the Balkans
amounted to much in the way of business. I differed with this.

On the way back to our headquarters we passed the equipment of an American armored division drawn up alongside
the road. It included tanks and light armored vehicles and

---

[6] This was Harold J. Laski, the Left-wing professor of political science, who as
chairman of the executive committee of the British Labour Party was then playing a prominent role in its intellectual leadership. Forrestal seemed to have a
mild obsession with Laski; there are numerous references to him and to his
writings in the diary.

must have extended for about three miles. Commodore Schade
said the Russians were much impressed by it. There came back
to my mind the President's remark about Stalin's observation
about the Pope: When Churchill suggested that the Pope
would still be a substantial influence in Europe, Stalin snorted
and said, "How many divisions has the Pope got?". . .

[The United States, in July of 1945, had the armored divisions
     and the Russians apparently were "impressed." Unfortunately the
     divisions were soon to vanish in the great demobilization, and
     much of Forrestal's subsequent career was to revolve around the
     anguished problem of how to deal with an ominous world-power
     situation when one's own power had been laid aside.
         On the Monday Forrestal breakfasted with the President—to-
     gether with Eisenhower, Clay, Judge Samuel Rosenman, his own
     naval aides and others—and what he recorded of the talk was, in-
     terestingly enough in view of that meeting with the American
     armor, mainly about postwar military plans and policies. Later
     Forrestal again saw Byrnes and spoke to him about "Saudi Ara-
     bian oil."

30 July 1945   *European Trip*
     . . . I told him I thought it was a matter of first importance;
that we were spending and had spent many millions in Saudi
Arabia, and the British and not ourselves were getting the
benefit of it. I told him that, roughly speaking, Saudi Arabia,
according to oil people in whom I had confidence, is one of
the three great puddles left in the world, the other two being
the Russian Caucasus and the Caribbean. . . .

[This is a significant note, because it tends to explain the strong
     interest that Forrestal continued to take in all questions of Medi-
     terranean strategy and the basis of his attitude on the question of
     Palestine, which was later to involve him in much adverse criti-
     cism. In London a few days later Brendan Bracken (Churchill's
     close aide, who was then retiring as First Lord of the Admiralty)
     stressed the relationship between Palestine and world strategy.
     Bracken expressed "concern," Forrestal noted, "about the pledge,

[taken by some two hundred odd members of the new Parliament, to support the Jewish National Home. He said this could touch off a most explosive situation in the Middle East; that many millions of Arabs would be willing to fight immediately if such a program were set in motion. He said the Russians would probably welcome such disturbances, and that they were already moving most aggressively in Persia." Events were to dispute the worst of Mr. Bracken's fears, but these notes tend to clarify Forrestal's subsequent position.

After his talk with Byrnes, Forrestal left from Gatow Airport in mid-morning for a quick survey of Germany. In the Bremen area he saw the plants that had been developed for the mass production of schnorkel-type submarines—there were sixteen of these formidable craft on the ways at the Deschimage yard. At Kiel he encountered "Walther, a typical unreconstructed Hun," the industrial manager who had "had charge of the development and production of many of the jet propulsion devices and also of the use of H_2O_2 (hydrogen peroxide) for submarine fuel." He went on to Frankfurt and then to Berchtesgaden, where he visited Hitler's famous "Eagle's Nest" on its summit high above the Königssee, and so on to London, which he reached on August 2. There he saw Attlee, Bracken and others, but the interviews yielded little of lasting consequence. His plane landed him at Washington at 2:30 on the afternoon of August 7. The atomic bomb had been fired over Hiroshima the day before; the Soviet Union declared war on Japan on August 8. The end was at hand.

10 August 1945   *Surrender*

Captain Smedberg telephoned at seven o'clock that he had a very important message. He came out for breakfast and showed me a copy of a decrypted message from Tokyo to Japanese Ministers at Stockholm and Berne. . . . "Tokyo, August 10—The Japanese government today addressed the following communications to the Swiss and Swedish governments respectively for transmission to the United States, Great Britain, China and the Soviet Union: ' . . . The Japanese government are ready to accept the terms enumerated in the Joint Declaration which was issued at Potsdam on July 26, 1945, . . . with the understanding that the said Declaration does not comprise any demand which prejudices the prerogatives of His Majesty as a sovereign ruler.' "

Major Correa came to breakfast and we both went to the office at 8:15. I telephoned the President congratulations both on the indicated surrender of Japan and on his speech of last evening. I went to the White House at 8:40 to meet the President with the Secretary of State and Secretary of War, Admiral Leahy, John Snyder [then Director of the Office of War Mobilization] and the President's Naval Aide, Captain Vardaman, and Military Aide, General Vaughan. There was general discussion as to the Japanese message. It was agreed that we should await formal receipt of the surrender offer. Justice Byrnes raised the question of whether the offer accorded with our terms of "unconditional" surrender. Admiral Leahy thought it did but Byrnes felt that we might be exposed to the criticism that we had receded from the totality and severity of the Potsdam Declaration. I said that I felt this could be met by an affirmative statement on our part in which we could see to it that the language of surrender accorded fully with our intent and view.

The Secretary of War made the suggestion that we should now cease sending our bombers over Japan; he cited the growing feeling of apprehension and misgiving as to the effect of the atomic bomb even in our own country. I supported his view and said that we must remember that this nation would have to bear the focus of the hatred by the Japanese. . . . It was left that the Secretary of State would undertake the drafting of a message to be sent when, as and if the formal surrender came in.

[The Cabinet was summoned later the same day; the official text of the Japanese note had by that time arrived, and the President read it. Secretary Byrnes then read the answer which had in the meantime been prepared. This explicitly stated that the Emperor would be "under and responsive to the Supreme Commander of the Allied Forces."

10 August 1945   *Cabinet*

. . . Both the President and the Secretary of State emphasized the fact that they had used the term "Supreme Commander" rather than "Supreme Command" so that it would be quite clear that the United States would run this particular business and avoid a situation of composite responsibility such as had plagued us in Germany.

The President observed that we would keep up the war at its present intensity until the Japanese agreed to these terms, with the limitation, however, that there would be no further dropping of the atomic bombs. He said that he expected it would take about three days before negotiations were completed. He anticipated that we would find that Great Britain and China would acquiesce promptly in our views, but that Russia would not—in fact, he expected that we might not hear from Russia. He said we shall, however, act without them if we fail to hear from them and proceed with the occupation of Japan. . . .

He said he hoped that Mr. Snyder would call promptly a meeting to consider the disposition of surplus, and unless we moved on this promptly we would soon be overwhelmed by a very large volume of surplus products. . . .

[And Forrestal added another note on this same tremendous day:

10 August 1945   *Surrender*

Admiral King dispatched to Admiral Nimitz this morning a message apprising him of the receipt of the Japanese offer of surrender. The message started: "This is a peace warning."

[It was three years, eight months and fourteen days since the evening—of November 27, 1941—when the Navy had sent out its first alert, beginning: "This dispatch is to be considered a war warning."

There were a few remaining alarms and excursions. The crypt-analysis people came up on the 13th with "indications" of a

["probable attempt for an all-out banzai attack" by the Japanese; on the other hand, the Russians, "contrary to expectations," had promptly agreed to Byrnes' answer to the peace offer. There were problems of arranging for the occupation and final surrender ceremonies. But the world's second great war was over.

CHAPTER III

Foretaste of the Cold War

I

[The formal surrender took place on the deck of the U. S. S. *Missouri* in Tokyo Bay on September 2. The mood of sudden relief from long and breaking tension is exemplified by an amusing exchange a few days later of "Urgent: Top Secret" telegrams which Forrestal put into his diary. In the enthusiasm of victory someone let out the story of how, in 1943, Admiral Isoroku Yamamoto, the Japanese naval commander-in-chief and architect of the Pearl Harbor attack, had been intercepted and shot down in flames as a result of the American ability to read the Japanese codes. It was the first public revelation of the work of the cryptanalytic divisions, and it brought an anguished cable from the intelligence unit already engaged at Yokohama in the interrogation of Japanese naval officers: "Yamamoto story in this morning's paper has placed our activities in very difficult position. Having meticulously concealed our special knowledge we now become ridiculous." They were even then questioning the Japanese officer who had been responsible for these codes, and he was hinting that in face of this disclosure he would have to commit suicide. The cable continued: "This officer is giving us valuable information on Japanese crypto systems and channels and we do not want him or any of our other promising prospects to commit suicide until after next week when we expect to have milked them dry. . . ."

Washington answered with an "Operational Priority: Top Secret" dispatch: "Your lineal position on the list of those who are

[embarassed by the Yamamoto story is five thousand six hundred ninety two. All of the people over whose dead bodies the story was going to be published have been buried. All possible schemes to localize the damage have been considered but none appears workable. Suggest that only course for you is to deny knowledge of the story and say you do not understand how such a fantastic tale could have been invented. This might keep your friend happy until suicide time next week, which is about all that can be expected. . . ."

It was a mood which, for men in high office, could not last. There were too many pressing new issues, which the coming of peace had merely substituted for those of wartime. For a Secretary of the Navy the whole problem of military reorganization was obviously of primary importance among them. In June, Forrestal had assigned his friend Eberstadt to do a study of the broad subject. How broad it really was is well illustrated by a note on a luncheon meeting a month later.

18 July 1945   *Government*

I lunched today with Mr. Eberstadt and Mr. Walter Laves, who is preparing a study on the State Department for Harold Smith [the Director of the Bureau of the Budget]. We agreed on these things:

1. There must be some conscious place in the government for the making of policy.

2. There is need for much greater exchange of information and knowledge of what government policy is, so that all hands can move in conformity therewith.

3. There is need in the Cabinet for better administrative procedure—a secretariat and an agenda.

4. There is need in government for two grand divisions to head up (a) the creation and definition of national policy (State-War-Navy) and (b) a national body to examine and keep informed at all times on national resources for war—stockpiles, mobilization plans, etc.

5. It was agreed that this, if possible, should be done within the framework of the Cabinet and existing governmental organization.

[Experience was to show that it was easier to recognize these needs than to meet them. The Eberstadt report and the subsequent act provided much organizational machinery to achieve these basic ends, but as the crises deepened through later years the same cries for better and clearer policy formulation, for better intelligence, better administrative procedure, were still to rise. As Forrestal well knew, improved organization, however necessary, could never in itself be enough.

At Potsdam, as has been said, he had an opportunity further to explore the President's ideas when he breakfasted at the "White House" on the morning of his own departure.

30 July 1945   *European Trip*

. . . [The President] is in favor of a single Department of Defense, but I gather that his interest in it is not so much from the belief that it will provide greater efficiency in their [the Armed Services'] operations or procurement, but because of its relation to education and universal military training. His purpose is to wrap the entire question up into one package and present it to Congress. He talked a good deal of what he called the citizen sources of officers in both Services and of the destruction of "political cliques that run the Army and Navy." This seems to be a fixation with him, although he admitted that he hadn't had so much experience with the Navy. I raised the question of whether he thought any one man was good enough to run the combined Army, Navy and Air Departments. I said that my own experience had been that it took about two and a half years to have a fractional knowledge of the Navy alone. I also raised the question of what kind of men he would get in peacetime to be Under Secretaries of War, Navy and Air respectively [assuming that the posts would be subordinate to a single Defense Secretary]. He admitted some misgivings on these points.

His views on [military] education in general I gather to be these: He would have a common basic and beginning education for all officers, Army, Navy and Air Forces, on the general thesis that modern war is a composite and not separate business. He is particularly anxious to have all men who become officers spend at least a year in the ranks before doing so, so that they get an understanding of the attitude and problems of the ordinary soldier or bluejacket. I told him that his views fitted in to a large extent with our own thinking on postwar education. . . . So far as West Point and Annapolis are concerned, he said he regarded them more or less as finishing schools . . . for . . . specialist training. . . .

It was clear that most of his thinking was predicated upon his experience in the Army during the last war and in the National Guard since then. [President Truman had been a captain of field artillery in France in 1918.] He remarked that he had gone every year to a refresher training course and had read and thought a great deal about military problems. My impression is that he is not closed-minded nor will he hold rigidly to his own views.

Among other things, he remarked that he had long talks with Marshall on this subject, who was in complete agreement (!), that he hadn't talked with the Secretary of War but hoped that he would find him also in agreement, and hoped that I would be. I said that I was in agreement with the general principles of what he had said, but I was forced to say that I had great reservations about the practical possibility of any one man running a show as big, even in peacetime, as the combined Army, Navy and Air Force.

[That there would also have to be agreement from Congress on postwar military planning of any kind was soon painfully apparent. At the first Cabinet after the President's return to Washington it was clear that the tides of demobilization, which in the space of a few months were recklessly to dismantle what was at the moment the world's most powerful military machine, were already running strongly.

17 August 1945   *Cabinet*

. . . There was a discussion of the question of continuation of Selective Service.

The Postmaster General [Robert E. Hannegan], the Secretary of the Treasury [Fred M. Vinson had succeeded Mr. Mor-

genthau in this post in July] and Clint Anderson, Secretary of
Agriculture, all expressed the belief that Congress would not
permit the extension of Selective Service. Judge Patterson
[Under Secretary of War], speaking for the Secretary of War,
said the Army felt it should be continued, that they would
need from fifty to sixty thousand a month. He suggested lifting
the age limit to twenty-five. (Anderson told me privately that
he was absolutely certain Congress will repeal the act.) Leo
Crowley, at the end of the discussion, said he thought the realistic way to deal with the problem was to ask Congress to give
a sixty- to ninety-day period in which he could appraise and
take inventory of the situation, particularly as regards the total
number of troops required for the occupation of Japan, and
. . . he could then make his recommendations to Congress. . . .
    The net of the discussion was that the politically expert peo-
ple in the Cabinet seemed to have a very strong conviction that
Congress will vigorously oppose any extension and that it
would be unwise for the President to make a recommendation
which he knew in advance would be turned down. . . .
    Surplus Property: The Foreign Economic Administrator, Mr.
Leo Crowley, said that no one could do the surplus property
disposal job unless Congress ceased to exercise its kibitzing to
the point where everyone concerned in this endeavor was afraid
to move. Mr. Byrnes said he thought there was a dangerously
growing tendency in Congress to usurp executive functions and
mentioned as an example the Naval Affairs Committee's bill
of earlier this year which would prohibit the Navy from disposing of its own property without the consent of Congress.

[At lunch that day Forrestal picked up a footnote on history:

17 August 1945   *Hornbeck on Japanese Attitude*
    I had lunch today with Joe Grew. He talked a little about
Japan and his prewar appraisal of the Japanese attitude. It was
clear from his conversation that one of the people he blamed
for failure to get across to the State Department in general and
to Mr. Hull in particular the attitude of the Japanese was

Stanley Hornbeck [adviser to the State Department in 1941 and a specialist in Far Eastern affairs], who, he said, adhered to the belief that the Japs wouldn't fight. Grew said he felt that so strong was Hornbeck's wishful thinking on this subject that he doubted very much whether many of the messages which he (Grew) sent back to the Department warning on the prospects of war were ever seen by Mr. Hull.

[In planning for future organization it was of course necessary to consider how matters had worked in the past. In a talk with Admiral Edwards, Deputy Chief of Naval Operations, Forrestal got an interesting analysis of the Joint Chiefs of Staff system, supporting his own and the Navy's distrust of the proposal for a single, all-powerful Chief of Staff.

25 August 1945 *Joint Chiefs of Staff*

. . . Admiral Edwards said he thought it [the Joint Chiefs system] had been an extremely useful medium during this war. As against the criticism that it did not have a source of decision in a single man, he pointed out that had there been such a single decider we would probably still be about a year away from the end of the war, because:

1. General MacArthur's concept was to remain on the continent of Australia or in the adjacent islands until he had mustered greatly additional strength. He recalled the fact that he [MacArthur] was most unwilling to move in 1943, that it was the Navy's insistence on the prosecution of a vigorous war in the East that finally "pushed him off the cliff." Once he got off he found he could go all right.

2. MacArthur's mind was focused primarily on the return to the Philippines and he did not think much beyond that.

3. He was against, as was the Army here, the concept of the invasion and capture of the Marianas, the taking of which was essential to the reduction of Iwo Jima and Okinawa, and was essential for the securing of the flank of MacArthur's move north to the Philippines.

4. The taking of Guadalcanal was the result of the vigorous

pressing of this decisive action by Admiral King. The Army
did not like it. . . .

5. Conversely, Admiral Edwards pointed out that if any admiral had been directing the campaign in Europe, it was most
unlikely that his conception of strategy would have been sound.
In other words, the Joint Chiefs of Staff, while it was accused
of being a debating society, for that very reason probably was
the most practical and useful device that could have been conceived for the conduct of this war.

The theory of the swift and lightning-like instinctive, intuitive decision we had found had admirers during the early
successes of Hitler but the great intuitive brain laid a good
many eggs later on in the war. . . . It is a pretty good thing
for anyone charged with the responsibility of great decisions
to have to maintain his point of view before an earnest and
intelligent opposition.

[Two days after the formal surrender, the President showed that
     he was thinking of innovations of his own.

4 September 1945   *Cabinet Luncheon*

Lunched at the White House today. The President announced he was planning to hold Cabinet luncheons once or
twice a week; that he was very anxious to see to it that the
whole government was knit together as a working team and
that it functioned through the Cabinet. He hoped to accomplish this by a gradual absorption of the various extracurricu-
lum agencies as established during the war into the Cabinet
posts.

[The Cabinet luncheons were thereafter to become a regular
     feature, as many later notes in this diary show, though the order
     and teamwork for which the President hoped were not, perhaps,
     so easily to be achieved.

At the next meeting of the Cabinet proper they were considering the broad question of national military policy as a whole
and the difficulties it involved were well stated by the Foreign
Economic Administrator.

. . . Mr. Leo Crowley said that he had just returned from the Middle West and was sure that the country would be violently opposed to the continuation of any universal military training. He said the assumption was that we had fought a war now to get rid of war, that we had the atomic bomb and we had the San Francisco Conference and all the various affirmations of faith in the possibilities of an organization to create the foundations of world peace, and that universal training would create the inference that we didn't have faith in our own platform. To this Secretary Stimson made an eloquent rejoinder, the substance of which was that the only way we could convince the world we *were* serious about preventing another war was to show that we took our responsibility in that direction with great seriousness. I supported the Secretary of War's point of view and remarked that history showed that all new weapons always developed a countermeasure, beginning with what the Romans developed to counteract Hannibal's use of elephants. The President interjected Alexander in that first tank. Mr. Crowley's view continued to be, however, that no matter how much we felt as we did, the country would not support that point of view. Colonel Stimson rejoined that he did not accept that statement of cynicism about the good sense and the willingness of the nation to accept its serious responsibilities.

Public health: The President talked about public health, the lack of doctors, and the inadequacy of doctors and medical service in certain areas of the country. He said he proposed to send a message to Congress at some time on this subject which he knew would arouse the active opposition of the American Medical Association. . . . Fred Vinson observed that doctors would not go into areas where there weren't adequate hospital facilities, that therefore a hospital building program would have to go along with any health program. The President said that the statistics of the Selective Service showed a need for taking radical steps to re-establish the health of the nation.

[President Truman's prolonged battle with the American Medical Association over his proposals for a federal health system

[was to occupy much time, energy and newspaper space in the years ahead. But Mr. Crowley's report on the national attitude toward defense was perhaps of a greater long-term significance. This too hasty popular revulsion from the costs and ardors of defense was to hamstring official policy at every turn thereafter. Forrestal was sound in his suspicion that even the atom bomb— then already being trumpeted as the "absolute weapon"—might meet its countermeasures; though he could hardly have foreseen that one countermeasure would turn out, in the bitter fall of 1950, to be the expendable Chinese infantry masses, to which the atom bomb could make no useful reply.

Probably no one at that time realized the extent to which the atomic bomb—its potentialities, its limitations, the hopes and also the fears it aroused in our own people, the reactions both good and bad that it induced abroad in the minds both of our Western Allies and of the Soviet Union—lay at the core of the whole problem of postwar military policy. But no one, of course, could be unaware of the critical importance of the subject. At the Cabinet luncheon on Tuesday, September 18, the President told them that there would be a full-dress discussion of the whole question of atom bomb policy on the ensuing Friday, the 21st.

The Cabinet meeting on September 21 was "occupied entirely with a discussion of the atomic bomb" and was clearly fundamental in the formulation of American policy on this new and dread subject. The Cabinet was fully represented; there were also present John W. Snyder (then head of the Office of War Mobilization and Reconversion), Vannevar Bush, Leo Crowley, Paul V. McNutt (head of the War Manpower Commission), John B. Blandford, Jr., (National Housing Administrator) and Senator Kenneth McKellar of Tennessee, president pro tem of the Senate. The Acting Secretary of State, Dean Acheson, represented the absent Secretary Byrnes. The President called first on "the former Secretary of War, Mr. Stimson." Henry L. Stimson, twice Secretary of War and once Secretary of State, who had given the equivalent of at least two full careers to the service of his country, had finally sent in his resignation. His successor, Robert Patterson, the former Under Secretary, was not to be sworn in until

[September 27, but he represented the War Department at this meeting. It was Mr. Stimson's last appearance as a high officer of the government to which he had contributed so much.

The question was presented in the form of what should be "the policy of this government in making available information in our possession to other nations." Beginning with Mr. Stimson, the President went round the table. According to Forrestal's notes, the Secretary of Commerce, Mr. Henry Wallace, was "completely, everlastingly and wholeheartedly in favor of giving it to the Russians. Commented on . . . the statement that Russian ambitions in China, Korea and Mongolia have not yet been sufficiently defined for us to have trust. He said the real reason for the Chinese-Mongolian disaffection was that the Chinese were primarily a farming people and the Mongolians a cattle-breeding or livestock people. Science cannot be cribbed, cabined or confined; scientific knowledge is bound to spread over the world. He questioned the statement that the Russians were Orientals. He said that particularly in Mongolia they had a Western viewpoint in contrast to that of the Chinese. Failure to give them our knowledge would make an embittered and sour people." This trusting view was not shared by the others. It is clear that ideas had not yet fully crystallized (and that most of those present still had a very imperfect knowledge of the subject); and there were varying shades of emphasis given to the several factors that had to be weighed. Some, going on the assumption that it would be impossible to keep the secret anyway, were more inclined to favor publicity; others would "give them [the Russians] nothing until they have demonstrated a willingness to work with us."

The underlying attitude of nearly all seemed closely in accord with Forrestal's contribution. He made the point that the bomb and the knowledge that produced it were "the property of the American people," which the administration could not give away until they were very sure that it was the sense of the people that they should do so. He reminded them that in World War I the Japanese had been among our allies, like the Russians in World War II; that we had afterward made naval agreements with the Japanese which we had lived up to but which they had not, and that "the Russians, like the Japanese, are essentially Oriental in

[their thinking, and until we have a longer record of experience with them on the validity of engagements . . . it seems doubtful that we should endeavor to buy their understanding and sympathy. We tried that once with Hitler. There are no returns on appeasement." He added that "trust had to be more than a one-way street; just as certain nations were proposing to exercise trusteeship over certain areas of the globe on behalf of the United Nations, so it seemed to me that we could exercise a trusteeship over the atomic bomb on behalf of the United Nations and agree that we would limit its manufacture for use on such missions as the United Nations should designate."

The idea of a sole trusteeship (if that was what Forrestal had in mind) seems to have got no support, but the idea of submitting the matter for adjustment under the machinery of the United Nations became basic to subsequent American policy. And another idea—expressed in various ways by several participants in the conference—became equally basic. This was the idea that we should offer to publish our data in return for a proper *quid pro quo* from the Russians in terms of equal publicity and acquiescence in adequate regulatory measures. This Cabinet on September 21 laid the foundations upon which there were erected, in turn, the Lilienthal-Acheson report, the Baruch Plan and the United Nations majority program. As the Cabinet ended, the President, according to Forrestal's notes, "said he wanted to invite a memorandum from all hands summarizing the views they had expressed; he said he did not propose to act without the concurrence of Congress; that he had taken an obligation, however, to send a message with his recommendations. He said there would be another discussion next week at which he would announce his own conclusions."

Forrestal's notes do not show whether or not the President did announce a decision at the Cabinet of the following week, but he followed the advice, which several had tendered, to move slowly. His message to Congress of October 3, asking for the establishment of a domestic Atomic Energy Commission, made it plain that he would proceed to develop an international atomic policy only after prior discussion with Great Britain and Canada and then a thorough exploration of the field with other nations.

II

[On September 19 Forrestal appeared before the House Naval Affairs Committee to testify on Representative Carl Vinson's bill fixing the postwar size of the Navy. Vinson's purpose, as Forrestal told a correspondent,[1] was "largely psychological" since the Navy's own ideas on the subject were still fluid, but in supporting the bill Forrestal gave a clear statement of his own position: "Why should we maintain any Navy after this war? . . . First, the outstanding lesson of the past quarter-century is that the means to wage war must be in the hands of those who hate war. The United States should remain strong. Second, the Navy is a major component of that strength. . . . In the future as in the past the key to victory and to the freedom of this country will be in the control of the seas and the skies above them." And then he added, with a prophetic insight which the years were amply to confirm: "All this sounds as if I did not have confidence in the world organization for peace. I have. But that confidence can only be justified if, while these organizations are in the process of transfer from paper to living reality, all the world knows that the United States will not tolerate the disorder and the destruction of war being let loose again upon the world."

The secret and top secret reports Forrestal was at this time filing in his diary were sufficiently ominous of "disorder and destruction" in the new world. There was one from Warsaw: "Situation in Poland becoming increasingly serious" under Soviet pillage and Soviet absorption of the country. There was another from Ankara: The Turkish Foreign Office felt that either the "Soviets, like Hitler, have become victory drunk and are embarking on world domination," or else they were staking out huge claims all over the world in order to make good those in which they were really interested—among which Turkey probably had a top priority. To the Turks the future seemed dark but, they said, "we would rather die on Turkish soil than be deported to Siberia." There was a long War Department dispatch from Korea, describing the chaotically "impossible" situation that had resulted from "the splitting of Korea into two parts for occupation by

[1] To Sheldon Clark, president of the Navy League, 24 September 1945.

[force of nations operating under widely divergent policies and with no common command." Russian infiltration and looting, on top of all the legacies of war destruction, financial disorder, Korean political immaturity and the presence of the still undemobilized Japanese army, added up to an appalling situation. Other reports were summarized in a diary note: "Berry's [Burton Y. Berry, Foreign Service officer] dispatches from Bucharest and Harriman's from Moscow indicate that the Russians have no idea of going through with the Allied Nations statement of policy about Rumania, namely to permit the establishment of free and democratic institutions in Rumania. . . . [Ambassador Laurence A.] Steinhardt makes strong recommendations from Czechoslovakia against the complete withdrawal of American forces. He says this will be an open invitation to the Communists in the country and to Russian influence from without to take over." [2] And then at a luncheon Forrestal heard both an encouraging view of Soviet policy in China and some of the suspicions against the attitude of our own State Department in the Far East which were to rankle for years afterward.

28 September 1945   *Far East Relations*
I had lunch today with Ambassador [Patrick J.] Hurley, just back from China. . . . He recalled his conversation with Stalin [in April Hurley, returning to his post at Chungking, had passed through Moscow and had an interview with the Russian dictator] about the Russian attitude toward China. Stalin told him (1) that the Chinese Communists were not Communists in the Russian sense of that word; (2) that Russia desired to see a strong government in China and recognized Chiang Kai-shek as most nearly able to provide such a government and would therefore support it; (3) that Russia did not desire either revolution or anarchy in China, that their own problems in Asia were far too complex and difficult to desire such a condition.
He said a good many of the professional staff of the State Department . . . had not merely been of no help but a definite hindrance to him. He said that many of the American cor-

[2] Diary, 7 September 1945.

respondents . . . were communistically inclined, as well as many of the people in the State Department . . . who, he said, "felt no obligation for the United States except to draw their pay."

[At the Cabinet on the same day, however, it was the domestic labor situation which held first place in the discussion.

28 September 1945   *Cabinet*

The Secretary of Labor [Lewis B. Schwellenbach] led off with a statement that in his opinion we were facing very serious problems in connection with strikes arising out of the demand for wage increases to make up the difference between the war wages and the curtailed work week. He said the mood of the unions was to insist on everything that they asked for; that in New York City one of the important strikes was against a decision of the War Labor Board and not against employers; that we are now facing the issue of collective bargaining and whether it can continue on a voluntary basis or whether the government will have to ask for legislation for compulsory arbitration.

The Secretary of the Treasury [Fred M. Vinson] inquired what sanctions there were available to government to deal with recalcitrant and overdemanding unions.

The Secretary of Labor: Government could take away the benefits of the Wagner Act and deny to union leaders the right to treat on behalf of certain unions.

[It is interesting to find the Truman Cabinet facing thus early the issues which were later to give rise to the Taft-Hartley law, and to note the sympathy with which the President's advisers then spoke of a modification of the Wagner Labor Relations Act. When a Republican Congress, with the Taft-Hartley measure, finally enforced that modification, the President and his party assumed a pose of opposition. In the late summer of 1945, when the problem was apparent but when the matter had not yet become a political issue, their attitude seems to have been rather different.

[One of the fascinations of the Forrestal diary lies in the extent
. to which it shows how many of the problems which were later to
become acute were already fully apparent in these closing days
of the war and opening days of what too many assumed to be
peace. To Forrestal, the country was "going back to bed at a
frightening rate, which is the best way I know to be sure of the
coming of World War III." [3] He had started circulating among
his friends at this time copies of Kipling's celebrated "Tommy
Atkins," on the soldier's lot in peace:

> For it's Tommy this, and Tommy that, an' "chuck him out, the
> brute!"
> But it's "Saviour of 'is country" when the guns begin to shoot.

His old friend and mentor, Bernard Baruch, thought it "a
good piece" but added pessimistically: "This is my second round
trip into war, peace and the aftermath, and I can tell you that already I see nothing but a repetition of what took place after the
last war." Forrestal, suddenly interested in the arguments which in
the previous "aftermath" had led to the decline of American military strength, sent a memorandum to one of his assistants: "I
want someone to do a research for me on the things that appeared in *The Nation, New Republic* and *New Masses* ten years
before the war, against preparedness." Now, again, a great war
machine was being destroyed; the country was "going to bed";
even from Washington, as he wrote a friend, "all hands are pull-
ing out," and with the early winter he knew he was facing "a
great exodus" from the service of the "lawyers, accountants, business people, etc.," who had in fact been such vital cogs in the
war effort. Yet the problems and the perils were no less than before, and they all had to be faced as they came—from domestic
labor policy to Soviet aggression, from demobilization to the
atomic bomb. Fantastically different as they were upon the surface, all were intimately interrelated at bottom. A State-War-
Navy meeting in mid-October gives a vivid illustration of the
complex with which Forrestal and his colleagues had to deal.

---

[3] To Ralph A. Bard, 16 October 1945.

16 October 1945   *State-War-Navy Meeting*

1. *Rio Treaty*: Mr. Byrnes first raised the subject of the Rio Treaty to be concluded pursuant to the Act of Chapultepec. . . . He would like to have the comments of the Navy by noon on Wednesday. . . .

2. *Central Intelligence Agency*: Mr. Byrnes next raised the question of a central intelligence agency . . . responsible to a Council of Defense which would consist of the Secretaries of State, War and Navy. Mr. Forrestal pointed out that this was substantially similar to the Joint Chiefs of Staff proposal. . . . Mr. Patterson did not recall having seen the Joint Chiefs of Staff proposal, nor had Mr. Byrnes seen it. All of the Secretaries agreed with the principle of the proposal, that any central intelligence agency should report to the three Secretaries rather than directly to the President. . . .

3. *Czechoslovakia*: Mr. Patterson next raised the question as to whether or not two divisions should be left in Czechoslovakia. . . . He stated that the Czechs originally wanted the American troops to leave but now want them to remain because they have 150,000 Russian troops on their hands who apparently are going to remain for an indefinite time. Mr. Byrnes stated that the President had addressed a letter to Stalin on the subject, suggesting that the troops be withdrawn, but that it could not be delivered for the present as Stalin was away and it was being held. He suggested deferring any decision for a week or so.

4. *Russia*: This led to a general discussion on the question of the Russian attitude in Eastern Europe and the Balkans, and also in Japan. Mr. Byrnes recounted his experience with the Russians at the meeting [held in London in the middle and latter part of September] of the Council of Foreign Ministers in the matter of an advisory council for Japan. He stated that the Russians agreed to an advisory council rather than a control commission but then, after the British had been persuaded to go along on the principle of an advisory council, sought to withdraw from the arrangement. . . . Mr. Byrnes stated that he is going ahead with plans for the first meeting of the advi-

sory council . . . whether the Russians came along or not. He
stated that the British were in accord but were most desirous
of having India invited to participate. This he said could not
be done unless the Russians agree. . . .

5. *Demobilization*: It was agreed by all present that the
point of this discussion was . . . that it was most inadvisable for
this country to continue accelerating the demobilization of our
Armed Forces at the present rate. Mr. Forrestal pointed out
that at this rate there will necessarily come a point between
the present time and the time when the Army and Navy reach
their planned postwar strength at which neither the Army nor
the Navy will have sufficient trained men to be able to operate
efficiently. Mr. Forrestal stated that this was a situation of such
gravity that in his view the President ought to acquaint the
people with the details of our dealings with the Russians and
with the attitude which the Russians have manifested throughout. Mr. Byrnes demurred somewhat on this point, however.
He stated that he was a little dubious about the advisability of
such a procedure as it would give the Russians an excuse for
claiming that we had furnished provocation which justified
their actions.

6. *Atomic Energy*: Mr. Patterson next raised the question
as to discussions with the British and Canadians relative to
atomic energy. . . . This led to a discussion of the question as
to whether or not this country should make available to the
Russians information concerning atomic energy. . . . Mr.
Byrnes [who had been absent when the same matter was raised
at the Cabinet on September 21] indicated that he was most
strongly opposed to imparting any of this information to the
Russians. He stated that he felt that undue emphasis was being
given to the views of the scientists on this subject. He said that
while it was all very well for the scientists to say as they did
that science has no boundaries, that certainly did not apply to
either Mr. Molotov or Mr. Stalin; that in his view it is idle to
expect that we would be allowed any access for purposes of inspection of Russian factories producing atomic bombs when we
cannot even gain access to Hungary or Poland. . . . In response to Mr. Patterson's questions Mr. Byrnes stated that in

his view the Russians were quite serious in their demand for Tripolitania and were pressing it most strongly. . . .

[At the Cabinet meeting ten days later Secretary Byrnes gave a fuller report on the difficulties he had encountered at London.

26 October 1945   *Cabinet*

. . . Although [Byrnes said] Russia agreed on September 11 to the participation of France and China in discussions at the London meeting, Molotov recanted on this and insisted that he could not agree to their sitting. . . .

The Russians would not agree to the particular principle of disarmament throughout the conquered nations, the obvious conclusion to be drawn from this being that in their satellite governments they wanted to maintain sufficient armed force to implement their own wishes.

The Russians asserted the right to trusteeships of some of the Italian colonies in Africa. Molotov asserted he had Stettinius's agreement to this. Byrnes asked to see the letter, which turned out was written by Harold Stassen. The letter said that the United States was willing to agree that Russia was "potentially eligible" for consideration as an administrator of trusteeships of conquered territories. Molotov insisted that this language constituted an agreement. Byrnes undertook to explain the meaning of the words "potential" and "eligible" by saying that every citizen of the United States was potentially eligible to become President of the United States but that didn't mean he was going to get the job. . . .

Proposal had been made that Trieste be made a free port —the President interjected that he had suggested Switzerland as the trustee. The logic of the free port idea was so strong that Molotov had to agree at one session to its soundness, but he later retracted when Tito pointed out that that would not satisfy their [the Yugoslav Communist regime's] requirements.

The Russians mentioned $600 million as the sum of Italian reparations. . . . Byrnes said that this country did not propose to permit reparations to be exacted from a nation which we would have to support later on. . . . Molotov said they could make no progress until this country recognized Rumania. Byrnes responded that we couldn't recognize a country about whose government we knew nothing except that it (the Groza government) had been installed by Vishinsky, who gave the King two hours and thirty minutes to accept that unilateral announcement, and that when the King asked for another thirty minutes he was told that was not available. Byrnes said it was clear from the whole procedure at London that the Russian conception of a free government was not like ours. . . .

The Russians took advantage of the agitation here about MacArthur to inject this issue [the Allied Control Commission] on the same day that Acheson had censured MacArthur; said we were not punitive enough with the Japanese, were not destroying their industries, were permitting the industrialists to survive, were not taking prisoners. . . . Molotov continued to press . . . for a control commission on the pattern of Germany, which Byrnes pointed out had not worked very well. They wanted Japanese prisoners, and in fact they are now using Japanese prisoners to build the railroad to Port Arthur. Evatt [Herbert V. Evatt, Australian Minister for External Affairs] saw an opportunity for personal publicity and joined Molotov in the demand but was later called off by Bevin. . . .

[Byrnes ended by mentioning a letter he had recently received from Jan Smuts, South Africa's elder statesman and at that time Prime Minister, who had congratulated him on the London Conference as "the first ray of hope" since it "had drawn out into the open issues which would have to be faced ultimately and which could be faced now with a far less degree of trouble." But the whole session, with its grim implications, reminded Forrestal of the position, which Stimson had taken in April and which Forrestal had supported, that a firm agreement between the United States, Britain and Russia "on world problems" should precede the calling of the San Francisco Conference. The issues should have been dealt with earlier, on Stalin's realistic principle that "those who have the power should exercise it." One can clearly see in retrospect that it would have been better; whether it would also have been possible, even in early 1945, is a question

[which will probably long be debated. What was already apparent, as the autumn declined, was that one of those who "had power"—the United States—was not only uninterested in its exercise but was rapidly divesting itself of the power which it held.

At the State-War-Navy meeting on October 30 there was a long, but apparently not very fruitful, argument over the control system to be set up in Japan and over "the great difficulty of working out some agreement which will satisfy the British, the Soviet and General MacArthur." According to Secretary Byrnes, Stalin now did not want to put occupation troops in Japan "partly because he does not want to place them under an American commander." But would this in turn mean barring British and Australian occupation troops? "Mr. Byrnes did not think the British would care much, but said that Evatt certainly would—'Evatt wants to run the world.'"

There was one effort being made in those days to exercise global power—the Navy was engaged in ferrying Chiang Kai-shek's Nationalist troops northward to meet the Chinese Communist armies in Manchuria. Forrestal entered a copy of a telegram from the "COM 7th PHIB" (Commander of the 7th Amphibious Corps) reporting the landing of the Chinese 89th Division near Shanghaikwan. The Chinese were "well disciplined. Docile. Very young. No contagious diseases. Apparently first experience with plumbing and initially mistook urinals for wash basins and dark corners for heads [the ancient Navy term for a toilet]. Many seasick. Troops have left but odors linger." This was an amusing item, but there was not really much cause for amusement. In the first days of November McCloy got back from a global survey, and he was not encouraging.

5 November 1945   *Secretary McCloy*

Assistant Secretary of War McCloy got in today from Japan, completing his round-the-world trip. He said that there were three impressions that one got everywhere throughout the world:

1. The postwar problems are global; that is, the conditions of anarchy, unrest, malnutrition, unemployment, etc., which exist in Europe and the Middle East are duplicated throughout

Asia and Southeast Asia—the economic dislocations are profound and far-reaching.

2. The tremendous position and prestige enjoyed by the
United States is the one beacon of hope everywhere, but the
dependence upon us to be the salvation for all the ills of the
world may not be an unmixed blessing; the disappointment,
frustration and bitterness of the end of next winter may be in
exact proportion to the confidence expressed in us now.

3. The universal fear of the Russian colossus, both in terms
of the size of that country and the locust-like effects of their
occupation wherever they may be. . . .

III

[Our growing difficulties with the Russians were world-wide,
but over the next few weeks attention was to be focused primarily upon the tangled problems of the Far East. Forrestal had
wanted the President to take the full story of our relations with
Russia to the people; Byrnes had hesitated, and at the State-War-
Navy meeting on November 6 his viewpoint appeared more
clearly. They were again arguing as to whether Japan should be
occupied jointly by a composite force under MacArthur or by
United States troops alone. Stalin would not send Russian troops
to serve under the American, and Byrnes "understood" that he
felt the entire occupation should therefore be left to the United
States. The difficulty was that MacArthur wanted the help of
contingents from the other Allies. According to Major Correa's
notes of this meeting:

"Mr. Byrnes said that unfortunately General MacArthur was
not thinking of the effect on the rest of the world, that he was
naturally looking at the matter largely from the point of view of
the problem of Japan. Mr. Byrnes felt that Stalin's position was
sound and that the presence of other Allied forces could not but
be a source of considerable irritation. . . . Mr. Patterson pointed
to the earlier views of the Joint Chiefs of Staff and said that
he favored bringing in British, Chinese and Australian troops
and leaving the Russians out if they don't want to come. Mr.
Byrnes emphasized that the trouble is such a step is merely making for two worlds and preparing the course for another war. The

[Soviets believe that the rest of the world is ganging up on them and he considered it most important for the future peace of the world to try to work in cooperation with them. Mr. Forrestal said that to summarize Mr. Byrnes' viewpoint it is that if we have the British and Chinese but no Russians, world opinion would oppose this arrangement, and furthermore a certain school of our columnists would make a great to-do over our failure to include Russia. Mr. Byrnes emphasized that Stalin feels that he has been completely ignored on the question of Japan and said by way of illustration that in his conversation with Harriman it was the only question that he [Stalin] wanted to discuss."

McCloy, who was present, concluded that the only choice was for the United States to assume the whole occupation burden. But even in this relatively minor matter they were already feeling the paralyzing consequences of demobilization. If the Allies did not participate we should have to find an additional hundred thousand men for the duty. "There was some discussion of the unfortunate effects of our rapid demobilization and the pressing problem of how we will get our Army unless the universal service bill is passed. Mr. Patterson said that under the voluntary recruiting system the Army has obtained only fifty-one thousand so far and most of these are old regular Army men. Of course MacArthur would be happy to have a purely American force, but the rate of demobilization presents a real question."

Forrestal, much later on, was to express his doubts as to whether Mr. Byrnes sufficiently understood Soviet ideology. He was entering one example of that ideology in his diary next day —in the form of a copy of a telegram from the MacArthur headquarters, reporting that the Russians had begun to remove the generating machinery from the great Yalu River hydro-electric plants in northern Korea. These plants were, said the telegram, among the world's largest; half the output went to Manchuria, "therefore Chinese have interest," and the other half to Korea, supplying thirty per cent of the power used in the American-occupied zone below the 38th parallel. The telegram called for "strong representation" to the Soviet government to "desist."

As November began, they had been worrying about the Japanese occupation and about Korea; as it ended, the far more vast,

[more baffling and more enduring problem of China itself had
arisen in an urgent way.

20 November 1945   *State-War-Navy Meeting*

At the meeting with Byrnes and Patterson this morning the
question of our future policy in China and Manchuria arose.
Wedemeyer [Lieutenant General Albert C. Wedemeyer, then
commander of United States Forces in China] has asked for
instruction, his present directive being first to keep troops in
China to accomplish the disarmament of the Japanese and to
provide for their repatriation up to the point when he considers the Chinese National government troops alone can carry
out this mission. In his original cable of last Friday he put the
decision up to the Washington government. This morning's
cable to him made clear that we were looking to him for a recommendation on the latter point, namely whether the Chinese
Nationalist government troops had the capability of carrying
out the *disarmament and return to Japan of Japanese in Manchuria.*

Patterson pointed out that this was consistent with the rest
of our policy in Asia, namely, to get the Japanese back to their
home islands, and that we would be inconsistent if we departed from that as far as the substantial number of Japs in
Manchuria is concerned. There is strong pressure to bring Americans out of China, particularly the Marines. If we do, we invite
a vacuum of anarchy in Manchuria, and it is obvious that into
that vacuum ultimately either the Japanese or the Russians will
flow. At the moment of course it will be the Russians. In this
connection I referred to a conversation with Admiral Mitscher
on Sunday, in which he pointed out that in any future war
between a combination of Russia and the Asiatic powers the
manpower available to such a combination would be so tremendous and the indifference to the loss of life so striking that
it would present a very serious problem to this country.

[Here, in very nearly its full form, was the dilemma that was to
bewilder the Truman administration from that day onward. Mitscher's, and Forrestal's, prevision was to be tragically confirmed

[just five years later, in November of 1950, when that huge and expendable Chinese manpower, conscripted in the service of Communism, rolled down upon our armies in northern Korea. But at the end of 1945, when it seemed difficult to find even a hundred thousand men for the occupation of Japan, and when all the popular pressures were demanding the withdrawal of the Marines we then had in China, what could be done?

The whole problem was, moreover, complicated by another factor that was again and again thereafter to vitiate effective policy. In the answering cable to Wedemeyer (a copy of which Forrestal included in the diary) it was made clear that while the State Department wanted to help the Nationalists under Chiang Kai-shek to get the Japanese out of China, "it does not wish to support the National government directly against the Communists." The Chinese Communist armies under Mao Tse-tung were at that time less well organized and far less well armed than they were later to become. But the State Department, impressed by the backwardness, corruption and unpopularity of the Nationalists under Chiang Kai-shek, convinced that Mao's Communists represented an important popular movement and that the United States could not openly combat it without suffering disastrously under the charge of "imperialist meddling," wished to stay clear of the struggle between Chiang and Mao. This telegram clearly recognized the difficulty: even to help Chiang get the Japanese out would "result in some collateral aid or prestige in favor of the National government vis-à-vis the Communists," yet "conversely withdrawal now" of American troops "may mean substantial frustration of a policy we have long supported which contemplated unifying China and Manchuria under Chinese National forces." They were never, throughout the succeeding years, to find the answer to that one. The State Department's answer at the moment was that the United States would transport no more Chinese Nationalist troops to Manchuria and "will not support the National government vis-à-vis the Communists except in so far as necessary to get the Japanese disarmed and out of China"; but its weakness seems to have been apparent, from the urgent concluding demand upon Wedemeyer to give his views.

[Major Correa's more extensive notes of this meeting show
that it came back at the end—as so many discussions of high
policy inevitably did that winter—to the swift evisceration of our
armed strength. "Mr. Patterson said that on November 1 he had
written a memorandum . . . to Mr. Byrnes pointing out that
under present accelerated demobilization plans, by next April
we will have in Europe only some four hundred thousand men.
He said that, viewed strictly as a police force, he thought this
number was adequate for the occupation of Germany and Austria. The same thing is true of Japan. . . . In China we are faced
with the same reduction and the same problem. In addition to the
numerical decline in our forces, the loss in their fighting prestige
is even greater. He said that he realized that these forces were
not sufficient to have an effective influence on our over-all national policy. He knew that the State Department, no doubt, considers it highly important to maintain adequate military strength,
but unfortunately Congress is on the other side. In connection
with War Department appropriations they are saying that if the
Army will demobilize fast enough, present appropriations will
last. . . . Mr. Byrnes said it unquestionably reduces the influence
of the United States if we have our men scattered all over. Mr.
McCloy pointed out that even where we have troops now the
emphasis is all on the question of withdrawal. Mr. Byrnes said
that the situation in China worried him considerably more than
that elsewhere."

It was at this time that Forrestal pasted in the diary a clipping
from the *Washington Post*; "Russia," the headline said, "Will Not
Disarm," and the story, under Moscow dateline, was about a
new campaign that had been launched to secure re-enlistment
of Soviet noncommissioned officers—a campaign in language
leaving "no doubt that disarmament plays no part in the present
plans of the Soviet leaders." But the country failed to grasp the
critical nature of the time. That rush to disarm in late 1945 was
surely one of the most expensive economies—in terms of life and
effort as well as of money—in which the United States ever in-
dulged.

Wedemeyer had been asked for his advice; he now proceeded
to give it in a series of long telegrams, exhaustive in their analy-

[sis of the situation but, when it came down to what could or should be done about it, little more illuminating than the State Department had been. Under date of November 20 his final recommendations were *either* to withdraw all troops at once *or* to announce continued military and economic support for Chiang. On the 23rd he emphasized that it would be impossible to support Chiang and at the same time stay clear of the latter's war with the Chinese Communists; "such United States support to the National government will definitely involve American forces in fratricidal warfare. There can be no mistake about this. . . . If the unification of China and Manchuria under Chinese National forces is to be a U. S. policy, involvement in fratricidal warfare and possibly in war with the Soviet Union must be accepted and would definitely require additional U. S. forces far beyond those presently available in the theater to implement the policy." This was a question he thought should be decided by the State Department.

On the 26th Forrestal entered in his diary a summary, compiled by an assistant, of State Department dispatches on Russian policy as they were coming in from all around the world. Everywhere, from Western Europe to Korea, they drew an unrelieved picture of Soviet highhandedness, unilateral action and aggressive pressure. It was also on November 26 that there was completed a long "Memorandum for the Secretary of State" for joint signature by Secretaries Forrestal and Patterson, setting forth the military Departments' considered conclusions on the problem of China.

This document was not—one must admit in retrospect—a model of either clarity, conciseness or decision. It was very long; it already showed the symptoms of that "on-the-one-hand-on-the-other-hand" disease which was to blight so many documents on Chinese policy in the ensuing years, and it skillfully handed the fundamental issue—which the State Department had passed to Wedemeyer, which Wedemeyer had returned to Washington—back to the State Department. "The State Department," in the words of one of the many subparagraphs of the paragraphs on "conclusions," should "provide a definitive policy to cover the period of the next few years in China." There is nothing to show

[what Forrestal's specific contribution to the whole may have
been. But there was a certain amount of iron in the verbiage,
and one may safely infer that Forrestal was in favor of putting it
there. Recognizing that it was impossible to support Chiang
against the Japanese without also supporting him against the
Chinese Communists, the memorandum firmly elected to accept
the risks of the latter course. It considered that the reports of
Communist military strength were exaggerated (which at that
time they probably were) and felt that from the long-range view
"the most important military element in the Far East favorable
to the U. S. is a unified China, including Manchuria, friendly to
the U. S. This is the best assurance against turmoil and outbreak
of war in the Far East." The specific recommendations were to
keep the Marines in North China "pending clarification of U. S.
political policy," in spite of the admitted danger of involvement
in "fratricidal strife"; to lend every aid to Chiang in getting the
Japanese repatriated, and to try to get an international agreement on China and Manchuria among the major powers, including the U. S. S. R. The memorandum ended with a prescient
paragraph:

It appears that if Manchuria and perhaps North China are
not to pass to Chinese control but rather pass to Soviet control
or separate states under its domination by a progression of
circumstances, then Russia will have achieved in the Far East
approximately the objectives Japan initially set out to accomplish. The impact of such piecemeal action, uncoordinated internationally, on the U. S. and the world at large would, in the
long run, probably be at least as grave militarily as any situation likely to arise due to continued U. S. support of the National government, also uncoordinated internationally. Whatever U. S. action is determined upon, it appears serious consideration should be given to consultation with other powers concerned.

[But it was too bold and forthright a position for those times.
The Marines, to be sure, remained in China temporarily; but
there is little to suggest that the State Department ever managed

[to provide a "definitive policy to cover the next few years in China." Next day there came a suprise.

27 November 1945   *Cabinet Luncheon*

Hurley's Resignation: At the Cabinet luncheon today the single topic of discussion was the resignation of Pat Hurley as Ambassador to China, charging the sabotage of his work for reconciliation between the C. C. P. (Chinese Communist Party) and Generalissimo Chiang Kai-shek. His action was a complete surprise to both the President and the Secretary of State, both of whom had the impression that he had agreed to return to China.

After lunch, in discussing the question of his possible successor, Clinton Anderson, the Secretary of Agriculture, said he believed the appointment of George Marshall would take the headlines away from Hurley's resignation the following day. I seconded Anderson's suggestion, and it was the general consensus that he would make an able ambassador. The President said he was reluctant to put additional tasks on Marshall, who had earned a rest after five arduous years. He confided to us that the place he had in mind for him was chairmanship of the Red Cross. It was pointed out, however, that Marshall could take the China assignment as a Special Envoy of the President on a temporary basis. Later in the day the President telephoned Marshall and he accepted.

[Thus it was decided to keep the Marines for a time in China, and thus George C. Marshall, the wartime Army Chief of Staff and the nation's outstanding soldier, was launched upon the diplomatic and administrative career in which five years later he had still to find a "rest." But nothing had really been determined. These decisions marked not an end but only another difficult beginning with the insoluble problem of China and the East.

IV

[This whole episode must have left a considerable impression upon Forrestal. The military weakness which paralyzed our policy can only have reinforced his convictions as to the necessity

[for power; while the hasty, disconnected and piecemeal way in which policy decisions of far-reaching implications were here taken drove home the need for a thorough overhaul of the whole mechanism of policy formation, by which that power would have to be directed.

Ferdinand Eberstadt had completed his report on military reorganization at the end of September, and Forrestal had transmitted it to Senator Walsh, the chairman of the Naval Affairs Committee, in mid-October. At the same time proposals for the general reorganization of the Executive branch were again in the air, and the subject came up at a Cabinet early in November.

9 November 1945   *Cabinet*

There was a discussion at the Cabinet this morning on the proposed government reorganization bill. The Senate committee has made thirteen or fourteen exceptions, including the FDIC [Federal Deposit Insurance Corporation], ICC [Interstate Commerce Commission], SEC [Securities and Exchange Commission], and the Army Engineers.

Secretary Byrnes and Senator McKellar said that it would be impossible to get any reorganization bill through without allowing certain exemptions; particularly, mention was made of the Army Engineers, Mr. Byrnes observing that the Army Engineers could not be included in a reorganization bill, no matter if the Secretary of War and even the President were to issue instructions, because of their strength on the Hill. At this juncture I remarked that I couldn't refrain from suggesting that it might be a desirable thing to consolidate the Army Engineers with the Army.

I also suggested that the need for government reorganization be carried to the country and that cabinet members refer to it in their speeches. I said particularly I believed it was possible to convince business of the need for this reorganization because business was coming up against the ineptitude and inadequacies of such organizations as the SEC, ICC and the Federal Trade Commission. It continued to be the view, however, of Mr. Byrnes and others that it would be impossible, no matter what amount of public exposition was done, to overcome the special prerogatives of certain legislative pets.

[A day or two later Forrestal left another entry in his diary as "A footnote on single department of defense."

14 November 1945   *South America*

. . . Admiral Edwards advised me this afternoon that the Army was in pell-mell haste to equip all the South American countries with armaments—ground forces, air and navy—on the grounds that this is necessary to carry out the concept of the regional arrangement for reciprocal defense.

I talked to the Secretary of State over the telephone and he seemed unaware of what was going on. I remarked that it seemed to me that this was a matter which should be considered, and a decision made, only at the highest level. Otherwise we might be promoting a series of wars in South America. . . .

[The President had told Forrestal when the latter saw him at Potsdam in July that he intended to "wrap the entire question" of unification "up into one package and present it to Congress." [4] Mr. Truman was now preparing his message to that end, and on the 21st he called in the representatives of the Navy viewpoint.

21 November 1945

Meeting with the President this morning, Senator Walsh, Carl Vinson, Admiral Denfeld [Vice Admiral Louis E. Denfeld, then Chief of Naval Personnel] and myself.

The President said he didn't like the concurrent resolution stating the size of the Navy. He said that was a usurping of executive functions. He finally agreed after some discussion to permit the legislation dealing with personnel to be passed by the Congress. . . .

Senator Walsh and Mr. Vinson told the President they hoped that he would not undertake to introduce a bill for unification

---

[4] See p. 88.

of the Services, Vinson saying that it would not pass either this winter, next winter, or the winter after. The President said he proposed to send a message which would not impair the Navy as an entity, but that in the meantime the Navy was entirely free to continue the presentation of its case. I told the President I had no brief in behalf of the Navy, that what I wanted was the best answer for the country; that I felt he had not yet had an opportunity to consider the real merits of the case and that I hoped before he sent his message he would give such consideration.

In connection with the discussion of the size of the postwar Navy I interjected the statement that the reason for delay on the Joint Chiefs of Staff directive of last August to outline for him the postwar strength of the Army, Navy and Air Forces was the fact that the Army had consistently delayed action on this, which they said could not be acted upon until the larger question of unification had been decided. I said the fact was that we had our case very thoroughly in order and the Army did not, but we were being blamed for being forehanded. . . .

[In his own studies of the unification question Forrestal had been much impressed by British experience. One consequence of his readings in this field was an interesting estimate of Winston Churchill's strategy.

2 December 1945

In reading Sir Maurice Hankey's description of the work of the British War Cabinet I recalled the fact that Winston Churchill was extremely skeptical of the success of the *Overlord* operation—the D-Day invasion of the Norman coast on June 6, 1944. It is doubtful whether . . . this operation would have been undertaken when it was if it were not for American pressure. . . . One factor in Churchill's reluctance may have been his readiness to listen to Air Marshal Harris, who always believed that Germany could be brought to surrender by mass bombing.

Churchill's conservatism, which is the outgrowth of the very heavy British casualties in World War I, may have been a salutary brake on American initiative in 1942. . . . Churchill's eyes were always on the Mediterranean, and he was always endeavoring to secure American support in his plans for the invasion of Europe either through the Balkans or by an expedition up the Adriatic and into the Balkans. . . .

It is clear now that it was not timidity or lack of boldness on Churchill's part that influenced him to bring this pressure, but rather his fear of the spreading influence of Russia throughout the entire Balkan peninsula and his desire to have American troops, jointly with the British, appear in those countries as the conquerors of the Germans.

[Meanwhile the public debate over unification was growing in intensity. The Eberstadt report, arguing for a "coordinated" rather than a "unitary" system, was thoroughly reasoned and was making considerable impression.

14 December 1945

Lunched with Arthur Sulzberger [Arthur Hays Sulzberger, publisher of the *New York Times*]. He spoke of his talk yesterday with Admiral Nimitz and complimented the Navy on the preparation of the booklet; said he thought we were making definite progress with the public in that we were dissipating the idea of merely stubborn opposition to the merger and had succeeded in showing that it was a much deeper problem than simply the merger of the two Cabinet offices. He said he would welcome an answer to the *Times'* editorial criticism. I told him that I had invited Patterson, Eisenhower and Nimitz to lunch with me Monday, and he was very much pleased with that.

Among other subjects: He remarked that he had just had a letter from Brooks Atkinson, *Times* correspondent in Moscow, to the general effect that the only thing "these people recognize is stark force; they have no respect for the normal human weaknesses, such as justice, kindliness, affection, etc." (This is particularly interesting in that Brooks Atkinson, the correspondent in question, had a definite intellectual Leftist leaning when he went to Russia.)

He said the *Times* would continue in support of the China policy; he was very much impressed with the need for an organizational pattern of government similar to that of the British Civil Service. He inquired about Hankey's book—I am sending him a copy. . . .

18 December 1945   *Cabinet Luncheon*

. . . *Unification*: The Postmaster General said he thought the President was making a mistake to send down the message on unification of the Armed Services, that the chairman of the Senate Naval Affairs Committee was opposed to the measure and the chairmen of both the Military and Naval Affairs Committees of the House likewise. Hannegan said he felt that the President was inviting an unnecessary fight which he might lose, with the resultant loss of prestige. The President said he felt it was his duty to send the message because it represented his conviction; the Navy had had an ample opportunity to present its case, that nobody had been muzzled. I said that that was true with the exception that (a) the Navy's case had not yet been fully presented and (b) the committee before which it had been presented was a highly prejudiced body which had reached a conclusion in advance. I said it reminded me of a lawsuit I had once where our firm was being sued for $15 million in the Ohio courts. We went to Akron to argue a preliminary hearing on whether what was known as constructive service was valid, when our lawyer, Joe Cotton, dining in the Akron Club, overheard the Judge who was scheduled to have the hearing the following day say to his associates that he certainly intended to have an impartial hearing but he hoped those New York s.o.b.'s would lose.

At this juncture the President interjected that he did not intend now to cut off discussion or to muzzle anyone. I later checked with the Postmaster General and Judge Patterson as to whether they had the same understanding of the President's remarks and they said they did. Later in the day I told Judge Rosenman of the conversation, about which he expressed great surprise.

I suggested this afternoon to Admiral Nimitz that we handle

the situation by instructing naval officers that it was not appropriate for them, once the message had been sent to Congress, to make public appearances in opposition, but that we considered ourselves free to present our untrammeled point of view to the committees of Congress, such as the Naval Affairs Committees of the House and Senate, when they begin hearings.

19 December 1945   *Unification*

Commander [Clark M.] Clifford told me this morning over the White House telephone that the question of the attitude of either the civilian secretariat of the Navy or of military personnel in response to questions before congressional inquiries had come up at the morning conference with the President and that the following precept for their conduct had been reached:

If the witness is of the opinion that the proposed consolidation of the Army and Navy is undesirable he should state at the beginning of his testimony that he understands it is the announced policy of the administration to favor such a proposal, but that his Commander-in-Chief has announced his willingness to have all witnesses express their personal views on the subject without restraint. Having made this announcement, the witnesses are then free to give their opinions, backed up by such facts as they wish to adduce, with vigor and clarity.

[The President sent in his unification message on December 20. It represented a defeat for Forrestal's and the Navy's point of view. The President flatly rejected the Joint Chiefs of Staff system, under which the Services had operated throughout the war and which Forrestal and Eberstadt had made the core of their own plan of unification; "this kind of coordination," Mr. Truman said, "was better than no coordination at all, but it was in no sense a unified command." The President insisted on a single, overall Chief of Staff—the arrangement Forrestal so much feared —and made it clear that the single Department of Defense which he envisaged would be closely centralized, with the existing Departments reduced to subordinate level and headed only by Assistant Secretaries. But if the message was a defeat, it was by no means a total defeat. When Forrestal had talked with the Presi-

[dent in June [5] there had been much in common in their broad
ideas; and the long message, extensively analyzing the problems
of military policy in a democratic society, echoed a great deal for
which Forrestal had been fighting.

The President recognized the importance of power: "Now that
our enemies have surrendered it has again become all too apparent that a portion of the American people are anxious to forget all about the war," but "the future peace of the world will
depend in large part upon whether or not the United States . . .
is willing to maintain the physical strength necessary to act as a
safeguard against any future aggressor." To meet such responsibilities, it was necessary to plan our military forces "as a whole,"
and to relate the plan to our supporting resources in "manpower
and raw materials." Nor was a merely military program enough;
"it must be supported in peacetime by planning for industrial
mobilization and for development of industrial and raw material
resources where these are insufficient. Programs of scientific research must be developed for military purposes. . . . The findings of our Intelligence Service must be woven into all of these."
The President mentioned the importance of coordination between the military and the Department of State in the formulation of higher policy.

With all of this Forrestal could thoroughly agree; it was very
close to his own thought through the preceding months. When
the President went on to specify that the Services should retain
their individual identities, that the Navy in particular should retain its shipborne aviation and that the Marine Corps should "of
course" be continued as an integral part of the Navy, it became
apparent that the basic objectives were more or less the same.
The President's answer to the problem of how to attain them
was "consolidation" of the Services; Forrestal's was not, but already it was more an issue of degree than of kind, of method
rather than of substance.

It was an issue, moreover, in which Congress rather than the
President would be the final judge.

---

[5] See pp. 62-63.

22 December 1945   *Unification*

Senator McFarland [Ernest W. McFarland, Democrat, of Arizona] called on me this morning to express the hope that the Navy was not too downhearted about the President's message. He said that there were still many people in the Senate, including himself, who had grave doubts as to the wisdom of consolidation, particularly on the loss of morale involved in such a step.

I told him the greatest help he could be to us would be to assist Senator Walsh in his efforts to insure that the bill was referred to the Naval Affairs Committee for consideration as well as the Military Affairs Committee. He said he had already talked to Senator Walsh on this and would continue to be of as much help as possible.

I told the Senator that we proposed to continue the preparation of our case for presentation to Senator Walsh's committee and that it would be a most careful and exhaustive examination of all the factors involved in the Army's proposal. I told him we would assign an officer to keep him advised of the development of the case as it went along and to facilitate his own study on the matter.

[The battle was to be fought before Congress and the public through the next eighteen months. At the moment Forrestal had time for a note on past history.

27 December 1945

Played golf today with Joe Kennedy [Joseph P. Kennedy, who was Roosevelt's Ambassador to Great Britain in the years immediately before the war]. I asked him about his conversations with Roosevelt and Neville Chamberlain from 1938 on. He said Chamberlain's position in 1938 was that England had nothing with which to fight and that she could not risk going to war with Hitler. Kennedy's view: That Hitler would have fought Russia without any later conflict with England if it had not been for Bullitt's [William C. Bullitt, then Ambassador to France] urging on Roosevelt in the summer of 1939 that the Germans must be faced down about Poland; neither the French nor the British would have made Poland a cause of war if it had not been for the constant needling from Washington. Bullitt, he said, kept telling Roosevelt that the Germans wouldn't fight, Kennedy that they would, and that they would overrun Europe. Chamberlain, he says, stated that America and the world Jews had forced England into the war. In his telephone conversation with Roosevelt in the summer of 1939 the President kept telling him to put some iron up Chamberlain's backside. Kennedy's response always was that putting iron up his backside did no good unless the British had some iron with which to fight, and they did not. . . .

What Kennedy told me in this conversation jibes substantially with the remarks Clarence Dillon had made to me already, to the general effect that Roosevelt had asked him in some manner to communicate privately with the British to the end that Chamberlain should have greater firmness in his dealings with Germany. Dillon told me that at Roosevelt's request he had talked with Lord Lothian in the same general sense as Kennedy reported Roosevelt having urged him to do with Chamberlain. Lothian presumably was to communicate to Chamberlain the gist of his conversation with Dillon.

Looking backward there is undoubtedly foundation for Kennedy's belief that Hitler's attack could have been deflected to Russia, but I think he fails to take into account what would have happened after Hitler had conquered Russia. Would he have been content to stop? Nothing in his record indicates that that would have been the case, but rather that having removed the threat to his eastern frontiers he would then have exercised the options open to him to construct a European German-dominated system to which he later gave expression after overrunning France.

Kennedy said that the Russian demand for incorporation of Estonia, Latvia and Lithuania into the U. S. S. R. was the stumbling block, in the spring of 1939, to an understanding between Russia and England. The fundamental difficulty of England, however, was that if they backed Germany . . . they were then faced with a greater Germany, a weakened France, and a relatively defenseless England, whereas an alliance with Russia and the ultimate destruction of Germany would present England with precisely the problem that they now have, namely, a vacuum of power in Central Europe into which Russian influence would flow.

V

[Neither in planning for the future, however, nor in reminiscences of the past, could they long escape the menace of the present and of the problems that Soviet policy forced upon them. At the State-War-Navy meeting on November 27 the Forrestal-Patterson memorandum on China was up for discussion. Dean Acheson, now Under Secretary of State, felt that it did not cover the whole field. Forrestal commented "that he is convinced that we cannot 'yank the Marines out of northern China now,' but he said that he feels that the situation is not adequately understood by the public in this country. He inquired whether we could not talk the matter over realistically with the Russians." Byrnes was "puzzled" over what to say to the Russians, but after much discussion came up with a suggestion which was in fact to be followed with the Marshall mission of the following year: "Mr. Byrnes said that, taking everything into account, perhaps the wise course would be to try to force the Chinese government and the Chinese Communists to get together on a compromise basis, perhaps telling Generalissimo Chiang Kai-shek that we will stop the aid to his government unless he goes along with this. It might be well, he said, to tell Russia what we intend to do and to try to line them up with this policy. Mr. Patterson stated that it is in his opinion clearly in our interests to see China united under Generalissimo Chiang Kai-shek if that is possible."

Another aspect of the Soviet problem was made clear at a White House meeting on December 4. Senator Brien McMahon of Connecticut, chairman of the special Committee on Atomic Energy, had appeared with a list of questions concerning the number of atomic bombs in existence, costs of the atomic projects, and so on, for which the Congress wanted answers.

4 December 1945   *Atomic Energy*

. . . The President said that it is impossible for him to approve release of this information to the Senate Committee because among the thirteen members it was almost a certainty that one would consciously or otherwise let some of this information become public. He said that he was trying very hard to come to an agreement with the Russians but that the timing of Senator McMahon's request was unfortunate; that he was trying to find a basis for an understanding which would give him the confidence that an agreement reached with the Russians would be lived up to. He said he did not have that feeling at the moment, nor did he have it so far as the French were concerned. He feels that the agreements we make with the British, the Dutch, and the Chinese will be respected, but that there is no evidence as yet that the Russians intend to change their habits so far as honoring contracts is concerned.

He said if the Senate Committee insisted upon the information it would of course have to be given, but he wanted to make clear what he considered to be the risks involved. Judge Patterson spoke very strongly against giving the information and I supported him. . . .

[Forrestal continued to enter copies of confidential reports on Soviet activities in his diary. There was a summary report from Mark F. Ethridge, publisher of the Louisville *Courier Journal*, who had been in Rumania and Bulgaria under State Department auspices; it drew the picture—now familiar to Forrestal if not to the public—of forcible Soviet infiltration and domination. The United States, it said, "is faced with the alternatives of continuing its policy of adherence to the position taken at Yalta and Potsdam or of conceding this area as a Soviet sphere of influence." But as to how the United States could enforce the first alternative, this report, like so many others, was silent. There were dispatches from Arthur Bliss Lane, American Ambassador to Poland, on the working-over which the Soviet secret police were giving to repatriated Polish soldiers. Forrestal entered a note on Korea:

19 December 1945   *Korea*

State Department dispatch from Korea dated December 11, 1945, suggests desirability of abandoning international trustee-ship for Korea if adequate specific guarantees for unification and independence can be obtained from U. S. S. R. . . . . It might be more realistic to bypass trusteeship and seek guarantees directly. . . . In absence of Russian cooperation a possible solution would be to have U. S. trusteeship for South Korea and U. S. S. R. trusteeship for North Korea under U. N. O. to end mutually with withdrawal of troops and invitation to U. N. O. membership after five years, with free movement of persons and goods between zones in meantime. This should be last choice, however.

[In fact, there was to be no trusteeship, no cooperation and not even any "free movement between zones." Americans even then were still far from having taken the full and grisly measure of the force with which they were dealing. But for Forrestal there came a brief Christmas interlude. On December 23 he departed for Palm Beach; on the 29th he left Palm Beach for a short inspection trip to the Caribbean and Panama. He was still at work—in Panama he heard a complaint from the Army general in command about "an unclear definition of command responsibility in the Canal Zone Act of 1912"—and there were numerous inspections. But for the moment he appears to have enjoyed a breathing space. On January 7 he was back at the Washington grindstone.

CHAPTER IV

Problems of Unification

I

[Characteristically, Forrestal had given his moments of leisure in
the South to consideration of the broader, more basic issues with
which they were all trying to deal, and his first diary entry for
the new year appropriately enough set down some of his reflec-
tions.

2 January 1946   *American Foreign Policy*
   I finished today reading the hundred-page document prepared by the State Department in response to a suggestion
originating with the State-War-Navy Committee: What is
American Foreign Policy?
   This paper of the State Department undertakes to set down
American policy in every part of the globe. It is a little vague
in parts but nevertheless represents a substantial step forward
in the effort to obtain an integrated statement of our objectives
and policies in regard to other nations. Throughout it there is a
little over-free use of the words "culture," "democracy," "peace-
loving nations" and other clichés which have become common
through both public and intragovernment statements. Nevertheless even these clichés reflect the aspirations of the United
States.
   They also, however, underline the difference between the view
of Russia and ourselves (with Britain more or less in the middle
of the road) on methods for securing peace: the Russian thesis
being that the framework for peace and terms within it should

be evolved by the three nations having power—namely, the U. S. S. R., U. S. and Great Britain—and then inviting the nations not having such power to participate if they choose; the American point of view, on the contrary, which runs through this document, is that *all* nations professing a desire for peace and democracy should participate.

One cannot help but be struck by the tremendous task that is involved in the implementation of American policy; they are the difficulties that always confront the liberal and reasonable mind in attempting to construct a workable pattern for international relationships in the complex of racial, religious and vastly different social-political traditions and habits. Palestine is an example. . . . Our task is further complicated by the fact that we are trying to preserve a world in which a capitalistic-democratic method can continue, whereas if the Russian adherence to truly Marxian dialectics continues their interest lies in a collapse of this system. Possibly it should not be stated that their interest lies in the collapse, but [one should rather] re-examine the Marxian belief that the capitalistic system, by the evolution of economic determinism, is due to collapse and that the sooner it occurs the sooner can be established the global communal system which the logic of their dialectics predicts.[1] . . . Note . . . Walter Lippmann's suggestion that the task of statesmanship is not to try necessarily to secure democracy for *all* the world, but to discover the means by which . . . democracy and Communism . . . can find a way of living together.

[Forrestal had been filling his diary with reported instances of Soviet aggression and domineering, but he was not yet sure in his own mind of the purposes which might lie behind them. This note reflects his growing feeling that it was necessary to dig deeper than anyone in the administration seemed to have done into the real moral and philosophical foundations of "this sullen, sinister Bolshevik state" (as Winston Churchill was later to call it) if American policy was ever to find a sound guide.

Professor Edward F. Willett of Smith College had assisted in

---

[1] Forrestal's dictation was a little involved in this sentence; the editor has altered it slightly to give what seems to have been the sense.

[the research work for the Eberstadt report; on Eberstadt's recommendation, Forrestal had already enlisted him to make such a study. On his return to Washington, Forrestal forwarded some of Willett's preliminary findings to Walter Lippmann.

To Walter Lippmann, 7 January 1946
Dear Walter:
Your piece of last month . . . is responsible for the enclosed notes. They are preliminary to a study . . . on (1) the nature of the Russian state philosophy, both in terms of historical and dialectical materialism; (2) whether the long-term Lenin-Marxian objectives still hold; and (3) the possibility of accommodation between the democratic and communistic systems.

There is no place in government where such a study has been made—at least I have been unable to find one—and it seemed to me important that it be made as objectively and coldly as possible, because to me the fundamental question in respect to our relations with Russia is whether we are dealing with a nation or a religion—religion after all being merely the practical extension of philosophy.

[Sending another copy of the Willett paper to Henry Luce, Forrestal remarked: "I realize it is easy to ridicule the need for such a study as I have asked Willett to make, but I think in the middle of that laughter we always should remember that we also laughed at Hitler." [2] Forrestal took a close interest in the Willett study on "Dialectical Materialism"; the final result was never printed, but Forrestal sent many copies in mimeograph form to his friends. While he thus strove, however, after a firmer basis for the use of American power, the power itself continued to evaporate. "Demobilization troubles" was the main topic at the Cabinet on January 11.

11 January 1946   *Cabinet*
The President expressed concern over the events of the last ten days; said he had gone into the system and method of

[2] To Henry R. Luce, 6 January 1946.

demobilization and was satisfied that with some gaps it had been done efficiently and thoroughly. The Under Secretary of State [Acheson], representing the State Department, said it was a matter of great embarrassment and concern to his own Department in their conduct of our foreign affairs.

I said that I thought the President should get the heads of the important news services and the leading newspapers—particularly Mr. Sulzberger of the *New York Times,* Roy Roberts, Palmer Hoyt, the Cowles brothers, John Knight, plus Roy Howard and Bob McLean of the AP—and state to them the seriousness of the present situation and the need for making the country aware of its implications abroad. I said these were all reasonable and patriotic men and that I was confident that if the facts were presented we would have their support in the presentation of the case. The President agreed to do so.

I also suggested that the heads of the broadcasting systems be called in and that a canvass be made of the important radio commentators. The best medium for this is the Association of Radio News Analysts—H. V. Kaltenborn, Lowell Thomas, John Vandercook, George Fielding Eliot, Bob Trout, Robert St. John, Johannes Steel, Raymond Gram Swing and other representative men of that profession—which has a weekly luncheon in New York.

Secretary Ickes suggested that the State Department arrange a nationwide hook-up to present the impact of the over-rapid demobilization on our foreign policy. . . .

[Here again was the idea of going frankly to the country with the true seriousness of the international position. What action was finally taken the diary does not show, but certainly in early 1946 there was no such trumpet call as Forrestal clearly had in mind.

A note at this time is a reminder that Forrestal had his own career to consider; but it is interesting how rarely this subject ever appears in the diary. Forrestal, as has been said, was always thinking of laying down his job and always responding to what he felt to be his duty to continue. Notes of the following kind are few but suggestive.

21 January 1946   *Politics*

Justice [William O.] Douglas dined with me this evening and proposed that I have a definite stand on either the New York State governor or Senate nomination next autumn. He said he felt confident that I could get either. I told him that I had concluded to get out of public life and stay out when I had quit as Secretary of the Navy. He strongly urged that I reconsider, which I said I would, but added that I felt that my conclusion would be the same. He said the alternatives for nomination for governor were Farley, Jackson, Mead or myself; that if I decided to stay out of the race for governor I could undoubtedly get the nomination for the Senate, and with reasonable chances of success.

[Another exasperating instance of confusion in policy-making —the kind of confusion Forrestal was hoping to eliminate—now arose. Secretary Byrnes was in London for the first meeting of the United Nations. One of the problems under discussion was that of trusteeships for the former mandated islands, over which Forrestal had been so exercised the year before. There suddenly appeared a cable from Byrnes asking whether he could make a statement to the effect that the United States would be prepared to trustee these islands "either under ordinary trusteeship arrangements or as strategic areas."

Acheson, as Acting Secretary, got the President's assent to such a statement and cabled back the authorization without consultation with the military Departments. When Forrestal heard about it he at once entered his protest.

21 January 1946   *Trusteeships*

The Under Secretary of War (Kenneth Royall) and I saw the President at 3:30 this afternoon with reference to . . . Mr. Byrnes' message to the President asking permission to announce that the United States would turn mandated islands in the Pacific over to a trustee when, as and if the trusteeship system of the U. N. O. is perfected.

Royall and I said that we thought it was a most unwise and precipitate decision and requested the President to tell Byrnes not to make any such statement. He said that the message had gone today requesting Byrnes not to commit this country to any definitive position; it was not clear to me, however, whether he meant that Byrnes was not to make any statement.

I told the President that I think that Acheson's method of securing his approval to Mr. Byrnes' request was not consistent with our general ideas of cooperation between War, State and Navy, and rather in my opinion was a desertion of the general idea of cooperation by getting hasty decisions out of him on behalf of a particular point of view, and I told him I propose to make such a representation to Acheson in very strong terms. He said he hoped I would. . . .

This incident is a reflection of the rapidly vanishing determination in America to see to it that we do not repeat the mistakes of 1918-19 when the formerly German-owned islands of the Pacific were turned over to Japan and Australia—those north of the Equator to Japan, those south to Australia—under a secret agreement between England and Japan without American knowledge until after it was a *fait accompli*. It is a case for the greatest concern to see this tendency developing so soon in the attitude of the State Department.

22 January 1946   *Trusteeships*

In light of the above sequence of events . . . I told Dean Acheson, Under Secretary of State, this morning that I thought it was highly important that we not permit the habit of the weekly meetings of the Secretaries of State, War and Navy to lapse, even if the heads of the Departments were away. I said I thought the tempo at which events were moving now made it more important than ever for us to make sure that there were no slips between us.

I also talked with Mr. Geilfuss, Admiral [Thomas B.] Inglis and Admiral Souers on the question of a more accurate and faster observation of the "eyes only" messages sent by State.

[The trusteeship question was also to have political repercussions. Secretary Byrnes was back from London at the end of January and he made his report at a Cabinet luncheon.

29 January 1946   *Cabinet Luncheon*

. . . Byrnes recited his difficulties with Senator Vandenberg
and John Foster Dulles, who, spurred on by General Kenney
[George C. Kenney, then U. S. air representative on the U. N.
Military Staff Committee] during conversations on the way
over on the boat, let word leak out that there was dissatisfaction
with the American policy and position on trusteeships. He said
that toward the end Vandenberg found his position unsatisfactory and was looking for a way out, mainly on the ground that
he was being accused by his colleagues at home of having
turned an appeaser. Byrnes said that the fact had to be faced
that Vandenberg's—and for that matter Dulles's—activities
from now on could be viewed as being conducted on a political
and partisan basis. . . .

Byrnes said in general the Russian attitude continued to be
that they would like to discuss stability and peace with the
United States alone, although from time to time admitting
Great Britain to the conversations. It was for this reason, he
said, that after having done so a few times at the beginning
he had discontinued the practice of having private meetings
with the Russians on various questions. They were always
eager to do so, he said, but he felt it was provocative of bad
feeling among the rest of the United Nations. . . .

[That same day Harry Hopkins, Franklin Roosevelt's close friend
    and confidant, who had been a central figure in so many critical
    negotiations of the war years, died in New York. Forrestal en-
    tered the newspaper clipping in his diary, and his appointment
    calendar for the following morning, January 30, bore the unusual
    notation "President Roosevelt's birthday." But the diary itself
    made no other comment.

    A conference a few days later concerning certain confidential
    negotiations with the British produced a handsome tribute to
    their stocky Foreign Minister.

8 February 1946   *Meeting*

. . . Byrnes gave it as his opinion that we could not be in the
position of doubting the good faith of Britain. He said he was

confident that so long as Bevin was in his post as Foreign Minister there would be no possibility of such a breach. He said that he could conceive of a case arising where such a promise might not be lived up to completely through no fault of the Foreign Office, but as long as Mr. Bevin was in the Foreign Office he didn't believe this could happen. He said that Bevin had lived up completely and wholeheartedly to his agreements—he had debated vigorously and sometimes harshly before entering into them, but having once committed himself he would carry out his contracts to the full.

13 February 1946   *Atomic Bomb Tests*

There was a meeting at the White House this afternoon. *Present*: The President, Byrnes, Patterson, Eisenhower, Nimitz, Leahy and myself.

The President said he wanted a commission appointed to see the atomic bomb tests [which were to take place that summer at Bikini atoll] in order to meet the criticisms that were being raised to the effect that the tests would not be objective, that they were under the control of the military and would therefore be conducted in a way to establish the conclusions that the military hoped would result. The President quoted from a letter he had from Secretary Wallace, the tenor of which was along the lines indicated. In the discussion that ensued Admiral Leahy took occasion to make a sharp criticism of some of the provisions of the McMahon bill [the basic measure that established the civilian Atomic Energy Commission in control over the field], which he said carried an implication of distrust of the Armed Services and proposed to turn over the making of one of the most effective weapons of war to a civil commission which would dole out its product, if it decided to make any, as it saw fit.

The President in response to an observation of mine said he was aware that Senator McMahon was out to get publicity for himself, but observed that he (the President) had to be sure that this test met all of the crackpot criticism and that not only would it need to be objective but we had to convince the public it was objective. We advised him of the evaluation group of civilians which Admiral Blandy was proposing to invite [to the test], and the suggestion was made that this same group, plus some additions from the House and Senate, could be used as the basis for a commission appointed by the President to report directly to him. . . .

17 February 1946   *Justice William O. Douglas*

I had a conversation this evening with Mr. Justice William O. Douglas on the President's request that he accept the position of Secretary of the Interior. I said I hoped he would accept it. I put my case on three grounds: (1) his patriotic duty; (2) the forum it would give him; and (3) the great service he could render as a practical nexus between the liberal and conservative elements of the government. I said I had great respect for Henry Wallace but found it very difficult to talk to him in practical language, or at least to have any feeling that he understood what I was talking about, whereas Douglas, I felt, even though he might differ with my views, had a common-sense approach to problems of government. . . .

Douglas' reply to my persuasion in general was an expression of doubt as to whether the President really wanted him or whether he was viewing the appointment as an expedient to rescue him from inconvenient political embarrassment. I suggested that he talk quite frankly with the President on this point in order to clarify it.

II

["Incidentally," Forrestal said in this same note of his conversation with Douglas, "I asked him if he had read Stalin's speech and if he had what was his impression. He said, 'The Declaration of World War III.'" On February 9 the Soviet dictator had delivered in the guise of an "election" speech a major pronouncement of the most ominous kind. Implying that a peaceful international order was "impossible under the present capitalist development of world economy," he had announced a five-year program of industrial and armament expansion on a huge scale. It called for trebling the Soviet output of iron, steel and coal and nearly doubling oil production "to guarantee our country against any eventu-

[ality." Forrestal was often to cite this pronouncement thereafter;
he continued his searchings into the true nature of Soviet philosophy and policy, but this speech and the program it laid down
came close to convincing him that there was no way, as Lippmann
had hoped, in which democracy and Communism could live together. It is clear that from this time on he felt increasingly that
policy could not be founded on the assumption that a peaceful
solution of the Russian problem would be possible.

The problem itself was certainly growing no easier. On the
15th Forrestal mentioned a dispatch from Lieutenant General
John R. Hodge, commanding the American forces in Korea.

15 February 1946   *Korea—Trusteeship*

. . . [Hodge] notes that the Russians are now improving
materially in behavior in their Zone and through clever propaganda are seeking to appear as saviors of the thirty million
Korean people.

Hodge feels that the Russians have no thought of unifying
the Korean nation while U. S. forces remain and thinks that
the North and South will never really be united until Russia is
sure that all Korea will be communistic. He questions our ability to stem the propaganda and controlled military maneuvering
of the Soviets.

We are opposed by a strongly organized, ruthless military
machinery designed to appeal to the millions of uneducated
Koreans. The U. S. must do likewise and not be satisfied with
dealing with wealthy U. S.-educated Koreans. He urges that
these ideas be passed to State and that it be impressed on State
that he must be kept informed and that it might be worth
while to consider some of the information and recommendations which he has sent in.

[A few days later Forrestal entered in his diary a copy of a long
dispatch from the American chargé d'affaires at Moscow, Mr.
George F. Kennan, who was later to become more widely known
to his countrymen as one of the ablest and most discerning minds
in the State Department. Here Kennan analyzed the backgrounds
and deeper springs of Soviet policy, its purposes and methods,

[with a remarkable insight—it was exactly the kind of job for which Forrestal had looked vainly elsewhere in the government —and went on to discuss its probable course in terms which everything in the succeeding years has tended only to confirm.

The whole document even today is of absorbing interest. After summarizing the official Soviet propaganda, with its implications of inevitable conflict, and after noting how completely its premises were contrary to the obvious facts of international relations, Kennan asked what this might mean. "It indicates that the Soviet party line is not based on any objective analysis of the situation beyond Russia's borders; that it has, indeed, little to do with conditions outside of Russia; that it arises mainly from basic inner Russian necessities which existed before the recent war and exist today."

He went on: "At the bottom of the Kremlin's neurotic view of world affairs is the traditional and instinctive Russian sense of insecurity," stemming from the days when the Russians were a peaceful agricultural people living on a vast, defenseless plain in the neighborhood of fierce nomadic tribes. To this, as Russia grew and came in contact with the West, was added a fear of "the more competent, more powerful, more highly organized societies" which the Russian rulers there encountered. This latter sense of insecurity, Kennan shrewdly noted, was one which afflicted the rulers rather than the Russian people, "for Russian rulers have invariably sensed that their rule was relatively archaic in form, fragile and artificial in its psychological foundation, unable to stand comparison or contact with political systems of Western countries. For this reason they have always feared foreign penetration, feared direct contact between the Western world and their own, feared what would happen if Russians learned the truth about the world without or if foreigners learned the truth about the world within. And they have learned to seek security only in patient but deadly struggle for the total destruction of rival power, never in compacts and compromises with it."

It was no "coincidence," Kennan continued, that Marxism, which "had smoldered ineffectively for half a century in Western Europe," should have come to a blaze for the first time in such a setting. Only in this land, which had "never known a friendly

[neighbor" or any balanced internal equilibrium of social forces, could there thrive the Marxist doctrine of insoluble social conflict. After the Bolshevik regime was established, the dogma "became a perfect vehicle for the sense of insecurity with which the Bolsheviks, even more than previous Russian rulers, were afflicted. In this dogma, with its basic altruism of purpose, they found the justification for their instinctive fear of the outside world, for the dictatorship without which they did not know how to rule, for the cruelties they did not dare not to inflict, for the sacrifices they felt bound to demand. In the name of Marxism they sacrificed every single ethical value in their methods and tactics. Today they cannot dispense with it. It is the fig leaf of their moral and intellectual respectability."

Stripped of the Marxist justifications, Kennan continued, the masters of the Soviet Union would "stand before history, at best, as only the last of that long succession of cruel and wasteful Russian rulers who have relentlessly forced the country on to ever new heights of military power in order to guarantee the external security of their internally weak regimes." It was for this reason that no one should underrate the importance of the Marxist doctrine in practical Russian policy. In clinging to this dogma, Kennan went on, which represented "the outside world as evil, hostile and menacing but as . . . destined to be wracked with growing internal convulsions until it is given the final *coup de grâce* by the rising power of socialism," the new rulers were basically expressing only the centuries-old movement of "uneasy Russian nationalism," in which "conceptions of offense and defense are inextricably confused." But equipped with the apparatus of international Communism, that movement had become "more dangerous and insidious than ever before."

On top of all this, said the Kennan analysis, "we have the unsolved mystery as to who, if anyone, in this great land actually receives accurate and unbiased information about the outside world. In the atmosphere of Oriental secretiveness and conspiracy which pervades this government, possibilities for distorting or poisoning the sources and currents of information are infinite. . . . There is good reason to suspect that this government is actually a conspiracy within a conspiracy; and I for one am reluc-

[tant to believe that Stalin himself receives anything like an objective picture of the outside world."

Proceeding from the foundation of this analysis, Kennan foresaw very accurately the course that Soviet foreign policy was in
fact to follow—the constant pressure to infiltrate, disrupt and
paralyze the West through the covert arms of the international
Communist organization, and to exploit every success thus obtained through the pressure of Soviet diplomacy on the official
level. Kennan predicted that the Russians would participate of-
ficially in any international organizations in which they de-
tected "an opportunity of extending Soviet power or of inhibit-
ing or diluting the power of others." In the United Nations,
Moscow saw not a "mechanism for a permanent and stable
world society, founded on the mutual interest and aims of all nations, but an arena in which the aims just mentioned can be favorably pursued." The Russians would leave the U. N. (as later
they did, in effect, for a time) whenever they felt that the organization was embarrassing or frustrating their pursuit of "power
expansion"; they would stay with it (as still later they were to return to it) if they felt that their withdrawal would fail to split the
unity of the other nations or render U. N. ineffective.

None of this, it must be remembered, was as obvious in February 1946 as it later came to seem. To any thoughtful mind this
analysis must, if accepted, have ended all hope of establishing
conventional or "normal" international relations with this dark
dictatorship, hag-ridden by the ghosts of the Russian past; it rendered foolish the ideas—which were to flourish popularly for long
after—of settling everything by concessions, by a meeting of the
"heads of state" or by some similar form of reasonable give-and-
take around a peaceful conference table. It made imperative the
discovery of some new, quite different and more effective approach on the part of American policy.

As Kennan posed the problem, "we have here a political force
committed fanatically to the belief that with the U. S. there can
be no permanent *modus vivendi,* that it is desirable and necessary
that the internal harmony of our society be disrupted, our traditional way of life be destroyed, the international authority of our

[state be broken, if Soviet power is to be secure. This political force has complete power of disposition over the energies of one of the world's greatest peoples and the resources of the world's richest national territory. . . . In addition, it has an elaborate and far-flung apparatus for the exertion of its influence in other countries. . . . Finally, it is seemingly inaccessible to considerations of reality in its basic reactions. For it, the vast fund of objective fact about human society is not, as with us, the measure against which outlook is constantly being tested and reformed, but a great grab bag from which individual items are selected arbitrarily and tendentiously to bolster an outlook already preconceived. This is admittedly not a pleasant picture. The problem of how to cope with this force is undoubtedly the greatest task our diplomacy has ever faced and probably the greatest it will ever have to face."

Kennan's ideas of how this might be done accorded very closely with those Forrestal had already been developing. "Gauged against the Western world as a whole," Kennan wrote, "the Soviets are still [this was early in 1946] by far the weaker force. Thus their success will really depend on the degree of cohesion, firmness and vigor which the Western world can muster." The first step was to study and recognize the Soviet force for "what it is"; the second was to tell the American public the truth, just as Forrestal had advocated. "We must," said Kennan, "see that our public is educated to the realities of the Russian situation. I cannot overemphasize the importance of this. . . . I am convinced that there would be far less hysterical anti-Sovietism in our country today if realities of this situation were better understood by our people. There is nothing as dangerous or as terrifying as the unknown. It may also be argued that to reveal more information on our difficulties with Russia would reflect unfavorably on Russian-American relations. I feel that if there is any real risk here involved, it is one which we should have the courage to face, and the sooner the better." But he thought that there was little to be risked. His suggestions, for the rest, were for "courage and self-confidence," for the greatest possible improvement in the "health and vigor of our own society" and for putting

[before the peoples of the world a "much more positive and constructive picture of the sort of world we would like to see than
we have put forward in the past."

Kennan's report was made in answer to certain queries from
the State Department. He thought the issues raised were of "such
urgent importance, particularly in view of recent events," that if
his answers deserved any attention at all they deserved it at once.
He consequently put the whole document, running to something
like eight thousand words, on the cables. Its significance so impressed the naval attaché in Moscow that he sent a separate
message to the Chief of Naval Operations recommending its
study to the Navy Department. The attaché felt that the American people, reared in the democratic tradition, had not remotely
understood "utter ruthlessness and complete unscrupulousness of
Soviet ruling clique. Its breath must be literally felt on back of
neck before really appreciated." And he added that while most
of the documents on Russian policy which had emanated from
Washington in the past two or three years were "impressive in
their intellectual scope and logical conclusion," they seemed lacking in "conviction"; in short, "wishful thinking still potent force in
conduct of our relations with U. S. S. R."

But caution still ruled; there was no great campaign of education or basic realignment of policy, and it was not until a year
later that President Truman was to raise the first (and even then
still rather tentative) alarm with his message asking aid for
Greece and Turkey in their battles against Communist infiltration. The governing mood at the time is suggested by an episode
attendant upon General Marshall's assumption of the embassy to
China.

27 February 1946   *Consul at Dairen*

An exchange of dispatches between Marshall and Admiral
Cooke [Deputy Chief of Naval Operations] relating to the
question of an American consul setting up shop at Dairen
[the Soviet-held port in Manchuria]. Marshall questions the
wisdom of his going in by destroyer on account of the implications of military power. . . . Cooke replies that it is perfectly normal for the United States to have a consul at Dairen.

. . . He suggests sending a consul in . . . a merchant-type ship such as Liberty or Victory, but having a man-of-war always within hailing distance by radio. If we back down on this action it seems to me we enter into a long road of appeasement such as we did in our failure to exercise the right of entry to the Japanese mandated islands after the last war.

[As Secretary of the Navy, Forrestal's power to control major policy was naturally limited. But he was now planning an important move that did lie within his competence and that sprang equally from his realization that appeasement had become impossible and from his knowledge of basic world strategy.

28 February 1946   *State-War-Navy*

. . . I asked Byrnes if he was agreeable to the Navy preparing plans for a task force in the Mediterranean. He said to go ahead, with the suggestion that it might accompany the battleship *Missouri,* which will take home the body of the late Turkish Ambassador [who had died at his post in Washington]. . . .

[His experience with the Navy had trained Forrestal to think strategically in global terms; the idea of establishing a naval squadron in the Mediterranean (as the infant Republic had done a century and a half before) had already occurred to him, and the Mediterranean Task Force, which in fact resulted from this initiative, was to have a greater influence on the history of the succeeding years than is always realized. It was to buttress Turkish resistance to the seeping advance of Soviet power; it was to appear as a suddenly important prop for the President's Greco-Turkish aid program of the following year, and it doubtless played its role in saving Italy from Communist engulfment. Forrestal was planning to apply power, in advance, where power economically used could bring disproportionately great rewards. But few thought as he did at the time, and the old problem of bringing coherence and direction into the vast and sprawling processes of government as it was being conducted was still acute in his mind.

7 March 1946   *Secretariat in Government*

I reflected again today on the tremendous need for a
linking-up and cementing secretariat in the American government. Varieties of subjects turn to the mind as work for such an
organization. For example, the American shipbuilding industry
is being allowed to go into doldrums for the lack of energetic
attention. At the instance of the Navy Department that Department and the Maritime Commission joined in a study by
the Harvard Business Administration School on the shipbuilding industry and its corollary, the shipping industry. This was
forwarded to the President with the recommendation that he
name a board similar to the Morrow Board to consider ways
and means of ensuring that America retain the appropriate
percentage of the world's sea-going commerce. On this committee there should be business, labor, and government representatives. I am sending a copy today to the Secretary of Commerce [Wallace] on the assumption that the name of his Department at least implies an interest in such a subject. The
main point however is that it is illustrative of the kind of work
that a secretariat should perform—a check-up on things un-
done. In business that check-up is provided by the profit and
loss statement. In government it can be provided only by individual men with imagination, initiative and tact—and
driven not by the profit and loss statement but by the desire
to see government perform its function.

As I write this it occurs to me that I have never heard the
head of the Department of Commerce put forward any views
that indicate a desire to help business. I shall look today at the
charter and precept of that Department.

Another example of this need is the St. Lawrence Waterway.
I was asked to sign a letter giving views on a project about
which I had practically no information and no convictions.

[At the Cabinet next day the discussion, after ranging over a
   number of other topics, touched on a different aspect of the
   complex problem of modern government.

8 March 1946 *Cabinet*

. . . *General Motors Strike*: Schwellenbach reported little progress on the General Motors strike. He said Reuther [Walter P. Reuther, of the United Automobile Workers] was making it very difficult to get a settlement and was trying to force the President to use his prestige in backing up the Union's demands. He told him Reuther was able to start strikes but hadn't shown any ability to settle them, that he was using this particular strike to further his own ambitions to be president of the United Automobile Workers. [Reuther was elected to the office in that month.] The President said he would not permit his office to be used in the fashion Reuther wanted and that while the latter had made many attempts to have him by-pass Schwellenbach he did not intend to do it.

[On the tenth Forrestal had two long interviews which shed much light on the whole problem of the times as he saw it. The first was at luncheon.

10 March 1946 *Russia*

Lunched with William Bullitt and Admiral Leahy. Bullitt most disturbed about the Russian situation and urgent in expressing the hope that the President will create some small group to make an appraisal and evaluation of American policy vis-à-vis Russia, with particular reference to the balancing of our capabilities with our commitments—in other words, to what extent we can back up our notes with action.

I said that this was only a part of the problem, that there must go along with any such program a similar one to inform the country of the facts, of the complete impossibility of gaining access to the minds of the Russian people, of piercing the curtain of censorship which is drawn over every area they occupy. I also said that it would be most difficult for this group to function without the danger of some infringement upon the responsibilities of the State Department.

Leahy said there was also the practical difficulty of getting sufficient of the President's time to deal adequately with the problem.

Bullitt said that the notion that the Russians had to have the Dardanelles for reasons of commercial egress through warm water had no substance. He said there could be only one objective in the effort to establish Russian influence on the Mediterranean littoral and that was to be able to sit athwart communications of the British Empire.

[The same afternoon Forrestal had a long talk with an even more eminent statesman. On March 5 Winston Churchill had delivered his celebrated speech at Fulton, Missouri, calling for an Anglo-American alliance against the Soviet Union. He was now back in Washington.

10 March 1946   *Russia—Unification*

1. *Russia*: At three o'clock saw Churchill and was with him for an hour and a quarter. He was very gloomy about coming to any accommodation with Russia unless and until it became clear to the Russians that they would be met with force if they continued their expansion. He agreed with my analysis that we are dealing not only with Russia as a national entity but with the expanding power of Russia under Peter the Great plus the additional missionary force of a religion. He mentioned the fact that in his own immediate entourage he had had two men—I inferred they were scientists—to whom they had to give terms of life imprisonment because they had taken blueprints and other secret documents and delivered them in person to the Russians in London. He said these men had no feeling that they were bound by patriotism or duty to their country but felt that they were acting according to the dictates of a much higher moral code. (He said there was considerable consolation in the victory of Bevin because Bevin was able to talk more firmly and clearly to Russia than he could have, by virtue of being a Labour government.)

2. *Task Force in the Mediterranean*: He was very glad of our sending the *Missouri* to the Mediterranean but was very much disappointed when I told him that the plans to have this ship accompanied by a task force of substantial proportions had been abandoned. He said that a gesture of power not fully

implemented was almost less effective than no gesture at all. He said that to make the gesture effective the entire task force should sail into the Sea of Marmara.

He said that the thing for the United States to consider was what its position would be after the Russians had the Germans, as he put it, "nobbled," with France fairly well inoculated now with Communism, the Russian influence having flowed across Germany into Holland and Belgium, and the lifeline of the British Empire broken—in brief, we would then have to deal with the Russians alone.

Referring to the Russians, he said they had no understanding of such words as "honesty," "honor," "trust" and "truth"—in fact, that they regarded these as negative virtues. They will, he said, try every door in the house, enter all rooms which are not locked, and when they come to one that is barred, if they are unsuccessful in breaking through it, they will withdraw and invite you to dine genially that same evening.

3. *Unification*: I talked with him at some length about unification. I said that I greatly feared the attempt that was now being made to consolidate the civilian Departments of War and Navy under one administrative head. He said he felt very strongly there should be a single Minister of Defense, but he agreed with me that he should perform a staff and coordinating function rather than an administrative function. He laid stress on the great usefulness which had been performed by the Imperial General Staff in peacetime between World War I and World War II and on the practical value it developed when it became the Secretariat to the War Cabinet during World War II. I told him that Mr. Eberstadt had made a study for the Navy of the whole subject of defense and that the germinal basis of his plan was the minute by Lord Hankey on the operations of the Imperial General Staff in England. He said that a Minister of Defense would have to be practically the alter ego of the President with power to resolve disputes between Departments, to provide common procurement where necessary, and to see to it that there was a maximum of inter-Service education and coordination.

I told him I would send him a copy of the Eberstadt report

and would be very glad to have his comments and criticisms.

4. *Fulton Speech*: He was very pleased with the reaction to his Fulton speech and anxious to get my view as to whether it had been beneficial or otherwise.

5. *Rhetoric*: At the end of our talk he spoke of the trip we had made together through England in March and April of 1941, just at the end of the period of bombing. I reminded him of the question I asked him in Manchester after one of his impromptu speeches. I had told him then that whenever he started one of his long and involved comments that I worried as to how he was going to finish his sentence. His response was that he learned early in his speaking career not to worry about where the verb came. He was reminded, he said, of a somewhat similar question he put to Lord Balfour when he first started in Parliament. When he asked Balfour how he delivered his peroration, Balfour's reply was, "After covering what I want to say, when I come to the first sentence that has a grammatical ending I sit down."

III

[Since the President's message of December 20, calling for the consolidation of the Armed Services and the creation of a single Department of Defense, the seeds of a bitter and distracting controversy had been germinating. A special subcommittee of the Senate Military Affairs Committee, consisting of Senator Elbert D. Thomas of Utah as chairman, with Senators Warren R. Austin of Vermont and Lister Hill of Alabama, had retired to draft a measure in response to the message; it was not yet known what its proposals would be, but the arguments of military officers and their respective civilian supporters in Congress and the press were already becoming acrimonious.

It is impossible to rehearse here all the intricacies of this issue. In rough summary, one may say that Secretary of War Patterson and the Army generals wanted consolidation because they feared that otherwise the ground Army would be neglected under the greater glamour and popularity of the Air Force and the Navy. The Army Air Force wanted independence from the War Department and a coequal status with the Navy and the ground

[Army; since no one would approve three separate and rival Departments, its best means to this end was to accept a single overall Department within which the three branches would be on equal footing. The Navy bitterly opposed consolidation, as it feared that it would be at a dangerous disadvantage against the Army-Air Force coalition; it feared the loss of the Marine Corps to the Army and that the Air Force might take over its aviation, which had become, of course, an indispensable element in naval warfare. Forrestal's position, as should be clear from this record, was less extreme than that of many of the admirals. Basically he was trying to find some middle ground on which the efficiencies, economies and coordinated direction of a unified system could be achieved without sacrificing the advantages—and all later experience was to suggest that they are very real if not absolutely vital advantages—of Service individuality and autonomy. It was not an easy position to make clear, even to some of his own supporters. In mid-March, the Thomas subcommittee had still not yet produced its bill, but there had already been much high-level discussion of the draft it had worked out.

14 March 1946   *Unification*

I had a conversation this morning with Senator Thomas about the unification. I reported conversations Mr. Eberstadt and I had had with Judge Patterson and repeated to him, as I had with Patterson, that I could visualize the merits and the good results of unification provided that the so-called Secretary of Common Defense and the men around him were limited to staff and coordinating functions and did not get into administration. I said that if that principle could be accepted we could make rapid progress. He launched into a disquisition on the merits of the conception of the Secretaries *for* War, Air, and Navy and their relation to the four functional Assistant Secretaries, but I said I must continue to express the view that this was a totally impracticable and unworkable arrangement. He said he could not recede from what he called progress they had made by going back to earlier prints, and I gained the impression from him that he was trying to convey to me the thought that he was acting under orders from the President.

For this reason I told him I had a similar discussion with the
President and outlined to him precisely what I was saying over
the telephone now—namely, the distinction between the decisive and coordinating duties of a Secretary of Common Defense as distinguished from the attempt to make him a giant
administrator.

[Two days later Forrestal was speaking to the President him-
     self. The conversation again showed that the two were actually
     not so far apart as was popularly supposed.

18 March 1946   *Unification*
I talked with the President at length about unification this
afternoon. I told him that Eberstadt and I had had talks with
Judge Patterson and I had told Patterson that it was my
opinion that the Thomas bill was completely unworkable, and
that in its present form, while it might pass the Senate by a
slight margin, it was certain to fail in the House. I said to the
President that Admiral Nimitz and I both felt that there were
things that ought to be done by way of coordination and some
unification of the Services and that I was very fearful that in
the way things were drifting presently that nothing would be
done, which would be bad.

I outlined to him our conception of the kind of responsibility
and duties that the Secretary of Common Defense or Office of
Common Defense would have, namely, coordinating and staff
functions—one man with a small group of highly competent and
able people to dig into those things requiring resolution and
decision, but not getting into administration. The President did
not seem to draw this line as clearly as it was in my mind, but
I think at the end he began to grasp what I was talking about.
I referred to the Thomas bill, which provides for a Super-
Secretary, an Under Secretary, and the four functional Assistant
Secretaries, with three *so-called* Secretaries for War, Air and
Navy stuck off in an annex with neither responsibility nor
power.

I said that Patterson and I both had some misgivings about the Ground Forces being extinguished by the efforts of the Navy and the Air Forces. The President concurred and said what he was really afraid of was that we would have a repetition of the situation in England. In other words, the Royal Air Force movement with all of its consequences. I told him that I thought if I were in his place I would in a week or ten days tell both Services it was time to call a halt to the propaganda discussion and lobbying, and I said the Navy would make this stick but I didn't think the Army could, particularly the Air Forces. He concurred and said that the Air Forces had no discipline. At the end of the conversation I suggested to him that he might get Admiral Nimitz and General Eisenhower for an extended talk with him. I said the fewer people were there the better, that he would get further with those two than he would with a large meeting. I told him that if we arrived at a compromise which the Navy believed in that I believed we could sell it even to Mr. Vinson [chairman of the House Naval Affairs Committee], but it would have to be something that we could really put our hearts into.

[The Thomas bill was not, however, to be made public until the following month. In the meantime there was a curious interlude concerning the forthcoming tests of the atomic bomb at Bikini atoll. With the enormous and elaborate technical machinery already in motion, Secretary Byrnes suddenly asked for a postponement of the operation on the grounds that it might have a bad effect upon the disturbed world situation and particularly upon the United Nations Security Council meeting, which was about to be held. Forrestal drafted an extensive memorandum for the President on the impossibility of holding up the undertaking: "There have been upwards of twenty thousand men actively engaged on it for the last two months," and the large corps of scientific personnel involved were leaving government for their university work in the fall. At the Cabinet on March 22 the President asked for comments. Vice Admiral W. H. P. Blandy took notes of the meeting.

. . . Secretary Wallace said he thought the Christmas holidays would be a good period for holding the tests, but Secretary Forrestal pointed out that months of continuous effort were needed. Secretary Wallace also said he could not see why more than the deep underwater test was necessary, as it was estimated to be the most effective; but Secretary Forrestal remarked that ships were in port a large part of the time, even in war, and it was desired to find out what would happen to a group of ships under those conditions. Vice Admiral Blandy said also that while the deep underwater test might have the greatest effect on the ships themselves, the surface or shallow underwater explosion would probably throw the most radioactive water over the ship, thus having the maximum effect upon the combination of ships and men.

Secretary [of the Interior] Krug said he thought the tests could be held in January, as the scientists would come back then if offered enough money.

Secretary Byrnes asked Vice Admiral Blandy how important the Navy considered the tests. The latter replied that he understood they were held to be of great importance by the Joint Chiefs of Staff; that for the Navy, it was necessary to know what changes in ship design, in tactical formations, and in the spread of ships in a harbor might be essential in the event the atomic bomb was not abolished by international agreement and we had to fight an atomic war. The Ground Forces also would learn much about the advisability of redesign of many items of equipment which would be exposed on the decks of ships; while the Air Forces wanted to know to what extent an enemy's naval vessels would be profitable targets for U. S. use of the bomb.

The President then said it was essential for the Congress to be in Washington at the date set for the first test, and he neither desired to have them away at the bomb tests then, or hold the tests without inviting them. However, he had no objection to commencing the tests on July 1, and unless there were further objections, that would be his decision. No objections were made.

[On April 4 the Army, engaged in some preliminary unification of its own, announced the abolition of the horse cavalry and its merger with the armored forces.

5 April 1946   *Cabinet*

. . . Secretary Patterson said that he had gone to Fort Riley, Kansas, yesterday to dedicate a hall to the memory of General Patton and the President might have picked a better day on which to abolish the cavalry. The President recalled that General Pershing was a cavalry officer and that for ten or twelve years after the last war many Army officers spent a great deal of their time proving that the cavalry had won the war and he didn't want that to happen this time. He remarked parenthetically, "I don't know just what bearing this has on unification."

[The Thomas bill as it was finally introduced on April 9 had been described as a "compromise," but the Navy did not so regard it. At his press conference on April 11 the President spoke severely of the Service opposition to this administration measure. Mr. Truman may have been acting on Forrestal's suggestion of the previous month that he "call a halt to the propaganda," but the correspondents interpreted his words as a "vehement" denunciation of the "naval lobby." Controversy grew even more embittered than before, and it seemed increasingly doubtful that the Thomas bill could pass the Congress. On the 17th the President summoned Forrestal for a conference on the subject; Forrestal made memorandum notes of the points he wished to present. These notes explained that he did not entirely share the Navy's apprehensions as to Naval Aviation and the Marine Corps. His concept of a single Secretary of Defense was that this officer should be "the source of decision on moot questions"; he should "lay down procurement policies, plan the budget" and "ensure coordination both on military and civil level." He then set down his view of the "chief difference between Army and Navy: the Army feels that everything will flow once the bill creating a single Secretary and Chief of Staff is passed. We believe it has to be thought through more carefully than that. Navy sees need for

[continuation in peace of the functions of Byrnes, [Fred M.] Vinson and [Donald M.] Nelson, an alter ego for the President. The difference is that the Common Secretary under Navy conception would have a small but highly capable staff; that he would not run a department. Army feels that putting him at the head of a department gets the answer.

"The Navy's fears quite frankly are: that the Navy's very real fear is that once this bill is passed in its present form, the Navy is merely another arm, and that is the Army intent."

The President, when these views were presented to him, seemed (as Forrestal had thought in the previous year) far from "closed-minded."

17 April 1946   *Unification*

. . . We had a most satisfactory interview with the President. He listened attentively and with great interest to the Navy views.

I share the President's wishes that discussion of unification be confined, henceforth, to appearance before congressional committees.

The President is not taking sides either for or against the Army or Navy. He simply wishes to get the best organization possible for the national security. I share that wish as, I am sure, do all thinking citizens.

Speaking personally, I am for unification. The form it takes is for the President and Congress to decide, and the Navy is not foreclosed from presenting its view.

[Unfortunately this was not the end either of the primary issue over unification or of the secondary problem of "propaganda" by the Armed Services, either directly or through their respective friends in Congress and the press, in favor of their diverse views. Actually the "propaganda" came in about equal proportions from all sides; in the popular mind, however, and perhaps also in the President's, it was the Navy which seemed the recalcitrant, objecting to an efficient and economical modernization of the military system for reasons of petty Service ambition or prestige. The charges of insubordination on the one hand, and of "gag

[rule" on the other, only exacerbated the issue and clouded the validity of Forrestal's real and fundamental argument—which was that this was a major question of national policy, to be solved by the basic tests of what would really work best in the national interest, rather than in the narrower light of jealously rival Service claims and particularisms.

Later history was to go far to justify Forrestal's and the Navy's stand in this controversy; the price of making that stand, on the other hand, was—as can be seen in retrospect—to postpone adequate consideration of the great policy issues confronting the nation. Until this paralyzing row between the Services on the form of military organization had been settled, it would be impossible to lay down any long-range military plans or policies, to determine properly the size or structure of the military machine to be maintained, or to face with any consistency and forethought the underlying politico-military problems which that machine existed to meet. It is hardly too much to say that the battle over unification —for which "all hands," to use one of Forrestal's favorite naval phrases, were about equally responsible—delayed the nation for a year or two in grappling with the already dire state of world affairs.

IV

[Forrestal was under no illusions as to how dire it had become. Writing in these days to his old friend and business mentor, Clarence Dillon,[3] he observed: "The Commies are working their heads off in France, the Balkans, Japan and anywhere else where they happen to have access. They have the advantage of a political medium in the CP [Communist Party] in each country. Furthermore they are not interested in preserving, but rather the opposite. Which makes it tough for Uncle Sam. In my opinion we are now facing a far more serious business than we ever faced in the thirties. I hope it is not too late to deal with it."

Among the summaries of State Department dispatches that Forrestal retained in his diary at this time was one of a Moscow telegram. General Walter Bedell Smith, who had been Eisenhower's Chief of Staff, had now replaced Harriman as Ambassa-

---

[3] To Clarence Dillon, 11 April 1946.

[dor to Moscow, and in early April he succeeded in securing a two-hour interview with Stalin. Smith tried the "cards-on-the-table" approach; the most important question to the United States, he said at the opening of the interview, was "what does the Soviet Union want and how far is Russia going to go." He was not conspicuously successful; to Smith's questions Stalin replied "at length" with countercharges and some "bitter" comment, and when Smith asked point-blank whether the Russian thought that the United States and Great Britain were united in an alliance to thwart Russia, Stalin "replied in the affirmative." The interview, to be sure, "ended very cordially," with Stalin reaffirming his desire for peace, but it seems to have contributed little toward that end; Stalin explained that he could not accept the President's invitation to visit the United States since "his doctors tell him he must not travel and keep him on a strict diet."

On the day that Bedell Smith was talking to Stalin, Senator Claude Pepper of Florida was talking to the Senate; Forrestal also had extracts from this effort copied into his diary. Senator Pepper, answering Winston Churchill's Fulton speech, was anxious that no one should "gang up" on Russia; all he wanted was that the United States should "not become a guarantor of British imperialism." His recommendation for a foreign policy was that the United States should take the lead in calling a Big Three conference to settle everything; and that before the conference convened we should "destroy every atomic bomb which we have" and smash every facility for their manufacture. In face of such stark contrasts of attitude, statesmanship was not easy. In the Cabinet on the 19th Secretary Byrnes described the difficulties which the Russians were putting in the way of a peace treaty with Italy. The discussion continued:

19 April 1946   *Cabinet*

. . . The Secretary said that his negotiations in the field of foreign affairs were greatly embarrassed by the public utterances of people in the Congress and even in the Cabinet. He cited specifically Iceland, where our efforts to get air bases had been aborted to a considerable degree by the statements and speeches of Secretary Wallace and Senator Pepper; Wallace's in particular having been quoted by the Premier of Iceland as robbing him of any success in the advocacy of bases for the United States. He pointed out to our chargé that he could have little hope of ceding base rights to the United States when important elements in our own country were against such action. . . .

I spoke briefly in support of . . . Byrnes' statement. With reference to the latter I said it seemed to me most inappropriate for a member of the Cabinet to make independent comments on foreign policy which was being conducted by one of his colleagues. I further said that in view of the Secretary's analysis of the forthcoming conference, steps should be taken to see that the country is properly informed of the problems that face him, of the attitude of Russia, so that if and when the breakdown occurs he may not be exposed to violent attacks by his own countrymen, at least by those of his own countrymen who follow the "party line." I said I would be very glad to make such a speech and make it as explicit as he wanted it made.

[Forrestal did make the speech, on April 29, before the Foreign Policy Association of Pittsburgh. First, however, there was a brief break when he went down to Norfolk to receive the President aboard the giant aircraft carrier, U. S . S. *Franklin D. Roosevelt,* and demonstrate the powers of naval aviation. From this excursion a memento survived—a printed place card on which was scribbled in the President's holograph: "Thanks for a grand time, Harry S. Truman." The basic cordiality of the relationship seems to be indicated not only by the sentiment but by the fact that Forrestal had the card pasted in his diary, which contains no other mementos of the kind.

Forrestal had the note-cards from which he spoke at Pittsburgh copied into his diary; they show that he fulfilled his undertaking to be "explicit." The Russians, he held, had in no way withdrawn from their thesis "that the capitalistic and communistic concepts could not live together in the same world," and he added a quotation from Stalin's February 10 speech to prove it. Another card echoed his concern of two years before over the

[policy of "morgenthauing" Germany and Japan; it noted "the
great problem created by the policy of the dismemberment of
Germany and the . . . controversy about the Emperor in Japan,"
and the danger of the resultant power "vacuums" thus laid open
to the relentless pressure of Soviet expansion. He noted four of
these vacuums: in Central Europe, in the Middle East, in
China and Japan, and in India and Indonesia. There was really,
he added, no "enigma" about Soviet policy in view of its history
since the Bolsheviks established their control in 1921; Russia "is
always pushing, receding when rebuffed, but like a great tide
seeping in elsewhere if there is an opening."

A further card explained "what Byrnes is faced with" in his effort, at the meeting of the Council of Foreign Ministers which had
by that time convened at Paris, to get an Italian treaty. "The
Russian desire to drag their feet. . . . We want to make a
peace treaty with Italy—Russia wants delay." He tried to drive
home to his listeners the dangerous and dynamic nature of the
whole problem of foreign policy, and he illustrated with an idea
that experience had driven deeply home in his own thought:
"No finality to the stream of history—no black and white decisions. The stream of history always flowing and problems between nations never ended. American tendency—to try to get
finality and quick decision of age-long problems: China, India, the
Middle East. (How fast can we settle our own Negro problem?)
The relation of Military Power to Diplomacy. Power is needed until we are sure of a reign of law."

Here was more than a mere warning; here was an active concept of the vast issues of the day, rooted in a careful analysis of
the true springs of Soviet policy. On the day of this address, as it
happened, Secretary Byrnes in Paris was disclosing the American
offer to Russia, Britain and France of a twenty-five-year treaty of
guarantee to assure the continued disarmament of Germany. This
was to be the last major American diplomatic effort based upon
the contrary estimate of Soviet policy—on the assumption that
the Soviet Union was in fact primarily motivated by its fears of
outside attack and could therefore be brought back into a cooperative relationship with the West by guarantees against such

[fears. Forrestal by that time could have had little faith in the success of the *démarche;* it was actually to prove of no effect.

How far the situation had already deteriorated is shown by a curious episode in early May.

Friday Night—3 May 1946   *French Situation*

The Secretary of War called me this evening to say that a message had come in from McNarney [General Joseph T. McNarney, commander of United States Forces in Europe] asking for permission from the War Department to dispatch troops from the American area in Germany to France should there be an attempted overturn of the government by the Communist wing, following the voting on the proposed new French constitution Sunday.

The analysis of the situation is that Duclos and Thorez, Communist leaders, are divided in opinion as to action to be taken in the event of defeat of the proposed constitution. Duclos is against precipitant and violent action. Thorez disagrees and is in favor of a *coup d'état.* Should his view prevail, McNarney is fearful of the thirty thousand American soldiers (who are all service troops) who are now in France guarding property valued at around $2 billion.

Acheson was strongly opposed to the message that the War Department proposed to send to McNarney. They [the War Department] suggest that our troops would avoid any conflict with the French but would protect our property and lives of our guarding personnel. The State Department recommendation was that we should advise American forces in France merely to call on French authority for protection of our property and interpose no resistance and evacuate if it seemed that the French were going to use force.

Saturday—4 May 1946

Patterson, Acheson, Admiral Leahy and I, plus Captain Clifford [now Naval Aide to the President], met with the President at ten o'clock. He said that he had already sent the message proposed by the Army but wanted to listen to the Under

Secretary of State present his view. Acheson said it was the view of the State Department that we should avoid anything that would involve interference in the affairs of another country.

Patterson and I both took the position that to leave our service troops in France without protection might result in inviting assaults upon them which we would be in no position to resist.

Patterson pointed out that the American property in France includes substantial amounts of munitions of war which might be seized and used by the Communists in their revolutionary action.

After listening to the statements of the people present the President said he would abide by his position of the previous evening.

[As it turned out, there was no Communist *coup d'état* in France, and this particular problem solved itself. But when Leahy came back in early June from a quick trip overseas, his report was not encouraging.

3 June 1946   Lunch with Admiral Leahy just back from England
The English are very much worried and fearful about Russian action in Europe. American and British forces in Germany would be totally incapable of stopping any Russian advance toward the West. Churchill very bitter indeed about the failure of the Attlee government to maintain the British position in Egypt and the decision to surrender India. He fears bitter fighting and bloodshed in India and describes the situation as a cowardly surrender of the results of two hundred years' fighting by Englishmen.

Bevin frank and communicative; Attlee not. Bevin's belief that what is right—in this case, the granting of autonomy to Egypt and independence to India—will ultimately prove to be for the good of England. . . .

The following is summarized from Beetle Smith's dispatches today from Moscow:

. . . Ambassador Smith in Moscow believes that the U. S. S. R. (a) is determined to maintain domination over its "satellite regimes," despite the powerful local resentment against and opposition to these regimes; (b) is prepared to go to "almost any lengths" to achieve this end; (c) has not set any definite limit to its objectives in Europe; and (d) will be limited in its actions only by its own capacities and the opposition it encounters.

[Meanwhile, however, Forrestal's thoughts and energies had been largely diverted to his more immediate and urgent problem —the reorganization of the Armed Services.

The Thomas bill had been the creation of the Senate Military Affairs Committee. In a tactical move, Senator Walsh, as chairman of the Naval Affairs Committee, secured authority at the end of April to hold his own hearings on the measure. These hearings, conducted in public through the first weeks of May, immediately brought the fires of controversy, which had been smoldering behind the curtains of official reticence, to a fine blaze. Forrestal appeared before the committee on May 1. Actually, his testimony was a reasoned, and very reasonable, exposition of his own and the Navy's views on the bill. His central point was that the Thomas bill, while setting up an organizational structure, had not really thought through any of the specific and very practical problems of organization with which that structure would have to deal; though much more elaborate than the simple proposals originally advanced by the Army, it still rested on the premise of "merge now and organize later." The validity of this point was to become apparent two years afterward, when it unexpectedly fell to Forrestal's own lot to try to solve the concrete problems of organization with no more than an organizational plan to work with. In retrospect his criticism of the Thomas bill seems both moderate and thoroughly sound.

But the press, which had not been party to all the behind-the-scenes discussion, was inclined to take a sensational view. The Secretary of the Navy, according to the *New York Herald Tribune*'s report, served notice today that the Navy will use every means in its power to defeat a pending merger bill which is backed by the Army and has received a tentative nod of approval from President Truman"; and the White House correspondents seemed surprised when the President at his press conference next

[day told them a little testily that the Secretary of the Navy had had a perfect right to say what he did and that the President had authorized him to say it. At any rate, as the Walsh hearings continued to fan the controversy, it was obvious that something would have to be done; and on May 13 the President called a conference of all concerned.

13 May 1946   *Unification*

Met at the White House with the President this afternoon with Patterson, Leahy, Spaatz [General Carl Spaatz, the new Commanding General, Army Air Forces], Handy [General Thomas T. Handy, Deputy Chief of the Army General Staff], Norstad [Major General Lauris Norstad, Assistant Chief of the Air Staff], Nimitz [at this time Chief of Naval Operations], Sherman [Vice Admiral Forrest P. Sherman, Deputy Chief of Naval Operations], Nash [Captain Frank C. Nash, special assistant to the Secretary of the Navy], Clark [the Attorney General] and Vaughan [Major General Harry H. Vaughan, Military Aide to the President]. The President said he would like the Army and Navy to get together to identify their points of agreement and disagreement with regard to legislation looking to coordination of the two Departments. He said he was not prejudiced in favor of one Service or the other—what he wanted was a balanced system of national defense with particular reference to the integration of the budget. He said that about $6 billion a year of our national income would have to go to the service of the national debt and that, of the balance remaining, not more than one-third could be allocated to national defense and this would mean the most careful screening of requirements.

The President asked Admiral Leahy his views and Admiral Leahy said he thought something could be worked out provided the proposed bill eliminated the single Chief of Staff. He said his experience during the war had convinced him that the idea of a single Chief of Staff was dangerous—that had he wanted to secure power for himself during the war he could have arrogated a great deal to himself. [As Chief of Staff to the President, and only member of the Joint Chiefs of Staff without direct command responsibility over a specific Service, Admiral Leahy's wartime position had in it the rudiments of that of an over-all single Chief of Staff.]

The President said that while he would not be too much concerned if the nation could always count on having someone like Admiral Leahy in the position, he felt nevertheless that the idea was a dangerous one, that it was too much along the lines of the "man on horseback" philosophy, and that he had finally made up his own mind against it.

Admiral Leahy added that he thought the sphere of activities of naval aviation could be worked out by agreement. On the future position and scope of the activities of the Marines, he stated that he was inclined to agree with the views of General Eisenhower. [In a press statement from Tokyo the day before, evoked by certain Marine testimony before the Walsh committee, Eisenhower had said that while he did not favor maintaining two different armies with the same missions, he would be "the last" to advocate the "abolition" of the Marines.]

When the President asked the Secretary of War for his comments, Patterson replied that he and I had tried to get together several months previously but had been unable to do so, partly, at least, because he had felt so strongly on some of the points at issue. Patterson added that he still felt the greatest efficiency would be obtained by the formation of a single Department, with a single Secretary and a single Chief of Staff. As to the latter, however, he said that he was not prepared to "jump into the ditch and die for the idea." Patterson stated further that he would be glad to make another effort to get together with the Navy. I said that I would likewise to glad to make another try, and Admiral Nimitz and General Handy added their concurrence.

At first the President indicated that he would like to have our report by May 24. I pointed out that General Eisenhower was not expected to return to Washington from his Pacific trip until the 23rd or 24th, and that I thought he should be in on our discussions. Patterson replied that he knew Eisenhower's views, that they coincided with his own, and that therefore there was no reason to delay the report on such an account. However, after Admiral Leahy expressed his opinion that Eisenhower's counsel would be most helpful, Patterson concurred, and the President stated that he would extend the time for the submission of the report to May 31. . . .

[The battle was very far from over, yet this meeting represented a decisive victory for Forrestal, largely reversing the effects of the defeat he had suffered in December with the President's initial message on unification. Later Forrestal was to be criticized on the ground that there was a certain lack of iron in his methods. Yet here his chosen tactics of patient pressure, persuasion and, above all, a thorough grounding in the essentials of the problem and a complete understanding of all the factors that were involved in it, had paid off. The President had come around to the view that a single Chief of Staff was "dangerous." It was Secretary Patterson, who had taken a much more stiff-necked attitude, who in the end had to confess that he would not "jump into the ditch" for principles that Forrestal had patiently exposed as unsound. Forrestal, when it was necessary, *was* ready to "jump into the ditch," as subsequent events were to prove, because he knew that he stood on principles that were firmly based in study and analysis. If in the end Forrestal was largely the winner in the unification fight, it was because he had thought more deeply, because he had enlisted Eberstadt and others to think for him, because he had looked at the real and central problems involved rather than accepted quick solutions which under the test of time and events could not stand.

In another way this was a significant meeting. It was here that President Truman for the first time laid down the arithmetical approach that he was to adopt toward the military budget in the ensuing two years. After fixed charges had been met, the Armed Services were to get no more than one-third of the remainder. It was a parochial view, with which (it must be said) most Americans in the late spring of 1946 would have agreed. First you paid your debts; then you decided how much you could afford for the vast business of government; then you determined how much of this latter sum you could spend on defense and foreign policy.

[The idea that the necessities of defense and foreign policy might impose their own imperative demands would not sink in until some years later. The President was to cling for a long time to this idea of a "ceiling" on defense costs (nor was Forrestal himself unsympathetic to it), and the result was to be another complex battle in 1948. But that was more or less in the future. Until the unification issue was settled, nothing else could be done.

The day after the White House meeting Forrestal, Patterson, Nimitz and Eberstadt met to take stock. They found that the area of agreement was actually very large. The Army had "no objection" to a Council of Common Defense (which was to come out as the National Security Council in the final legislation), to a National Security Resources Board, to a Central Intelligence Agency or to a Military Munitions Board. Secretary Patterson had "definite reserves" on a central research and development agency but was willing to accept the continuance of the Joint Chiefs of Staff. Mr. Patterson still favored a single Chief of Staff, but after what the President had said the day before he was now willing not to "press the point." Mr. Patterson even yielded on the basic organization, to be composed of "three autonomous Departments," Army, Navy, Air, each to be headed by a civilian secretary of Cabinet rank and a military commander. Only one major point of difference remained, and that was over the powers to be given to the single over-all Secretary, or "Director," of Defense.

14 May 1946   *Discussion with Patterson*

. . . There was a difference of opinion as to what his powers and authority should be. Secretary Patterson expressed a preference for giving him full power and responsibility for the administration of the three military Departments, but was willing to limit the Director's action by a specific provision that the maximum administrative autonomy be left to the Departments.

Secretary Forrestal and Admiral Nimitz were not prepared to accept this. [Eberstadt took the formal notes of this meeting.] While agreeable to such a Director, they felt that his powers should not extend to administration. In their opinion his powers should be similar to those of the chairman of the War

Production Board and the chairman of the Office of War
Mobilization and Reconversion. . . .

[The situation is perhaps made clearer by Forrestal's own note
on this meeting.

14 May 1946   *Lunch with Patterson*

Lunched with Patterson today in my office—talked two hours
on consolidation. He holds out for a single Department with
what he calls a straight line of command, Chief of Staff under
the Secretary, with all orders flowing down through him to
the three components, Army, Navy and Air. He said he did not
see much use for civilians in this organization except on essentially civilian matters such as public relations (it was rather
astonishing to me to see the extent to which his mind had
been pervaded by Army thinking). I said I could not agree to
anything which would involve the destruction of the integrity
of the Navy. By that I meant its ceasing to have the status of a
separate entity rather than merely a branch, its own Secretary
having a seat in the Cabinet and access to the President.

With the entrance of Eberstadt we finally got down to talking specific business, but when Eber [the nickname by which
Eberstadt was known to most of his friends] undertook to
enumerate what the powers of the Secretary would be, Patterson objected, said he didn't like that approach but rather the
creation of the job and allocation of the broadest kind of
direct control over the three subsidiary Departments [again,
it would seem, an instance of "merge now and organize later"].
I said we would never agree to *administrative control* over the
Navy. That we might consider the word "supervise" but that
was as far as we could go.

On most other points there was no great disagreement. Patterson conceded that the single Chief of Staff concept was out
although he reiterated his belief that was a sound way to run
the war.

[The meetings continued, in the effort to meet the President's
deadline of May 31. On the 21st Forrestal and Eberstadt met

[with Patterson and W. Stuart Symington, Assistant Secretary of War for Air. Symington asked whether the Navy would support the proposed separate Department of Air; Forrestal answered that "there were two positions for me to choose between—one of opposition, and the other of saying it was not our business as to what the Army chose to do with its Air Forces." Eberstadt asked whether, if the Navy acquiesced in the separate Air Department, the others would accept the Navy's concept of the powers of the over-all Secretary of Defense, but he got no definite answer.

The Cabinet on Friday, May 24, was given over entirely to the sudden major crisis precipitated the afternoon before by the beginning of the greatest railroad strike in the nation's history, bringing virtually every railroad in the country to a halt. Forrestal had ready a memorandum detailing what the Navy had done in preparing to supply air, water and motor transport to cope with the emergency; the strike was, however, brought to an end next day. Meanwhile, May was running out, and, despite their best efforts, Patterson and Forrestal had failed to bridge the last gap remaining between them. In their joint letter to the President of May 31, while outlining the very considerable measure of agreement that had been achieved, they were forced to turn in a divided report on the basic organizational form. The Army insisted on a strongly centralized Department of Defense under a Secretary, with the existing Departments (though each would still have a civilian head) reduced to three coordinate "branches" of subordinate status.

The Navy, on the other hand, favored unification, but only "in a less drastic and extreme form." It assented to a separate Department of Air; it would prefer, the letter said, to see the Army integrate its air component with its surface forces in the same way that the Navy had done, but that was the Army's problem, and if the choice were between one Department or three, it would choose the three. But it wanted to retain full Department status for the Navy with Cabinet rank for its Secretary. Over the whole establishment it would place a "presidential deputy with clearly defined powers of decision over specific matters." There were two other important points of difference. The Army wished to concentrate in the Air Force full responsibility for "the mili-

[tary air resources of the United States," excepting only ship and water borne aircraft and certain minor service aviation, which would be left to the Navy; the Navy insisted, on the contrary, that it must retain control over the land-based aircraft needed for reconnaissance, antisubmarine warfare and the protection of shipping. Finally, the Army wished severely to limit the functions of the Marine Corps in amphibious warfare.

The issue was now in the hands of the President, and he called a meeting on the subject on the afternoon of June 4, at which Eisenhower was present along with the two Secretaries and the military and naval chiefs.

4 June 1946   *Meeting with President*
    . . . The Army presented through Patterson and Eisenhower its views. Patterson repeated the usual Army arguments for unification—economy, unity of command, elimination of jealousies, etc. Eisenhower's argument was not very germane to the subject. It dealt mostly with the question of inequities between Army and Navy allowances for foreign duty.

Both Patterson and Eisenhower went to great pains to emphasize that no matter what the President's decision was to be, they would accept it cheerfully and loyally and do their best to support it. . . .

After I had read my statement, Nimitz volunteered that, of course, the Navy would also loyally carry out the President's decision. I had made no such observation, but later on I said that, of course, whatever the President decided, the Navy would abide by the decision. I realized that Patterson's and Eisenhower's remarks flowed from the realization that the President was already pretty much on the Army's side of the case and they had nothing to risk in volunteering such a statement. I was considerably entertained by Patterson's saying at the end that he greatly regretted the impression that this merger was something the Army was trying to "put over." I refrained from observing that it would be quite difficult to have any other impression inasmuch as it had been the Army's promotion from the outset.

[On rereading this entry two or three weeks later Forrestal
added a further note:

My own conduct in this matter has been governed by three
main considerations: (1) to try to keep the Navy intact as a
Service as distinct from a merely subordinate branch of a vast
Department; (2) to obtain the improvements in our national
defense organization which the war indicated should be made
but without sacrificing the autonomy of the Navy; (3) to discharge my responsibilities to the President as a member of his
Cabinet, which means that I must go as far as I can in accepting and promulgating his views, always having the alternative,
when I can no longer do so honestly, of resigning. . . .

[The President let it be known to the public that he would review the issue and would shortly embody his conclusions in a directive which he would expect all the Services to observe. On
June 15 he did so, simultaneously releasing the two Secretaries'
letter of May 31, his own long reply, and a letter to the chairmen
of the military and naval committees of the Senate and House,
laying down a twelve-point program on which he believed unification should be established. As Forrestal had anticipated, the
decision, although representing an obvious attempt at compromise,
was a substantial defeat for his own and the Navy's views. The
President was firm for a single Department of National Defense
under a Cabinet Secretary. Under him there would be three "coordinated Services," each to have its own civilian "Secretary."
These last would not be members of the Cabinet; they would, on
the other hand, sit in the proposed "Council of Common Defense" (which became the National Security Council) and thus
have "opportunity to represent their respective Services to the
fullest extent." The President accepted the Navy's view as to
the mission of the Marine Corps; on the other hand, he balanced
this—and it was by far the most damaging aspect of the decision
—by allotting to the Air Force land-based planes for naval reconnaissance, antisubmarine warfare and protection of shipping.
Forrestal was well aware of the disastrous nature of this last

[decision. The history of the war was full of examples to prove
the vital need for naval control over land-based aviation used
in support of naval operations—only the night before he had
been reading an account of the naval catastrophe off Savo Island in August 1942, which demonstrated the Navy's utter dependence on air reconnaissance—and he knew that this much of
the "directive" he could not accept.

But if the decision was a defeat, it was again—as in the preceding December—by no means total defeat. The Army's simple
plan to "merge now and organize later" had been left far behind.
The single, all-powerful Chief of Staff had been eliminated. Forrestal's patient work had forced both a sounder and broader analysis of the true problem on all concerned; and the President's
support of all the larger agencies of integration which he and
Eberstadt had urged—from a National Security Council down to
a Munitions Board or Research and Development agency—constituted a very considerable monument to Forrestal's efforts. For
the rest, there was still the Congress; and there was a final
weapon which he had already hinted that he might use—the
weapon of resignation. Four days after the decision had been published he saw the President.

19 June 1946   *Meeting with President*

I talked to the President this morning at 10:15. I told him
that I did not wish to send him any letter in response to his letter about unification until Admiral Nimitz's return. (I informed
him that it was the opinion of all my civilian assistants that his
letter reflected a very earnest and sincere attempt to reconcile
the different views that had been presented to him and to get
the best answer for the country.)

I told him that in the letter that we proposed to send we
would stress the fact that his communication showed how
beneficial it had been to give this subject thorough study and
that the Navy was gratified that many of its ideas had found expression in his message. Our letter, I said, would express
gratification also for his emphasizing the fact that he desired
that any man who was to be the over-all head of national de-

fense should not run counter to the concept of *autonomy* and *integrity* for the Navy.

I said that Admiral Nimitz was concerned that the President's statement created the impression that we were foreclosed from expressing opinions on any bill that was sent in. I told him that I was confident the President did not maintain that—that we should be free to express our views on any particular parts of any legislation so long as we kept within the framework of his major objectives. He agreed fully to that view.

I said that the Navy Air people were greatly disturbed over that passage in his letter which dealt with the land-based reconnaissance planes. I said the Navy felt so strongly as to be fanatic about it, that they *must* have the means to carry out their mission. I said that it was my impression that his language did not intend to convey a denial to the Navy of sufficient land-based planes for reconnaissance and "search and strike" purposes. He confirmed this [which seems a little surprising in view of the explicit language of the directive].

I told the President of my visit to New York and a conversation with Wilbur Forrest of the *Tribune*—that I had urged the *Tribune* to be moderate in criticism of his message, that I felt that a very long road had been traveled toward reconciling the conflicting views of the Army and Navy, and that while I had been against the single Secretary all along, and while it was hard to shake myself loose from those misgivings, I thought the essence of the matter was this: whether or not a law could be written which would clearly leave the Secretary of the Navy free to run his own Department without kibitzing from above and while at the same time giving the Secretary of National Defense the global authority to make decisions on broad issues.

I told the President that the Navy had very sincere misgivings and apprehensions about the "mass play—steam roller" tactics of the Army. He said he was fully aware that there were foundations for those misgivings but that he intended to see that any such tactics were not successful.

In conclusion I told the President that my general view of

Cabinet members' responsibilities in supporting and securing orderly government was this: That he support policies of his President up to the point where he encounters sincere and *major* disagreement. That he should then ask to withdraw from the Cabinet.

I remarked parenthetically that I didn't take myself overseriously in this whole matter and that I had no illusions that my resignation, if it occurred, would have any earth-shaking consequences. I said I was simply trying to avoid following in the footsteps of Mr. Ickes! [The former Secretary of the Interior had proffered his resignation in what he apparently intended as a mere gesture and had been somewhat surprised to find it accepted.] . . .

[The hint of resignation had been made explicit. But there, for the moment, the matter rested. Congress was already approaching its adjournment date (it finally rose on August 3), and there was little likelihood of unification legislation in that session. Forrestal himself was to leave on June 24 for a trip that was to take him first to the test firing of the atomic bomb at Bikini and thence on around the world. It was to take another year before all the unification issues were finally worked out into a completed act; and it would take much longer than that before all the actual problems, which Forrestal knew to lie beneath those issues, would find an answer. Many are unanswered still.

CHAPTER V

The Cold War Grows Warmer

I

[Absorbed though he was in the unification controversy, Forrestal had by no means forgotten the greater problems and perils which all military policy exists (or should exist) to meet. He had not laid aside his idea for a Mediterranean squadron, and in early June he was talking to the Secretary of State about it.

6 June 1946   *Secretary Byrnes*

I talked to Secretary Byrnes this afternoon about sending casual cruisers unannounced—not as a fleet or a task force, but in small units—into the Mediterranean so that we may establish the custom of the American Flag being flown in those waters. Secretary Byrnes concurred entirely with the idea and said the visit of the *Missouri* [to Turkey] had been most effective and had produced most satisfactory results (a statement which was confirmed in conversation today with Mr. Walter Lippmann). . . .

10 June 1946   *European Situation—Russia*

I talked with the Secretary of War this morning and told him that I felt he should ask for a meeting with the Joint Chiefs of Staff and possibly the Secretary of State to discuss the situation in Europe. I gave it as my own opinion that in spite of certain disturbing indications the Russians would not move this summer—in fact at any time. I further gave it as my own view that in our position we could not fail to take notice

171

of certain warnings that were coming through almost daily in the dispatches from Europe. The most recent one on Monday from Caserta as of Saturday expressed misgivings about the situation in Venezia-Giulia.

I expressed the same view in a subsequent conversation with Admiral Nimitz and he suggested that Patterson and myself attend a meeting of the Joint Chiefs of Staff on Friday of this week. . . .

[Such a meeting was actually called next day by the President, with the Secretaries and the Joint Chiefs present, to hear an Army "appreciation and estimate" of the European situation. It was ominous: "Russians have been reducing their forces in the Balkans but adding to their forces in the North German plain. Qualitatively a substantial improvement in the latter during recent weeks. British and American forces inadequate for resistance." Nor was there much else, in Turkey, France or Spain (Spain, it was noted, had about six hundred thousand men "used mainly for garrison and repression"), on which to rely. In the event of crisis, Eisenhower thought, the American troops in Germany would withdraw probably to Hamburg, and he "thought that they would be able to get away without serious loss"; but Leahy, just back from London, disagreed. What, if anything, they decided, Forrestal did not record.

A day or two later he was listening to the perhaps somewhat embittered views of Sumner Welles, who until his resignation in 1943 had been Under Secretary of State under Roosevelt and Hull.

13 June 1946   *Sumner Welles*

In conversation with Sumner Welles at a dinner at his house this evening . . . Welles and I had a conversation about Russian relations.

Welles said that he thought the situation had now deteriorated so far that it would be most difficult to correct and bring back to balance. He said that a firmer policy toward Russia, had it been initiated in 1945, would have saved difficulties we now face. I made the observation that I thought our firmer policy toward Russia would have had to start much earlier than that—to be specific, before the invasion of Normandy. Much to my surprise, Welles said that had been his view, that he had expressed it to Mr. Roosevelt, who concurred, but that he had no success with Hull, who, as he phrased it, wanted to rely on the linger-and-wait policy of a domestic politician, with the result that instead of shaping events he had permitted events to shape him.

Welles was most pessimistic about the future of Europe and its ability to resist the momentum of Russia.

[But Forrestal was about to set off to see for himself. He left Washington by air on the evening of June 24; was in San Francisco next day and left the same evening for the Central Pacific. He witnessed the atomic explosion at Bikini on July 1 (his account adds nothing to the many since published) and went on by way of Guam to Manila. After the inevitable formalities and festivities, he continued next morning to Shanghai and finally to Nanking, where General Marshall, in his capacity as Ambassador to China, was striving to deal with the vast problem of Communism in Asia, which had been so abruptly handed to him.[1] Forrestal went straight from the plane to a luncheon with Generalissimo Chiang Kai-shek, which was given over to "polite exchanges and no business" until General Marshall appeared.

7 July 1946   *Trip—China*

. . . General Marshall came in afterward, and we talked for a short time at the Generalissimo's house and on the way to the airport. Marshall said that the Central government [of Chiang Kai-shek] was in a very strong position in Manchuria due to the victory of General Tu Yu-ming at Changchun. He said this general had moved with boldness and decision in a situation where most of the other of Chiang's military advisers had told him that the CP [Communist Party] Army was too strong to defeat in Manchuria.

He said that the truce of January which froze up the units

---

[1] See p. 113.

of both military forces, that is the CP and the GWO [the Kuomintang—in other words, Chiang's Nationalists], wherever they
happened to be at the moment, had worked to some extent in
favor of the Communists. It had interfered with the plan of
moving the Marines from the duty of guarding the railroads
because the Central government armies could not be moved to
take up that duty.

Marshall said the negotiations [these were the negotiations
the Ambassador was trying to promote between the Kuomintang and the Communists, looking toward peace between them
and Communist participation in the government] had taken a
very sharp turn for the worse. He was at that moment in
conference with the GWO group. He said if his worst fears
were realized and the negotiations broke down, he would recommend a period of withdrawal—and by that he included the
withdrawal of the Marines—and that the U. S. then take two
or three months for reappraisal and re-evaluation of its policy
toward China.

[Forrestal flew on to Peking, where he got an idea of how grave
     the results of such a course might be from the American Com-
     missioner, Walter S. Robertson.

8 *July 1946* [2]   *Trip—China*
After dinner at Marshal Li's I skipped the entertainment
which they put on for our senators and congressmen. Came back
to talk to Robertson. Robertson reiterated what he had said
earlier that the Marines had been the chief stabilizing force in
China. That without them last winter would have been chaotic
because the Communists undertook to prevent the delivery of
coal from Manchuria and from Central China by their
guerrilla operations against railroad communications. He said
undoubtedly the CP was very well organized in the technique
and tactics of Moscow, that they had no idea and no sense

---

[2] This entry bears the date of the 7th, but the context seems to make it clear
that the conversation took place on the 8th.

of responsibility for the vast economy of China. They were out to accomplish a revolution and would be satisfied with nothing short of a complete expropriation of the land of the owning farmers.

He said he thought one mistake was that the Nanking government did not use northern people to govern in the northern cities and provinces. (T. V. Soong denied this in my conversations with him the following day. . . .) Robertson forecast that if America withdrew from China, the Russians would surge in and flood Manchuria and North China. [Brigadier] General [Omar T.] Pfeiffer of the Marines confirmed this statement later; American withdrawal would mean Communist domination of all Manchuria and China down to the Yangtze River.

Robertson said that he had been told by a missionary of an incident which the missionary had seen with his own eyes: of the burying alive of seventy small landowners who had refused to agree to the expropriation of their land.

[Forrestal flew back to Nanking on the 9th for a long but not particularly illuminating talk with T. V. Soong, then Chiang's Premier; he returned the same afternoon to Peking on his way to Tokyo.

10 July 1946   *Trip*

Left the Cathay Hotel at 8:30. Rode to the airport with Admiral Cooke [now commander of the 7th Fleet]. Admiral Cooke said that his principal reason for advising that I visit Tokyo was to get from MacArthur further impressions of the Russian pressure throughout Asia. He said the Chinese had told him that the Russians now had in Shanghai and its environs about the same number of agents as the Japs had back in the thirties, that they were coming in almost daily in the guise of merchants, café entertainers and even through the medium of the Greek Orthodox Church. He said that he felt we should keep the 7th Fleet as a fleet in being in the Western Pacific, and that should mean that there be a competent amphibious force to operate with it. This he felt should be trained at Guam: i.e., one Marine division. . . . Any operations in the Pacific would probably not be on a vast scale but rather on the order of sporadic fighting and calling for speed rather than mass in dealing with them.

He expressed the view that the Chinese had within themselves the making of a great nation—that they were very much like ourselves in the degree to which they prized personal liberty and the freedom of the individual, but that they have not yet learned the principles of management necessary to provide a cohesive administration which would give a stable order within which individual people could really have the benefits of freedom. The CP doctrine of course is the opposite, that freedom is not of great importance provided the masses have the ownership of all the elements of industrial and agricultural production. America's contribution to China would be the training of the Chinese in the business of management and administration.

[July 10 was a long day. With Admiral Cooke's very perceptive remarks in his mind, he took off from Peking; he was at Atsugi Airport, Tokyo, by three o'clock, and on the drive in through the ruins of Yokohama and Tokyo he heard something of the Navy's work in the area from Vice Admiral Robert M. Griffin, commander of Naval Forces in the Far East. Forrestal was surprised to learn that the Navy had repatriated some four million Japanese troops to Japan and about one million Chinese, Koreans and others from Japan to their homelands; and that there were still some two million more to be moved. "It is clear," he noted, "here as elsewhere, that if anything the requirements of the Navy for the next year were under, rather than over, estimated. In the postwar planning inadequate consideration was given to the support needs of the 7th Fleet, of the occupation of Japan and of other activities incidental to the surrender. . . ." He hurried on, to inspect various naval installations, and to arrive by six-thirty at MacArthur's headquarters for an hour's talk with the Supreme Commander, Allied Forces in the Pacific. MacArthur made a number of points:

. . . 1. To get reparations settled—let the Japanese know definitely what they are to pay so that their industry can begin to revive. Japanese economy must be set up on a basis that will enable the people to work and produce sufficient export balances to provide the . . . food and clothing which they do not themselves produce. . . .

2. To get a government established which will permit the development of the concepts of liberty and freedom which are the American way of life. He summarized the political-economic picture in Japan as that of a nation of eighty millions of people of whom ten million were masters and seventy million were slaves. . . . He said he believed nobody in Japan was happier in his emancipation than the Emperor. . . .

He said the Russians were trying and were continuing to try to infiltrate into Japan but they have made no progress yet. . . .

The Russians don't want the re-establishment of Japan as an industrial nation, at least until they can be sure that they can control it. Japan, he said, must be regarded as the western outpost of our defenses. While the Central government in China might not be the best in the world, and while Chiang Kai-shek might be all the things he was accused of being, nevertheless they were on our side and they should be supported. He thought that Marshall had somewhat oversimplified the Chinese problem and the possibility of a near-term solution.

He greatly appreciated the support he had had from Secretary Byrnes but had a very dim view of other people in the State Department. . . .

The two great ideas which he said he believed America could oppose to the crusade of Communism were (a) the idea of liberty and freedom, and (b) the idea of Christianity. He had just read the evening before, he said, the account in the New Testament of Gethsemane, of the ordeal and agony of Christ, and he felt he had never been fully able to understand why it was described in such detail, but having witnessed the agony and distress of the world in recent years, he now felt that it was there for us to learn a lesson from; that Christ, even though crucified, nevertheless prevailed.

He expressed great admiration for Secretary of State Byrnes' handling of our relations vis-à-vis Russia in the past year. . . . He was critical and contemptuous of what he called the Left-wing writers in the American press. They were, he said, playing the game, whether consciously or not, of the Communists against the interest of their own country. . . . The success he had had with the native population, he pointed out, would diminish and dwindle very rapidly if the time ever came when they were denied a subsistence level of food and where they felt no hope for the future. . . .

[Forrestal's day was still not done; he went on to a dinner with the high military and naval authorities, and a talk with George Atcheson, who had been sent out as a diplomatic adviser with the rank of Minister and with whom Forrestal was "very favorably impressed." Of Atcheson, he noted, "he is quiet, not overdogmatic, fully aware of the magnitude of his problems, entirely loyal to MacArthur and fully aware of the underlying issues between us and Russia."

It was nearly a year and a half since Forrestal had last encountered General MacArthur and had heard him insisting, amid the ruins of newly recaptured Manila, that the Russians would have to be induced to come into Manchuria with sixty divisions if we were to conquer Japan.[3] The picture he now carried away of the General presiding over the ruins of Tokyo, reading the New Testament, and excoriating those who might wittingly or unwittingly be playing the Communist game in China, is undoubtedly arresting—in itself and in its contrasts with other parts of the long and tangled record. But it made the Soviet problem itself no less menacing.

Forrestal took one day for sightseeing in Japan; on July 12 he was in Okinawa, and on the 13th he arrived in Calcutta after a stopover at Bangkok and a bad half-hour trying to get into the Dum Dum Airfield through heavy storms and cloud at five hun-

[3] See p. 31.

[dred feet. There was a dinner that evening at Government House "with Governor General and his wife, Sir Frederick and Lady Burrows. He is a former engineer, one of the early pioneers of the Transport Workers Union in England. Obviously he does not think very much of India or the Indians. But he is finding out that the imperialistic policies which the Labour Party criticized in England so violently are not easily corrected overnight." Since Forrestal took off early next morning to the westward, it is not surprising that his notes on the vast issues of the Indian subcontinent contain little more than a traveler's hasty data. But he seems to have employed the eight-and-a-half-hour flight from Calcutta to Karachi on July 14 in summing up his impressions so far.

14 July 1946   *Impressions on Trip around the World*

Japan: MacArthur is doing splendid work in Japan. He has the respect and almost the admiration of the great bulk of the population, but these he may not hold if he is unable to provide the country with reasonable direction and hope. Japan's economy needs to be restored as quickly as possible. . . . Japan will need the most careful study by the United States to be sure that when the Americans get out her position as a nation is sufficiently clear so that she cannot be led in some other direction.

China: Marshall doing a splendid job and working up to the limit of his capacity. I have the impression that he may have been a little overoptimistic about the ability of anyone to get an agreement that will not come unstuck when the architect of agreement leaves China. We will have great need for tolerance in dealing with China. . . . One thing is clear—that the Marines were the balance of order in China during the last six months. The consolidation of government in China will have to travel a long road. The National government is deficient in trained administrators. . . . The Communists have had no experience in modern industry and have apparently only one objective, and that is the agrarian revolution. . . . Soong, the Executive Yuan or Prime Minister, is probably the ablest man in government, but he is under sustained attack as a grafter, exploiter, etc. Whether the Central government is venal or not, however, MacArthur's view is that it should be supported because "they are on our side."

Philippines: My impressions of Roxas [Manuel Roxas, President of the Philippine Republic] very favorable. Seems like an honest, decent and patriotic man. . . .

India: The solution for India, like China, will be a long-time development. . . .

The Middle East: America has lost very greatly in prestige in the Arab world by our attitude on Palestine. The British say that they cannot do all they would like to for the Arabs because of the pressure that we were able to exert in connection with the British loan. . . .

American Representatives Abroad: The very superficial impression I had wherever I went leaves me with deeper convictions than ever about the necessity of strengthening the quality of men going into our government service. . . .

I think the President and Secretary of State might do well to have a traveling representative to report to both on conditions throughout the East because whether we like it or not we are now, and will have to continue to be, a factor in the Far East. People out there feel very remote from the seat of government. . . . The British will, and quite justifiably, use the blocked sterling accounts to the fullest extent in retaining domination of the Far East trade. They are reluctant to have American visitors, for example, in Singapore—I was told that the airfield would not take my C-54 plane but discovered later that was not the case. It may be that we should not oppose this tendency because this Eastern trade is so essential to Great Britain, but it ought to be a conscious policy. . . .

General: . . . A great need for the world is to get back to work and let business and international trade start again. There is a vast amount of trade in the Far East which is now lying dormant—they can produce many things of an individual character which would find a sale in America and which would provide the balances to enable them to buy from us—small handicraft articles, etc.

[Forrestal dined at Government House in Karachi on the evening of the 14th, left for Cairo, left Cairo next morning and was in Rome by five o'clock on the 15th. On the way he encountered "a most unusual character," Frank O'Brien, a correspondent of the Associated Press, "native of Kansas, graduated from the Missouri School of Journalism, married to a Turkish girl, has four-year-old son who now speaks Turkish, French and German." O'Brien, who had been in Rumania, told him that "he was violently disillusioned about the Russians. . . . It was perfectly clear to him that the Russians were using precisely the same tactics as the Nazis, except more violent. He said they would keep pressing until stopped by war."

Forrestal spent but one night in Rome; it was enough for him to hear the now familiar story in another version. The American chief of the Allied Control Commission for Italy, Rear Admiral Ellery W. Stone, told him that the recent disposition of the Trieste problem had been "most upsetting to Italy and had very greatly lowered the prestige of the United States in Italy"; and on the way to the airport next morning the admiral was "again very blue about the situation both in Italy and the Middle East. He said the general opinion was that Ben Cohen [Benjamin V. Cohen, then Counselor of the State Department] was the influence on Byrnes' staff which advocated surrendering everything to Russia in order to avoid war. He said it was his own view that . . . if we fought Germany because of our belief that a police state and a democratic state could not exist in the same world, it must necessarily follow that we could not afford to lie down before Russia. He said that Freeman Matthews [American Foreign Service officer, then Political Adviser to the Council of Foreign Ministers] had told him that at the conference in Washington between Admiral Schuirmann, Matthews, Dean Acheson and Ben Cohen, Cohen had advocated giving Russia the Tripolitania trusteeship and permitting her to fortify the Dardanelles."

Forrestal was in Berlin by one o'clock that afternoon. He was to stay only two hours, but in the talk he had with the American commander, General Lucius D. Clay, the shape of many things to come was already discernible in dim outline.

16 July 1946   *Trip—Berlin*

His [Clay's] theory is that we should be firm with Russia but should be very polite at the same time. He cited as an illustration the difficulty he had with Russians in kidnaping German prisoners from trains under American cognizance. After a number of these incidents he had finally taken himself to see his opposite Russian member [of the Allied Control Commission], Lieutenant General Sokolovsky, to whom he had said that he, Clay, would be constrained to put guards of fifty soldiers with machine guns on each of our trains with instructions to shoot anyone who boarded any train or interfered with its operation. He pointed out to the Russian that such an incident would be unwelcome in both his country and Russia. Throughout his conversation he was consistently polite and thoroughly earnest. Shortly after his visit the Russians issued an order forbidding any train-jumping or kidnaping. Clay expressed it as his view that the Russians did not want a war and that we should find it possible to get along with them. I asked him if he would continue to think so if the Russians mean what Stalin had said in his February 10 speech, namely, that the world revolution was still on. He admitted that that must necessarily condition what he had to say. . . .

So far as Germany is concerned, he thought it was essential that Germany be brought back to some kind of economic stability where she could export enough to buy the necessities of life. . . . He said that the chief trouble with the conduct of the Allies toward Germany now was that all agreed on denying Germany its heavy industries but were not willing to provide the markets for the German light industries upon which she could support herself. He mentioned that Eastman Kodak, for example, would vigorously oppose the development of a German camera industry in the United States. . . .

[The crisis over Germany and the Berlin Blockade were still at this time nearly two years in the future. Clay's policy of polite firmness had worked in the matter of the "train-jumping"; but the fact could scarcely conceal the dangerously exposed nature of our position in Berlin, especially as both our military power and our

[willingness to use it continued to evaporate. Forrestal evidently felt that the strain was beginning to tell on Clay himself, for on his return to the United States a few days later he dropped a memorandum to the Secretary of War: "I think you should order General Clay to take a ten-day or two-week holiday—nothing else will make him do it—and if he doesn't get some break he runs the risk of blowing up entirely. . . ."

Forrestal was in Stockholm the same evening. One is hardly surprised to find that he excused himself from the dinner which the American chargé d'affaires had arranged—in the preceding seven days he had been to no less than five official dinners, plus lunches, cocktails and even an official breakfast or two, on three continents and a couple of islands—for there must have been limits even to his athletic constitution. But next morning he was playing golf with the chargé and by dinnertime was back to the routine, with a formal gathering at which he discussed "the Swedish parliamentary system and the single Department of Defense" at length with a number of eminent Swedes. The Swedes, he learned, "are obviously uneasy about the proximity and power of Russia" and still, despite their close geographical association, felt that they did not understand the Russians. But he was told that Sweden had no domestic Communist problem of her own.

He was in London on the evening of the 18th. This time he was let off; he had dinner "with Mrs. Forrestal and Captain Smedberg," his aide.

In London the round of official functions resumed, beginning with a lunch on July 19 with the King and Queen. There was a naval dinner that evening which included A. V. Alexander, First Lord of the Admiralty, and Sir John Cunningham, First Sea Lord (the British equivalents of the American Secretary of the Navy and Chief of Naval Operations).

19 July 1946   *Trip—London*

. . . Conversation with Alexander and Cunningham after dinner indicates a deep concern of the British over future relations with Russia and equally deep concern that their ties with the United States remain very close. Both Cunningham and Alexander were disappointed that we did not go through with the proposal to have Mitscher's 8th Fleet train in the Mediterranean. . . .

[Next day Forrestal had a meeting with Rear Admiral Thomas B. Inglis, the Chief of Naval Intelligence, "who briefed me on the results of his intelligence trip through Europe." These were, in effect, that his own intelligence officers were so burdened with official, social and commercial duties that they were not of much use for intelligence, and that there would have to be a "closer integration of relationships of State, War and Navy. The State Department inclined to hold aloof from military people and to be unaware of the very great influence that the Navy particularly can exercise in Europe. Its prestige is high, the record of its accomplishments in the Pacific is widely known and its personnel in general have been disciplined and of good conduct. . . . The Navy people need direction if they are to be effective—Bieri, for example, did not know whether the State Department approved of his being at Trieste or not." This evoked a letter the same day (20 July 1946) from Forrestal to Rear Admiral B. H. Bieri, commanding the American Naval Forces in the Mediterranean, which is of interest as showing Forrestal's own basic approach to the naval problem.

Inglis, the letter said, had pointed out "that there were still some deficiencies in the working relationships between Navy and State. And that in particular you were not entirely clear whether the presence of our ships in Trieste was in conformity with American policy or not." Forrestal said he would raise the matter with Byrnes when he got back, and continued: "It is one of my strongest-held beliefs that our diplomatic and military policies must be closely matched. . . . For your own information, it is my hope that the American policy will be to have units of the American Navy sail in any waters in any part of the globe. I am anxious to get this established as a common practice so that the movements of our ships *anywhere* will not be a matter for excitement or speculation. It was with that in mind that I had at first proposed to have the 8th Fleet conduct its spring exercises in the Mediterranean itself. . . . If you feel you need a further clarification of American policy I suggest that you raise the

[question with Admiral Nimitz and we will try to get you a prompt answer."

The round of contacts continued.

22 July 1946 *Trip—London*

Lunch with Ambassador Harriman [Harriman had become Ambassador to Great Britain in April]. He said that all through the British government there run these two main notes: a passionate desire for military and diplomatic cooperation with the U. S. coupled with the fear of our economic power. The British are desperately afraid of another U. S. depression, which they think might lead to world disaster. Chief deficiency of their Labour government is their lack of knowledge in broad practical fields of administration and management. They have probably bitten off more than they can digest in the nationalization of the steel industry.

Harriman said he thought one of the great dangers in countries where there is a strong Communist Party was the preferential ballot, which results in giving the Communists a place in the government from which they can operate and rob the democratic elements of power to govern. . . . When Tillon became Minister of Defense in France as a result of a deal which allocated this among some other Cabinet posts to the Communists, he was able to infiltrate a substantial number of Russian sympathizers in both the officer corps of the French Army and the enlisted personnel. . . .

Meeting at three o'clock with Sir Hastings Ismay, Secretary of the Council of Imperial Defence [roughly the equivalent in the British system of what is now the American National Security Council]. He said that he was at work now on a White Paper which would "tidy up the mechanism of the defense organization constructed during the war." Their minds were not yet clarified but in general they were working along the lines of the U. S. Navy plan [the Eberstadt report], i.e, with an individual on the top limited to broad powers of decision and supervision rather than administration and with the heads of the three Services having autonomy under him. He would probably be called the Minister of Defence and be the only one to sit in the Cabinet but would not mess in the details of internal administration of the Departments. . . . Ismay thought his [Ismay's] function [as Secretary of the Council of Imperial Defence] was the most important function but that it should be carried out by a man relatively obscure and not desirous of power. He feels there is a need for the closest kind of link between the defense program and diplomatic objectives. . . .

As the British envision it, the Prime Minister, the Foreign Secretary and the Minister of Defence will be the committee of the Cabinet dealing with all matters referring to foreign affairs and military operations. . . . Ismay said . . . it is a cardinal principle that they do not expect to write legislation which will successfully solve all the many problems that flow from this reorganization. He said that it was rather their idea to make a beginning and then make subsequent readjustments . . . as events and practical considerations dictated.

Saw an old friend of mine, Sir Edward Peacock, who expressed the view that the present Labour government would be in for five years. . . . Peacock said the chief deficiency of the existing government was lack of experience in either business or government—that Strachey's [John Strachey, Minister of Food] mishandling of the bread rationing was an example.

[Forrestal went out for golf next day with Sir Oliver Lyttleton, who had been Minister of Production under Churchill, and the two fell to philosophizing. Sir Oliver felt that the Labour government, after carrying its nationalization program to a few basic industries, would then propose to let the free enterprise system function elsewhere; but the trouble was that "they had no idea of how that system functioned," with its risk enterprise and managerial techniques. "I said that was one of the chief handicaps of business—its failure to explain to the public what management meant." In any business, he went on, each department —labor, design, production, sales, accounting—thought itself the most important, but "there still remains that imponderable element which provides the synthesis for all of them, namely, management, which is the ability to handle people, to select leaders and to exercise judgment.

["I said I was impressed in looking at Europe and Asia by the same factor in government, namely, management. That it was easy to wreck management of governments through war and anarchy but it was damn hard to re-create them." It is a good statement of the philosophy toward both business and government which Forrestal was often to express and on which his administrative methods were founded.

His trip was now nearing its end. A few minutes after noon on July 24 he landed at the Washington Airport. In just short of thirty days he had been around the world, getting a quick view for himself of its huge, intricate and ominous problems. He sent regrets for a reception that evening, and his appointment calendar for the next day is a blank. But a diary note intimates that he spent it, characteristically, reading Walter Bagehot's *English Constitution.*

I I

[Everywhere around the vast periphery of the Eurasian continent the situation had been the same; everywhere there was the same sense of a relentless pressure—acute in some places, latent but no less menacing in others; everywhere there had been need for firmness, action, strength and coherence of policy in meeting this extraordinary threat. What was everywhere demanded was a far closer coordination of the diplomatic and military arms; more and abler men in our foreign services; better use of the politico-military instruments we possessed. We should strengthen the 7th Fleet in the Far East; we should keep the Marines in China; we should put naval power into the Mediterranean; we should be watchful of our sinking prestige on half a dozen threatened fronts. Such were the lessons Forrestal had brought back in his diary notes. But the country in mid-1946 was not in the mood for either realism or exertion.

26 July 1946   *Cabinet*

I reported to the Cabinet on my impression of the atomic bomb test and said we were satisfied that both the "A" and "B" tests would be productive of important results, not merely of a military character but also [would] yield information of

a collateral scientific value. I said that personally I had some
doubts whether the third test, from a military standpoint, was
necessary. [The third test of the Bikini series was never made.]

I spoke about China: We could shortly expect acceleration of
Russian propaganda that America should get out of China,
should cease to back Chiang Kai-shek with munitions and
money—in other words, turn the Far East over to Russia. The
Marines were in very exposed positions on the railway lines
between Peiping and Tsingtao and between Peiping and Chin-
wangtao. The Chinese should take over responsibility for the
guarding of these railway lines, but they will not do it until
they are forced to by the withdrawal of the Marines. . . . I
said I was not suggesting the withdrawal of the Marines from
China but rather consolidation of them into a compact force
which would be able to take care of itself. Leaving Americans
in the exposed positions along these railways was a dangerous
invitation to trouble and unfair to the boys themselves.

After the Cabinet meeting I showed the President and the
Secretary of State a map of North China giving the precise
location of the Marine outposts. . . . The Secretary of State
asked whether Marshall was not fully aware of the situation. I
said he was but that he was so preoccupied with the main question of trying to get a permanent peace arrangement between
the Communists and the Central government that he was unwilling to do anything to disturb the chances of agreement. I
proposed that I would draft a tentative message to Marshall
focusing the problem and asking him to give immediate and
serious consideration to a proposal that the Marines be relieved
of this railway guarding duty and allowed to withdraw, so that
they would form a compact and militarily effective striking
force, under which conditions I felt confident . . . that they
could take care of themselves.

26 July 1946   *Palestine Question*

After the Cabinet meeting today talked with Byrnes, Patterson and Snyder [now Secretary of the Treasury] about the
Palestine-Arabian-Jewish question. Jews are injecting vigorous
and active propaganda to force the President's hand with refer-

ence to the immediate immigration of Jews into Palestine. Two
areas have been agreed upon—one for the Arabs and one for
the Jews, with the Arabs getting the less desirable land. The
problem is complicated by the fact that the President went out
on the limb in endorsing the Barkley-Krum [*sic*] report saying
that a hundred thousand Jews should be permitted entry into
Palestine. Substance of the agreement reached in London between the American, British, Arabian and Jewish leaders is the
division of areas of land referred to above, plus agreement to
have the number of Jews specified to enter Palestine when, as
and if the settlement reached has been accepted by the Jews
and Arabs.[4]

[It was the Far East, however, which bulked much larger in
Forrestal's notes. At the next Cabinet it was again the leading
topic.

2 August 1946   *Cabinet Meeting*
    . . . Dean Acheson, at the President's invitation, gave a re-
port on the present situation in China. He forecast that there
would be attacks on our policy with a view to determining us
by the force of public opinion to withdraw the Marines.[5] He
said the Marines had been necessary in China to provide for

---

[4] This note, which is both obscure and garbled, has been included in order to
follow the development of Forrestal's position on Palestine, one of the controversial aspects of his career. The year before, the President's rather offhand
demand for the immediate opening of Palestine to Jewish immigration had led
to the appointment of a Commission of Inquiry of representative citizens, six
American and six British. In April the commission turned in its report, which
recommended the admission of a hundred thousand Jews but coupled this with
certain political recommendations. The British took the position that the report
must be considered as a whole, and that they could not acquiesce in the admission of the immigrants until its political provisions were also accepted. Bartley
C. Crum, one of the American signatories of the report, was particularly vocal
in insisting that the immigrants should be admitted forthwith. The President
appointed Byrnes, Snyder and Patterson as a Cabinet committee to consult with
the British on the matter. The resultant plan, calling for the partition and
federalization of Palestine, had not been formally published on July 26, but
presumably it is this plan to which Forrestal refers. It never became operative.
[5] This sentence, also garbled in the original, has been reconstructed in accordance
with the apparent meaning.

the orderly evacuation of a million-odd Japanese soldiers and of many hundreds of thousands of civilians. This had been accomplished, and the reason for the Marines being in China now was to support policy and efforts of General Marshall to bring about order, a constitutional government and a unified National Army. He said it was true that the existing Nationalist government of Nanking was not all that could be desired and that Marshall was not getting any great help in his endeavors to secure peace. But he felt that we should back Marshall up to the limit until he himself has said that there is no longer any hope of gaining his objective and that it is time to come out and reconsider our position in China and our general policy in the Far East.

The Secretary of Labor [Schwellenbach] said he saw no reason why we should continue to interfere in the affairs of China and if they wanted to have a civil war they should have it, but that we should not be in the position of trying to impose any form of government on any nation. To this I responded that if we came out of China, Russian influence would flow in and over the country; that whether we liked it or not, conditions of this order and of civil war in China could not be permanently acceptable to the United States because they were an invitation to some other power or group of powers to come in and dominate China; that, I said, was what happened in the thirties, and it is precisely that which will happen in the forties except that Russia will be substituted for Japan. Mr. Schwellenbach said that in view of my statement and the recent date of my visit to China he would withdraw his objection, but that ninety days from now, if the conditions were the same, he would not be willing as far as he was personally concerned to endorse the continuance of American intervention in China.

[Secretary Schwellenbach's attitude (and perhaps Under Secretary Acheson's as well) was very typical of the times. It was difficult for Americans in mid-1946 to grasp the idea that they might not always be able to control events and that events might control them. It still seemed a matter of choice whether we left the Marines in China or withdrew them. If Marshall's mission

[failed we would then "reconsider" and think of something else; Schwellenbach would consent to leaving the Marines for another three months, but if the situation had not improved he would then withdraw them. It was the essence of Forrestal's position that we were confronting a desperate danger here and now; that if we could not now develop an effective and workable policy there would be no time to "reconsider" at leisure later on, that if we needed the Marines in China at all, then a further deterioration of the situation would make the need for them not less but all the greater.

It was not a popular attitude at that time, when people were just getting back to the pleasures and profits of civil life, when they were tired of warlike exertions and were willing to leave the future—when they thought about it at all—either to the United Nations or, in extremity, to the atomic bomb. But Soviet pressure was not to be denied. Almost immediately there was another instance, this time over the Dardanelles.

At Potsdam the Western powers had agreed with Russia that there should be a revision of the international convention controlling the regimen of that famous and strategic waterway. The Soviet Union had now suddenly advised the Turks of the terms on which she proposed that the revision should be made. It is unnecessary to go into details; it is enough to say that the note plainly implied Russia's intention to take over control and fortification of the Strait for herself, at the same time reducing Turkey to the status of a minor or satellite partner in the enterprise. On the 14th Forrestal was at the State Department for a conference with Acheson and various military and diplomatic officials.

14 August 1946   *State Department*

. . . It was agreed that it was desirable to canvass the United States policy and decide now whether this country proposed to take a firm attitude on the Russian *démarche* or whether we should do as we have in the past—protest, but ultimately give in. . . . It was agreed that the Under Secretary of State and the Under Secretary of War [Kenneth C. Royall] and myself should see the President at 3:30 Thursday afternoon, August 15.

15 August 1946   *Meeting with President*

Meeting with the President at 3:30. Dean Acheson stated the background of U. S. S. R.'s note of this week to Turkey. . . . The Under Secretary of State said that the War, State and Navy Departments had canvassed the situation thoroughly—that it was the view of the State Department that the Russian note and its last three demands on Turkey reflected a desire to control and dominate that country; that acceding to these demands would be followed next by infiltration and domination of Greece by Russia with the obvious consequences in the Middle East and the obvious threat to the line of communications of the British to India. He said that he felt that this trial balloon of the Russians should be firmly resented by the President with the full realization that if Russia did not back down and if we maintained our attitude it might lead to armed conflict. The President replied that he was perfectly clear we should take a firm position both in this instance and in China; that we might as well find out whether the Russians were bent on world conquest now as in five or ten years.

The Under Secretary of War recommended that in view of the seriousness which the State Department attached to the position we planned to take, steps should be undertaken to inform the country of the background of the decision, particularly of the implications contained in the Russian note. I added further that we should set in motion machinery to see to it that people on the [*New York*] *Times* and [*New York Herald*] *Tribune* and other newspapers should be briefed on the factual background.

[The President was firm; as it turned out, there was no showdown then and diplomacy was able to deal with the Dardanelles question. Yet the episode remains as a vivid example of just those weaknesses in policy formation and direction which Forrestal, with his larger unification plan, was striving so hard to eliminate. Here was the sudden, surprise development (that might have been foreseen); the hasty, *ad hoc* convening of a committee to deal with it (none of the top policy-makers except Forrestal was

[present); the referral to the President, who had to be "briefed" on the simplest background elements of the situation; then the quick decision which—correct and forceful though it was—was still taken with no real consideration of the means available to back it up and no preparation of public opinion for the grave implications that it might have carried. It is a clear illustration of what Forrestal had in mind when he argued, as he ceaselessly did, for a closer integration of the political and military arms, for a coordinated defense structure, for higher organs of intelligence, policy-formation and decision that could foresee such crises, could relate them to long-term, basic policies and could provide the means for surmounting them with full public knowledge and understanding. Admittedly the actual organs established by the unification act of the following year were to fall considerably short of these desiderata in practice. But the need was real; and we do not know how far the instrumentalities which Forrestal was so earnest in initiating may ultimately develop under the hammers of experience and necessity.

III

[On other fronts there was no cessation of stress and crisis. Two letters of these days give Forrestal's estimate in informal terms. One was to Palmer Hoyt, publisher of the *Denver Post*, the other to James Warburg, who was then writing numerous articles on Germany.

To Palmer Hoyt, 14 August 1946
Dear Ep:
This is an interim contact. When do you plan to come East? I would like to give you Forrestal's summation of the world in three words—"not so hot."

I hope you continue to back up James F. Byrnes and don't fall for the line of getting the Americans the hell out of China. The issues involved there are complex, deep and not curable by Monday morning, but one thing is inescapably clear: we have an interest in Asia and we cannot afford to abdicate it. . . .

To James P. Warburg, 20 August 1946

Dear Jimmy:

Not for publication: I certainly agree with you that the German problem is the key to the whole question of destruction or peace—although I would probably, as a result of my recent travels, add China, Japan and India to that category.

[The world was "not so hot." In China the situation continued rapidly to deteriorate, and on August 10 General Marshall had been obliged to admit publicly that an agreement between the Nationalists and Communists seemed impossible, though his mission would continue. In Greece, Soviet pressure was rising to ominous heights.

There was another brief interlude for Forrestal on August 18 and 19, when he made one of his fast inspection trips. He was in Newport on the afternoon of Sunday, the 18th, where he had a twenty-minute visit with the President aboard the latter's yacht, the *Williamsburg;* he left for Norfolk, where he arrived at eight o'clock for dinner; was up at six-thirty on Monday to witness the joint assault landing exercises by Annapolis midshipmen and West Point cadets at Little Creek, Virginia (an early effort at unification in military education); left Norfolk about ten-thirty for Washington and thence flew to Mitchel Field, Long Island, where he landed in time to reach Bernard Baruch's house for a luncheon given in honor of the latter's seventy-sixth birthday. At lunch he sat next to Mrs. Andrei Gromyko (the wife of the former Soviet Ambassador to the United States recently appointed permanent delegate to the Security Council), "who," Forrestal noted, "is now occupying the former Ogden Mills estate in Woodbury. They both inquired for news of Mrs. Forrestal and they seemed to recall with much pleasure their dinner at our house with the Stimsons two years ago. I had the feeling quite definitely that they both felt quite lonely and would like to break the fence which exists between the Russians and any community in which they live, but which I presume they are prevented from doing by the policy of the Russian government." He motored on that evening for a dinner at the house of Mrs. Grant Harkness at East Hampton, where he spent the night, and

[returned to Washington for an appointment at ten-thirty on Tuesday, August 20. On the two days he had been away, August 18 and 19, Yugoslav fighters had fired on one American airplane near or over their territory and shot down another with the loss of its crew. Yugoslavia had not at that time thrown off her status as a Soviet satellite; and another crisis was at hand. It loomed behind a conversation in which Admiral Nimitz had discussed the still thorny problem of Pacific command with General Eisenhower, at that time Army Chief of Staff.

21 August 1946   *Admiral Nimitz*

Admiral Nimitz came in at 3:00 to report on his conversations with Eisenhower.

Pacific command: Eisenhower agreed that subject to the embarrassments of the MacArthur situation, a wise disposition of this question would be to make a Western Pacific Command extending from the main islands of Japan through the Ryukyus and including the Philippines, and a Pacific Ocean Command —the rest of the Pacific—to be under a naval officer, namely Towers [Admiral John H. Towers, Commander-in-Chief, Pacific Fleet].

Eisenhower agreed with Nimitz that the whole question of the command setup over the globe should be considered and a definite decision arrived at as soon as the President returns. . . .

They talked in general about the command situation in the event of a war with Russia. Eisenhower's view was that the land commander in Europe would be an American. . . .

Eisenhower gave it as his view that the Russians would not take steps leading to immediate war. He said he could not for example conceive of the shooting down of two planes over Yugoslavia as being a *casus belli*. . . .

[On August 21 "Acheson called the Joint Chiefs of Staff" to discuss ways and means for providing fighter escort to American planes on the Austrian-Italian route near Yugoslavia. It brought up the whole question of what we had with which to back the very strong protest note we were sending to the Tito government in Yugoslavia.

22 August 1946   *JCS Meeting*

. . . Dispatch from Conolly [Admiral Richard L. Conolly, recently appointed commander of United States Naval Forces in European Waters] stated that the presence of the American warships and particularly the *FDR* [U. S. S. *Franklin D. Roosevelt,* giant carrier] in the Mediterranean, he thought, would be a tremendously helpful and stabilizing influence.

Later this afternoon I asked Admiral Ramsey [D. C. Ramsey, Vice Chief of Naval Operations] to prepare for me a brief of our naval capabilities in the event of trouble in Europe. The Fleet is stripped down as a result of our rapid demobilization to a dangerously low point of efficiency although it is beginning to climb again in this respect slightly since July, which was the nadir of our effectiveness. Probably our strongest unit is Cooke's 7th Fleet, but Ramsey pointed out that if there were trouble with Russia it would be reasonable to assume that equivalent difficulties would arise in the Far East and therefore necessitate keeping our units in those waters. We have a very large number of vessels in the *active* fleet which cannot go to sea because of the lack of competent personnel. When Admiral Barbey [Vice Admiral Daniel E. Barbey] wanted to move the *Catoctin* [command ship used at the Little Creek maneuvers] last Monday, he had to get personnel from all the other ships in Norfolk in order to be able to proceed, and even then the ship had a minor accident.

Ramsey estimated the Army's available strength for application in Europe as being 460 fighters of which possibly 175 could be called really trained first-line pilots and about 90 bombers.

23 August 1946   *Talk with Acheson*

I talked to Acheson this morning and told him I was very apprehensive about our capabilities to meet any sudden emergency in Europe; that the tone of our notes to Yugoslavia was quite strong and that it seemed to me it was incumbent upon us—the State, War and Navy Departments—to make an evaluation of what we had to back those notes with. . . . Acheson agreed that this was important and said he would himself make a formal request to Joint Chiefs of Staff for such a review. . . .

[Yet in spite of such serious concerns, the pressures for budgetary economy were as strong as ever. In response to them, the President had taken the unusual step of ordering the Services to make drastic reduction, not in their future budget estimates but in their current spending. In mid-August Forrestal had written his friend Paul Shields:

To Paul V. Shields, 13 August 1946

I am still planning to get down to Southampton some day before the end of the month—I'd had my mind set on the middle of this week, but the President's $700 million cut in our funds for this year washed up that idea. He had to do something drastic to bring the budget more nearly into balance but I hope it's not symptomatic of other cuts to come. The state of the world and the happenings in Paris do not make me feel like putting the pistols away just yet.

[It is curious to find John R. Steelman, then Director of the Office of War Mobilization and Reconversion, discussing the budget question with Forrestal on August 27 as if it were in a wholly separate compartment of policy. The Navy had sent a letter to the President outlining "reductions it proposed to make in order to effect the $650 million reduction in expenditures in 1946-47 as directed by the President." Forrestal pointed out that if they had to make the cuts, it was desirable to start canceling the contracts right away, and this the Navy had decided to do. "Mr. Steelman made no comment one way or the other, but I took it from his failure to interpose an objection that he was agreeable to our decision." Yet it was only three days later that the Joint Chiefs of Staff were discussing the strategic situation in terms which made military budget reductions of any kind almost grotesque.

3 September 1946   *Admiral Ramsey*

Admiral Ramsey reported to me today that at the meeting of the JCS with the British Army and Navy representatives in Washington which took place last Friday [August 30], there was a general discussion of the question I raised a fortnight ago, namely, what this country and the British had available with which to meet an emergency should it arise. It developed that no very definite plans had been evolved because no one had raised the question. Admiral Leahy kept insisting that there should be specific and definite answers, particularly in the way of clear and precise planning for movements in Europe and for support.

The British agreed that they would send over their top planners from the Army, Navy and Air Forces and that the meeting should be held in Washington. They were, however, most apprehensive about security and felt that the meeting should be on an informal basis. To this the JCS agreed.

The most important problem would be how to get McNarney's people [the American occupation troops] out of Germany and how to support British and Americans in the Trieste area. . . .

[Forrestal's questioning insistence on considering capabilities along with commitments had here planted one of the seeds from which, at long last, the North Atlantic Pact and its military organization were to grow. In retrospect, one is struck by the calm and rather theoretical way in which the military chiefs in 1946 approached issues which Forrestal even then knew to be urgent and which one would suppose ought to have been the military men's first concern. But they were, at all events, beginning to realize the direct connection between military economy and military obligations. Forrestal himself, together with Patterson, attended the JCS meeting on September 5 when they again discussed the matter of "conversations with the British planners on British-American action when, as and if." Eisenhower went on to bring up the President's order for a reduction in expenditures.

5 September 1946   *JCS Meeting*

. . . Eisenhower expressed apprehension about the cuts in spending in 1946-47. He said the Army's budget presentation had been made on the most economical basis possible and that the spending cuts which had been imposed as a result of Steelman's suggestion to the President would make it practically impossible for the Army to operate. He said they were particularly bothered by the fact that a good deal of the money that would be paid out this year would be for contracts that had been completed prior to June 30, 1946. And that, therefore, the money would not represent current working capital. He said it looked to him as though the amount they would have for this year would be nearer $3.5 billion rather than the $7 billion contained in their budget figure. I said we are having the same experience plus the additional fact which troubled us, namely, that the Budget Bureau's estimate of Navy's cash withdrawals from the Treasury was considerably below what our figures were. . . . I said it seemed to me that we would have to ask for a meeting with the President to be sure that he understands the full implication of the current *spending* cuts that we are putting into effect.

["When, as and if" anything had to be done, it seemed increasingly unlikely that we, to say nothing of the British, would have anything with which to do it. The Secretary of the Navy apparently felt that he needed the help of a riper wisdom. After a State-War-Navy meeting on the 11th, Forrestal again boarded his plane.

11 September 1946   *Meeting with Stimson*

This afternoon I flew up from Washington to see Henry Stimson at Syosset [Long Island]. I recalled to his mind his efforts, in which Grew and I joined, at the San Francisco Conference of a year ago last spring to postpone [the conference] until the question could be resolved as to whether Russia really wanted to work toward world peace with the United States and Britain. I said that the conduct of Russia since that time tended to make me feel that we would have made little progress. Stimson

said that that might have been so but that in all his actions
. . . he had been motivated by the desire to find out the extent to which they would join with Britain and ourselves in
making a stable world.

He said the way things had now developed he thought we
should not delay in going forward with the manufacture of all
the atomic missiles we could make.

He expressed deep misgivings about the labor situation in
the country and said that such "conspiracy" against the public
interest would have to be dealt with just as the big business and
other compulsions against the public interest had been dealt
with. He said there were adequate precedents both in our own
law and in old English common law to deal with such conspiracy.

I V

[Beneath these formidable problems of international policy
there lay always the domestic problem of military and governmental reorganization to meet them. It had been left in mid-
June with the President's "directive" on unification and Forrestal's
intimation that if it came to a clear issue of conviction he would
have to resign. But when Forrestal met in mid-August with Eberstadt, Leahy, Clifford (the President's Naval Aide) and other
Navy leaders, it appeared that the situation was not as serious as
that.

14 August 1946   *Question of Unification*
. . . Mr. Eberstadt expressed his view that the Navy's position on this subject could now be brought into consonance with
the President's wishes, the only question being the phrasing of
language which would accomplish his objective of a so-called
single Department, and ours the preservation of the integrity
and economy of individual Services. It was agreed that Admiral
Leahy and Mr. Clifford would present the Navy's ideas to the
President at the morning meeting on Thursday.

[On August 27 Forrestal gave a dinner aboard the U. S. S. *Sequoia*—the naval yacht provided him which he often used for

[such meetings—for Secretary Patterson, Eberstadt, General Handy and Assistant Secretary of the Navy W. John Kenney. The purpose was to find out whether the Army would assent to the suggestion that the President, by executive order, should put into effect the many agreed points in the unification plan, leaving the controverted issues to Congress.

27 August 1946   *Unification*

. . . Judge Patterson expressed willingness to go along with such an idea although he said it was not a cure for the central problem. It was clear from his conversation and Handy's that the Army still adheres to the conception of unification as a single boss with both decisive and administrative authority.

I said I would not be willing to go along if Patterson felt it [the proposal for an executive order] was a concession to the Navy. I said it was Eberstadt's suggestion and as a matter of fact I would regard it as weakening the Navy's present situation because the obvious follow-up would be "you have gone thus far, why not go the whole hog and finish the job by having a single man at the head?"

Handy said he could not understand why, if we were willing to move along the lines of these eight [agreed] points, we wouldn't do the whole business right now. My answer was that there was a fundamental difference between the Army's and Navy's ideas of unification which apparently had not yet been made clear; that we recognized the following areas in which the power to decide by someone other than the President was needed:

(1) The assignment and allocation of commands, which automatically involves the resolution of command disputes.

(2) Missions and means.

(3) Components of the several forces.

(4) Cognizance over new weapons and their development.

(5) Decisions on money.

(6) Common policies on personnel.

I said furthermore that we must not confuse the two areas of discussion, the first being . . . to find out whether the Army and Navy would follow the suggestion of implementing the eight agreed-upon points and the other being the deeper issue of whether we would accept the Army's view of a single Department, a one-man boss or nabob who is to be the supreme military civilian in the government.

Judge Patterson and Handy both referred to our ROTC bill [a matter of Army-Navy dispute at the time], to the failure of the Joint Chiefs of Staff to agree on the composition of the forces in the Army and Navy which was asked for as of a year ago now, as striking examples of why a single boss was necessary. I said all the things that they have mentioned could have been resolved through the medium of an active Secretariat but that Patterson had never been willing to go along with this suggestion. I said frankly that we had the feeling that the Army wanted to drag its feet to show that no progress was possible until their view was accepted.

The meeting finally wound up with Mr. Eberstadt securing the agreement from Patterson and myself to designate someone to work with him in the working up of the executive order.

Throughout the evening it was quite clear the Army has not surrendered any of its objectives—they brought up all of the old points—that naval units have never been under Army command in the Pacific; that Nimitz, Halsey and other naval commanders had been in thorough agreement on the merger but had been dissuaded from that view by the influence of King; that the Navy was ambitious to be the *sole* instrument of national defense; that the Marine Corps was an unnecessary duplication of Army units (Patterson, recognizing, I think, that attacking the Marines is politically unprofitable, was careful to say what high regard he had for the Marine Corps), the failure of the Joint Aeronautical Board in the last twenty years ever to reach any solid agreement, the failure of the Joint Chiefs of Staff to resolve the questions of command, composition of forces, etc.

[The subject recurred at the State-War-Navy meeting on September 4.

4 September 1946   *State-War-Navy Meeting*

. . . I mentioned Mr. Baruch's letter to me requesting that the State Department be informed of our effort to put into effect the eight areas of agreement arrived at by the Army and Navy . . . last spring. Patterson agreed but made the observation that while the signature was Baruch's, he thought the language was undoubtedly Eberstadt's.

[At the Cabinet on September 6 the President announced that the Joint Chiefs of Staff had recommended postponement of the third atomic bomb test firing, originally planned to follow the first and second Bikini tests. There was no objection, and the postponement was decided on. At this meeting there was also a political note of interest.

6 September 1946   *Cabinet Meeting*

. . . There was a general political discussion about the forthcoming election with a request on the part of the Postmaster General [Hannegan] that all Cabinet members do whatever they could to support Democratic candidates and to hold themselves free for speeches, particularly in the four closing weeks of the campaign. The Postmaster General stated that he realized that the Secretaries of War and Navy could not take active part in a political campaign, in which the Secretaries of War and Navy heartily concurred.

[Forrestal saw the President on September 9 and told him frankly that he hoped to put a unification bill into the new Congress that would provide for a "small executive office acting as his Deputy" at the head of the military establishment with powers of decision in the six fields he had listed to Patterson a few days before. The diary does not give the President's comment; but the latter called a meeting the next day to go over the whole question.

10 September 1946   *Meeting with President*

Meeting at the White House with the President. *Present*: General Eisenhower, Admiral Nimitz, Admiral Leahy, Mr. Clifford, **Patterson** and myself. President stated the purpose of this meeting was to consider plans for the introduction of merger legislation in the next Congress. He recalled the fact that the Army and ourselves had agreed on eight out of twelve points in our conversations of last spring; he said he proposed to have a bill drawn in his office by Mr. Clifford and Admiral Leahy, that that would become then the doctrine of the administration, and after it had been mulled over by all interested parties he would expect support for it in the Congress. [This seems a curious repetition of the general course adopted with the "directive" of June, which had not been notably successful.] He added that he did not propose to carry out the suggestion of Senator Thomas that the eight agreed-upon points be implemented by executive order, feeling that this assumption of executive powers might militate against the possibility of getting legislation passed at the session. He then asked for an expression of views, admonishing all hands that everyone was expected to "take his hair down."

Patterson said that he was in accord with the President's program, that he was still confident that unification could not be achieved by committees or boards or coordination, that he was willing to have the law specify that a Secretary of Common Defense limit himself as much as possible to broad matters of policy and so far as possible not interfere in the administration of the respective Services.

I said that unification could be accomplished, in my opinion, by the creation of Office of Deputy to the President, called the Secretary of Common Defense or Office of Common Defense or what you will, [but] . . . limited to providing a source of decisions on these fundamentals:

    (1)   Missions and means.
    (2)   Cognizance of weapons.
    (3)   Composition of forces.
    (4)   Finances.
    (5)   Resolution of command disputes.
    (6)   Personnel (training, education and recruiting).

I said that such a man should not try to get down into the administration of each Department, and by that I meant he should not have the power to oust a bureau chief in the Navy or the head of a branch in the Army. I said I also wanted to make it clear that while I recognized that the genius of our government made it necessary for the President to have the support of his Cabinet members, I could not get myself into the position of agreeing to support by testimony before committees of Congress a bill which did violence to the principles which I outlined above. I said I recognized clearly that a member of the President's Cabinet should support his policies and that therefore I did not wish to set myself up as any source of embarrassment to him in the carrying out of his policies, and that, if I could not support with conviction and sincerity a bill introduced by the administration, I would have to ask him to accept my resignation. The President said in response to this that he expected no such necessity need arise.

Eisenhower repeated what he had said at earlier meetings that the broad principle of a Secretary of Common Defense should be accepted with the details left to be worked out afterward.

He said he could not conceive that the Navy need fear any actions following such legislation would impair its ability to perform its mission.

I was again constrained to say that the Navy *did have* deep apprehensions as to what would happen to it under such a plan as the War Department has proposed. I said it *did* fear that the Marines would be subject to great restrictions and that the Navy would be denied the use of the means to carry out the missions which only it fully comprehended.

Admiral Nimitz expressed himself as being in accord with the views of the Secretary of the Navy with relation to the duties and responsibilities of the Secretary of Common Defense. He later asked that a draft of the proposed bill be made available to the Secretary of the Navy for examination.

[A week later Forrestal had Field Marshal Montgomery (Viscount Montgomery of Alamein) to dinner; the latter told him that the British had now worked out their own military reorganization proposals. Retaining full administrative authority for the

[three existing Service Secretaries, and providing a Minister of
Defense simply as a deputy to the Prime Minister with powers
to coordinate and resolve disputes, this plan accorded closely
with Forrestal's views. "Monty" told him that it would be "fatal"
to merge the Services or to combine the administrative and coordinating function in one person. And he added a comment of
particular interest to Forrestal: "He agreed that the failure of the
Germans to appreciate sea power, and therefore the strategic
importance of the Mediterranean, lay at the root of the decision
they made in 1941 to abandon the Mediterranean campaign, just
as they were about to win it completely, for the adventure into
Russia."

At all events, Forrestal had now made his position clear to the
President, and the President had responded that he did not "expect" that the Secretary's resignation would be necessary. Under
this somewhat veiled assurance, the preparation of a new unification bill went forward; and as it did so there suddenly supervened a celebrated blunder of the Truman administration—an
episode which, whatever else one may think about it, would
seem vividly to illustrate the imperative necessity for the kind of
unification on the higher policy levels for which Forrestal had
been pressing.

On September 12 the Democrats were to open their political
campaign in New York with a "beat Dewey" rally, under auspices of strongly Left-liberal coloration, at which the principal
speakers were to be Senator Pepper of Florida and Henry Wallace, the Secretary of Commerce. Both were to address themselves to foreign affairs. The Secretary of State, Mr. Byrnes, was
at the moment in Europe. When the advance copies of the Wallace speech were circulated—speaking severely against any alliance with "British imperialism" and laying down a "soft" policy
toward Russia that appeared to amount to a division of the world
into two great spheres of influence and turning the larger over
to the Soviet Union—it seemed to many that this represented
a complete reversal of the entire course of the Byrnes foreign
policy. To make matters worse, Mr. Wallace had included the
statement that the President had read and approved his speech;
and when the reporters at the White House press conference on

[the 12th asked the President about this, he gave them to understand both that he had read the whole speech and that he thought it exactly in line with the Byrnes policies. A dramatic account of what followed is given in a memorandum to Forrestal from the Under Secretary of the Navy, John L. Sullivan, which Forrestal later entered in his diary.

At six o'clock in the evening Sullivan, together with Captain Robert L. Dennison, then an Assistant Chief of Naval Operations, arrived at the office of the Acting Secretary of State, Will Clayton. There they found a gathering including Clayton, James W. Riddleberger, acting head of the Division of European Affairs, and Loy Henderson, head of the Division of Near and Middle Eastern Affairs. Sullivan's memorandum continues:

12 September 1946   *Memorandum to the Secretary*
. . . They appeared extremely dejected and handed us a copy of a speech to be delivered this evening by Secretary Wallace at Madison Square Garden. Captain Dennison and I read the speech and agreed with the State Department representatives that if this speech were given by Secretary Wallace with the approval of the President it would in a large part repudiate the foreign policy which this country has been trying to establish for the last year.

In response to my question Mr. Clayton stated that the speech was to be delivered at 7:00 p.m. Washington time. I then inquired whether or not this speech had been submitted to the Department of State, and the reply was negative. I asked when they had gotten it and learned that at 1:00 this morning Riddleberger at a bridge game overheard a correspondent refer to Wallace's speech on foreign policy. Clayton advised me that the State Department's transcript of the speech had been received at 3:00 [presumably this means 3:00 p.m.] but that he was busy on an UNRRA matter and had no opportunity to read it until a few minutes before six. I asked him if he had protested to the White House and he answered in the negative.

I then suggested that he call the White House and see if: (a) the speech could be stopped; (b) the White House could prevail on Secretary Wallace to delete the last sentence in the sec-

ond paragraph on page 5 in which Secretary Wallace stated
that the President had read these words and said they represented the policy of his administration.

[After some telephoning in search of various presidential aides,
     they finally got hold of Charles G. Ross, the President's press
     secretary. The memorandum goes on:

. . . Mr. Clayton . . . expressed the opinion that Secretary
Byrnes would be very much disappointed. Later in the conversation he said that Secretary Byrnes would probably feel
that the ground had been cut out from under him.

Feeling that Mr. Clayton's conversation with Mr. Ross was
not sufficiently forceful to produce a last-minute effort to stop
or change this speech, I asked Mr. Clayton if I could talk with
Mr. Ross.

I told Mr. Ross that I recognized it was too late to change
the speech in toto but I considered it imperative to remove
the sentence in which Secretary Wallace quoted President Truman as approving the speech as representing the foreign policy
of this country. I expressed the opinion that the President
could not possibly have read this speech and approved it. Ross
sent for a transcript of the press conference this afternoon and
said that he was afraid that the President had told the newspapermen that he had approved it. I then pointed out to Mr.
Ross that if this particular sentence to which I referred was
deleted from the Wallace speech the President might then be
able to say, "I scanned through his speech hurriedly and the
parts of it which I read were quite consistent with the foreign
policy of this country as enunciated by Secretary Byrnes. Obviously there were some parts of the speech which I did not
see and could not have approved."

Mr. Ross asked me if I felt it would be necessary for the
President to qualify his approval. I stated that in my opinion
if this speech were delivered in its present form the President
would be obliged to repudiate either Secretary Wallace or Secretary Byrnes.

I then stated that there were four or five particularly objec-

THE COLD WAR GROWS WARMER

tionable phases of the speech and as an illustration I read him
the first paragraph on page 8 in which Secretary Wallace stated
that "we are still armed to the hilt. Our excessive expenses for
military purposes are the chief cause of our unbalanced budget." I stated to him that of course such a statement as that in
the light of present Russian military might could not be permitted to go unchallenged. I further observed that, if there was
so much in this speech which leading members of the administration would be called upon to repudiate, I was afraid the
Republican National Committee would seize upon this speech
as evidence of the disintegration of the administration from
within.

Mr. Ross said that he did not know what could be done at
this late date but that he would try to talk with the President
and do what he could.

Secretary Patterson arrived at about 6:20 and after reading
the speech stated that he thought the speech was pretty bad and
might cause some stir for six or seven days but he did not believe the situation to be as serious as Mr. Clayton and I believed.

Before 7 o'clock Mr. Clayton had three or four further conversations with Mr. Ross which appeared to be inconclusive to
us who heard just one side of the conversations. Mr. Clayton
remarked that Ross was noncommittal as to whether or not he
had discussed the matter with the President and we agreed it
would be unwise and useless to press Ross further on this
point. . . .

[Sullivan adds that they tried to hear the speech over the radio
but that it was not broadcast in the Washington area. The effect
—heightened by the considerably more extravagant remarks of
Senator Pepper and by the vociferously pro-Soviet sentiments of
the audience, which actually forced Wallace to drop from his
prepared text some of his qualifying criticisms of the Soviet
Union—was enormous and certainly justified all of Sullivan's
fears. Mr. Byrnes' protests from Paris were prompt and vigorous.
The President made several unconvincing efforts to gloss it all
over and retain both Wallace and his supporters and Byrnes and

[his foreign policy, but the Secretary of State finally made it clear
that either he or Wallace would have to go. "You and I," he mes-
saged the President on the 19th, "spent fifteen months building a
bipartisan policy. We did a fine job convincing the world that it
was a permanent policy upon which the world could rely. Wallace destroyed it in a day." [6] Next day the President announced
that he had asked for Mr. Wallace's resignation.

Sensational and disturbing as this affair seemed at the time,
the net result was no doubt to draw the real lines more clearly
and to firm and strengthen the Truman administration's foreign
policy. At a State-War-Navy meeting on September 25 there appeared the germ of ideas which were to lead to important results
in the following year. Up to this time the United States had, in
general, been trying to meet the vast international problem of
war relief on a nonpolitical basis, through its contributions to
UNRRA (United Nations Relief and Rehabilitation Administration). The difficulties this might entail in an increasingly divided
world were rather sharply brought home by the Yugoslav crisis,
in which it appeared that American resources were going by
way of UNRRA to the direct or indirect support of a regime
which had begun to shoot down our own airplanes. In the meeting on the 25th, "Mr. Clayton read a dispatch from Mr. Byrnes,
expressing the view that we must help friendly countries, particularly Turkey and Greece, in every way and refrain from assist-
ing countries who either from helplessness or otherwise are opposed to our principles." Patterson and Forrestal "strongly endorsed those views." And at the same meeting Forrestal urged
that a "State Department draft covering military assistance to
foreign governments was unduly restrictive"; it should be so
broadened that it would make possible military aid to Turkey.
Here was the concept of giving political precision to our use of
our economic and military resources; a concept that first took
important shape in the "Truman Doctrine" of Greek-Turkish aid,
and was to broaden very rapidly thereafter.

More important at the moment, ten days after Wallace's dismissal Forrestal was at last able to announce the consummation

[6] James F. Byrnes, *Speaking Frankly* (New York: Harper & Bros., 1947), pp. 239-
242.

[of an effort on which he had long been working—the re-establishment, as a permanent policy, of American naval power in the Mediterranean.

30 September 1946   *Diary*

We released a statement tonight for publication on Tuesday morning [October 1] giving the relating [relevant?] naval policy in regard to the maintenance of American units in the Mediterranean.

The gist of it was: Units of the American Fleet have been in the Mediterranean and will continue to be there in the future to (1) support American forces in Europe, (2) carry out American policy and diplomacy, and (3) for purposes of experience, morale and education of personnel of the Fleet.

This document was written at my direction in order to provide a clear and simple statement to the country on what our policy in the Mediterranean is. It was cleared with the Department of State, which in turn cleared it with the White House. It is typical, in my opinion, of the kind of statement which we should make from time to time to the American public so that there will be no misapprehension. Furthermore, in my opinion it is due the public so that they may know clearly what our policies involve. I think a similar statement should be made about the presence of the Marines in China.

[While it may in form have been simply an "explanation" of an existing state of affairs, it was widely received as a decisive new development of American policy. While American men-of-war were no strangers in the Mediterranean, they had usually gone there, as elsewhere, on the grounds of "courtesy visits," "special service" or similar reasons. "The Forrestal statement," in the words of one newspaper account,[7] "formally linked naval operations with American foreign policy for the first time." That was, precisely, Forrestal's intention.

---

[7] *New York Herald Tribune*, 1 October 1946.

CHAPTER VI

Setting New Courses

I

15 October 1946   ***Bureau Chiefs Meeting***

Averell Harriman came to a meeting of the Bureau Chiefs this morning and talked about European affairs and particularly about our relationships with Russia.

He was not overpessimistic. He said that he did not believe the Russians would provoke war in the near future, but there was a chance of finding an accommodation which would be the foundation for peace provided they realized we would not make an unending series of concessions and that they must expect resistance to any extreme demands or conduct. He said that each time they tried something, such as they undoubtedly did in letting the Yugoslavs shoot down our pilots, our reaction should be immediate, sharp and firm.

He said he thought we did not place as much value as we might on the sending of notes, that we were a little apt to regard them as rather futile instruments of diplomacy when, as a matter of fact, they could be very powerful in the formulation of world opinion. . . .

[In domestic affairs at this time, the administration was finding much stronger grounds for optimism. At the Cabinet on the 18th the discussion turned on the effects of the President's withdrawal a few days before of the last of the wartime price controls—the results seemed most favorable—and then went on to the political campaign.

18 October 1946   *Cabinet*

. . . There was general discussion of politics with Hannegan
reporting a substantially more optimistic attitude throughout
the country. He mentioned some of the critical states as being
Missouri, Kentucky and Pennsylvania.

He said that Lehman was anxious for Averell Harriman and
myself to speak in New York State and that we had to counteract
the visits of some of the more willing but unwelcome helpers
in his campaign.

[Now, however, an old problem in Forrestal's own field returned—the problem of conserving the legitimate strategic interests of the United States in the Pacific island bases under the
United Nations trusteeship system. Forrestal had been very skeptical of the trusteeship idea the year before, but had acquiesced
in the decision to set up the general system first and then write
trusteeship provisions broad enough to fulfill American requirements in areas of strategic significance.[1] The time had now come
to draw up the terms under which the Pacific bases should be
offered as trust territories to the United Nations, under the desig-
nation (specifically provided for in the Charter) of "strategic
areas." The President called a meeting of top State, War and
Navy representatives on October 22 to discuss the subject.

22 October 1946   *Trusteeships*

. . . The President's statement at the outset was along the
lines . . . that the form of a contract on trusteeships would be
agreed upon by the United Nations Organization first, and then
we, the United States, would offer the mandated islands for
trusteeship under that form. Both Nimitz and I expressed concern that if the procedure were reversed or even if the two things
were talked together the result would be that those who were
charged with the drafting, on behalf of the United States, might
be led into a situation where they would surrender piecemeal
the position which now has been very clearly stated by the Joint
Chiefs of Staff and which is entirely satisfactory to them.

---

[1] See pp. 44-45.

In view of Admiral Nimitz's understanding, I am sending this entry from my own diary plus Admiral Nimitz's memorandum to the Secretary of State, who is entirely in accord with the Joint Chiefs of Staff representation but who in the press of other duties may not be able to supervise the draftsmanship of his own subordinates. A situation might arise where there was a leak to the effect that the intransigence of the military was blocking the good intentions of the State Department.

There is a definite drive on now toward (1) disarmament, (2) spreading of the thesis that the JCS are running American foreign policy, and (3) against Mr. Byrnes' policy in general. It is my prediction that this drive will be greatly intensified during the next six months and may even have the unwitting help of elements in the Republican Party such as Taft, Taber, Knudsen, etc., whose services will be enlisted on the side of economy.

Admiral Nimitz stated it as his considered opinion, speaking as Chief of Naval Operations, . . . that the sovereignty of the ex-Japanese mandates should be taken by the U. S., . . . that the ultimate security of the U. S. depends in major part on our ability to control the Pacific Ocean, that these islands are part of the complex essential to that control, and that the concept of trusteeship is inapplicable here because these islands do not represent any colonial problem nor is there economic advantage accruing to the U. S. through their ownership. . . .

[Forrestal did not confine his anxiety about the "drive for disarmament" to his private papers, as a couple of letters show.

To Quincy Bent, 21 October 1946

This [taking community leaders as guests for cruises in men-of-war] is not related to any particular publicity program but is simply an effort to provide long-term insurance against the disarmament wave, the shadows of which I can see already peeping over the horizon.

To Dr. Philip Marshall Brown, 22 October 1946

. . . There are many signs of a gathering drive to cut down our Armed Forces and to persuade the people that we should haul out of Europe and out of China as well. . . .

However, don't be discouraged. I am confident there is a sound core of American opinion, not very vocal but with an instinctive awareness of dangers. If I didn't think so I should be very skeptical indeed of the future.

[In the latter part of October Forrestal departed for an inspection of the White Sands, New Mexico, base and other western installations. Byrnes reached him by telephone at the Hastings ammunition depot in Nebraska to say that the Navy proposal—to get a hard-and-fast strategic trust contract first and only then offer the former Japanese islands under it—"would put us in an impossible position before the world on the matter of trusteeship."

30 October 1946   Telephone Conversation with Secretary Byrnes

. . . He then read to me a statement that he proposed to make which was to the effect that the United States proposed to offer the mandates or trusteeships but upon terms to be stated unilaterally by the United States. I suggested that the language of this be reversed, that the first statement be that the United States was going to submit the text of the contract and after that was approved make the offer of the islands. Byrnes said this would open us to charges of hypocrisy in our professions of faith about the United Nations. I told him that I recognized that he had great problems and I would not undertake to deny him freedom of action but that . . . my great concern was that having made a statement along the lines of what he had just read to me, Dulles [John Foster Dulles] or some of his associates on the advisory committee of the American Delegation [to the United Nations] or some of Byrnes' own assistants would get caught in a negotiation about the form of our trusteeship agreement with resulting dilution and weakening of our original position. He said he was mindful of that view, of my fear, but that he proposed to handle this matter himself and he would see to it that this would not happen. He said,

furthermore, that the American statement was going to be communicated not to Dulles or the advisory committee, but to the
Security Council of the United Nations itself. Byrnes said he
proposed to see the President tonight and get his agreement.

[In the upshot the issue was skillfully resolved for the time be-
    ing by a presidential statement on November 6, saying that the
    United States proposed to place the former Japanese mandates
    under trusteeship but under the terms of a trust agreement to be
    submitted later. And in the latter part of the month Forrestal was
    to receive firm assurance that his views would not be disregarded.

26 November 1946   *Trusteeships*
    I talked to Secretary Byrnes in New York last night. He re-
ferred to the trusteeship question and he said he was disturbed
about Dulles' talking to the press as much as he had. The Secretary of State said he proposed within the next two weeks to
make a careful and considered statement on the whole matter
of trusteeships. He repeated that he had very much in mind
his pledge to us that whatever form the final agreement took,
the Navy wanted something that was tantamount to sovereignty
at least until the United Nations had become a going concern.

[This particular problem was, however, still only one facet of
    the larger issues which had constantly to be kept in mind. The
    State-War-Navy meeting on November 6 showed the steady de-
    velopment of American policy in the Near East.

6 November 1946   *State-War-Navy*
    . . . Upon my inquiry Acheson said that the broad outlines
of extending our policy in order to permit further assistance to
Turkey were as follows:
    (a) The United Kingdom should furnish arms to Turkey
and Greece. If the British can't, we should give the British the
arms needed to make the transfer.
    (b) We should extend credits not to exceed $10 million to
Iran for the purchase of arms.
    (c) No further exceptions to the current policy will be

made unless essential to the national interest. These matters were discussed by Byrnes and Bevin in Paris and will be further discussed in New York. . . .

Acheson said that the U. S. position on disarmament [a subject the Russians were then vigorously pressing in the United Nations] was confused and that he was communicating with Byrnes and Baruch [who had been appointed as American representative on the United Nations Atomic Energy Commission] on it. He thinks that Molotov's proposal on world-wide disarmament can be used to point up the fundamental obstacles blocking international acceptance, such as Russian positions on inspection [of atomic weapon development], exchange of information, etc. The State Department's present position is that the U. S. should not be drawn into a general disarmament discussion but should make it clear that such discussions are contingent upon international acceptance of accessibility of territory for inspection and a free interchange of information. Baruch intends to press for a vote on the atomic energy control to focus attention on the Soviet's stand. I mentioned that satisfactory conclusion of peace treaties should also be included in any such statement of policy. . . . Acheson said he thought the point could be worked in.

[A day or two later Forrestal entered in his diary the gist of an intelligence report on Soviet atomic strategy. This represented Soviet policy as one of pressing for disarmament and outlawry of atomic weapons on the world stage while refusing to allow any inspection of Russia's own atomic activities. The result would be to create a world opinion that would force the Western powers to disarm and drop their atomic development, permitting the Soviet Union to continue its own atomic operations while the West slept. Forrestal made no comment; but this kind of thing cannot have diminished his own restless yearning for a greater unity, coherence and precision in democratic policy. Meanwhile the election of November 5 had come and gone; contrary to Mr. Hannegan's hopes, the result was the celebrated 80th Congress, in which the Republicans would hold majority control of both Houses, making the problem of unity more formidable than ever.

[Forrestal brought up the subject with the President a few days
later.

16 November 1946   *Annapolis*

Visited Annapolis today with the President. He was in good
form and I think had a most enjoyable time.

I took the occasion to refer again to a subject which I have
talked to him about from time to time, namely, the need for
sincere nonpolitical cooperation between the Congress and the
Executive in the next two years. I repeated what I had said
earlier, that I thought there were in the Senate a substantial
number of men of good will with whom he could work in certain areas which ought to be nonpartisan: labor legislation,
foreign affairs, Palestine and national defense. He agreed to the
principle, but I am a little depressed by the fact that he seems
to feel that not much will come of such an attempt, that political
maneuvering is inevitable, politics and our government being
what they are.

[Here, perhaps, the President was wiser than his Secretary of
the Navy. It was again a case of a confrontation of two able men,
with the same national problems at heart, approaching them
from different viewpoints—the one from a political, the other
from an administrator's, background. Forrestal was many times
to recur to the idea that politically intricate problems—that of
Palestine in particular—could be solved by taking them "out of
politics." He never did, one feels, reach a sound or satisfactory
answer for the riddle of the proper place of partisan politics in a
democratic society. Few others have.

II

[Forrestal's diary records a variety of matters in these fall days.
At a State-War-Navy meeting on November 20, Acheson, in
response to Forrestal's inquiry, said that State had developed a
policy on disarmament; the essence of it was that "we shall take
a strong attitude to make the Soviets face up to their position on
international control of atomic energy, which by denying rights
of inspection, etc., blocks all progress on this matter." A little

[later there was a note on the activities of Elliott Roosevelt, the late President's son, on his journey through Moscow.

22 November 1946   *Elliott Roosevelt*

Ambassador Smith reports that Elliott Roosevelt, in the presence of the Soviet guest of honor, made the following observations to U. S. journalists at a reception given in Moscow by an Embassy OIC [Office of International Information and Cultural Affairs] staff member: (a) foreign correspondents have as much liberty in the U. S. S. R. as they do in the U. S., where Soviet cultural representatives are subjected to "humiliating" treatment; (b) the Danubian question is no affair of the U. S., which did not go to war to restore the international regime; (c) it is proper for the U. S. S. R. to insist on a joint regime with Turkey for the Dardanelles in which the U. S. S. R. would "naturally play a leading role"; (d) the U. S. and U. K. should insist on internationalization of the Dardanelles only if they were willing to permit the same for the Panama and Suez Canals; (e) the U. S. S. R. would not be interested in building up Communism in states along its borders if the U. S. and U. K. were not pursuing their "present expansionist policies"; (f) the U. S. and U. K. have often broken their word as given at Tehran, Yalta and Potsdam, but the "Soviets have never broken theirs"; (g) the U. N. is being used by the U. S. merely to further its own "selfish ambitions"; (h) Soviet officials admit that some things are wrong with "Soviet as well as U. S. foreign policy" and hope the two countries will compromise their views. [The party for Elliott Roosevelt was "off the record," but the substance of Ambassador Bedell Smith's report of his remarks had leaked into the American press, causing something of a minor scandal. It is believed that this summary of Smith's dispatch is the fullest account of the incident so far published.]

25 November 1946   *White House Luncheon*

Lunched today at the White House. Some discussion of the coal strike and a report by the Attorney General [Clark] of the events in Federal Court this morning. [Judge T. Alan Goldsborough had ordered John L. Lewis, president of the United Mine Workers, to stand trial for contempt of court on the ground that he had refused to comply with a court order looking toward suspension of the coal strike then in progress.] I could not help but think that if we had acted on the suggestion made in late spring of a study of the whole field of labor legislation with a view to determining what changes needed to be made in existing labor law, we would be in a better position today.

I have the feeling that opinion on labor has not been focused beyond the loose generality of criticizing Lewis and other labor leaders. I am fearful that if the public pendulum swings against Lewis too sharply it may encourage certain elements in the country to demand, and possibly get, restrictive and overpunitive labor legislation which would be dangerous.

25 November 1946

Message from London this morning. State Department recites the growing uncertainty in Britain of dependability of U. S. in foreign affairs. This plays into the hands of those Left-wing members of the Labour Party in England who are criticizing Bevin for cooperating too closely with the U. S. It is precisely the thing that the Russians would like to see—the derisive [divisive?] forces begin to erode Anglo-American understanding.

29 November 1946   *Cabinet*

Discussion at the morning's Cabinet: . . .

3. *Disarmament:* The President said he would state his position on disarmament and asked for expressions of opinion or if there were any in disagreement with those views. His position was this: That he would be in favor of disarmament once the major questions involved in a global plan were disposed of, such as inspection of manufacturing of munitions, manufacturing facilities of atomic energy resources, etc.; that he was not willing to place this country in the position which it had been placed in by the 1922 [Naval Disarmament] Conference, namely, that of a unilateral disarmament with the

resulting weakening of our position in the world. All hands at
the Cabinet agreed completely with his statement.

The Acting Secretary of State, Acheson, added the comment that he thought Senator Austin,[2] who was pressuring for
a declaration of American policy on this subject, had been
frustrated, misled and confused by the Russian maneuvers
since last spring, in their effort to get off the hook of their
refusal to accept the principle of inspection on atomic energy.
He said that it should be made clear to Austin by the President,
as it had been by Byrnes, that the American position was that we
were quite willing to support any disarmament program provided that it was a universal one and did not result in our stripping ourselves of our weapons while others retained them. . . .

Mr. Harriman made the observation that it was fortunate
that Bevin held precisely the same views as those expressed by
the President, although efforts were being made currently by
certain groups in his own Party to embarrass him in the
affirmation of such a policy. . . .

[At the Cabinet on December 6 there was a further note on
Austin's trials in the United Nations. The matter of a permanent
site for the United Nations came up. "The Russians," Forrestal
noted, "have aroused Senator Austin's indignation to the point
where he says he is unable to exercise judgment. Specific reason
is the bitter Russian attack made yesterday on Senator Austin by
Saskin, who charged Austin with conducting lobby operations on
behalf of San Francisco, a city to which, he said, the Russian
delegates would not go." The President said that he had no preference between San Francisco and Philadelphia, though he leaned
to the latter.

Through these weeks, however, Forrestal's own chief preoccupation was with the tangled issues of unification. In September
the President had said that he would have a bill drawn in his own
office by Clark Clifford (formerly Naval Aide, now appointed as

---

[2] Warren R. Austin, Republican of Vermont, had been appointed in June Permanent Representative of the United States on the Security Council; the appointment was not, however, to take effect until the conclusion of his Senate term in
the ensuing January. In the meantime he was acting as adviser to the Acting
Representative.

[special counsel to the President) and Admiral Leahy. Progress was evidently slow; and on November 12 there was a conference at Forrestal's Georgetown home, including Symington, Assistant Secretary of War for Air; Vice Admiral Arthur W. Radford, Deputy Chief of Naval Operations (Air); Major General Lauris Norstad, Director of Plans and Operations, War Department General Staff; and Vice Admiral Forrest P. Sherman, Deputy Chief of Naval Operations (Operations). According to Admiral Sherman's notes of this meeting, there was a considerable area of agreement. All appeared to accept a Secretary of Defense with "full authority to take such action as he considered required for effective coordination of the three Departments" but with his staff "sharply limited in number in order to make certain that he could not undertake any detailed administration." Symington thought he should have power to remove the Secretaries of the three Departments; Forrestal thought this would not be "feasible" but that the Defense Secretary should have a large hand in the selection of the subordinate secretaries to begin with.

They agreed on the composition of a National Security Council and discussed the possibility of adding a smaller group, which later in fact became the War Council. There seemed to be less clarity of view on the Joint Chiefs of Staff and the structure of military command; but all appeared to accept the principle that the Chiefs should continue to be the military commanders of their respective Services; that some means short of the President would have to be supplied for resolving differences between them, and that this function should lie with the Secretary of Defense. There also "appeared to be no dissent from the concept that the Marine Corps continues as is."

Sherman's memorandum continues: "*Naval Aviation.* Mr. Symington explained that the Army Air Forces actually feared that the Navy might set up a strategic air force of its own and threaten their existence. He was told by Radford and me that there was no such danger but that the Army was openly advocating the extermination of the patrol land-plane component which is essential to naval efficiency. Both Mr. Symington and General Norstad agreed unmistakably to the continuance of naval patrol land-plane squadrons for antisubmarine warfare, and

[we agreed to Army preparation and training to augment naval antisubmarine squadrons when needed." Norstad and Sherman were to draft a statement of the agreed principles as the basis for "the legislation about to be drafted by Clark Clifford." In the matter of the missions of the Marines and Naval Aviation, which it was not deemed necessary to include in the statute, the agreement would be submitted for presidential approval.

Up to this point the discussions had turned primarily on the form of unification; here they were confronting the question of substance which the form would determine. The questions of the Marines and Naval Aviation were of course not new, but as they moved into the foreground Forrestal seems to have come to a new understanding of their significance.

2 December 1946   *Unification*

Met Sunday [December 1] with the Assistant Secretary of War for Air, W. Stuart Symington. Conversation about unification. I told Symington two central issues appeared to be left. First, the character, scope and depth of the authority of the over-all Secretary of Defense, and second, the definition of the missions of the three components of the Armed Services.

We talked particularly about land-based Air. I said no sensible person in the Navy ever entertained any idea about the creation of a strategic air force in the Navy. By the same token, I said there were very strong fears of the Army's desire to roll up Naval Air and get control of all aviation under the Army Air Forces. I remarked that the Army's approach to this whole question had been most unfortunate—that it had been unilateral and nonconsultative. The Collins Plan [a plan for a simple merger, drawn up by Lieutenant General J. Lawton Collins and advanced by the Army early in the proceedings], I said, had been put in the form of a bill without the consultation of the Navy, and then we were expected to go down and say we are in favor of it. I reminded Symington that if he looked at the bill today in the light of what had occurred since, it was clear what a monstrosity that bill was, and yet we were accused of stodginess, lack of cooperation and almost disloyalty because we expressed that view.

Symington expressed the opinion that the case for unification would find a more favorable reception in the next Congress than in the last. I agreed that their [the Army's] tactical position was better but I expressed some doubts as to whether the economy argument would hold, particularly when the record of the last war showed that the Air Forces, instead of using the facilities of others, had insisted upon the creation of their own hospitals, medical corps, engineer forces, etc.

At the end Symington said it might be possible to get the Army Air Forces to agree to a statutory assignment of certain land-based components to the Navy for antisubmarine and reconnaissance work provided this was limited to a moderate percentage of the total land-based big planes of the AAF. It was left that we would consider meeting again on Wednesday.

[Before that meeting Forrestal instituted some research on the Army's attitude toward the Marines, and a memorandum of one of his assistants, composed of excerpts from General Eisenhower's Joint Chiefs of Staff papers, was not reassuring. According to these extracts, Eisenhower could see no reason why Congress should fix the strength of the Marines. The "emergency development of the Marine forces during this war should not be viewed as assigning to the Navy a normal function of land warfare, fundamentally the primary role of the Army." There was, the General had granted, "a real need for one Service to be charged with the responsibility for initially bridging the gap between the sailor on the ship and the soldier on land." He recognized the need of "a force within the Fleet to provide small, readily available and lightly armed units to protect United States interests ashore in foreign countries," and to fulfill the functions of interior guard in ships and shore stations. But "once Marine units attain such a size as to require the combination of arms to accomplish their missions, they are assuming and duplicating the functions of the Army and we have in effect two land armies." He therefore recommended that "Marine units not exceed the regiment in size, and that the size of the Marine Corps be made consistent with the foregoing principles." And he urged, again, that the Marine Corps should be maintained "solely as an adjunct of the Fleet," to

[participate "only in minor shore combat operations in which the Navy alone is interested," with "major amphibious operations" to be undertaken in the future only by the Army.

When Forrestal met with Symington again on the Wednesday, they seemed to make no progress.

4 December 1946   *Unification*

Lunch with Symington, Norstad, Radford and Sherman. The net result of this lunch was to bring out more clearly how difficult it would be for us to come to an agreement with the Army Air Forces on any unification program. Admiral Radford brought out very clearly and sharply the feeling on the part of officers in Naval Aviation that the granting of Department status to the AAF is a first step in much larger and more ambitious plans of the Air Forces to take over the whole business of national defense. Radford particularly aroused Symington's and Norstad's ire by asking what foundation there was for the Air Forces to believe that there was a place in the war of the future for a strategic air force. He pointed out that it was extremely dubious whether big bombers could be used effectively against any country unless they had fighter cover. He said that the experience of strategic bombing commands in their attacks on Germany in 1944 brought this out very clearly. He cited the very heavy losses in the months of August and October 1943—the raids on Schweinfurt and Regensburg on the days of 17 August and 14 October when American losses were so high that the whole question of air attack on Germany hung in the balance. He reminded Norstad that the Air Forces had to make most clamorous demands for sufficiently long-legged fighters to provide fighter cover.

He said that from his own experience in the carriers off Japan he was confident that the B-29s against the kind of fighter opposition that our Navy could have offered would never have been able to break through to bomb Japan by day. As to night operations, he was not prepared to be so categorical. Norstad replied that the B-29s could bomb from 40,000 feet whereas the fighters could not get up above 38,000, which was the farthest distance at which antiaircraft fire, even our own, was effective. Radford's answer was that bombing from 40,000 feet was extremely inaccurate and unsatisfactory except for aerial [area?] bombing.

The meeting broke up with a feeling on my part that we were farther away than ever from reaching an agreement.

[Forrestal lunched next day with Admirals Sherman, Denfeld and Mitscher, then commanding the 8th Fleet.

5 December 1946   *Unification*

. . . Mitscher gave expression to just about the same views as Admiral Radford had voiced the day before. He said that for twenty-five years Naval Air had been trying to protect itself both within the Navy and outside the Navy. . . . They had to resist the attempt in 1925, shortly after Mitchell's attack [the celebrated General William A. ("Billy") Mitchell], of the Army Air Forces taking them over. He said this was always the object of Army Air—complete control of all the air forces in the country . . . and cited what had happened in England. . . . After the RAF took over, the Royal Navy had no freedom either in design or procurement, they had given up reconnaissance and antisubmarine work [to the RAF], no pilot was ever given command of a carrier of the Royal Navy. . . . The absorption of the Naval Air Arm by the RAF robbed British naval airmen of any chance for a career and of prestige in their own Service. . . .

[Mitscher said that the Army Air Force was already raiding the Navy for able young flyers, and "in this connection," Forrestal added, "I had a report later in the day that a lieutenant commander, one of our best pilots with a splendid war record in the Pacific, had been approached by the Army Air Forces with an offer to make him a lieutenant colonel in that organization if he would transfer." At the new "Air University" at Maxwell Field, Forrestal heard, officers "openly proclaim their ultimate objective to be complete domination of all military air activities in the United States."

Forrestal, always careful where the Legislative branch was con-

[cerned, took steps to put his views before the Republican leaders who would organize the new Congress. On December 10 he lunched with Senators Wallace White of Maine and C. Wayland Brooks of Illinois, telling them that he would "like to get their advice on how the Navy should handle itself on the question of unification." Both told him that Senator Chandler Gurney, Republican of South Dakota, would probably head the new Committee on the Armed Forces. Forrestal feared that Gurney was already committed to the Army side of the case; the others thought him still open-minded, and Forrestal was in fact to work closely with Senator Gurney throughout the next two years.

Forrestal was concerned about the progress of the Army's "publicity program." General George C. Kenney, then heading the Strategic Air Command, was very active as a proponent of an independent Air Force. "I asked Brooks," the diary note continues, "whether he thought Kenney would make much progress if he went out to see Bertie McCormick of the *Chicago Tribune*, as we understood he was going to do. Brooks said he didn't think so and said that McCormick had made a speech in favor of the Marines three weeks ago. . . . He thought there was no chance of McCormick coming out in favor of unification."

Two days later Forrestal saw an even more influential Republican leader.

12 December 1946   *Unification*

Had lunch today with Senator Taft. He himself brought up the question of the organization form of the Armed Forces. . . . I said that I had no violent feelings about it except that I wanted everything that was done to be done with deliberation and effort and not before examination of the problem. . . . I had acquired another set of misgivings about unification which stemmed from the feeling I had that even the top command in the Army had no true appreciation of sea power or what control of the sea meant. . . .

I said I had been here now over six years and I regarded my knowledge of the Navy itself as only fractional; that any man who came in to run the three branches of War, Navy and Air couldn't possibly have any knowledge of what he was supposed to do and he would ultimately be in the hands of the Chiefs of Staff, which, I said, was my impression of what the Army wanted. . . .

Taft's son was in the Navy and he showed considerable knowledge of what I meant when I talked about the easy assumptions of the Army regarding control of the sea.

Regarding Air—I told him that the development of the Air arm was probably the most uncertain of all in modern war; that the phrase "guided missiles" was a misnomer because the missiles were not guided and it looked like a long time before they would be. When they were fully developed it would be a question then whether the airplane became a guided missile or the guided missile an airplane. Senator Taft said he would be here continuously from now on and we agreed that we would talk again before the first of the year.

[The diary records no further details of the unification discussions until January 3. Forrestal came away from the Cabinet meeting that day with Secretary Patterson.

3 January 1947   *Cabinet Meeting*

. . . Judge Patterson rode back with me from Cabinet to the Navy Department. He said he was much disturbed in the growing evidence of bitterness between the Services and mentioned the fate of the Japanese Army and Navy, referring particularly to a book by Kato. He said that if the Army and Navy officers went down to testify in a mood of bitterness and hatred, they would do serious damage to the Services and the national defense. I replied that he was simply stating what I had stated right along, that unless the two Services were honestly and thoroughly back of a plan for integration and coordination, it would not be successful. In fact, it would produce the opposite of the result we were after.

I told him that I had discovered a depth of feeling in Naval Aviation which had been very surprising to me—that it was not merely a question of the battleship admirals and the older men but of the younger ranks of officers—which had impressed me as quite dangerous. I told him that it came from various segments of Naval Aviation who remembered that they had had to fight hard *within the Navy* to get recognition and *outside* of it to retain their independence against the assaults of the Army Air Forces.

Patterson said he was not rigidly or stubbornly committed to any one plan, that he was quite willing to be flexible on the question of roles and missions, and that everything that was done heavyhandedly or without the freely given support of the officers of all Services would not be successful. His concluding remark was "they must have the attitude that they're all truly brothers in arms."

I told him that was precisely the attitude of Admiral Nimitz and Admiral Ramsey and both had been at great pains to prevent the growth of bitterness within the Navy, and that I knew the President and he and I could rely on their efforts to create precisely the atmosphere which he indicated. But I said it was difficult to create such an atmosphere when we had such speeches as were made by General Armstrong at Norfolk, some excerpts from which I quoted to him.

He spoke highly of Admirals Nimitz, Ramsey and Sherman.

The whole conversation was in an entirely different key and tenor than any talk I've ever had before with Patterson. He said he had not paid much attention to the conversations that Symington had had with Norstad and Sherman.

[This "new key" was evidently productive of results. Forrestal's appointment calendar over the next couple of weeks shows numerous meetings which must, from the persons present, have been devoted to unification, and on January 11 the whole day was given over to the subject. But there was no further diary note until January 16.

16 January 1947   *Unification*

Admiral Sherman, Symington and Norstad agreed today on the final draft of the letter [to be signed by the two Secretaries] reconciling the Army and Navy views on the integration of the Armed Services. Talked to Clark Clifford at the White House, who wanted to make an immediate release,

but I insisted that that not be done until I had an opportunity
to inform the principal Navy friends in the House and Senate—Senators Robertson, Byrd, Tydings, Brooks, Russell and
Austin, ex-Chairman Vinson of the Naval Affairs Committee,
Cole, etc., in the House. I said this was desirable not merely
from the standpoint of the Navy's obligation to these men, but
also by way of enlisting their sympathetic cooperation in
the future.

The documents were released to the newspapers at 6:00 p. m.

[These documents recorded a climactic milestone in a long,
arduous and earnest effort. One, the joint letter from the two
Secretaries to the President, was in the form of a sequel to their
joint letter of May 31, 1946,[3] in which they had reported disagreement on four important points. They were now completely
agreed on all aspects of the proposed legislation. Their recommendations—calling for a single Secretary of Defense with coordinating powers, for a National Security Council, a smaller
War Council, a National Security Resources Board, a Central Intelligence Agency, and a command structure headed by the Joint
Chiefs of Staff—in general accorded with the principles for
which Forrestal had begun to search in the middle period of the
war and which he had since so firmly argued for and upheld. It
was agreed that the allocation of specific roles and missions
among the three proposed Services should be dealt with not by
law but by executive order, and a second document presented an
agreed draft for such an order. Here the wording was less exact,
although again the draft order represented an acceptance, in the
main, of Forrestal's and the Navy's position. The Navy was given
primary responsibility for its own land-based reconnaissance and
patrol aircraft and the Marines were accorded primary responsibility for the techniques of amphibious warfare.

For Forrestal it was a very considerable success; but it was not,
as he well knew, a final victory. The newspaper reaction on
January 17 was highly favorable; but it remained actually to draft
a bill and get it through Congress. "It is," Forrestal noted in his

---

[3] See pp. 164-65.

[diary on the 17th, "most important that this drafting work be watched very carefully. I think we still have to face continued efforts on the part of the Army to enforce their conception of a single Department and a single Chief of Staff, each of which, in my opinion, would be disastrous." As it turned out, the bill was finally passed in midsummer in substantially the recommended form. The sound and satisfactory division of roles and missions was, however, to prove a more obstinate question; the draft executive order, clothed in the vagueness common to most products of compromise, was insufficient to settle the intricate problems involved, and, as Secretary of Defense, Forrestal was to find himself still struggling with them nearly two years later.

III

[A few days before Christmas Forrestal entered a note in his diary that sheds an interesting light not only on the President but on Forrestal himself, and on the relations between the two men.

20 December 1946   *The President*

Last night the President came to dinner with Secretary of State Byrnes, Averell Harriman and a few others. Before dinner I showed him a copy of the *New Republic,* which I said I was going to give Jimmy Byrnes for Christmas. In it was a caricature of Senator Taft with a picture of his father in the background. Senator Taft and his father were represented in a caricature fashion. The President laughed at the caricature of Senator Taft but expressed himself that it was not in good taste and an impropriety to caricature an ex-President who is dead.

(I make note of this because it served to strengthen the impression I have had of the President's traditionalism and his sense of the importance of sustaining the dignity of government. His remarks to the Commission on Universal Training this morning reflected much of the same feeling, plus a deep and obviously very sincere devotion to the government and the people of the country.)

[A little earlier there had been an amusing anecdote concerning the British Foreign Minister.

8 December 1946   *Bevin*

Dinner last night at the British Embassy with Bevin and the British Ambassador [Lord Inverchapel]. Asked about Bevin's health, which apparently is good. He told the story about his conversation with a sculptor who wanted to make a bust of him to be put up in one of the London squares. Bevin stated he didn't take to the idea very kindly—he didn't see much point in having a marble bust of himself in Trafalgar Square for the pigeons to sit on.

[And it was also about this time that Mr. Harold Ickes stirred Forrestal to a rare, satiric outburst. The former Secretary of the Interior had renewed, in his newspaper column, the old feud between Interior and the Navy over control of the Pacific Islands. "High in the moral stratosphere," Forrestal observed in a memorandum, "Mr. Ickes, bathed in the serene light of his own self-approval, emanating the ectoplasm of conscious virtue, views the motives of most men as mean and vulgar, with, of course, one notable exception. If I should send a commission to the Pacific islands to report to me on . . . the current results of naval administration they will all be yes-men. . . . Mr. Ickes, among other things, is an expert on yes-men. He has taken pains to have a satisfactory number around him. . . . For tolerance, understanding, wisdom and devotion to the cause of human freedom, I believe the admirals, when called upon for their final accounting before their Maker will not have to step aside, unless Harold Ickes does it by force." And having thus relieved his feelings, Forrestal characteristically left the memorandum in his private files.

Other sidelights on men and issues are scattered through the papers for these days.

13 December 1946   *Cabinet*

The President said that he had been asked by the War and Navy Departments to raise the question of a program for

Civilian Defense in the event of war. He said his impression was that this matter had not been particularly successfully handled in the last war and while it may be premature to start talking about it now, he realized it was something which should have attention. . . .

16 December 1946   *Cabinet Luncheon*

The Secretary of State [Byrnes] gave an account of his negotiations the last month in the Council of Foreign Ministers with particular reference to the peace treaties. [The Council had met in New York at the beginning of November in an effort to complete the drafting of the treaties.] He said that about three weeks ago he summoned Molotov to a private meeting with him. In that conversation he told Molotov that he had come to the conclusion that there was little hope of arriving at any settlement of the peace treaties and that he had decided to advise Molotov to that effect. . . . Molotov was obviously surprised at this attitude and attested that he was not as pessimistic as Byrnes, to which the latter replied that he was quite willing to be shown the reason for any optimism. . . . The net of it was, after a long conversation, that Molotov said he would produce specific proposals on all the questions in dispute and would bring them to Byrnes very quickly, which he did. . . . [Byrnes] said that there was one particular amendment that he was most anxious to get with Russia—this amendment being one which denied to a nation the benefits of any treaty which that nation refused to sign, and had reference, of course, to the Yugoslavian statement that they would not sign the Italian treaty, and having got this he was not anxious to see Molotov alone again because, every time he saw him, Molotov pressed very strongly for some further concessions to Yugoslavia which he (Molotov) said he was under great pressure to obtain. . . .[4]

Mr. Byrnes said that Molotov had told him . . . that Russia would have to be in on any decisions concerning the Pacific islands wherever fortifications were involved, and he would

---

[4] The Forrestal notes on this have been condensed, as Mr. Byrnes' own more extended account of the incident appears in his *Speaking Frankly,* pp. 152-55.

want to ask what we propose to do with mandates in that connection. At this, Byrnes responded that he would like to know what the Russians proposed to do about the Kuriles and Sakhalin. These islands, Molotov said, could not be included because they were already the subject of previous agreements. Mr. Byrnes said he regarded nothing as being subjected to previous agreements and we would have to bring them into the field of discussion. During this particular conversation Molotov kept returning continuously to his question as to what we proposed to do on U. S.-held islands in the Pacific, and each time Byrnes responded by asking what he proposed to do about the Kuriles and Sakhalin.

Byrnes confirmed with Dulles said as to the Russian attitude, namely, that any trusteeship agreements affecting the Pacific islands would have to be referred to the Security Council, where the Russians could exercise their veto power.

Secretary Byrnes' conclusion was that he saw a long road of argument ahead on trusteeships but that as far as he was concerned he was in no rush to have any trusteeship agreement made definitive and that he didn't see that any great harm would come to the world if they were never consummated. I said I concurred fully in this attitude.

The President mentioned the reports in the morning's newspapers of the deficiencies in the grain crop in Russia, the Ukraine, and that there were rumors of unrest within Russia because of short rations. He said he believed this accounted, to a large extent, for the Russian attitude of intransigence on many questions; that they had taken note of the irritation and dissatisfaction manifested in this country on UNRRA, particularly the congressional attitude, and that it must have become clear to them by now that they, as well as others, would have to look to the United States as the sole source of relief on the question of food. . . .

24 December 1946   *Cabinet Luncheon*

Lunch at the White House yesterday. It was interesting that . . . the Secretary of State reported to the President a visit he had had from former Secretary of War Stimson in which the latter had said to him that in view of the conduct and general attitude of the Russians since the cessation of hostilities he saw no reason to be in any particular hurry to give them any information about atomic energy or the atomic bomb. . . .

[Forrestal's own field of military policy presented two aspects, intimately related yet residing, under our governmental system, in two separate compartments. One was unification—involving long-term military statesmanship—the other was the military budget for the coming year, involving the immediate and present provision for military strength, on which alone the long-term policy could be established. In mid-October Forrestal had talked about it with James E. Webb, Director of the Bureau of the Budget.

16 October 1946   *Budget*

I asked Mr. Webb, Director of the Budget, this evening what was the next step in the consideration of the military budget— did he expect the Army and Navy to get together to present a single budget? . . . His reply was that he could only suggest that the Army and ourselves make sure there were no duplications in our two budgets, and second, that we consider submitting to him alternative budgets for 1947-48 with a definition of the effects of these budgets in terms of Fleet efficiency and capabilities.

He said he desired us to have an opportunity to submit any views along these lines that we wished before he went to the President with his own idea of what to recommend to the Congress for national defense in fiscal 1947-48.

[It may seem a somewhat curious way in which to fix the level of defense needs, but the diary does not recur to the problem through the next few weeks. Often Forrestal made no mention in his diary of questions which must have been absorbing his time and energies at the moment—for it tended to be a record of what

[he might forget rather than of what he was certain to remember. His letters show his concern at the time with the budget question.

Memorandum to the President, 18 November 1946

This is partly gossip and most of it you probably already have.

At the meeting of the Steering Committee of the House, I am told, Republicans decided to go ahead with the consolidation of committees as provided in the La Follette-Monroney Act and also that they would resist any attempt to emasculate national defense. (I confess I find it difficult to reconcile this with the public statements of Bob Taft and John Taber [Republican of New York, who was to become chairman of the House Appropriations Committee in the new Congress].)

To Edward H. Hopkinson, 7 December 1946

. . . There is great danger of repetition of the pattern which developed after the last war, apparent already in the contradictions inherent in wrapping up a balanced budget and a decreased tax rate. That these are sometimes accompanied by reaffirmation of necessity for remaining strong isn't much consolation.

[Whatever the arguments that may have gone into it, the budget, including the military sections, was complete by December 20.

20 December 1946   Cabinet

The President announced the completion of the budget and said he had listened to all those, including the Army and Navy, who felt the sums allocated to their Departments were insufficient and had weighed these against Treasury estimates of governmental income next year and had decided to let the proposals of the Bureau of the Budget stand. He pointed out that fixed charges of government now were over $20 billion. With Army's and Navy's total around $11.5 billion, it was obvious, he said, that there wasn't any great leeway left for the general business of government.

The Secretary of the Interior made two observations. A protest against the methods by which people down the line in the Budget not much above the status of clerks make allocations within Departments between various bureaus and offices of that Department, and the other being a general observation that he felt the federal budget should be divided between monies going into current operating expenses and those sums representing the investment of capital funds, so to speak. . . . I associated myself with his remarks about the budget, pointing out, however, that any such division would have to be done with the greatest care because at some future time it could become a device through which a dishonest government could hide its spending, as had been the case occasionally in France.

(With reference to the people in the Budget, in my talk with the President yesterday I said that we had been quite uneasy under Harold Smith's administration of the Bureau, about the fact that a young man recently a seaman second class in the Navy, who had been a student of administration at the University of Colorado, . . . had been making up our figures. The President then, and at this morning's meeting, said he wanted to get that type of person out of the government service.)

The President expressed the hope that all members of the Cabinet would support the budget as submitted, because otherwise, he said, we would expose ourselves to sniping from the Republicans, particularly in the House.

After the Cabinet the President, Patterson and I went to a meeting of the commission the President has named to make a study on universal military training.

[On January 17, the day that the Army-Navy agreement on unification was published, Forrestal saw Senator Chan Gurney, the new chairman of the newly established Committee on the Armed Services (in which were combined the functions of the old Military Affairs and Naval Affairs Committees). They talked both unification and the budget and made arrangements for contacts with the Navy on these matters. As for the budget:

17 January 1947   *Meeting with Senator Gurney*

. . . He particularly inquired what our relations were with
the Budget, whether we were going to suffer from their paring
of the appropriations. I said, of course we were going to suffer—
that we were fully aware of the tightness of the national budget
as a whole and that we were fully aware that we had to try to
cooperate with the President and the Congress in an endeavor
to achieve a balanced budget; that wherever we met with a
denial of funds for a particular purpose, which we thought
would be dangerous, such as fuel oil, we would ask the President for permission to recite those troubles to the appropriate
committees.

[At the Cabinet on January 24 there was a new member present. James F. Byrnes had resigned as Secretary of State on January 7; he had been succeeded by the stocky figure of General of
the Army George Catlett Marshall, whom the President, a little
over a year before,[5] had been reluctant to send to China because
he had "earned a rest." At the Cabinet, the topics discussed were
not of first importance—they opened with a consideration of the
foot-and-mouth disease in Mexican cattle—but the new Secretary
of State was not left unaware of the complexities of his position.

24 January 1947   *Cabinet*

. . . Before the Cabinet I spoke to Marshall about the suggestion of Senator Robertson last evening that presentations of
our military position as related to our international obligations
and responsibilities be presented to the Appropriations Committee chairmen of the House and Senate along with the chairmen of the Armed Services Committees and the Foreign Affairs Committees by the Secretary of State, the Secretaries of
War and Navy and the professional military leaders. Marshall expressed some fear that if he did this job it might be
misinterpreted as an effort by him to introduce immediately
a military factor into his work and that if it became known
publicly would immediately result in the charge that policies

---

[5] See p. 113.

were now being dictated solely on military considerations. I suggested that this might be met possibly by having Jim Byrnes do the briefing on the diplomatic front, and Marshall was in agreement on this, although I suspect it will take some urging to get Mr. Byrnes to do it. . . .

[Here again was an example of Forrestal's constant effort to link our diplomatic commitments with the military capabilities which we could muster to fulfill them; it is ironic (although a real tribute, perhaps, to our democratic concepts) that a stumbling block now lay in the fact that for the first time in our history we had a Secretary of State who had been a professional military man.

The adjustment of the military budget to the real military needs on the one hand, and to the legitimate claims of the civilian economy on the other, was never an easy problem. It would have been easier for Forrestal personally if he had not been so sensitively aware of both horns of the dilemma. He already had a vivid appreciation of the Soviet menace and of the imperative necessity that the United States should make itself strong throughout the world; he shared, at the same time, the fears of the President and of other able men lest there be a limit to the strains which could be placed on the normal American peacetime economy without risking the destruction of everything that the military establishment existed to defend. In January he was writing to his friend George Rentschler: "There is no question we have to get all the economies we can because the country simply cannot stand continuance of the heavy budget which is ahead of us next year, but with the present state of the world I for one do not want to see the economy attained at the expense of our ability to move, and move fast." Other letters conveyed the same dichotomy of thought:

To Admiral R. E. Schuirmann, 2 February 1947
. . . There is unease throughout all the Services. The government faces a Herculean task in the effort to bring its budget into balance. There will be the usual hue and cry about lowering our military expenditures, although everyone

wants us to remain strong enough to maintain our proper authority and balance in the world. General Marshall probably
has the hardest job of all, as all the considerations I have
named affect the success of his mission.

However, the tenacity of the human race and its ability to
take it, I suppose, will see things through. . . .

To Charles Thomas, 24 February 1947

As you know, I never object to scrutiny if it is objective,
factual and conducted by intelligent people. Nor do I question
the methods of those Republicans in the House and Senate who
think we ought to have a cut. God knows I am fully aware of
the terrific task which this country faces if it is to keep a free
economy and a free society. But the next eighteen months look
to me to be about the most critical that this country has ever
faced, and to deny Marshall the cards to play, when the stakes
are as high as they are, would be a grave decision.

[The appropriation bills for fiscal 1948 were to go through in
accordance with the ideas of the Bureau of the Budget. That did
not, of course, settle the vast issues implicit in the problem of
the military expenditure. As with so many other subjects in these
transition days, the decisions on the military budget in the winter
of 1946-47 were to prove only beginnings, not conclusions.

IV

22 January 1947   *Atomic Energy Committee*

Visit this morning from Senator [Bourke B.] Hickenlooper
[Republican of Iowa], who is chairman of the Senate's Com-
mittee on Atomic Energy [actually the Senate-House Joint
Committee], and the Secretary of War. Hickenlooper ex-
pressed a good deal of concern about the impression which his
committee has of a growing disinclination on the part of the
Atomic Energy Commission named by the President (Lilienthal,
Strauss, Waymack, Bacher and Pike) to communicate with the
Military Liaison Committee which was specified in the organic
act dealing with atomic energy. Admiral Parsons [Rear Admiral
William S. Parsons, member of Military Liaison Committee]

participated in the conversation and expressed the view that some of the attitude which Senator Hickenlooper was concerned about came from the realization by Lilienthal and his associates of the tremendous power and responsibility which had been put upon his, Lilienthal's, committee. . . . The general tenor of Senator Hickenlooper's remarks would lead to the conclusion that he and his Senate associates are very much concerned about a pacifistic and unrealistic trend in the Atomic Energy Commission.

29 January 1947   *State-War-Navy*

. . . General Marshall explained that the other members of the Security Council were unanimous in the belief that the Council should go ahead with the discussion of the general problem of disarmament. He believed that other nations would take a solid vote against us should we propose otherwise. He said Senator Austin and Mr. Baruch shared the view that it would be unwise for us to eliminate the atomic bomb until other matters in the field of regulation of armaments were well along. Admiral Nimitz suggested that in view of present circumstances U. S. position should be that committee discussions should be directed toward the problem of *how* and *when* to regulate armaments rather than *what* to regulate. He said that the important thing was to establish methods of inspection and control, and also to establish criteria of world conditions, such as conclusion of peace treaties and establishment of forces under the Security Council as prerequisite to undertaking general disarmament. There was complete acceptance of these views after considerable discussion. . . .

I pointed out that there was imperative need for informing the public of the vital issues involved in considering regulation of armaments. I suggested that once discussions in the Security Council appeared to hold out a plan for a disarmed utopia there would perhaps be irresistible public pressure to adopt such a plan forthwith, regardless of world conditions which for some time will require existence of force to accomplish stability. There was general agreement with these views.

2. *Korea*: Mr. Patterson said that the Korea problem was

the single most urgent problem now facing the War Department. There was a lack of railroad, power and fertilizer in the area and there seemed to be no leadership of political ability among the Koreans. There has been no cooperation at all between the Russian and U. S. Zones, and all agreed that an approach to U. S. S. R. by this government at this time would likely lead nowhere. There was general agreement to Mr. Patterson's proposal that congressional action should be sought by the War Department to obtain funds for the rehabilitation of Korea. . . .

[At the Cabinet on February 7 Forrestal opened a question of which all of them were to hear a great deal in the ensuing months.

7 February 1947   *Cabinet*

. . . I raised the question as to the locus in government of any means to counteract Communist propaganda, not merely throughout the world but in our own country. I said it took different forms—that the objectives of the Communist Party as published in the *Daily Worker* would find support from divers sources (for example, one of their objectives is drastic reduction in military expenditures, and in this the Republican Party, at the moment, is cooperating). . . . Harriman joined me in emphasizing the need for countermeasures. Marshall stated that he was relying very largely on the development of the United States Information Service as sponsored by the State Department and said that he felt the only countermeasure that would really be effective was the creation of a record for truth and accuracy by the United States, which in the long run would establish a record of confidence throughout the world. For this reason he proposed to have the USIS confine itself in the strictest manner to factual rather than subjective substance. Patience would be required to have this become a powerful medium throughout the world. I said I was not concerned so much with the world as I was with our own opinion and recalled to his mind that the Nye Committee, headed by a Republican isolationist, was staffed by Communist attorneys and

that it had much to do with the curtailment of our own
armaments industry in the period 1936 to 1939. . . .

[Forrestal went on the same day to a luncheon at which the
subject recurred.

7 February 1947   *Congressman Brown of Ohio*
I had lunch today with Clarence Brown of Ohio, one of the
influential Republicans of the House (member of the Rules
Committee and the Committee on Expenditures) and Arthur
Krock [columnist and editorial writer for the *New York
Times*].

Among other subjects discussed was the question I raised at
Cabinet this morning: How to counteract external propaganda and how to get facts about our governmental policies,
objectives, etc., before the world, but most important, before
our own people. Krock very strongly supported the USIS,
which Brown criticized sharply, expressing lack of confidence in
the way it had been directed, the way funds had been spent.
He made specific reference to photographs in the current number of *Look* magazine, which reproduced exhibits of American art which were being sent to other countries. He said that
if he wished to, with the aid of this magazine article he could
completely eliminate all funds for the USIS. Krock said the
program should not be judged by one mistake, that Marshall
could be trusted to see that proper policies were established
and wise use made of money obtained from Congress.

Krock said that Marshall had made a most effective presentation at a gathering at which he (Krock) was present, of the
need for universal military service, with particular reference
to Marshall's statement that the sums spent for our occupying
troops alone would be more than sufficient to cover the cost of
the UMT program. Brown's response was that one should be
realistic and face the fact that there was not the slightest chance
of getting universal training through Congress. He expressed
the view that thought and attention should be given to alternatives such as development of intramural athletics in schools,

close liaison between the Armed Services and industry,
adequate program for development of technicians. I said that
the Navy was moving along all of these lines and I believed
the Army was also. . . . I said that sometime we would have
to look to him for a defense of these activities, . . . that at
some time in the not-too-distant future I foresaw the recurrence
of attacks such as the Nye investigation, to prove that the
Army and Navy and American business were combining on a
neo-fascist program of American imperialism, thought domination, etc.

I believe that Congressman Brown is worth a good deal of
attention not merely for his position in the Republican Party
but also because, as proprietor of a chain of eight newspapers
in Ohio, he is a pretty good reflector of public opinion.

19 February 1947   *State-War-Navy*

. . . I supported the position that the United States has a
continuing need to apply force at a distance and suggested that
changed conditions would be taken into account by measures
such as the redesign of submarines and the redesign of ships to
permit the carrying of guided missiles. General Marshall expressed his desire to be kept fully informed of naval and military problems. He and Secretary Patterson emphatically support the need for universal military training, but I expressed
a doubt that it would be voted by the Congress.

[Yet to this, as to all similar politico-military problems in this
period, there was inevitably a theoretic cast. While there had
been hope of getting an agreement between the Chinese Nationalists and the Chinese Communists; while Byrnes had been
struggling in London, Paris and New York to find, through firmness, some *modus vivendi* that would enable us to live in peace
with the Soviet Union; while responsible American legislators
could still think "intramural athletics" a sufficient contribution to
military preparedness, and even the Service Secretaries could
hesitate, with the Budget Bureau, over the economic costs of
genuine power, the basic power problem could be only dimly
seen. Its grim imperatives, however clearly sensed, still came to

[the ablest minds in academic guise. At the Cabinet lunch of February 24 there struck the first warning gong, announcing, distantly as yet, the harsh realities which were to overwhelm us through the succeeding years.

24 February 1947   *Cabinet Luncheon*

Lunch today with the President. Just before it Marshall showed me a memorandum which had been handed to him by Acheson as he left his office, saying that the British Ambassador had called this morning at the State Department for the purpose of informing the United States government that Britain could no longer be the reservoir of financial-military support of Turkey and Greece. Such support, he said, would involve expenditures of about $250 million in the current year and Britain simply could not afford it. Marshall said that this dumped in our lap another most serious problem—that it was tantamount to British abdication from the Middle East with obvious implications as to their successor.

Marshall also told me that Bevin had called him yesterday to ask that he, Marshall, request the Russians for a postponement of the Moscow Conference to April 15 because the northern Russian ports were closed and he, Bevin, could not fly on account of his heart. Marshall said this particular situation had been met by the Russians' finding it possible to clear the northern ports of ice with ice-breakers. . . . He said that . . . he had told Bevin . . . that he would support Bevin's request for a postponement but that he would not initiate it. He recited the incident not so much for the facts concerned in it but because he considered it so remarkable that Bevin should have asked him to make the request of the Russians.

At lunch the President recited certain figures about the budget and expenditures. He said that the budget scheduled to go to the conference for fiscal 1945-46 prior to the end of the German war, totaled 106 billion. He said that after VE-Day and just prior and subsequent to VJ-Day, rescissions were effected totaling 40 billion. Actual spendings in 1945-46 were 62 billion. For 1946-47 they were 41 billion and for 1947-48, his present project, they would be 32 billion. He said that

there had never been in the history of any country such sharp
and drastic cutbacks from conditions of war. His objective, he
stated, was to reach a postwar budget between 25 and 30 billion but that this would have to be accomplished gradually
and not by disorderly and drastic measures.

[Below this last entry, on the same page, there appears a note
without further explanation: "'Ideology' is the figleaf for Soviet
respectability," a quotation, whether consciously or not, from
George Kennan's analysis of the year before.

25 February 1947   *British Empire—World Picture*

I saw Gordon Rentschler, [Winthrop W.] Aldrich and [Rus-
sell C.] Leffingwell separately last evening. All are thoroughly
aware of the explosive possibilities in the general world situation with particular reference to the British Empire. Leffingwell, in particular, is thoroughly familiar with the background of the British economic situation; he feels that some
of the conditions put around the American loan were so
stringent as to make it of dubious value to them. He refers to
the provisions which deal with their ability to use their
blocked sterling balances and also, I gathered, to certain restrictions which are consonant with our free-trade principles. . . .

Rentschler particularly is quite familiar with the British
Empire world picture. He said that information he had from
the head of the jute industry in India was there might be no
export of jute from India next year, which would mean almost
complete cutoff of bagging for the next sugar pack. He said
that he had talked to Linlithgow, former Governor General
of India, who was extremely gloomy.

[Meanwhile the draft of a unification bill had finally been com-
pleted. Forrestal had not ceased his efforts in this matter; on
February 6 he, with his Under Secretary, Sullivan, and Admiral
Sherman, had dined with the "76-77 Club, being a club of Re-
publican members of those Congresses." He had repeated the
Navy's position, and found that "the majority of the people at the

[dinner were inclined to be against any merger, although all had a general idea that economies could be effected by joint procurement. However, my sense of the meeting was that a good deal of their opposition is based on the general desire to oppose any Democratic proposal. I said that this agreement and the President's approval of it was a completely nonpolitical, nonpartisan accomplishment." The draft bill as it now emerged from the White House seemed satisfactory to him. "We hope and expect," as he noted on February 27, "that it will have the general support of all hands throughout the Service. Any officers and men holding different views are completely free to express those views when called upon to testify before the appropriate committees of Congress."

For the moment, however, the international situation, now rapidly centering on the question of aid for Greece and Turkey against the heavy pressures of Communist threat and infiltration, seems to have been Forrestal's first concern. A couple of weeks before he had made a suggestion to Marshall regarding support for China; and on February 27 he wrote the Secretary of State to explain this proposal for a mission to China "comprising men of practical knowledge (not necessarily economists or so-called fiscal experts) in the field of government finance, national banking, industrial production, transportation and agriculture. . . . I believe American business would do its best to provide people of competence and experience." It was on that same day, February 27, according to newspaper accounts, that Marshall at a closed meeting at the White House laid the real gravity of the Greco-Turkish question before the congressional leaders. Forrestal's ideas were even more applicable to the rescue of Greece and Turkey than to that of China, and in the next few days he was actively spreading them.

3 March 1947   *Lunch—John Snyder*

Lunched today with John Snyder [Secretary of the Treasury]. Talked to him about my beliefs that if we are going to have a run for our side in the competition between the Soviet system and our own, we shall have to harness all the talent and brains in this country just as we had to do during the war. I said I felt very strongly that the world could only be brought back to order by a restoration of commerce, trade and business, and that would have to be done by businessmen. Specifically that meant that in Germany and Japan people would have to recapture the hope of being able to make a living. That would have to be done by the restoration of trade between countries, which in turn meant the ability of Japan, Germany and other affiliates of the Axis to get back to work. I said that I thought we should see that any financial help extended was accompanied by American supervision. Domestically we shall have to do all we can to encourage and not discourage business. That would have to take the form of wise taxation, freedom from unnecessary prosecutions, etc.

4 March 1947   *Lunch—Cabinet*

Lunched today with Marshall, Patterson, Anderson, Clark, Harriman, Schwellenbach, Ambassador Douglas [Lewis W. Douglas, Ambassador to Great Britain], Mr. Webb, Director of the Budget, and Senator [William B.] Umstead [Democrat of North Carolina].

I repeated a good deal of what I had said at lunch yesterday to John Snyder and last night to Ambassador Douglas. Douglas said he thought the present situation in Greece would be watched all over the world as a manifestation of whether the rest of the world could look hopefully to us or would have to turn to Russia.

Marshall said that before we could approach the problem from the standpoint of getting the help of business there would have to be a lot of work done by a planning staff. I agreed that was necessary but I said there also would be need for avenues of communication between government and business; that the job could not be done by government alone or by business alone, but would have to be done jointly, and that labor would also have to be in the picture.

5 March 1947   *Clark Clifford*

I talked today with Clark Clifford, the President's counsel, along the lines of my luncheon of yesterday and Monday. We are going to prepare a memorandum for the President which will endeavor to bring into sharper focus the central problem—which is: Which of the two systems currently offered the world is to survive, and what practical steps need to be taken to implement any policies that the government may establish.

Clifford said that he thought the most important thing was the development of a mechanism by which the Executive and Legislative branches of government could function. This, he thought, was particularly important because of the existing fact that different parties were in control of these two branches.

[Forrestal went on the same day to a luncheon with some of the House Appropriations Committee. The newspapers that morning had carried Marshall's preliminary statement on Greece and Turkey: "The problems involved are so far-reaching and of such transcendent importance that any announcement relating to them could properly come only from the President himself."

5 March 1947   *House Appropriations Committee*

The chairman of the House Appropriations Committee, Mr. John Taber, and other members lunched today at the Navy Department and afterward listened to a presentation by Admiral Nimitz, Vice Admiral Sherman, Admiral Turner, Assistant Secretary [of the Navy W. John] Kenney, Rear Admiral [L. C.] Stevens [Assistant Chief, Bureau of Aeronautics], General [Alexander A.] Vandegrift [Commandant of Marines] and myself, in a measure outlining the present Fleet dispositions, tasks, personnel and material requirements, etc. Admiral Sherman gave a general outline of the world military picture from a naval standpoint. The talk of the committee and the questions of its members were mainly directed toward Russian expansion, especially to the extent to which the United States proposed to try to occupy places in which British influence, power and military strength were collapsing.

Representative [Frank B.] Keefe of Wisconsin wanted to know whether this presentation by the Navy was in the nature of implementing Marshall's statements to the Congress on

Greece—in other words, whether it was a part of a general propaganda picture. Vice Admiral Sherman was able to reply that his paper had been written some ten days to two weeks in advance of the deterioration of the Greek situation. Keefe spoke rather vehemently on the need of conveying to the American people what the true situation on our relations were with Russia so that we would not repeat the experience of pre-Pearl Harbor. . . .

In my statement to the members of the Committee I said that the Navy was fully aware of the great task laid upon the Congress in trying to secure enough revenue to meet the tremendous burden which the country had to carry; that there were a lot of colliding objectives in the national mind; the five-day week, six-hour day, high wages, low prices for manufactured goods, reduced taxes, a balanced budget, debt reduction, a large and strong Army and Navy, a firm foreign policy including firmness with Russia but keep-out-of-war. I said it was easy to have these objectives but not so easy to secure their fulfillment and that even naval officers were not economic fools and recognized the fact that by forfeiting a sound economy at home we could stumble into state socialism just as successfully as if we had marked our course for that harbor.

The attitude of the committee was one of keen interest although I do not believe that the presentation very much affected Mr. Taber's determination for cuts. There is no doubt but that developments in connection with Greece have made Congress begin to do even more serious thinking on the subject of the United States position as the great stabilizer in international affairs. There was no anti-British talk, but on the other hand a good deal of questioning as to how much further we would have to go in Greece in taking up her responsibilities.

[The climax was now rapidly approaching:

7 March 1947   *Cabinet*

At the Cabinet meeting this morning the President . . . went into a lengthy discussion of the Greek question. He said that he was faced with a decision more serious than had ever confronted any President; that he wanted to have the facts put forth before the Cabinet, have a full discussion of them and then to talk ways and means of procedure.

Acheson outlined the position of Greece and Turkey. The British, he said, had agreed to continue their military commitments in Greece for the next three months at a cost of about $8 million a month but at the end of that time they would have to pull out. He said that the Greek government was not a satisfactory one to us; that it contained many elements that were reactionary; that much of the success of the Russian propaganda was due to the knowledge the people had of corruption and inefficiency.

With regard to Turkey, he said the situation was much better; that the Turkish economy . . . was healthy but that the continued Russian pressure was compelling Turkey to maintain an army of six hundred thousand men which was a great drain upon their resources and would in the course of a few years lead to bankruptcy.

Harriman said that he agreed with the observations about the character of the Greek government but we must remember that they were among the first people to fight the Germans, that the country was overrun, their communications, transportation and other elements of an organized society completely wrecked.

The general consensus of the Cabinet was that we should support Greece to the extent that we can persuade Congress and the country of the necessity.

In my remarks I said that what was occurring was simply the manifestation of what had been in process of development in the last four years; that if we were going to have a chance of winning, we should have to recognize it as a fundamental struggle between our kind of society and the Russians' and that the Russians would not respond to anything except power. I said that it would take all of the talent and brains in the country, just as it had taken all of them in the war, and that these abilities and talents should be harnessed in a single team. By that I meant that we would have to turn to business if what we are talking about is in reality holding out the hope of people in stricken countries that they again may make a living, and the way to provide a living for them will have to be opened up by business. Government alone cannot do the job and business cannot do it unless it has the full-out support of government both inside and outside, and by that is meant the lifting of as many restraints and time-consuming irritations as possible so that businessmen have time to devote themselves to the real problem.

At the end of the discussion the President appointed a committee headed by John Snyder, including Harriman, Patterson, Acheson and myself, to lay out a program of communication with leaders throughout the country and particularly of the plan for laying the facts before a selected group of business people. I said this selection should be made most carefully; that simply a conventional and well-advertised gathering of big shots was not what we wanted—we had to reach men who were active in business and who would have to do the job.

8 March 1947   *Meeting with Snyder*

Meeting at John Snyder's office which continued the discussion of yesterday at the Cabinet. *Present:* Acheson, Patterson, Harriman, Schwellenbach. Snyder undertook to take steps to inform selected groups of our diplomats of our problems in Europe particularly, of course, referring to Turkey and Greece. Acheson said it would be necessary to have working parties comprising experts in government, communications, transportation, taxation, etc., go to Greece or other countries which we proposed to help; he thought it advisable to follow Marshall's plan of having someone in Washington as a backer-up and local agent to see that things needed are done here.

[At the Cabinet luncheon on Monday the President told them that he would make "a very explicit statement on Turkey and Greece" two days later. That day, Wednesday, March 12, he appeared before Congress to read his message asking $400 million to provide economic and technical aid and weapons for the two countries. This much had been anticipated. What was striking was

[the firmness and frankness of the language which he used and the breadth which he gave to the policy thus announced—a policy of helping free peoples everywhere "against aggressive movements that seek to impose upon them totalitarian regimes," of "supporting peoples who are resisting attempted subjugation by armed minorities or by outside pressures." The Soviet Union was nowhere mentioned by name, but the message was universally received as marking a basic reorientation of United States policy toward Russia; some even went so far at the time as to call it "the beginning of World War III." It was hardly that, but subsequent events—leading on through the Marshall Plan, the defense of Berlin, the Atlantic Pact and the Korean War—only confirm the contemporary impression that with the so-called "Truman Doctrine" American policy had reached a crucial turning point. How much Forrestal's thought and counsel may have contributed to it there is, obviously, no way of knowing; but at least the new course ran closely parallel to the moral, strategic and tactical ideas which Forrestal had long been developing.

The new course had been set. The problem of providing the strength to follow, to sustain and to vindicate it remained.

CHAPTER VII

Soviet Policy and American Defense

I

[In a note of January 21, shortly after Byrnes' resignation as Secretary of State, Forrestal had confided to his diary that "in my opinion accommodation with Russia could only be secured if we continued the firmness and resolution which Mr. Byrnes had displayed during the last year; that any negotiations with Russia had to be predicated upon a thorough awareness of the unbending determination of the Russians to accomplish world Communization." In March, on the eve of the President's enunciation of the "Truman Doctrine," Forrestal was writing to Paul C. Smith, publisher of the *San Francisco Chronicle*:

To Paul Smith, 10 March 1947

It is my opinion that world events may move within the next six months at almost the same speed as they did in 1940. Marshall has the equipment in terms of orderliness of mind and capacity to deal with them. The only areas where I am not sure about his equipment are, first, the economic background, and second, awareness of the nature of Communist philosophy. However, he learns fast.

[Events were moving on many fronts, both foreign and domestic. The beginnings of a subsequently famous feud are recorded in a couple of notes of early March.

8 March 1947   *Lilienthal Appointment*

After dinner with McCloy—went to Senator Ferguson's house [Homer Ferguson, Republican of Michigan] where there were Knowland [Senator William F. Knowland, Republican of California] and Saltonstall [Senator Leverett Saltonstall, Republican of Massachusetts] and others. Knowland reported disturbing news about the Lilienthal appointment, said they had new information but of rather dubious character on some of his appointments.

[The President had nominated David E. Lilienthal, chairman of the Tennessee Valley Authority, as chairman of the new (domestic) Atomic Energy Commission. His confirmation was then before the Senate, which gave its assent in the following month. Senator Hickenlooper, mentioned below, was in later years to wage determined war on Mr. Lilienthal and his administration of the atomic energy operations.

9 March 1947   *Lilienthal Appointment*

Senator Hickenlooper came to my house and expressed great disturbance over the intransigence and inflexibility of Lilienthal in trying to create an atmosphere which would make it easier for Hickenlooper and others who were going to vote for his confirmation. He said that Lilienthal had taken on Marks [Herbert S. Marks, general counsel of the Atomic Energy Commission] at a salary of $14,000 a year which he was entitled to, which he thought was outside the intent of the act, although legally proper. Also, he said that he had not had his appointees screened by the FBI before naming them.

At his suggestion I talked to the President that evening, transmitting his ideas, and also to Lewis Strauss.

[The day after the President's message on Greece and Turkey, Forrestal was talking with Herbert Hoover—not about the Balkans but about Germany.

13 March 1947   *Meeting with Hoover*

Meeting at 2:00 p.m. at the Department of Agriculture with Harriman, Anderson, Patterson, Acheson and ex-President

Hoover. Hoover said that the burden of Germany upon the American taxpayer could not be lifted until the ceiling on German heavy industry was lifted. He pointed out that Germany had provided the heavy industry for most of Europe, now there was a great dearth of capacity for making tractors, electrical equipment, etc., that everybody was turning to us for these supplies. . . . Harriman pointed out that to meet the demands for steel alone we would have to add about six to ten million tons to our present American steel capacity, then we would be exporting this steel to nations which could be supplied from European steel capacity and that we would wind up with an overexpansion of our own steel industry. I also referred to the depletion of our prime ore reserves, which the war had proved were by no means inexhaustible.

I said that the observations that Mr. Hoover had made about Germany . . . applied with equal force to Japan. I also pointed out that this restoration could only come about if people who had been the managers of business were permitted to return to their jobs. He confirmed this and said that as a matter of fact, while the Russians were yelling about denazification in the American Zone, they were seducing industrial technicians and engineers on their side of the border by offering them high pay and special privileges. One engineer . . . who had been working as a Nazi suspect as a day laborer in the American Zone had been offered by the Russians the managership of the Siemens and Halske plant in Berlin, an offer which he accepted. He is now living in his own house, being paid a substantial salary.

[But the main subject at the moment was the policy toward Greece and Turkey. Earlier this day, Forrestal had appeared before the Senate Foreign Relations Committee, in a closed session.

13 March 1947   *Greece and Turkey*

Appeared with Acheson and Patterson today before the Foreign Relations Committee. Intensive discussion of the President's message. Acheson outlined the needs of Greece and the related needs of Turkey. . . . He said that these countries were complements and functions of each other. If Greece succumbed . . . Turkey would be encircled and could not hold out indefinitely. He said Greece . . . had had her Civil Service completely demolished during the German occupation. The government was inefficient—in many cases corrupt. The British have had 80,000 troops in the neighborhood of Salonika and have had a military mission comprising as many as 1300 officers and men. The Greeks have about 100,000 poorly trained soldiers. The dissident guerrillas number about 12,000. [Sic: it seems a low figure.] General Lincoln of the Army said that a combination of tactical aircraft and trained soldiers would probably be able to handle the guerrillas.

Vandenberg [Senator Arthur H. Vandenberg, Republican of Michigan] said that one difficulty he would have on the floor of the Senate would be in answering the question as to why this matter was not referred to the United Nations. Senator Smith [H. Alexander Smith, Republican of New Jersey] spoke rather strongly to the same point. Senator Connally's answer [Tom Connally, Democrat of Texas and ranking minority member of the Foreign Relations Committee] was that the United Nations could not handle the question; that the implementation of their military police force was a long way off and that it would be an idle thing to take such a step. Vandenberg responded that he realized there would be no concrete result but that it would make the inadequacy of procedure through the United Nations manifest. . . .

Acheson said the Greeks [obviously the Turks are meant], a nation of twenty-five million people, had a sound agrarian economy but were under great pressure because they were compelled through the war of nerves waged by Russia to keep about six hundred thousand men under arms. They had only a small air force, about three hundred planes, very little modern armor or mechanized equipment. Patterson said it was roughly what you might call "a 1910 army."

I spoke in general terms on the importance to the United States of the Mediterranean, of the fact that the American Navy practically had its birth in the Mediterranean through the necessity of sending ships in 1797 to make war on the pirates of the Barbary Coast in order to protect our merchant marine. I also reminded the committee of the fact that last summer, when the Russians began making their representations to Turkey on the Dardanelles, the appearance of American war vessels in the Mediterranean was followed by the first amiable utterances of Premier Stalin in late September.

[The strategic insight which had led Forrestal to work patiently in the preceding year for the re-establishment of an American Mediterranean squadron was already beginning to pay off. From this time on, few, if any, voices were to be raised against the presence in that strategic sea of the "storm-beaten ships" on which the Soviet armies might never look but whose influence they were nevertheless to sense in more ways than one.

Over the ensuing two weeks—occupied with problems of the naval budget, unification and many other matters—Forrestal made no diary notes. But at the State-War-Navy meeting on March 26 there were matters interesting enough to record. Warren Austin, now Permanent Representative of the United States on the Security Council, was there and discussed the United Nations' work on atomic energy control.

27 March 1947   *State-War-Navy*

Meeting held 26 March 1947. . . .

Mr. Austin stated that he felt that considerable progress with the Russians had been made [in regard to atomic energy]. However, the Russians' stand on specific issues could not be determined and would only come forth when specific proposals come up for consideration of the [Atomic Energy] Committee.

I cautioned that public opinion might become oversanguine if too great importance was placed on minor conciliation by the Russians and stated that in the proposed aid to Greece and Turkey apparently a large part of the public was of the opinion, due to overstressing the United Nations' capability, that the United Nations could handle a problem of this nature. The growth of similar misconceptions with regard to the atomic energy problem should be avoided.

Mr. Lilienthal stated that control of production of atomic energy for industrial purposes could not be separated from the control of production of atomic weapons. . . .

The Secretaries were in general agreement that Senator Austin should endeavor to bring up at first priority in the Atomic Energy Committee the matter of establishing a charter for an international agency for inspection, supervision and control of atomic energy. . . .

[At the next State-War-Navy meeting the subject recurred. (Forrestal was present, but the notes this time were taken by an assistant.)

3 April 1947   *Atomic Energy Commission*

. . . Senator Austin voiced again his definite optimism with regard to progress in the treatment of the atomic energy matter in the United Nations. . . .

Mr. Osborn [Frederick Osborn, Deputy Representative on the U. N. Atomic Energy Committee] was in general agreement with Senator Austin except that he did not breathe the same degree of optimism. However, he did think that if agreement was reached on the minor and semi-important issues, changing world conditions and world opinion might force Russia to accept agreement on a complete control of atomic energy. . . .

Mr. Acheson pointed out the relatively little progress to date on atomic energy and stated that worthwhile progress on major issues was essential for determination of our future national policy. . . .

It appears that the question of differences of opinion resolved to whether it was best to come to grips with the main issue at an early date or postpone it to a future date. The Secretaries in general favor an approach to meet the real issues involved at the earliest feasible time.

Senator Austin brought up the idea of the War and Navy

Departments taking the positive approach for formulating a plan for quantitative reduction of armaments. It was pointed out that this matter was under consideration and that any definitive stand would be dictated by progress of political stability and world confidence. It was further stated formulation of peace treaties for Germany and Japan and decision as to U. N. security forces were prerequisites for determination of the extent of reduction and regulation of armaments.

[The Cabinet next day, April 4, dealt with a strange mélange of issues, curiously typical of the way in which democratic government, even at the height of its most serious crises, is so often forced to operate. One of them was the Greco-Turkish question; but there were others—a telephone strike (on which Schwellenbach reported "no progress in negotiations"), and problems raised by two perennial sources of trouble, John L. Lewis, the president of the United Mine Workers, and Henry Wallace, late Vice President and Secretary of Commerce. Mr. Lewis had just called out his four hundred thousand mine workers for a six-day stoppage "in memory" of the hundred and eleven miners who had lost their lives in a mine disaster at Centralia, Illinois; and he was attacking the Secretary of the Interior, "Cap" Krug, on the ground that the Interior Department's Bureau of Mines had paid inadequate attention to mine safety.

4 April 1947   *Cabinet*

. . . Krug reported that Lewis would continue to make violent attacks upon him and upon the administration about the mine disaster. The President remarked that Lewis had never displayed any interest on measures looking toward mine safety. Krug confirmed this. . . . He said Lewis had boasted that he would *get* Krug first, Clark second and the Navy third, and that he would wait until 1948 to get the President. . . .

Acheson reported the action of the Senate [Foreign Relations] Committee yesterday which unanimously approved extension of American aid to Greece and Turkey. He said the State Department had come to the conclusion that Vandenberg's amendment [in effect giving the United Nations the power to suspend the aid program if it should find it to be unwise or unnecessary] as altered was satisfactory to them. He expressed concern about the attitude of Senator George [Walter F. George, Democrat of Georgia] who, he said, had expressed strong criticism of Britain in presenting the Greek-Turkish problem to us on a crisis basis and that we had permitted ourselves to be rushed into an action without full consideration. He said George had reserved to himself the right to bring up on the floor of the Senate the proposal to amend the proposed bill postponing implementation of it for sixty days, during which time the United Nations will be given a chance to act. This undoubtedly reflects some of ex-Secretary Byrnes' opinions.

I inquired if we had our plans made for a man to head the American mission to Greece. It is to be offered to Walter Gifford. The President seemed optimistic that he would accept— an optimism which I said I did not share. Moses' name [Robert Moses of New York] was mentioned as an alternative, and both Patterson and I told Acheson we thought he would do it well. [Actually the President had been asked at his press conference the day before whether Moses would get the job, and had replied in a terse negative. Forrestal was apparently right about Gifford; the appointment finally went to Dwight P. Griswold, former Governor of Nebraska, who had been serving with the Military Government in Germany.]

Acheson reported receipt of a cable from the American Ambassador in London [Douglas] expressing concern over the contents of Wallace's proposed speech next week in Britain. Wallace's speech will deal with, first, Middle Eastern oil; second, the bellicosity of the American attitude toward Russia; and, third, American bypassing of the United Nations. Douglas is to speak himself at the Pilgrims' Dinner in London later in the month, in which he will discuss the American position without direct reference to Wallace's speech. Douglas suggested having Herbert Agar, an American now resident in London, make a direct reply to Wallace. Harriman thought this should be done. I inquired why we had not denied Wallace a passport and why we should not do so now. The President felt that to deny an ex-Vice President and an ex-Cabinet member the right of travel abroad would expose us to severe criticism. I said I would prefer to take the criticism than permit Wallace to interfere with American policy. The Attorney General suggested that it might be even better to weigh carefully the re-entry of the gentleman in question into the United States.

[Forrestal noted the same day the results of a gossipy dinner with Mr. Byrnes, now exercising the immemorial prerogatives of the statesman out of office.

4 April 1947   *Dinner with Byrnes*

Had dinner last night with Jimmy Byrnes. He is critical of the Greek-Turkish policy on the general line that the administration is not smart in opposing Vandenberg's effort to save face for the U. N. and also in not identifying the American action in Greece as a flat and direct counter to Communist expansion. He also said that if the British withdrew their troops we had only a small unit of Army and Navy officers to go for staff consultations with the Greek Army. The loss would be highly detrimental to American prestige. He said he thought the United Nations Commission on Greece should immediately make an interim report; otherwise, when Molotov was free of some of his present problems, he would make an effective and destructive attack on American action, on the grounds that the Russians had agreed to the British plea for U. N. examination of the facts about Greece and we had then proceeded to act before a report had been received. . . .

[Forrestal had another talk with Byrnes at the end of the month.

30 April 1947   *Hon. James Byrnes*

Jimmy Byrnes came in this morning and in talking about the Russians he said they are "stubborn, obstinate and they don't scare." I reminded him of our conversation about two years ago when he chided me for being too extreme in my views about the Russians when I told him that [when] he harbored the illusion that he could talk in the same fashion with the Russians that he could with the Republican opposition in the Senate he was very much mistaken. At that time I told him that when he spoke, so to speak, using language in a third dimension, the Russians spoke in a fourth, and there was no stairway.

Byrnes said the whole Russian system was shot through with great emphasis on class and rank. One amusing sidelight of the last Moscow meeting, he said, was the segregation of Connally and Vandenberg from him and his assistants. They, the Senators, being of a lower order in the Russian mind—consequence, Messrs. Connally and Vandenberg were considerably burned up.

[At the Cabinet on April 18 they were concerned with such things as the telephone strike and the cost of living, but the implications of the policy on which the country had been embarked by the "Truman Doctrine" were not absent from their minds.

18 April 1947   *Cabinet*

. . . I said that in view of the feeling that our support for Greece and Turkey might be the forerunner of many other and very much larger economic political actions in other parts of the world, we should make a study of what may confront us in the next eighteen months. I mentioned Lippmann's thesis that there will be a series of economic disasters in Europe which could produce profound repercussions here. (Lippmann predicts that the British loan will be either exhausted or the exhaustion point will be in sight by the end of 1948, that French hard-money requirements will be deficient by one billion dollars, that Italy will need half a billion dollars and that, in addition, great demands will continue to be put upon us by China, Japan and Germany.)

Secretary Acheson said SWNCC [State-War-Navy Coordinating Committee, composed of Assistant Secretaries of the three Departments] now had such a study under preparation and that a paper should be available in the near future.

[From this entry it is evident that what was to become the Marshall Plan was already taking shape upon the horizons of the
future. A few days later Forrestal was at a long luncheon which
ranged widely, not only over the future but over the past.

25 April 1947   *Pentagon Luncheon*

Lunch at Pentagon Building today [at this time the offices
of the Secretary of the Navy were not in the Pentagon but in
the Navy Building in Potomac Park] with Judge Patterson,
General Eisenhower, General Spaatz, Admiral Nimitz.

General Eisenhower spoke of the difficulty of the association
and relation of military strategy to political action. As a soldier
in Europe concerned with only one job, mainly that of getting
the war over as quickly as possible, he had to take issue with
Churchill's thesis of an invasion from the south—that is, at the
head of the Adriatic. He said Churchill had vitally opposed the
operation which was the landing in Southern France. He had
always to contend with Churchill's skepticism as to the speed
with which the American power that Eisenhower commanded
could be used to disseminate [disperse?] and smash the enemy.
In early 1944 Churchill said that if Eisenhower could seize the
proposed bridgehead, Granville, on the Cherbourg Peninsula,
. . . and then mass his forces for the subsequent frontal assault
on Germany, which he figured could take place . . . in the
spring of 1945, it would have been one of the most brilliant
military operations in history. When Eisenhower replied to
him, "But, Mr. Prime Minister, we beyond any question will
be at the Rhine by Christmas," Churchill's comment was that
it was all very well to be optimistic but one must keep within
the framework of reality.

. . . Eisenhower commented that one gap in Churchill's
thinking was that the British had had no idea of how to exploit the use of air power and smashing of troop resistance on a
vast scale. One reason for the holding back of American troops
from thrusting into eastern Germany and taking Berlin . . .
was Churchill's profound conviction that the American forces
would not be ready to do so, and that therefore when he got
the Russians' agreement on what he calls the Linz-Eisenach-

Stettin Line, he, Churchill, thought he had conceived [received?] a great concession. When as a matter of fact agreement on that line prevented the Americans from going a hundred and fifty miles deeper into German territory, which they could have done with ease. . . . [Here the diary records Eisenhower's account, already quoted,[1] of President Truman's desire at Potsdam to get the Russians into the Pacific war.]

Judge Patterson complained about the drain upon Army resources in the form of occupation troops with particular reference to Korea. He said that the fact that Americans were still compelled to do an occupation job in that country was not only a great drain on its appropriations but also was the source of unceasing complaint from parents of the enlisted men who were unhappy, dissatisfied and bored. . . .

Eisenhower gave it as his considered opinion that the Russians would not initiate a war, short of stupidity or blunder, short of five years. In the interval, however, they would continue to export their one commodity, the composite of chaos, anarchy and confusion. The Russians, he said, would not be concerned by any loss of life among their own people; during the last war they kept no records of the dead, of their casualties; there were no personnel records in any of the Russian armies; when they wished to clear minefields they did it by human bodies rather than by any mechanisms; in short, in their conduct of war they were guided by an utter and ruthless disregard for the lives of their soldiers.

Admiral Nimitz expressed the view that Italy was a country of great importance to the United States; that we should do everything to help in its rehabilitation and to extend all possible assistance in the restoration of Italian military forces. . . .

At the conclusion I said it was manifest that American diplomatic planning of the peace was far below the quality of the planning that went into the conduct of the war. We regarded the war, broadly speaking, as a ball game which we had to finish as quickly as possible, but in doing so there was comparatively little thought as to the relationships between nations

---

[1] See pp. 78-79.

which would exist after Germany and Japan were destroyed. The United Nations was oversold; sound in concept and certainly the only hope for improvement in the world order, it was built up overextravagantly as the solution to international frictions that had existed for centuries. Now there is a danger of its being cast aside by the American public in a mood of frustration and disappointment.

[As this luncheon was being held at the Pentagon, the Council of Foreign Ministers was concluding, in Moscow, another long and largely fruitless attempt at peacemaking. Secretary Marshall had set out for the Soviet capital early in March, hoping to get an Austrian peace treaty written and to secure at least general agreement on the principles governing a peace treaty with Germany. He was back in Washington for the Cabinet luncheon on the 28th, with scant success to record in either direction.

28 April 1947   *Cabinet Luncheon*

The Secretary of State reported on the Moscow Conference:

Two underlying motifs ran through all the conversations with the Russians—first, money, and second, reparations out of Germany, i. e., in terms of production. . . . The Russians have found that the taking of physical assets does not get them the result they want in terms of goods. Even taking of management personnel with the plants does not suffice because the trained labor is not available in Russia.

Concrete accomplishments regarding Germany as between Britain and America: first, agreement on raising the level of German industry; second, agreement on one central city in which executive headquarters will be located. . . .

We must be very careful to preserve our good relationships with the "fringe" countries in Europe—Belgium, France, Denmark, Norway, Sweden, Holland, etc., because otherwise Communism can infiltrate into all of them.

His conversation with Stalin:

He recited to Stalin a long list of proposals and communications which had been addressed to the Russians and to which we had not received any answer. He said such conduct was not merely discourteous but that it amounted to an attitude of contemptuousness, and if their design was to earn our ill will they were going about it most successfully. Stalin, in response to the list of items Marshall raised, commented that was "sloppy government" but then he referred to the Russian request for a loan from the United States which he said had been made two years ago without any answer having been received as yet from us. At this juncture Bedell Smith interposed that an answer had been made about a year ago, which, however, represented a year's delay. . . .

There has been a notable lack of any central planning on American policy. Marshall has undertaken to correct this by the creation of a planning group which will work directly under him and outside the departmental framework. He feels the need of a central policy in terms of which any representative of the State Department can think and speak when he is away from Washington. George Kennan will head one part of this central planning group and a man named Davies who has been in China another.

At the end of the luncheon Secretary Anderson said that Marshall's observations about the need for planning in the State Department was equally applicable to the Cabinet and the rest of government. . . . [As an example he cited a recent case of conflict of policy between Agriculture and State over wool tariffs.] Anderson reminded the President that both he and I had been urging this for some time and that he felt the need for it was of the most immediate character.

The President said that he was in full accord; that it was simply a question of adjusting personalities, finding the right man, etc. . . .

I asked Marshall whether he had the impression from the British that the present government was more or less overwhelmed by the scale and depth of its own problems. He replied that they were trying a great experiment without very much management skill either in government or out of it in charge of things; that they had had added to those considerations the fact of the unexpected weather disaster of this winter. [An unusually severe winter with much heavy snow had materially hampered Britain's economic recovery in early 1947.] . . .

I said [to Marshall] that I was very glad that he was setting up this planning organization because in the use of our vast resources and present power we were up against the factor of time which conversely was on the Russian side; that we *had* the ability to be a catalyst in the restoration of world economy but it had to be done very fast and using all the talents in the country, which means business management as well as proper governmental policy. . . .

II

[Concerned as he was by these major problems of policy and governmental organization, Forrestal was wrestling in these weeks with his own more immediate issues of military program and Service unification. In a meeting on April 2 he argued the naval budget with Representative John Taber, chairman of the House Appropriations Committee.

2 April 1947   *House Appropriations Committee*

At the conclusion of an hour-and-a-half talk Mr. Taber said, "Couldn't we make some cut in the 1947-48 budget appropriation figure; that he didn't know where it should be made but he felt sure that some cuts could be made without doing injury to the power of the Fleet." Both Nimitz and I told him that the trouble was that until the de-activation of our ships was completed every cut would produce more spending. . . . I told Taber . . . that if there were any reduction in naval funds it would have to come from Mr. Taber as a decision by him; that I could not be in the position of accepting or approving such a cut, and I added that this was more than simply a speech because I knew how strongly the naval people had argued with the Bureau of the Budget and the President against reductions in our submittal of the budget, and that the President had told us, as well as others in the government, not to do any padding but to give him a hard-pan figure which we could defend.

Taber said he understood my position fully.

[While Forrestal was thus defending the Navy against congressional economy, on one hand, a new danger seemed to arise, on the other, through the committee hearings on the unification bill. General Eisenhower appeared before the Senate Armed Services Committee on March 25 and Under Secretary of War Kenneth C. Royall on April 15. Naval opinion was thrown into a state of alarm when (as Forrestal summarized it in a later diary note) "General Eisenhower . . . said, in effect, that he was sorry there wasn't a single Chief of Staff but he hoped that that development would come in the future, and when Under Secretary Royall, in response to questions, had very specifically underlined his assumption of the broad and almost absolute powers of the Secretary of National Defense to reallocate functions and duties of the Services." On the day of the Royall testimony Forrestal dined with Senator Millard E. Tydings, Democrat of Maryland, a member both of the Armed Services and Appropriations Committees.

16 April 1947   *Senator Tydings*

Had dinner last evening with Tydings, who talked about the unification bill. He thinks it can get through the Senate although he was not familiar with recent developments following Ken Royall's testimony—that is to say, he has not talked with Chairman Gurney or Senator Saltonstall. I told him of my conversation with General Vandegrift and the misgivings that the Marines and Naval Aviation had developed after reading General Eisenhower's testimony, and also yesterday that of Mr. Royall. He said he would not be too much disturbed because he felt that these objections could be met by letting the protagonists of the Marines—Byrd, Robertson, *et al.*—and of Naval Aviation put in protective clauses. I said this did not conform with the policy of the administration and that I myself did not think they were necessary although I would have to confess I was somewhat shaken by the recurring evidence of the Army's intransigence in regard to the chain-of-command concept (when, as a matter of fact, during this war they had not been able to issue a single order to MacArthur—and they couldn't now). I said my whole attitude in the bill was that unless the civilians who were named to the various jobs outlined would work together in complete harmony, the operation of the bill would be a mess. And by the same token, I said that unless the Services were led by officers who were determined to make the thing go, there would be the same chance of a mess. I said the difficulty I had all along was the Army's genial assumption that by writing a chart and drafting a law you could get discipline, when as a matter of fact I had seen very little of it in the Army itself. Cooperation and harmony take constant effort and work as well as imagination to foresee the things that will create friction.

[This last is an admirable statement of Forrestal's philosophy of administration and of the methods which he constantly sought to apply. And his foresight in this instance was to be only too fully justified in the following year, when one of the great difficulties in launching the unified military system proved to be the inability of civilian and military heads alike to see that system as a whole and "make the thing go."

This conversation ended on a different subject: labor legislation. The new Congress, under its Republican control, was now at work on what was to become the Taft-Hartley Act, modifying the Wagner Act in the direction of placing certain restrictions on union labor. The diary note continues:

We then switched to labor and the Senator expressed the strongest hope that the President would let fall some indication of the area of his acceptance of labor restrictions so that his friends in the Senate could battle and if necessary compromise intelligently. He gave it as his view that the President should try to see that a bill was sent up to him which was not too bad, which he could sign with expressed reservations. If he vetoed any labor legislation that was sent up, Tydings felt that the political results would be damaging, although he realized that it was not easy for him to sign such a measure in the light of the Case bill [2] veto. He kept reiterating that he hoped that I would try to give his point of view to the President and not let him be stampeded into a last-minute veto without very deep consideration.

[As for unification, it was clear that the whole issue was again in difficulties. Forrestal talked with Clark Clifford by telephone on the 17th; Clifford "complained" of General Vandegrift's attitude and said he could not understand how, after agreement had been reached all around on the draft bill, there could still be opposition to it from the Services. Forrestal intimated that it was the Eisenhower and Royall testimony which had reawakened all the Navy's fears. In the end he arranged a luncheon discussion for the 18th.

18 April 1947   *Unification*

Lunched today with Senators Gurney, Robertson, Tydings and Saltonstall, Mr. Clifford and Admiral Sherman. (After lunch Judge Patterson and Mr. Sullivan came in.)

At the opening of lunch I made a hasty recapitulation of the present unification bill in the Congress. I said that while I had the impression that it might go through the Senate, it might have hard going in the House. . . . To my mind, I said, the question of whether definition of functions was included in the law or not was of no consequence, but that (a) the Marines felt very strongly that it should be in and (b) the White House felt equally strong that it should not be in. . . .

Mr. Clifford stated his reasons for believing that it was of great importance that the law as enacted have loose rather than overprecise language so far as the mission of each of the Services is concerned.

Senator Saltonstall disagreed, saying that he would like to point out very closely and respectfully that the Marines occu-

---

[2] This bill, introduced by Representative Francis H. Case, Republican of Iowa, provided for a five-member labor-management mediation board, a sixty-day cooling-off period, and provisions for holding employers, unions, or employees accountable for infringement of contracts or restraint of trade. It was vetoed by the President and the veto was sustained.

pied a unique and singular place in the hearts of the people
and that, whether or not Congress did anything about it, the
people would. Tydings said it was not a matter of logic but of
emotion and that all that would be necessary, particularly in
the House, would be for someone to get up on his feet when
the bill was under debate and say that logical arguments about
the bill were all very well but that, after all, "these young
men, thanks to their traditions and their fighting history, were
the troops that we needed to take Mount Suribachi."

[The unification hearings dragged on; Representative Taber
continued his efforts to reduce still further the already drastically
reduced military appropriations; there was still much confusion on the larger issues of policy. Under the circumstances,
to design a really effective and adequate military policy was
scarcely possible. Early in May Forrestal was talking with Sen-
tor Owen Brewster of Maine about Middle Eastern oil supplies.

2 May 1947   *Lunch—Senator Brewster*
    . . . I said that Middle East oil was going to be necessary
for this country not merely in wartime but in peacetime, because if we are going to make the contribution that it seems
we have to make to the rest of the world in manufactured
goods, we shall probably need very greatly increased supplies
of fuel.
    Brewster said that . . . Europe in the next ten years may
shift from a coal to an oil economy and therefore whoever sits
on the valve of Middle East oil may control the destiny of Europe. He expressed considerable misgivings about the capacity
of American forces to keep Russia out of Arabia if they decided
to move there. I replied that I would not undertake to make
any military evaluation of the possibilities of such defense but
that we should not forget that the logistics problems of the
Russians would be considerable and that their industrial capabilities were still limited. It is doubtful if they have much yet
in the way of modern planes for mass production, beyond the
Stormovik, which is the general utility fighter-bomber used in
the last war.

[At the State-War-Navy meeting a week later the question of Korean aid came up.

7 *May 1947*   *State-War-Navy*

. . . Mr. Patterson reiterated that we should get out of Korea at the earliest possible time. He stressed the expense to the U. S. and the insignificance of the strategic and economic value of Korea. General Marshall did not agree with these views.

[And even the policy of our British ally was a source of doubt and difference. At this same meeting:

General Hilldring [Major General John H. Hilldring, then Assistant Secretary of State for Occupied Areas] explained that the proposed dispatch cable to General Clay was designed to advise that the U. S. shared his fears that the establishment of a Bi-Zonal Economic Council [in Germany] might result in socialized industry. . . . I said that the government should make it clear that we do not propose to endorse socialization in Germany under any circumstances and this should be communicated at the highest level. . . . [Forrestal added a further note:] It is clear that the British policy is determined by their desire to impose a socialized economy and government in their Zone. I said that this was distinctly contrary to American policy and belief and that we [it?] would not win support for the British in Congress or of the American public; that at some point it would have to be made clear to the British at the highest levels that they were operating their economy on three and a quarter billion capital obtained from this country, and that they would probably need additional working capital, and that we did not propose to have our money used to implement a German system contrary to our own ideas, and particularly if the Germans themselves did not want it. Judge Patterson raised the point that we might have difficulty in case the Germans did vote to nationalize industry.

[But while the necessity for clearing up the unification controversies and establishing the new machinery of diplomatic and

[military coordination can only have seemed more pressing
than ever, it appeared more and more doubtful in early May
whether any bill could be passed in the current session.

9 May 1947   *Unification*

Lunched today with Mr. Eberstadt, Admiral Sherman and
Mr. Sullivan. Mr. Eberstadt testified before the Armed Services Commitee of the Senate this morning. His evaluation of
the prospects for unification are as follows:

Unless there are specific saving clauses for the Marines and
Naval Aviation and a definition of the powers of the Secretary
of National Defense the bill will fail to pass. He said that with
the saving clauses for the Marines and Naval Air there was
about an even chance of getting a bill, but without the single
Secretary of National Defense. He gave it as his view that the
testimony of Eisenhower and Royall had been destructive; the
first principally because he had not given serious study to the
proposed legislation; Royall's because it had so clearly revealed
that the Army had not surrendered its view that what was
wanted was a merger and not unification or integration.

In order to get a single Secretary there would have to be
agreement between Patterson and myself and others in the
Army and Navy as to the necessary language, but even then it
would take concerted selling effort by all hands to get the desired result.

[A more immediate and disturbing danger, however, was represented by Mr. Taber's determined effort to slash the Navy budget,
already at paralyzingly low levels. Forrestal was quoted as saying
that the reductions being proposed would virtually immobilize
the Navy, leaving the nation without any active fleet whatever.
Nevertheless the naval subcommittee of the Appropriations
Committee, under Representative Charles A. Plumley, Republican of Vermont, voted a tentative ten per cent cut on May
9, and the full committee adopted it on the 16th. Forrestal wrote
to the Commander-in-Chief of the Pacific Fleet:

To Admiral Louis E. Denfeld, 16 May 1947

We are in the middle of our worries about appropriations—had word today that Mr. Taber's committee had cut us by $378 million. Should this stand, it could, of course, be most serious, but I am hopeful that when the bill goes into conference with the Senate Committee (Senator Saltonstall is chairman of the naval subcommittee of the central Appropriations Committee of the Senate) this very disastrous cut will be adjusted.

[Saltonstall did not, as matters turned out, disappoint him; but the Navy's tendency to go over the head of the House Committee ruffled some feelings. Forrestal was always adept and diligent in his relations with Congress, and the care he took to smooth the situation was very characteristic of him.

26 May 1947   *Meeting—Representative Plumley*

I went to see Congressman Plumley this morning to express our regret at failure to communicate our disagreement on the Navy budget through the chairman of the Appropriations Subcommittee, Mr. Plumley himself. He disavowed any irritation and said the irritation was mostly Mr. Taber's. He indicated that he felt that Mr. Taber was trying to do too much of the work by himself without sufficient delegation among his subcommittee chairmen. He said he was fearful that this would make such an accumulative strain on Mr. Taber's health that there was danger he might not be able to stand the burden of the work he was assuming.

I said that with Mr. Taber's approval we would do our utmost to see that any conversations with or communications to the chairman of the full committee would be reported to Mr. Plumley.

We therefore did not relish implications in Mr. Taber's letter of lack of frankness on our part.

I told Mr. Plumley that we planned to present our case to the Senate subcommittee and would rely on a conference committee of the two Houses to correct omissions that we consider to be really dangerous.

III

[As summer approached amid these internal worries and disagreements, the world situation continued only to deteriorate. In
the latter part of May Secretary Marshall moved to bring one
troublesome matter to a head.

21 May 1947   *State-War-Navy*
. . . General Marshall brought up the subject of the articles
given Russia under Lend-Lease, the return of which we
should now request. He said that the size of the list [of articles
to be reclaimed] submitted by the War and Navy Departments
was such as to preclude any chance of a successful negotiation.
He said the Russians would have in their minds arrangements
we had made with England—in this case we permitted the English to retain many items which were usable for war purposes.
The Russians know what these articles are, generally speaking,
and will resent quite bitterly any pronounced increase, on a
comparable basis, over what we got back from England. He
referred particularly to the submarine chasers and PT-boats—
202 of the latter and about 150 of the former.

I said that I viewed our position as this: That the Navy
should say to the State Department what we felt should be returned, from a *military* standpoint; that, however, the State Department was charged with problems of a wider nature in the
field of diplomacy and that having given our views to the State
Department it was up to them to make the decision. General
Marshall replied that he realized he would have to take the
rap before Congress on the decision arrived at but requested
the War and Navy Departments to reconsider their lists and
submit new ones in the light of this conversation.

[At a luncheon with McCloy, Sherman and others a week later
the interest was, for the moment, historical. McCloy "said he was
writing a piece for *Foreign Affairs* on the major strategic decisions of the war" and asked opinions as to what these were.
After discussing a number of the major decisions—to land in
Normandy, to concentrate the Fleet before Midway and so on—

[McCloy mentioned the decision to use the atomic bomb against Japan. Forrestal queried this.

29 May 1947   *Luncheon*
. . . I raised the question of whether this did turn out to have been a sound decision or not, in view of the exchange of dispatches between Sato in Moscow and the Japanese Foreign Office[3] which, by mid-July 1945, clearly indicated the hopelessness of the Japanese situation. I also put in on the possible negative side the decision to go through with the *Anvil* operation [the landing in southern France, 15 August 1944] rather than following Churchill's plan to attack at the head of the Adriatic, on the grounds that this permitted Russia to overrun the Balkans and the Yugoslavs to take a position in Venezia Giulia. Sherman disagreed and said the right counterstroke to the Russians would have been to permit the American Army to exploit their gains thoroughly at the head of the Danube; that they could have flowed down the Danube Basin and pushed American strength into the Balkans from the top rather than going up from beneath. McCloy made the observation that Churchill's plea for the attack in the Adriatic was based on the losses that would be sustained rather than on political motivations.

[Another lunch a few days later left behind it a rather striking summary of Forrestal's politico-economic philosophy.

4 June 1947   *Lunch with Ambassador Ali*
Lunched today with the Indian Ambassador [M. Asaf Ali]. He described for me the plans of the Indian government for economic development of the country. He said they proposed to have three great areas of development more or less under government control if not ownership: (1) national defense, (2) public utilities (power development), (3) railways and communications (these are already government-operated in the main). . . . Outside of these areas he looked for a free enter-

---

[3] See pp. 74-75.

prise and said that the country would need American technicians and experts.

I asked him how he expected to get the technicians and who
in the government would be competent to run the enterprises
on which they were supposed to give expert advice. I told him
that the development in this country had been accomplished
through business, which was composed of many different factors: promoters, bankers, engineers, salesmen and so forth.[4]

It is obvious that Mr. Ali has the same illusions about the
development of an economy as many academic thinkers. He assumes that technical skills can be disassociated from the various
elements that went into the development of our economy. Like
all such people, he places great emphasis on engineering and
fails to grasp the fact that management is a synthesis of all the
elements that I have mentioned above.

We talked about exploitation. I asked him what guarantee
American capital would have against exploitation by Indians
of it—that exploitation went both ways. Capital might unduly
and unjustly exploit a country by *taking out* more than it put
in, but there was another kind of exploitation which was the
expropriation of capital investments on the easily salable theory
that they represent foreign influence, contribute nothing and
live on the dividends of absentee ownership.

[But even as they talked a new period was opening in the his-
    tory of international economic and political relations. On the day
    after this luncheon Secretary Marshall, journeying to Cam-
    bridge to receive an honorary degree at the Harvard commence-
    ment exercises, delivered the address which was to form the
    starting point of the Marshall Plan. Forrestal made no direct
    comment in his diary on this decisive development, but its in-
    fluence was soon apparent.

    On June 13 Forrestal lunched with an old friend, Robert A.
    Lovett, who had just been appointed to succeed Dean Acheson
    as Under Secretary of State. The actual transfer of office was not

---

[4] Cf. his conversation with Sir Oliver Lyttleton, 23 July 1946, pp. 186-87. This was
an old idea with Forrestal.

[to take place until July 1; technically Lovett was still at this
time a "special assistant" only, but he was already involved in
those problems of organization in government which had worried
Forrestal and Anderson and, it would seem, nearly every high
governmental officer forced to struggle with the increasingly
lush jungles of federal administration.

13 June 1947   *Lunch with Admiral Sherman
                                  and Under Secretary Lovett*

Lunched today with Admiral Sherman and Under Secretary
Lovett of the State Department. Lovett recited the difficulties
of getting the Department organized. He said that the preceding Secretaries of State had made almost no progress in the creation of a rational organization. With the result that while
there were many good men in the Department, the means for
using their abilities were extremely limited. His chief immediate difficulty is acquisition of sufficient facts to determine
policy. He agreed with me that means of securing public backing, through the press and all other agencies, of Marshall was
most important.

He regards the statements as to what Europe must have in
terms of financial support from the United States as premature, unrealistic and not based on facts. He said the $5 billion
figure had apparently been reached by subtracting the total of
imports from Europe to the U. S. from the total of U. S. exports. His feeling is that much smaller sums applied in critical
areas such as the Ruhr do far more to re-create European economy than a general scattering of charity and largesse.

[Lovett, as the event was to prove, was mistaken in his idea
that Marshall aid could be limited to small sums; so was Forrestal
mistaken in the idea he later expressed at a Cabinet luncheon[5]
that "there was no chance of Russia's *not* joining in this effort."
Where there was no mistake was in the realization that a new
departure had been made and in the sense of a new tension in
the international air.

---

[5] Diary, 23 June 1947.

18 June 1947   *Conversation with Admiral Nimitz*

. . . I asked him if he knew what steps this government was prepared to take in the event of a Russian *démarche* in Europe —and I mean by that the communization of Italy and France and Russian aggressiveness toward Austria. I said that I did not expect such a development but that we should know our course of action in case it should happen that way. . . .

[At the Cabinet two days later there was a strictly domestic interlude.

20 June 1947   *Cabinet*

. . . The President announced he was going to veto the labor bill [the Taft-Hartley bill]. Anderson and I both registered dissent with the decision, and in particular expressed regret that there had been no Cabinet discussion of this matter such as had occurred on the price controls, on the portal-to-portal pay and on the tax bill, all of which discussions had been productive of a unanimity of view and which enabled members of the Cabinet to support with vigor the President's position.

I recalled our experiences during the war with the Brewster strikes, with the Allis-Chalmers strike, and I called attention to the fact that it was well known there were many Communists in the CIO organization. I recalled the experience of the French in the thirties, during which constant concessions by the Socialist government to labor resulted in the atrophy of French industry and in leaving the country almost defenseless before the German attack. I said it might sound fantastic to express fears of anything of a similar nature happening here, but expressed my view that it was not impossible. That if the present international situation should deteriorate further the Communists had available many instruments of sabotage and disturbance which they would not hesitate to use.

After the Cabinet the President apologized for the fact that there had not been full discussion in the Cabinet and said he would take pains to see that there was no repetition of such a situation. [But he nevertheless vetoed the bill, which was, of course, immediately repassed over the veto.]

[Forrestal could not forget the international situation in dealing even with so domestic a problem as labor legislation; and at the Cabinet lunch a few days later he returned to the question he had first opened with Admiral Nimitz on Wednesday the 18th.

23 June 1947   *Cabinet Luncheon*
. . . Just before breaking up I asked permission of the President to pose a question which I had put to the Secretary of State last Thursday: What does this country do, politically or militarily, if it is confronted during this summer with a Russian *démarche* accompanied by simultaneous coups in France and Italy? The President replied that we would have to face that situation when it arose, and he then said that he and General Marshall had been talking about it just prior to lunch. He said that he was afraid the answer would have to be found in history—of the struggle between the Romans and Carthage, between Athens and Sparta, between Alexander the Great and the Persians, between France and England, between England and Germany. He *hoped* that the present situation would not have to be answered the same way—that he saw some ray of light in the indicated Russian willingness to join France and Britain in making a constructive response to General Marshall's invitation. . . .

[A couple of days later Forrestal got a gloomy view of the European scene from Richard R. Deupree, industrialist and chairman of the Army and Navy Munitions Board, who was just back from Europe.[6] "Very gloomy about the whole European picture, particularly England. That country in a state of complete and super control which was resulting in the atrophy of all business effort. Deupree's view is that we should send money to Europe only in return for raw materials, and that none of our own raw materials should be expended to provide the export of finished goods."

[6] Diary, 25 June 1947.

[Even Lovett was still arguing for strictly limited aid under the
Marshall proposals.

26 June 1947   *Cabinet Lunch*
    . . . After lunch Lovett asked for a meeting with Snyder and
myself in which he advanced his thesis that there had been
much too much loose talk about the vast sums to be advanced
by the U. S. to European countries without any exact examination of how this help was to be extended and the conditions
under which it would be extended. Snyder rejoined that he
was very fearful Marshall would get himself out on a limb,
particularly if his supporters such as Ben Cohen continue to
make unrealistic statements as to what this country would have
to do (Cohen, in his Los Angeles speech, had referred to the
figure of $5 billion a year as necessary to prime the pump of
European economy). Lovett said that the prerequisite of the
re-establishment of economic stability was the creation of fiscal
stability within the individual countries of Europe. . . . [For-
restal recalled the work of the Dutch banking syndicate after
World War I which led to the mitigation of the effects of
the astronomical inflation in Germany through establishing the
Rentenmark as a basis for international exchange.] Lovett said
that his experts in his own bank [Brown Brothers Harriman
& Co.] had studied a similar proposal and had come to the conclusion that if a dollar credit from one and a half to two billions
were created for this kind of operation it would be adequate
to begin the restoration of the normal economic and business
functioning of the European economy.
    Snyder said he was very much concerned lest Marshall get
himself out on a limb by references to such astronomical sums
as had been referred to after his Harvard speech, with a resultant freezing of sentiment in Congress against *any* further
American attempts at help to Europe, simply because it was
too vast a project to be undertaken without dangerously weakening our own economy.

[If the event is to be taken as the test, then Cohen was more
nearly right here than either Lovett or Snyder, since, after thor-

[ough examination of the whole problem, aid was finally voted on a level of about $5 billion a year. Nor was this more than a beginning of the vastly larger strains which the struggle with Soviet Russia was to impose upon our economy, without any evidence of "dangerous weakening" in the latter.

But foresight, even for the wisest, is never so easy as hindsight. Facing the new problems, as they all were, Forrestal spent a retrospective evening about this time with Sumner Welles, in company with V. K. Wellington Koo, the Chinese Ambassador, Walter Lippmann, Elmer Davis, General Matthew B. Ridgway (who was to reach top command in the Far East, replacing General MacArthur, in 1951) and "Mr. Curtis of Boston."

21 June 1947   *Mr. Welles*

. . . Welles made these statements:

1. That there *was* a plan in the State Department to deal with postwar situations.

2. That Hull was responsible for the failure of any implementing action of this plan to redress the obvious imbalance in favor of Russia which would be in existence when the Germans were beaten. He quoted the Army's and the JCS insistence that a separate peace between Russia and Germany could be fatal—he said that this had to be the foundation of State Department policy.

3. That the greatest calamity in the United States was the appointment of Byrnes as Secretary of State.

4. That the State Department was fully aware of the meaning and significance of Russian ideology—this in answer to my observation that when I became Secretary of the Navy I found there was in existence nowhere in the government any critique of Russian objectives in terms of the underlying philosophy of dialectical materialism.

In regard to his observations about Russia, I said I did not see how he could fail to include Mr. Roosevelt in any appraisal of responsibility for our postwar situation; that he had named Hull and permitted the continuance of an organizational setup that was fundamentally unsound—I was referring to the friction in the Department of State between Hull and Welles. His

strictures on Mr. Byrnes were based upon the negative results
of Byrnes' visit to Moscow in 1945 and the commitments of
Americans in action in Europe which he seemed to feel flowed
out of that visit.

IV

[At this juncture an old problem returned. Its name was China.
The Marshall mission of the preceding year had ended in failure;
the Marines had first been concentrated and then withdrawn; the
United States had retired to "reconsider" its policy; even Mr.
Acheson had left the State Department. Unfortunately no
amount of "reconsideration" or changes of personnel could
change the basic factors of the Far Eastern problem, which
seemed to become only more and more insoluble. It arose at a
State-War-Navy meeting on June 19, which began with a discussion of the level of industry to be allowed to Japan. This involved the question of reparations, and in turn of General Mac-
Arthur, who wanted to make reparations a "unilateral" decision
by the United States. But that was only the beginning. It appeared that the British and Australians were "becoming increasingly suspicious that the United States was interested in restor-
ing Japan to economic soundness in order to have her as a bulwark against Russia." The conclusion was that the Secretary of
State should tell the British and the Dominions that "the United
States could not indefinitely continue to pay out $350 million a
year to support the necessary food level of the Japanese." That
led to considerable more talk about food supplies for both Japan
and Germany, and so to a discussion of the British desire to so-
cialize Germany. Clay wanted a directive on the subject; and
while the British were reportedly propagandizing for socialization, insufficient coal was being produced from the Ruhr. "I proposed," Forrestal says in his diary note, "that the British permit us
to send an American team of management into their area and
that the coal would be forthcoming. Marshall said such an action
would mean the fall of the British Labour government at home. I
replied that there might be some falling in our own government if we had to continue to pay out vast sums which we are
now paying to support German economy and feed their people."

[But the final note on this meeting seems possibly more significant that any of the foregoing.

19 June 1947   *State-War-Navy*

. . . Admiral Denfeld was present and reported his impressions of China, which were, in general, those of a continuing and general disintegration with the clear indication that the Russians will come in as we go out.

[At the Cabinet on June 23 "there was some conversation about China."

23 June 1947   *Cabinet Luncheon*

. . . Marshall said he had been searching for and inviting some suggestions of some positive action that we might take. He referred to the mistake of the Generalissimo in discharging General Sun about a year ago after he had won a notable victory in the north against the Communists and replacing him with Tu Li-ming. In this connection I told Marshall that the Chinese Ambassador at dinner Saturday night had told me that the Generalissimo had restored Sun to command. Marshall said he hopes this was true.

The Chinese are apparently starting another drive around town to enlist further help for the Nationalist government, using particularly the danger of Communism as their chief argument. Snyder said that he had had four or five invitations in the last ten days to dine with the Chinese Ambassador. . . .

[At the State-War-Navy meeting on June 26 the "first and only subject was China."

26 June 1947   *State-War-Navy*

. . . Secretary of State stated that he had been searching for a positive and constructive formula to deal with the Chinese situation which, he said, showed every sign of disintegration. We were confronted, he said, by the dilemma created by the incompetence, inefficiency and stubbornness of the Central government—qualities which made it very difficult to help them.

He cited the military ineptitude of their leaders, the cashier-
ing of the only generals who had produced successful cam-
paigns, the instability of their leadership and the appalling lack
of an organization to deal with the vast and complex economic
and social problems of China.

Penfield [James K. Penfield, Deputy Director of the Office
of Far Eastern Affairs], who had just returned after a ten-day
tour of North China, reported increasing evidences of failure
and disintegration. . . .

I made the observation that we could not draw entirely
oblique conclusions about China today without realizing that
part of the antipathy, which Marshall had quoted was now
mounting in China, derived from the Yalta Agreement in which
we gave away certain of the sovereign rights of China in order
to get the Russians into the war. . . . Marshall agreed that
this unfortunate fact was a substantial factor in the present rising unpopularity of the U. S. A. in China.

I gave it as my view that we should continue to supply support and ammunition to the Central government troops, pointing out that this was in consonance with the commitment we
had taken with that government along with Russia, that no
matter how difficult the situation became we should not withdraw entirely from China. . . .

Secretary Marshall had to leave the meeting to go to New
York but at the conclusion asked all of those present to endeavor to submit to him some basis for a constructive program
toward the existing Chinese government.

[It was to prove a tough order. At the next Cabinet meeting
    Marshall put the problem even more clearly.

27 June 1947   *Cabinet*

. . . The Secretary of State outlined the situation in China
and the dilemma facing this government:

(a) Whether to continue to supply armament and arms
to the Chinese National Army—failure to supply armament
would in effect be disarming them by such denial. The War
Department has a substantial amount of 7.92 ammunition

which was manufactured for the Chinese Army and which is not suited to American weapons.

(b) Interpretation by the Russians and certain elements in this country that the furnishing of ammunition and other arms is a continuance of intervention in Chinese domestic affairs. In other words, taking part in a civil war.

(c) The impression created in China of announcement of withholding of the $500 million Export-Import Bank loan. (Attempt is being made to balance this impression by pushing the Export-Import Bank to make loans for specific projects. . . .)

[At the same Cabinet, Marshall raised a problem from the German front. He recalled that about a year before General Clay had suspended the transfer of German industrial plants to Russia, and the other victor powers as well, because of Russia's failure to live up to her part of the Potsdam Agreement; the policy had not, however, produced any correction of the Soviet attitude. Forrestal's note continues:

Clay now desires to resume delivery to the Western Allies of reparation plants, but to continue withholding them from Russia. This would be contrary to an agreement between Marshall and Bevin in Moscow, in which apparently Molotov was advised. I suggested, and I had the support of Anderson and Harriman, that the *entire* question of plant transfers be held in abeyance. I pointed out that we were now talking about lifting the steel production of Germany from 7.5 million tons agreed upon a year ago to 11,200,000 tons, and I predicted that within a year we would be trying to lift it to 15 or 20 million, with a corresponding increase in other German industries. The decision was taken to advise Clay that *all* transfers would be held in abeyance. Marshall pointed out that to deliver to the Western Allies and refuse to deliver to Russia would be unnecessarily provocative of Russia at a time when we were both publicly and privately trying to secure their cooperation. He further said that he was fully sympathetic with Clay's difficulties but after all he was the person who had to handle negotiations with them and that he was trying to avoid clashes on lesser issues in order to be sure that these minor considerations did not destroy the chance of the larger hope of getting a concert of intent and action with Russia.

Harriman made the observation that it was his experience that any conciliatory moves toward Russia were always construed as appeasement rather than the implementation of a sincere desire to work together.

[Dining on the following evening with Representative John D. Lodge (Republican of Connecticut), Forrestal gave a further interesting estimate of Marshall's basic policy. Lodge, a member of the Foreign Affairs Committee, was dissatisfied with what he felt to be a want of frankness on the part of the State Department and was thinking of introducing a resolution calling for a protest note to be sent to the Polish government.

28 June 1947   *Congressman John Lodge*

. . . I suggested that he talk to Marshall and Lovett about this before he did it. I said that I thought it was important that as little as possible occur in Congress to embarrass these two men at the present time. I said he should keep in mind the fact that the great objective that Marshall had was to ascertain whether cooperation with Russia was possible or not, and to show to both the world and our country that every effort had been made on our part to secure such cooperation so that we should have the support of public opinion in whatever policy we found it necessary to adopt thereafter. I said I was confident all other considerations were secondary, in Marshall's mind, to this. I said he should keep in mind the fact that there had been no real organization in the State Department, that Byrnes had had to deal with vast problems on a day-to-day basis and had never been able to address himself to organization.

Lodge said that the people he regarded as most intelligent and progressive on his committee were Judd of Minnesota, Fulton of Pennsylvania, Javits of New York, Don Jackson of

California, Mrs. Bolton [of Ohio], and Karl Mundt [of South Dakota]. He thought that a luncheon or dinner between Lovett and Judd, Fulton, Jackson, Javits and himself would be productive of results.

[But however sincerely and high-mindedly Secretary Marshall might strive for cooperation with Russia, the Communist advance, particularly in the Far East, was growing only more and more ominous. On July 3 Forrestal breakfasted with William C. Bullitt, who was about to leave for the Far East and who thought the condition of China "to be most alarming." He lunched the same day with a Marine officer who had just returned from the area.

3 July 1947   *Situation in China*

. . . Lunch with General Howard, presently commander of the 1st Division of the Marine Corps, which has been withdrawn from China.[7] He said that aggressive attitude and actions on the part of Russia increased, in his opinion, almost in direct proportion to the degree of American withdrawal. In reply to my question he stated his belief that it would be a serious mistake for us to withdraw completely from China, even though the forces we had left there were very small. He said the situation in the large cities during the coming winter would be most severe because of lack of coal, the transit of which over the railway lines from the north would become increasingly difficult. . . .

The Communist tactics are in general on the hit-and-run order, although of late months they have been somewhat bolder and have indicated a willingness to take on fairly large-scale engagements. There are indications of improvements in the divisional organization, and for the first time, recently, the Nationalist government troops encountered steady battery fire from 75s [field artillery], indicating the possession of a substantial amount of this ammunition.

---

[7] This was Major General Samuel L. Howard, USMC. He had commanded the 4th Marines at Corregidor and spent the rest of the war as a Japanese prisoner.

[In another diary note of about this time Forrestal indicated
that he thought it "most regrettable" that the abilities of Major
General Leslie R. Groves, who had been military commander of
the atomic bomb project, were no longer being employed in this
field.[8] The general's name was brought up at a Cabinet luncheon
a few days later.

14 July 1947   *Cabinet Lunch*
    . . . The Attorney General [Clark] reported he had had a
visit from David Lilienthal, chairman of the Atomic Energy
Commission, on Saturday, at which Lilienthal charged General
Groves with the spreading of stories inimical to the AEC, particularly with reference to the lack of security, as brought out
in recent days by the announcements of theft of top secret information at Los Alamos. The Secretary of War said he was
confident that there was no substance in these stories, that
Groves had conducted himself with complete propriety so far
as any remarks about the AEC, or its chairman, or the lack of
security.

[Forrestal's own ideas about armament in general are well illustrated by a letter he wrote at this time to his friend Ralph
Bard, who had served under him as Under Secretary of the Navy
and was now Deputy American Representative on the United
Nations Commission on Conventional Armaments.

To Ralph A. Bard, 11 July 1947
    . . . The thing that I think we have to hammer home is the
fact that there is practically *no* basis for any realistic talk about
disarmament until the Russians have made it manifest and
clear that they want the substance and not merely the sham of
peace in the world. By this I mean cooperation in a swift conclusion of treaties with Germany and Japan, and real cooperation in the economic and social reconstruction of Europe. If
they don't mean business along these lines, I know you will
agree that even the talk of disarmament is highly dangerous,

---

[8] Diary, 8 July 1947.

because of the American tendency always to take for granted that other nations have the same objectives as ourselves. . . .

I am most apprehensive of our people's mistaking the *discussion* of disarmament for the fact. There is plenty of evidence that this tendency is already underway. (Did you know that Mike Robertson was teamed up with Jo Davidson in a group to prevent World War III? ! ! !). . .

[And Forrestal must have responded sympathetically when Bernard Baruch argued a few days later for a far more activist policy toward the Russians.

15 July 1947   *Meeting—Bernard Baruch*

Met with Mr. Bernard Baruch, Eisenhower, Patterson after lunch. Baruch feels that we must begin to use immediately all possible economic measures in our relations with Russia. By this he means pre-emptive and preclusive buying of scarce commodities. He would, for example, buy the entire surplus of the Cuban sugar crop. He would also buy coffee and send gold to other countries in exchange for their raw materials. . . .

[Through all this Forrestal had been engrossed with his immediate problems of the naval budget and unification. As for the budget, the House had agreed to the Taber economies and sent them to the Senate in May. In June Senator Saltonstall, as chairman of the naval subcommittee of the Senate Appropriations Committee, worked out an astute compromise, based on an increase of $177 million in the new funds to be voted, balanced by a cutback in old funds already appropriated, mainly for shore establishments and construction. While total expenditures would actually be less under this Senate proposal than under the House bill, more money would be available for the active fleet. On July 11 House and Senate conferees agreed on a bill following virtually the terms of the Saltonstall compromise. A spending budget of about $4 billion was not great in comparison with later ideas of the real need, but the fact that it was no worse was another victory for Forrestal's patient and careful methods. On the 17th he wrote to Mr. Taber.

To Representative John Taber, 17 July 1947

Now that the smoke of battle has cleared away on the Navy Money bill for 1947-48, I wish to send you my appreciation for the hard work that you and your staff put in with us on this task. We did not always see eye to eye—it has been my experience that the seeker after funds and the provider of them usually do not—but even in our differences we always had courteous and considerate treatment from you.

It is my strong belief that intelligent cooperation between committees of the Congress and the Executive Departments of the government is best secured by free and continuous exchange of pertinent information between them. . . .

[The long battle over unification was also building to its climax. Early in June the Senate committee had finally sent the bill to the floor, but the House committee was still holding exhaustive hearings. On Wednesday afternoon, June 25, Forrestal gave a party at his Georgetown home for a lengthy list of congressmen (of both parties), Cabinet officials and naval officers and their wives. One topic was the President's veto of the Taft-Hartley bill; "all expressed regrets," according to Forrestal's note, "at the temper of the President's veto message," but at the same time "all were united in expressing good will toward the President and none challenged the honesty of his belief, although some had the feeling that it was a 'lawyer's brief' rather than his own opinion." Doubtless more interesting to Forrestal at the moment was Representative James Wadsworth's report "that he had been able to force Hoffman's hand [Representative Clare E. Hoffman of Michigan, chairman of the Committee on Executive Expenditures, to which the unification bill had been referred in the House] and cut short hearings on the unification measure—such hearings will now end next Tuesday. . . . I told Wadsworth, Admiral King was now ready to endorse the Senate bill, and Wadsworth thought this might be the reason that Hoffman had decided not to call him."

Later the same day Forrestal had Senators Saltonstall and George for supper aboard his naval yacht, the U. S. S. *Sequoia*. "Senator George repeated his warm personal feeling toward the

[President and expressed regret that there was so little consultation between the President and some of his old associates in the Senate. He thought that some of the opposition in the Congress to the President was unnecessary. . . ." [9]

By the beginning of July, with the unification bill successfully pried out of the hands of Mr. Hoffman's committee, its passage began to seem certain. It had been shaped, slowly, skillfully and patiently, very largely in accordance with Forrestal's ideas. A major work was reaching its completion; and Forrestal, who had so often expressed his desire to leave government service, was facing a moment when he might gracefully do so. One of the diary's rare notes on party politics, occurring at this time, may possibly hint at such an idea.

15 July 1947 *Lunch—Paul Fitzpatrick*

Lunch today with Paul Fitzpatrick, New York Democratic chairman. He said that the situation in that state was disintegrating from the standpoint of the Democratic Party chiefly because of the failure of the party in Washington to support the local chairman. O'Dwyer [William O'Dwyer, then Democratic Mayor of New York], he said, was not helpful. There is now no organization such as Tammany used to be in New York with its associations and links upstate, and no one man to whom anyone could talk in the party in New York City. He felt that the state was not hopelessly lost to Dewey [Thomas E. Dewey, the Republican Governor of New York who was to run for President the following year], but unless some steps toward organization were taken it would be most difficult to carry. He pointed out that unless it were carried, history indicated the strong possibility of failure to elect any Democratic candidate.

[Both history and Fitzpatrick were wrong in this case; Dewey carried New York in 1948 but Truman was re-elected.

From other sources there is little doubt that Forrestal was seeing the end of his career as an appointive official. And then a new factor suddenly supervened. As early as mid-July it was publicly

---

[9] Diary, 25 June 1947.

[reported that Judge Patterson, a "logical" choice to fill the new
post of Secretary of Defense, had submitted his resignation from
the government and that Forrestal would be appointed. Patterson resigned on the 18th, the day before the House passed its
own version of the unification bill. If Forrestal had any official intimation that he was to be the nation's first Secretary of Defense, his diary gives no hint of it; but it was at once generally
assumed that the appointment would go to him. Another week
went by while the House and Senate versions of the bill were
adjusted in conference.

On the 22nd Forrestal was lunching with Saltonstall, Sherman and Clifford; apparently they were talking over the executive order which was to accompany the enactment of the law.

22 July 1947   *Lunch—Unification*

We discussed unification and in particular the question of
several clauses in the form of definitions of rules and measures
[roles and missions] for the Navy, Navy Air and Marine Corps.
I told Senator Saltonstall that my reasons for regarding these
reservations as of little consequence were derived mainly from
my experience in business. I said that "there were very few
occasions that I could recall where the language of the mortgage had made the bonds good."

[There was to be more than one occasion in the future on which
the "language of the mortgage" was to prove an inadequate answer to the intricate problems of Service missions, but at all
events the Senate adopted the conference report on July 24, the
House on July 25; and Congress was to adjourn next day. Not
until then, at the last moment and under curiously dramatic circumstances, did the President definitely declare his choice.

Forrestal was at the White House on the morning of July 26.
The President's aged mother, Mrs. Martha E. Truman, was sink-
ing in her last illness and the President's plane was ready at the
National Airport to take him to her in Missouri. He was waiting
only to receive the engrossed copy of the unification bill from the
Capitol.

26 July 1947   *Conversation—President Truman*

Talked with the President. The President told me he proposed to send my name up as Secretary of Defense. Bob Patterson wouldn't take it. He said he had talked to him about it, but Patterson was so hard put to it for money that he felt he was unable to stay longer in government. I told the President I would have been very happy to serve under Patterson for as long as I could be useful to both of them. The President repeated that Patterson could not be considered for the reason stated.

He said he would like me to have my offices in the Pentagon. He was critical of some of the people in the Navy and Air Force who, he said, had not gone along with him after the agreement of last January had been reached. He specifically mentioned Admiral Nimitz and General Vandegrift. I said in the case of the first officer he was in a most difficult position in the Naval Service, and that in my opinion if it had not been for his endorsement of the legislation we would not have had the result we got.

I asked the President whether he intended that control of the military establishment should be in civilian hands, because I said that was the way I proposed to exercise the powers in this job. He repeated most emphatically that that was his concept and that I had his full approval in proceeding on that basis.

He asked me about the posts for Air and for the Navy. I said Mr. Sullivan was obviously the man to succeed me, and as regards Symington, that I felt he was an able man, the only reservation I had was whether two people who had known each other as long as he and I had could work successfully together. I said one's friends were frequently more difficult as partners than strangers.

We talked for about forty-five minutes, the President then being in a position of awaiting receipt of the unification bill from Congress before he took off for his mother's bedside at Grandview, Missouri. Among other things I asked him how he accounted for Hitler's decision to make war in 1939

when he actually had in his hands all the cards necessary to
dominate Europe. He replied that the man had simply become
drunk with power. He said he thought Hitler had made two
great mistakes: (1) The decision to attack Poland; (2) Failure to invade England after the fall of France. The President remarked that Hitler was terrified at this event—something which Eisenhower showed five years later could be done.
I remarked that there was a vast difference between the two
cases, that Hitler had the troops but lacked the ships, and I
could not help but think at the time that it illustrated the
work that we had to do to impress on him the fact that the
crossing of a body of water is not a casual business.

[Ultimately, the President departed for the airport; and he was
already on board his personal plane (popularly known as the
Sacred Cow) when, shortly after noon, the bill was finally
rushed to him there by the Congress officials. He signed it sitting
in the plane; he also signed the executive order defining the roles
and missions of the Services, and he signed the nomination of
James Forrestal as Secretary of Defense. The nomination was
sped back to the Senate as the plane took off. Over Cincinnati
the President learned that his mother had died about half an
hour after he left the Washington airport.

Forrestal, for his part, went to lunch with Robert Lovett,
whom he found greatly disturbed over a message of that morning from Bevin, saying that Britain was virtually bankrupt. Lovett
"was deeply concerned because he doubted if this country would
be willing to produce the sums necessary" to maintain Britain's
world position. The note continues:

26 July 1947   *Lunch—Robert Lovett*
    . . . He spoke of the lack of planning for peace in the State
Department and the casual and off-the-cuff decisions of the
late President, and referred to Churchill's remark that at Yalta
he had been dealing with the "shell of a man" and not the
man himself.[10] Lovett added that the great political error in

---

[10] One might, perhaps, compare this with Mr. Stettinius's report at the time (see
p. 35) that Churchill was "going through some sort of a menopause."

the postwar period was the failure to insist upon the writing of peace treaties while our troops and military power were still evident in Europe. Nothing, he said, could have stopped the American forces which were at that time deployed in Germany.

[It was hardly, one may think, a happy introduction to the immense new responsibilites which were descending upon Forrestal's shoulders. But the die was now cast; yielding, as he had done before and was to do again, to the belief that it was his duty to serve, Forrestal had made his decision. The Senate was prompt. As the President's plane winged westward, the nomination was sent to committee. It was favorably reported the same afternoon, and in the early hours of July 27, in an end-of-session jam, Forrestal was confirmed as Secretary of Defense by a voice vote a few minutes before adjournment.

CHAPTER VIII

First Secretary of Defense

I

[The new machinery of unified, though not unitary, defense had been authorized; the arduous and complex task of setting it up and putting it in motion had fallen upon Forrestal's shoulders, and it was to occupy his time and energies for months to come. As the interview in which he was offered the appointment showed, he was to approach the task in good accord with the President, but not, perhaps in complete agreement. He had been Mr. Truman's second choice; the interview left him with the feeling that the former field artillery captain still failed to comprehend sea power, while he was to be given a Secretary of Air about whom he had misgivings. It was Symington himself who at one point had suggested that the Secretary of Defense should have power of removal over the Department Secretaries;[1] Forrestal had opposed this, urging that instead the Defense Secretary should have a large hand in their appointment, to begin with. His doubts as to his ability to work with Symington were now put very diplomatically; they were not acceded to, and the results were to be unhappy. No reservations, however, clouded his letter to the President.

To the President, 28 July 1947
My dear Mr. President:
    The fact that we have a bill which, as you have expressed it, gives us the beginnings of a national military policy for the first

---

[1] See p. 222.

time since 1798, is due first and last to your own patience, tact and knowledge of legislative procedures. With the exception of Clark Clifford, I know probably more than anyone else how much restraint you had to exercise under trying and sometimes provoking circumstances. I believe the result will justify your forbearance.

As I told you Saturday, I will do my best to live up to the confidence you have reposed in me. If I fail, I know it will not be because of lack of support from you.

[The appointment brought Forrestal to a new apex of popular acclaim. Of all the congratulatory letters that came flooding in, he entered only one—from Myron C. Taylor, an old friend who was then serving as personal representative of the President at the Vatican—in his diary.

27 July 1947 *Congratulations—Myron Taylor*
Sunday
Killingworth, Locust Valley, Long Island
Dear Jim:
Congratulations on another great honor—stepping stones in a great career. May this one lead to world peace. If that is impossible, then to effective war and enduring peace in timely sequence.

Sincerely,
/s Myron Taylor

[The fact that this letter alone found place in the diary suggests how closely it expressed Forrestal's own concept of his responsibilities. Equally revealing are the many letters he wrote in acknowledgment. His most frequent expression was in the form: "Thanks for your note. I hope I can justify your confidence. I will do my best. . . ." (To Representative Jay LeFevre, Republican of New York, 29 July 1947.) But to his older associates he expressed the doubts that accompanied his sense of dedication: "This office," he wrote to Robert Sherwood on August 27, "will probably be the greatest cemetery for dead cats in history," and the note recurred.

To W. Stuart Symington, 29 July 1947

. . . If I don't do this job well I certainly can't blame lack
of support—although, as you observed this morning, honey-
moons are soon over and roses are soon followed by bricks.

To Walter Dunnington, 30 July 1947

I hope it is patriotism and not egoism that makes me continue in this life—one never can be sure. Of one thing I am
sure, however, and that is that this is my final contribution. At
the end of the year both the Army and the country will probably be grateful for that.

To Dean Mathey, 4 August 1947

. . . When I finish this assignment my public service is ended,
period. You have got to like politics if you want to be successful
in it, and I frankly don't.

To A. L. Barach, 5 August 1947

Thanks for your note and your good wishes. I shall certainly
need the latter—and probably the combined attention of Fulton Sheen and the entire psychiatric profession by the end of
another year!

["The difficulty of government work," he said in another letter
of this time (to Ernest Havemann, an editor of *Life*, 26 August 1947), "is that such work not only has to be well done, but
the public has to be convinced that it is being well done. In
other words, there is a necessity both for competence and exposition, and I hold it is extremely difficult to combine the two
in the same person." And he added later in this letter one of his
favorite dicta: "The removal of human frictions is a substantial
part ["90 per cent," he often put it] of administration, whether
it is in government or business." Finally, in still another letter,
he stated at greater length his concept of the problem before him.

To William C. Potter, 2 September 1947

. . . I have no illusions that anyone down here can do much
more than see that too many blocks are not put in the way of the

country's effort and power, because it is the country that does the job. My chief misgivings about unification derived from my fear that there would be a tendency toward overconcentration and reliance on one man or one-group direction. In other words, too much central control—which, I know you will agree, is one of the troubles with the world today. A lot of admittedly brainy men believe that governments, history, science and business can be rationalized into a state of perfection. These ideals all come out of the same hat, whether it is one worn by a German, a Russian or a Stafford Cripps! . . .

[It was in this mood and with this attitude toward his own role in the undertaking that Forrestal took up his new responsibilities. As these letters well show, his was a character more complex, more subtle and more sensitive than was generally supposed. In appearance and often in manner he seemed grim, tight-lipped and pugnacious; he did not suffer fools easily and he could at times be abrupt. Yet his whole approach and method were actually at the farthest remove from those of the narrow-minded administrative martinet; he had a deep and discerning distrust of dictation in any form, even his own, and his constant impulse was to understand and to adjust rather than to rush to conclusions and issue orders. Believing that nine-tenths of administration lay in "the removal of human frictions," he advanced to a task fraught probably with more various kinds of human friction than any other in government.

Actually, although appointed and confirmed, he did not even take the oath of office until nearly two months later, preferring to wait until the first elements of the new mechanism could be installed. In the meanwhile, the international pressures that the new defense structure would have to face seemed to grow only more and more serious.

4 August 1947   Lunch—Secretaries Marshall, Harriman, Snyder
Lunch today with Marshall, Harriman, Snyder. Marshall expressed his deep concern with the implications that might be drawn from the withdrawal of British troops from Greece and Italy. He has wired Bevin in strong language, protesting against

the British action in presenting the United States with such decisions as the one of last February advising us that we would have to accept the responsibility for Greece and this most recent one of complete withdrawal from southern Europe. He asked Douglas to inquire of Bevin whether this indicates a fundamental change in British policy. Bevin replied to this in the negative.

Harriman gave it as his analysis that the decision of the Attlee Cabinet on troop reduction was influenced substantially by the pressure from the extreme Left. . . . He gave it as his view that they would have small hope of getting additional help from the United States unless they faced up squarely to their problem, which essentially is that of inducing their people to go back to hard work. He thought the spectacle of Britain endeavoring to carry out the drastic program of nationalization and socialization of industry could not be underwritten by Americans.

Snyder reported that in Rio the British were building a very impressive and magnificent million-dollar embassy and that the Brazilians could not understand why we loaned money to Britain and denied it to Brazil.

Marshall asked me to explore the possibility of stepping up gradually our naval forces in the Mediterranean and also of increasing the frequency of [naval] visits to Greek ports. He said he was most anxious to avoid anything in the nature of bluff, in other words, of making a gesture on which we could not go through, but he felt it might smoke out the depth of the Russian purpose to adhere to the line of intransigence which they have taken.

Saw Admiral Conolly, who was here from London, in the evening and he reported on the serious and far-reaching character of the British economic crisis.

8 August 1947   *Cabinet*

Secretary Marshall made a brief presentation of the world situation.

Conditions both economically and politically critical in Britain, Greece, France, Italy. He expressed sharp resentment of the British action in precipitating *now* their decision for troop withdrawal from Greece, pointing out that they had substantial numbers in Japan, Germany and elsewhere which could be reduced without any effect, and also pointing out that the announcement of the decision for the withdrawal from Greece was timed to occur the day after the Russian veto in the United Nations of the proposal for a continuing border commission on the Greek-Macedonian-Yugoslav frontier.

The British decisions and actions were obviously conditioned by political considerations at home, principally the desperate struggle for survival of the Labour Party.

Harriman, asked for his views, expressed himself as being most concerned over the course of British policy. The extreme Left-wingers, Laski-Zilliacus-Crossman [2] group, have been pressing:

    (a)   To reduce British military strength.

    (b)   To get out of Greece.

    (c)   To push even more vigorously on nationalization of industry.

It is a serious question whether we should underwrite the stability of a government whose objectives seem to be moving farther to the Left as they lose the support of even moderate Liberals. . . .

He [Marshall] read a monograph on Palestine in which the conclusion was drawn that the British are not keeping troops in Palestine on account of their oil interests in particular. Aside from the normal British doggedness in sticking out a difficult and unpleasant situation, he thought there was no particularly strong British desire to retain the mandate over Palestine. There were, he said, many different views among the Jews in this country as to the conduct of the various elements now active in Palestine. [The Palestine terrorist organizations were at this time taking a prominent place in the news.] The British withdrawal, he felt, would be followed by a bloody struggle between the Arabs and Jews. (Lovett feels that in the first instance the Jews would be successful, owing to their superior

---

[2] Konni Zilliacus and Richard H. S. Crossman, an editor of the *New Statesman and Nation*, both Labour Members of Parliament.

weapons, but [added that the Arabs would reply with a protracted and bloody guerrilla war].)

The President interjected at this time that he proposed to
make no announcements or statements upon the Palestine situation until after United Nations had made its finding. He said
he had stuck his neck out on this delicate question once, and
he did not propose to do it again. (He referred to his statement about the desirability of the British admitting a hundred
thousand Jews, made in the autumn of 1945.) . . .

[Forrestal's deepening interest in the Palestine dilemma was
     closely related to the strategic importance of Middle Eastern oil
     supplies. At the next Cabinet the oil question came up in a some-
     what different context.

15 August 1947   *Cabinet*

There was some discussion of prices and the President expressed interest in the Attorney General's program for an inquiry into the present high price level. The Attorney General
reported that they had been able to secure a reduction in the
price of soap by conference with the three main companies
producing soap. I inquired of Mr. Clark: "If the companies
reduced prices in cahoots, would you still sue them?" [The reply is not recorded.]

The Acting Secretary of State, Mr. Lovett, reported a growing apprehension on his part, flowing out of the increasing
tendency toward "austerity" programs in Britain, which he
said he expected to spread to other countries. If it did so, he
felt it would finally communicate itself to the Western Hemisphere and would defeat the American efforts for international
free trade. The so-called dollar shortage is really a production
shortage. England is not producing what it needs, is trying to
make up the difference by reduction of imports and stimula-
tion of sales to so-called sterling areas. . . . The Secretary of
War said this problem was highlighted by Germany [where
coal production per man was 15 per cent or less than that in
the United States]. . . . He said he thought it was high time,

regardless of the Russian charges of American imperialism, to have American business management go into Germany to facilitate the production of Ruhr coal.

I said that we didn't need to wait for the development of this tendency in the Western Hemisphere, that it was already here, and cited a piece in this morning's *Wall Street Journal* on Mexico, which is also complaining of the "dollar shortage." The fact is that Mexico has substantial oil deposits which could be developed if American companies undertook the job. Oil is in short supply. It would create dollars for Mexico, but the Mexicans show little interest in taking advantage of this national asset because of their political feeling that once having expropriated American oil properties, they would be admitting failure of their nationalization of the oil industry.

Lovett said that he expected the effects of this "disease" to begin to appear here about October, and to reach its full force by next March. . . . Schwellenbach, the Secretary of Labor, asked why it was that England was in such a difficult position if it was a fact, as the statisticians reported, that their production was now above 1938. Lovett and I explained to him that the present British difficulty arose largely from the fact that income from shipping and foreign investments, which formerly had produced the $2 billion annual deficit between what they exported and what they bought, had been wiped out during the war.

I made the comment, in addition, that a corollary of the disease that Mr. Lovett mentioned would be the spread of another disease in this country, which, as a point of fact, is already developing: "Let Europe go." I said that there would be a resurgence of isolationism, that the isolationists would claim that we were wrong to have fought Germany and exterminated Hitler, thus finding ourselves in a much worse position—that of the Russians swarming over Europe and no balance of power available to check them.

[The extent to which all their problems were interrelated is well exemplified by the Cabinet meeting on August 29, at which

[Palestine, the British economy, Marshall Plan aid, power resources and even Democratic politics in the Northwest all
came up.

29 August 1947   *Cabinet*

Lovett reported on the foreign situation. . . . On the negative side he placed the increasing complexity of the Palestine
situation. . . . He said that the tendency in the General Assembly toward taking decisions by majority vote could consti-
tute a danger to the United States. There was some indication
of a lash-up between the Asiatic peoples and those of the Middle East on a color-versus-white basis. He said while much emphasis had been placed upon the distress and commotion
among the Jews, there was an equal danger of solidifying sentiment among all of the Arabian and Mohammedan peoples
against us.

The Paris Conference [of prospective recipients of American aid] . . . had been getting down to fairly solid work. He
read parts of a cable he had sent . . . in which he had underlined the fact that what the sixteen nations assembled at Paris
agreed upon must not merely be a shopping list on the United
States.

The President agreed with Lovett that when the European
nations had completed their studies and we had completed ours
it would probably be necessary to summon Congress back to
Washington, although he said it was a prospect he did not contemplate with pleasure.

Snyder reported on the recent financial conferences with the
British. The basic difficulty with Britain is not the lack of mod-
ernized mining technique and machinery but rather difficulties
that spread through their whole economic structure. . . . The
crux of the whole matter is that men will only work for incentives, and the British are not producing the incentives, except in the form of dog races, soccer matches and horse racing.

Harriman reported on his recent visit to the Northwest. He
said a primary issue out there was going to be a greater need for
power. The government has taken commitments to provide this
increased power; the private power companies for that reason

have not increased their plants, and the net result is going to be a shortage, out of which political capital can be made.

Democratic leadership in the Northwest has a serious problem in handling the Communist infiltration into the party organization. They are fully aware of the problem but do not find it easy of solution.

[Meanwhile the situation in Greece continued to deteriorate.

31 August 1947   Greek Situation—Meeting with Robert Lovett
Visit this morning from Lovett, Under Secretary of State, who outlined to me a paper which he said would be delivered to me as Secretary of Defense within the next week or ten days, dealing with our next course of action in the event of a Communist take-over in Greece. The paper points out that we have to accept the fact that the original concept of one world, upon which the United Nations was based, is no longer valid and that we are in political fact facing a division into two worlds. (This was the subject of an exposition made at the War Department yesterday by the State Department people and which Eisenhower spoke about yesterday afternoon.) Congress, Lovett pointed out, placed restrictions upon the use of American troops in Greece; and testimony of Judge Patterson and Dean Acheson was always in the sense, and several times specifically stated, that our aid was to go mainly for economic reconstruction and would be military only to the extent of advice and consultation. In passing the Greek-Turkish Aid law we had imposed upon ourselves and had advertised to the world three conditions under which we would withdraw: (1) At the request of a legally constituted Greek government; (2) at the request of the United Nations, on their taking over of our responsibility; (3) on our own decision if we concluded that our efforts were not getting results.

He said that what he was concerned with was that we should initiate practical steps now to meet all contingencies which might be created by withdrawal, such as, for example, seeing to it that we get into the country *now*, operatives who will provide sources of information to us and trouble for the other side; plans for the setting up of a government in the island of Crete which we would recognize and which would be the base for operations of this character.

I said that before we proceeded to this kind of planning I thought we should take all the steps possible to prevent Greece going Communist and that the first of these steps should be the calling by the President, on his return, of the congressional leaders, to advise them of conditions in Greece and to seek their advice on the question of sending American forces into the country. I said that whatever decision was taken, whether it involved action of this kind or withdrawal, should be shared in by Republican leaders, otherwise the President would be exposed to a most difficult domestic political situation next year. Lovett conceded this point and said he had already taken steps to secure the help of John Foster Dulles in a more active fashion in the United Nations. In the event of further trouble in Greece and the continued veto by Russia and Poland of the submission of the report of the border commission or a proposal to have a continuing mission to solve the problem—it was his plan to go to the General Assembly on the request of the Greek government under Article 51 (threat to peace, actual disturbance, or active aggression). He was fairly sanguine over getting positive action out of the General Assembly, with only one reservation, and that was the support of Britain. I said this was fundamental to everything we were now talking about and we had better get it clarified at the earliest possible moment. He said he had made this the subject of an "eyes only" message to Lew Douglas this morning, suggesting to Douglas that he make one or two very frank speeches for internal consumption in Britain.

Lovett agreed that the Russian signing of the peace treaties last week[3] was undoubtedly related to their belief that they

---

[3] The peace treaties with the five former German satellites—Italy, Finland, Hungary, Rumania and Bulgaria—negotiated at the Paris Conference in 1946, were formally signed on February 10, 1947. They were ratified on various dates thereafter by the defeated powers. The reference here is to the ratification by the satellite regimes of Rumania and Bulgaria on August 22 and 25 respectively.

had extended and consolidated their grip on the Balkans. He did not believe, however, that this was a sudden decision—they have always said they expected to sign by September 1, but (in his opinion) they have always had the feeling that they would have their position consolidated in the Balkans by that date. He believes, however, that even if they succeed in all their objectives, the possibility of keeping the resulting framework together will not be altogether easy, and that they will find that exposure of their people to the same guerrilla tactics which they are now employing in Greece will make their position very uneasy. . . .

[Washington's irritation over London's policy in Greece, reflected in so many of Forrestal's diary entries during this period, was paralleled by London's irritation over Washington's policy in the other Mediterranean trouble spot, Palestine.

4 September 1947   *Cabinet Lunch*

At the end of the lunch Hannegan [Postmaster General] brought up the question of the President's making a statement of policy on Palestine, particularly with reference to the entrance of a hundred and fifty thousand Jews into Palestine. He said he didn't want to press for a decision one way or the other but simply wanted to point out that such a statement would have a very great influence and great effect on the raising of funds for the Democratic National Committee. He said very large sums were obtained a year ago from Jewish contributors and that they would be influenced in either giving or withholding by what the President did on Palestine. . . . I pointed out that the President's remarks on Palestine of a year ago did not have the expected effect in the New York election. [It was added] that the President was prompted to make the statement by Rabbi [Abba Hillel] Silver of Cincinnati [actually of Cleveland], who was neither a Democrat nor friendly to Truman, and said that the net effect of the President's observation was to make the British exceedingly angry, particularly when it was coupled with the rejection by the Grady Com-

mittee Report.[4] It amounted to a denunciation of the work
of his own appointee. It also resulted in Secretary of State
Byrnes washing his hands of the whole Palestine matter, which
meant that it was allowed to drift without action and practically without any American policy.

[On September 10 Forrestal got some interesting views on the
   domestic political situation from Harold Stassen.

10 September 1947   *Harold Stassen*
  . . . He [Stassen] gave it as his own opinion that he was
gaining vis-à-vis both Taft and Dewey and that his tactics of
discussing the issues of the day had forced both of his opponents into an earlier discussion of central issues than they had
planned or wanted. He said the current poll in Iowa showed
him gaining and Dewey slipping. He felt the result of yesterday's election in Pennsylvania, where the issue of the Taft-Hartley law was posed, gave a different index of the public thinking
on the labor question than Mr. Truman had expected. With regard to Europe he felt that the country was ahead of Washington in its willingness to support a strong and constructive policy
in Europe, but that more leadership and more facts needed to
be given. The country would support the implementation of
our Greek policy even to the extent of sending troops. He has
great confidence in Griswold's integrity and courage [Chief of
the American Mission for Aid to Greece] although he has not
seen him in any post of difficult administration.
  He expressed confidence in General Marshall and asked me
to send him his regards.

[Forrestal lunched the same day with Marshall.

10 September 1947   *Lunch with Marshall*
  Lunch today with Marshall, Harriman, Baruch, Lovett, and

[4] See p. 189n. When, in the previous summer, the President appointed his special
Cabinet Committee on Palestine, Henry F. Grady, a San Francisco businessman
(later our first Ambassador to India), served as chairman of the deputies who
conducted the actual negotiations with the British.

Kennan. Purpose was to get Baruch's views on the extension of help to Europe. He expressed a strong disinclination to continue American aid unless we had more facts and figures on which to base judgment. He believes both the British and French have assets which they have not yet disclosed. . . .

Lovett tried to emphasize the critical nature of the food problem and that a relatively small amount of the total wheat that we consumed in this country would mean the difference between collapse of the present Italian government and its salvation.

With regard to the British, Lovett said: There had been a great deterioration in the ability and quality of the British governmental staffs, that the people in the present government had displayed a recklessness in dealing with the July monetary crisis that amounted almost to anarchy. They are focused on the goal of establishing a pattern of life for Britain based on the Labour Party philosophy, and are willing to accept almost any penalties to achieve it. They do not tell their own people the truth. One of our difficulties in dealing with them on uranium is that they have made public promises that atomic energy can provide a solution for all of Britain's fuel problems, against the fact that it is already clear that use of atomic energy for fuel and power is a number of years in the future. . . .

Part of the problem, he said, was the British desire to preserve the validity of the pound sterling as a medium of international exchange. They had practically invited the draft on sterling which culminated in the crisis of mid-July. . . . Baruch repeated the suggestion that he has made before that whatever additional credits are given to any of the European countries, including Britain, they should be advanced through a consortium of American businessmen to an equivalent consortium of business people . . . in the countries which we desire to aid. This would keep it on a private rather than a governmental level. He said it was clear to his mind that it *is* to our interest and that he was willing to pay a very high price for it, but that we must have more facts. . . .

Lovett did not agree that if Britain went it meant an irreparable loss. That is, he . . . did not think that it followed

inevitably that Britain's collapse meant the collapse of the rest
of Europe. . . .

[They were wrestling, as the summer waned, with many issues,
  doubts, possibilities, uncertain future considerations. At this moment, however, real and immediate crisis suddenly loomed, a
  crisis that was to propel Forrestal himself into his new office.

15 September 1947   *Italian Peace Treaty*
  The Italian Peace Treaty became effective today. A line between Yugoslavia and Italy was originally determined by a
crayon drawing on a map. When surveying parties undertook
to establish this line in precise fashion it was found that it would
go through the middle of cities and villages. A resurvey was ordered, the result of which, territory-wise, was disadvantageous
to the Italians. American Ambassador Dunn [James C. Dunn,
Ambassador to Italy] telephoned the State Department that adherence to this line was against the national interests of Italy,
that it could be used to great advantage by Togliatti, the Communist leader, and probably would mean the fall of the De
Gasperi government. Army people replied that any attempt to
alter the line at this late date would almost inevitably result in
fighting, with the strong possibility that American troops
would be projected into the middle of it with obviously un-
foreseeable consequences. State then said it would adhere
to the original line but made it clear that it was a War Department decision. The War Department people refused to accept
this responsibility, saying that they were merely acting as trans-
mitters of the judgment of the Joint Chiefs of Staff to the
State Department, to the effect that the consequences of war had
to be considered a possibility if the line was altered. The State
Department finally agreed to accept the JCS paper in this
spirit.

[Here was a vivid example of just that kind of disconnection
  in policy which the new defense structure had been devised to
  overcome. That real dangers were involved was apparent before
  the day was out.

15 September 1947   *Admiral Wooldridge*

Wooldridge [Rear Admiral Edmund T. Wooldridge, Assistant Chief of Naval Operations] came in to see me this evening to say that the State Department had just had a message from Ambassador Dunn to the effect that Yugoslavia informed General Lee [Lieutenant General John C. H. Lee, commanding Mediterranean Theater of Operations] that they proposed to occupy Trieste. Lee, after consultation with Ambassador Dunn, who in turn communicated with the State Department, replied that if they did he would resist with all the force at his disposal.

I asked Wooldridge to check with Admral Nimitz on the wisdom of concentrating our naval forces—with particular reference to the aircraft carrier *Leyte* which is now at Smyrna.

I talked to Under Secretary Lovett of the State Department, who confirmed the information I had received from Wooldridge. He said the State Department was lodging a note of protest to the Yugoslav government in Belgrade. I asked him whether the British were taking parallel action. He said he assumed that they would because half of the troops in Trieste, although under Lee's command, were British. . . .

[President Truman at the moment was returning on board the U. S. S. *Missouri* from a visit to Brazil. As the crisis developed it seemed essential that the Secretary of Defense should assume his office.

16 September 1947   *Clark Clifford*

Clark Clifford informed me that he had yesterday afternoon radioed the President the central facts of the situation in Trieste and the Yugoslavia-Italian line. The President responded during the night with instructions that I should be sworn in immediately and take action to see that all available reinforcements were provided for General Lee. In the light of the failure of any worsening developments today, Clifford said he has decided to take the responsibility of not proceeding on this schedule and has cabled the President that conclusion with supporting reasons.

[Forrestal was sworn in at noon the following day, September 17, as first Secretary of Defense; Sullivan and Symington were sworn in on the 18th as the new Secretaries of the Navy and of Air. The Trieste crisis passed, and there is no further reference to it in the diary. But the President's prompt order to "provide all available reinforcements" for General Lee left behind it an obvious and embarrassing question: What reinforcements, in fact, did the United States possess against menaces which were now apparent in nearly every quarter of the globe?

II

[Since his confirmation, Forrestal had of course been occupied with the problems of setting up the new Military Establishment. A memorandum of August 18 to Royall (now Secretary of the Army) noted "a few subjects that I would like to talk over with you sometime at your convenience"; they included the correlation of the Army and Navy Reserve Officers Training Corps programs, the use of the Office of Naval Research by the Army and Air Force rather than the creation of new research offices by the other two, and "a detailed and carefully thought-through plan" for universal military training. "I have the impression," he added to the last, "that this has not yet been done. I think it will need to be done if it is to be effectively and successfully presented to the public."

At the end of August he was discussing plans for the organization of the Joint Staff (which the unification act had provided to serve the Joint Chiefs of Staff) with Major General A. M. Gruenther. Gruenther, who was to prove a valuable and able military administrator, was leaving his post as a deputy commandant of the War College to head the new body.

29 August 1947   *Lunch—General Gruenther*

. . . [Gruenther] made the observation that there was a fundamental difference in thinking between the Army and the Navy on the question of a Staff versus Committee system of arriving at decisions. I concurred, but I said the difference went deeper than that, that one had to realize and take into account a number of considerations: for example, the vast difference in the conduct of war on land masses and the kind of war that was fought in the Pacific; the inherent organizational differences between Army and Navy derived from the fact that the smallest unit the Army could employ was a division, whereas the Navy was accustomed to operating either a single PT or a task force of a thousand ships, and for that reason always had to be flexible. Gruenther admitted that there was this basic difference, both as regards the character of war and the character of organization.

I pointed out that the concept of the chain of command and the single commander simply could not operate in the South and Southwest Pacific where commanders were a thousand or two thousand miles apart, where communications were sporadic and unreliable, and where the fighting was of the most dispersed and varied character. I said I had the feeling that Eisenhower had no conception of the Pacific war and that our thinking in terms of planning for another war might have to be quite different from the planning and thinking for any aspect of the recent war. . . .

[On the day that Clifford told him that he should immediately take the oath, Forrestal was confronting further problems of adjustment raised by the act.

16 September 1947   *Lunch—General Norstad*
                                       and Admiral Ramsey

General discussion about the functions of the National Security Council—its relation to the President, the Cabinet, and to the Bureau of the Budget.

Norstad confirmed my impression that State under Acheson's leadership had been very dubious about the creation of the council and would undoubtedly try to castrate its effectiveness. It was his view, however, that it was an essential link because so many decisions that now had to be made were a composite of military and political questions. He did, however, express considerable misgivings about the extent of military participation in diplomatic decisions. This flowed, in his opinion, from the paucity of trained people in the State Department and the consequent necessity of drafting people from the military to fill in the gap. Continuance of this practice he regarded as not in the interests of the Military Establishment, which in due course would come to be attacked as exercising too powerful an influence upon our foreign policies. The actual facts of the matter, he said, were contrary to public impression—it was usually the military people who had to hold back the sporadic and truculent impulses of political people and diplomats who do not realize the consequences of aggressive action. He cited for an example the incident of last September when Yugoslavs shot down American fliers. Acheson was all for an immediate and aggressive use of American Air fighter power over Yugoslavia. Norstad at that time had to point out to him that such a demonstration would inevitably mean war and we would be exposing relatively green and untrained pilots to a superior and competent enemy. I said this was an example of what I believed the Security Council should be for: To make a careful examination of situations and incidents and to avoid "stumbling into war." The opposite, I said, was the *Panay* incident [in 1937, when Japanese airplanes sank the U. S. S. *Panay*, a river gunboat, in the Yangtze], where we should have seen to it that we went to war—if we had it would probably have avoided World War II.

[Again, at a buffet luncheon the next day for the heads of the new organization, Forrestal realized that the National Security Council might bring friction.

17 September 1947   *Meeting at 1:00 P. M.*

It is apparent that there is going to be a difference between the Budget, some of the White House staff and ourselves on the National Security Council—its functions, its relationship to the President and myself. I regard it as an integral part of the national defense setup and believe it was so intended by the Congress. As I have said earlier I regard it also not as a place to make policies but certainly as a place to identify for the President those things upon which policy needs to be made.

[At this buffet luncheon Forrestal had called together all of the key figures in the new National Military Establishment. Together they formed a kind of dramatis personae of Forrestal's administration, and as such it is worth listing them. Those who attended were: the three Service Secretaries—Royall of the Army, Sullivan of the Navy, Symington of the Air Force; the three military chiefs—Eisenhower, Nimitz and Spaatz and the head of their joint staff, Gruenther; the heads of four of the new national Military Establishment boards—Arthur M. Hill of the National Security Resources Board, Thomas J. Hargrave of the Munitions Board, Vannevar Bush of the Joint Research and Development Board, and Admiral Sidney W. Souers, executive secretary of the National Security Council; the President's special counsel, Clifford; the chief of the Central Intelligence Agency, Rear Admiral Roscoe H. Hillenkoetter; and Forrestal's own three assistants, Wilfred J. McNeil, Marx Leva and John H. Ohly.

A number of them were present at a meeting a few days later devoted to further discussion of the role of the National Security Council.

22 September 1947   *Meeting with War and Security Councils*

Meeting in my office today, following present: Royall, Symington and Sullivan, Eisenhower, Nimitz, Spaatz, Souers, Gruenther and Leva.

I said the purpose of the meeting was a preliminary discussion of procedures in the War Council [composed of the four Defense Secretaries and the three Chiefs of Staff] and in the Security Council, what category of subjects the War Council should discuss and what form they should be transmitted to the Security Council. The question arose as to whether the Security Council should make positive recommendations as to matters of policy and to whom they should make them. Secretary Royall stated that the council *should* make such recommendations. I expressed the view that we would have to be most careful to avoid (a) the appearance of either duplicating or replacing the functions of the Cabinet, and (b) giving the public the impression that our foreign policy was completely dominated by a military point of view.

I reported a conversation I had this morning with [Under] Secretary Lovett of the State Department on the question of Italy—whether if upon evacuation by American troops there should be subsequent formation of a Communist republic in the north, we should encourage an invitation from De Gasperi's government to send a military mission to Italy to reconstitute their army and otherwise put them in a position to resist Communist domination. I said that Lovett had made the statement that neither he nor the State Department was in a position to evaluate our capabilities in this direction. I had responded, I said, that by the same token the military Services were in no position to determine national policy on such a matter; that it was our job only to state the capabilities and then await instructions. Lovett said because of this mixture of interest between our two sides of government, it was obvious to him that such a subject afforded an example of what kind of business should come before the Security Council. I agreed and set some time during Friday for such a meeting.

Other subjects discussed briefly were Korea, the United Nations Police Force, and the work of the Committee on the Reduction of Conventional Armaments.

[Forrestal took time out in these days for one of his reminiscent lunches with former Secretary Byrnes.

18 September 1947   *James F. Byrnes*

Lunched today with Jimmy Byrnes. We talked about Russia and American policy from 1943 on. He said one of the difficulties, he thought, after Roosevelt's death, was that Stalin did not like Truman and had told him (Byrnes) so. I made the observation that Mr. Truman was the first one who had ever said "no" to anything Stalin asked—that he had good reason for liking FDR because he got out of him the Yalta Agreement, anything he asked for during the war, and finally an opportunity to push Communist propaganda in the United States and throughout the world.

[The Atomic Energy Commission had been rigorously separated by law from the Military Establishment; but inevitably its operations came within the purview of the Secretary of Defense. The deepening atmosphere of suspicion and disagreement surrounding its activities was evident from a visit on September 23 of Lewis Strauss, a member of the commission. Strauss was worried over a recent action of the AEC (against which he alone had voted) in releasing information on isotopes to other nations. Forrestal had no scientific knowledge as to the possible importance of the information but he was disturbed by "the fact that the AEC had acted without first checking with the Joint Chiefs of Staff. . . . I told him that the impression I had from members of the Military Liaison Committee with the AEC was a very unhappy one; they felt that, contrary to the public statements of Dr. Lilienthal as to cooperation, we were actually getting none."

Another organizational problem was involved in the appointment of Bush as head of the Resources and Development Board. When Forrestal took him to see the President the latter made some pungent observations on the trials of his office. Bush was under the impression that he did not have the full backing of the President in scientific matters because of a difference between them the year before over the National Science Foundation bill.

25 September 1947   *Meeting with President*
. . . The President objected to this bill mainly because it removed from him the right of naming the head of the foundation, which he felt was transgression of the prerogatives of the presidential office. Dr. Bush mentioned this at his meeting with the President today and pointed out that in the handing out of federal funds the President would need the advice of some professional body to protect him against the importunities of states and regions of the country on a political basis. I supported this view. . . . The President interpolated the remark that the Chief Executive of the United States had to spend most of his time soothing the sensitivities of the people he wanted to get to work for him. He mentioned the fact that he had spent fifteen minutes this morning listening to a man he had asked to

head up the Food Conservation program as to where he would rank as to protocol, this matter seeming to the individual concerned to be paramount to the job that he was asked to do. In short, the President said, the President of the United States has to spend a good part of his time saluting the backsides of a large number of people. . . .

[On September 26 the National Security Council held its first meeting, thus laying the cornerstone, as it were, of the new defense structure.

26 September 1947   *National Security Council*

First meeting of the National Security Council. *Present:* Royall, Sullivan, Symington, Hillenkoetter, Hill, Souers, Lovett and myself [in addition to the President].

Souers outlined the general scheme for organization of the Security Council. The President indicated that he regarded it as *his* council and that he expected everyone to work harmoniously without any manifestations of prima-donna qualities. I said that it was my conception of the Council that it would serve as an advisory body to the President, that he would take its advice in due consideration, but that determination of and decisions in the field of foreign policy would, of course, be his and the Secretary of State's. . . .

Admiral Hillenkoetter then presented a thumbnail review of the world situation in the order of priority of importance.

I then told the President that we had agreed yesterday that Mr. Lovett should present a review of one situation which he regarded as a typical example of the kind of subject upon which the Security Council's advice and thought would be useful to the State Department, namely, Italy.

Italy is in the middle of a struggle between the Communist Party on the extreme Left, the conservatives on the extreme Right, with the government of De Gasperi now in power representing the middle of the road. Togliatti leads the Communists and is mainly active in the north, where twenty-six million out of forty-five million Italians live. He has a working arrangement with Nenni, the leader of the Socialist Party.

Nenni he described as being under the delusion that he could "control" the Communists. Lovett sketched various situations which, if they developed, would call for quick decisions by the United States (decisions which he hoped could be pondered over in advance so that they would not be made under the frenzy and fury of last-minute crisis): If the Communists in the north should seize power and set up a so-called People's government, invite Tito to "help them maintain order," and then threaten the De Gasperi government in the south, what does the United States do?

He pointed out that our failure to act would mean the negation of any effort we had made in Turkey and Greece for the obvious reason that Italy lies athwart the line of communications to those regions. Furthermore, he said the whole position in the Middle East would be threatened to the extent that, with the line of communications through the Mediterranean dominated by a Russian satellite, both Iran and Iraq and Saudi Arabia would have to reassess their position vis-à-vis Russia.

[The National Security Council's own first meeting thus clearly defined its function. Echoes of the initial misgivings could be heard as late as the presidential campaign of 1948, however, when the Republican candidate, Governor Dewey, attacked the preponderance of military figures in foreign-policy making. Ultimately the law was changed, dropping the Secretaries of Army, Navy and Air Force from the council.

III

[Lovett's citation of Italy as a case in which quick decisions, which should be carefully pondered in advance, might have to be made was given only as an example; there were many others he might have chosen. A pregnant one came up at the Cabinet luncheon on the 29th.

29 September 1947   *Cabinet Lunch*

. . . Secretary Marshall said that he was giving close study to the question of getting out of Korea, that to many of his people in the State Department it seemed that the Russian offer to withdraw provided we did might be an opportunity. Harriman raised the question of whether we could get out without loss of face. That, Marshall said, was the aspect of the question to which he was giving most serious thought.

I said that at a meeting between the other Secretaries and myself this morning we had agreed, in view of the international situation, that we should play down the tendency to overzealousness and overtruculence by either Army or Navy officers or civilian representatives of the Departments. Marshall concurred wholeheartedly, said that in his opinion Vishinsky's speeches [Andrei Y. Vishinsky, then Deputy Foreign Minister of the Soviet Union and head of its United Nations delegation] were the best arguments we had to our own people and for that matter other nations; that if we could resist the temptation to respond in kind he felt we could get universal military training without much trouble.

I asked the President whether it would not be possible to lift the Jewish-Palestine question out of politics.

The President said it was worth trying to do although he obviously was skeptical. Anderson asked me what I would do if I were in the other party. I said that if I were in the other party I would listen patiently to the impact of this question on the security of the United States, and if it was dangerous to let it continue to be a matter of barter between the two parties, I felt confident that I would try to put it on a national and bipartisan basis.

[This last idea was one that had evidently been growing on Forrestal. He had opened it, in a more general way, to the President after the November election;[5] the latter still seemed as dubious of it as he had been on the earlier occasion, but Forrestal at least had his implied permission to try it. For months he was to pursue, with the greatest earnestness and persistence and at considerable cost to his own standing, the hope of taking Palestine "out of politics." Unfortunately the hope was vain; Palestine was "in politics" on both sides of the party line and (as

[5] See p. 218.

[had already been made evident) in the most direct and material way.

6 October 1947   *Cabinet Lunch*

. . . Hannegan brought up the question of Palestine. He said many people who had contributed to the Democratic campaign fund in 1944 were pressing hard for assurances from the administration of definitive support for the Jewish position in Palestine. The President said that if they would keep quiet he thought that everything would be all right, but that if they persisted in the endeavor to go beyond the report of the United Nations Commission there was grave danger of wrecking all prospects for settlement. Hannegan tried to press him on this matter but he was adamant.

[There is much about Palestine in the later pages of the diary. In evaluating Forrestal's position, it must not be forgotten that he had a very immediate sense of official responsibility in the matter. Three days after this Cabinet lunch he appeared before the Senate Committee on Small Business. At a time when American small businessmen were clamoring for steel, the administration had licensed the export of twenty thousand tons to build a pipeline in Saudi Arabia, and the committee had questioned the decision. Forrestal's testimony showed one major consideration which lay behind his whole attitude on Palestine.

9 October 1947   *Arabian Pipeline*

. . I took the position that because of the rapid depletion of American oil reserves and an equally rapidly rising curve of consumption we would have to develop resources outside the country. The greatest field of untapped oil in the world is in the Middle East. . . . We should not be shipping a barrel of oil out of the United States to Europe. From 1939 to 1946 world oil reserves . . . went up about 60 per cent while American discoveries added only about 6 per cent to ours. Until there were indications of new fields of substantial magnitude in the Western Hemisphere, I said, pipe for the Arabian pipeline should have precedence over pipe for similar projects in this country.

[And the Palestine issue, of course, intimately involved our relations with the Middle East and its oil supplies.

It was also at this time that Forrestal took up another activity, of more lasting effect than were his efforts to "depoliticize" Palestine. His appointment calendar shows that on September 29 he attended the first meeting, at the White House, of what came to be known as the Hoover Commission—the Commission on Organization of the Executive Branch of the Government. On October 6 he dined with Ex-President Hoover, the chairman, and discussed matters of organizing the work. Though Forrestal served as an active member of the commission throughout its deliberations he made almost no further references to the subject in his diary; and the few which do appear in no way suggest how largely the commission, established under the Lodge-Brown Act, owed its very existence to Forrestal.

Actually Forrestal was the catalyst that precipitated the Lodge-Brown Act. Having listened at dinner one evening to Senator Henry Cabot Lodge's ideas on government reorganization, Forrestal next morning sent his assistant, W. J. McNeil, whose ideas on the subject Forrestal knew and approved, to Lodge's office. Before McNeil left the Senator, the legislation that was to create the Hoover Commission had been written. Forrestal was offered the vice-chairmanship; but because he had his hands full organizing his own new job he declined, suggesting Dean Acheson instead.

Though Forrestal always insisted that he had no taste for politics, politics—in the larger sense and of many different kinds—were of course an inseparable part of his daily task. On October 6 he was in conversation with the President over various military appointments, a conversation that got farther afield before it was over. The President indicated that he wished to change his Naval Aide and added that "he wanted to find a place for Vaughan"—Major General Harry H. Vaughan, his Military Aide—"but until that time he would continue. In general I gathered his desire was to have one officer of top rank, such as ma-

[jor general, with three aides of captain and colonel rank below."
The entry continues:

6 October 1947   *The President*
. . . He asked me who I wanted for the Navy as CNO
[Chief of Naval Operations] and I told him the choices remained the same: Ramsey, Blandy and Denfeld; that I was
somewhat concerned about Denfeld's political activity. I told
him that I had had solicitation from a wide variety of sources,
including Jim Farley. However, it is obvious that the President would find Denfeld the easiest of the lot to work with.
[Admiral Lewis E. Denfeld was to receive the appointment,
which in turn was to have a somewhat unhappy ending.]
For the Army he agreed that Bradley was the obvious selection [General Omar N. Bradley, then heading the Veterans'
Administration], that he was unable to move Bradley until he
had someone to take his place at VA. This he found difficult. He
mentioned Hershey [Major General Lewis B. Hershey] and
Louis Johnson; thought the latter would do a good job if he
disassociated himself from his Legion connections, which he,
the President, thought he might find it difficult to do.
With regard to Eisenhower's presidential flirtation, he said
he had been amused to have Ike tell him upon his return from
Japan that he thought the President would have to face the
prospect of MacArthur's returning here in the spring to launch
a campaign for himself; on the other hand, another visitor to
MacArthur had returned the message from MacArthur warning the President that Eisenhower would be a candidate for
the presidency!
The President remarked that everybody seemed to get either
"Potomac fever" or "brass infection."
He remarked that he looked forward with deep misgiving
to another four years after 1948 in the White House. And that
if it were not his duty to run again in the face of world conditions, the delay in getting the peace treaties with Japan, Germany, Austria, etc., he would like to step aside.
He said he wanted to get a place for Vaughan, and that, having accomplished that, he would have taken care of everyone.

[At a dinner in New York a week later (it was an impressive affair, in memory of the celebrated Democratic Governor of New York, Alfred E. Smith) Forrestal found himself again involved in politics.

15 October 1947   Conversation with Governor Thomas E. Dewey

Sat next to Governor Dewey at dinner in New York last night. He started out by saying that the Food Conservation program was a failure and a farce. I challenged him sharply on this. . . . I said I could assure him it was nothing faked or insincere; that I had been in enough of the discussions to be confident of that, but I pointed out that any conservation program dealing with food was a highly complicated business and could only be made thoroughly effective after several months of both operation and planning. He said the administration had known and had had ample time to do the planning, that the shortage was apparent last summer. I replied that estimates of grain crops were always variables. . . .

He is obviously concerned about General Eisenhower's candidacy, and certain that he, Eisenhower, could dispose of it very quickly if he wished to and cited Marshall's action. He said Ike was obviously campaigning. He thought, however, that Eisenhower's boom had been launched too early and that the general did not realize how complicated his position would become the longer the boom is permitted to continue. Politics look very simple to the outsider whether he is a businessman or a soldier —it is only when you get into it that all the angles and hard work become apparent. . . .

I had the impression that he was, in general, in accord with the conduct of our foreign policy.

[Foreign policy, of course, was always with them. An ominous new development came on October 5, when Moscow with considerable fanfare announced the creation of a Communist Information Bureau to coordinate the activities of international Communism in the satellite countries, in France, Italy and elsewhere. This was widely accepted as an avowed revival of the old Com-

[intern (Communist International), which ostensibly had been "dissolved" in 1943; its effect, in the West, was that of a renewed declaration of "cold war." At the Cabinet of October 10 Lovett, "speaking for the State Department, complimented all agencies of government for the long hours and willing attitude which they had put in in facilitating" the Department's work, particularly in its study and organization of Marshall Plan aid. Lovett "went on to say that he felt confident that if American resources could be made available promptly, no great amount of money would be required in the immediate future to meet the challenge of the Soviets as implied in their reactivation of the Comintern."

Forrestal went on the same day for a lunch with Lovett, Bedell Smith, Robert D. Murphy (then political adviser in Germany with rank of ambassador), General Clay and others. Forrestal asked Bedell Smith whether the Russians wanted war; in answer, Smith cited a reply which he had heard that Stalin had made to a similar question: "Stalin said, we do not want war but the Americans want it even less than we do, and that makes our position stronger." The Ambassador went on to quote some recent Soviet oratory which certainly did not sound peaceful.

The extent to which the atomic bomb was slowly emerging as a pivotal point in American politico-strategic thought is indicated by an entry a few days later on a meeting with Ralph Bard—who represented the United States in the U. N. negotiations over conventional armaments—Lovett, Eisenhower and Gruenther. Bard felt himself hampered by the Joint Chiefs of Staff position that there should be no further discussion of conventional armaments until atomic weapons had been dealt with. "Eisenhower made the point, which Bard had apparently not heard before, that it would be dangerous" to proceed with conventional armaments "until the Russians had agreed to a workable plan of inspection," since if we agreed to a plan for conventional weapons without rigid inspection requirements the Russians could move for the application of the same formula to atomic weapons. In Eisenhower's opinion, "any agreement about atomic weapons without enforceable methods of inspection would be most dangerous for the U. S. Bard saw the point." It is interesting that he had not al-

[ready seen a point which a year or two later would appear obvious to everyone.

Other policies were gradually changing under the relentless pressure of the "cold war." At the end of October Forrestal was lunching with Souers, of the National Security Council, Royall and George Kennan, whom Marshall had made head of his State Department policy group.

31 October 1947   *Luncheon*

. . . Kennan said our policy needed adjustment with respect to Spain and Japan. In the first instance, he felt that we should direct our representatives at the United Nations not to join in any further attempt to discredit the present government of Spain—in other words, to reverse our policy. The Mediterranean cannot be considered without considering Spain and the question of transit through the Straits of Gibraltar. With respect to Japan, he said it had become clear to him at the end of the summer that the socialization of Japan had proceeded to such a point that if a treaty of peace were written and the country turned back to the Japanese it would not be possible, under the present economic machinery, for the country to support itself. This would mean it would go through a period of economic disaster, inflation, unbalanced budgets, resulting possibly in near anarchy, which would be precisely what the Communists would want. The social policy had been carried out by a man named Welsh, formerly of the OPA [Edward C. Welsh, chief of the anti-trust and cartel division of Allied Headquarters in Tokyo], and was of such a character that it was totally impossible for any business in Japan to plan for the future. The most vicious feature of the de-Zaibatsuing process in Japan was the regulation contained in the present directive that all plants, businesses, over a certain size were to be sold to small buyers, not on the basis of their worth but on the basis of what the buyer could afford to pay, with the result that a fifteen-thousand-dollar plant might be sold for seven-fifty. Another almost equally vicious feature is a provision by which labor unions are to elect the boards of directors and control management. This, of course, would make it impossible to run any business.

[That this analysis made a vivid impression on Forrestal is evidenced by a letter of a few weeks later.

To R. T. Stevens, 13 December 1947

. . . I have just recently discovered that some ex-OPA boys have been writing up laws for Japan which in certain respects impose state socialism on that country—which is a fine way to keep them permanently busted and would ultimately lead to economic anarchy. . . .

[Through all this, Forrestal had of course been much occupied in getting the defense system going. The Security Council had been launched on September 26, not without certain doubts and jealousies. Similar difficulties on a lesser scale confronted its companion, the National Security Resources Board. Here was another issue of "roles and missions," particularly involving the already established Munitions Board. Forrestal outlined his own ideas in a memorandum in mid-October.

13 October 1947   *Meeting with*
                          Secretaries of Army, Navy, and Air

. . . I stated my view of it as expressed in the following memorandum:

The National Security Resources Board has the responsibility for preparing directly, or through such agencies as it may select, general plans for industrial, military and civilian mobilization of the country in the event of war. It must deal in terms of the entire economy as distinguished purely from the needs of the military alone. . . .

The Munitions Board has two separate and distinct functions: (1) to coordinate *currently,* among the three Services, procurement and related matters, with the objectives of economy and efficiency of operation; and (2) to plan for and implement those portions of an industrial mobilization program which re-

late specifically to the National Military Establishment, i. e.,
the military aspects of industrial mobilization. Insofar as the
second function is concerned, the Munitions Board is very
much in the position of an advocate of the Services' requirements.

Mr. Royall said . . . that this arrangement, while theoreti-
cally correct, might not work out well as a practical matter. He
said he would like to point out two things: (1) the desirability
of confining the Resources Board's activities to planning rather
than to operations; and (2) the desirability of having contacts
with industry occur through only one source—which he felt
should be the Munitions Board.

[This day was no busier than many others, but as a small tribute to what our public servants go through, it is perhaps worth
looking at Forrestal's calendar for Monday, October 13. The
meeting about the Resources Board and Munitions Board was at
10:00. At noon there arrived twelve cadets from the Mexican
Military Academy. At 12:30 Senator Brewster of Maine appeared, to talk about an investigation he was undertaking into
the industrial mobilization for the war and a lot of other complicated subjects. Forrestal had to make a lunch at the White
House at 1:00 (the President and Cabinet were presenting a silver platter to former Secretary of War Patterson, "soldier and
able servant of his country"), so he took Brewster along with
him in the car to finish the conversation. The conference of the
morning reconvened at 2:30, this time with Chairman Hill of
the Resources Board present. At 4:00 Mr. Lilienthal of the
Atomic Energy Commission arrived, with the draft of a press release in which he proposed to announce that a second series of
atomic tests would be held at Eniwetok. (This brought vigorous
protest from Lovett, in which Forrestal concurred, and no publicity was given to the Eniwetok tests until after they took place
in the following spring.) At 6:00 there was a reception at Blair
House for the Mexican cadets. Neither diary nor calendar shows
what he did that evening (by long habit Forrestal often used his
free evenings for reading), but promptly next morning (between
an appointment with the head of the Central Intelligence

[Agency and a ceremonial presentation of a sword to Eisenhower at the Netherlands Embassy) he saw Chairman Hargrave of the Munitions Board.

14 October 1947   *Mr. Hargrave*

. . . I told him of our discussion yesterday with Mr. Hill. He said he did not know what all the "shooting was about" in connection with the setting up of Mr. Hill's National Resources Board. I told him that there was no shooting, that I was sure that he and Hill would work out together the areas of their respective cognizance and responsibility. But that, based upon my experience with WPB [the War Production Board of World War II], what I had derived from talking with Mr. Baruch, that I felt it was important even between two good and reasonable men to have it clear at the outset precisely what their respective fields of work were; that most of the trouble at WPB had arisen from the lack (a) of clear definition of responsibility and (b) of clear lines of authority *before* men went to work.

[Forrestal continued with a recollection that was to have timeliness in 1951, when Charles Wilson was summoned to head a new war mobilization effort.

I recalled particularly a conversation I had had with Charles E. Wilson of General Electric, who described that omission as the principal reason for difficulties that he encountered. I pointed out that the directive given by President Roosevelt to Mr. Nelson [Donald M. Nelson, wartime director of WPB] in March 1942 had been global in its extent and character, but that Mr. Nelson, for one reason or another, some of which I had good sympathy with, had permitted a lot of his authority to leak away—notably in the fields of food control, transportation control and the direction of solid and liquid fuels. I arranged for Mr. Hill and Mr. Hargrave to get together this afternoon.

[NSRB raised other problems.

30 October 1947   *Cabinet Lunch*

. . . I submitted copy of a directive, which it is Arthur Hill's desire for the President to sign, directing all other government Departments and agencies to furnish such information as the chairman of the National Security Resources Board (Hill) shall ask for. The principal objection seemed to be that such a directive would bypass the authority of the heads of the Department or agency and would, in effect, negate his authority. General Marshall said the same issue had come up when General Dawes was made the Director of the Budget [Charles G. Dawes, appointed first Director of the Budget in 1921]. He then wanted authority to require every Cabinet officer to, in effect, report to him on all budgetary matters. . . .

[The NSRB problem was cleared up, for the time being at any rate, at a White House meeting early in November.

5 November 1947   *Meeting at White House—*
                              National Security Resources Board

At four o'clock today meeting at the White House of Clark Clifford and Messrs. Anderson, Snyder, Hill, Schwellenbach and Assistant Secretary [C. Girard] Davidson of Interior on a proposed draft of an executive order setting Arthur Hill up in business.

The two points under discussion were power of the chairman of the National Security Resources Board to obtain information from government agencies and Departments, and, second, whether the chairman would be considered as deriving his authority from the President or whether his authority would be voted to him by the board. The final agreement was based on some modification of the language of his prerogatives for securing information (basing the order on the use of the word "request" rather than "order"), and with regard to the second point, agreeing on the text of a resolution which would be passed by the board at its first meeting, vesting the powers of the board for action in the chairman.

[So the matter was left. Experience was to prove that Secretary Royall's doubts as to the adjustment of theory and practice were well founded. NSRB's position was never, perhaps, sufficiently well defined. In hindsight it is easy to see that one difficulty resided in the fact that when the unified system was being devised the intimate connection between current operations and planning for a hypothetical future "emergency" was insufficiently realized. The distinction between plans and operations, current and future, proved difficult to maintain as the "cold war" deepened in intensity, and in the new mobilization of 1950-51 NSRB did not take a prominent place.

There were few occasions, Forrestal had observed, "where the language of the mortgage had made the bonds good." A War Council meeting on October 21 indicated that the language of the executive order on "roles and missions" (issued together with signing of the National Security Act) was unlikely to settle all the bitter issues of Service rivalry. Though the ensuing diary entry does not specifically say so, the issue here was apparently over Marine Aviation—perhaps also over the tactical use of Navy carrier aircraft.

21 October 1947   *War Council*

. . . Mr. Symington raised the question of tactical air. Said that the Air Forces had agreed to the unification bill on the assumption that tactical air would remain with the Air Forces. I said I had no idea opposite to this idea but I did want to make sure that tactical air takes into account dispersed and scattered operations such as we had in the Pacific. I remarked to Eisenhower that his operations in Europe had been over vast land masses and he dealt always with masses of men and material, whereas in the Pacific operations were scattered and varied greatly in size, but that from my own observation close-in support of aircraft was vital for troops in these operations. General Spaatz said it was a mistake to try to differentiate between strategic and tactical aircraft since to a certain extent they were used interchangeably and both depended on the same installations, supply systems and overhead. General Eisenhower

and General Spaatz were asked to prepare a paper addressed to
the question of whether all elements in the Services were satisfied with the allocation of tactical air to the Air Force. In doing so, I asked them to take fully into account the operations at
Leyte Gulf and Okinawa, and other similar Pacific operations,
and to get the advice and experience of persons who participated in them.[6]

[Forrestal was pressing for effective unification on a number of
fronts. In a memorandum to Admiral Sherman (25 October) he
asked for a "one-page digest of your ideas of the basic difference
in organization between Army and Navy, with particular reference to flexibility and movements of masses." Within two weeks
he was asking Gruenther to arrange "a forum . . . on the general question of command; the difference in Army and Navy concepts." He asked Hargrave (27 October) for "a comparison of
Navy procurement during the war, and the Army." Within six
weeks of taking office Forrestal had thus opened up studies of
command organization, tactical air power, industrial mobilization
and war procurement. But the mood in which he met his problem is indicated by a letter of this time to a retired admiral.

To Rear Admiral W. B. Young, 23 October 1947

I have gone somewhat slowly because I believe in the theory
of having things to talk about as having been done rather than
having to predict them, and as you know from your own experience this is a complex business and morale and confidence are
easy to destroy but not easy to rebuild. In other words, I want to
be sure that any changes we make are changes that accomplish
something and not merely for the sake of change. I want to operate with as small a staff as possible on the theory that the

---

[6] In the Pacific war naval carrier-borne aviation had on occasion been very
effective in support of land operations. The Marine Air component, specifically
trained in close support of ground troops, had proved a valuable tactical element
not only in the operations of the Marine divisions but in Army operations, in the
Philippines and elsewhere, on occasions in which the Army's own Air Force,
which had paid less attention to close ground support, was less successful. The
same situation recurred in Korea in 1950.

more people you have around the less time you have yourself to think—and to work.

[Forrestal believed in going slowly in order to go surely, but he also knew that time was growing shorter. At the War Council meeting on November 4 Gruenther announced "that he and his staff were working on a new strategic plan which they hope to have ready to present to the Joint Chiefs of Staff on Wednesday a week—November 12." The need for sound planning was growing urgent.

On the last day of October Forrestal summed up his view of the world situation in a letter to the Ambassador to Poland.

To Stanton Griffis, 31 October 1947

It looks to me as if the world were going to *try* to turn conservative but the difficulty is that between Hitler, your friends to the east, and the intellectual muddlers who have had the throttle for the last ten years, the practical people are going to have a hell of a time getting the world out of receivership, and when the miracles are not produced the crackpots may demand another chance in which to really finish the job. At that time it will be of greatest importance that the Democratic Party speaks for the liberals, but not for the revolutionaries.

CHAPTER IX

"Playing with Fire"

I

[Early in 1951—nearly two years after Forrestal's departure from office—a question was put in the House of Commons as to whether "the equal partnership between America, Britain and Canada over the development and use of atomic energy still subsisted." It gave rise to the following colloquy:

"Mr. Attlee [the Prime Minister] said there was a wartime partnership between the United States, the United Kingdom and Canada for the development of the atomic weapon. By agreement between the three governments, the nature of those wartime arrangements had not been revealed on grounds of public policy. The position of the United States administration in many of these matters was now regulated by legislation enacted in the United States since the end of the war, and the wartime arrangements had been modified accordingly, but partnership between the three countries for certain purposes in the atomic energy field continued.

"Mr. Churchill said there was an agreement about this matter in the war. Now that that agreement, as he understood it, had been revoked by the Prime Minister and the government, was there any reason why its terms should not be stated in public?

"Mr. Attlee said he could inquire into that matter, but it would have to be agreed with the United States government. At present he was precluded by the agreement from announcing what the arrangements were. . . . It was a rather complicated and

[delicate matter which he would like to discuss with Mr. Churchill." [1]

Forrestal's diary notes show that during the latter part of 1947
he took an active and influential part in the "modification"
mentioned by Mr. Attlee of the wartime arrangements. Unfortunately it is possible to make little more than passing reference to
the episode here, since, as the Attlee statement also indicates, the
matter was still under a high-security classification in mid-1951.
The existence of the wartime atomic agreements with Britain
and Canada is well known. Mr. Churchill described in his mem-
oirs the joint decision by himself and President Roosevelt to proceed with the atomic development, the actual work to be concentrated in and carried out by the United States; he added that an
initial "basis of agreement" was settled at their conference at
Hyde Park in June 1942. Sherwood's *Roosevelt and Hopkins*
reports that the matter was discussed again at Casablanca early
in 1943; the British felt that the Americans were not living up to
their agreement to make the atomic development a cooperative enterprise, particularly in the matter of the exchange of information, and Churchill entered into a correspondence on the
subject with Hopkins. The difficulty seems not to have been adjusted, however, until Churchill came to Washington in May
1943 and secured a new undertaking from Roosevelt: "The President agreed that the exchange of information . . . should be
resumed and that the enterprise should be considered a joint
one." [2]

In August 1943, at the time of the Quebec Conference, the so-
called Top Policy Group, which had been entrusted with the general overseeing of the American effort, was associated with the
corresponding British and Canadian officials in a Combined Policy Committee, directly responsible to the President and the
Prime Minister. [3] That there was a more formal agreement at
Quebec has since been made evident. In June 1949 Senator Hick-

---

[1] *The Times* [London] 31 January 1951.
[2] Winston S. Churchill, *The Hinge of Fate* (Boston: Houghton Mifflin Co., 1950),
pp. 381, 809; Robert E. Sherwood, *Roosevelt and Hopkins*, pp. 703-704.
[3] Henry L. Stimson and McGeorge Bundy, *On Active Service in Peace and War*
(New York: Harper & Bros., 1948), p. 614. The date, August 1943, is given in an
article by William L. Laurence in *The New York Times*, 20 July 1949.

[enlooper, prosecuting his charges against the AEC of "mismanage-
ment," asked the investigating committee to secure the production of certain documents. Among those asked for were "the
Quebec Agreement, the Hyde Park *aide-mémoire*" and "the paper
stating the position of the United States and the United Kingdom
of January 1948." [4] The committee decided not to demand these
particular documents at the time, but the fact of their existence
became in this way a matter of public record.

It was the paper of January 1948, embodying the agreed modifications of the wartime undertakings (later publicly referred to
as the *modus vivendi*), which Forrestal took an active part in
negotiating. He first appears to have heard of the Quebec Agreement from Senator Hickenlooper in July 1947. Hickenlooper
brought the matter up again in the following month, expressing
his concern over certain aspects of the Roosevelt-Churchill commitments, and Forrestal promptly took steps to inform himself
about these documents. As Secretary of Defense his official responsibility in anything concerning the atomic bomb was, of
course, immediate and direct; and his diary notes show that he
was soon in contact with the State Department on the matter.
He learned, what was not publicly known until some two years
later, that "there was a restriction in the Quebec Agreement
upon certain actions" that was "undoubtedly binding upon us." [5]
In early November he participated in a meeting of the American side of the Combined Policy Committee, taking the place of
Mr. Stimson, who, as Secretary of War, had been the principal
representative of the military Departments on the original Top
Policy Committee. The British, he found, were themselves dissatisfied with the working of the secret agreements—again they
were "irked" over the old matter of exchange of information,
which even the published Attlee-Mackenzie King-Truman Agreement of November 1945 had failed to clear up. At the same time
it was becoming apparent to the American representatives in the
United Nations that there was no hope of securing an international agreement on atomic energy in any visible future, which

[4] *The New York Times,* 2 June 1949.
[5] These are the words of Senator Brien McMahon, speaking on the floor of the
Senate, 10 July 1950, *Congressional Record,* Vol. 96, p. 9763.

[made it more urgent to regularize the position between ourselves and the British. It was clearly the appropriate moment in which (as Forrestal elsewhere expressed it) to "tie up the loose ends of casually drawn agreements of the past" and, in general, to clarify the whole relationship.

The diary shows that the various questions involved were very thoroughly canvassed with the AEC, with congressional leaders of both parties and with members of the Joint Congressional Committee on Atomic Energy before the American officials met in early December with their British and Canadian counterparts in the Combined Policy Committee. Forrestal was impressed with the importance of stepping up bomb production—an importance which he felt was being "emphasized by current events." His notes show that he was concerned to remove the "restriction" of the Quebec Agreement; to assure the maximum efficiency and security of manufacture and get an adjustment as to the exchange of information which, within appropriate security limits, would make optimum use of the knowledge available on both sides of the Atlantic in "a partnership which should have meaning backed up by fact." As was later publicly stated in the Senate, the *modus vivendi* was concluded at a final meeting in Blair House in January 1948; among other things, the Quebec restriction "which was undoubtedly binding on us . . . was removed from the *modus vivendi*," while the agreement provided "for the exchange of information in nine specified areas having to do with health and safety and certain other things which are deemed not to pertain to military information." [6] There is nothing in the diary notes to suggest that any serious difficulties arose in the course of what seems to have been a rapid and harmonious negotiation; nor is there anything to imply that Forrestal was other than satisfied with the new terms of "partnership" which emerged.

II

[These negotiations with Britain and Canada had been carried on against a background of international affairs that was still obscure. As the winter of 1947-48 approached, the outlook

---

[6] Senator McMahon, 10 July 1950, *Congressional Record*, Vol. 96, pp. 9762, 9763.

[seemed in some respects encouraging, in others ominous. At a
Cabinet in early November Secretary Marshall had presented a
striking summary of the world situation as it then appeared.

7 November 1947   *Cabinet*

. . . The Secretary of State read a paper on the present international situation. Outstanding conclusions: The advance of
Communism has been stemmed and the Russians have been
compelled to make a re-evaluation of their position. The consequences will depend to some extent on their internal economy
and internal political strength. If they conclude the situation
is becoming desperate, particularly internally, they may be
driven by the dynamism of their own situation to precipitate
civil war in Italy and France this winter. Another possibility,
and a very likely one, is the stepping up of the tempo of the
guerrilla activity in Greece with the possibility here of more
definite aggression. Tito is an unpredictable and explosive
factor in this situation because the degree of his adherence to
the Politburo discipline is not known. Up to now it has been
the Kremlin policy not to permit the Greek affair to get into
what the military people call the "artillery phase"—that is,
where troops would actually be supported by artillery fire.

Another factor of uncertainty is the extent to which American aid becomes available to, and effective in, Europe. If the
program of European aid appears to be in the process of becoming effective, this may also accelerate a Russian *démarche*.

Marshall noted the one section in Molotov's speech[7] at which
he referred to the fact that apparently some people inside of
Russia still believe that the capitalistic system was not through.
He said that the State Department was pondering the significance of this statement (Harriman later said it was quite clear to

---

[7] On November 6, at a ceremony in the Bolshoi Theater in Moscow commemorating the thirtieth anniversary of the Bolshevist seizure of power, Molotov delivered
a truculent speech, vehemently attacking American "imperialism." It was in the
course of this speech that he declared: "In expansionist circles of the U.S.A. a
new, peculiar sort of illusion is widespread—faith is placed in the secret of the
atomic bomb, although this secret has long ceased to exist." This was the first
authoritative indication that the Western monopoly of the weapon might be at
an end.

him that the proper interpretation of this language was that another purge was in prospect). Marshall said that the United Nations as a platform and forum for Russian propaganda was in a state of decline, and that it was entirely possible the Russians might decide to quit it. He said the warmongering speeches of Vishinsky had had some propaganda effect, and he raised the question as to whether or not answers should be made. I gave it as my view that answers *should* be made and that they should be very carefully planned. He said he is speaking in Chicago on November 17, just prior to going to the London Conference, but he proposed to limit his remarks at that time to a factual exposition of the present international picture. It was suggested, and the President concurred, that Vandenberg be given the necessary material to make a response to Molotov's speech of yesterday.

Marshall referred to the present status of China as one of critical instability; it is a situation with which we shall have to deal as best we can, maintaining the American interest to the best of our ability. The Middle East he referred to as another tinder box. I repeated my suggestion, made several times previously, that a serious attempt be made to lift the Palestine question out of American partisan politics. I said that there had been general acceptance of the fact that domestic politics ceased at the Atlantic Ocean and that no question was more charged with danger to our security than this particular one.

Marshall stated that the objective of our policy from this point on would be the restoration of balance of power in both Europe and Asia and that all actions would be viewed in the light of this objective. At this juncture I repeated my inquiry about the review of the levels of industry in both Japan and Germany; I said that the policy of restoration of balance of power must necessarily be related to the elements of balance of power and those elements must include obviously the two nations which we have just destroyed.

At the conclusion of Marshall's remarks Harriman raised the question again of adequate control on critical materials going to Russia and also the reconsideration of the level of industry in

Germany. I supported him in this position but said that any
such reconsideration would obviously have to be coupled with
some kind of partnership with the French, who were extremely
sensitive to any idea of re-establishing the military potential of
Germany.

[Forrestal went on to a luncheon the same day with Loy Henderson of the State Department and others; and here, in a kind of
footnote to Marshall's presentation, he heard of certain British
views of the subject. Bevin, he was told, "was thoroughly aware
of the vital importance of the Middle East to the existence of
Britain and would make every effort to cooperate with us in
maintaining its integrity. . . . There were four countries the independence of which from Russia was vital to our joint security;
Greece, Turkey, Iran, Italy. . . . The fall of the Middle East
would virtually mean the end of England as a power"; and Henderson was inclined to agree. The British, it was said, "did not
want to stay alone in Palestine; they didn't want to engage in a
war with either the Jews or the Arabs." As for India, it was a
British view that "the Indians, particularly the Hindus, were
extremely loath to see the British leave—that within the past
forty-eight hours Nehru had importuned Mountbatten not to go
to the Princess's wedding because they were so fearful that some
crisis would develop in his absence." (Lord Mountbatten was
then Viceroy, and Princess Elizabeth, the British heiress pre-
sumptive, was to be married on November 20.)

Such was the situation as it seemed to them. In his own field
Forrestal had already (at a War Council meeting on November
4) moved to begin the study of three large subjects that only the
unified Defense Department could deal with and which the times
were making increasingly urgent: a system of civilian defense,
a program of psychological warfare, and an over-all program
for the civilian components (National Guard, Reserves, student
training corps, etc.) of the Armed Services. Much thought and
labor was to be spent on all three before concrete results were
achieved.

The President meanwhile had settled the question of high
command.

12 November 1947   *The President*

Talked with the President this afternoon on command setup in the Army and Navy and various other subjects. He agreed to the naming of Admiral Denfeld as Chief of Naval Operations and at the same time told Admiral Blandy [that he had done so], with a limitation of this office to two years. Admiral Denfeld agreed to this arrangement regardless of whether it was put on the statute books or otherwise. The President had Admiral Blandy come in and told Blandy he had given careful consideration to Ramsey, Denfeld and Blandy and had great difficulty making a selection because they were all men of such high ability, but had finally come to the decision in terms of age and position on the lineal list.

Later he told me he had a successor for Bradley in the VA and that immediately after the naming of Bradley's successor he proposed to have Bradley go over to the Army with the idea that it would accelerate the change in the Chief of Staff. He did not want to ask Eisenhower to withdraw but he thought he would take the hint.

[This proposal gently to nudge the Chief of Staff, the conqueror of Germany, into other fields has its amusing side, but the conversation led the two men into a more serious vein in which the characters of both and the attitudes with which they faced the formidable future seem well exemplified.

I told him I would like to make a statement saying that under no circumstances would I accept the nomination for the vice-presidency. He said he wished I would not go quite so far out on the limb, but to make a statement more on the order of Marshall's. He said as far as he himself was concerned he would be delighted not to run again if it were not for a sense of duty which compelled him to do so. He said there was little satisfaction outside of the reward of service in the presidency— that his "baby," as he called her, Margaret, was limited—had her entire life conditioned by the fact of being the daughter of the President; that his nephew who is named after him had to live an entirely different type of life, and as a matter of fact all those in close relationship to him had to accept something other than a normal life out of respect for the office that he held.

There is no question in my judgment as to the complete sincerity of the President that the only thing that holds him to this grinding job is the sense of obligation to the country and, secondarily, to his party.

[Nor can there be any question as to the complete sincerity with which Forrestal flung himself in the course of this winter into his campaign to take Palestine "out of politics." On November 6 he buttonholed J. Howard McGrath, Senator from Rhode Island, and Democratic National chairman. Forrestal repeated his arguments that "no group in this country should be permitted to influence our policy to the point where it could endanger our national security." McGrath was not encouraging; he "replied by saying that there were two or three pivotal states which could not be carried without the support of people who were deeply interested in the Palestine question. I said I would rather lose those states in a national election than run the risks which I felt might develop in our handling of the Palestine question." Forrestal was persistent. At the end of the month he tackled McGrath again.

26 November 1947   *Lunch—Senator McGrath*

Lunch today with Senator McGrath. Prior to it I had him read the secret report on Palestine prepared by CIA.

I said to McGrath that I thought the Palestine question was one of the most important in our American foreign policy, and that if we were talking about lifting foreign affairs out of domestic politics, there was nothing more important to lift out than Palestine, with all its domestic ramifications. I said the Palestine-Jewish question was similar to the Eire-Irish question of forty years ago and that neither should be permitted to have any substantial influence on American policy. McGrath answered that he realized how serious the situation was and said he would like to come back and read more carefully the CIA documents.

[Forrestal derived several points from McGrath's conversation. In the first place, Jewish sources were responsible for a substantial part of the contributions to the Democratic National Committee, and many of these contributions were made "with a distinct idea on the part of the givers that they will have an opportunity to express their views and have them seriously considered on such questions as the present Palestine question." There was a feeling among the Jews that the United States was not doing what it should to solicit votes in the U. N. General Assembly in favor of the Palestine partition. (To this Forrestal objected that it was "precisely what the State Department wanted to avoid; that we had gone a very long way indeed in supporting partition and that proselytizing for votes and support would add to the already serious alienation of Arabian good will.") McGrath said that "beyond this the Jews would expect the United States to do its utmost to implement the partition decision if it is voted by the U. N., through force if necessary"; and he was considering suggesting to the President that, in the event of partition, the President should invite a group of leading Jewish citizens to form a committee to go to Palestine "and work out a peaceful and effective arrangement with the Arabs." As to the use of force, McGrath thought "it might be worth while to have the Gallup Poll or some other opinion-reporting agency make a spot check" as to whether American opinion would favor supporting a partition decision with American troops, either alone or as part of a U. N. force. "I said," Forrestal's note continues, "I hoped that Senator McGrath would give a lot of thought to this matter because it involved not merely the Arabs of the Middle East, but also might involve the whole Moslem world with its four hundred millions of people—Egypt, North Africa, India and Afghanistan."

On Saturday, November 29, the General Assembly voted 33 to 13, with 10 abstentions, to partition Palestine into two independent states. The vote, one of the few in the U. N. on which the United States and the Soviet Union stood together, was received with satisfaction by Jewish opinion. Lovett brought up the matter at the lunch on Monday.

1 December 1947   *Cabinet Lunch*

. . . Lovett reported on the result of the United Nations action on Palestine over the week end. He said he had never in his life been subject to as much pressure as he had been in the three days beginning Thursday morning and ending Saturday night. [Herbert Bayard] Swope, Robert Nathan, were among those who had importuned him. . . . The Firestone Tire and Rubber Company, which has a concession in Liberia, reported that it had been telephoned to and asked to transmit a message to their representative in Liberia directing him to bring pressure on the Liberian government to vote in favor of partition. The zeal and activity of the Jews had almost resulted in defeating the objectives they were after.

I remarked that many thoughtful people of the Jewish faith had deep misgivings about the wisdom of the Zionists' pressures for a Jewish state in Palestine, and I also remarked that the *New York Times* editorial of Sunday morning pointed up those misgivings when it said, "Many of us have long had doubts . . . concerning the wisdom of erecting a political state on a basis of religious faith." I said I thought the decision was fraught with great danger for the future security of this country.

The President referred to the limitations put under our participation in the implementation of the Palestine partition (that he had repeatedly made the statement that American armed forces could not be used toward this end); however, I fail to see how we can avoid meeting that issue if participation by our forces is asked by the United Nations; (in other words, if we are asked to contribute our prorated share of an international force to carry out the United Nations decision). . . .

3 December 1947   *Lunch—Mr. Byrnes*

Lunch today with Jimmy Byrnes. We talked Palestine. Byrnes recalled the fact that he had disassociated himself from his decision of a year ago to turn down the Grady report[8] which recommended a federated state for Palestine or a single

---

[8] See p. 310.

Arabian state. He said the decision on the part of the President to reject this recommendation and to criticize the British for their conduct of Palestinian affairs had placed Bevin and Attlee in a most difficult position. He said that Niles [David K. Niles, administrative assistant to the President] and Sam Rosenman were chiefly responsible for the President's decision; that both had told the President that Dewey was about to come out with a statement favoring the Zionist position on Palestine, and that they had insisted that unless the President anticipated this movement New York State would be lost to the Democrats.

I asked Byrnes what he thought of the possibility of getting Republican leaders to agree with the Democrats to have the Palestine question placed on a nonpolitical basis. He wasn't particularly optimistic about the success of this effort because of the fact that Rabbi Silver was one of Taft's close associates and because Taft followed Silver on the Palestine-Haifa question. I said I thought it was a most disastrous and regrettable fact that the foreign policy of this country was determined by the contributions a particular bloc of special interests might make to the party funds.

Byrnes spoke about the Ruhr. . . . He said that in his opinion it would be fatal if the Russians were permitted to join in a quadripartite scheme for the management of this area. Byrnes recalled an incident when he and Molotov had a few drinks late at night—Molotov had indicated that he was willing to give up practically anything else to get such an arrangement in the Ruhr. (This was in response to one of Byrnes' questions after about the third highball, when he said, "Mr. Minister, I would like to know what you would *really* like in Europe.") . . .

[Within a week Forrestal made his first attempt to enlist Republican support for a nonpartisan policy on Palestine. On December 10 he called on Senator Vandenberg; the Senator pointed to one obvious difficulty—"that there was a feeling among most Republicans that the Democratic Party had used the Palestine question politically, and the Republicans felt they were entitled to make similar use of the issue." Vandenberg himself had tried to keep aloof from the matter, but he quoted Stassen's remark, " 'if

[Republicans were to cooperate on foreign policy they would
have to be in on the take-off as well as in the crash landing.' "
Forrestal was to find Governor Dewey even less encouraging.

13 December 1947   *Gridiron Dinner*

At the Gridiron Dinner tonight I spoke to Governor Dewey
about Palestine and posed to him the question of getting nonpartisan action on this question, which I said was a matter of
the deepest concern to me in terms of the security of the nation.
The Governor said he agreed in principle but that it was a
difficult matter to get results on because of the intemperate
attitude of the Jewish people who had taken Palestine as the
emotional symbol, because the Democratic Party would not be
willing to relinquish the advantages of the Jewish vote. He
said he had become very cynical about entering into "gentle-
men's agreements" after his experience in the 1944 campaign,
when he said he had a clear agreement with FDR not to bring
the question of the use of force by the United Nations, and the
American participation in the use of such force, into that campaign. Shortly after this agreement was entered upon, he said,
FDR introduced that issue into his speech before the Foreign
Policy Association in New York City on October 27.

I said I was fully aware of all of the past actions and attitudes, political and otherwise, which would make a nonpartisan approach to this question difficult, but that I
considered I would be derelict in my duty if I did not try, and
that I knew that any engagements that the President entered
into he would live up to most scrupulously. I said I was not
authorized to speak for him beyond the fact that he had
agreed to let me present my view of the matter before Republican leaders. Senator Vandenberg was sitting next to
Dewey at dinner and after the dinner I asked the Senator if
Dewey's attitude had been at all responsive. Vandenberg's reply was, "Responsive but skeptical."

At the same dinner Lovett was importuned by Felix Frankfurter on the subject of Palestine and upon his (Lovett's) refusal
to enter into discussion Frankfurter became annoyed and
Acheson [Dean Acheson, having left the State Department,

was at this time in private practice] reported to Lovett afterward that he, the Justice, had been offended. Lovett's conversation was very brief: he said he had had enough of Palestine for a time and did not want to hear of it again.

(In my conversation with Dewey I responded to his comment that we were already committed to an unfortunate course, and to his inquiry as to what we could do now, I said there would inevitably be two things coming up: (1) the arming of the Jews to fight the Arabs (2) unilateral action by the U. S. to enforce the decision of the General Assembly.

At this point Vandenberg interjected to say that on the question of unilateral action he was completely and unequivocably against such action because it would breed in his opinion a wave of violent anti-Semitism in this country.)

[For the time being Forrestal let the subject drop; but he was not easily discouraged, and he was to return to the crusade in the new year.

Early in December Forrestal was still considering what military moves could be made "in the event of a *coup d'état* in the north of Italy"; while it had been definitely planned to make an Air Force and Naval Air demonstration over that country on December 14. But at a luncheon discussion on December 9 with Souers, Hillenkoetter and others, the "general feeling [was] that the French crisis had reached a peak and the worst [was] past," while the head of CIA "felt confident" that Italy would not succumb to the Communists.[9] The skies were momentarily, perhaps, a little lighter; yet the basic facts remained unaltered, and in a letter of this time to Chan Gurney, chairman of the Senate Armed Services Committee, Forrestal gave his own penetrating analysis of the broader problem.

Gurney had sent him a newspaper editorial (from the *Vermillion Plain Talk*) arguing that in Europe we had but two alternatives: to stay in force, using many more troops than were there at the time, or to get out. Forrestal thought neither was the answer. "Certainly," he wrote, "we cannot default Europe to Russia" —to do so would be to invite attack "within the next two decades"

[9] Diary, 9 December 1947.

[by a totalitarian land colossus armed with all the sea and air power which the whole of Europe could, under authoritarian management, produce. But neither, considering the limits of our own strength, could we simultaneously finance European economic recovery, European rearmament and a defense of Europe by American forces. "As you know, I hold that world stability will not be restored until the vacuum created by the destruction of German power and the weakening of the power of Western Europe has been filled—in other words, until a balance of power has been restored in Europe." Such a balance would include military strength, but "I believe that economic stability, political stability and military stability must develop in about that order." Forrestal then gave his own significant concept of American politico-strategic policy.

To Chan Gurney, 8 December 1947

. . . At the present time we are keeping our military expenditures below the levels which our military leaders must in good conscience estimate as the minimum which would in themselves ensure national security. By so doing we are able to increase our expenditures to assist in European recovery. In other words, we are taking a calculated risk in order to follow a course which offers a prospect of eventually achieving national security and also long-term world stability.

If we refuse to take such a calculated risk we will be forced into one of the two unacceptable alternatives of the *Vermillion* editorial and the problem will not approach solution during the years immediately ahead.

During those years—of which the exact number is indeterminate—we will continue to have certain military advantages which go far toward covering the risk. There are really four outstanding military facts in the world at this time. They are:

(1) The predominance of Russian land power in Europe and Asia.

(2) The predominance of American sea power.

(3) Our exclusive possession of the atomic bomb.

(4) American productive capacity.

As long as we can outproduce the world, can control the sea

and can strike inland with the atomic bomb, we can assume certain risks otherwise unacceptable in an effort to restore world trade, to restore the balance of power—military power— and to eliminate some of the conditions which breed war.

The years before any possible power can achieve the capability effectively to attack us with weapons of mass destruction are our years of opportunity.

[In Forrestal's thought, the atomic bomb had already moved into the center of the international equation. (He had apparently not been impressed by Molotov's veiled, if boastful, warning of the month before.) He was still uncertain whether the country would be resolute in the bomb's use; at the time we were still bound by the secret Quebec Agreement with Britain and Canada, and even months later, long after the agreement had been adjusted, he was asking every casual visitor to his office whether in his opinion the public would support the employment of the bomb in the event of a major war. Whatever Forrestal's doubts on this score, he was willing, because of our supposedly exclusive possession of atomic weapons, to accept a policy which was cutting our other forms of military power virtually to impotence in order to finance European economic and political recovery and stability.

It was a calculated risk. Events, unhappily, were within a few months to force a revision of the calculation.

III

[Involved as he was in establishing the unification machinery and making a start on such over-all problems as civilian defense or the consolidation of activities, Forrestal seems not to have spent much time on the preparation of the individual Service budgets for the coming fiscal year. There are, at any rate, few references to this vital subject in the diary for the latter part of 1947. On August 4 he had written the President: "This acknowledges your memorandum of August 1 in reference to the budget for 1949. I fully realize the difficulties with which you will be faced next year in bringing national income and expenditure figures into balance and assure you of my support in carrying

[out your instructions." There was no serious effort to raise the
levels to which Service operations had been reduced; and the
new budget was being designed on about the same pattern
that the current one had assumed after Forrestal's tussle in the
spring (on the Navy's behalf) with Mr. Taber. That the budget
concealed bitter issues of Service rivalry, which were later to become serious, was hinted at a luncheon on November 8, when
he saw Gruenther and his own administrative assistant, W. J.
McNeil, who had special charge of budgetary matters. Gruenther
said "there was a general impression throughout the Army and
Air Force, but particularly in the latter, that the amount of
money provided for the Navy was disproportionate to the tasks
of the Navy and its use in a future war. The Air people, he said,
made the point that plant, weapons and ships of the Navy
were far out of line with the existing material strength of the
Air Force. I pointed out what is of course obvious, that this
was merely because we had to build a tremendous Navy during
the war and that this gives us a present plant which *is* of great
proportions. The fact is that we have it, and certainly I would
doubt that any sensible person would suggest our sinking this
force." [10]

The budget which the President was to present in January
called for an estimated expenditure on national defense, in the
fiscal year ending June 30, 1949, of a trifle over $11 billion. They
were then, of course, in the fiscal year 1948. In spite of Mr.
Taber's slightly pathetic hope that *something* could be cut out of
national defense without reducing efficiency, expenditures were
running at about the level which the previous budget had envisaged.[11] To the American public, recalling the last peacetime

---

[10] Diary, 8 November 1947.
[11] A table will perhaps make the matter clearer. Here are the actual and estimated *expenditures* (not appropriations) as presented in the two budget messages
of January 1947 and January 1948:

EXPENDITURES (in thousands)

		Actual 1946	Estimated 1947	Estimated 1948
1947 Message	National Defense	45,012	14,726	11,256
	Total	63,714	42,523	37,526

[military budgets in 1939 and 1940, it seemed a very high level indeed; and Forrestal appears to have been willing to acquiesce in that view. The fact that even $11 billion a year was insufficient, under all the circumstances, to provide any really formed, available and effective military power in the actual contexts of current world affairs only became apparent—and then under dramatic circumstances—in the ensuing spring.

In mid-December Secretary Marshall returned from still another exhausting and largely futile meeting of the Council of Foreign Ministers. It had been held this time in London; the purpose had been to secure peace treaties for Germany and Austria.

19 December 1947   *Cabinet*

The Secretary of State reported on the London Conference.

He said Molotov approached the meetings with the thesis that the Foreign Ministers should proceed immediately with the drafting of the treaty for Germany, putting, in Marshall's language, the cart completely before the horse, because the writing of a treaty with Germany could not be carried out until the boundaries of the German state, the character of its government and many other matters were first determined. The Russians conducted their negotiations almost exclusively with an eye toward German opinion. Molotov used every opportunity to endeavor to give the Germans the impression that they, the Russians, were anxious to see a unified and autonomous Germany but that in this effort they were being blocked by the British, French and Americans.

He became increasingly abusive as the meetings proceeded, and Marshall kept repeating to him that he, Molotov, knew that Marshall knew that Molotov's statements were untrue in the minds of their authors. Toward the end Bidault [the French Foreign Minister] and Bevin were even more annoyed than the Americans but were very chary about calling for adjournment.

		Actual 1947	Estimated 1948	Estimated 1949
1948 Message	National Defense	14,281	10,746	11,025
	Total	42,505	37,728	39,669

Marshall finally took the opportunity at the end of one of Molotov's most abusive statements to say that the conduct of the Russian Foreign Minister and his remarks were of such a character as to make it impossible for him or his colleagues to have any respect for the Soviet Union.[12] This seemed to take Molotov aback, Marshall's analysis being that it would be considered as a loss of face at home and with possible serious consequences for himself.

The Secretary of State said that the French, British and Americans were proceeding to develop plans for the consolidation of the three zones. . . . He next dealt with the question of the Ruhr. . . . The French were most anxious to start immediately on discussion of the Ruhr, the British opposing; the real reason behind the British opposition was that they were fearful that if the French got what they wanted as regards the Ruhr they would be most difficult to deal with on other matters.

Molotov's charges, he said, dealt with such things as the allegation that the Americans and British were making vast profits out of Germany, coupled with refusal of the Russians to give any statement as to what they had taken out of their Eastern Zone. . . . On reparations he said the Russians advanced the unique argument that extraction of reparations from Germany would actually help the country to get on its feet. I remarked at this point that it sounded like Thurman Arnold's statement during the war that the indictment of officials of munitions-making firms in the U. S. was a very valuable stimulant to production. . . .

[At this point the Christmas holidays were approaching and Forrestal allowed himself one of his rare vacations—which he characteristically devoted, in part, to an inspection of the Air Force installations at Eglin Field, Florida, and Maxwell Field, Alabama. Maxwell, the seat of the new "Air University," and its associated large-scale testing and maneuvering ground at Eglin were the paint-fresh centers of Air Force gospel and doctrine—

---

[12] It is interesting to compare this episode with Secretary Byrnes' rather similar experience of a year before (see pp. 233-34).

[roughly the equivalent of the Army's Command and Staff School at Leavenworth or the Navy's War College at Newport. The visit evidently left him with some reservations. He was struck by what seemed to him the immaturity of the officers who had been brought to high command by the spectacular development of the Air Force; as he put it in a letter a few weeks later to Admiral Sherman: "One of the real difficulties is becoming more manifest every day: the gap in the Air Force of wise and experienced leadership in the upper ranks. Ten or even five years from now they will be all right." [13] Nor had the aviators, he felt, really faced up to the implications of their own doctrine. "The most urgent strategic and tactical problem," he noted in his diary on December 31, "to be solved by the Air Force is the question of usefulness and capabilities of the long-range bomber against jet fighter and radar defense. Upon the answer to this question, which may not be completely found until actual wartime, may depend the outcome of future wars." In this note Forrestal was touching on questions that went to the heart of the military policies to which the country was being committed, and that later gave him much concern. His own views were to vary from time to time, and perhaps he was never satisfied with his own conclusions.[14] But neither were others; and even two years later the capabilities of the heavy bombers were still a matter of bitter technical dispute, as was shown by the so-called "B-36 controversy."

Forrestal was back in Washington in time to attend the customary Cabinet meeting for the advance reading of the President's annual message on the state of the Union. This was, of course, the beginning of a presidential year; the message was centered largely on domestic political and economic issues, and Forrestal expressed some mild reservations.

6 January 1948   *White House*

Meeting at the White House at 4:00 to read the President's message. The Secretary of State made the observation that he felt it was a little overweighted on the side of sweetness and

---

[13] To Vice Admiral Forrest P. Sherman, 14 February 1948.
[14] See p. 538.

light and not enough blood, tears and sweat. I had previously said that I thought all the objectives outlined in the President's speech were highly desirable and laudatory, but that some reference ought to be made to the amount of hard work on the part of all hands necessary to attain them. There was a passage about getting a college education for everyone. I offered it as my belief that the really serious question was the lack of proper secondary education, that a lot of them who went to college simply wasted their time, and that in the Service we had found great deficiencies in the training in simple mathematics, ability to write legibly and with clarity of expression, and that as a matter of fact in the case of a good many university graduates their education was not much use in preparing them for military service or for that matter for any other practical work. There were several passages about the low standard of living in this country on the part of many millions of families and the foreboding of a coming depression, both of which I remarked would be excellent propaganda for the Kremlin. Some of these passages were modified.

7 January 1948   *Address by President Truman*

1:30. To the Capitol to hear the President's address to Congress. Speech political. Response not hostile but definitely restrained.

[Forrestal in the meanwhile had returned to his anxieties over the oil supply, the strategic significance of the eastern Mediterranean and the Palestine question.

6 January 1948   *Breakfast with Mr. Jennings*

Breakfast with Mr. [B. Brewster] Jennings, president, Socony Vacuum of New York. He told me that his company and associate companies—that is, Texas, Standard of California and Standard of New Jersey—had made up their minds to suspend work on the pipeline and collateral developments in Saudi Arabia because of the disturbed condition in Palestine and the indications of its continuance. The investment program of these companies over the period of the next few years contemplates an expenditure of around $400 million.

I told Jennings I was deeply concerned about the future supply of oil for this country, not merely for the possible use in war but for the needs of peace. I expressed it as my opinion that unless we had access to Middle East oil, American motorcar companies would have to design a four-cylinder motorcar sometime within the next five years.

Later in the morning talked with Mr. Robert McConnell [industrialist and engineer who had served in various posts in government during the war] who has just been in Germany. He came in to see me with a vigorous expression of the thesis that it would be a basic mistake to reactivate the coal industry of the Ruhr. He said that an oil economy would produce greater efficiency at lower cost [and would have various political advantages]. . . . I said that his reasoning was sound and I would accept his engineering conclusions, but I found it difficult to understand its practicality in light of the present situation in Palestine. He said his remarks were made without reference to that situation. . . .

[A brief entry of the following day hints at the importance the Near East was assuming in strictly military planning.

7 January 1948   *Meeting—Admiral Souers—*
                                        Bases in Mediterranean

11:45. Meeting with Admiral Souers on the paper that we drafted as a result of Sunday's conference with Secretary Symington and General Spaatz on the question of air bases in the Mediterranean.

(Later today General Gruenther said he thought the question of air bases in North Africa implies a narrow limitation on our needs in the event of war. He said that what we were really talking about was bases in the Eastern Mediterranean and in the Middle East.)

[At lunch on January 9 Forrestal heard from Loy Henderson more about the "very great pressure" that "had been put upon

[him as well as Mr. Lovett" to get active American solicitation for
U. N. votes for the Palestine partition. "He said Felix Frankfurter
and Justice Murphy had both sent messages to the Philippine
delegate to the General Assembly strongly urging his vote." At
the Cabinet a week later Forrestal had an opportunity to state
his own case, which he did with earnestness, traversing the same
ground he had gone over with Brewster Jennings. "There was,"
says his diary note, "a general discussion of oil. Krug reported
a 50 per cent increase in the use of fuel oils since prewar. . . .
We are now importing about 450,000 barrels a day against exports of a similar amount. . . . The simple fact is that while
production has doubled since 1938, demand has gone up even
faster." Forrestal argued that without access to the Middle Eastern pools, the Marshall Plan could not succeed, we could not
fight a war and we could not even maintain the tempo of our
peacetime economy; without Middle Eastern oil we would have
to convert "within ten years" (he here doubled the period) to
four-cylinder cars. Marshall asked whether South America could
not meet the need if its restrictive laws against American capital
were modified. He thought that at the forthcoming Bogotá trade
conference it might be possible to "explain the situation" to the
Latin American representatives and to suggest how their laws
"could be adjusted to permit the ingress of American capital,
management and skill." Forrestal's comment was pointed. The
diary continues:

16 January 1948   *Cabinet*
. . . I said that the real need was the appointment of ambassadors with some business experience and background as
well as negotiating skill, who would vigorously and continuously push the interests of American business. I cited the
case of Mexico and the deficiencies of an amiable but untrained personnel. There are substantial oil deposits in Mexico
but the Mexicans expropriated foreign oil properties ten years
ago, have since found themselves unable to develop and produce oil through government operation, with the result that
today Mexican production is only about in balance with her
internal consumption. . . .

Harriman outlined his program for export controls and pointed out that it would meet head-on with the economic section of the State Department who were crusading for the pattern of international trade agreements, reciprocal trade, etc., sponsored by Will Clayton. Harriman said these were desirable objectives in a more orderly world but were not applicable now where a large section of the world was on a cartel [basis] and under rigid control. He was particularly apprehensive that oil machinery would go to Russia through the satellites who would pay for it in gold. . . .

Krug and Attorney General Clark stressed the seriousness of the oil situation, Clark stating that New York in two months would have practically no oil and Krug saying that the situation was the result not only of increased use but of such considerations as allocation of steel for refineries, drilling equipment and so forth.

I took the opportunity to remark that it seemed to me this provided us an excellent platform and material with which to emphasize to the people the overriding importance of access to Middle East oil reserves. . . .

[In his campaign on Palestine Forrestal had met with no more success from the Republican leaders than from McGrath, his own party chairman. He now made a determined effort to enlist the State Department. On the morning of January 21 he drew up a paper which he proposed to show that day to Under Secretary Lovett. " 'Bipartisan foreign policy,' " it began, "and 'domestic politics end at the seaboard' have come to be accepted components of the policy of both parties. It is doubtful if there is any segment of our foreign relations of greater importance or of greater danger in its broad implications to the security of the United States than our relations in the Middle East." On these premises it would be "stupid" to allow the situation to develop in such a way as either to do "permanent injury to our relations with the Moslem world" or to end in a "stumble into war." The paper went on to explain: "I have had permission from the President to make an informal attempt to secure Republican agreement on the broad general principle that the Palestine

[question will not be permitted to breach the premises in the
first two paragraphs. I have had some encouragement from Senator Vandenberg, accompanied by skepticism as to the ultimate
outcome, somewhat less encouragement from Governor Dewey,
and complete agreement as to the desirability of the objective
from various other Republicans, not in the leadership, such as
John Taber, James W. Wadsworth, Dewey Short and Everett
Dirksen." On the Democratic side, he added, he had encountered a realization "of the importance and danger of the situation"
but a consciousness that a substantial part of the Democratic
funds came from Zionist sources inclined to ask in return for "a
lien upon this part of our national policy."

Consequently, the paper continued, "it is suggested" that the
Secretary of State should take up the matter with the President.
Admitting that the country was now committed to the U. N. partition plan, Forrestal foresaw two dangerous issues that might
arise before the political conventions in June, as result of pressures to give or sell arms to the Jews in Palestine, or (in the very
probable event that U. N. would be unable to implement its decision) to force the United States to implement it unilaterally.
He had discussed the question, the paper concluded, "with a number of people of the Jewish faith who hold the view that the present zeal of the Zionists can have most dangerous consequences,
not merely in their divisive effects in American life, but in the
long run on the position of the Jews throughout the world."

Forrestal saw Lovett the same day and showed him this
paper; Lovett "agreed in general with the conclusions" and then
produced a paper from his side which had just come "from the
Planning Staff of the State Department." This, as Forrestal paraphrased it, concluded that the U. N. partition plan was "not
workable," adding that the United States was under no commitment to support the plan if it could not be made to work without resort to force; that it was against American interest to
supply arms to the Jews while we were embargoing arms to
the Arabs, or to accept unilateral responsibility for carrying out
the U. N. decision, and that the United States should take steps
as soon as possible to secure withdrawal of the partition proposal.

[Lovett, according to Forrestal's memorandum, made the general comment that the use of the U. N. by others as a propaganda platform was complicating our conduct of foreign relations. He felt that our dealings with the Arabs and Jews "would be greatly facilitated if we did not have to conduct every negotiation practically within the framework of the United Nations," which the Russians were using to inject themselves into a situation in which they had no legitimate interest. Forrestal felt that the State Department was "seriously embarrassed and handicapped by the activities of Niles at the White House in going directly to the President on matters involving Palestine." His memorandum continues:

I gave it as my view that the Secretary of State could not avoid grasping the nettle of this issue firmly, and that it was too deeply charged with grave danger to this country to allow it to remain in the realm of domestic politics. I said I had first proposed to try to carry the policy myself in negotiations between Republican and Democratic leaders . . . but I had come to the conclusion that it was neither appropriate nor proper, and that it would have to be done under the aegis of the Secretary of State. . . .

He said he had had two significant telephone calls this afternoon, one from a congressman of New York inquiring if it were true that the President was about to lift the embargo on the sale of arms to the Jews, and the second a call from Niles at the White House, relaying a message from Morris Ernst of New York, expressing the hope that the embargo would be lifted. Lovett said he had then called Matt Connelly [Mathew J. Connelly, one of the President's secretaries] at the White House and asked him to give a message to the President, requesting . . . that he not release any such statement without first advising the State Department.

[Incidentally, this same meeting with Lovett produced the diary's only hint that Forrestal may have been interested in providing private funds to assist the political battle against Communism

[in Europe. It is, however, no more than a passing reference, by no means clear. This subject does not recur in the diary; there is, on the other hand, a great deal about Palestine in the ensuing days. The seriousness of the military considerations involved is indicated by an entry of January 24: "Lunch today with General Gruenther. We talked Palestine." Gruenther left no doubt as to the Joint Chiefs' realization of the possible effects which future developments of the Palestine situation might have upon their strategic plans. Again on January 28 Forrestal was discussing the subject with Herbert Feis, the economist and former adviser to the State Department. Forrestal brought up "the impression I had of schisms among the Jewish people themselves on the wisdom of projecting the United States into the politics of the Middle East. . . . He discounted the dangers of this and said he felt sure that a policy of firmness by the United Nations would dispose of Arab resistance." Feis was ready to agree that politics should end at the seaboard, "but expressed the opinion that the desire for a national Jewish state was a matter of deep and emotional concern to the Jewish community in the United States."

Next evening, January 29, Forrestal with some of his assistants met with Dean Rusk, Loy Henderson and others from State to discuss the problem. Henderson took the position that the vote of the General Assembly for partition amounted merely to a recommendation, not a final decision of the United Nations itself, and that American support of the recommendation was predicated upon the assumption that it would prove "just and workable." Forrestal asked whether there was not already sufficient evidence "to support a statement that unworkability of the proposed solution would justify a re-examination." Henderson thought that there was. Actually American policy was to be "re-examined," and reversed, more than once in the tangled succeeding history.

Fortified by Henderson's analysis, Forrestal was forceful to the point of bluntness with another visitor a few days later.

3 February 1948   *Meeting—Franklin D. Roosevelt, Jr.*

Visit today from Franklin D. Roosevelt, Jr., who came in with a strong advocacy of the Jewish State in Palestine, that we should support the United Nations "decision," and in general a broad, across-the-board statement of the Zionist position. I pointed out that the United Nations had as yet taken no "decision," that it was only a recommendation of the General Assembly, that any implementation of this "decision" by the United States would probably result in the need for a partial mobilization, and that I thought the methods that had been used by people outside of the Executive branch of the government to bring coercion and duress on other nations in the General Assembly bordered closely onto scandal. He professed ignorance on this latter point and returned to his general exposition of the case of the Zionists.

He made no threats but made it very clear that the zealots in this cause had the conviction of trying to upset the government policy on Palestine. I replied that I had no power to make policy but that I would be derelict in my duty if I did not point out what I thought would be the consequences of any particular policy which would endanger the security of this country. I said that I was merely directing my efforts to lifting the question out of politics, that is, to have the two parties agree they would not compete for votes on this issue. He said this was impossible, that the nation was too far committed and that, furthermore, the Democratic Party would be bound to lose and the Republicans gain by such an agreement. I said I was forced to repeat to him what I had said to Senator McGrath in response to the latter's observation that our failure to go along with the Zionists might lose the states of New York, Pennsylvania and California—that I thought it was about time that somebody should pay some consideration to whether we might not lose the United States.

[Here is an excellent statement of Forrestal's basic motives in a matter which was to involve him in more criticism than any other of his actions in his nine years in Washington. But he went on that same day to lunch with an older, wiser and certainly far more experienced mind than that of the younger Franklin Roosevelt. Bernard Baruch in effect warned him to go slow.

Had lunch with B. M. Baruch. After lunch, raised the same question with him. He took the line of advising me not to be active in this particular matter and that I was already identified, to a degree that was not in my own interests, with opposition to the United Nations policy on Palestine. He said he himself did not approve of the Zionists' actions, but in the next breath said that the Democratic Party could only lose by trying to get our government's policy reversed, and said that it was a most inequitable thing to let the British arm the Arabs and for us not to furnish similar equipment to the Jews.

[It was on this same day, also, that Forrestal received a telephone call from Winthrop Aldrich, chairman of the Chase National Bank in New York, who had been discussing Palestine, evidently at Forrestal's instigation, with Governor Dewey. Dewey, Aldrich said, was very much interested in Forrestal's campaign on Palestine; he thought Forrestal was doing just right; he was in entire sympathy and would cooperate in any way for the best interests of the country. Dewey, Aldrich continued, suggested that any discussions of cooperation be handled through the Secretary of State and John Foster Dulles. It is just conceivable that there echoed in Forrestal's mind a remark of Dewey's he had noted in the preceding fall:[15] "Politics look very simple to the outsider whether he is a businessman or a soldier—it is only when you get into it that all the angles and hard work become apparent." At all events, Forrestal answered cheerfully into the telephone: "I appreciate that a lot, Winthrop. It's a long road, but that's a good beginning. . . . I think he is correct. I think that from now on it ought to be in channels that are, let's say, more correct."[16] And from that time on he left Palestine largely to those other, "more correct" channels.

He sent a transcript of this conversation to Marshall, and on February 7 he drew up a memorandum for the President summarizing his findings. "Eisenhower," according to a concluding paragraph of this memorandum, "told me yesterday that effec-

---

[15] See p. 326.
[16] Telephone conversation with Winthrop Aldrich, 3 February 1948.

[tive U. S. participation in a Palestine police force would involve about one division with appropriate supporting units." But apparently the paper was never submitted. Forrestal probably had to admit to himself that Baruch was essentially right. The crusade to take Palestine out of politics, high-minded as it was in its inspiration, had insufficiently grasped the powerful emotional factors involved. It was accomplishing very little of practical value; it was at the same time impairing Forrestal's own usefulness and bringing down on the Secretary of Defense a volume of criticism to which Forrestal could not, in fairness, subject that office. Forrestal made two appeals to Marshall, on February 12 and 18, to find a "nonpartisan" policy. But these ended his active efforts toward that end. He never changed his opinion; while his interest in Palestine never flagged—it could not, since the area was too deeply involved in every strategic and logistic calculation that he was required to confront. Occasionally and with vehemence he continued to speak of the strategic importance of Palestine and of the danger of letting domestic political maneuvers determine our course there. But his proselytizing in the matter was at an end.

IV

[In the meantime General Eisenhower had taken the President's "hint" and on February 7 he was to transfer the office of Chief of Staff into the hands of Omar Bradley. He had also reached a more important decision, which he confided to Forrestal on January 22.

22 January 1948   *Conversation—General Eisenhower*

General Eisenhower talked with me this morning, after the meeting of the War Council, about his political situation. He said that he had come to a decision that he would not permit his name to be considered for the presidency, and showed me a letter which he had written to send to Mr. Finder of New Hampshire [Leonard V. Finder, publisher of the *Manchester Union Leader*] who had informed him of the entry of his, Eisenhower's, name in the New Hampshire primaries. I remarked to General Eisenhower that the language of his letter was conclusive and meant that he was definitely out of politics. He agreed and said that was his intention.

He added that he had spent a great deal of time in the composition of the letter and that his only misgiving had been that a construction could be put upon it of its constituting a refusal to respond to a duty, around which, he said, his entire life had been built. He remarked that there were many youngsters in the country who, whether with reason or not, had made him more or less a symbol of the duties and obligations, as well as the opportunities, open to American youth, and he was truly worried about the responsibility of, in effect, telling them that there was a limit to any man's conception of his obligation to respond to the call of duty. He said that was why he had put in a paragraph about the danger of letting political considerations influence the conduct and actions of men in the high command in the Armed Forces.

I told him that his letter would put him in a position of tremendous influence, above the battle, and that in this role he could still perform a great service to the country. There is no question in my mind as to his complete sincerity or that his letter reflects the outcome of a genuine moral struggle with himself.

He said that he had had the help of nobody in the course of the composition of the letter and had come to me because he didn't know anybody else that he could turn to for advice. I told him that I thought the letter, both in its content and in its style, was splendid, and I would not recommend changing anything in it.

[Eisenhower released the letter the following day, and it had the effect that its author had intended.

After his talk with the general, Forrestal flew to Chicago to deliver an address the same evening. The experience was to produce some sharp and revealing comment.

23 January 1948   *Address at Commercial Club, Chicago*
Dinner at the Commercial Club of Chicago last night impressed me with the continued remoteness of people of the

Midwest on international affairs. People like General [Robert E.] Wood, reflecting, of course, to some extent, Bert McCormick, Sewell Avery, etc., still hold to the view that (a) our participation in the war was a mistake; (b) that we can work out our own salvation independently of what happens elsewhere in the world. For this reason I did not talk directly about the Marshall Plan. I went into the necessity for the reconstruction of the balance of Europe and of the balance of military power throughout the world, and pointed it up in terms of our oil supply—that over half of the world's known reserves of oil are now in the Middle East, and that we have less than half in the Western Hemisphere, although we are producing and supplying 80 per cent of the world's total consumption. . . .

The Commercial Club is an excellent audience although it has somewhat of the complacent atmosphere of the successful businessman—Merle Trees of the Chicago Bridge and Iron Company; James Forgan of the First National Bank; Sewell Avery, Bob Wood, Fowler McCormick (somewhat less stuffy than the others); Jack Knight of the *Chicago Daily News*; Charlie Freeman of Commonwealth Edison; Chauncey Borland, etc. They are not, however, stupid people, and for that reason I am going to try to have General Eisenhower go out sometime in the spring, to speak. I think they all recognize that we *do* have an interest in the future of Europe, but have a vague idea that in some fashion it is possible to get a purely business solution for Europe's troubles.

I was deeply impressed with Mayor [Martin H.] Kennelly [of Chicago]. Although a Democrat, he has the solid backing of even the most conservative elements in the community. . . . He dislikes the intrusions upon his privacy that are imposed by his job, which I am convinced he is doing out of a sense of duty. There is a general impression that a deal has been made between Republicans and Democrats which will deny the governorship to Adlai Stevenson, although everyone admits that Green [the Republican incumbent] is not a strong candidate. [Here, as so often in 1948, the crystal balls were clouded; Stevenson was not only nominated and elected in November, but Illinois was carried in the process for Truman.]

I had the general impression that in spite of being of an opposite political party, the President continues to hold the respect of these men, although, of course, they take a sharply critical view of his message to Congress. I didn't find any great interest in MacArthur, except from a *Chicago Tribune* reporter.

[These were the familiar preoccupations of domestic politics, to which, of course, no competent administrator could remain indifferent. But already events were building toward a new crisis in the field of military and foreign policy which was to stand in retrospect as certainly one of the major turning points, and possibly a decisive turning point, in the history of the "cold war."

The Forrestal papers by no means tell the whole story of the crisis that arrived suddenly in March of 1948. They do shed a good deal of light upon its backgrounds, insofar as the American aspects are concerned; and they make it clear that it was an episode as complex as it was unforeseen and unpremeditated. To understand the events which were to ensue in March it is necessary to look first at the prior history.

By the latter part of January it was already beginning to appear that the nation would be compelled to some reappraisal of its military policies. It was faced with growing perils on nearly every front. The President had submitted his $11 billion expenditure budget for the national defense; to many it seemed a colossal amount of money, but it was being largely absorbed in the enormous "overhead" of a stand-by military machine, yielding very little actual military strength available for current contingencies. Even to intervene effectively in Palestine would require a "partial mobilization." There was much reason for considering means to increase our military weight upon the world stage, and at the Cabinet on January 30 the President brought up an old and favorite proposal.

30 January 1948   *Cabinet*

The President invited discussion of universal military training. I said the principal suggestion I had to make was that there be a concentration in the National Military Establishment of responsibility for securing suggestions for embodiment in the legislation from other government agencies. I expressed the hope that there would not be too many of these, because of my feeling that to get any legislation through at this session was going to require steady effort and a good deal of legislative skill. I was particularly gratified to have Oscar Ewing, the Federal Security Administrator, say that he felt that any extraneous action such as social training would weaken the chances for the bill, and that, therefore, they should be excluded. It was his opinion that the bill could only pass on the grounds of being a military necessity. I expressed complete agreement with Mr. Ewing and said I hoped we would not be burdened with any of the kind of suggestions that Mrs. Roosevelt had tried to promulgate several years ago when the subject first came up— in the field of training in its broad social sense.

Marshall spoke with great vigor as to the necessity of the UMT Program and made the point that it could not be considered as a matter of arithmetic. Just as in the case of ERP [European Recovery Program, i.e., Marshall Plan aid], he pointed out that the money spent on the UMT program would convince the world that we were ready to follow through on our policy at all times and thereby would in the long run result in the saving of very large sums. Once the world *was* convinced of that fact, it would then be possible to begin the re-establishment of some kind of political balance and stability throughout the world.[17]

[A week after this meeting General Eisenhower retired from active duty as Chief of Staff; in going, he left behind him, at Forrestal's request, a memorandum of grave implications. The General of the Army expressed himself on many subjects—the

[17] The Diary contains another, more colloquial note on this meeting: "Cabinet this morning. I said that at best the course of UMT legislation in the present Congress would be quite rocky and that burdening the bill with a lot of collateral considerations would greatly weaken its chances of passage. I said that I thought calling it a universal service bill was not helpful, that this was an idea that Mrs. Roosevelt had introduced and would seriously prejudice its chances of success. Ewing, much to my surprise, agreed with this. The President said the deletion of the word 'military' had been considered advisable a year ago but he was quite willing to consider the emphasis on military aspects."

[proper role of the Marine Corps, the danger that the Joint Chiefs of Staff might become "fly-speckers," the desirability of commissioning a few outstanding officers in the Armed Forces rather than in any one of the three Services; but his major theme was the weakness of the United States Army. It was already a hundred thousand men short even of its authorized strength and was still dwindling; the "modest Emergency Force of 2⅓ divisions" maintained in the continental United States was below strength. "One of two things will now happen," Eisenhower observed; either there would have to be action to hold the Army at the existing level or it would continue to waste away until the occupation of Germany and the Far East would be no longer possible "and the areas involved would have to be abandoned to chaos and Communism."

It was this inability to maintain Army strength through recruitment that formed a main argument for UMT. But manpower deficiencies were only a part of it. "The problem of matériel," Eisenhower wrote, "is hardly less serious. . . . With certain negligible exceptions, we have purchased no new equipment since the war. Consequently we cannot arm even the few regular combat troops with new weapons developed late in the war but which had not achieved large-scale production. Obviously we have not been able to equip them with weapons developed since the war."

The true consequences of this situation were not to come fully home to the American people until the outbreak of the Korean War, nearly two and a half years later. It is a coincidence that on the day Eisenhower left office, February 7, Communist elements in South Korea precipitated a wave of sabotage, strikes and riots that may be regarded as one of the earliest engagements of the subsequent struggle. But in early 1948 Korea still seemed only one menace, and a relatively remote one, among many. On February 12 there was a significant meeting of the National Security Council.

12 February 1948   *Meeting—National Security Council*

At today's meeting of the Security Council (*Present*: Marshall, Sullivan, Whitney [Cornelius V. Whitney, Assistant Secretary of Air], Hill, Draper [William H. Draper, Jr., Under Secretary of the Army]) discussion dealt with our position and policy in Greece, Turkey, Italy, Palestine and China.

With respect to Italy, decision was reached to expedite the shipment of all available and surplus arms under the general plenary of the President.

With respect to the sending of military assistance to the Greek government in the form of U. S. troop units, reference was made to the letter from the Joint Chiefs of Staff . . . to the effect that dispatch of any American forces to Greece in sufficient numbers to be of consequence would involve a partial mobilization by this country. . . . The question . . . was referred back to the JCS for further study.

With regard to Greece, there was discussion of various alternatives, including (a) withdrawal; (b) sending of American forces; and (c) standing pat on present policy. The Secretary of State asked what was the opinion of the meeting as to the size of forces that could be sent by this country without involving major political considerations. I said that any dispatch of forces would raise serious questions, but for purposes of discussion the largest unit that could be sent without too much commotion would be something on the order of a Regimental Combat Team of Marines.

The Assistant Secretary of the Air Force at this point observed that the Air Force was most desirous of conducting flight training operations in as many strategic areas as possible and suggested that as a compromise there might be some flights of B-29s to Greek airfields which might accomplish at least a part of the purpose in mind in considering the dispatch of ground forces. The Secretary of State indicated interest in this latter suggestion and it was decided to proceed along those lines.

With reference to Palestine, the Secretary of State said that a paper had come to him this morning from his Department outlining three alternative courses as a guide to American policy. They are (a) direct abandonment of American support for the recommendation of the General Assembly; (b) vigorous support for the forcible implementation by the Security Council of that recommendation, which would involve the use of substantial American forces, either unilaterally or jointly with Russia; (c) an effort to refer the question back to the General Assembly and attempt to reshape the policy, not surrendering the principle of partition but adopting some temporary expedients such as a trusteeship, or a joint Anglo-French-American mandate with a revision of the partition decision along the lines of the original British cantonal plan.

The Secretary of State observed that these were simply the statement of alternatives and that none of them carries as yet the approval of the Secretary of State.

With reference to China, Marshall read two documents [which he intended to submit to the Senate and House Foreign Relations Committees]. . . . The gist of both is that we regard the China problem under present conditions of disorder, of corruption, inefficiency and impotence of the Central government as being practically unsolvable; that we cannot afford to withdraw entirely from our support of the Chiang Kai-shek government and that neither can we afford to be drawn in on an unending drain upon our resources. He will recommend to the Congress a sum of about $550 million for aid to China, to be administered by the director of the European Recovery Program.

At this juncture I made the observation that it seemed to me the Secretary of State would have increasing difficulty in dealing with the problems and complexities of our foreign affairs in this highly political year, unless he would have the support on an informed basis of both parties and of the candidates of both parties. Concretely, I suggested that he try to get Vandenberg to invite Taft, Stassen, Dewey and Martin to meet with him at Blair House and make an exposition of the entire field of our foreign policy, with particular reference to Palestine and the Middle East and to the fact that any serious attempt to implement the General Assembly's recommendation on Palestine would set in train events that must finally result in at least a partial mobilization of U. S. forces, including recourse to Selective Service.

At this juncture Secretary Marshall made some remarks on

the question of universal military training. He said that the trouble was that we are playing with fire while we have nothing with which to put it out. He questioned whether we should bring this Greek situation to an issue of the use of troops. On the other hand, he felt that if we appear to be weakening we will lose the game and prejudice our whole national position, particularly since we are now involved in the European Recovery Program.

[In a brilliant phrase Marshall had here stated the whole dilemma. We were playing with fire while we had nothing with which to put it out. On nearly every front we were facing essentially the same grim alternatives: to withdraw, to attempt to stand pat on positions obviously untenable, simply to confess (as Marshall suggested in the case of China) that the problem was "unsolvable," or to take vigorous action—for which the means and trained men did not exist.

What was to be done? Primarily, no doubt, this was a question for the newly unified structure of politico-military administration. Unfortunately the loosely "coordinated" system of unification on which Forrestal had insisted was in practice failing to unify.[18] The Air Force had already manifested its dissatisfaction with the division of the restricted budget.[19] "The process of unification," Forrestal observed in his letter to Admiral Sherman of February 14, "proceeds, but not always at an even pace—three steps forward and about one backward, I would say." There was no really unified military policy or even strategic plan to which the diplomats could appeal under a situation such as Marshall had set forth. And a more or less fortuitous factor had entered to complicate the problem of developing one.

In the previous year the President had appointed his Air Policy Committee, under the chairmanship of Thomas K. Finletter, to make a civilian review of the whole question of aviation policy; a parallel Joint Congressional Aviation Policy Board under

---

[18] To grant this is by no means to say that the monolithic system advocated by others would have worked even as well. The matter might be argued at length; but to the editor it seems most unlikely that the unitary system would have worked at all.

[19] See p. 352.

[Senator Owen Brewster had been set up to study the same subject. Since the closing days of World War II the Air Force had
been arguing vociferously for a permanent Air Establishment of
seventy regular air groups (with numerous National Guard and
Reserve groups in addition)—a goal much higher than the fifty-
five groups allowed under the Truman peacetime military budgets. The Finletter report had been made public on January 13. It
accepted the Air Force estimate of seventy groups as a measure
of the need; in effect, the congressional board was to do the same
when its report appeared a few weeks later.

The Finletter report had made a wide public impact, but it
was not particularly helpful in the specific situation Marshall laid
before the National Security Council on February 12. By its
terms of reference, the Finletter Commission had concentrated
upon air policy, not military policy as a whole; while its attention was plainly focused on a possible future "all-out" war with
Russia rather than on the immediate military requirements of
the moment. However necessary in the long view, atomic bombers were obviously no substitute for ground troops in the policing of Palestine or, say, the protection of Korea; and while a
demonstration by B-29s might be helpful in Greece, it was not
a very effective answer to the particular military menaces there
confronting us.

The acutely felt want was for currently useful ground forces.
What was "lamentably clear" to Forrestal, as he put it some days
later, were "the limitations of our military power to deal with
the various potentially explosive areas over the world" there
and then. The want was so acute that on February 18 there was
a formal review of the situation before the President at the
White House. In the presence of Marshall, Forrestal, Royall and
the full membership of the Joint Chiefs, General Gruenther
gave the President a summary presentation showing how appalling the "limitations" actually were.

18 February 1948   *Meeting—White House*

. . . General Gruenther made a presentation concerning our
available military strength balanced against present and possible
commitments:

STRENGTHS—1 FEBRUARY 1948

	Actual	Budget Authorization	Congressional Authorization
Army	552,000	560,000	669,000
Navy	476,000	526,000	664,000
(includes USMC	79,000	87,000	108,000)
Air Force	346,000	362,000	382,000

Deployments of Major Army Elements

Far East: 140,000 against requirement of 180,000. (Includes 20,000 in Korea as of 1 March 1948 against requirement of 40,000. Department of Army has cut Korea allotment to 30,000.)

Eucom: 98,000 against requirement of 116,000. (In addition, 10,000 in Austria and 5,000 in Trieste.)

Zone of Interior [U. S.] operating 155,000 against requirement of 166,000. This figure does not include the General Reserve.

The total Army shortage will be 165,000 by the end of 1948. The Navy has an acute personnel shortage now which requires the immobilization of 107 ships, but this condition is expected to improve by July 1. The personnel situation in the Air Force is satisfactory.

In Korea JCS face major problem how to secure 10,000 additional troops needed urgently by Hodge [commanding in Korea] for critical period ahead. Choices are: (1) Japan, where already under strength; (2) send Marines; (3) take from General Reserve.

Status of Army Reserves and Marines is:

	Peace Authorization	Actual
82nd Airborne Division	12,200	13,300
2nd Inf. Division	11,400	7,300
(T/O strength [i.e. full war strength] of Inf. Div. is 15,900)		
Combat Command A	2,380	2,000
Task Force and Corps Support		24,000
		46,600

(Usually referred to as 2⅓ divs. Will be reduced to 40,000 by 1 July 1948)

Marine Corps—Equiv. of 2 divisions
in 11 Battalion Landing Teams:

2 BLT's	Tsingtao	2,600
2 BLT's	Guam	4,800
2 BLT's	Camp Pendleton	5,100
1 BLT	On station, Medit.	1,080
1 BLT	En route	1,080
2 BLT's	Camp Lejeune	8,000
1 BLT	Quantico	1,400
		24,060

General Gruenther touched on the possible explosive points in the world, identifying them as Greece, Italy, Korea and Palestine, stating that if a commitment were made in any one of these areas it would probably reduce our reserve to a dangerous degree.

He stated that the British have now in Palestine on the order of 57,000 troops and gave estimates of what would be required to implement a forcible application of the United Nations General Assembly recommendation as from a minimum of 80,000 troops to a maximum of 160,000. . . . [Gruenther here gave some conclusions, derived from war-game studies, as to the communications lines the Russians would have to use if they participated in a Palestine occupation.]

He also gave a brief description of the Emergency Plan, pointing out importance of Middle East to such a plan. . . .

He emphasized that the employment of anything more than a division in any area would make partial mobilization a necessity.

I raised again with General Marshall in the presence of the President the suggestion I had made earlier—that Marshall talk with the leading candidates and leaders of the Republican Party in order to bring them into possession of the military facts of the Middle East, its strategic importance to this nation and the profoundly dangerous situation which would result from the loss of our oil and strategic positions in the Middle East and/or Russian penetration into that area. The President expressed some doubt as to whether such a procedure could be kept in confidence. I said it seemed to me that the matter was of such vital importance that we were constrained to take the chance. My specific suggestion was that we invite Dewey, Stassen, Taft, Howard McGrath, Vandenberg and [B. Carroll] Reece for a briefing by Marshall, Lovett, Gruenther and Bradley.

[Here was the problem. There were not enough ground troops to implement even the existing emergency war plan; to send anything more than a division anywhere would necessitate partial mobilization, while even the small authorized strengths were wasting away for lack of recruits. UMT had been the ground Army's established answer. Marshall, both then and thereafter the chief and unwearied proponent of UMT, saw in it an act of dedication, a gesture of determination, "clear evidence to the world," as he repeatedly argued, "that we did not propose to abdicate our responsibilities in Europe or anywhere else in combating the rising and spreading tide of Communism." [20] But it also had a more direct bearing on the immediate problem. It was believed that UMT, with its various Service options, would encourage recruiting for the Regular Army—thus at least saving the small authorized formations—and would fill the skeletons of the reserve components. "Up to the present time," as Forrestal had already written February 10 to Chan Gurney, chairman of the Senate Armed Services Committee, "we have not found any feasible alternative to UMT as a means of providing the necessary trained personnel for the National Guard and the Reserve." But Gurney had not been encouraging. On the 16th he had called, together with Saltonstall, another member of the committee, to say that "they had reached a conclusion they should not start hearings on universal military training until they had a more precise statement of the cost of UMT and its relation to other components of the military budget." [21]

[20] Diary, 4 March 1948.
[21] Diary, 16 February 1948.

[To work up cost figures was obviously not difficult; to relate
them to all the other aspects of the military budget was another
matter. There had never been any real integration of the Army's
plan (UMT), the Air Force plan (seventy groups) and the
Navy's plans. The Finletter report had given great encouragement to the always ardent advocates of "air power"; and Gurney's
hesitation may have reflected a feeling—it was soon to become
very prominent in congressional opinion—that massive expansion
of the Air Force could serve as a substitute for the unpopular
universal training system. Unification was failing to unify; and
the executive order [22] in which, at the time the act was passed,
the President had defined the roles and missions of the three
Services was proving quite inadequate to still the disagreements
among them.

In a letter to Eisenhower on February 21 Forrestal threw
out an idea for getting the Joint Chiefs away from Washington
now and then on a long week end; "the difficulty with this
town," he wrote, "is the constant interruptions from various
sources with constant failure to get any time for sustained thinking." Sustained thinking by the Joint Chiefs was becoming more
and more imperative, and Forrestal was to act upon his own
idea perhaps sooner than he had intended. In a memorandum of
February 27 he advised the President that he had "informally"
let the Joint Chiefs know that he would like to have their decision on the roles and missions of the Services by March 8, adding, "I propose then to make my own decisions. . . . . From the
standpoint of budget considerations, the present world situation
and public opinion, I think I cannot do anything else than press
along the lines indicated."

There were of course many other problems in these days. One
was the perennial issue over German plant deliveries and the
German level of industry. Forrestal was consistent in his opposition to the further weakening of Germany; and when the
subject arose at the Cabinet on February 13 he argued that "it
was unrealistic to talk about ripping up plants in Germany with

[22] See p. 296.

[one hand and then rebuild and re-establish them with the other
hand with the European Recovery Plan." The President gave his
view at a luncheon on the 16th.

16 February 1948   *Lunch—White House*

. . . Marshall said that a number of delicate situations were
involved [in the question of plant deliveries]—not merely relationships with Russia but also with England and France, particularly the latter. The President said he did not want to be
in the position of defaulting on the Potsdam Agreement on
reparations, under which 10 per cent of the Western Zone of
Germany's plants were to go to Russia without any counter-
payment, and 15 per cent to go on a payment-in-kind basis.
The President vigorously asserted that he did not believe in the
Morgenthau Plan for Germany and had never supported it, but
by the same token neither did he want to see Germany rebuilt.

It was finally decided to approve Marshall's memorandum
which provides for a re-examination of plants in certain categories, such as agricultural chemicals, friction and ball bear-
ings, light steel and aluminum.

[Still another source of trouble was casting deepening shadows,
as appears in an entry for the 24th.

24 February 1948   *Lunch—Atomic Energy Commission Matters*

Conversation with Senator Hickenlooper, and subsequently
lunched with Hickenlooper, Arthur Hill and Quincy Bent [vice
president of Bethlehem Steel Company].

The Senator said he had come over to give expression to certain rather vague misgivings which he was experiencing in
connection with the Atomic Energy Commission and its activities. He could put his finger on no one action or policy, but
said that the character and number of the speeches which
Lilienthal was making, the emphasis upon the future possibilities of atomic power as a source of energy for industrial and
general purposes, and his constant reference to control of atomic

energy by "the people," all made a pattern with ultimate indicated objectives as follows: (1) The indispensability and
therefore the perpetuation of Mr. Lilienthal in power; (2)
the general underlying idea of statism.

He said that outside of Lewis Strauss there was no one on the
commission of any great practical ability, although undoubtedly
Bacher [Robert F. Bacher, AEC member] was a good scientist.

He was disturbed by the fact that there had been practically
no advances made in the art since the dissolution of the Manhattan District and he was further concerned that the one man
who had brought the Manhattan District to successful completion was no longer in this field of work, namely General
Groves. . . .

[In a conversation a few days later with Rear Admiral John E.
    Gingrich, the AEC's Director of Security, Forrestal was to hear
    further doubts; the Admiral was disturbed by "the lack of proper
    security and surveillance measures for atomic materials," and
    the "lack of practical industrial-business direction in the com-
    mission's activities." He cited the Brookhaven Laboratory proj-
    ect on which $40 million was spent "under the control of nine
    universities." Forrestal did not record his comments.[23]

    Forrestal could also find time for other matters, familiar to
    every father of a boy in college.

To Peter O. Forrestal, 1 March 1948
Dear Pete:

I just had your report marks for the First Semester. I imagine
they were not entirely satisfactory to you, but I am confident
you will be able to buck them up for the next term by a little
planning and application to the subjects in which you are low
Third Group. I was glad to note that you had a Second in
mathematics. If you can maintain such a standing in that subject, there is no question but what the others can be lifted in
proportion to the time and concentration you invest.

All of which is heavy paternal stuff—and I might add that I

---

[23] Diary, 3 March 1948.

hope you won't look up my own marks in the files, because they
were not so hot.

As ever,
/s/ Dad

[Unfortunately, in the press of great events the diary could
rarely if ever record such winning glimpses of the personal side
of Forrestal's character. And events were now to begin to move
with dramatic speed.

It was on February 24, and against the background of the
various concerns which have just been described, that one of
the world's "explosive points"—though not one of those which
Gruenther had listed—blew up with a shocking suddenness.

CHAPTER X

The March Crisis

I

[On February 24, 1948, an armed and violent Communist *coup d'état* abruptly seized power in Czechoslovakia. Communist "action committees" roamed the country, suppressing all possible opposition; the Communist Premier, Klement Gottwald, formed his new Cabinet the next day, and the Czechoslovak Republic, which from its foundation at the end of the First World War had been a model of successful democratic governance in Central Europe, was subverted at a stroke into a satellite Communist dictatorship, or "people's democracy," on the already familiar pattern. Throughout the West the shock was profound. The methods used did not differ greatly from those which had already been applied in the Balkans and elsewhere; this was, however, the first forcible Communist conquest of a strongly based free government, and in the eyes of most Western publics it put an altogether new light upon the power, ferocity and scope of Communist aggression.

Forrestal made no diary entries during the next few days, and there is no specific diary reference to Czechoslovakia. His appointment calendar, however, is unusually full of engagements with high military and diplomatic officials; he lunched with the Joint Chiefs of Staff on February 25 and with the State and Army leaders on the 26th; he saw Gruenther, Bush of the Research and Development Board, Hillenkoetter of CIA, Whitney of the Department of Air, Souers of NSC and officials of the Budget Bureau in these days, and it is scarcely possible that

[Czechoslovakia failed to figure in the discussions. Neither is it surprising that the first diary note subsequent to the crisis should have dealt with the altogether different subject of China, for it was clearly a moment inviting a stock-taking of our position all around the world.

1 March 1948   *General Wedemeyer*

Meeting this morning with General Wedemeyer [who had returned from the Far East to become Director of Plans and Operations, Army General Staff]. I asked him his view about China and our present policy. It is obvious that he feels it is unrealistic and that Marshall is not facing up to the problem because he has a feeling of frustration and failure. Wedemeyer said that when he first met General Marshall after the latter's appointment as ambassador he, that is Marshall, had shown him the directive written for him by the State Department (John Carter Vincent and Company), the objective of which was a government based upon a coalition of the Kuomintang Party and the Communists. Wedemeyer said he had informed Marshall immediately that such an objective was impossible of attainment because of the completely differing nature of the two organizations and the fundamental fallacy of assuming that there could be political association with any Communist group without ultimate absorption by it. He said the present Army representative in China, Major General David G. Barr, is polite and loyal, a good officer, but almost entirely lacking in force.

[Italy was another possible "explosive point," as Forrestal heard on the following evening when he met with Representative John Lodge and Alberto Tarchiani, the Italian Ambassador. The Ambassador was concerned about the election to be held on April 18. "He said the Communists were spending from twenty-five to thirty millions of dollars in addition to lire brought in from Yugoslavia. He said De Gasperi [the Premier] would not give in as Beneš [President of Czechoslovakia] had done, that the Italian people, he was confident, did not want Communism, but that there was an undercurrent of fear which made the

[outcome unpredictable—the same kind of fear which had made
many who did not believe in Mussolini join his party. . . . I
asked the Ambassador about the loyalty of the Army and he said
there was no question as to the loyalty of its top command, but
that there might be some Communist infiltration at the lower
levels." [1]

The administration's first concrete response to the Czech overturn seems to have been an effort to push through UMT. On
March 2 Forrestal lunched with the Secretary of State.

2 March 1948   *Lunch*

Lunch today with Marshall, Lovett, McCloy [at this time
president of the International Bank] and Souers. The Secretary
of State reported a meeting he had this morning with members of the Armed Services Committee of the Senate, Senators
Gurney, Saltonstall, Bridges, Byrd, Hill and Kilgore.

Saltonstall told him that it would be impossible for the
Senate committee to make any progress unless he, Marshall,
made it clear to the country through either a speech or statement, which would have wide circulation and receive broad
attention, of the relation of universal military training to his
conduct of foreign policy. Subsequently Senator Gurney called
me to say that the visit had been most interesting and had impressed people like Senator Byrd and Senator Bridges. The
Secretary of State said he believed the Armed Forces would
have to modify their ideas of what they needed to implement
universal military training. He recalled the fact that when he
got Selective Service through [in 1940], the Army had practically nothing to implement it whereas now we at least have
the camps, buildings and so forth. The important thing from
his point of view is to get the adoption of UMT in order to
make inescapably clear both to our friends and non-friends
that there is continuity, firmness and will behind our foreign
policy.

He said that Bridges at the end of the conversation told
him he should be sure that the Armed Services, and in par-

[1] Diary, 2 March 1948.

ticular the wives of leading officers, be brought into line. The Senator mentioned a dinner which he attended last evening at which he said the wife of an officer had expressed the strongest views against UMT. I gave it as my opinion that the command in both the Air Force and the Navy were now solidly behind UMT—that the Navy had been lukewarm about it originally but were now convinced that even they had to have it, and that the Air Force, possibly a more recent convert, was also ready to give more than lip service in support. I mentioned the fact that I had talked about it this morning with Mr. Symington, who was anxious to make any contribution he could to a renewed campaign on behalf of such a bill. . . .

Both Secretary Marshall and Under Secretary Lovett are now ready for him, Marshall, to take the lead in renewing the drive for UMT either through the occasion of a speech in California on 19 March or before the Senate Armed Services Committee, or possibly the entire Senate. (After the manner of his, Marshall's, appearances before the entire Congress during the war.)

On my part, I agreed to get hold of the appropriate people in the Army to endeavor to bring our figures within more reasonable limits and also to try to have them reconciled with Navy and Air Force figures.

There was some consideration given to a joint effort by Marshall and myself to get a concurrent resolution through the House and Senate giving approval immediately to the principle of UMT, linking the implementation to a subsequent bill, the thought being to capitalize on the present concern of the country over the events of the last week in Europe.

Senator Gurney called me up after lunch to say that his meeting with the Secretary of State had been excellent and to advise me that he was calling me and the three Service Secretaries and the Chiefs of Staff before his committee on Monday morning to tell us that we had to get a more realistic approach from a budget point of view. . . .

[On the day after this meeting there was a development of an alarming kind, recorded only in a terse note:

3 March 1948   *Submarine Sighting—Eniwetok Atoll*

Word today from Eniwetok that there was affirmative identification of a non-U. S. submarine with schnorkel on the surface in the neighborhood of Eniwetok.

[It was at Eniwetok atoll that the second series of atomic tests (of which there had been no public announcement) was to be held in the following month.

It can only have increased an already rising tension. In a telephone conversation with Representative Walter G. Andrews that day, Forrestal had agreed that the President would have to give serious thought not simply to UMT but to a revival of Selective Service. On March 4 Forrestal called on Senator Walter F. George of Georgia, ranking minority member of the Finance Committee, member of the Foreign Relations Committee and one of the most powerful of the conservative Democratic senators. Forrestal wanted George and some of his colleagues to hear a "presentation of the world situation by a member of the Army Staff" (presumably this was Gruenther's summary as given at the White House two weeks before). It is an example of Forrestal's constant care for congressional relations, and at least suggests that already the administration was realizing that more would be required in the way of rearmament than UMT.

4 March 1948   *Meeting—Senator George*

. . . I mentioned particularly Palestine, and said that many people were saying we should implement the recommendation of the General Assembly with vigor and promptness, who did not realize the fact that the deployable Army troops left in this country total less than 30,000, to which might be added 23,000 Marines, whereas the British had to employ 90,000 troops merely to *police* the Palestine area, without trying to impose any political partition or to create a new state. . . .

The people I have in mind [to hear the proposed presentation] are Senator George, Senators Millikin, Baldwin, Robertson (Wyoming), Knowland, Hickenlooper, Ives (?), Byrd, Vandenberg and Gurney if they choose to come, Saltonstall and Cabot Lodge (?).

I said I didn't want to have it so large as to take on the character of a sales talk or a persuasive presentation—I had merely been so impressed with this particular global recital that I felt it would be both interesting and instructive to people like himself—that in fact I felt it my duty to make such facts available.

[Tension was rising. The Czechoslovak *coup* had spread a sense of nervousness and excitement through the free world. Washington, already alarmed by the perils it faced and its powerlessness to meet them, had clearly begun to move in the direction of a more effective military policy. And then on March 5 there arrived a top-secret telegram from General Clay in Berlin, which fell with the force of a blockbuster bomb. Forrestal copied the text in his diary:

5 March 1948   *War—Likelihood in near Future*
                                      —Message from Clay

FROM CLAY EYES ONLY TO CHAMBERLIN [LIEUTENANT GENERAL STEPHEN J. CHAMBERLIN, DIRECTOR OF INTELLIGENCE, ARMY GENERAL STAFF]

FOR MANY MONTHS, BASED ON LOGICAL ANALYSIS, I HAVE FELT AND HELD THAT WAR WAS UNLIKELY FOR AT LEAST TEN YEARS. WITHIN THE LAST FEW WEEKS, I HAVE FELT A SUBTLE CHANGE IN SOVIET ATTITUDE WHICH I CANNOT DEFINE BUT WHICH NOW GIVES ME A FEELING THAT IT MAY COME WITH DRAMATIC SUDDENNESS. I CANNOT SUPPORT THIS CHANGE IN MY OWN THINKING WITH ANY DATA OR OUTWARD EVIDENCE IN RELATIONSHIPS OTHER THAN TO DESCRIBE IT AS A FEELING OF A NEW TENSENESS IN EVERY SOVIET INDIVIDUAL WITH WHOM WE HAVE OFFICIAL RELATIONS. I AM UNABLE TO SUBMIT ANY OFFICIAL REPORT IN THE ABSENCE OF SUPPORTING DATA BUT MY FEELING IS REAL. YOU MAY ADVISE THE CHIEF OF STAFF OF THIS FOR WHATEVER IT MAY BE WORTH IF YOU FEEL IT ADVISABLE.

[Again the diary makes no comment on this alarming telegram. But that it did cause intense alarm among those in Washington who were aware of it is now well known, while its influence seems clearly traceable in the events of the next few days.

[The Clay telegram came on a Friday. Gurney had called his
meeting of the Armed Services Committee and the military
heads on the subject of UMT for the following Monday; its purpose, he had said to Forrestal, was "to tell us that we had to get
a more realistic approach from a budget point of view." [2] When
the meeting took place there were, to be sure, plenty of objections voiced to UMT on budgetary and other grounds. But the
result was a unanimous committee decision to proceed forthwith on hearings on the measure.

8 March 1948   *Armed Services Committee*
   . . . The objections, chiefly voiced by Senator Byrd, although shared to some degree by Senator Saltonstall, were as
follows:
   1.   The ultimate amount of the money involved in UMT
is around $4 billion. To add this to the already large sum ap-
propriated for military purposes would mean a $50 billion na-
tional budget, which would wreck the country.
   2.   So far as the effect on Russia and the rest of Europe
is concerned on the passage of UMT, the passage by the Senate
and rejection by the House would not merely rob the discussions of any value in the implementation of our foreign policy,
but would actually weaken that policy because it would show a
split in the country which would be interpreted as a vote
against war or against our determination to resist the overrunning of Europe.
   3.   The effect of the Finletter report and of the Brewster-
Hinshaw Board [this was the parallel Congressional Aviation
Policy Board which had reported on March 1] has been to convince the country that by a substantial increase in appropriations for Air, there would be no necessity for UMT. . . .
   Senator Morse said he felt there was a need for a review
and presentation to the country of the facts about the world
situation and our present military weakness. He said he had
spoken in many parts of the country over the past few months
and wherever he went he encountered the impression that

---

[2] See p. 385.

there was no real or serious danger of war, and that while the Russians were truculent and difficult, the situation would be ironed out without breaching the peace.

[The diary does not say so, but according to news reports at the time the committee was told, in answer to the objections, that UMT had become "not only mandatory but necessary." The committee unanimously voted to start hearings. Forrestal told reporters after the vote that "events are making progress for us," [3] and it is not difficult to guess what event he had in mind. "The atmosphere I'd say is considerably improved," he said to Robert Cutler two days later, "the improvement derived from other events that one can't take much pleasure in. I think the political aspect of it is much better." And he added, "It is always the difficulty of not being hysterical and at the same time giving them the grim facts, and the facts are grim enough." [4]

Events were making progress; yet at the meeting with the committee there had already appeared the shadow of what was to become an embittered controversy, seriously hampering the course to rearmament. The Finletter and Brewster reports had fostered the notion that by increasing expenditures on Air, "there would be no necessity for UMT." Actually—and it was a weakness in the administration position—UMT was scarcely a more relevant answer than Air expansion to the pressing immediate need, which was for some readily available forces, not to fight a possible future third world war but to deal on the ground at that time with the "various potentially explosive areas," as Forrestal put it, out of which alone the danger of a future world war could come.

The need for better Service integration and consistency of basic strategic plan was urgent. Forrestal had already told the President that if the Joint Chiefs did not produce decision on the roles and missions of the Services, he would make some decisions himself. On March 10 he informed his press conference that he was summoning a prolonged meeting, outside of Washington, of the Joint Chiefs of Staff to thrash out the whole controversy over

---

[3] *The New York Times,* 9 March 1948.
[4] Telephone conversation with Robert Cutler, 10 March 1948.

[missions and to decide "who will do what with what." If they
failed, he said, "I shall have to make my own decisions"; and he
added—it seemed almost as an afterthought—that the Services
were now agreed that some form of compulsory military service
was a necessity. It was no longer a question of whether or not
to adopt UMT; if there were no UMT there would have to be a
revival of the draft.[5] The meeting of the JCS was actually convened on the following day at Key West.

It was also on March 10 that Jan Masaryk, Foreign Minister of
Czechoslovakia, son of the country's first President and liberator,
and a figure well known and well liked in all Western capitals,
fell to his death from a window of his official residence. According to the official announcement, he had committed suicide. The
event added enormously to the initial shock of Czechoslovakia's
subversion.

II

[The conference—it lasted from the 11th to the 14th of March—
to which Forrestal summoned the Joint Chiefs (Leahy, Bradley, Denfeld and Spaatz) and their aides, in the seclusion of the
Key West Naval Base, marked the beginning of the effort to rebuild the Armed Forces of the United States. It also marked the
first really serious attempt to grapple with the paralyzing divisions between the Services and to re-form the Military Establishment as a whole into a genuinely integrated team, designed to
meet the actual rather than the theoretic military problems confronting the country. Both efforts were to progress, unevenly
and with many difficulties and discouragements, down to the outbreak of the Korean War in 1950.

Forrestal prepared some terse "Notes for Friday—Opening of
Meeting," which he later entered in his diary. They are sketchy,
but they clearly show the searching significance which he saw in
the seemingly technical question of "roles and missions." "We
must be guided," the notes began, "by the National Security Act,
but I don't want the impression that we are engaged in legalistic
discussions." The Navy, they continued, would keep its own air

---

[5] *New York Herald Tribune,* 11 March 1948.

[power but would have to realize that budget limitations might compel it to "make-do" with help from others; that it would, for example, have to give Air Force crews training in antisubmarine work and the close support of amphibious landings. The notes go on:

11 March 1948   *Notes for Friday*

. . . 3.   There should be certain studies inaugurated now looking to reciprocal use of personnel in the event of emergency. For example, I doubt if the Navy will require the number of pilots that were in training at the end of the last war. *Question*: Could any of these be made available to meet deficiencies of the Air Force?

4.   *Question*: What is being done about joint amphibious training operations between Army and Marines and Navy, so that techniques and tactics will be identical?

5.   *Question*: Are there any plans for the use of Marine commanders with Army units on tactical maneuvers?

6.   Function of strategic bombing is the Air Force's.

7.   The Navy is to have the Air necessary for its mission, but its mission does not include the creation of a strategic air force.

8.   Both Services, that is, Navy and Air Force, have to give much more thought and help to the third Department, the Ground Forces, who are the catch-all for the unwanted and unglamorous jobs.

9.   The mission of the Navy which was inescapable in the Pacific war was the knocking out of enemy-held land bases which were unreachable by land-based Air. I should like to see some study given to the possibility of passing surplus Navy air power into the Air Force when such missions are no longer necessary. For example, the closing phases of the Japanese war. . . .

[Without a clear definition of the responsibilities of the several Services, without plain answers to these questions on the integration of function, no intelligent division of military manpower, munitions or money could be made.

[As the discussion got under way on Friday there arrived a dispatch from the Secretary of State, advising them of still another area of tension and carrying, incidentally, an early suggestion of the North Atlantic alliance which was later to take so important a place in American military planning.

12 March 1948   *International Situation—Russian Expansion*

Dispatch from Marshall today reflecting deep apprehension on the part of Great Britain over the evident intention of the Soviet Union to bring immediate pressure upon Norway to negotiate a pact similar to that which they are now asking of Finland. Bevin makes three proposals:

(1)   Build around the five-nation (U. K., France, Benelux, etc.) pact.

(2)   A plan for Atlantic security.

(3)   A Mediterranean system of security.

Bevin suggests a meeting in Washington between British and American representatives early next week.

[Apparently, the Joint Chiefs had not reached a point where they could consider such larger possibilities as these. At Key West they continued to thrash out the issues of inter-service relations. Even here they seem not to have answered all of Forrestal's penetrating questions, but by Sunday noon (March 14) they had arrived at certain "broad, basic decisions." The diary summarizes them as follows:

1.   For planning purposes, Marine Corps to be limited to four divisions with the inclusion of a sentence in the final document that the Marines are not to create another land army.

2.   Air Force recognizes right of Navy to proceed with the development of weapons the Navy considers essential to its function but with the proviso that the Navy will not develop a separate strategic air force, this function being reserved to the Air Force. However, the Navy in the carrying out of its function is to have the right to attack inland targets—for example, to reduce and neutralize airfields from which enemy aircraft may be sortying to attack the Fleet.

3. Air Force recognizes the right and need for the Navy to participate in an all-out air campaign.

[With this decided, there was still a half-hour left before lunch. Gruenther brought up a Staff paper that would otherwise have awaited their next meeting. This paper laid down five propositions: The joint war plan of the Joint Chiefs called for larger Armed Forces than Congress had authorized; existing forces had shrunk to levels below even those which had been authorized; therefore voluntary enlistment was a failure; UMT could not furnish additional men fast enough; therefore the Joint Chiefs should recommend immediate re-enactment of the draft law. The conference accepted the conclusion, and Forrestal's summary ends:

It was concluded that it is now necessary to ask immediately for a restoration of Selective Service.

It was concluded that an immediate examination of atomic energy matters is required, including the decision on whether or not now is the time for turning custody of the weapons over to the Armed Services.[6]

[Though the diary does not mention it, it was also decided, according to a subsequent public statement of Forrestal's, to request the President to ask a supplemental appropriation from Congress "in order to bring our total strength up to the point where it more nearly met the realities of the world situation."[7]

Forrestal left Key West the same afternoon. He stopped overnight at West Palm Beach and did not reach Washington until Monday afternoon. It was not until 5:15 that day that he reported to the President. His account of the Key West decisions included one or two additional points: "Navy not to be denied use of A-bomb"; "Navy to proceed with development of 80,000-ton carrier and development of HA [high altitude] aircraft to carry heavy missiles therefrom"; and he also reported that the Joint Chiefs were of the opinion that custody of the completed atomic

---

[6] The Diary note bears the date 11 March 1948, but covers the whole conference.
[7] Address to the American Newspaper Publishers Association, 22 April, *New York Herald Tribune*, 23 April 1948.

[bombs should be turned over to the military. "I said the condition of readiness of these weapons was highly uncertain—that what a civilian might think was ready would be a long way from readiness for battle use."

More important at the moment than his own report, however, was what Forrestal learned. The President, already advised of the Joint Chiefs' conclusion that revival of the draft was essential, had a couple of hours before announced a dramatic decision.[8]

President Truman had an engagement of some weeks' standing to speak at the St. Patrick's Day dinner in New York City on March 17, and he had intended to use the occasion for a plug for UMT. The Joint Chiefs' demand for Selective Service had put the matter into a much more serious context. According to Forrestal's diary note:

15 March 1948   *Meeting with the President*

The President said he was going to deliver a message to Congress on Wednesday going all out for Selective Service and UMT. He said the original idea had been that he would make reference to this in the St. Patrick's Day speech that evening, but Marshall had felt that that was not a proper forum. We have arranged to have the UMT initial testimony-taking deferred until Thursday, when Marshall will be the first witness.

[In changing his "forum" the President had changed to one that would give his remarks the very maximum of solemnity, urgency and effect. The news of Monday afternoon that he was taking the unusual course of addressing a joint session of the House and Senate two days later (in addition to making an important policy speech in New York the same evening) came with a sensational impact. It is reflected in Forrestal's diary note of the next day.

16 March 1948   *International Situation*

Papers this morning full of rumors and portents of war. Wallace in New York interview yesterday charged that United

---

[8] The announcement was given out at the White House at 3:35 p.m. *New York Herald Tribune*, 16 March 1948.

States was fomenting war and the Czech *coup* was an act of desperation by the Communists to which they were driven by threat of a Rightist *coup*. Nothing could be sillier, but such statements, even from Wallace, will have their effect. The fact is that this country and its government are desperately anxious to avoid war. It is simply a question of how best to do it. If all Europe lies flat while the Russian mob tramps over it, we will then be faced with a war under difficult circumstances, and with a very good chance of losing it.

It is inconceivable that even the gang who run Russia would be willing to take on war, but one always has to remember that there seemed to be no reason in 1939 for Hitler to start war, and yet he did, and he started it with a world practically unprepared. Our effort now is to try to make the Russians see the folly of continuing an aggression which will lead to war, or, if it is impossible to restore them to sanity, that we at least have a start which will enable us to prevent our being caught flat-footed as we were in 1941.

[Since General Clay's telegram of ten days before, the intelligence services had been working at high pressure. Not until this Tuesday, March 16, was the CIA able to hand the President a brief combined estimate by State, Army, Navy and Air Force, saying that war was not probable within sixty days; and not for another two weeks was CIA able to extend even this tenuous forecast of peace.[9] In the meantime, even before the President's message had been delivered, there was already evidence that the decisions of Key West would be insufficient to control the quarrel over the allocation of the rearmament effort for which everyone now assumed that the President was about to call.

16 March 1948   *Press Release—Key West Conference*
Secretary Symington called this morning to say that Norstad and Spaatz were not in agreement on the press release to the effect that there had been agreement in all major areas at Key West. I said I believed this referred to the preamble or statement of philosophy. I subsequently talked to General Spaatz

---

[9] Diary, 23 December 1948, which gives a summary report of the March crisis.

and asked in what things there was not an agreement. He then referred to the preamble mentioned above and said the basic question was whether there were to be two air forces, with separate training, separate Service commands, etc.—in other words, whether there is to be one air force or two, with all the duplication resulting from the latter.

I said what he really had in mind was a modification of the law, and he agreed that was the case. I then said that was a matter for Congress, that I had to administer a law and not try to contort the present law into a different concept than Congress had authorized.

I said what General Spaatz was talking about would involve going to the Congress for a change in the legislation, and he agreed that was the case. I said I was not going to get into a discussion on that point because we had a law that was given us by Congress and it was up to us to carry it out.

[In the midst of all this, Forrestal had a meeting the same morning with the House leaders; he was to testify before the House Appropriations Committee in the afternoon.

16 March 1948   *Speaker Martin—Key West Meeting*

Meeting today at the office of the Speaker of the House, with Congressmen Andrews [Walter G. Andrews, Republican of New York, chairman of the Armed Services Committee] and Halleck [Charles A. Halleck, Republican of Indiana, majority floor leader].

I gave a brief résumé of the conclusions and agreements reached at Key West, and in particular laid stress on the fact that while it would be desirable to build up our Air Force, additions to our air power alone without accompanying increase in the components of the Army Ground Forces and the Navy might give us an unbalanced military organization and an illusory sense of security

[Forrestal made no note on his meeting with the House Appropriations Committee in the afternoon, but from the newspaper

[accounts it seems clear that his effort was to secure a sound allocation of whatever rearmament funds might become available.

Next day, March 17, Forrestal with the rest of the Cabinet
joined the President in the Oval Room of the White House and
accompanied him to the Capitol. The message was remarkably
forceful. For the first time the President identified the Soviet
Union as the "one nation" that was blocking all efforts toward
the writing of a peace and was aggressively threatening the free
world. We must, he said, meet "this growing menace." He described at some length the development of Soviet policy. "It is
this ruthless course of action," he continued, "and the clear design to extend it to the remaining free nations of Europe, that
have brought about the critical situation in Europe today. . . .
I believe that we have reached a point at which the position of
the United States should be made unmistakably clear. . . . There
are times in world history when it is far wiser to act than to hesitate."

The message was, and was widely assumed to be, a ringing call
for a serious effort at military rearmament to meet a situation
that had been deteriorating alarmingly in the preceding weeks.
Yet specifically the President asked for only three things:
prompt enactment of the Marshall Plan program for European
economic aid; the adoption of UMT as "the only feasible means
by which the civilian components of our Armed Forces can be
built up to the strength required"; and the "temporary" re-enactment of Selective Service "in order to maintain our Armed
Forces at their authorized strength." The draft, in other words,
was recommended simply as a means of filling the existing
ranks; there was no proposal to enlarge the low authorized scale
of the regular establishment, and the sole increase of military
strength which the President, in terms, suggested would have
gone only to the reserve components, and to them only in the long
run, through the slow operation of UMT. The situation had been
stated with great vigor and effectiveness; the response in Congress and the country was highly favorable, and both public and
congressional opinion was prepared for a considerable additional
effort of rearmament. But no considered, consistent and agreed

[program to guide such an effort existed; and it was not until nine
days later (on March 25) that Forrestal was able to present a
concrete plan, with facts and figures, to the Senate Armed
Services Committee. In the meanwhile, the only specific proposals that had been generally publicized were those of the Finletter and Brewster Committees calling for a seventy-group Air
Force; and the many ardent advocates of "air power," both in
Congress and out, were assuming that rearmament should begin
there.

The day after the President's message Forrestal found proof
of its impact.

18 March 1948   *Armed Services Committee on UMT*
                                      and Selective Service

Ten o'clock meeting with [Senate] Armed Services Committee on UMT and Selective Service. The most surprising
fact developed were the questions asked by Senator Kilgore
[Harley M. Kilgore, Democrat of West Virginia] and Senator
Morse [Wayne L. Morse, Republican of Oregon]. Senator
Morse's questions in particular were sharp and pointed with
relation to the overhanging threat of Russia in Europe, and
reflected a pronounced and surprising change in attitude. The
same could be said of Senator Kilgore although his questioning was somewhat less well conceived.

[Forrestal made few diary notes during these days. There is a
record of a somewhat cryptic telephone conversation with Representative Walter G. ("Ham") Andrews on the 18th, concerning the preparation of a draft bill. There was, Forrestal suggested at one point, "something more than meets the eye. I think
our friend General Vaughan has been doing a little bicycle work."
There are also two diary notes on atomic energy matters.

18 March 1948   *Lunch—General Spaatz, Mr. Leva*

Lunch with General Spaatz and Mr. Leva [one of Forrestal's
assistants]. General Spaatz brought up the question of atomic
energy with particular reference to the custody of weapons
and their surveillance.

19 March 1948   *Secretary Royall* et al.

Meeting at Secretary Royall's office with Admiral Strauss, Dr. Ernest O. Lawrence of the University of California, Dr. Irving Langmuir of GE, and Colonel Kenneth D. Nichols. Lawrence's proposal was a plan to use AE in a different form and deny the use over great areas such as cities and industrial centers, etc., to massed population, but do it in a way that would not expose such populations to extermination.

[A few days later Forrestal got another reaction to the international situation.

23 March 1948   *Dinner—Walter Winchell, Secretary Symington*

Dinner tonight with Walter Winchell and Stuart Symington. Winchell had a copy of his Sunday night radio address in which he addressed a message to Stalin to the general effect that America did not want war, would do its utmost to avoid it, but on the other hand would not tolerate a repetition of the events that led to Hitler's attempt to gain power over all of Europe. He said he had had a thousand telegrams within an hour after its delivery. He also said that the chief of the Russian Intelligence in New York City, V. M. Sobolev, had called up within an hour after its delivery to see if he could get a transcript.

He said one story which the Wallaceites were circulating and giving great emphasis to was that President Truman had had an indirect indication from Moscow that Marshal Stalin would be glad to meet him (the President) in Sweden, and that the President had turned this down.

[If the diary entries are few in this period, the appointment calendar is again filled with high-level meetings with military and congressional authorities as the administration program was worked out, and for six o'clock on the evening of March 24 there was scheduled: "Final 'dry run' of presentation to Senate Armed Services Committee," which was to take place the following day. He was already feeling pressure to drop the unpopular UMT proposal. Representative Leon H. Gavin, Republican

[of Pennsylvania, called him to urge that he abandon UMT and
concentrate instead upon the draft; his answer is of interest.

Telephone Conversation with Leon H. Gavin, 24 March 1948

. . . Forrestal: Ambassador Douglas was here at lunch and
he said the most dangerous thing for this country is to get the
impression that this is a temporary period of tension. He said,
"I think this will be with us for the next decade." You can't
keep this country on a draft Army basis indefinitely, and the
only thing that would get you off the hook of the Selective
Service is some form of UMT. . . .

[In a long day before the Armed Services Committee on the
25th Forrestal, supported by his three Service Secretaries and
their three Chiefs of Staff, presented the administration program
—"a specific program," as he phrased it, "which is solely designed
to achieve one great objective: to avert war, whether it be open or
covert."

In an opening statement of striking power and bluntness he
described the international situation as he saw it. He compared
it with that of 1914 and of 1939 and placed the aggressive policies
of the Soviet Union squarely beside those of Hitler and Mussolini.
"The record," he said, "shows that despotism, whatever its form,
has a remorseless compulsion to aggression. . . . Today another
power, wearing the false mask of freedom for the people, seeks
to spin its web over all Western Europe." As against the very
great military forces of the Soviet Union, he argued, the West
also had immense political, economic and spiritual reserves; but
to avert an ultimate war under disastrous circumstances they had
to be given some military effect then and there. "Now is the
time to let the world know that our fields will not lie fallow,
but that we shall keep them planted for a quick harvest of
strength and will, not next year or next month, after the rich
prizes of northern Italy and the Ruhr and Sweden and France
may have fallen, but now."

To this end he proposed a program for "a balanced strength
in manpower—on the ground, on the sea, in the air." He di-

[vided the program sharply into two parts (this contributed to clarity, although it plainly exposed UMT to separate defeat): "the short-term, which looks to the immediate strengthening of our regular forces; the long-term, which looks to the provision of adequate reserves."

Here it was for the first time made plain, as it had not been in the President's message, that what was asked was not simply the maintenance but the immediate increase of the regular establishment. For this, the "short-term" program, Forrestal requested an increase of 349,500 men, from the actual total (as of March 1) of 1,384,500 to 1,734,000, these to be supplied by Selective Service. With recommended increases in equipment, weapons, aircraft and other items, the total cost would be $3 billion, over and above the $11 billion expense budget already presented for the coming fiscal year.

All three Services were to benefit under the program, but the accent was preponderantly on the ground forces, where the actual want was most acutely felt. Of the additional manpower, 240,000 were to go to the ground Army and 11,000 to the Marines—together, nearly 72 per cent of the total asked. A sum of about $775 million was asked for the procurement of new aircraft and for air research; this, however, was to be divided between the Air Force and Naval Air. The Air Force would receive additional men and means to fill out its existing fifty-five-group organization; there was no provision to increase it to the desired seventy-group goal. For the "long-term" program, Forrestal proposed the adoption of UMT to fill the reserve components; the costs of this would be additional, although the budget had already requested $600 million to initiate the system.[10]

Symington and Spaatz had appeared with the others in support of what was presumably a carefully balanced and mutually agreed program. Under questioning by the committee, however, they did not conceal their conviction that the Air Force should be given its seventy groups; Symington, at least, did not

---

[10] *The New York Times,* 26 March 1948.

[hesitate to leave the plain inference that the Air Force had been overridden by the other arms. Symington estimated that the full seventy groups could be provided for a further $800 million. Forrestal was recalled for further questioning.[11]

From the record of his diary and papers, already given, his position would seem to be plain. It was from the want of ground troops (and supporting tactical aviation) as revealed in Gruenther's analysis in February that the whole movement toward rearmament had originated. At Key West and elsewhere he had repeatedly emphasized the needs of the ground Army and the importance of integrating the other arms and Services with it into currently effective military forces. As he was to insist then and later, he had no objection to an Air Force of seventy groups; but with the Military Establishment already seriously unbalanced, in his eyes, by its lack of tactical components, he did not want to see the Air Force still further enlarged at the expense of the "unglamorous" elements whose weakness was the source of our current embarrassment and helplessness. It was the reason for his constant stress on a "balanced" military structure. One may observe that the experience in Korea two years later seems amply to confirm the soundness of the position. However that may be, he now told the senators that an establishment based on a seventy-group Air Force, with the other arms in proper proportion, would cost, not the additional $800 million of Symington's simple estimate, but more like $15 billion in addition. The discrepancy between the two figures produced an instant confusion; and as the hearing ended that day there had been precipitated a damaging and often passionately embittered controversy.

Forrestal went back to his office that day and shot off two one-sentence queries to General Gruenther; they well illustrate the quickness with which he grasped the essential implications of the day's events.

Memorandum: To General Gruenther, 25 March 1948

Have the JCS a plan of what is required in the way of collateral support for the Air Force seventy-group program?

---

[11] *New York Herald Tribune,* 26 and 27 March 1948.

Memorandum: To General Gruenther, 25 March 1948

Have the JCS made any evaluation of the desirability of endeavoring to equip the armed forces of nations in Europe, specifically those of France, Belgium and Holland?

[If Congress wanted seventy air groups, it was necessary to know at once what should go with them; and if Congress was not going to furnish the essential ground forces, they would have to be found somewhere else.

III

[The brickbats had inevitably begun to accumulate. "This office," he had written to Robert Sherwood the year before, in the glow of popular acclaim over his appointment, "will probably be the greatest cemetery for dead cats in history";[12] and the dead cats were duly arriving upon his doorstep. He had already come under heavy criticism for his activities in the Palestine question; the Air Force controversy was to subject him to much more. "After all," as he wrote to Peter Grace early in March, "one cannot expect to be liked by everybody when there are decisions to be made or a policy to be formed"; and he said in the same letter that "when I quit it will not be in response to the pressure or the criticism." "I don't particularly mind the criticism," he wrote to another correspondent, "but it is nonetheless heartening to hear from someone who is in agreement." [13] He thanked another for sending him "John McClain's piece in the *Sun*. Its implications are far beyond what I deserve, but among the slings and arrows that come from other directions, I am grateful for this balance." [14] And to McClain himself (of the New York *Sun*): "I am afraid that your column will make the taxpayers believe that they have someone with more steel than the old frame contains; however, I will do my best to live up to the picture."

His answer to still another friendly letter, from Senator Robertson of Wyoming, gives a suggestive glimpse of his attitude, five

---

[12] See p. 299.
[13] To the Reverend Stewart M. Robinson, 24 March 1948.
[14] To Charles H. L. Reilly, 30 March 1948.

[days after the Senate Armed Services Committee hearings, on
Service unity.

To the Honorable E. V. Robertson, 30 March 1948

. . . I am grateful that you think the job is well done, but
I am forced to tell you that it was no one-man accomplishment.
It was only possible because of the cooperation and understanding of three broad-minded and patriotic men: General
Bradley, Admiral Denfeld and General Spaatz, combined with
the talents and real ability of Major General Gruenther in
achieving resolution of differences.

The course is not yet smooth by any means, and I don't want
to give you the impression that our troubles are all behind us.
We have, however, made a beginning, and with good will
from all quarters will be able to improve it. . . .

[The day after the Senate committee hearings a brief diversion appeared from an unexpected quarter.

26 March 1948

Secretary of State Marshall called me this morning to say
that he just had word from the White House that Franklin
Roosevelt, Jr. was going to make a statement this afternoon, to
the effect that the Democratic Party would have to draft General Eisenhower as its nominee for the presidency, and asked
me for my suggestions. [The sensational factor here, of
course, was the implication of revolt, led by the late President's
son and namesake, against the Truman leadership.] I said I
would be glad to talk to young Roosevelt myself but doubted
whether this would be effective and suggested that I inform
General Eisenhower and see if he would care to talk to him.

I called General Eisenhower and he was very reluctant to call
[Roosevelt]. He said that if I called Roosevelt I could quote
him (General Eisenhower) that he would be greatly distressed
at any such move and public declaration.

Senator McGrath told me that my calling would not affect
young Roosevelt because he was very set in his ideas and was
determined to go ahead.

I called Eisenhower about 2:15, reported these facts to him, and he said that he would be willing to call. He called back in about ten minutes and said that he had got hold of Roosevelt and said that any action of this kind now, in the middle of very delicate situations in various countries abroad, could have the most dangerous consequences and might negate American policy. He said that he would personally urge in the strongest possible terms that any statement which might be interpreted abroad as implying failure to support the President at this most critical time or to indicate deep and serious splits in public opinion would be detrimental to the country. He said he was making this observation without reference to any political considerations, particularly as they affected himself; that he had tried to make himself clear on that point when he made his public statement some weeks ago. That he meant what he said then and was sorry that people didn't believe him, but it still continues to be true.

[In spite of this urgent advice, "young Roosevelt" went ahead with his plan; fortunately the repercussions in both international and domestic politics were less serious than they might have been or even, perhaps, than Mr. Roosevelt had expected.

Palestine, meanwhile, continued as a constant and embarrassing problem. American policy had now shifted to the advocacy of a joint Anglo-French-American trusteeship, which Austin was about to present to the United Nations. On the 29th Lovett telephoned: What could Austin say if he were asked what forces the United States would contribute toward the policing of such an arrangement?

29 March 1948   *Conversation with the President and*
                 Under Secretary Lovett re Palestine Trusteeship

. . . I said that at the moment we did not have such forces available and that I did not see how we could escape making an effort to contribute.

I then talked to the President who said he did not want to make any firm commitment to send troops into Palestine, but

I told him what Lovett's problem was and that he was simply trying to get something affirmative for Senator Austin to say in case he was cornered. The President then said that he felt that if we had to respond [we could say] that we would participate in the implementation of the trusteeship mandate . . . up to the limit of our ability. I then called Mr. Lovett and reported my conversation with the President and suggested to him that he write out the precise language which he proposed to have Senator Austin use and send it to the White House so there would be no possibility of a misunderstanding. He said that that was what he was in the process of doing.

[On the next day Forrestal was doing some missionary work for the military program with union labor.

30 March 1948   *Luncheon—Philip Murray*

Luncheon with Philip Murray [president of the CIO], Edward F. McGrady [a former Assistant Secretary of Labor and an expert on labor relations] and Secretary of the Army Royall for discussion of UMT and Selective Service. Mr. Murray said he was bound by an action of the CIO annual convention last year in which "a strong and unequivocal position was taken against a peacetime draft." He said that had to continue to be his position. McGrady raised the question of whether the executive committee (or Council) of the CIO could not properly review such a decision of the convention if there were a radical change in circumstances. Mr. Murray agreed that that was always possible.

He said that the CIO was making progress in weeding the Communists out of its organization but were encountering substantial difficulties from the United Electrical Workers and some other unions. In response to my question he said he regarded the conversion of Joe Curran of the NMU [Joseph Curran, president of the National Maritime Union] as genuine.

[From a British visitor next day he heard an echo of the recent atomic energy negotiations and received an interesting glimpse, at the same time, of British press relations.

31 March 1948   Breakfast—Admiral Sir Henry Moore, Royal Navy

Breakfast this morning with Admiral Sir Henry Moore [who told him he was acting for Lord Portal, head of the British Atomic Energy Group]. The purpose of his visit was to advise me that in order to put an end to rumors and guesses, some of which were appearing in the British press, about a change of policy by the British on the manufacture of atomic weapons, the government would shortly, either through a speech of a Cabinet member in the House, or elsewhere, state that the government was proceeding with rearmament and the construction of modern weapons, including guided missiles, atomic weapons, etc. The British press will be alerted by what they call a "D" Notice some days prior to the announcement and will be asked not to emphasize the atomic part of it, and, as always, they expect to get full cooperation from the press. . . .

[This breakfast with Sir Henry was Forrestal's last untroubled
    meeting that day. For at this moment fresh and seemingly deadly
    crisis struck. General Clay's fears of imminent war in Germany
    had not so far been borne out. But now the Russians made an
    alarming move. It was the beginning of the Berlin blockade.

31 March 1948   Meeting with Secretaries Royall and Symington,
                Generals Bradley, Eisenhower and Spaatz, Admiral
                Denfeld, Messrs. Lovett, Beam and Thompson.[15]

Subject was a dispatch received from Clay to the effect that he had just received a communication from Lieutenant General M. I. Dravotin that in the interest of greater efficiency in the handling of affairs of the Russian-occupied portion of Germany, a new system of inspection and validation of personnel coming into, or leaving, the Russian Zone would be instituted as of April 1. In effect this means that the Russians assert the right of inspection of material coming in by either train or truck to the Berlin area and the right to examine the

---

[15] Jacob D. Beam, chief of Division of Central European Affairs, and Llewellyn E. Thompson, Jr., chief of the Division of Eastern European Affairs, State Department.

credentials and the belongings of personnel (the previous practice had been for the American commander to provide the Russians with his manifest of goods shipped into the Zone and a roster of the personnel, the Russians accepted in good faith the word that the latter's credentials were in order). Clay asked for instructions. He proposed to issue orders to American personnel aboard such trains to prevent the Russians from coming aboard and shoot if necessary. Subsequently the text of the letter of the Russian general came in and while the intent of annoyance and embarrassment to General Clay and his personnel is apparent, the wording was not as truculent as could be inferred from Clay's first message. The following suggestions were considered:

1.   That the President send a message to Stalin pointing out that implementation of the Russian proposal might create an incident which might be provocative of war.

2.   That he call into conference the majority and minority leaders of the House and Senate.

3.   That instructions be sent to Clay endorsing his proposed action, with a qualification that he be told that his guards would not use their weapons except in self-defense.

4.   It was also suggested that immediate communication be had with the British to see whether they had taken action identical to ours and given similar instructions to their train guards.

At Mr. Lovett's suggestion the proposal to have the President address a communication to Marshal Stalin was discarded because it would add disproportionate emphasis on this incident and might convince the Russians that they had secured precisely the effect they were after.

The President on his own initiative decided against calling in congressional leaders because (1) it would become immediately known, and (2) it would add unnecessarily to the creation of a war hysteria.

The question of concerted action was disposed of by a ticker announcement that the British did not propose to stop running their trains and that they would maintain armed guard personnel on them.

[There was a continuous series of conferences throughout the
day. Clay was given his orders to bar the Russians from the
trains; this he did, and the Russians retaliated by stopping the
trains themselves at the border points. Cargoes of food were
actually flown into the Western sectors of Berlin on April 1—a
faint prevision of the later famous airlift. The episode was to
prove, however, only the first brush of the cat's paw. On April
1 there arrived an estimate of "Soviet Intentions" from the American Embassy in Moscow; this gave the Soviet Armed Forces
the "capability" of overrunning Europe but not of carrying war
"to the Western Hemisphere," and concluded that "the Soviet
Union will not deliberately resort to military action in the immediate future but will continue to attempt to secure its objectives by other means." [16] On April 2 CIA felt able to extend its
estimate that there would be no war beyond the sixty-day period of its March 16 forecast, though this time the Air Force was
unwilling to concur.[17] But the Russians in the next day or two re-
laxed their restrictions on Berlin's traffic; some trains began to
move, and the crisis, despite the uneasiness which it left in its
wake, appeared to pass. It was not until midsummer, after some
three months more of these irritating and tentative tactics, that
the blockade was clamped down in earnest on the Western sectors of Berlin.

IV

[In the meanwhile there were still many problems, aside from
those of the budget, involved in getting the new machinery
of the National Security Act in motion. The current tensions
lent a particular urgency to those centered in industrial mobilization. Forrestal held a luncheon meeting on April 1, with Snyder
(Treasury), Attorney General Clark, Krug (Interior), Anderson
(Agriculture), Lovett and others. Various suggestions were advanced: that "someone start now planning the organization of a
skeleton WPB," in which Krug said he would be glad to help;

---

[16] Forrestal entered a later précis of this report in his diary under the date of 21
October 1948.
[17] Diary, 23 December 1948, when Forrestal entered the summary account of the
March crisis.

[that they should start financial planning, of which Snyder said that "it was important to get the RFC back into business for the purpose of making loans for raw materials"; that they should explore questions of substitute materials or substitute material sources; that they should "organize the various statistical services that will be required in any war effort, such as the Bill of Material Plan which was necessary for the successful operation of the Controlled Materials Plan" in the previous war; that they should reconsider the policy of the War Assets Administration in disposing of war plants which might better be retained. "Lovett and Krug both raised the question of stockpiling and said an immediate effort ought to be made not only to get more money for stockpiling purposes, but to extend economic assistance to countries . . . which were the source of usable raw materials." Arthur S. Barrows, Under Secretary of the Air Force, made an interesting reference to "specific bottlenecks on such a vital item as jet engines. He said in this case the blades and buckets were the tight items, both of which involved highest quality heat-resistant alloy steels." Memoranda of this discussion were sent both to Hill of the NSRB and Hargrave of the Munitions Board; many of these matters were to cause much thought and argument over the ensuing months.[18]

Nor was even the relatively lesser matter of policing a possible Palestine trusteeship settled as yet. Lovett was still appealing for a concrete estimate of what would be required; as a result of his request there was a special Sunday meeting on April 4 of the Joint Chiefs, their principal planners, Air Force and State Department officials, which Forrestal attended. Dean Rusk, director of the State Department's Office of Special Political Affairs, put the dilemma succinctly. "If we did nothing," he said, according to Forrestal's notes, "it was likely that the Russians could and would take definite steps toward gaining control in Palestine through the infiltration of specially trained immigrants, or by otherwise capitalizing on the widespread, violent civil war that would be likely to break out." Moreover, Rusk added, "the slaughter of thousands and perhaps hundreds of thousands" in Palestine which might result would create the gravest problems for the

---

[18] Diary: Memoranda to Arthur Hill and Thomas J. Hargrave, 1 April 1948.

[United States. "In the event of such developments the United States might be forced to intervene, and intervention under those circumstances might require a substantially larger force than the force required simply to support a trusteeship."

But the main difficulty (as Forrestal well knew) remained: we had no available forces. The Joint Chiefs gave their opinion that even if the trusteeship were undertaken under a truce by Jews and Arabs, the extremists on both sides would be unlikely to respect it; we would still be faced with the "possibility of extensive violence by irresponsible groups," and to meet this "a minimum of approximately 104,000 troops would be required" to start with. (It had been concluded only a few weeks before that the United States could not send more than a division—about 15,000 men—anywhere without "partial mobilization.") The Joint Chiefs added a comment particularly significant in view of the rising controversy over air power: they "felt that the particular type of operation was one which required almost exclusively ground troops rather than any substantial air components." The meeting ended on another equally significant but almost pathetic note: "It was suggested that the British might undertake to hold the fort alone pending the augmentation of our forces following the adoption of Selective Service." [19]

Palestine was not, in the end, to call for occupation by American troops. But the situation made it only more urgently necessary to clear up the developing snarl over the Air Force appropriations and get the rearmament program under way. A hint of the rising difficulties may, perhaps, be read in a memorandum of April 5 to Symington: "Don't send any letter to Senator Gurney without first checking with me." [20] But a letter of the same day to John Taber, chairman of the House Appropriations Committee, shows that Forrestal himself was working to smooth the troubled atmosphere. One very practical limiting factor on any plans for Air Force expansion was the capacity of the existing industrial plant to meet suddenly increased demands for aircraft. In this letter to Taber there appears for the first time the idea of making all proposed appropriations for aircraft pro-

[19] Diary, 4 April 1948.
[20] Memorandum for Secretary Symington, 5 April 1948.

[curement immediately available in order to start work at once, save time and discover what bottlenecks might exist. He wrote next day (in a slight mixture of metaphors) to the chairman of the United Aircraft Corporation.

To Frederick B. Rentschler, 6 April 1948

. . . It is obvious we cannot, without wrecking our economy, go to a war-production basis, and yet we have to see there is enough in the hopper to get the industry off the ground. I talked with both the House and Senate Appropriations chairmen and I believe there is a reasonable chance that we can get made available for immediate contract authorization all the aircraft part of the 1948-49 budget, together with the aircraft part of the $3 billion supplemental which the President sent in last week.

[On April 8 Forrestal, backed by a presidential request, laid this proposal before the House Appropriations Committee. He issued a public statement at the same time, repeating that he was neither for nor against the seventy air groups, and revealing the fact that the Joint Chiefs had the matter under study; he also repeated his warning that to increase the Air arm would require large corresponding increases in the Army and Navy. The President heartily endorsed this position at his press conference.

In retrospect, it would seem that if the only object were the prompt and sound expansion of the Air arms, the proposal to proceed at once with appropriations already in sight was a logical, indeed a necessary, one. But the whole subject by this time was suffused with emotion. Hampered by his inability to lay the full facts of the international and strategic situation before the public, Forrestal had failed to make clear the real issues, and the new proposal unquestionably only confused still further a public already pretty badly at sea. Many took it as simply an effort to "head off" the seventy groups.

Forrestal was frequently before the committees in the next few days. On the 12th, when he appeared before the House Armed Services Committee, Representative Carl Vinson, now the rank-

[ing minority member and an old coadjutor of Forrestal's from the days when Vinson had served as chairman of Naval Affairs, announced that he would move to amend the new aircraft procurement bill by adding $922 million for the seventy-group Air Force. At the same time Congress, in its enthusiasm for air power, seemed to be losing what slight interest it had ever had in UMT. When Forrestal saw Representative Taber next day, the Appropriations chairman told him that "Mr. Vinson had taken the bit in his teeth on the subject of seventy air groups and might be able to get a substantial increase through the House. He [Taber] was highly critical of the Air Force presentation of figures and of their overstatements." [21] Vinson with two associates followed Taber into the office within the hour.

13 April 1948   *Meeting—Congressmen Vinson,*
                                      Paul Kilday, Lyndon Johnson

Meeting this afternoon with Congressman Vinson, Congressman Paul Kilday [Democrat of Texas] and Congressman Lyndon Johnson [Democrat of Texas]. Mr. Vinson said that he and his associates, plus a large number of Republicans, had decided that they would support the authorization of the seventy-group Air Force and insist upon the addition of funds to implement it, to the $3 billion supplemental now before the Congress. I pointed out to them that I was not against the seventy-group Air Force and that it was simply a question of proceeding in an orderly way to arrive at the funds necessary to implement it, to be sure we knew what we were buying, and not act in a way that would give any possible enemy the idea that we were hysterical or overfearful. He replied that if the additional funds were not voted now, it would not be possible to do so later in the session. I questioned this, but he stuck to his point. I said the important thing was getting orders into the plants with the greatest possible speed so that they could begin their planning, and also so that as their subsuppliers received subcontracts from them, the effect on the economy would be apparent, and tight spots and bottlenecks would be revealed.

---

[21] Diary, 13 April 1948.

I said I was particularly concerned about the Army—that the Navy had its ships and its strong, well-organized Reserve, but that both in terms of the personnel necessary to support an enlarged air program and also trained and usable troops to seize or hold bases overseas, the Army situation was alarming.

Subsequent to Mr. Vinson's call, I talked to Chairman Taber, Congressman Andrews and to John McCormack.

[Forrestal talked to Vinson next day, urging him to reach some adjustment with Taber. Vinson "suggested a compromise on sixty-five groups, to which I replied that I would rather talk about money, because I regarded the group concept as a rather fluid and flexible thing, and that my concern was to see that we had an orderly examination of the effect of the impact of these new demands on the economy in order to prevent runaway inflation." [22] He also talked to Taber again that morning, and the latter raised a matter which was to have many later reverberations. Taber "particularly mentioned the B-36 [the giant, six-engine "intercontinental" bomber], of which, he said, the Air Force had originally planned to procure a hundred planes and had then cut the order to thirty. In this connection I said that I felt constrained to tell him that I regarded this as a wise decision— that the B-36 had been built for World War II and that the change in the order was simply an effort to find out if it could be adapted to the changed conditions of a future war." [23]

Meanwhile Symington and Spaatz had repeated before the House Armed Services Committee their demand for the seventy groups; while General Bradley, following them to the stand next day, now added to the uproar by reverting to what the Army had originally asked—a total force of 822,000 men rather than the 782,000 provided under the Forrestal program. Presumably Bradley reasoned that if the Air Force could jump the traces the Army could do likewise. Bradley put the true situation rather more clearly, perhaps, than Forrestal, with his diplomatic insistence on "balance," had done, when he bluntly said that the 822,000-man requirement, providing for twelve full-strength

---

[22] Diary, 14 April 1948.
[23] A diary note of 14 April appended to the entry for 13 April 1948.

[divisions, "is necessary at this time, whether we have fifty-five groups, seventy groups or any other number of groups." But in so doing, as the leading military critic, Hanson W. Baldwin, observed, "he emphasized inferentially the cleavage of the Armed Services in strategical concept, intelligence analysis and personalities. . . . 'Unification' becomes a joke when the Secretary of the Air Force goes over the head of the Secretary of Defense and of the President himself." [24] The House, at any rate, was in no mood for the niceties of strategic theory; on Thursday, April 15, by a vote of 115 to 0, they amended Forrestal's consolidated aircraft procurement bill to add $822 million for starting a seventy-group Air Force, and then passed the whole by 343 to 3 and sent it to the Senate.

While these fires of enthusiasm and controversy were raging in public, Forrestal was struggling in private with the Joint Chiefs. By Monday, April 12, they had at last achieved a tentative answer to the question he had shot at them three weeks before: What would be required in the way of collateral support for a seventy-group program? Gruenther was to point out to them (as he later told Forrestal) "that the draft letter that they had tentatively agreed on Monday had caused you a certain amount of indigestion, in connection with certain parts of it. They recognized that that was probably true." [25] At any rate, the formal report was laid before him on Wednesday, April 14. There was adroitness in its solution for the multiple dilemma. "Based solely on military considerations," the Joint Chiefs unanimously reported, "it is the opinion of the Joint Chiefs of Staff that the administration should advocate a balanced Military Establishment commensurate with the seventy-air-group program for the Air Force." It was their "unanimous" judgment that such an establishment should include an 837,000-man Army in a total force of over 2,000,000, and they put the additional over-all cost at $9 billion instead of the $3 billion of the Forrestal program. But the report continued: "The Joint Chiefs of Staff recognize, however, that the phasing (of this balanced Army, Navy and Air Force program) must be made responsive to such other factors as the

[24] *The New York Times,* 15 April 1948.
[25] Telephone conversation with General Gruenther, 18 April 1948.

[capability of the aircraft industry to expand, the impact of the cost of the program on the national economy and the calculated risk which can be accepted in the light of changing world politico-military situations." [26]

Under the circumstances, this left the "phasing" as the obviously vital question. In a session on Thursday the Joint Chiefs wrestled with it, without reaching a conclusion. The week end came. In the comparative calm of Sunday (April 18) Forrestal was busy on the telephone. His assistant, McNeil, told him he doubted that the Joint Chiefs would have their answer by Tuesday "because I think they are going to have a terrific battle, and I would encourage them to submit a split paper rather than a watered down, unanimous decision." Forrestal agreed, and raised another question. He had suggested to the Joint Chiefs the possibility of getting a supplemental of $5 billion instead of $3 billion; now the House vote of $822 million for the seventy-group Air Force threatened to consume nearly half of such an addition— assuming that they could get it from the Budget Bureau and Congress. The conversation continued:

Telephone Conversation with W. J. McNeil, 18 April 1948

MR. MCNEIL: That's correct, although you know Taber put a hooker in that bill.

MR. FORRESTAL: I know. With that hooker, I'm not so sure we ought not to let her go through.

MR. MCNEIL: By adding one more year to it.

MR. FORRESTAL: I didn't get that one-year part.

MR. MCNEIL: Well, when this bill was written originally the authority was available immediately, and was good till June 30th, 1949; then Taber, in this same amendment, added 822 and lengthened the period one year, till June 30th, 1950.

MR. FORRESTAL: So they have until then to make the contracts?

MR. MCNEIL: That's correct. . . . He could only have done that with the idea of saying, okay, I'll go along with the increase, but in the back of my mind I'm expecting it to last twice as long.

---

[26] Forrestal's statement of 21 April, *The New York Times*, 22 April 1948.

MR. FORRESTAL: The real hooker is the President's control, isn't it?

MR. MCNEIL: Definitely. There are two or three hookers in there, but none of them is so bad.

MR. FORRESTAL: With that in it I'm not so sure we should oppose the bill.

[As passed, the bill was to make the spending of the money dependent on a presidential finding as to "necessity"; with this "hooker," the control over the $822 million would still be in Forrestal's hands, and that problem became less serious. He talked next with Gruenther, who told him that the Joint Chiefs would meet for two and a half hours next day and in an all-day session on Tuesday, in order "to go over the program of each Service, seventy-group-wise, money-wise and every-wise, where they are to find out and analyze, criticize and knock the —— out of each other's budgetary programs." [27] Senator Chan Gurney was next on the telephone. "These men," Forrestal told him, "are meeting again tomorrow morning for three hours, and I would like to keep their noses in this until I get an answer that has some meaning to it. . . . I have asked two kinds of questions, in addition to those that I had already addressed to them: number one, their recommendation for the division of that part of the supplemental $3 billions which does not deal with aircraft procurement; number two, what they would divide, how they would divide, an increase of $5 billions. . . . Then I have got to get the President to decide what he is willing to ask the Congress for. I'd like to keep their noses at this job until I get the thing back from them, because I do not want to go down there with speculative and unfirm answers." And again in the same conversation: "But this Air thing doesn't scare me, Chan; I won't say that they have shot their bolt completely, but people like Baruch who understand this whole business of mobilization, the thoughtful people, are doing some thinking about it." [28]

The climax came at the Monday JCS meeting, which Forrestal attended.

---

[27] Telephone conversation with General Gruenther, 18 April 1948.
[28] Telephone conversation with Chan Gurney, 18 April 1948.

19 April 1948   *Meeting of the Joint Chiefs of Staff*

Conclusion of a discussion about money and appropriations, particular reference to the split-up of 3 billions supplemental to the 1948-49 budget, it was clear that there could not be an agreement reached within the framework of these figures.

We therefore went into a study.

I asked the Army and Air Force at that point to ascertain how near they could come to their objectives with the addition of a half-billion dollars. General Spaatz estimated that with 273 millions additional, the Air Force could activate all of its seventy-group program except for two troop carrier groups and two light bombing groups. These estimates were later revised to 180 million.

With reference to the proposed addition to the supplemental bill in the House of 822 millions, I remarked that that was an entirely different matter, that the purpose of this meeting was to reach an agreement upon the funds available under the ceiling imposed by the budget plus what additional amount I hoped to be able to get.

I said General Spaatz and Mr. Symington would have to decide for themselves later on as to the testimony that they would give on this other subject.

[Laying the "other subject" to one side, the Joint Chiefs settled for an expansion of the original program by $481 million, making a total supplemental of $3,481 million (and a total military budget for 1948-49 of about $14.5 billion). On Wednesday morning, April 21, Forrestal, accompanied by James Webb, Director of the Budget, by Bradley, Denfeld and Spaatz, and by McNeil, laid this conclusion before the President. Forrestal was told to assemble the details and submit them through the Budget Bureau, but meanwhile he was authorized to lay the program before Congress.[29] He did so the same afternoon, with a long, formal statement and testimony before the Senate Armed Services Committee.

If scarcely a complete account of what had been going on, this was at least the clearest statement of the situation that had

---

[29] Calendar, 21 April 1948; statement, 21 April 1948.

[yet been laid before the public. Forrestal quoted the Joint Chiefs' conclusion, "based solely on military considerations," that what was required was a "balanced" establishment based on seventy air groups, with a two-million-man force and a $9 billion supplemental appropriation. He also quoted their proviso that the "phasing" of such a program would have to be "responsive to such other factors" as economic realities and changing world politico-military situations. The purely military estimate, he said, was "their job"; he intimated on the other hand that the phasing was the job of the civil administration and the Congress. Consequently he had asked the Joint Chiefs a "supplementary" question: "Granted the military desirability of the $9 billion program, what program would the Joint Chiefs recommend—in the general vicinity of $3 billion—as the most effective military program within the limits of the funds that will probably be available to us?"

He had, he said, received their answer to this the previous day (again he emphasized that it was "unanimous," thus firmly nailing the Air Force to the new platform); he had submitted it to the President and had received authority to present it to the committee. He then described the $3,481 million supplemental program, calling for a total force of 1,795,000 men. Its results in terms of manpower may best be put in tabular form:

	Final agreed program	Less than JCS program by:	More than original program by:
Army	790,000	— 47,000	+ 8,000
Navy	552,000	—116,000	+ 0
Air Force	453,000	— 49,000	+53,000
Total	1,795,000	—212,000	+61,000

It would, Forrestal explained, permit the expansion of the Air Force from fifty-five to sixty-six groups; but would accomplish this largely through reactivating moth-balled B-29s rather than through the construction of new aircraft.[30]

---

[30] Statement of 21 April, *The New York Times*, 22 April 1948.

[The battle was far from over. But so far Forrestal, relying on his favorite methods of patience, tolerance and gradualism, had carried his main points. As the table indicates, the Air Force was the principal gainer from the four weeks of controversy since the introduction of the original program. It had been given enough men for eleven extra air groups, which would virtually complete its program (it had no great interest in the four primarily tactical groups of troop carriers and light bombers that were deferred), although it had not been given the money to equip them with new planes. It did have large amounts of money for re-equipping and maintaining the existing fifty-five groups, and there was the promise of the House's $822 millions even for the new ones. All this was reasonably apparent at the time. What the public could not so easily grasp was the measure of Forrestal's accomplishment.

He had averted the danger that the whole rearmament effort would be swept, by the public enthusiasm for "air power," into an expansion of the Air Force, which might be necessary for fighting a third world war but was of little use in the current job of preventing one. He had secured the critical essential—an increase in the ground forces and a beginning on their re-equipment—and he had secured it in a way that committed the Air Force to its support and in such a form that Congress would have to accede and would, moreover, have to accept Selective Service if it was not to stultify itself. He had done even more. Hanson Baldwin's verdict that "unification becomes a joke" was well warranted at the time; but actually Forrestal had for the first time enforced the rudiments of a genuine unification upon the Services. The "hookers" on the aircraft procurement bill insured orderliness in whatever industrial mobilization might be undertaken. And Forrestal had got all this within budgetary limits which he believed the President would agree to. He knew that the President was very reluctant to support major and dislocating armament programs (of the kind that Mr. Truman was later compelled to ask for in 1950 and 1951) and that the country was unprepared for them. Forrestal himself was unprepared at the time to accept such risks of "explosive inflation," as is indicated

[by his frequent statements that greatly enlarged military budgets would "wreck the economy."

In doing all this he had been obliged, in effect, to sacrifice UMT, which never had much chance after his April 21 statement. He was willing to defend Symington and Spaatz in public and in his correspondence; summing it all up in an address to the American Newspaper Publishers Association in New York on April 22, he made it plain that although he had disagreed with them they had had the right to testify as they did, and had done so with his approval. The situation was confused and confusing, and the public was inclined to mistake Forrestal's gradualism for failure. It did not clearly see that what he had actually done was to keep American military policy on course —a course which, however stormy it was to prove, was to lead to invaluable results only two or three years later.

CHAPTER XI

The Effort to Rearm

I

[The fact that there was another aspect to the problem of defense has already appeared, fragmentarily, in this record. In the midst of the Key West discussions Marshall's telegram had arrived, reporting Foreign Minister Bevin's proposal for a "plan for Atlantic security" to be built around the five-power Brussels Pact.[1] One of Forrestal's first queries, after the presentation on March 25 of the original rearmament program, was whether the JCS had any plans to equip European defense forces.[2] At the height of the argument over the domestic military program this important subject had recurred.

9 April 1948   *Conversation—General Gruenther—*
                    Western European Pact

General Gruenther informed me today of the progress of the conversations between the British and the United States staffs on European security.

1. The five nations concerned in the Western European Pact are extremely anxious for the United States to associate itself with that pact. The present American attitude is that the President should make a fair statement giving his blessing to the organization of the five-nation alliance but without formalizing it in the form of a treaty or even a protocol. This

---

[1] See p. 392.
[2] See p. 403.

would not be satisfactory to the Europeans. A curious fact is that Canada is equally as strong as Britain for the formation of the alliance. More understandably, Mr. Spaak, of Belgium [Paul-Henri Spaak, Foreign Minister], also supports it most strongly.

2. The British have always held to the view of what they call the three pillars of strategy: Britain itself, the Mediterranean and the sea lanes. To these they now add a line in Europe which they consider to be the present line and the time for announcing Allied policy concerning which, to be now.

[On April 22, the day after Forrestal's presentation of the revised military program, the subject was before the National Security Council. The extreme delicacy with which it was approached is indicated by the fact that this diary note ("ribbon copy only") is one of the very few in which Forrestal designated the participants only by initials.

22 April 1948   *National Security Council*

Meeting of the National Security Council at the White House today. *Subject*: Western Union.

"L" outlined tentative proposals for as nearly concurrent action as possible by the Senate and the President, not in terms of a treaty, but a statement that we were willing to consider, under Article 51 of the United Nations, steps looking to the construction of a regional agreement, if it proves to be in the interests of the security of the United States. The tactics would be to have this action initiated by the Republicans and to have the ball picked up immediately by the President, who would state his interest in the plan and make some further appropriate comments.

"R" raised the question of whether this was not provocative, whether it did not raise the fear in another mind even if one did not presently exist. "L" pointed out we were trying to get this group to say what they would do to help themselves in addition to taking help from us, and that this proposed step was part of that action. It was designed to indicate to anyone that there would be a price to any decision to overrun—that it would not be simply a walk-in.

[At the Cabinet next day Lovett first reported that the atomic energy negotiations in the United Nations had "come to a point of standstill." The discussion then turned to the fundamentals of Soviet-American relations.

23 April 1948   *Cabinet*

. . . Mr. Lovett spoke of meetings which he and Bohlen [Charles E., or "Chip", Bohlen, Counselor of the State Department] have had recently with Panyushkin [Alexander S. Panyushkin, Soviet Ambassador] and members of the Embassy staff. These conversations have taken the form of apparent probing by the Russians as to our real position vis-à-vis the Russians. They asked, for example, at the first meeting between him and Bohlen and Llewellyn Thompson, whether America really intended to stay in Europe. The Americans at the meeting restated the question and said that the real question is: Do the Russians mean to push beyond the line of their troops' advance at the end of the war?

Mr. Lovett summed up the position of Russia in his opinion as being of a dual nature at the moment: (1) constant probing to find out the solidity of our intent; and (2) a reflection of their own fear of a preventive or aggressive war on our part. Two things he felt were contributing to their motivations— the overexcitable statements, some by military people, on a preventive war, and the activities of Henry Wallace and his proposal that the President sit down with Stalin and make a world agreement.

He read a cable, which is to be sent to Bedell Smith, outlining in general terms our position and our desire for accommodation with Russia plus our apprehension that any meeting between the heads of the states would prove as futile and as nonproductive as in the past. Smith was asked his opinion as to whether a communication addressed to Stalin along these lines —namely, that America has no aggressive intent but neither did she intend to let Russia dominate Europe—should be sent

by the President or should be explored on a personal basis by
Smith himself. . . .

   After Cabinet I talked to Mr. Lovett about the implications
of the Western Union conversation which we had at the Security Council yesterday, when he related the substance of conversations between France, Britain, Belgium, Holland, Denmark, *et al.*, on the question of Western Union and the political
and military implications thereof. This morning I asked him
how far we were getting committed to such countries on a
military basis. He said the whole point of the conversations was
that we wanted to make it clear that we were not willing to become bound to an unequivocal contract to come to their assistance unless and until they manifested a desire to help themselves. Such assistance by us, he said, would of course have to
take the form of some kind of lend-lease. I asked him what he
would guess the total of arms procurement might be, and he
replied, "Not less than $3 billion."

[Such demands from Europe would, of course, only aggravate
   the already acute dilemma between unpreparedness and inflation.
   On April 24 Forrestal dictated two memoranda. The first considered the "economic factors"—employment already at 50½ million with the prospect of reaching 62½ million by July, "the
   highest in history," and leaving "practically no employable without a job"; and the demands for ERP, atomic energy and expanded armament which would fall upon "this tight economy."
   These were "very great pressures," as he wrote at this time to
   Mrs. Ogden Reid, thanking her for an editorial in the *New York
   Herald Tribune* supporting his stand; "we have to keep America
   militarily strong, but we have to be sure she does not become
   economically or socially impotent in the process." [3] The second
   memorandum considered the probable impact of these economic factors on the fate of the defense program in Congress.

24 April 1948   *Alternate Courses*

   1. The President wishes to adhere to UMT program.
   2. There is some chance, in my opinion, of getting the

---

[3] To Mrs. Ogden Reid, 28 April 1948.

"marriage bill" (Selective Service and modified UMT) by in the Senate. Very doubtful in the House.

3. The administration, through me as Secretary of Defense, took the action which initiated the acceleration of aircraft procurement appropriations. The House added 822 millions to the sum total of the Air figure in the original 1948-49 budget and the aircraft item in the supplemental.

4. Senator Bridges opens hearings in the Senate on this latter bill on Monday. He will try to get it on the Senate calendar before the Armed Services Committee gets its bill on UMT and/or Selective Service to the floor. This will be legislation to the Appropriations Committee, which is diametrically opposite to the spirit of organization. [Presumably Forrestal meant the spirit of the recent reorganization of congressional procedure.] It would undertake to prevent lawmaking through appropriations.

General Conclusion: There is not the slightest chance, in my opinion, for UMT to come up before the Armed Services Committee of the Senate if the Appropriations Committee passes the 822 millions additional Air Force procurement.

(Both Byrd and Saltonstall will insist on the projection of figures into future budgets which would come to around 16.5 to 17 billions in 1948-49, 18 billions in fiscal 1949-50 and 20 billions in 1950-51.) . . .

Alternative Courses of Action:

1. Permit the 822 millions to go through with its amendment giving the President the responsibility of certifying [that] contracts made are in the national security interest, which will be used by opponents of UMT to defeat that measure on the grounds that the two together will lead to a $22 to $23 billion budget within three or four years.

2. Oppose the 822 million additional sum. To make this opposition effective it will have to be joined in by all segments of the Military Establishment. Air Force opposition can be based on the statement that they are not withdrawing from their belief in a permanent peacetime seventy air groups but are willing to accept the compromise of the immediate

augmentation and permit time for study of the long-term program in relation to other demands on capacity.

[If Forrestal entertained any real hope that the Air Force would be so accommodating, it was quickly disabused. When Symington and Spaatz appeared before the Senate Appropriations Committee they repeated their demand for the full $822 million; the Senate accepted it (though retaining the "hooker"), and in early May sent the bill to the President. There remained only the first alternative—to abandon UMT—and at the Cabinet of April 30 Forrestal explained the situation.

30 April 1948   *Cabinet*

. . . I reported to the President that the Armed Services Committee of the House had called us for hearings on Monday on their Selective Service bill—Chairman Andrews having stated that they proposed to pass a Selective Service bill as such and then endeavor to get the UMT measure before the House directly afterward. I said I was somewhat less sanguine than Mr. Andrews on the possibility of doing this. I said my position would be that the President had expressed dissatisfaction with the Senate-modified version of the Selective Service-UMT bill but had expressed a willingness to take it as being the best he could get, and that in his view it was a workable and practical thing; that I would support this position but would emphasize the fact that we must have some immediate means of augmenting the Armed Services, particularly the Army, and for that reason a Selective Service Act was necessary, and that we would then continue to support and advocate a UMT measure.

I also referred to the morning-paper comments on the possibility of renewing lend-lease for the Western Union [at his press conference two days before Marshall had revealed that military lend-lease for Europe was under consideration], and asked whether it might not be wise to let something get out on this subject to indicate the extent of further demands which might be imposed upon the national economy. The President and Secretary of State thought this would be premature, although the latter said he realized that his own remarks . . .

had already provided the foundation for speculation on the subject. . . .

[There was certainly not going to be money enough for everything, and in effect UMT here went by the board. Nor was rearmament (as Forrestal well knew) simply a matter of dollar figures in the budget. To rouse the country and its representatives to a real military effort was a many-faceted problem. Bernard Baruch had been campaigning before congressional committees and elsewhere for the adoption of a "stand-by" plan for genuine industrial mobilization, and at the end of April Forrestal was on the telephone with Byrnes about it.

Telephone Conversation with James F. Byrnes, 28 April 1948

MR. FORRESTAL: Arthur Hill and Eberstadt have worked up a document to go to the President along the lines of our conversation. . . . First, the immediate things that need to be done . . . and, second, Bernie's complete control of the economy—which Bernie is wonderful at advocating ex cathedra, so to speak, but it may not be quite so easy politically.

MR. BYRNES: It is not. . . . I'm sure that B. M.'s statement —so far as the Congress is concerned—made a bad impression.

MR. FORRESTAL: Yes.

MR. BYRNES: And you would have a terrible uphill fight. It seems to me that you have so much trouble with your own crowd that you can't pick on that thing, when it has already been tried out by him. . . .

MR. FORRESTAL: Also, of course, Bernie is very adept at the art of making his recommendation and advice so global that he can say, "I told you so."

MR. BYRNES: Everything. I talked to [Senator] George, and somebody else on the committee—I think Vandenberg; you remember that Van said that he'd covered the waterfront? . . . And B. M. didn't like it.

MR. FORRESTAL: That's right. . . .

MR. BYRNES: Make it as narrow as you can; that's the way you may hope to get something. But I notice those fellows, the newspapers, quoted you and Bradley as referring to the allocation principle before some committee two days ago.

MR. FORRESTAL: Well, yes. . . . I simply said . . . that these dollar figures have no meaning unless they were accompanied by a relatively small number of sanctions and priorities that give you the right to get the plant capacity to produce the items you are talking about, and the dollars for which you are appropriating. . . . The impact of these present programs—I mean by programs ERP, the military supplemental, Maritime Commission and the Atomic Energy, which everybody forgets about and yet is 800 million for procurement— . . . needs the addition of from 7.5 to 15 per cent [of current production] in various categories to make them effective. . . . You add onto that what they are talking about now, the lend-lease for the Western Union in Europe of 5 or 6 millions, billions, and you have a barrel that is completely full now, and one blow of the hammer is going to bust the bungs on it. . . .

["One blow of the hammer is going to bust the bungs." It was this fear which had underlain Forrestal's attitude on the seventy-group Air Force, his proposal to split off and advance the aircraft procurement appropriations in order to test out the bottlenecks, his insistence on "orderly" mobilization planning and the patience with which he had finally secured the agreed $3,481 million supplemental program. And now, as others also began to realize the danger, the whole work was suddenly threatened from an unexpected quarter.

On April 21 the President had given only a qualified approval to the compromise supplemental program; while authorizing Forrestal to lay it before Congress he had also required that the details be worked up and submitted through the Budget Bureau. On May 6 Forrestal received his first, and rather staggering, intimation of what the Budget Bureau and its Director, James E. Webb, proposed to do with it.

6 May 1948   *Budget Meeting*

Meeting this morning with Budget.

Present: Mr. McCone [John A. McCone, industrialist who frequently assisted as consultant], Mr. McNeil, Budget Director Webb and staff.

Re our discussion of the military budget, Director Webb presented an analysis of the $3.481 billions in supplemental Service estimates, which the Bureau of the Budget review had reduced to $3.1 billions. This analysis showed a build-up from the proposed $15.5 billions in cash appropriations and authority in fiscal 1949 to around $18.2 billions in 1952, and if prices continue to rise, possibly to $20 billions, which would mean a $50 billion budget for the nation. . . .

Mr. Webb proposed that the current supplemental be reduced from the $3 billion-odd to about $2.5 billions, suggesting that we reconsider the military strengths and that we reduce the structure to a point where the requirements for cash appropriations and authority could be held to $15.3 billions in 1950 and level off at about the $15 billion level.

The reduction proposed by Webb was predicated on going back to a base of fifty-five air groups for fiscal 1949 and on a deferral of some vital parts of the Navy program, particularly on Naval Aviation and antisubmarine warfare components, as well as some reduction in Army matériel support.

Question: Is the world situation such as to warrant appropriations on this order at the present time?

I said that I believed that I would have to support the larger program which required $3.1 + for fiscal 1949 because of my belief that the next eighteen months to two years were a critical period in our relations with Russia.

Webb raised the question: Can we carry out such a military program, support ERP, provide a merchant marine program and implement the atomic energy plans without having available the controls and sanctions [over the civil economy] which it seems very doubtful that we will get in this election year?

My position was that the authorization of the larger military program was still essential and probably could be accomplished with certain pre-emptive authority but not necessarily requiring across-the-board controls.

[Suddenly it appeared that it was Mr. Webb who was in control of American military policy rather than the Secretary of Defense. A long, appended memorandum outlined "action taken on

[questions raised by Mr. Webb," several of the many items noting "Webb's decision" on disputed points. This memorandum indicates the ways in which the Budget Bureau proposed to cut the $3.48 billion supplemental to $3.1 billion. Some of its suggestions, such as cutting out "$18.5 millions for radar fence equipment" or reducing the sums for ship conversion by two-thirds, were serious; in the main, however, these proposals looked only to paring down and tightening up the agreed program, and Forrestal appears to have accepted them. It was the further proposal, to slash the program itself by another five or six hundred million through "reconsidering the military strengths," going back to the fifty-five-group basis, deferring vital Naval Air and anti-submarine components and cutting down on the desperately needed Army re-equipment, which was cataclysmic. Forrestal had already learned that it was impossible to get from the Joint Chiefs an agreed division of any sum less that the $3.48 compromise. Aside from its specifically military effects, the Webb program, by reopening the whole question with all its painfully adjusted issues, would overthrow all the results of weeks of patient work.

Webb had also introduced the idea (it had already occurred to the Senators) that all these military programs represented only beginnings which were bound progressively to grow; and had suggested that the whole military "structure" be reduced to such a point that it would "level off" at about $15 billion a year. This was the first proposal of a hard-and-fast ceiling on military spending, and therefore on military strength; literally applied, it would have been tantamount to freezing available strengths about where they then stood. Forrestal had to know at once whether Webb was speaking for the President. There was an "off-the-record" White House meeting next morning, including Marshall and Snyder, Souers, Steelman (the President's assistant), as well as Webb, Forrestal and the President.

7 May 1948   *Meeting at White House: 1948-49 Budget*

. . . I said that I had asked for this meeting in order that there might be full discussion with the President as to what his objectives were in lifting the financial sights on the 1948-49 budget. The President asked the Secretary of State to comment.

Marshall said the policy of this country was based upon the assumption that there would not be war and that we should not plunge into war preparations which would bring about the very thing we were taking these steps to prevent. He said he had always regarded UMT as the best manifestation to Europe—both as to the Western friendly countries and the Iron Curtain countries—of the continuity of our policy and of our determination to continue our position in European matters.

The President approved the statement of the Secretary of State and said he wished to make it very clear to all present that the increases on which he had given the green light through certain augmentations in the budget were not to be construed as preparation for war—"that we are preparing for peace and not for war."

He also pointed out that the very people in Congress who would now vote for heavy Air appropriations are those who a year from now would deny anything to the Armed Forces, and that if we permit the military budget to rise to proportions that cut too deeply into the civilian economy, the ones that will suffer in the long run will be the Armed Services. That, he said, is precisely what he is trying to avoid, and he is sure the advice he is giving, as well as the statement of policy that he is outlining, is sound.

[Forrestal entered no comment on this in his diary. At best, it was confusion worse confounded. He had been willing to sacrifice both the extra air groups and UMT precisely because neither was of value except as preparation for a possible future war. He believed that to "prepare for peace" one first of all needed some available tactical forces with which to control the current situations out of which alone a great war would come;[4] while his whole course had been motivated by a desire to avert just the situation to which the President pointed—in which Congress, after whooping through big appropriations for "air power," would then deny anything to the other branches. But under the

---

[4] Perhaps his clearest statement of this view was given in his New York address on 22 April; he again made it plain in his letter to Marshall, 31 October, 1948; see pp. 508-510.

[circumstances there was nothing to do but wait until the President's policy was outlined.

Forrestal was accustomed to keep his inner emotions under a tight control; while believing, as he did, that government was 99 per cent persuasion, he was schooled in the arts by which persuasion is facilitated. For those reasons it is not always easy to infer his true inner attitude toward the President. But it is of interest that in a farewell note at just this time to Clinton Anderson (who was leaving the cabinet), he spoke of "the time that we were associated in working for the best Boss that I have ever known." [5]

II

[Through all this, Forrestal had been serving as a member of the Hoover Commission on the organization of the Executive branch, which he had helped to set up. In early May a decision of importance was reached. The commission had originally excluded Forrestal's own Department from its survey, on the ground that it was too newly established to permit of useful judgment; but amidst the confusions and controversies that had arisen it was not surprising that the idea of extending the study to the Department of Defense should have been advanced, or that Forrestal should have welcomed it. At a commission meeting on May 10 [6] it was decided to go ahead, and a "task force" for the purpose was presently set up under Ferdinand Eberstadt.

Forrestal was already feeling the need for a somewhat stronger hand and firmer legal position than the Security Act had accorded to the "coordinating" Secretary of Defense (in this the Hoover Commission was later to agree), and in May he sought to get Bradley as his "principal military adviser." Both Bradley and Royall demurred on the ground that the general could not be spared as Army Chief of Staff, "particularly in view of the possibility of a change in administration next November." Talking about it with Gruenther, Forrestal learned that there were other reasons as well.

---

[5] To Clinton P. Anderson, 11 May 1948.
[6] Diary, 10 May 1948.

11 May 1948   *Conversation—General Gruenther*

. . . In commenting on the reluctance of General Bradley
to make this change in his status, General Gruenther remarked
that it was regrettable that back of this and other decisions was
the determination of the Army and the Air Force sharply to
reduce the appropriations for the Navy. One of the reasons, he
said, advanced by Mr. Royall against Bradley's taking his place
on my staff was the fact that anyone who stood in that relation
to the Secretary of Defense would have the obligation of a 40
per cent cut in the Navy budget and obviously it was not desire-
able for the Army to incur the Navy's displeasure which would
follow upon a decision.

[Obviously they were still a long way from unity of either
spirit or strategy. On this same day, however, Forrestal was relieved of one worry when Lovett let him know that a renewal of
lend-lease was still far in the future.

11 May 1948   *Conversation—Mr. Lovett*

. . . [Lovett] has been exploring with Senator Vandenberg
and other members of the [Foreign Relations] Committee the
character and extent of United States association with the
Western Union, with particular reference to the reservations
in the Senate legislative record regarding the United States
participation in regional pacts. He stated his belief that between Vandenberg and himself he would be able to work out
a practical method of approach. This will rest on the fundamental concept that the Western Union nations must display
energy and competence in the perfection of their own plans—
standardization of equipment, reactivation of their military organizations, etc.—before we give any indication of the scope or
degree of our support. He has stated to the Western Union
nations that they should be mindful of the history of ERP, that
Secretary Marshall had invited the sixteen nations associated
as beneficiaries of ERP to get together and project plans for
greater economic cooperation, increased trade, etc., after which
the United States would address itself to the consideration of a
statement of their requirements.

In answer to my question whether this excluded any near-term possibility of a demand upon the Military Establishment for a substantial lend-lease program, he said that the only programs which would be considered at the moment were such as would implement the so-called Title VI part of the ERP bill (subsequently stricken out). Such programs would be of a limited character. . . .

[By the 13th the President was ready to give his outline of military budget policy; and he summoned Forrestal, the three Service Secretaries, the three Chiefs of Staff (Hoyt Vandenberg had just succeeded Spaatz as head of the Air Force), Webb and McNeil to the White House.

13 May 1948   *Meeting at White House: 1948-49 Budget*
. . . The above people met with the President off-the-record today at 3:30 in order that the President might outline . . . the basis for certain augmentations at this time in the military strength of the United States: to indicate that the increase was for the purpose of demonstrating a continuing firmness in world affairs, with the thought that we were preparing for peace and not for war.

The President read from a memorandum, which he stated would be kept on file in his office as the minutes of this meeting. In general, the memorandum outlined the President's fiscal policy. In summary, this policy is that the augmentation of our military strength should be gradual and not precipitate and that the Services should not increase their personnel and build a "structure" which would require in excess of $15 billion to maintain during the fiscal year 1950. The President stated that he desired to have a re-evaluation of our military position made in September and in December, in order to determine the point where we should level off our increased strength.

[The memorandum had actually been written by Forrestal's assistant, McNeil, to the President's and Webb's specifications, and had then been edited by Webb. Forrestal entered the text in his diary. "My [the President's] statement before the Con-

[gress on March 17," it began, "represented the action which I took on the Joint Chiefs of Staff recommendation that Selective Service was necessary to maintain or augment the military man-power strengths of the Armed Forces—principally the Army. It was realized that occupation forces in Korea had diminished to a point where it was doubtful if we could continue to main-tain troops in that country. The occupation forces in Japan and Germany were at a minimum. It was realized that the Army was continuing to lose its strength at the rate of about five thousand per month, and that our mobile forces available for movement abroad or for home defense were only thirty thousand."

The President, the directive continued, had contemplated no more than "the development of a military posture which would give evidence of continuing firmness in world affairs." This, the President had thought, could be done on a total strength of no more than 1,734,000 men at a supplemental cost of $1.5 billion. When the Military Establishment had indicated that it needed much more than this, the President had consented "to go along with a program of $3 billion." Then Forrestal had returned with the compromise program of $3.481 billion; and "on the basis of the information then available, I did not feel that I could ap-prove a program of this kind without qualifications," although he had authorized Forrestal to give the program to Congress.

The review, the directive went on, had now been completed; it had, of course, emphasized the heavy impact of the military program (along with ERP, atomic energy and similar items) on the economy, and had developed the fact that to maintain the contemplated augmented strengths would require much larger sums in the future. The Military Establishment was asking a total (including stockpiling) for fiscal 1949 of about $15.5 billion. A continuing level of about $15 billion, the directive concluded, was about all the economy would stand, and "unless world con-ditions deteriorate much further" the President did not propose to exceed that ceiling. To do so, the directive pointed out, would be to end with a total national budget of about $50 billion a year, "and this amount is several billion dollars more than the estimated income at present tax rates. We would be in a position where even with full employment, business good, and the tax

[rates still at a very high level, we would be required to resort to large-scale deficit financing." But if the year-end strengths contemplated under the 1949 program were attained, and no more than $15 billion were available for fiscal 1950, a "demoralizing demobilization" at the end of fiscal 1949 would be the inevitable result.

The Budget Bureau had slashed the $3.481 billion supplemental to $3.17 billion without, the President considered, impairing "the essential elements of the program"; but he thought that the program itself was still more than should be asked of Congress at that time. Nevertheless, "taking other factors into consideration" and remembering the uncertainty of the world situation, he was willing to submit this supplemental on one condition—that the Armed Forces did not spend it! This was the President's rather original solution for the dilemma between maintaining the full program and reopening all the issues of strategy and Service rivalry which Forrestal had striven so hard to adjust. Specifically the President's condition was "that administratively we do not, in the next eight months, create a military structure which would require in excess of approximately $15 billion for the next fiscal year. I do not want immediate action taken toward the activation of all of the units contemplated—and by that I mean such things as Army training camps, Naval Air stations and air groups."

The directive continued to prescribe the review he wanted in September, "to see if administratively we should not place a ceiling on our program at less than we contemplated in this supplemental"; and the second review in December, before the final submission of the fiscal 1950 budget, to determine whether strengths should be limited to what could be supported within the $15 billion ceiling. The President noted the "hookers" provided in the aircraft procurement bill and strongly intimated that he would use them. Finally, "as Commander in Chief," the directive concluded, "I expect these orders to be carried out wholeheartedly, in good spirit and without mental reservation. If anyone present has any questions or misgivings concerning the program I have outlined, make your views known now—for once this program goes forward officially, it will be the administration

[program, and I expect every member of the administration to support it fully, both in public and in private."

So Webb's viewpoint had largely won. The policy had been established of a fixed $15 billion ceiling through the "next fiscal year," which would not end until June 30, 1950—a date, as it turned out, which did not arrive until six days after the outbreak of the Korean War. The compromise program of April 21 was to be eviscerated. In a formal letter to the Secretary of Defense on June 3, the President defined the initial effects of the ceiling policy. "Since," he wrote, "you are to review the entire military program in September and again in December, I consider it necessary in the meantime to place limits on the activation of the various components." Pending the September review, these limits required that the maximum strength to be reached by September 30, 1948, was not to exceed an aggregate of 1,494,000 in the event that no draft act was passed or, if Congress enacted Selective Service, of 1,539,000. The latter figure was still 256,-000 short of the agreed program of April 21; it was actually only 165,000 more than the low reported by Gruenther in February.[7] The President was to dispose of the House's seventy-group Air Force by announcing that the $822 million should "not be spent" without his approval; the Congress, meanwhile, was itself disposing of UMT, which was never voted. It might seem that the whole momentum generated by the March crisis had been dissipated against the rock of social and economic costs in an election year. As Forrestal himself put it in a letter to Marshall a couple of weeks later, an apparent slackening in the tension with Russia, together "with the political stresses of an election year, have combined, I believe, to produce a dangerous complacency on the part of certain elements in the country." [8]

Yet it should not be overlooked that Forrestal had also conserved some very important gains. He was to secure a re-enactment of the draft—probably the most vital point of all—and he had maintained the principle of a "balanced" force, averting the dangers of either a hypertrophy of the Air Force or of a retreat into the remote and somewhat hypothetical defenses of

---

[7] See pp. 375 and 419.
[8] To George C. Marshall, 29 May 1948.

[UMT. He had kept military policy on course; and all the intervention of the Budget Bureau had done was to reduce the speed. It was a drastic and perhaps a dangerous reduction, to which Forrestal never acquiesced. Yet he was acutely aware of the economic problem that had dictated the President's decision; and there were not one but two ways of meeting the resultant situation. One, of course, was to get the President to raise his limit; the other was to compel the military to review their own plans, improve the real efficiency of their vast machinery and get a greater degree of "usable" military strength out of the budgetary limits imposed. Forrestal was to devote himself to both endeavors throughout the rest of his career.

Even Selective Service was to be jeopardized in an unexpected way, as an entry for this same day shows.

13 May 1948   Difficulties in Getting Legislation in a Political Year
. . . The President sent his message on Civil Rights to the Congress on 2 February 1948. This produced a bitter reaction from the South. Problems flowing from it:

As a result of the President's message there have been certain developments in the Senate Armed Services Committee's attitude on Selective Service, which have elements of danger.

Senator Russell [Richard B. Russell, Democrat of Georgia] on Tuesday proposed an amendment to the Selective Service-Draft law which was about to be voted upon by the Armed Services Committee . . . to the effect that each individual drafted into the Armed Services would have the right to say that he preferred to serve in a unit of his own race. The Armed Services Committee rejected this amendment after the appearance of Secretary Royall and myself, but Senators Wilson and Russell voted against sending the bill to the floor and Senators Byrd, Hill and Maybank abstained from voting. The result may be a bitter fight on the floor. The Russell amendment will probably be beaten . . . but . . . Senators Russell, Maybank and others . . . may decide upon a filibuster which will prevent passage of the bill. . . .

The motivation for Senator Russell's amendment extends from the fact that he is up for re-election this year and he must therefore be clearly and strongly on record against the spirit of the President's Civil Rights message. In the process there is a chance that great damage may be done to our program for the re-creation of adequate national defenses.

[Forrestal was to express his "serious concern" over this snag in a memorandum for the President on May 28 and in a long letter to Marshall of the same date; but this threatened filibuster did not develop. The draft act was to encounter further difficulties, but all were eventually overcome.

I I I

[Meanwhile one issue on which Forrestal had spent much energy reached an abrupt denouement.

14 May 1948   *Conversation—Mr. Lovett*

Lovett called me at 6:30 to say that at 6:15 this government had recognized the new state of Israel. He said this position had apparently been reached twenty-four to forty-eight hours ago and had been communicated to Marshall and himself at a meeting which was attended by Clifford, Niles and several others of the White House staff.

He said he expected severe fighting would ensue but that the Jewish Army was superior in equipment and training to the Arabs and could probably take care of themselves. Repercussions in other parts of the world where United States interests are affected, such as Egypt, Pakistan and North Africa, would probably be felt within the next few days.

[Evidently the President and the White House staff had taken Palestine out of the hands of the State Department as firmly as they had taken the military budget out of the hands of Defense. The fact was to be emphasized by another conversation with Lovett a month later.

23 June 1948   *Conversation—Mr. Lovett*

. . . [Lovett] said he was called at 4:20 yesterday afternoon by Clark Clifford, who said the President had asked him to call up Lovett and, through him, to name James G. MacDonald as Minister *de facto* to the Israel state. . . . [When Lovett questioned this on the grounds of MacDonald's identification with the Zionists and for other reasons] Clifford said he did not know anything about that but that the President had told him he did not want any discussion of the matter but to have action followed at once in the form of an announcement that afternoon by the State Department.

[So another die had been cast. Forrestal had a long conversation with Henry Morgenthau, Jr., at this time, going over much of the old ground,[9] but there is little reference to Palestine thereafter in the diary or the correspondence.

The always paramount issue of Soviet relations had at the same time taken a somewhat baffling turn. While Berlin continued to live uneasily beneath a mounting threat of blockade, Moscow had seized an opportunity for a "peace offensive." When in early May Ambassador Bedell Smith had acted upon his instructions[10] to put American policy plainly before the Kremlin, Molotov had adroitly twisted the intent and published the correspondence. The American government, said the Russian note, "declares that the United States has no hostile or aggressive intentions . . . and expresses the hope of the possibility of finding a way to the establishment of good and reasonable relations between the two countries. . . . The Soviet government can only welcome this declaration," leaving the implication that it was up to the United States to do the peacemaking. Henry Wallace, now Progressive Party candidate for the presidency, did not improve matters by addressing an open letter to Stalin, outlining Mr. Wallace's ideas of a peace and giving Stalin the chance to reply (May 17), cordially accepting the Wallace terms and thus putting the onus for the "cold war" even more firmly on the State Department. There was much worry in Washington next morning.

---

[9] Diary, 22 June 1948.
[10] See p. 424.

Discussion this morning with Sidney Souers about our position vis-à-vis Russia. He said he had told the President this morning that he, Souers, was deeply worried about the evolution of a pattern of confusion in the public's mind as a result of (a) Molotov's midnight announcement about the Molotov-Smith conversations, (b) Wallace's letter to Stalin, and (c) Stalin's answer on Monday night. I observed that one concrete result of these developments might be failure to secure the passage of Selective Service.

Eber [Ferdinand Eberstadt], who was present at the meeting, said the practical situation now was that the development and expression of our Russian policy was escaping from the formal channels of government into conversations between a private citizen and the head of another state. He said it seemed to him that all concerned within the government . . . should meet to discuss all angles of the Russian question. . . .

I then talked to Under Secretary Lovett to express a feeling of frustration at the success of the Russian propaganda. . . . Lovett deplored the ability of the Russians to capitalize on the ignorance of the American public but said he felt that the American position had been made abundantly clear ever since the statement of the Truman Doctrine of a year ago . . . , the exposition of the Marshall Plan, the general statement of our reasons for partially rearming and Marshall's statement . . . of Wednesday, May 5. . . . Russia's insincerity, he claimed, was made manifest on the very day that Stalin was writing in response to Wallace's suggestions, in the announcement of the failure to come to any agreement on atomic weapons [as well as in certain aspects of the reply itself]. . . . Mr. Souers said that he felt the President was getting forced into the position of apparently basing his actions on the expectation of war, whereas his aims were toward precisely the opposite objective.

[They would have been less worried had they known how soon the Russians, by finally tightening the noose on Berlin, were themselves to provide the best possible answer to Soviet "peace" propaganda. As it was, the President actually called a high-level

[meeting—Marshall, Forrestal, Lovett, Bohlen, Kennan, Harriman, Souers and Clifford—to consider the subject. He was about to leave for a Western speaking trip and wanted their ideas as to how to deal with the Soviet propaganda. The result was some high-level, and very interesting, thinking.

21 May 1948   *Meeting at the White House*

. . . Marshall started the discussion [by saying he had been reviewing a speech he was himself to make]. . . . He proposed to emphasize in his speech the necessity for continuity of policy and of the need for sufficient residual force to back up policy. He said that as a result of the unscrupulousness of Russian diplomatic methods and susceptibility of the American public to propaganda, the attention of the public had been diverted from basic issues to tactical methods. The criticism directed at the State Department had been on the question of their lack of alertness and skill in meeting the Russian techniques. During the course of the change the newspapers and the public had lost sight of the issues involved. They had forgotten that the objectives of American policy, as stated by the President and the Secretary of State, were the attainment of peace and economic stability throughout the world. They lost sight of the fact that the very breach of confidence implied by the unilateral release by the Russian Foreign Office of the Smith-Molotov conversations and the direct interference in American politics [implied by Stalin's response to Wallace] in themselves provided evidence of the difficulties in dealing with Russia on a normal and frank basis.

Lovett said that foreign policy, like a war plan, could not be stated in a single speech . . . but was a planned, continuing flow of actions and statements directed toward a central objective. . . .

Harriman said the public and the newspapers had failed to grasp the fact that [the Russian moves] were clear evidence that American policy, as initiated a year ago last winter and as expressed . . . in our firmness at various points of contact . . . had forced the Russians to a change of their tactics.

I gave it as my view that the country needed a constant restatement of our objectives and of the magnitude of our task, that we must not approach our international responsibilities in swiftly changing moods, that there was an American tendency to go from apathy to inertia, or as Scotty Reston [James B. Reston of the *New York Times*] said, "If you tell Congress nothing, they go fishing; if you promise nothing, they go fishing; if you tell them all, they go wild." We must have a resolute and firm attitude behind which we can advance on a solid front and not on a jagged and spasmodic line. We had to make it clear that ERP, our own rearming, our blessing to the Western Union and the indication of ultimate military aid to it were all parts of a pattern of world policy and that in moving toward these objectives we had to be sure that we remained socially sound and financially solvent; a busted benefactor, no matter how deep and sincere his beneficence, obviously can be of little use to any community.

Specifically, I said I was concerned . . . because of the changing tempo of the Congress and in the relaxation of tension. . . . On March 17 we could have had Selective Service through both Houses in three days. Today there is serious question about the passage of such a bill. . . .

Harriman reported a meeting of commentators and other newspaper people, including Ernest Lindley, last evening, in which he said, in response to their questions as to how the State Department came to bungle the Smith-Molotov exchanges, that he had taken the position that no foreign newspaper writers had the responsibility of clarifying the American position and are falling victims to Russian propaganda. [Harriman's meaning appears to have been that it was natural for foreign writers, without national responsibility, to fall victim to the Russian thesis, but not for the Americans to do so.] He said he took the position that *they* had a responsibility to identify such obvious propaganda methods as the Russians used when they left out of context certain remarks of Bedell Smith, to force a construction which suited their purposes.

Kennan, Lovett and Bohlen all felt that the initial success of the Russian propaganda was becoming less each day as the Russian communiqués became exposed to the searching analysis of the more intelligent writers.

[A few days later Forrestal lunched with Dwight Griswold, chief of the mission to Greece, and Stanton Griffis, Ambassador to Poland. Griswold told him that conditions in Greece were "substantially improved"; Griffis felt that the Poles, though violently anti-Russian, were on the whole "well fed and satisfied" with their Communist government—to go from Moscow to Warsaw was "like going from the slums to the Ritz"—and he had seen no signs anywhere of imminent war.[11] When he breakfasted with Griffis next day, the latter told him that he was about to be offered the Egyptian Embassy, although he would have preferred Spain. "Finds it difficult to understand how we can talk about the control of the Mediteranean at one end and ignore the other points, now that we have no Ambassador in Spain." Forrestal agreed about Spain but told him that Egypt was important too.[12]

A memorandum worked up by Admiral Wooldridge from diplomatic reports from London and the Near East, which Forrestal thought important enough to enter in his diary, cannot have diminished his belief in the significance of the Eastern Mediterranean. It was couched in terms of the deepest Navy-blue gloom: "U. S. prestige in the Middle East has suffered what may be irreparable damage. . . . Sharp cleavage in relations with U. K. . . . Arabs are not bluffing. . . . Problem transcends the age-old conflict between Jews and Arabs, and is worldwide in its repercussions," and so on.[13] But events, fortunately, were to prove that the situation was not quite so dire as that.

There remained to get the draft bill through, and Forrestal went to work on the Republicans. On May 30 he had Senator Taft at his home. "I said that without Selective Service our defense establishment might really become a hollow shell as a re-

---

[11] Diary, 25 May 1948.
[12] Diary, 26 May 1948. When in 1951 ambassadorial representation was restored, Griffis received the appointment to Spain.
[13] Diary, 31 May 1948.

[sult of the competitive wages offered by industry, the 'peace' campaign of Wallace and many other considerations; that it was very doubtful whether the Services, and in particular the Army, would be able to bring their strengths up to required levels." But Taft was encouraging, and so was Gurney when Forrestal repeated the conversation to him next day. The talk with Taft incidentally elicited another indication of the already widespread belief that Mr. Truman could not survive the approaching election.

31 May 1948   *Conversation with Senator Taft*
. . . I told Senator Taft that I hoped whoever became the nominee of the Republican Party in next month's convention would immediately assign several members of his staff to make a study of the national defense establishment, the duties of which were now so complex and involved such large sums of money that it was one of the most serious questions the country had to face. He agreed and said that the decision on the allocation of funds between the Services was probably the most serious job in government. He said there was a general impression in Congress of waste and extravagance in military spending because of the lack of any criterion by which efficiency could be proved or disproved.

[Forrestal also appealed to the Senate Democrats for help on the draft bill; they were also encouraging, but he found them quailing, like everyone else, before the costs of military strength, and inclined to flee into hopes for disarmament. The luncheon group included Leslie L. Biffle (staff director of the Minority Policy Committee) and Senators McGrath, Scott Lucas (minority whip), McMahon, Tydings, George and Kilgore.

2 June 1948   *Luncheon at Capitol—Selective Service—*
Disarmament Possibilities
. . . Impression is that Republican leadership will secure a vote on Selective Service, although Langer's [William Langer, Republican of North Dakota] determination to couple Civil Rights with Selective Service is still a danger. Biffle told me

that he believed that they had the necessary votes to secure a tabling of such an amendment. Senator Russell, according to Tydings and Biffle, is disposed to modify the character of his proposed amendment. . . .

Senator McMahon said that he had recently read a speech that Senator Tydings made in the Senate about a year and a half ago about disarmament. . . . He had advocated the U. S. taking a strong position on a general world disarmament which would, of course, carry with it inspection and other essentials of a real disarmament program. He and Senator Tydings proceeded to explore the possibility of a bold and dramatic statement by the President, inviting the world to a genuine disarmament conference outside the framework of the United Nations. The purpose would be to re-emphasize the fact of Russia's unwillingness to disarm, starting with the atomic bomb, or of bringing the pressure of world opinion on her to accept *real* disarmament.

I do not believe there is much practical possibility of such a movement developing at the moment, but this conversation reflected a basic, although latent, search for a disarmament formula. Senator McMahon stated there were now nineteen million people throughout the world under arms, and both he and Tydings referred to the rising curve of arms expenditures in the United States as well as other countries.

[Senator McMahon was long to pursue, without success, his restless search for a disarmament "formula." But meanwhile the Senate adopted the Selective Service bill (omitting UMT entirely) on June 10 by 78 to 10; the House promptly followed suit, and after the breaking of a final filibuster in the Senate the bill went to the President on June 19. Forrestal was careful to express his thanks to all the principal leaders concerned, but most cordially of all, perhaps, to Senator Gurney.

To Chan Gurney, 11 June 1948
Dear Chan:
My hat is off to you on the result in the Senate. As I told you over the telephone, it is a great tribute to your tenacity and

patience, and everyone in the Armed Services is most grateful
—not merely for the result itself but for the size of the favorable vote. . . .

[Thus the curtain was rung down upon the dramatic passage
which had begun with the March crisis some three and a half
months before. It represented the first effort to rebuild the
Military Establishment, the first serious attempt to grapple with
the underlying issues of unification and the first important test of
the new machinery for national security as established by the act
of 1947. In each respect the results were mixed; they were also
complex and difficult properly to evaluate. Forrestal had not
gained in popular esteem. Yet his answer to an appreciative note
from a friend was essentially correct.

To Roger W. Cutler, 12 June 1948
     . . . It is always helpful to have the old troops rally around.
In spite of all the commotion there is substantial progress being
made on the foundation of this structure, but there is work
which has to be done before the ornaments become visible.
Furthermore I want to be sure we do not destroy existing organizations until we are sure of what is going to replace them.
Nothing could be more fatal at this juncture of world affairs.

[Some of the "ornaments," few though they still were, did unquestionably become visible in the tragic summer of 1950. And
perhaps the most penetrating comment on the episode was Forrestal's own, in a letter to Hanson Baldwin.

To Hanson W. Baldwin, 16 June 1948
     . . . I haven't the faintest idea what I am going to do when
I get out of here—I never have planned my life except at the
beginning when it was necessary to get enough money to eat
and pay debts.
     With regard to unification, the most substantial accomplish-
ments are of an unspectacular character. There are things that

had to be done before superficial problems are tackled: the creation of an efficient and clear-headed approach to the budget. The 1948-49 budget was already in last September, so the plans, in my judgment, had to be for the 1949-50 budget. On that I believe the foundations are laid for a rational and logical method by which the Joint Chiefs of Staff will participate in, and share, responsibility. This is the greatest central problem of unification, and everything else, more or less, stems from it. In other areas the ancillary bodies created by the Security Act of 1947 had to be brought into being and staffed. . . . There is, of course, the Central Intelligence Agency, on which, I am sure you will agree, if one is to secure improvement, one must undertake to secure it without fanfare, and that I believe we shall be able to do. . . .

There is, of course, a great additional spate of things that have to be done, most of which are all obvious to you. The coordination of publicity will have to be brought together into one central spot and there will have to be a more vigorous approach to stockpiling. Much more detailed planning has to be done, through the National Security Resources Board and the Munitions Board, regarding the relationship of our raw materials, manpower and industrial capacity to our war capabilities.

Two fields I almost forgot are of the highest importance: civilian defense and special weapons, including atomic energy and B. W. [Biological Warfare]. . . . There will be some public announcements in the near future.

[In all these basic matters—of more critical significance in the long run than current budget levels—progress was being made. But the core of the whole problem, as Forrestal clearly saw after the almost grotesque experiences of the spring, lay in the budget, in the manner of its construction, in the responsibility for its allocation and for its adjustment both to logical strategic plan and to the nonmilitary limitations which could not be disregarded. By June 23 he had prepared the rough draft of a memorandum for the three Secretaries which clearly defined the issue and indicated what he intended to do about it.

23 June 1948   *Rough Draft*

Subject: Formation of the 1949-50 budget.

1. Preparation of this budget is the most important business facing the Military Establishment in the next ninety days.

2. I have asked the Joint Chiefs of Staff if they wish to accept the responsibility for advising me upon the division of funds within the limitations, and under the ceiling, of the global sum given us for military purposes by the President. The Joint Chiefs of Staff indicated they are willing to accept that responsibility.

3. In the event that they do not agree, however, and past history does not give any guarantee that they will, I must have some source of advice from men, both with experience in their Services and sufficiently advanced in rank to be free from the normal subjectivity and prejudices of the individual Services.

4. I therefore request that the following individuals be detailed for service in my office from 15 July to 15 September:

    From the United States Army—Lieutenant General W. H. Haislip

    From the United States Air Force—General Joseph T. McNarney

    From the United States Navy—Admiral W. H. P. Blandy
                                 Captain Arleigh A. Burke

5. Will you please see that the appropriate orders are issued to the officers named.

[While this particular proposal was not put into effect, it led to the appointment by the Joint Chiefs of a board of three high-ranking "budget deputies," composed of General McNarney, Vice Admiral Robert B. Carney, and Major General George J. Richards. This body, which came to be known as the McNarney Board, was to toil from mid-August onward upon what was, in effect, the gigantic task of rationalizing the huge, sprawling and divided American military machine.

CHAPTER XII

The Berlin Blockade and the Atomic Bomb

I

[The Republican National Convention of 1948 met in Philadelphia in the latter part of June. The Russians, as if to exploit the customary American absorption in such events, chose the week of the convention to end the cat-and-mouse game they had been playing with Berlin and finally clamp down a complete blockade upon the city. On June 24, the day that Thomas E. Dewey of New York was nominated for the presidency, they halted what little rail traffic was still running and with this and other measures left only the dubious possibilities of air transport standing between some two million Berliners and starvation. Forrestal stopped after the Cabinet next day to meet with the President, Royall and Lovett. The discussion turned on the controlling legal rights and undertakings; and it is a little striking to find how vague the position still was, although Soviet pressure had been mounting against Berlin for three months.

25 June 1948   *Berlin Occupational Agreement*
 . . . Lovett [*sic*: the context suggests that it should be Royall] stated that in the records of the War Department there were certain dispatches which indicated there had been an exchange of messages between Stalin and Roosevelt in connection with the four-power occupation of Berlin. He said there was an indication there had been a message from Hopkins to Roosevelt recommending agreement to Russian occupation of

Berlin (sometime in 1944), provided that the United States
had free access to that area. It is believed there followed an exchange of messages between Stalin and Roosevelt in which
Stalin agreed, in principle, to the stipulation that the United
States should have complete right of entry of persons and goods
into the Berlin area; that Stalin replied to this message with
one of his own, stating that he agreed in principle but that the
terms would be worked out by the Russian, American and
British commanders in the field. Apparently this was never
done, although it is General Parks' recollection [presumably
Major General Floyd L. Parks, chief of the Public Information
Division of the Army Special Staff, who in 1945 had been the
first commander of the American military sector in Berlin] that
in conversations between Eisenhower and the Russians there
was a clear verbal agreement in the sense of the above. . . .

Lovett observed that the casualness of this procedure
stemmed from the attitude prevailing at that time in the minds
of Roosevelt, Stimson, Hopkins, Eisenhower, etc., that we
would have no trouble in dealing with the Russians.

[But the present was more urgent than the past; the legalities
less important than the problem of what to do. On Sunday, the
27th, there was a conference in Royall's office of Forrestal, Lovett, Royall, Sullivan, Bradley, Norstad and a number of other
State, Defense and military officers. Once more they found themselves facing the now wearisomely familiar dilemma: to fight, to
get out or to try to stand on some uneasy middle ground.

27 June 1948   *Berlin Situation*
    . . . Discussion proceeded on the assumption that with ex-
isting food stocks, plus supplies which might be brought in by
air, serious food shortages would not occur for approximately
thirty days, and the German population could perhaps be fed
for sixty or more days if dried foods were introduced. The
three possible courses of action discussed were the following:
    1.   Decide now to withdraw from our position in Berlin, in
concert with the other Western powers, at an appropriate time
in the future, presumably when a constituent assembly for a

Western German government is called on September 1, and plan accordingly.

2. Decide at this time to retain our position in Berlin by all possible means, including supplying Berlin by convoy or using force in some other manner, such action to be only as a last resort after utilizing all diplomatic and other means to stay in Berlin without force to avoid war, but accepting the possibility of war as a consequence if necessary.

3. To maintain our unprovocative but firm stand in Berlin, utilizing first every local means, and subsequently every diplomatic means, to obtain recognition and assertion of our rights while postponing ultimate decision to stay in Berlin or withdraw.

Secretary Royall felt that a decision should be reached now concerning our ultimate position, since our actions in the immediate future should be patterned in the light of this decision. There was considerable discussion concerning (a) the effect of withdrawing from Berlin on our position in Europe, on the spread of Communism and on the success of the European program as contrasted with (b) remaining in Berlin under the stress of consistently recurring crises and frequent humiliation, or (c) running the risk of war through efforts to supply Berlin by force. There was also preliminary discussion of the various steps which might be taken, on the one hand either to minimize or cover our withdrawal from Berlin, and on the other hand to augment our position vis-à-vis the Russians. Consideration was given to whether two B-29 squadrons now in Goose Bay should proceed to Germany, and as to whether it would be advisable to base two B-29 groups in England.

Definite conclusions reached at the meeting were the following:

1. That State and Civil Affairs Division should prepare a currency paper for transmittal to Clay which might be used by him as a basis for resuming discussions with Sokolovsky.

2. That Secretary Royall, Mr. Lovett and I should meet with the President the next morning and present the major issues involved for his decision, and that in the meantime De-

partments of Army and State should prepare a short statement
of the possible alternative courses of action and the arguments
in favor and against each.

3. Clay's reaction should be obtained as to whether two additional B-29 squadrons should go to Germany.

4. A proposed dispatch to Ambassador Douglas, which was
read by Mr. Lovett, was approved with the modifications here-
inafter noted.

5. Douglas should be informed that we saw no particular
merit in CCS [Combined Chiefs of Staff] discussions.

6. Douglas should be asked to explore the possibility of basing two B-29 groups in England.

[This entry is striking in a number of ways. Where, one is
forced to ask, was all the elaborate machinery which had been
set up to deal with just such situations—the CIA, which was supposed to foresee and report the approach of crisis; the National
Security Council, which was supposed to establish the governing policy; the War Council, which was supposed to transmit the
policy to the military so that they should have their plans set up
to meet the requirements?

The Berlin crisis had been long in the the making; but when
finally it broke, the response was this *ad hoc* meeting at
4:00 p.m. on a Sunday afternoon in the Pentagon, which by-
passed the formal machinery of the Security Act to take large
(if rather vague) politico-strategic decisions—incidentally over-
looking in doing so the potentialities of the airlift, which was actually to be decisive. Its findings, at all events, went direct to the
President, at 12:30 next day.

28 June 1948   *Meeting at White House—Berlin Situation*
              Present: Lovett, Royall and myself.

Lovett recited the details of the meeting at the Department
of the Army, Sunday afternoon. When the specific question was
discussed as to what our future policy in Germany was to be—
namely, were we to stay in Berlin or not?—the President inter-
rupted to say that there was no discussion on that point, we
were going to stay period.

[Secretary Royall, according to the note, expressed "some concern" as to whether the problem had been fully thought through; he did not want the United States committed to a position under which we might have "to fight our way into Berlin" unless the possibility was clearly recognized and its consequences accepted. The President's rejoinder was "that we would have to deal with the situation as it developed," but that the essential decision was "that we were in Berlin by terms of an agreement and that the Russians had no right to get us out by either direct or indirect pressure."

According to a memorandum on this same meeting which Royall sent to Bradley (a copy of which Forrestal entered in his diary), the President "expressed affirmative approval of sending the B-29s to Germany. Mr. Lovett announced casually that he assumed that the other two groups of B-29s would go to England. . . ." At the Pentagon the afternoon before, they had already decided to sound out both Clay and the British as to the B-29s; Clay's reaction was prompt and in the affirmative, and, somewhat to the surprise of the Americans, so was that of the Foreign Office. As for Clay, there was nothing else available with which he could be reinforced. But by the time Friday's Cabinet came around there had been some second thoughts about basing the big bombers in Great Britain.

2 July 1948   Cabinet

General Marshall discussed the situation in Berlin.

He read a copy of a message which the State Department had drawn and proposes to send to Stalin. It recites both the legal and moral considerations for the Western Allies remaining in Berlin and reaffirms the determination of the Allies to stay there. . . .

The French and British both agree that a meeting of the Council of Foreign Ministers is not desirable at this time—that it would only lead to protracted discussions with probably the same sterile results of previous meetings of these personalities.

He reported the beefing up of the B-29 strength in Germany from one squadron to a group. He said that the British had been asked whether they would like to have two additional

B-29 groups proceed to Britain and that Bevin had replied in the affirmative. Douglas had been instructed to ask Bevin whether he had fully explored and considered the effect of the arrival of these two groups in Britain upon British public opinion, and he (Marshall) had to weigh the effect (a) on the Russians, and (b) of the implications and inferences to be derived from sending these groups to Britain. He said the effect on the Russians had to be balanced against the appearance to our own people of what might be construed as a provocative action. . . .

[The diary does not further explain the "implications" which Marshall had in mind; but some of them may be readily guessed. The B-29s were known throughout the world as the atomic bombers, and to put a strong force of them into British bases would be to bring them within striking distance of Moscow. The sudden exigency of the Berlin affair was, throughout the ensuing weeks, to compel much serious reappraisal of the bomb and of its real place in American policy and strategy.

Even in the matter of the B-29s for Britain, decision was not finally reached until mid-July. In the meanwhile, of course, there were always other problems. The Cabinet on July 9 brought a foretaste of one for which the United States would be long in finding a sound answer.

9 July 1948   *Cabinet*

The Secretary of State referred to a message which had come to the Department of the Army from Under Secretary Draper, suggesting that the State Department consider making a favorable response to an approach from the Tito government for re-examination of relations on Eastern-Western trade, commercial relations with the U. S., etc. The Secretary of State felt it was not wise to take that step at the present time because no one could foresee as yet the ultimate outcome of the current breach between Russia and Yugoslavia. . . .

[Since Marshall, with his belief in UMT, had been less than helpful in Forrestal's efforts to build up the active troop strength,

[the latter may have taken a wry satisfaction in a subsequent observation.

The Secretary of State expressed the hope that the Military Establishment would not find it necessary to be quite so explicit as to the substantial times that must elapse before the recent decision to augment our military position would become effective.

He said that repetitions of such statements would emphasize our present weakness and add to the difficulty of negotiations with Russia. He added that they might actually delude the Russians into a hasty action because they would not appreciate how much we could speed up our mobilization under pressure.

[On July 15 the National Security Council gave its verdict in the matter of the B-29s. Forrestal summarized the reasoning in his diary.

15 July 1948   *Sending of B-29s to Britain*
Summary of considerations affecting the decision to send B-29s to England:

1. It would be an action which would underline to the American people how seriously the government of the United States views the current sequence of events.

2. It would give the Air Force experience in this kind of operation; it would accustom the British to the necessary habits and routines that go into the accommodation of an alien, even though an allied, power.

3. We have the opportunity *now* of sending these planes, and once sent they would become somewhat of an accepted fixture, whereas a deterioration of the situation in Europe might lead to a condition of mind under which the British would be compelled to reverse their present attitude.

[Marshall and Forrestal went on to report these findings to the President, who told them that he had "come independently to the same conclusion." The diary continues:

15 July 1948 Meeting—the President and Secretary Marshall—
Atomic Bomb

. . . The President was chipper and in very good form and
obviously pleased with the results of his speech at the [Dem-
ocratic National] Convention last night. (At an earlier brief
meeting with Secretary Royall and myself he made the observation that he had not, himself, wanted to go as far as the
Democratic platform went on the Civil Rights issue. He said
he had no animus toward the delegates from the Southern
states who had voted against the Civil Rights plank and against
his nomination. "I would have done the same thing myself if I
were in their place and came from their states.")

[However, the decision to send the atomic bomb carriers raised
     questions, more serious than those of Democratic politics, about
     the bomb itself.

I informed the President this morning that I asked for a
meeting with him for the next week to discuss the question of
custody of atomic weapons. I said I did not propose to ask him
for a decision on their use because I felt confident his decision
would be the right one whenever the circumstances developed
that required a decision. He then remarked he wanted to go
into this matter very carefully and he proposed to keep, in his
own hands, the decision as to the use of the bomb, and did not
propose "to have some dashing lieutenant colonel decide when
would be the proper time to drop one."

I said I had found in the military no thought of denying him
freedom of action on this subject but that there was a very
serious question as to the wisdom of relying upon an agency
other than the user of such a weapon, to assure the integrity
and usability of such a weapon. I said, however, I did not think
it appropriate to argue the merits of the case unilaterally but
that I thought it needed a decision at an early date.

[On Monday, the 19th, there was a special meeting on the Ber-
     lin problem. The airlift by that time had begun to demonstrate
     its power; immediately the situation was a trifle easier, but the
     long-term possibilities were formidable.

19 July 1948   *Meeting with the President—Berlin Situation*

Meeting this morning at 11:45 with the President and Secretary of State.

Marshall outlined the situation in Berlin to the President and the various courses open to the United States and the Allies. He said that we had the alternative of following a firm policy in Berlin or accepting the consequences of failure of the rest of our European policy. He recited that our policy had been successful in Greece, in Italy and in France; that the Soviets had been reversed in Finland and had been severely shaken by the Tito incident. Russian activity was the manifestation of the success of our policy.

He felt there was some chance of containing the Russians in Western Europe, and in the light of this fact I said I felt constrained to point out there was a definite limitation on our ability in the event of Russian military aggression. I reminded him that our total reserves were about 2⅓ divisions, of which we could commit probably about one division with any speed. The Army build-up would not come along until next spring or summer. He responded by saying that we were much better off than in 1940 and felt that we could encourage the French and other Europeans by supplies of token weapons.

The President, at the conclusion of the discussion, said our policy would remain fixed; namely, that we would stay in Berlin until all diplomatic means had been exhausted in order to come to some kind of an accommodation to avoid war. . . .

[Forrestal was evidently less confident than Marshall as to what could be done with "token" arms and European troops. However, General Clay, when he flew in two days later for consultation, did not seem particularly pessimistic. Forrestal dined with him on the evening of his arrival.

21 July 1948   *Dinner with General Clay*

Highlights:

1.   He said he was confident that three weeks ago he could have put through an armed convoy without difficulty. Chances of difficulty now somewhat greater but still believes it could be

done without creating a crisis. Chances will get slimmer as the Berlin impasse assumes greater proportions in the press and becomes subject of an increasing number of diplomatic exchanges; the obvious reason is that these klieg lights bring the situation into a focus of world opinion which makes it more and more difficult for the Russians to withdraw from a position so publicly taken.

2. Chances of war today about one in four.

3. Does not agree that we have to assume the immediate overrunning of France.

4. Believes the French will fight and that twenty good divisions could hold up the Russians at the Rhine.

5. German people unequivocally on the side of the U. S. and will do all in their power to help.

[Hopeful as this was, the fact remained that there were not "twenty good divisions" in Europe; and if the one chance in four should be fulfilled, the United States could barely supply one division as reinforcement. The emphasis which this put upon the atomic bomb was obvious; and the meeting which Forrestal had asked on the custody of the weapon had been held that morning.

21 July 1948   Meeting at the White House—Atom Bomb Custody

Meeting at the White House today with the President, members of the Atomic Energy Commission, Secretary Royall, Secretary Symington and Mr. Carpenter [Donald F. Carpenter, an executive of the Remington Arms Company], the latter the chairman of the Military Liaison Committee of the National Military Establishment (liaison with the Atomic Energy Commission), David Lilienthal, chairman of the AEC, and his four other associates.

Subject of the meeting was the presentation of a formal request of the National Military Establishment for an executive order from the President turning over custody of the atomic bomb to the Military Establishment, the chief reasons being (1) that the user of the bomb, who would ultimately be responsible for its delivery, should have custody of it with the accompanying advantages and familiarity, etc., which this would bring, and (2) concentration of authority—unified command.

Lilienthal based his objection to the transfer of the bomb on the broad general theory that the atomic bomb was not simply another weapon but an instrument of destruction which carried the widest kind of international and diplomatic implications; that the law which created the AEC dealt with certain constitutional relationships of the President; that actually greater efficiency in terms of surveillance, further developments, etc., could be had by leaving custody with the AEC.

The President made the observation that the responsibility for the use of the bomb was his and that was the responsibility he proposed to keep. He said he would reserve decision.

[After the Cabinet meeting two days later (which was wholly devoted to Mr. Truman's domestic program) the President held Forrestal back to tell him what the decision was to be. "He told me that he would make a negative decision on the question of the transfer of custody of atomic bombs and said that political considerations, at the immediate moment, had influenced this decision. He indicated that after election it would be possible to take another look at the picture." [1] In the course of a public statement of the next day (July 24) he declared that he regarded control of all aspects of the atomic energy program, "including research, development and the custody of atomic weapons," as functions of the civilian authorities. So that ended, for the time being, the question of custody; the AEC would retain physical possession of the weapons. Yet the point was at most a technical one; it did not settle the larger issues of both strategy and policy which were arising around the bomb. On the 28th Forrestal lunched with Marshall, Royall and Bradley.

28 July 1948   *Lunch—Use of the A-Bomb in War Planning*

. . . I said in view of the tensions in the European situation that I felt it was difficult for me to carry out my responsibilities without resolution of the question whether or not we are to

---

[1] Diary, 23 July 1948.

use the A-bomb in war. I observed also that it seemed to me that the Secretary of State had a deep interest in this, because, if there were any questions as to the use of this weapon, he was automatically denied one of the most potent cards in his pack in negotiation.

Bradley said the question was actively in the JCS. . . .

[Forrestal's note continues in terms which leave no doubt that he himself believed it necessary to draw war plans based on the assumption that the atomic bomb would be used as well as plans based on the assumption that it would not be used.

I I

[The emergence of the atomic bomb as the real core of American military strength—as, indeed, about the only form of military strength which remained after the evisceration of the April "balanced" program—had an unfortunate side-effect in exacerbating the rivalries between the Services. The compromises at Key West and in the budget discussions had imposed at best only an uneasy truce. Forrestal had defended Symington's right to testify for a bigger Air Force before the Finletter Board and the congressional committees; but he had already had occasion to rap his Air Secretary over the knuckles for his extracurricular activities in that direction.[2] It must have been with both surprise and exasperation that Forrestal read, in the *New York Times* for Sunday, July 18, a report of the "gloves-off talk before five hundred aviation engineers" which Symington had given at Los Angeles two evenings before.

"It was learned," said this report, "that on Mr. Symington's arrival in Los Angeles by plane last night, he was handed a prepared speech—presumably as approved by higher quarters in the Department of Defense—which had been wired here and laboriously manifolded for distribution. Considering it as too inconsequential to deliver, it was stated, he summarily rejected it and spoke 'off the cuff' with frequent undisguised tinges of acerbity.

---

[2] Memoranda for Secretary Symington, 4 and 8 May 1948.

["Assailing 'ax-grinders dedicated to obsolete methods' of warfare, who contended that large Air appropriations might 'unbalance' the three Services, Mr. Symington declared air power
should be put in balance not with the Army or the Navy, but
with the power of potential enemies, and that 'the American people have put their money on air power.' . . . No department
store, he asserted, could obtain financing for a line of merchandise with such a disjointed program as that pursued by the
Armed Services. Referring evidently to recent controversy over
defense appropriations, Mr. Symington said, 'Why should the
American taxpayer be forced to finance a plan unapproved by
the Joint Chiefs of Staff?' "

There was more of the same. Forrestal pasted the clipping in
his diary on the back of the following entry:

18 July 1948   *Speech by Secretary Symington*
I sent this message today to Mr. Symington:
"If the account of your speech in Los Angeles on Friday evening, as reported by Gladwin Hill in today's *New York Times,* is
accurate, it was an act of official disobedience and personal disloyalty.

"I shall await your explanation."
I called on the President this afternoon and told him I
would have to ask for Mr. Symington's resignation unless he
could provide a satisfactory explanation of his conduct in Los
Angeles. I said I did this with reluctance but I had come to
the conclusion it was the only possible course. The President
agreed and asked me to report to him on the conversation.[3]

[If the report was correct, the speech—with its undisguised and
even disingenuous attacks on the Secretary of Defense—would
seem to have well warranted dismissal. Yet on the following
evening Forrestal was dining with Symington, Sullivan and Royall in seeming amicability. Apparently what he was trying to
do was to get at the root causes of the Air Secretary's conduct.

---

[3] A notation shows that the entry was not actually dictated until 3 August.

It became clear that the area of disagreement between the Air Force and Navy Air is not necessarily very wide but it is quite deep. It deals fundamentally with the concepts of so-called strategic warfare, and this boils down to use of the atomic bomb. The Navy is willing to concede, according to Sullivan, the responsibility of strategic warfare to the Air Force but is not willing that it, the Navy, should be denied the use of the atomic bomb on particular targets.

Royall expressed his view to Sullivan and later to Symington that the Navy should accept not only the "dominant interest" of the Air Force in the atomic bomb but also their practical control of it. It, the Navy, should be subservient to the Air Force in any use the Navy makes of this weapon—there is an analogy in antisubmarine warfare, which, he said, was obviously the field of the Navy both as to offensive and defensive measures, but in which the Navy would obviously in wartime call upon the Air Force for such help in the form of air reconnaissance as it could offer in meeting this responsibility.

It seemed to me that this might be settled by:

1. Assigning the atomic bomb to the Air Force on the basis of dominant interest.

2. Limiting Naval Air use of it to (a) sorties upon strategic targets at the direction of the Air Force; (b) sorties upon purely naval targets.

3. Accept a principal of "dominant interest" with right of appeal by the Navy, first to the Joint Chiefs of Staff and to the Secretary of Defense.

[Here was an attempt, at least, to come to grips with the real trouble. How Symington explained away the Los Angeles speech is not stated; but Forrestal was both a genuinely tolerant man and one who disliked sharp, personal showdowns. He had often exasperated his staff by his endurance of dissents that bordered on disloyalty. Now, at any rate, when he reported to the President (as he had promised to do) he glossed over the whole affair.

23 July 1948   *Conversation with the President—*
                                  Resignation of Secretary Symington

I had a conversation with the President after Cabinet this morning, in company with Mr. Symington. I told the President that following my visit with him on last Sunday, I had decided to ask for the resignation of Mr. Symington if the version of his remarks . . . proved to be correct.

Since then, I told him, Mr. Symington had related extenuating circumstances in terms of arrival in nonusable form of the speech corrected in my office, that he had the copy of his original remarks, which he had shown me, plus the fact that he denied having made any impromptu remarks.

I also said that in view of the fact that I had expressed to him my dissatisfaction with Mr. Symington's conduct, I wanted to be sure that he was fully informed on the subsequent developments.

[Forrestal was still following his maxim that "removing human frictions" is 99 per cent of the art of government. But in his field the number of "frictions" was enormous. By this time the Hoover Commission "task force," under Ferdinand Eberstadt, was digging into the defense system and in the process affording an opportunity for the revival of the old demands for a completely centralized structure under unitary and dictatorial direction. Forrestal was now in a position to profit by such powers, but he clung to his original conception. A memorandum of this time (July 22) to his assistant, John H. Ohly, "for use before the Eberstadt Committee," stresses his conviction that "the Departments should retain autonomy, and with that, prestige, not merely in order to increase the position and prestige of the individual secretaries, but . . . to spread the burden of work which would fall upon this office. . . . In general, my policy is to let the Department having the dominant interest in any particular situation carry the ball, giving support to that Department where necessary." But this belief in Departmental autonomy put a greater responsibility upon the Secretary of Defense to secure underlying unification of strategic plan, policy and outlook.

[On the 28th he had a long conversation with the new Air
chief, Hoyt Vandenberg, seeking to resolve the developing Navy-
Air Force competition over the new weapon.

28 July 1948   *Conversation with General Vandenberg*
    I asked him what he thought of the idea of bringing General
Spaatz and Admiral Towers [long a leader in Naval Aviation]
back to active duty to assist in defining the issues involved in
the differences between the Navy and the Air Force on the use
of the atomic bomb. He said he saw no objection to it although he felt that the paper which the Air Force would submit to me through the Joint Chiefs of Staff would clearly
identify the issues, which revolved primarily around the question of responsibility for strategic warfare, which he conceived
would be the responsibility of the Air Force. This specifically
means that the Air Force, if granted this responsibility and
if made the executive agent for the Joint Chiefs of Staff in
that field, would be the sole source of authority on missions involving use of the A-bomb. He expanded on this thesis to say
that this decision would have a profound and far-reaching effect on future weapon programs; that obviously the country
could not afford to spend $15 or $20 billion a year continuously on its military establishment.
    I remarked that there were these fundamental psychoses,
both revolving around the use of air power:
    1.   The Navy belief, very firmly held and deeply rooted,
that the Air Force wants to get control of *all* aviation;
    2.   The corresponding psychosis of the Air Force that the
Navy is trying to encroach upon the strategic air prerogatives of
the Air Force. (He denied that the Air Force had the first objective in mind, although that is what General Spaatz has said
to me in private conversation.)
    I told him that my view was that while I was solidly behind
the Air Force in its claim for predominance in the field of
strategic air warfare, I would not extend that to denial to another Service of the development of a weapon which it thought
it needed in its own particular field. I mentioned the construction of carriers from 1942 on—a decision which met with strong

opposition from the battleship admirals in the Navy and equally violent opposition in the Air Force, particularly from General Knerr [Colonel, later Major General Hugh J. Knerr], who wrote a series of articles in 1942 to prove that the aircraft carrier was of no use. Subsequent events proved that it was the determining factor in the strategic air war in the Pacific. It was Halsey's carriers which shot down four hundred Japanese aircraft in a single day on their way to interdict the landing of the Marines at Saipan. [Actually it was not Halsey but Admiral Spruance who commanded in this action.] It was from the fields established on Saipan that the B-29s were able to deliver the A-bomb on Japan.

I said I was against the development of a new fleet of supercarriers by the Navy but I felt it was most important that one such ship, capable of carrying the weight of a long-range bombing plane, go forward.

I suggested that had we had the A-bomb in 1942 and a plane capable of carrying it from the *Hornet,* Doolittle's flight over Japan in April of 1942 might have aborted the Japanese war effort.

I remarked that there were serious misgivings about capacity of the heavy ship to survive against new weapons now in the process of development (such as the guided heavy aerial bomb with homing impulse, guided to its target), but that the perfection of such missiles would probably not occur within another five to ten years and in the interval I believed the carriers would remain a valuable method of waging warfare.

He said the whole matter, of course, came down to a question of money and that the nation could not afford to continue spending money for two duplicating programs, particularly when one involved the use of obsolescing weapons. At this juncture he remarked that it was very difficult to tell now what would be obsolescent five years from now—development in the field of antiaircraft weapons might make the large bombers as obsolescent as the battleship. I said I agreed with him on the necessity for coming to an early decision on the particular question before the Joint Chiefs of Staff, and if they were not able to decide it, I would.

[Clearly Forrestal was something less than satisfied. Vandenberg had spoken diplomatically, but the tenor of his remarks (as of those attributed to Symington at Los Angeles) was unmistakable. It all came to "a question of money"; Vandenberg implied that what money was available should go into strategic air, and as Forrestal had already noted,[4] "this boils down to use of the atomic bomb." So great a commitment to one weapon was at least questionable, and on August 9 Forrestal decided to call on Spaatz and Towers. "For my benefit in trying to resolve areas of disagreement in procurement planning for the future," his directive read, "it is requested that you set down your fundamental concept of strategic warfare as it might have to be waged in defense of the United States. There is obviously no disagreement that air power, in one form or another, will be a major factor in any strategic warfare of the future. Current discussions and differences . . . concern themselves with the most effective and economical means of applying air power against the enemy. . . . I think it is desirable to do two things: (1) point up the issues involved; (2) recommend the decisions which should be made on these issues."

It was a question, the directive continued, "of evaluating these new weapons, their capabilities and their control." Had the Key West decisions left "uncovered areas"? Did the carrier have a useful role in strategic air operations? Should the Air Force have operational control over all atomic weapons? Should the Navy's use of such weapons be limited to targets prescribed by the Air Force and purely naval targets? Forrestal ended by saying that he would consider making public their report; "it might well be that expositions by two such known and reliable experts in the field would usefully explain to our people the difficulties and alternatives we face in trying to plan the nation's safety."[5] In the end no such public findings emerged; but Forrestal was to take many of the implicit problems to another "out-of-Washington" meeting of the Joint Chiefs, at Newport later in the same month.

---

[4] See p. 464.
[5] Memorandum for General Spaatz, Admiral Towers, 9 August 1948.

[Meanwhile, behind all such problems, there was, of course, the Berlin crisis to lend them urgency. Negotiations had now got under way in Moscow; as in virtually every negotiation with the Russians since the mid-period of the war, the first results were amazingly hopeful, and State was giving away to that initial optimism which apparently never failed to deceive Western diplomats throughout the era. Bedell Smith was carrying the brunt, supported by Mr. Frank Roberts for Britain and the French Ambassador, Yves Chataigneau, and at the War Council on August 3 "Chip" Bohlen presented a glowing report of their achievements. The evening before, he said, Stalin and Molotov had agreed "to lift the blockade," desiring in return only "an arrangement which will prevent currency disorder in the Russian sector" and a meeting of the Foreign Ministers to take up the "broad problem of the future of Germany." The diary note continues:

3 August 1948   War Council—Ambassador Smith's Meeting with
Stalin and Molotov

. . . Smith reported both Molotov and Stalin in an extraordinarily amiable and cooperative mood. They gained the impression the Russians do not want war. Stalin and Molotov agreed to a joint communiqué describing the results of the conference. Bohlen said the Russians mentioned the Ruhr repeatedly throughout the conversations but Smith and his colleagues kept insisting they could not be committed to any specific agenda for the meeting of the Council of Foreign Ministers. Bohlen also reported on his conversations in London last week with Bevin, whom, he said, he found in a highly volatile and explosive condition. . . .

Bohlen regards the outcome of the conversations in Moscow last evening as highly satisfactory. He believes it indicates that the Tito incident and other reverses in Europe have greatly modified the Russian attitude. The success of the airlift over Berlin had a tremendous impression upon the Germans. As a result of U. S. propaganda the Russians, he feels, have lost tremendously in terms of prestige and good will in Germany, possibly to an irrecoverable degree.

[Just a week later, unhappily, Mr. Bohlen was a sadder and
wiser man.

10 August 1948   *Dinner—Mr. Bohlen*

Bohlen said that conversations in Moscow were taking an
unsatisfactory form; that the Russians were insisting upon language which would lift all restraints [on Berlin's communica-
tions] put into effect after June 19 [but would thus leave many
unacceptable restraints imposed prior to that date]. . . . The
nature of the Russian proposals throughout carry the implication that the four-power occupation and control of Germany is at an end, and acceptance of their language would, in
effect, mean that the U. S. was a vassal staying in Berlin by suf-
ferance rather than by right. . . .

[Forrestal got a "briefing" next day at which he was told of
"a message from Bevin expressing strong disapproval of the language as submitted by the Russians" and suggesting that Smith
and his two colleagues "should see Molotov promptly," and "if
Molotov should prove obdurate they should ask to see Stalin
again." [6] It was also on the 11th that there came an echo of Forrestal's anxieties over Palestine, in the form of an urgent request from the State Department for a detail of enlisted men
from the Mediterranean Fleet to assist Count Bernadotte, the
United Nations mediator. It was an appended document that
was of interest:

11 August 1948   Palestine Situation with Relation to that in Berlin
. . . In this connection there is a copy of a message from
London, reporting Ambassador Douglas's conversations with
Bevin. The latter is deeply disturbed about the situation in the
Middle East. He foresees that the Russians will do everything
possible to incite a renewal of fighting. . . . In brief, Bevin
foresees that if the Russians are unsuccessful in their efforts in
Berlin they will immediately step up their efforts to exploit the
chaos and disorder in the Middle East, if the U. S. and U. K. fail

---

[6] Diary, 11 August 1948.

to stand firm, he said, on vital matters in regard to Palestine and the Middle East. In general, both nations will suffer a defeat just as profound and just as dangerous to their future security as would be involved in any reverses in Germany.

[Forrestal had reason to know that his problems—and they were the nation's problems—were literally "global," every difficult issue everywhere dovetailing into some other more difficult one on some other front. It was not until some weeks later, however, that he was to become deeply involved in the Berlin muddle.

In the meanwhile, there was more trouble over the exchange of atomic information with the British. This incident was to be rather throughly aired in the Senate two years later. From what was then said it appears that at the end of July 1948 Dr. Cyril Smith, an AEC scientist, had been dispatched to England with a letter from the AEC Director of Research containing a list of subjects on which he was to exchange information. Dr. Smith had been gone nearly two weeks when a copy of his letter of instructions came into the hands of Rear Admiral John Gingrich, then the AEC Chief of Security. The admiral spotted one of the items for discussion—"the basic metallurgy of plutonium" —as going far beyond what he considered the limits allowed under the *modus vivendi*. Chairman Lilienthal and two other members of the commission happened to be out of Washington, but the admiral appealed to Commissioner Strauss, and the latter in turn laid the matter before the only other AEC member available, Sumner T. Pike, who was acting chairman.

Recollections later differed as to the exact sequence of events thereafter; but it is clear that Strauss felt that Pike was unduly slow to take alarm. Strauss called in Senators Hickenlooper and Vandenberg. The metallurgy of plutonium, as Hickenlooper later put it, "is the metallurgy of explosives of an atomic bomb"; the senators were as much concerned as Strauss and they went directly to Forrestal. The Secretary of Defense called in Vannevar Bush and Don Carpenter, head of the Military Liaison Committee, and as a result of the consultation informed Pike that the Defense Department "regarded the conveyance of this information as extremely serious and to be halted if humanly

[possible." When on August 12 Pike finally called Dr. Smith by
transatlantic telephone, he was "touring Scotland" and unavail-
able; but they got hold of him next day. Then it turned out that
he had not yet had opportunity to discuss the basic metallurgy of
plutonium with the British scientists, and he was told to drop
that one item from his agenda.[7] The British appear to have gone
ahead, without benefit of Dr. Smith's information on plutonium
metallurgy, to develop bomb manufacture on their own. At all
events, it was reliably reported in March 1951 that they were
building their first bomb and asking permission of the United
States to test it on the Nevada range.[8]

At the moment when this affair occurred, Forrestal was about
to leave for a short trip to Canada. It was just a little over a year
since he had been confirmed as America's first Secretary of Defense. His stewardship had certainly raised more and deeper
problems than it had settled; there was vital unfinished business
in his every important field of responsibility. But there had been
a substantial measure of achievement too. When a magazine
writer asked for material for an article on unification, Forrestal
responded with a memorandum to his newly appointed director
of public relations, Harold Hinton.

This memorandum listed such things as the consolidation of
military air and sea transport, the work of the McNarney Board
looking toward sounder budget procedures, an appeal Forrestal
had made to the National Security Council for clearer guidance
as to basic military policy,[9] and decisions, about to be confirmed,
for clearer allocation of roles and missions among the Services.
And as a final accomplishment, Forrestal added Hinton's own appointment as public relations director, "which obviously cures
all problems with the press, public and Tass!"

Much else had been done which could not then be given out
for magazine publication; in addition, there had been all the
work of setting up and staffing the new Security Act agencies
and instituting their many studies of everything from civil de-

---

[7] *Congressional Record,* Vol. 96, p. 9757-58, 9762, 9771-72.
[8] *The New York Times,* 18 March 1951.
[9] See pp. 492 and 509.

[fense to biological warfare, from industrial mobilization to weapons evaluation.

For all the controversy it had been far from a fruitless year. Forrestal departed for his Canadian trip, by way of Quonset, Rhode Island, on Friday, August 13.

III

Forrestal was never a party politician, and the 1948 presidential campaign left little trace upon his diary or in his letters. He lent a hand now and then with the fund-raising, but he made no speeches, and it seems clear that he assumed, along with innumerable others, that the Republicans would win in November and that his own public career, consequently, would doubtless come automatically to an end in the ensuing January. He thanked a friend for suggesting otherwise but added "by next January I will have finished eight and a half years in this town and that will have been enough. That is a firm decison." [10] Regardless of the election, he had convinced himself (as he had more than once before) that he would not continue; "no matter what the outcome in November," he wrote to another, "the end of this year will be the end of my bureaucratic career." [11] "Both for the sake of the country and for myself," he wrote to still another, "I assure you that [to continue beyond the end of the year] would not be wise, and, under no circumstances, could I be induced to continue." [12] And to another who had suggested "a session in the woods," he said that he didn't believe he could "get around to it until the end of this year when I am going back to the woods for good." [13]

Probably the truth is that Forrestal was incapable of "going back to the woods." The Canadian visit centered on the dedication of a plaque at Ogdensburg, New York, commemorating the Ogdensburg Declaration of Mutual Defense agreed there eight years before by President Roosevelt and Prime Minister Mac-

---

[10] To Samuel A. Perkins, 2 August 1948.
[11] To Guy P. Gannett, 30 July 1948.
[12] To Edward H. Little, 7 August 1948.
[13] To Robert W. Martin, 2 August 1948.

[kenzie King. But despite the inevitable ceremonial parties and dinners it was no junket. Forrestal met with the Cabinet Defense Committee at Ottawa on Monday, August 16, and they went over much ground: "They expected Russia to continue its pressure. . . . The Russians did not desire war. . . . The atomic bomb, while a formidable weapon, will not be a determining one. . . . Canadian emphasis was upon the creation of a high-quality, highly trained, small but compact striking force. . . . They are giving a good deal of thought to a radar screen although the very great costs involved make it a problem difficult of solution. . . . The Canadian defense organization is built on a functional basis —personnel, procurement and operations. . . . There are no Under Secretaries to represent the particular Services." [14] What most struck Forrestal, with his own recent experiences vis-à-vis Congress and the President fresh in his mind, was the Canadian governmental structure. He entered a separate note on the subject.

18 August 1948   *Meeting—Defense Committee*
                                        of the Canadian Cabinet

One of the deep impressions that I had as a result of this meeting was the contrast to the functioning of our own government. In this group there were the incoming Chief of State, Mr. L. S. St. Laurent, who will succeed Mackenzie King as Prime Minister; the Under Secretary of State for External Affairs, Mr. L. B. Pearson, who will succeed to St. Laurent's job as chief of that Department; Minister of Trade and Commerce C. D. Howe; Minister of Defense Brooke Claxton, and the three Chiefs of Staff. . . .

This group not merely was the Defense Committee of the Cabinet . . . but they also represented the control of the Canadian Parliament, because they are the chosen Ministers of the Liberal Party, which is the party now prevailing in power, as well as the chiefs of their respective government agencies. Therefore expressions of policy at this meeting are the statements of a responsible government.

---

[14] Diary entry dated 18 August 1948.

The link between the military and the civilian government is obviously provided by the presence of the three military Chiefs of Staff. The Cabinet Secretary provides the link between this particular committee and the entire Cabinet.

I talked afterward to Mr. A. D. P. Heeney, the Cabinet Secretary, and he advised me what I had already suspected, that there was a central secretariat pool in the Canadian government from which the secretaries of the various Cabinet committees are drawn. These men . . . provide a central nexus for insuring a common procedure throughout the entire government.

By contrast, in the American Cabinet the appointees of the President are responsible to him but their main job is to sell Congress. They do not speak for the government in the sense of reflecting party control of the Legislative branch. Therefore, the decisions they take are decisions only in the sense of an effort to merchandise a particular idea to the really controlling power, the power of the purse. In the formation of our military budget, for example, the power of the Secretary of Defense is really one of recommending to the President what he thinks should be spent in what proportions between the various Services. After he has made such a recommendation it is a free-for-all before the Appropriations Committees . . . who, if they are of an opposite political control, are quite apt to take particular delight in altering the budgets sent up by the Executive.

[In his patent envy of the Canadian system Forrestal no doubt overlooked the price which the Canadian Ministers had to pay for their assured authority—they had run for and been elected to Parliament, something not required of American Cabinet officers and something which Forrestal himself would never have desired to do. But his view of the Canadians' methods confirmed him in the shrewd conclusions he had already reached: the key to sound defense policy was responsibility, and the key to proper responsibility lay in the budget.

Forrestal was back in Washington on Tuesday evening, the 17th. On Friday afternoon he took off for the Quonset Air Station near Newport, Rhode Island, whither he had summoned

[the Joint Chiefs to wrestle once more with the problems which the Key West Conference had failed to settle.

Spaatz and Towers meanwhile had turned in their report. They agreed that the Key West decisions were sound in themselves and should stand, but that they needed "interpretation." They agreed that "no sharp line can be drawn between strategic bombing and tactical bombing" and that the Navy should be equipped to bomb strategic targets within the area of naval operations, even though the Air Force had primary responsibility for strategic missions. Spaatz went even further and agreed that the Navy's "ability to perform some of its primary missions" required it "to provide for delivery of atomic bombs," thus inferentially approving the proposed giant carrier capable of launching atomic bombers. They split only on the question of control of the bombs, Towers holding that "operational control of such weapons should not be vested in any one Service," Spaatz insisting that control "should be vested in the Chief of Staff of the Air Force acting as executive agent of the Joint Chiefs of Staff." The report scarcely covered the broad and basic fields suggested by Forrestal's directive, but there had been little time for that.[15]

Forrestal, the Joint Chiefs and their aides arrived in Newport for dinner Friday evening, August 20; the conference, held in the Naval War College, lasted through luncheon on Sunday, August 22. Forrestal's assistant, John Ohly, prepared a memorandum of the decisions taken, which was entered in the diary. "Control and Direction of Atomic Operations" headed the list. "It was agreed that, as an interim measure, . . . the Chief, Armed Forces Special Weapons Project [would] report to the Chief of Staff, U. S. Air Force." Since the Special Weapons Project handled the atomic bomb, this gave the desired operational control for the time being to the Air Force. "It was agreed to postpone any decision concerning the permanent future organization for the control and direction of atomic operations until the current study of the Military Liaison Committee [the link between the Armed Forces and the AEC] could be completed."

---

[15] Memorandum for Secretary Forrestal, 18 August 1942.

[The second decision clarified the term "primary mission" as used in the Key West agreement. In the fields of its primary missions (such as strategic bombing by the Air Force) each Service, it was now declared, "must have exclusive responsibility for planning and programing," but "in the execution of any mission . . . all available resources must be used. . . . For this reason, the exclusive responsibility and authority in a given field do not imply preclusive participation." The Air Force, in other words, was obligated to utilize any strategic bombing capabilities the Navy might develop. The Joint Chiefs added that this clarification was not to be regarded as "in any wise a victory or defeat for any Service," and they agreed so to explain it to their respective Services and to the public. This settled the immediate Navy-Air Force quarrel, which was not again to become acute during Forrestal's tenure of office. But the delicacy of the balance achieved suggests why his successor's decision to cancel the Navy's big "atomic" aircraft carrier had so violently unsettling an effect.

In a third decision the Joint Chiefs agreed that "the establishment of a weapons evaluation group is desirable and necessary." Here was another thorny subject. Sound military evaluation of available or prospective weapons systems was not only of first importance in guiding research on, and development of, the new instruments of war, but bore directly on all the current controversies as to bombers vs. fighters, air vs. surface and so on. An evaluation group would have great power; and its establishment had been held up by an argument as to whether it should be controlled primarily by the civilian head of the Research and Development Board or be directly under the military control of the Joint Chiefs. On this point "no final decision was reached"; it "appeared to be the consensus" that the group should be organized directly under the Joint Chiefs, but that the latter should "call upon Dr. Bush to organize the group and get it operating."

The conference further agreed that Forrestal should add "a small military group" to his office to keep him in closer contact with the Services; and there were decisions on one or two other miscellaneous matters. One of the last items on the Newport agenda was, however, one of the most important.

["It was agreed that it was imperative immediately to establish a stationary Western European Headquarters behind the Rhine. . . . (As to related matters, see separate memorandum for the record for decisions with respect to command.)"

The separate memorandum shows that Forrestal and the Joint Chiefs worked out two entire systems of unified, international command for Western Europe. One was for "immediate" use; the other for use "in the event of war." After clearance by President Truman and the State Department, the "immediate" plan would be urged upon our European Allies; and it was in fact followed by the appointment of Field Marshal Montgomery as Commander-in-Chief for Western Europe. The plan "in the event of war" was "for United States information only at the present time." It provided for "a Supreme Allied Commander-in-Chief (West) who should be an American," and sketched out other provisions, none of which took effect until the appointment of General Eisenhower as Supreme Commander in December 1950. There was no reference to this subject in the press release issued on the conclusion of the conference.

The Newport Conference had made progress; but Forrestal returned to Washington under no illusions that it had solved the manifold problems of a unified military policy. "I see at last the end of a long road as far as I am concerned," he wrote to a friend, "but it looks, however, as if the closing months are going to be the toughest." [16] To another, he stated the essential issue succinctly: "The difficulty stems mainly from money. . . . Each Service knows the magnitude of its own responsibilities. The simple fact is, however, that the economy simply cannot stand fulfillment of all the requirements without the nation accepting very substantial deficit financing." [17] Always vividly aware of these economic limitations, Forrestal took a greater interest, perhaps, in the building of firm economic and political foundations for a war effort than he did in current controversies over programs and "missions." A few days after his return from Newport he was writing a long letter to Arthur Hill, chairman of the

---

[16] To Edward J. Birmingham, 26 August 1948.
[17] To Franklin D'Olier, 26 August 1948.

[National Security Resources Board, presenting many aspects of industrial mobilization planning which he wished to see pressed. "This" he concluded, "is not a needling letter—as a matter of fact it is a self-needle as far as I am concerned. I am convinced we have to press with all of our energy from both sides of the river to get these results quickly. . . .

In a memorandum to Hinton a few days later (August 30) he was asking whether the Military Establishment should consider making plans for a re-establishment of "Byron Price's and Elmer Davis's jobs"—that is, for censorship and for war information—should the need arise, and was raising the question of psychological warfare. The true field of the Secretary of Defense's responsibility was enormous, complex and—for a sensitive mind—demanding in its every aspect, for nothing less than the safety and survival of the United States depended upon the adequacy with which those responsibilities were discharged. None could ever be neglected or forgotten. Yet with them there went even larger responsibilities in the formulation of current national policy. Over the next few weeks Forrestal's thoughts were to be largely absorbed, not by the details of defense organization, but by the Berlin crisis.

IV

["A note came in last night from Moscow," a diary entry of the 24th records, adding "the gist of the agreements" which it reported. The Russians were still attaching dubious provisos to their undertaking to lift the blockade. The entry continues:

24 August 1948   *Berlin Situation*
. . . The State Department and Clay, with whom and with Douglas telecon conversations were held all day, are very much disturbed about the apparent failure of Bedell Smith to insist upon inclusion in the communiqué announcing the results of the discussions of any reference to the juridical rights of the United States in the Berlin area. Lovett told me this afternoon that they have sent a message to Smith emphasizing the fact that some such reference would have to be made.

27 August 1948   *Meeting in Moscow—Berlin Situation*

Lunch today with Marshall and the Joint Chiefs of Staff less
Admiral Leahy. . . .

Smith, Roberts (U. K.) and Chataigneau have seen Molotov
and Vishinsky today. State expects to get a summary of the
results by six o'clock. State is concerned that Smith has not fully
grasped the importance of, and has, therefore, not registered
thoroughly and strongly, the American position on its basic
juridical rights to be in Berlin. He has been somewhat captious
in arguing with the Department on the line that they are being
unnecessarily meticulous.

The program, if agreement is reached on broad lines in
Moscow, would transfer the negotiations to the four military
governors in Berlin to work out details.

Lovett called me after lunch to express great concern about
Clay's ability to preserve his calm and poise in these negotiations. He said that he had the impression that Clay was now
drawn as tight as a steel spring. I suggested that Royall go over
to help him, but Lovett said this would be impractical because it would indicate a lack of confidence in Clay, through
sending over his superior, so to speak, to monitor and guide
him. I later talked to Royall, who agreed with Lovett's point of
view. . . .

[The transfer of negotiations from Moscow to the military governors in Berlin failed to improve matters. On September 3
Marshall told the Cabinet that "there was some improvement
of the atmosphere of the meeting yesterday but no improvement
in the attitude on the fundamental question on the control of the
Bank of Emission of Currency." [18] Two days later Forrestal gave a
Sunday afternoon to going over the dispatches.

5 September 1948   *Berlin Situation*

Digest of meetings between the four military governors of
Berlin, held in Berlin the last two days.

Russians are displaying a typical intransigence. Sokolovsky

---

[18] Diary, 3 September 1948.

is apparently trying to go back on the Moscow understandings in regard to the lifting of restrictions. . . . Clay takes a very gloomy view of the progress and of the Russian attitude. . . .

At the close of Saturday's meeting Sokolovsky announced that Soviet air maneuvers would be held in the Berlin area, beginning September 6. Clay remarked that such maneuvers would hold grave dangers of undesirable accidents and incidents. (Sokolovsky referred to these maneuvers as normal maneuvers of this time of year for the Soviet forces and observed that they had no other significance. Clay remarks in his message to Draper that in the four past summers no one has ever seen or heard of these maneuvers.) The British General Robertson [General Sir Brian Hubert Robertson, Military Governor] thanked Sokolovsky for providing the information and expressed the hope it would not interfere with the air corridors. To this Sokolovsky replied, "Certainly." Clay remarked he didn't know whether this meant "Certainly, yes" or "Certainly, no." He referred, in a subsequent remark to Sokolovsky, to "our agreed safety regulations," and "that there was sufficient air for any type and kind of air maneuvers without utilizing the corridors." To this Sokolovsky replied that no such air regulations existed and insisted that the Russians would have to use the corridors.

[Here was a threat to break up the airlift; it seemed as though crisis might again be growing acute. Next day was Labor Day, and Lovett took advantage of the holiday calm to come to Forrestal's office, with Bradley and Gruenther, for a review of the position.

6 September 1948 (Labor Day)   *Record of Conversation*

Mr. Lovett stated that he desired to review with Mr. Forrestal the current Russian situation. It is quite clear that an important Russian objective is the domination of Germany, the first step of which is the control of Berlin. The Soviets have made three errors of judgment [in understimating the determination of the American people, the capacity of the airlift and the temper of the Western Europeans]. . . .

This is the seventy-fourth day since the blockade. . . . The sheer duplicity of the Soviets during these negotiations is beyond the experience of the experts in the State Department, with the result that any future promise made by the Soviets is to be evaluated with great caution. It appears that they do not mind lying or even our knowing that they lie, as long as it is for the benefit of the state.

Two months ago key figures in the satellite powers were advised that "a great diplomatic victory" was about to take place in Moscow. In our talks in Moscow we arrived at certain arrangements with Stalin and Molotov only to find that in the final meeting Molotov and Vishinsky were extremely sour and disagreeable. Our estimate is that when they reported the results of their negotiations with the Western powers to the Politburo they were informed that they "had lost their shirts." [19] The objective appraisal of the results of their negotiations would reveal that the Soviets had gained very little, since we had agreed, on June 22, to the currency proposal and we have continued to maintain that we cannot be forced out of Berlin. The directive issued to the four governors has been completely disregarded by Sokolovsky. Three days ago he not only refused to lift the blockade but also tried to impose additional airlift restrictions. He has disavowed practically all of the four-power conference proposals agreed to by Stalin and Molotov.

It is Mr. Lovett's hunch—and he reiterates that it was only a hunch—that the Soviets do not want an agreement. They would just as soon have a break now unless they can get an

---

[19] It is curious how hard this notion died. Again and again, the recurrent contrast between the fair openings and sour endings of negotiations with the Russians was explained by Western statesmen on the ground that the Politburo had intervened to veto Stalin's or Molotov's initial generosity. It was the best answer Stettinius could find for the disappointments after Yalta. One encounters it as early as August 1942, when Churchill, reporting to his War Cabinet on his talks in Moscow, observed: "We asked ourselves what was the explanation of this . . . transformation from the good ground we had reached the night before. I think the most probable is that his [Stalin's] Council of Commissars did not take the news I brought as well as he did" (*The Hinge of Fate,* p. 489). Only slowly did it seem to dawn on the West that the Russians might be using a standardized technique.

agreement on their own terms. There are no intelligence estimates to support this conclusion, but Mr. Lovett feels that there is no other explanation for the extraordinary behavior of the Soviets. He stressed the difficulty of dealing with someone "whose head is full of bubbles."

Mr. Lovett emphasized the necessity of unity in government at this time. "Beadle" Smith has done an excellent job in the Moscow negotiations—better than probably ninety-nine out of a hundred who might have been selected. While he may not have the negotiation facility of Lew Douglas, he has the requisite toughness to deal with the Soviets under current conditions. . . . There has been a tendency to criticize him for failure to get this or that result, but Mr. Lovett pointed out that this criticism is not justified. He stated that it is very easy to "kibitz" the event critically from this safe distance, but that it is a very different matter when one is in the driver's seat.

[On the following day there was a special meeting of the National Security Council to consider the problem more formally. The President and all members of the Council were present.

7 September 1948   *National Security Council*

. . . Secretary Marshall and Mr. Lovett reported that the situation regarding the Berlin negotiations is discouraging and serious and that we are not making any progress. General Sokolovsky has flagrantly ignored the clear directive agreed to in Moscow and, instead of discussing technical arrangements, is challenging the basic principles which were agreed to with respect to quadripartite control of the Soviet currency in Berlin and the lifting of transport restrictions. The situation has been further complicated in the last few days by the riots and local troubles inspired by the Soviets, and there is a danger that the Soviets may cause the negotiations to blow up at any time.

The State Department . . . proposes to put to Molotov in Moscow the broad question whether the Soviets propose to live up to the Moscow agreement. If Molotov's answer is in the negative or is evasive, we will submit an *aide-mémoire*, listing our specific charges and announcing that we are referring the entire problem to the United Nations Security Council under Chapter VII of the U. N. Charter ["Action with Respect to Threats to the Peace, Breaches of the Peace, and Acts of Aggression"]. The State Department is now trying to bring the British and French in line with this proposed course of action. The President and the Council concurred in these proposals.

Mr. Lovett discussed the Soviet intention to conduct air maneuvers in the Berlin corridor and said that we have put them on notice that the airlift will proceed and that any interference will be at their own responsibility. It was agreed that unless the Joint Chiefs of Staff express an adverse opinion, the number of C-54s taking part in the airlift should be increased from 125 to 200.

Mr. Royall said that General Bradley is in communication with General Clay in order to plan appropriate protective measures which would, if possible, be nonprovocative. He also stated that under our evacuation plans, the actively loyal Germans in the Western sector came next in order of priority after United States dependents.

It was arranged to hold a meeting on the following day at which Secretary Marshall and the Joint Chiefs would be present in order to discuss emergency plans.

[This meeting (held at 10:30 next morning) was preceded by a two-hour telecon conference with Clay, with Bradley, Wedemeyer and, for the last half hour, Forrestal, sitting in on the Washington end. From Forrestal's diary notes, it largely hashed over the old ground, not really adding very much to what they already knew. At one point Bradley "raised the question of Clay's actions in the recent mob violence in Berlin. Stated he thought General Clay had handled the matter correctly by not sending in MPs, but questioned whether or not it was likely Clay would send in MPs on a subsequent occasion. Clay said he did not intend such action [because it would legalize Russian entry into the Western sectors] but added, 'You cannot live surrounded by

[force and bluff without showing that you have no fear of the first
and only contempt for the latter.'"

Forrestal left no diary note on the 10:30 meeting with the
Joint Chiefs, but the tangled situation did lead him to some re-
flection on the powers and responsibilities of the Secretary of
Defense.

8 September 1948   *Secretary of Defense*

I said to Mr. Royall this morning at the end of the telecon
conference with General Clay that this whole negotiation provided food for thought on the question of the concentration of
all authority and power in the Office of the Secretary of Defense.
I pointed out that these negotiations were of a nature that requires almost continuous attendance in order to follow the
threads between State and the Defense Departments. That if
it were all concentrated in my office I would have had to assign some particular person to do it, but that with all the
minutiae of detail in connection with the Bank of Emission,
with trade arrangements, etc., I would have had to maintain
daily and almost hourly familiarity. Furthermore, all discussions with State would have had to have been carried on by
me.

[There was further negotiation next day; and at the Cabinet
on the day after, Marshall summarized the state to which the
Russian tactics had reduced them all.

10 September 1948   *Cabinet*

Marshall reported on the Berlin-Moscow situation.

This is the seventy-ninth day of negotiations and all persons
concerned in it are close to a state of exhaustion—telecon conversations with Douglas in London ceased at 2 o'clock this
morning, which was 7 o'clock London time, and were resumed this morning at 8:30. This government is greatly har-
assed by the fact that there is no responsible government in
France. . . . Marshall's apprehension about [a further spinning out of "the Berlin Merry-Go-Round"] is that if it is per-

mitted to do so, it gives the Russians the chance of taking it to the United Nations rather than us, with all the opportunity created by the initiative and with all of the invective which they ordinarily use.

The present plan, assuming the French and British consent, is to present an *aide-mémoire* to Molotov, reciting the failure of . . . Sokolovsky to effect the agreements arrived at in Moscow and stating that unless a directive goes . . . to Sokolovsky instructing him to negotiate in the terms of reference created at Moscow . . . the Western ambassadors will report the fact back to their governments. The British, as Bevin is inclined to prefer, want to go back to Stalin and in this he will have French support.

Marshall's objection to this is that he would anticipate getting from Stalin merely a bland statement of generalities which would be followed by a continuance of the same delaying tactics—tactics which are entirely in favor of the Russians.

[The situation was harassing, dangerous and uncertain; and one of the greatest of Forrestal's own uncertainties had never been cleared up. It was nearly six weeks since he had declared that in view of the European tensions he must have a "resolution of the question whether or not we are to use the A-bomb in war." [20] The tensions were daily increasing and there had still been no answer. As this Cabinet broke up, Forrestal raised the question again with Marshall.

10 September 1948   *General Marshall—*
                              Negotiation with British Chiefs of Staff

Talked with Marshall this morning on the use of A and a conference with the President.

He suggested a meeting with the President at twelve Monday.
. . .

[At the meeting on Monday Forrestal got a reasonably plain answer.

[20] See pp. 461-62.

13 September 1948   *Meeting—the President*

Meeting at the White House with Secretary Royall and Generals Bradley and Vandenberg to make to the President the same presentation that Vandenberg made to the Secretary of State last week. . . . [The question was brought up] of a decision for use in an emergency. After a repetition of the briefing which Vandenberg had given to Marshall, the President said that he prayed that he would never have to make such a decision, but that if it became necessary, no one need have a misgiving but what he would do so. . . .

[Forrestal never again felt it necessary to raise the matter with the President. Of American public opinion he felt less certain. The next evening, at the home of Philip L. Graham, publisher of the *Washington Post*, Forrestal, Marshall and other high officers met with a large gathering of newspaper publishers and editors in order to brief them on the Berlin crisis, and Forrestal took occasion to pose the question of the bomb.

14 September 1948   *Meeting at Residence of*
                                Mr. Philip Graham—Berlin Situation

Meeting at Philip Graham's house. *Those present were:*

Arthur H. Sulzberger	*New York Times*
Geoffrey Parsons	*New York Herald Tribune*
Walter Annenberg	*Philadelphia Inquirer*
Paul Bellamy	*Cleveland Plain Dealer*
Paul Miller	*Gannett Newspapers*
Mark Ethridge	*Louisville Courier-Journal*
Roy Roberts	*Kansas City Star*
John Cowles	*Minneapolis Star-Tribune*
Wright Bryan	*Atlanta Journal*
William Mathews	*Arizona Star* (Tuscon)
Clayton Fritchey	*New Orleans Item*
Roger Ferger	*Cincinnati Enquirer*
Paul Patterson	*Baltimore Evening Sun*
William Block	*Pittsburgh Post-Gazette*
Palmer Hoyt	*Denver Post*
Robert McLean	*Philadelphia Bulletin*

John Knight   Knight Newspapers, Inc.
Paul Smith   *San Francisco Chronicle*
John Cline   *Washington Evening Star*
Secretary Marshall   Secretary Forrestal
General Bradley   Under Secretary Lovett
                          Mr. Bohlen

General Marshall, Under Secretary Lovett and Mr. Bohlen made a presentation of the sequence of events in Moscow and Berlin in the last six weeks. After dinner Mr. Bohlen read the text of the latest communication from Smith in Moscow, reciting the details of his and Roberts' and Chataigneau's conference with Molotov.

Chief impressions: Roy Roberts expressed the strong belief that the policy of our government should be so conducted as to make sure there would be no chance of any overt act prior to November 2. The rest of the group dissented from this view and took the position that our actions should be without reference to political expediency or elections, but Roberts could not be shaken in his opinion; unanimous agreement that in the event of war the American people would not only have no question as to the propriety of the use of the atomic bomb, but would in fact expect it to be used.

There were many statements to the effect that the opinion of the country was substantially ahead of Washington in its impatience with the Soviet government. None present expressed any desire for war—in fact, as was to be expected, quite the contrary, but there was strong evidence of a growing distaste for the actions of Russia.

[Through the next two months Forrestal was systematically to query men on both sides of the Atlantic as to the public reaction to be expected should the United States use the bomb. He never recorded a dissent from the "unanimous agreement" of this dinner meeting. Marshall was to quote to him a remark of John Foster Dulles that "the American people would execute you if you did not use the bomb in the event of war"; Clay said that he "would not hesitate to use the atomic bomb"; Winston

[Churchill, going even farther, told him that the United States erred in minimizing the destructive power of the weapon—to do so was to lend dangerous encouragement to the Russians.[21]

All this was reassuring as against possible eventualities, but it did not solve the immediate problem of Berlin. At the Cabinet Lunch on the 13th Marshall had been pessimistic.

13 September 1948   *Cabinet Lunch*

The Secretary of State reported on the week-end developments in the Moscow-Berlin negotiations. They were faced, he said, with constant and continuing difficulties with both the British and the French, neither being willing to go as far in firmness of language as the United States desired. . . . He looks forward with great apprehension to the meeting of the Council of Foreign Ministers. Lovett suggested this morning that both Byrnes and Vandenberg [the senator, not the general] accompany him, both for purposes of counsel and also possibly to speak in some of the debates. Dulles, he said, only wanted to talk on the basis of a lawyer's brief, whereas the debates in the Security Council sessions may call for a swift give-and-take and rough-and-tumble debate.

Marshall said that Bevin had sent him a personal cable over the week end. . . . Bevin's position is that he wishes, if possible, to avoid a break in the negotiations, which will send the issue to the U. N. Cripps participated with him in some of the week-end conversations and agrees with Bevin's position.

Marshall said that one of the difficulties in Britain was the fact that with Parliament out of session and a minimum of public exposition of the issues underlying the Berlin impasse, British opinion had not yet crystallized to the extent that ours had. I made the observation that in addition to this fact, Bevin was undoubtedly conditioned by the war-weariness of the British and their extreme reluctance to have to face the grim prospect of another war. (Marshall said that Bevin kept referring constantly to the fact that "they were in the front line.") I mentioned the report that General Saville had brought back from Britain, . . . that he reported the sense of a tre-

[21] Diary, 10 October, 12 November (pp. 523-24), 13 November (p. 527), 1948.

mendous reluctance to face any decision which might lead to conflict.

16 September 1948   Meeting—the President, Secretary Marshall
   . . . Marshall also mentioned the question of custody of the bomb. . . . The President said he was most anxious to withhold this decision until after the campaign.

I said I was still convinced that the physical custody of the weapon should be in the hands of the military. . . . I said that I did not feel that six weeks' time [until the election] would make a vital difference in our planning for use of the bomb, but that I would like to reserve the right to come back to him if those responsible felt it should be opened.

[Yet these days were at the same time bringing a certain relaxation of the tension. The negotiations in Berlin had reached a deadlock, but when the ambassadors took the issue back to Molotov in Moscow he seemed at least willing to continue talking. The American-British airlift had stepped its deliveries up to a level of five thousand tons a day, including large amounts of coal as well as food; and in celebration of American Air Force Day on September 18 they put a record seven thousand tons into the beleaguered city. It seemed probable that Berlin could be maintained indefinitely, while the negotiations would meanwhile go to the United Nations General Assembly, about to convene in Paris. Marshall took off for Paris on Sunday the 19th. Forrestal made a diary entry the same day:

19 September 1948   Meeting—Berlin Situation
   Meeting this morning with Royall and Draper.
   The most recent Russian note is in. As expected, it says that Sokolovsky acted in perfect accord àbout [with] the Moscow agreements between Stalin and the three Western ambassadors. The note was not satisfactory but at the very end of the conversations Molotov indicated his willingness to continue further conversations in an effort to reach an agreement.
   Royall made this point: that it would not be a good record to have broken on such a note—in other words, with Molotov still willing, apparently, to work out an accommodation.

I called Marshall just before he left and made the suggestion that, insofar as technical matters of trade, finance, etc., in the Berlin area are concerned, the Western powers might find it advantageous to suggest the creation of a neutral commission —Dutch, Swedes, Norwegian, Swiss, etc.—to deal with these matters.

[It was never found necessary to act upon this latter suggestion; and with it, Forrestal's direct preoccupation with the Berlin crisis dwindled. The crisis was to drag on, of course, throughout the winter and spring, but with steadily lessening chances that it would explode into war; and though Forrestal returned to it more than once in his diary, it was the diplomats who thereafter carried the principal responsibility.

Meanwhile the crisis had advanced the B-29 groups to British airfields; it had brought the atomic bomb plainly into the forefront of our military policy and had enforced some serious thought about the bomb itself in both Washington and London. Washington's fears of London's firmness were to prove unfounded. When Sir Stafford Cripps (then Chancellor of the Exchequer) visited Washington in early October, he told Forrestal that "Britain is placing its main reliance on the development of fighter aircraft to insure the security of Britain. Britain must be regarded as the main base for the deployment of American power and the chief offensive against Russia must be by air." [22] And when Forrestal visited Britain in November the Prime Minister told him that "there is no division in the British public mind about the use of the atomic bomb—they were for its use. Even the Church in recent days had publicly taken this position." [23]

---

[22] Diary, 3 October 1948.
[23] Dairy, 12 November 1948.

CHAPTER XIII

The Battle of the Budget

I

[The events of the summer had made only more urgent, and more complicated, the problems which would come to a head in the autumn, as Forrestal well understood, with the preparation of the budget for fiscal 1950. Forrestal was trapped between the refusal of the President, on the one hand, to go beyond the continuing $15 billion "ceiling" and the refusal of the Joint Chiefs, on the other hand, to allocate—and so take the responsibility for—any budget which could be kept remotely within that limit. Neither were the Joint Chiefs eager to grapple with the patently inescapable problem of "phasing" their military recommendations to the capacity of the civilian economy. The McNarney Board [1] had been laboring to correlate and scale down the separate and competitive demands of the three Services, but their progress was not too encouraging.

It left Forrestal facing some very large issues. How was the responsibility for "phasing" to be met? Were the strategic plans in fact sufficiently clear, coordinated and self-consistent to support the heavy budget demands? With so much of the emphasis already on the atomic bomb, what actually were the combat capabilities of the big bombing planes, in themselves and in relation to all the other weapons for which such huge amounts of money were being asked? As early as July 10 Forrestal had formally asked the National Security Council for "guidance" in formulating his views on requisite budget strengths—and as late

---

[1] See p. 450.

[as the end of October he was still to be waiting for an answer.[2]
He considered calling on Charles E. Wilson (whom the President
was to summon two and a half years later to head the entire war
mobilization effort) for help with the "phasing" problem; but in
September he was able to write Wilson that the Joint Chiefs
"have now come up with a plan so there is no need for a
needle," and he would not ask the industrialist to come on.
He explained later that "the JCS *did* come up with a plan. . . .
There was only really one major split decision which was on the
question of plan of construction of additional new, big carriers.
That question I had to resolve myself." [3]

Forrestal at the same time was thinking of a maneuver test
for the strategic bombers.

22 September 1948 War Game—National Military Establishment

I talked this morning with General Gruenther and Don
Carpenter, new chairman of the Munitions Board.

I told Gruenther I wanted to make preparations to set up a
war game on the capabilities of the big bombers to attack industrial targets in this country. He said that such a war game
would involve a tremendous administrative burden, with a
large number of people employed and a substantial amount of
material.

I said I realized that, but the stakes were so high that I felt
we had to do it, particularly as we were spending billions of
dollars on the purchase of aircraft, which, if they could not
carry out their mission successfully, would lead us to a series
of very dangerous assumptions. . . .

[The Air Force was very confident, as is shown by a signed
memorandum from Symington of October 5 which Forrestal
placed in the diary: "Re our conversation last night, I talked to
General Vandenberg this morning about his certainty as to
whether or not the bomb could be dropped where, how and
when it was wanted; and he told me again what he had already
told me; namely, he was absolutely certain it could be dropped

[2] See p. 509.
[3] To Charles E. Wilson, 9 and 18 September 1948.

[on the above basis." The maneuvers were not held; though a
year later there were still to be demands, in the so-called
"B-36 controversy," for maneuver tests of the conflicting Service
claims.

There were also, of course, the political aspects of budget-mak-
ing to be considered; evidently, they were being approached under the belief that the Republicans would win in November.

24 September 1948   *Luncheon—Budget, Preparation of*
Lunch today with Congressman Taber, General Bradley and
General Vandenberg.

Mr. Taber said that he would be in Washington sometime
after election and then would like to sit down with the
budget people in the Services to lay out plans. . . .

If Mr. Dewey is elected, he felt that the new administration
must have time to acquaint itself with the problems in connection with the budget. . . . He has proposed to Webb that in
the event of Mr. Dewey's election, he (Webb) invite some of
the new President's budget people to work with the present
budget organization in order that they might acquire needed
education and knowledge in the two and a half months' period
between election and inauguration. Mr. Webb has not, as yet,
reacted favorably to this suggestion. . . .

I said that I would like the privilege of submitting some supplemental appropriations early on in the new Congress; that
I was concerned about gaps that had shown up in the budget
hearings, particularly with reference to certain categories of
Army equipment, and that I thought it was of vital importance that such deficiencies be corrected as early as possible,
even before the consideration of the budget as a whole.

[A letter of this time well illustrates both Forrestal's own atti-
      tude toward politics and the pressures which the budget-making
      was now putting on him.

To William Gaston, 4 October 1948
I have delayed answering your letter because I was endeavoring to get clear in my mind on two things:

(a) Whether I would make any political speeches.

(b) Whether, even if I wanted to, I would be able to get away from this grind long enough to do it.

I am now clear on both. I have come to the conclusion that in my present position I should not get into politics. Second, even if I decided affirmatively I could not possibly get away until I have finished with the preparation of the 1949-50 budget, which is now in process, and which is a task which will extend over the next month.

I respect your willingness to take the rap of running for office, which is, after all, the acid test of whether many of us mean what we say when we talk about "taking an interest in government." I have always been amused by those who say that they are quite willing to go into government but they are not willing to go into politics. My answer, which has now become a bromide with me, is that you can no more divorce government from politics than you can separate sex from creation.

[Forrestal felt this last deeply; and perhaps it explains the rather striking lack of rancor with which in his many differences with the President he received adverse decisions which seemed politically motivated.

In the making of the military budget it was, of course, never possible to lose sight of the actual international problem which the Military Establishment existed to meet. On the day of Forrestal's lunch with Taber, Bedell Smith came in from Moscow.

24 September 1948   *Conversation—Ambassador Smith—*
                                                          Russian Situation

. . . Summary of his views: The Russians do not now want war, but that doesn't mean that they will go to all lengths to avoid one. They have the Oriental habit of misunderstanding the Western mind. . . . Their view is a long one. They accept the inevitability of ultimate conflict, but feel it may not come for five, ten, fifteen, fifty or even five hundred years. . . .

The Russians cannot possibly have the industrial competence to produce the atomic bomb now, and it will be five or even ten years before they could count on manufacture of it in quantity. They may well now have the "notebook" know-how, but not the industrial complex to translate that abstract knowledge into concrete weapons.

The atomic bomb by itself will not be a deterrent to their making war. They count upon their great diversification and their vast areas. . . .

The great mistakes were made during the war because of American failure to realize that military and political action had to go hand in hand. Both the British and the Russians realize this fact and that was what lay behind Churchill's desire to attack through the Ljubljana Gap. This might have prolonged the war six months to a year, but it would have prevented the Russian domination of the Balkans. . . . After Hitler's death in 1945, Jodl made a final attempt to persuade the Allies to make a separate peace with Germany. . . . The Russians were always terrified of this and they were equally terrified that we might push on through beyond Berlin and the Stettin-Trieste line. In 1945 Churchill wept when he was informed that we proposed to withdraw from territory we had conquered. The difficulty was that we were already committed by previous agreements arrived at between Mr. Roosevelt and Stalin, with Churchill the reluctant partner, to divide occupation responsibility on lines that suited the Russians. . . .

[Nor was Europe the only strategic problem affecting military plan. For months the Far East had taken little place in Forrestal's diary; now, however, there was a reminder that its problems also had to be considered in the design of the American Military Establishment.

5 October 1948   China—Probable Effects of U. S. Withdrawal from

I met Captain Bob Dennison [Robert L. Dennison, the Naval Aide] at the White House this morning and he expressed concern about China. He said he felt that if we ever withdrew from China—and by this he referred specifically to the current situation in Tsingtao—we would probably never get back in. I inquired as to the capabilities of carrier aircraft to operate against forces trying to take the port, and he said the roads of ingress to Tsingtao were so concentrated that it would be very easy to operate against any forces which did not have aircraft cover.

["There is no question," as Forrestal put it in a letter at this time, "that foreign policy is a function of defense and vice versa." [4] The trouble, under our system of intricately divided responsibilities and conflicting official preoccupations, was to bring the two into any kind of rational accord. The March crisis had emphasized the need for available tactical forces; and as a result of the re-enactment of the draft and the April supplemental program, total strengths had risen from the 1,374,000 of February 1 to 1,531,881 on October 1. The increase was scheduled to continue through the first half of 1949, but thereafter, under the operation of the Truman "ceiling" policy, strengths would have to be cut back again. (On the outbreak of the Korean War in June 1950 the establishment would actually stand at only 1,465,000.) Facing this situation, Forrestal on October 5 laid his intentions before the President.

He spoke first of the recommendations he proposed to make to the Eberstadt "task force" of the Hoover Commission. Fairly bitter experience had convinced him that the Secretary of Defense needed greater powers with which to control the unruly team over which he presided, although those for which he would ask were still very far from dictatorial. He believed that he should have the assistance of an Under Secretary; that there should be a responsible chairman of the Joint Chiefs (not, however, a single, all-powerful Chief of Staff), and that the language of the Security Act which limited the Defense Secretary to only "general" authority over the Departments should be amended by eliminating the word "general." (He added that he was developing Gruenther "as my principal military adviser rather than in the concept of a Chief of Staff.") As to whether the Department Secretaries should continue in that status or be reduced to Under Secretaries or Assistant Secretaries, Forrestal was undecided.

[4] To George E. Sokolsky, 2 September 1948.

[The President "expressed the strong view that they should be Assistant Secretaries."

These, however, were all long-run answers for the problems which the budget had brought into focus. The immediate and vital problem was the budget itself.

5 October 1948   *Conversation—the President*

. . . With reference to the budget, I said on the 14.4 billion ceiling limitation[5] we would probably have the capability only of reprisal against any possible enemy, in the form of air warfare, using England as a base. The Mediterranean would be ruled out. I said I proposed to submit a budget to him based on the 14.4 billion limitation, but at the same time we would proceed with another budget which would probably be on the order of 18.5 billion and which would be predicated on the attainment of capability of exploiting the holding of the Mediterranean LOC [line of communications]. With reference to this latter, he said he wished it to be held in reserve, that the fact of its presentation would be interpreted as a step toward preparation for war and that additional estimates could be kept in the form of supplementals, to be presented if and when the situation became more dangerous.

He remarked that he had talked with Marshall this morning and had asked Marshall to come back over the week end so that he, the President, could explore the international situation directly with him.

[It is striking that here is the first intimation, in the available record, of an attempt to design the Military Establishment in accordance with specific, definable capabilities and objectives. The $14.4 billion level would permit Air (which of course meant atomic) reprisals from Britain and nothing else; an $18.5 billion level would make it possible to plan to hold the Mediterranean as well, with the access to bases, Allies and resources which that

---

[5] The President's ceiling of $15 billion included $600 million for stockpiling raw materials. Forrestal did not regard this as properly a part of the military budget, and frequently used the $14.4 billion figure to express the President's ceiling. The two figures refer to the same thing.

[would give. No calculation of this kind had previously appeared in the argument. Obviously this is not to say that none had been made—Forrestal by no means put all that he knew into his diaries and letters—but nothing of the sort had been advanced in the policy and budget discussions of the spring, which had all been on a much vaguer plane of generalized "augmentation" of the forces. Striking as well is the President's reaction; since the announcement of the "Truman Doctrine" in March 1947, he had certainly been keenly aware of the importance of holding the "Mediterranean LOC," but he seems to have recoiled from this blunt translation of a vital national policy into its corresponding military and budgetary terms.

The day after this talk with the President, Forrestal attacked the other horn of his dilemma: the Joint Chiefs.

To the Joint Chiefs of Staff, 6 October 1948

I want to have it clearly established in your minds that I am expecting a definitive recommendation from you, as an entity, as to the division of funds in the 1949-50 budget—specifically, as to the allocations to the respective Services, under a ceiling of $14.4 billion.

I want this question disposed of before consideration is given to the need for supplemental appropriations or as to the division of such supplemental appropriations.

[Forrestal's strategy seems clear. The ex-captain of artillery in the White House was at best not overtrustful of the four-star generals in the Pentagon. It was essential to get a consistent and intelligible program, to which the Joint Chiefs "as an entity" would put their names, on the lower level of expenditure, in order to make a convincing case for expansions and supplementals beyond the presidential ceiling which Forrestal still hoped to get. In June the Joint Chiefs had agreed to accept the responsibility, though "past history" even then had left Forrestal with his doubts.[6] The doubts were now amply justified. The Joint Chiefs returned a flat refusal. On October 7 they replied through Fleet

---

[6] See p. 450.

[Admiral Leahy that they could agree on no program within the
$14.4 billion limit; they simply transmitted the separate and un-
correlated budget requests of the three Services—totaling, of
course, very much larger sums—thus dumping the whole problem on Forrestal's desk.

It was on the following day that Forrestal dropped a note to
the new President of Columbia University: "Dear Ike: . . . Will
you . . . let me know so I can arrange to set aside some time
in which we can talk fundamentals: policy, budget and our
whole military-diplomatic position." One can understand his impulse to seek General Eisenhower's experienced counsel.

Marshall had by this time returned from the Paris session of
the General Assembly, and on Sunday, October 10, there was
a special meeting in his office with Forrestal, the three Service
Chiefs of Staff, McNarney and Gruenther. Again, it would seem,
Forrestal was seeking to establish some firm connection between
foreign policy and its military arm; again, Marshall seems not to
have been particularly responsive to the acute problems of the
Secretary of Defense. Gruenther (who took extensive notes,
which Forrestal entered in his diary) and the military chiefs began by outlining the effect of the Truman ceiling on the
strengths of the Armed Forces; but Marshall, after "a few questions," plunged rather into a long report on the European scene.
According to Gruenther's notes:

10 October 1948   *Meeting with the Secretary of State*

. . . General Marshall had one central theme which he referred to repeatedly during his hour's talk, and that is his
strong conviction of the tremendous importance of furnishing
equipment—particularly ground equipment—to the Western
European nations. He stated that these nations are in a particularly apprehensive state of mind, "completely out of their
skin, and sitting on their nerves," and hope must be recreated
in them very soon. He concurs most enthusiastically with the
plea which General [Alphonse] Juin made, "I could arm a
million young Frenchmen, if I only had the equipment. You
must give us something to put in their hands." . . . If some-
how we could arrange to start shipment soon the psycholog-

ical effect would be electrifying and would furnish the stimulus to morale which is so sadly needed at this time. . . . Anything would do, even if we could give them nothing more than rifles. . . .

General Bradley asked the Secretary that even if we gave arms to Europe should we not have more than token forces in this country to give tangible evidence that we would be able to come to their assistance in the event of war. General Marshall replied that this, of course, was desirable, but from the presentation he had heard it was clear that we would have nothing but token forces to supply, and that he felt it was extremely important that intensive and immediate aid be furnished to the Western European nations.

When General Marshall discussed the budget he referred to the forthcoming planners' conferences with the British and stated that if we were embarrassed in these conversations by the meager forces that the contemplated budget would provide, he would suggest that we explain that we were considering the budget at a time when considerations other than those of national security were occupying the limelight; and that the situation would probably be better for supplementary funds after the election. In that connection, he stated, that of course the converse might be true if the Soviets should make any concessions which would indicate peaceful intentions on their part. In that event it would probably be extremely difficult to secure additional appropriations.

Secretary Forrestal stated that he was not particularly worried about the conference with the British planners, even if they had to cool their heels for a couple of weeks while we decided on a new strategic concept as a result of reduced forces which would be available because of the budgetary ceiling.

Mr. Forrestal stated that regardless of the political situation he wanted to be able to submit to the President an estimate of what the country needs in the way of a Military Establishment in the light of the current international situation. General Marshall replied that we must give careful thought to saving our manpower. . . .

(*Comment*: It is my [Gruenther's] distinct impression that

General Marshall, although sympathetic with the Chiefs because of the budget ceilings which have been imposed, was not particularly disturbed over the implications in the field of foreign relations. He certainly uttered no caveats which could be used by the Secretary of Defense in an appeal for more funds. Mr. Forrestal referred obliquely on two occasions to the probability that the reduced capabilities of our Armed Forces might prove to be an embarrassment in executing our foreign policy but General Marshall made no comment. He appeared reasonably confident that Congress would give relief. His prime concern was the prospect of equipment for the French. . . .)

[The conference ranged over many other matters. Marshall thought that "the Soviets are beginning to realize for the first time that the United States would really use the atomic bomb against them in the event of war." He was "most enthusiastic" about French Premier Robert Schuman; he was very cautious about Spain, because of the repercussion which any raising of that question would cause in France and Britain. He even mentioned a matter over which Forrestal had already experienced some concern. Marshall said "that the President mentioned to him yesterday that he was disturbed because he was finding on his trip that many people friendly to him referred to the 'military clique in Washington.' Mr. Forrestal suggested that a good deal of this agitation came from the pen of Mr. [Walter] Lippmann, who uses it as a continual theme song, but on balance he is not very much worried about it."

On the main issue of the military budget, however, Forrestal had clearly not got much help from the Secretary of State. There was nothing for it but to tackle the Service Chiefs in earnest. On the 15th of October he did so.

II

[Forrestal called a conference in his office on October 15. The Air Force was represented by its Vice Chief of Staff, General Muir S. Fairchild; the others included Bradley, Denfeld, Gruenther and Forrestal's assistant, McNeil. A stenographic record was kept, and Forrestal entered in his diary extracts from the trans-

[cript running to nearly eleven typewritten pages. In itself a remarkable picture of the actual processes of policy formation under our system, the transcript also makes clear what Forrestal was trying to do and admirably illustrates his skillful methods. He began with the President's $15 billion limit: "Of course, you have come up with a split paper on that. What I have been anxious to do is, first, to see what we could do on the 15 billion." He explained that there were two possible approaches to this problem (which the Joint Chiefs as a body had refused to face). One approach was, so to speak, functional; they could confine the plan "only to the mounting of the atomic offensive from Britain," and then see "whether you are going to try to do anything else. I take it that you haven't resolved anything yet." The other approach was to start with the empirical monetary limit "and then cut to that." This approach was "easier," but, Forrestal continued, "it is not satisfactory to me. Sixty-six per cent complements on board your ships in the Navy. That is breathing, but not moting. I want to get the flying time between the Navy and the Air Force a little more closely examined. . . . On the question of your pants, Brad, the seven pairs per man. In the Navy you have to have them, but I suspect you [the Army] have got to . . ." The sentence is unfinished in the transcript.

Once a division of a $15 billion budget was agreed upon, "the next step," Forrestal continued, was to take the Services' own concept of their needs. The McNarney Board had worked this figure down to a total of $23.6 billion. It was necessary to "see what between that figure and this $15 billion figure would give you a possible force that could jump off if war came. I should like to present those two, if I could, together. I do not know whether it is possible or not, but I am most anxious to say we have made a terrific effort to come under the 15 billion. You cannot have a satisfactory and usable military power under that ceiling. You can do a patchwork job. You cannot do a thorough one. The second figure—we cannot do everything we would like to do but it is a fairly practicable instrument to use." Forrestal, who understood the political problem much better than the military men appear to have done, urged them with eloquence to produce such an intermediate figure.

["Whether you can get that done in the next two weeks, I do
not know. I hope very much that you can, because if you could
come up in the Joint Chiefs—saying we are agreed upon this
second concept, whether it is 17.5 or 18 billion, and we will go to
the Congress and back this one, it would have a tremendous
effect for the country and a tremendous gain in stature for the
JCS, which I think is more important. I shall be out of here
within one, two or three months, but I think, as a citizen, it is
most vitally important that the concept of the JCS not lose face
with the country. I think it is a dangerous thing for the country
if it does. You accept to some extent a confession of inability to
get away from Service interests and look at the whole business
in the light of what the national interest is. That will be the
public interpretation of it."

What he was really asking them to do was to assume the cor-
porate responsibility for military policy as a whole which the
nation supposed that they were discharging. Bradley was first to
respond; perhaps, he intimated, the Army could prune its share
of the McNarney $23.6 billion figure to some such intermediate
level. Actually he had already told his people "to apply all these
things that we have unearthed [in the McNarney estimates]—
·buying seven pairs of pants, I think we can put it off. New automatic rifle is very desirable if we ever go to war, but I do not
think we can afford to put it in this year's budget. . . . Put that
down to the bottom. . . . The force requirements will be
squeezed out by squeezing out the extra pairs of pants and some
of that equipment." Forrestal entered a caution against squeezing
too much on equipment, but Bradley thought it could be done:
"Maybe Louie [Denfeld] can get along without a better destroyer and I can get along without a better gun. There are
things like that which I think we can squeeze out of that 23.1
figure and still have an 800,000-man Army."

Forrestal challenged them to clarify their thought in another
way; if, he suggested, the plan was based simply on an air offensive from Britain, would the Army and Navy require the
strengths they were asking? The discussion became somewhat involved. Bradley objected that to plan only for an air offensive was
to "put all your eggs in one basket," and the argument digressed

[into other considerations. But Gruenther brought them back to
the main point by observing that the simple air offensive from
Britain had never "for one moment" been regarded "as an acceptable concept"; it had merely been taken as a "very minimum"
in the effort to meet the $15 billion ceiling.

Here was the point Forrestal wished to drive home. He had
raised the matter "simply to bring out the absurdity" to which
the presidential ceiling led, when the problem was stated, as he
wanted the Joint Chiefs to state it, in functional terms. Only so
could they provide him with anything with which to argue
against the Budget Bureau. On the $15 billion limit they could
"certainly" mount an air offensive from Britain; but that was all
they could do, and in that case all the rest of the Military Establishment became useless. The result was an obvious absurdity—unless, as Gruenther added, "you are willing to gamble
on that [the air offensive]—that it will bring the end of the war."

Forrestal tried to emphasize the demonstration: "I want to say
to you men also that I am going to try to be in this as much as
I can myself, so I would appreciate attending any [JCS]
meetings. I am not there as a spy. My job is going to have to be
to convince the President and his successor, if there is one, that
we have taken every drop of water out of this thing that we
could find—we can't catch it all—but I have got to be able to
say that we have gone into this thing from the ground up and
prefer to go at it from the top down. . . . This is not any Ges-
tapo to try to produce evidence. . . . We are talking about three
things: maximum [the McNarney $23.6 billion] concept; mini-
mum—15 billion; intermediate one, which is what I want really
to get to ceiling. The ones I want work on, those that are the
two realistic objectives, are the intermediate and the minimum. I want to be able to state in broad terms what the maximum was—to have the competence to make an effective
and immediate reprisal if the Russians move, and that an intermediate one will enable us to make reprisals and at the same
time have the tables of organization and cadres to fill out
promptly."

The conversation digressed here into a debate over Mediterranean strategy. From this point on the transcript is so heavily

[cut that it is difficult to follow the thread of the argument, but the main lines are apparent. They discussed technical means of reducing the budget requests; it is plain that Forrestal tried to keep them firmly on the rails of concrete proposals involving functional military results, and at the end he brought them back to the main issue. The question had been raised of reducing ship complements. What would be the results? "That," said Forrestal as the meeting approached its end, "is what I want to know. I want to know what the consequences of that would be. In some things you can accept a lack and in other things you cannot accept any lack, and I want to be sure what their areas are. We will meet again when there is business to talk about that can get the case forward. What I want is what we get out of the 15 billion, and what I want these men to do is to agree what the distribution would be on the 15 billion. They failed to do that. I want to get what the results will be from the 15 billions of appropriations. Second thing is the intermediate field which enables us to have a healthy response to Russia."

In confronting the Budget Bureau and the President he would need firm, specific ground to stand on. But whether he would get it from the Joint Chiefs may still have seemed doubtful to him, despite the skill with which he had driven the lesson home.

"We are looking," Forrestal had said at one point in this meeting, "at a situation which is not war, but it certainly is a lot grayer than it was last May." When Clay presently returned to Washington to report, Forrestal breakfasted with him, together with various State and Army Department officials, on October 21. In Paris the six "neutral" members of the U. N. Security Council had busied themselves in finding a compromise formula —of somewhat uncertain implications—for settling the Berlin dispute, and word came that morning that the Russians had accepted it.

21 October 1948   *Breakfast with General Clay*

. . . Clay indicated that he felt this concession by the Russians might be the first step in a maneuver to follow the same pattern as they had in Korea: suggesting that all hands get out

of Germany. American agreement to such a proposal would
be tantamount to surrender of all he assumed we were fighting for in Europe: to prevent the taking over of Western Europe by Communism. The Russians already had an army of
200,000 people, either trained or in training, in their Zone.
There is no comparable armed strength in the Western Zone
because the French have consistently objected to the arming of
any Germans. The only thing that has kept Europe stable has
been the presence of the American Army and the airlift.
Withdraw that, Clay says, and you practically turn the show
over to Russia and the Communists without a struggle.

We are now winning the struggle but any of the suggestions
that had been current about getting out of Germany would be
the beginning of our losing it. The periphery theory advanced
by Lippmann and others—which contemplates the stationing
of garrison forces at the ports and on the rim of Germany—is
totally impracticable because there is no place in these areas
to put the number of troops that would be involved.

I said the most dangerous spot is our own country because the
people are so eager for peace and have such a distaste for war
that they will grasp for any sign of a solution of a problem that
has had them deeply worried. . . . We are meeting the President, with Clay and Royall, later this morning. I said to Royall
it was most important that we try to convince the President
he should not attribute undue significance to this proposal
and that Clay should say to him, as bluntly as he has said to
us, that any policy which contemplates withdrawal from Germany means withdrawal from Europe and in the long run the
beginning of the third world war.

[None of this made the problem of adjusting the military
    structure to the needs of policy any simpler. At the National Se-
    curity Council meeting that day, Forrestal spoke with apparent
    asperity of another disconnection in our policy-making. Accord-
    ing to an assistant's note, "Mr. Forrestal referred to the State
    Department request for four to six thousand troops to be used
    as guard forces in Jerusalem in implementation of the Berna-
    dotte Plan for Palestine. This unexpected request was an example

[of how the Palestine situation had drifted without any clear consequent formulation of United States policy by the NSC. Mr. Forrestal said that actually our Palestine policy had been made for 'squalid political purposes.'. . . He hoped that some day he would be able to make his position on this issue clear." [7]

The prerequisite to intelligent military policy was, here as elsewhere, intelligible and consistent national policy. Forrestal at this time got out two "top secret" State Department analyses of Soviet intentions and entered précis of them in his diary. One was the estimate of April 1, already referred to;[8] the other was an estimate of June 23, weighing factors in Soviet policy "affecting the nature of the U. S. defense arrangements." The second found, much as had the first, that "war is not a probability but is always a possibility." In the light of this, the analysis had concluded that it was "necessary that the United States maintain armed strength" to serve as "support for our political position; as a deterrent; as encouragement to nations endeavoring to resist Soviet political aggression" and in order to "wage war successfully in case war should develop." It had also suggested that an American defense policy "based on the maintenance of a permanent state of adequate military preparation is better than an effort pointed toward a given peak of danger." [9] In the budget discussion with the Chiefs of Staff only capabilities "in case war should develop" had been considered. This analysis, on the other hand, had not only stressed the importance of a permanently "adequate" defense structure, but had also put current "support for our political position" as the first function of such a structure. As October ran out, Forrestal made another effort to enlist Marshall's help, this time putting it in a formal letter.

To the Secretary of State, 31 October 1948

As you know, we have been engaged for a number of months in the preparation of a statement of forces on which to base a military budget for fiscal 1950.

At the risk of oversimplification, I would say that we have

[7] Diary, 21 October 1948.
[8] See p. 409.
[9] Diary, 23 October 1948.

two basic problems with respect to the size of the Military Establishment: One is the problem with which the Joint Chiefs of Staff have been dealing—namely, ascertaining the forces which we need in order to combat possible acts of aggression. Over and above this—and of greater importance in my opinion—is the problem with which you are concerned— namely, that we maintain sufficient strength to assist you in your difficult international negotiations, in order that peace may be maintained.

As you know, last spring the President set a limit of $15 billion as the tentative ceiling for the military budget for fiscal 1950. . . . You are, of course, familiar with the international background when this decision of last spring was reached. You will recall that you and I and the Secretary of the Treasury talked over the matter with the President, and at that time you made the statement that our plans should be predicated on the assumption that we were *not* preparing for a state of war.[10]

I think it is important to note that the ceiling . . . will not be adequate to maintain the level of forces which we are scheduled to attain at the end of the current fiscal year [30 June 1949]. . . . What I should like to have from you is your judgment on the following matters:

(a) Has there been an improvement in the international picture which would warrant a substantial reduction in the military forces we had planned to have in being by the end of the current fiscal year?

(b) Has the situation worsened since last spring and should we, therefore, be considering an augmentation of the forces that we were planning at that time?

(c) Is the situation about the same—that is, neither better nor worse?

On 10 July 1948 I addressed a letter to the National Security Council asking for guidance which would be of assistance to me in the formulation of my own views on the budget strengths that should be maintained. Up to the present time the National Security Council has not been able to give me a reply. I fully

[10] See pp. 431-32.

realize, of course, that these are questions which involve many imponderables, and that a letter in precise language is not an easy one to draft. I do feel, however, that I must seek every avenue of judgment in order to supplement my own. . . .

In addition to submitting a budget within the President's tentative ceiling of 14.4 billion, I feel an obligation to inform him of the weakening of our strength which this budget entails, in the opinion of the Joint Chiefs of Staff, and I am also considering sending the President, as my own recommendation, a proposal that he lift the ceiling to approximately 17.5 billion—which, in my opinion, while involving some risks, would provide us with forces capable of taking effective action in the event of trouble.

I am writing this letter to obtain from you as much guidance as possible in determining the degree of vigor with which I should support the recommendation which I propose to submit, as outlined above.

[An accompanying memorandum explained the effects of the budgetary limitation on troop strengths. The April program as finally adopted would "if fully implemented" provide on 30 June 1949 a total strength of 1,964,000 men [including 161,000 one-year trainees) and a sixty-six-group Air Force. The $14.4 billion ceiling would permit the maintenance in fiscal 1950 of an aggregate strength (including one-year trainees) of only 1,625,000 and a fifty-one-group Air Force. It was estimated that "to construct forces with a capability of effective reaction immediately at the outset of a war" would require an aggregate strength of 1,975,000 and seventy groups. The cost for fiscal 1950 would be about $21 billion. "Specifically, these estimates are based upon a war plan which—in the event of hostilities—would contemplate securing of the Mediterranean line of communications." The immediate program on which the Defense Department was working would come to about $17.5 billion and would provide strengths approximating those originally contemplated for the end of fiscal 1949.

At the time this letter was written, Marshall had already returned to Europe. Lovett promptly telephoned.

1 November 1948   *Letter to Secretary of State*

Lovett called me this morning to inquire as to the speed with
which I desire an answer to this letter. I told him that the important part of it obviously dealt with the larger amount,
namely, 17.5 billion, and that I would like to have Mr.
Marshall's view by 15 November in order to help me in
determining the degree of importunity that I put into my recommendation to the President. . . . [After promising swift
delivery of the letter] he said that in an effort to be helpful he
would make his own responses to the questions, observing
that to the first question, which was whether or not the international situation has improved sufficiently since last spring
to warrant a decline in our military strength, the answer is: no.
He remarked that he felt that the answer to the first question
pretty much provided the answers to the other two. In brief, he
would say that he would respond, no, to the first and third, and
make no comment on the second.

[But when Marshall's own answer came back from Paris a week
    later, it evaded the real issue by answering the third question—
    "Is the situation about the same?"—in the affirmative, and then
    returning to his familiar theme. The important task, Marshall in-
    sisted, was to rearm Western Europe. In the specific dilemma in
    which he was trapped, Forrestal was apparently to get little more
    help from the Secretary of State than he had been getting from
    the Joint Chiefs. But by the time the answer was returned there
    had been a dramatic reversal in the whole position.

III

[Not until October 26, exactly one week before the election,
    does the diary record any intimation that the Republicans might
    not, after all, be the certain winners; and even this intimation
    was disputed by a distinguished political commentator.

26 October 1948   *Conversation with Leslie Biffle*

Leslie Biffle told me that he thought the President had
made very substantial gains in the last two weeks. He thought
he would carry Massachusetts, Rhode Island and possibly Con-

necticut. The Senate, he thinks, will be Democratic by a majority of five, and thinks there is a possibility of the House also being Democratic.

On the contrary, I asked Arthur Krock [Washington correspondent of the *New York Times*] his view this morning and he saw no change. So far as the Senate and House are concerned, he thinks that "the hair will go with the hide"; in other words, Dewey's strength will counterbalance local tendencies.

[Other prophets were also seeing dimly. When Forrestal two days later had Admiral Hillenkoetter, the head of the Central Intelligence Agency, in for breakfast, the admiral was apparently "assuming Mr. Dewey's election." The intelligence chief also predicted "no war in the immediate future," in which he was right, and that De Gaulle would be "in power in France next March," in which he was as wrong as he was about Dewey.[11] Whatever the voters might do, Forrestal still seems to have considered his own public career as approaching its end, and there was much unfinished business. On October 7 he had appeared before the Eberstadt "task force" of the Hoover Commission, to testify for the strengthening (which he had already outlined to the President) of the powers of the Secretary of Defense. One of the "task force" members, the Chicago industrialist General Robert E. Wood, wrote to say that he had been "very much impressed" both by Forrestal's appearance and by the inordinate difficulty of the military problem in a capitalist democracy. Forrestal's answer put it well.

To Robert E. Wood, 18 October 1948

. . .There are no easy black and white solutions for the problems which face this country. How to secure the formation of capital necessary to our plant replenishment, how to secure a tax system which will provide the incentive and the opportunity for the individual acquisition of capital, how to balance between a military organization sufficiently formidable to give any other country reason to stop, look and listen, without at the same time its eating our national heads off—these

[11] Diary, 28 October 1948.

are segments of a very complex matter which must trouble any
citizen who understands it. . . .

[There has seldom been a better statement of the searching
    socio-political implications of the military problem in demo-
    cratic societies, which have rarely paused even to consider that
    the problem exists. Forrestal was not having much success in
    getting either the military or the civil arms of government to
    face these implications; but it is a measure of his stature that he
    was throughout acutely aware of them himself.
        The "task force" hearings had afforded a forum in which to re-
    vive the old demands for the absorption of Naval Aviation in the
    Air Force. Forrestal dictated a memorandum which was a
    shrewd and penetrating comment not only on air strategy but on
    the whole strategic problem.

27 October 1948   *General Notes on the Question Naval Air—*
                                                    Air Force

    1.   We now have in existence strategic air forces of great
potential power in terms of weight-lifting capacity and range.
The unresolved question, however, is whether unescorted big
bombers can penetrate to targets that have a vigorous fighter
defense.[12]

    2.   We also have in existence a nucleus of carrier aircraft and
in reserve an additional number of carriers which can provide
tremendous striking power.

    3.   Strategic air warfare is the assigned responsibility of the
Air Force with the proviso that they are to call upon Naval Air
for whatever help Naval Air can provide. It is my opinion that
if war came the Air Force itself would immediately, or shortly
after the outbreak, realize the diversionary possibilities necessarily of the aircraft carrier task forces.

    4.   No one knows the form and character of any war of the
future. War planning—so-called strategic plans—are largely an
intellectual exercise in which the planners make the best estimate of the form of a war against possible enemies. But the ac-

---

[12] Forrestal considered it "unresolved" in spite of the Air Force's confidence of
a month before. See p. 493.

tions of any enemy must, necessarily, profoundly affect any war planning. If one did not have an enemy, it would be possible to have a perfect plan that could be taken off the shelf for immediate execution, but unfortunately the enemy does not always conform. . . .

5. I do not believe that air power alone can win a war any more than an Army or naval power can win a war, and I do not believe in the theory that an atomic offensive will extinguish in a week the will to fight. I believe air power will have to be applied massively in order to really destroy the industrial complex of any nation and, in terms of present capabilities, that means air power within fifteen hundred miles of the targets— that means an Army has to be transported to the areas where the airfields exist—that means, in turn, there has to be security of the sea lanes provided by the naval forces to get the Army there. Then, and only then, can the tremendous striking power of air be applied in a decisive—and I repeat decisive—manner.

[Here was an answer—and its soundness was to be demonstrated in many respects by the Korean War—to most of the inter-Service arguments. But the Service rivalries remained, and so did the problem of keeping the battle within bounds. The Navy reacted with a natural asperity to the proposal to bestow its aviation on the Air Force, and Forrestal drafted a restraining letter to Sullivan.[13] Its theme was that while it was "entirely appropriate" for any Service to testify before congressional or other committees in defense of its competence to perform its missions, this should not extend to attacking the competence of another Service in its own field. Specifically, in defending its own aviation, the Navy should not attack "the capabilities of the bomber aircraft of the Air Force to penetrate enemy territory"; it should not indulge in "destructive criticism of a sister Service." The letter was drafted but not sent; partly, perhaps, because Forrestal realized that it dealt with but one aspect of a subject that demanded larger treatment.

At least since the exploits of the Air Force advocates in the spring, Forrestal had been concerned with the problem of con-

[13] Draft letter, 29 October 1948.

[trolling virulent inter-Service controversy before Congress and the public. In the summer he had brought Major General Walton B. Persons into his office as an over-all director of liaison with Congress; the hope was to institute some control over the rival Departmental legislative programs. In September a meeting of the War Council had been devoted almost entirely to the question of the vociferous retired officers, who frequently carried the inter-Service battle when orders or discretion had silenced those on the active list. The occasion was the somewhat testy autobiography of the redoubtable Marine general, Holland M. ("Howling Mad") Smith, about to appear serially in the *Saturday Evening Post*. Forrestal considered requiring that all such works be submitted for official clearance, as a basis not for disciplinary action but for "moral suasion"; but the Air Force representatives doubted the legality of such action and Bradley hesitated to deprive retired officers of this means of augmenting their diminished pay.[14] In October Forrestal raised the problem with two thoughtful journalists.

7 October 1948   *Luncheon with Hanson Baldwin and*
                              Walter Lippmann

. . . We talked about the general question of the control of speeches and writings by military personnel, either active or retired.

Mr. Lippmann said he rather doubted the efficacy and/or value of specific orders or directives. As an alternative he suggested the preparation of a very thoughtfully written paper, what he called "Testimony of Faith," which could go to the senior personnel of all the Services for their guidance. He said this should go into the question of our international relationships, the role of the military in our society, the relationships between the Services, etc. He said he saw many difficulties in the wise and effective application of any categorical orders.

[But Forrestal continued to ponder the question. On November 1 he released to the public an order tightening up the existing provisions for bringing the Departmental legislative pro-

---

[14] Diary, 21 September 1948.

[grams under his "central control." [15] Finally, on November 8, he issued a general order, in the form of a memorandum to all three Secretaries, based on his draft letter to Sullivan.

Memorandum for the Secretary of the Army, the Secretary of the Navy, the Secretary of the Air Force, 8 November 1948

From time to time the Services are called upon to testify before various congressional and other committees on matters covering a wide range of subjects. It is entirely appropriate in such a presentation for a Service to use the most persuasive arguments in defense of its competence to perform its missions. I think it is most inappropriate, however, and certainly not conducive to the spirit of cooperation between the Services, to permit such an exposition to develop into an attack upon, or criticism of, the competence, equipment or weapons of another Service.

I desire, therefore, that you take steps to insure that any report or presentation by a responsible official of your Service to an agency outside of the Military Establishment, which involves any criticism of another Service, he submitted to me prior to delivery. I recognize that occasions may arise where officers testifying before committees may be asked questions the answers to which may involve criticism of another Service. I am not issuing any instructions which forbid an officer to reply to such a query or which direct him to answer it in a certain manner. I strongly urge, however, that sympathetic consideration of the problems of the other Service be constantly kept in mind in responding to questions of this character.

It is obviously impossible for this office to monitor all testimony, presentations or other statements by individual Services. I shall have to rely on the development of an attitude which will find reflection in a disciplined restraint and moderation whenever other Services are concerned. This does not mean to imply that I do not welcome the freest and most vigorous expression of opinion and statements of belief within the Military Establishment itself, because it is only by such healthy

[15] *New York Herald Tribune*, 2 November 1948. The order was dated 29 October, the day he drafted his letter to Sullivan.

and objective critiques that we can avoid the danger of inertia and atrophy, but these discussions should be carried on within our own family and not outside it. . . .

[This very mild limitation was as far as Forrestal cared to go. His successor's experiences with a stricter "gag rule" would seem to confirm the wisdom of Forrestal's position.

In the meantime, however, Tuesday, November 2, had brought the presidential election. Mr. Truman departed for his home in Missouri in order to cast his vote and receive the returns; in his absence there was to be a special meeting of the National Security Council, called at his request, in the White House on Wednesday afternoon to "deal with the question of China generally and Tsingtao in particular." By the time the policy-makers convened, the election results, though not final, were sufficiently clear. "The hair," in Mr. Krock's phrase, had indeed "gone with the hide," though both were of a coloration opposite to what had been expected. President Truman had been re-elected and the Democrats had regained control of both House and Senate. In a sense they were all back at the old stand; and there was something drearily familiar in the NSC's indecisive conclusions on China.

The immediate question was what to do about the American forces at Tsingtao. The Chinese Communists had completed their occupation of Mukden on November 1 and had begun the march which was to carry them in the ensuing year across the whole face of China. A directive was worked out for the commander on the ground, Rear Admiral Oscar C. Badger, based on the idea that "arrangements should begin for the evacuation of dependents and the phasing out of our forces," but on the larger issues they did not get very far.

3 November 1948   *National Security Council*

. . . There was discussion as to whether a decision could be taken regarding Tsingtao in the absence of an over-all determination of our policy in China. . . . There was also inconclusive discussion of whether the shipments of supplies and equipment to the Chinese Nationalist government could be delayed and whether the distribution of supplies and equipment in China could be controlled.

No decision was reached on the general China situation, which will be studied further.

[In the abruptness of the political reversal there were many decisions which had to be "studied further." It obviously transformed Forrestal's entire personal and official problem. He had been expecting a probably automatic solution for the constantly vexing dilemma about resignation, by which he would go out gracefully with a defeated administration, under circumstances that would leave him no option but would imply no reflection on him. Now the administration had not been defeated; but it was doubtful whether he himself would survive, and he may well have begun to wonder if the administration any longer regarded him as an asset.

In his differences with the President over military budget policy, the latter's hand (and the hand of his Budget Bureau) had of course been greatly strengthened. The congressional committee chairmen, with whom Forrestal had been working so carefully over the past two years, would now all be changed; he would have to go over much of the old ground with new faces or with old faces now suddenly restored to power. Forrestal had antagonized important groups—the always numerous and ardent friends of the Air Force, the professional Democratic politicians who resented his refusal to participate in the party battle, influential sections of the Jewish community who resented his stand on Palestine, labor and "liberal" groups who thought him too closely identified with the industrialists. The newspaper columnists were already beginning to circle, vulture-like, for the kill; and soon after the election the more responsible Washington correspondents began to disseminate the speculation that when the President re-formed his Cabinet, Forrestal would no longer be a member. Among Forrestal's personal papers there is a scrapbook in which are entered samples of these newspaper predictions of his early downfall. And against all this, there was little or no real public understanding of what he had been trying to do and of the very great services he had rendered to the nation in

[the attempt. As he had himself written the year before, the difficulty of government work was that it "not only has to be well done, but the public has to be convinced that it is being well done." [16]

Forrestal wired the President his "congratulations on a gallant fight and a splendid victory"; and went down with the others to the Union Station on November 5 to greet the President's triumphant return. At 12:30 the same day there was a brief Cabinet meeting.

5 November 1948 *Cabinet*

Cabinet meeting today. The President said that he wanted his Cabinet members to go to work on the preparation of material for his policy message on the state of the Union which is due for delivery to the Congress on the first of January. He asked to have these suggestions available to him at the time of his return, in about two weeks.

[The President was leaving on Sunday, the 7th, for a vacation at Key West; and on Saturday he made it known that there would be no decision on Cabinet changes until he got back. Forrestal, called again to the White House the same day, had to run a gantlet of reporters; he told them "jokingly" that his resignation had been on file with the President ever since he had assumed office, and he did not intend to "reiterate it." [17] The President duly departed for his Florida vacation. A couple of days later Forrestal took off for a rapid, one-week flying trip through Western Europe.

IV

[For this final trip to Europe, Forrestal kept unusually extensive diary notes, partly, perhaps, because he had Gruenther (always exact and efficient, and who took some of the notes himself) along. The survey really began in Washington, in a conversation with Lewis Douglas and Allen Dulles, who were at his house for dinner on Saturday evening.

---

[16] See p. 300.
[17] *New York Herald Tribune,* 7 November 1948.

7 November 1948   *Conversation with Ambassador Douglas—*
Allen Dulles

Highlights of conversation with Ambassador Douglas last evening.

It is essential to get a settlement of the Berlin impasse. He believes that the Russians are equally desirous of it provided some face-saving formula can be found. He thinks that a solution may lie something along the lines of my suggestion that a neutral group . . . suggest a formula dealing with economic matters.[18] . . . The British have not yet solved the problem of costs, and it is doubtful if they *will* solve it in the next three or four years since the government is unwilling to face the political consequences of asking for more work and longer hours. . . . He is very deeply concerned about the Middle East, and believes the consequences of the creation of the Israeli state will flow for a long time. . . .

With regard to France: I gave him my view that we should not permit ourselves to become frozen into a state of aloofness from De Gaulle. . . . He expressed complete agreement in view of the fact that he believes De Gaulle will come to power in France within a matter of months.

Allen Dulles said he thought the greatest mistake in Mr. Dewey's campaign strategy was the failure to attack the Democratic record more vigorously. This stemmed from the failure to realize that they were the challenger and not the challenged. Among other areas in which they restrained Mr. Dewey was the sequence of diplomatic decisions at Tehran, Cairo and Yalta. They did not do so [*sic*] because they felt that injecting these issues into the campaign would have been destructive of the effort toward bipartisan foreign policy.

[On Tuesday afternoon, November 9, Forrestal, with Gruenther and two or three other aides, took off from Washington. The trip was doubtless due to a suggestion from Harriman, in the preceding month, that he should come over and see for himself the urgent necessity for getting ahead with Atlantic union and military aid; and on Wednesday evening he dined with Harriman

------

[18] See p. 491.

[and Marshall in Paris. His diary entry was dictated the following day.

11 November 1948   *Aid to France*

Marshall returned to the theme which he had developed in his last visit to Washington: the importance of making available, to France in particular, but also to other countries of the Western Union, arms on a sufficient scale to give these countries the feeling that we were back of them. . . . I made the observation, which was supported by Harriman, that we need to have a clear and focused policy, embracing political, military and economic matters. . . .

In a conversation with Harriman this morning, he returned to this subject and said there was a great need for coordination of our policies in these three areas, and that otherwise our strength would be frittered away without relation to the accomplishment of the result that fundamentally we are after: the re-creation of stable conditions throughout Europe. He said he believes that this idea could be sold on the basis of its being a sound investment—that money spent on a carefully thought-out and phased program would . . . have the result of lifting a great continuing burden from the American taxpayer. . . . Such a program could not, however, be imposed by fiat on these countries, all of whom are made even more sensitive by the fact of their poverty and present straits. . . .

11 November 1948   *Aid to France*

Conversation with M. Ramadier [Paul Ramadier, the Prime Minister] this evening. Central points of his conversation were:

France must be defended at or east of the Rhine. There is manpower sufficient for the creation of thirty divisions, but the French must have equipment. I asked whether this equipment could take the form of small arms, etc. He said that was not their need, but rather for heavy equipment—tanks, antiaircraft, vehicles. . . .

They are considering the building of carrier, to be finished in 1952. I said I hoped they would not divert too much of their effort to naval power, particularly in the field of aircraft car-

riers, of which we had plenty. I said I thought that France
should have a Navy as a symbol of its greatness as a power, but
that first things should come first, and it is obvious that the first
thing in this instance is Ground Forces. He agreed, but repeated that they lacked equipment. . . .

He said the great need was to convince the French nation
that the United States would keep a continuing interest in the
integrity of France. I said there were two components of this
—French integrity and American assistance.

[Next day, the 12th, he saw Herbert Evatt, Australian Minister
of External Affairs, who was in Paris. Evatt called because he
was worried over certain questions of security breaches which
had arisen among Australia, Britain and the United States, but
the conversation ranged widely. Evatt stressed the need for
"some instrument for dealing with the problems of Southeast Asia
as a whole"; he thought India was making great progress and
that Nehru would continue as a bulwark against Communism;
he admitted that some means had to be found to provide a liveli-
hood for the Japanese. But when he tended to be critical of American policy in regard to Berlin and to suggest that we were de-
parting from our original agreements, Forrestal appears to have
answered somewhat bluntly: "I replied that there had never been
anything equivocal or unclear about the American attitude."
Evatt indicated some misgivings as to whether we could indefinitely continue the airlift; "I assured him there was not the
slightest question on this point and that we both could and would
do so." [19] The interview over, Forrestal took off for England.

He was at Lakenheath in time for lunch and to inspect the
B-29 base now established there; and he was back in London
for a 4:30 call upon the Prime Minister and the Minister of Defence at 10 Downing Street.

12 November 1948   *Conversation with Prime Minister Attlee*
                        and Minister of Defence Alexander

. . . I asked both of them what their defense estimates would
be for next year. It was obvious that neither one wanted to

[19] Diary, 12 November 1948.

talk figures, and then I realized how secretive the British officials are about anything to do with finance before discussions in the House of Commons (it will be remembered that that was the cause of Mr. Dalton's downfall. . . .)

Alexander said that roughly the budget would be 50 per cent, or over, to the Ground Forces—this not entirely because they wanted it but because of their numerous overseas commitments. . . . He thought the long-range, high-speed bomber would play the largest part in the air warfare of the future.

Attlee said that there was no division in the British public mind about the use of the atomic bomb—they were for its use. Even the Church in recent days had publicly taken this position. . . . He considers it important to arm the French. . . .

[Forrestal went on to a conference of American officers at the Embassy in Grosvenor Square and finally to dinner with Ambassador Douglas and Winston Churchill. Douglas "had had a very bad day on the Palestine business, the most recent shift in the American position apparently having been" to back the Jewish demand both for the Negeb (under the U. N. decision) and for Galilee (under the conflicting Bernadotte decision.) With respect to Britain, the Ambassador was "quite concerned about the continued underwriting by the United States of British Labour political objectives," although he put it on the ground that the Labour policies would inhibit real economic recovery in Britain.[20] The conversation with Churchill turned primarily on the atomic bomb.

12 November 1948   *Atomic Bomb—*
                    Conversation with Winston Churchill

. . . [Churchill] deprecates what he feels to be a dangerous tendency to "write down" the atomic bomb, both as regards its effect on Russia and on Western Europe. He had been under the impression that this weapon, which destroyed the cities of Nagasaki and Hiroshima, was an extremely potent and destructive one, but if the Russians get the impression that it

---

[20] Diary, 12 November 1948.

is simply a substantial extension in damage potential to an ordinary bomb, it may well affect their conduct.

He has strong feelings about the prosecution of war criminals in Japan, notably the case of Prime Minister Tojo. He points out that Americans are going to need Japanese cooperation in the years ahead, and at this juncture, three years after the end of the war, to hang prominent people in that country seems to him stupid. . . . No ruler of a country can control the actions of his troops. On the same theory, both Roosevelt and himself would have been executed if the Allies had lost the war. . . . .

[The formal conference took place next day, when Forrestal, with Gruenther, met with Alexander and the three British Chiefs of Staff and their aides. They canvassed with thoroughness a wide range of subjects; the notes, taken by Gruenther, run to some seven typewritten pages and need only be summarized here. Alexander agreed with Forrestal that "there should be planning now by the U. S.-U. K. agencies for combined production problems in the event of war." The Minister of Defence intimated that in their war plans they had run into much the same difficulty which Forrestal had encountered in the spring. They had begun by planning on a "long-run" or future basis, like the American Services; now they found that the "cold war" with its possibility of "conflict on a short-range basis" demanded available Army troops in numbers much greater than "would fit into a long-range concept." Even the Air Chief, Tedder, agreed that "the Army role was very significant."

Alexander said "that he had high hopes of French revival, although, for the moment, they were completely shot, and his contacts with the French politicians left him with the impression that they have a definite fear complex." He thought the rise of De Gaulle a "definite danger and not an advantage." Later on there was "common agreement by the British that Italy's value from a military point of view is not significant"; they all recognized that country's geographical importance but did not think that the Italians should be given much, if any, military equipment.

[The British were frank in saying that they considered "that the United States is adopting a 'very sticky attitude' in the release of information to members of the Western Union. General Slim [General Sir William J. Slim, Chief of the Imperial General Staff] . . . cited the instance of the Dutch, who wanted to make a better land mine, only to find that the British could not give them that information because the U. S.-British agreement prevents it." They gave other illustrations, and Forrestal said that he believed a more liberal attitude was desirable and would have the matter examined.

"Lord Tedder stated that the two countries are engaged in the preparation of strategic plans for a war, but that those plans are utterly unrealistic because they do not include in sufficient detail the planning for atomic warfare." Forrestal felt that there were two questions involved; that for economic reasons manufacture (and by implication the information concerned with manufacture) should remain with the United States, but that there should be a freer exchange of strategic information.

"In response to a question by Mr. Forrestal, the British Chiefs of Staff stated that they believed that the Mediterranean-Middle East area could be held if we get forces there quickly enough. Lord Tedder stated that he felt that carriers would be able to operate in the Mediterranean, at least in the early stages of a conflict, and Admiral Fraser [Admiral of the Fleet the Lord Fraser of North Cape, First Sea Lord and Chief of the Naval Staff] agreed." As for the Far East, the British felt themselves committed to the limit in Malaya and unable to make any further contribution. When they got on the China problem Forrestal must have felt himself in a familiar atmosphere: "There was a general discussion on the China situation, with no conclusions of any importance."

On the question of an Atlantic pact, "the British made it very clear that they considered it essential that the U. S. sign a pact to support the Western European powers in the event of hostilities." They were asked what the effect would be if the United States failed to sign a pact but made substantial military shipments; they were unanimous in replying that this would be better than nothing but still "totally inadequate." The British wanted

[to put the American, Rear Admiral Richard L. Conolly, in complete charge of planning in the Mediterranean just as Field Marshal Montgomery was in charge of Western European plans; they also wanted to consolidate the American and British Missions in Greece under a single American head. Forrestal said that he would have all this looked into.[21]

After an hour and a half of it, they all adjourned for a luncheon at the American Embassy; and from lunch, Forrestal departed for the airport. He was in Berlin by dinnertime.

13 November 1948   *Dinner—Berlin*

. . . Arrived Berlin at 7:00 and dined with Bedell Smith, Ambassador [Robert] Murphy and General Clay. Smith said he was confident that the strongest deterrent to war was the building up of our own strength and at the same time the rearming of Western Europe. I asked him whether he would be willing to accept deficits in the American budget over the next several years in order to achieve this result. He said that he would, beyond any question. General Clay said he would not, because he felt that an unbalanced budget in the United States would have a serious impact in Europe, where it would be taken as a signal that even the United States was unable to cope with its fiscal problems and was on the road to inflation.

General Clay said there had been a tremendous upswing in the condition of Western Germany since the stabilization of the currency last spring. . . . Throughout Germany, and for that matter the rest of Europe, it is a race between Socialism and private enterprise. The British in their Zone, and some in ours who have academic inclinations toward Socialism, seize the opportunity of using their economic aid to further the development of the Socialist system, which Clay feels will lay a dead hand on the recovery of Europe.

After dinner Bedell Smith told this story:

Upon the death of Zhdanov [Colonel General Andrei A. Zhdanov, a leading member of the Politburo], the Argentine

---

[21] Diary, 13 November 1948.

government sent a conventional message of condolence to Moscow, at the end of which someone in the Buenos Aires office of the Radio Corporation of America added this sentence: "Hurrah! One more gone." The net result of this was that the Argentine government received no reply to their message and RCA immediately lost all of its facilities in Russia. Sarnoff [David Sarnoff, president of RCA] sent the most apologetic message to the Kremlin, had no reply, and finally, on the occasion of Smith's last visit to Washington, asked him to intervene. He had been unable to do so, but the RCA facilities were suddenly restored, because the Russians found that they had need of these channels of communication to get messages overseas. Bedell said he had had extravagant messages of appreciation from Sarnoff, who thinks it was due to the Smith diplomacy.

Clay gave it as his view that we were unduly apprehensive about the Russians. That we have built them up into a power which they do not possess. Is confident that they do not want war, but that if we get out of Berlin under duress, they will walk through Europe, and at least gain such power and prestige in France that France will crumble. Considers that even the limited forces now available to him in Germany can give a good account of themselves, and, with an increase in French forces, tactical air support and British willingness to commit their forces in France, the Russians could be held at the Rhine.

In the event of war, Clay would not hesitate to use the atomic bomb.

[The next day, Sunday, Forrestal flew to Frankfurt; there he got a firsthand view of the "extraordinary accomplishment" of the airlift and its ability to continue despite bad weather. In the afternoon he met with five German officials of the Bizonal Administration, finding that "all these people evidently have the highest respect for Clay and are anxious to cooperate with him." [22] Next day he motored to Heidelberg to visit the United

---

[22] Diary, 14 November 1948.

[States Army Headquarters, and the commander, Lieutenant General Clarence R. Huebner. Huebner, like Clay, was anxious to get a North Atlantic pact signed and to arm the French.

15 November 1948   *Visit to Heidelberg*

. . . Huebner's experience with colored troops is excellent. He is very proud of his Honor Guard, which is all Negro. He is ready to proceed with the implementation of the President's directive about nonsegregation down to the platoon level, and proposes to initiate this in the three cavalry regiments and the AA battalion up north, but does not want to do it if it is premature.

Believes very strongly that the French should have some tactical air, and that with tactical air a strong stand could be made. . . .

[Huebner added his own conviction that in the event of war an atomic bomb should at once be dropped where the Russians could observe its full potentialities, "because he believes the Russians have no knowledge of its effect." There were indications, he said, that even the pictures of the Bikini tests had not been shown in Russia.

After lunching with Huebner, the party motored back to Frankfurt, to take off from the Rhein-Main Airport at 2:30 for the United States, traveling in President Truman's plane, the *Sacred Cow*. They flew by way of Gibraltar, the Azores and Newfoundland, and reached Washington at 7:35 Tuesday evening, November 16, having covered over eleven thousand statute miles and the many conferences in almost exactly one week's time.

The return to Washington brought Forrestal back to the personal problem of his own future. The President was due back at the White House in a few days, but next morning (Wednesday, November 17) Forrestal telephoned him at Key West to ask, according to the President's staff, for an immediate interview. The President invited him to fly down for lunch next day. Forrestal met a normally busy schedule on Wednesday; in the course of it

[he dictated a letter to his friend Stanton Griffis, then Ambassador
to Egypt.

To Stanton Griffis, 17 November 1948

. . . We are very fortunate in having Mr. Truman, a man
who, while he reflects the liberal forces both in this country
and throughout the world, is nevertheless a conservative in the
real sense of that word—a conserver of the things we hope to
keep. . . . I will be away from here some time during the year.
Just when depends upon the legislative program and, of course,
the wishes of the President. . . .

[The reporters at his press conference that afternoon assailed
him on the matter of his resignation. "I am at the service of the
President," he answered. "The Cabinet is singularly and pecul-
iarly his business." [23] At 7:15 Thursday morning he took off
with Gruenther and Marx Leva for his luncheon with the President in Key West; at 9:15 that evening he was back in Washington.
   The diary makes no mention of this conference, and there is
nothing in the papers to indicate what took place. According to
Forrestal's associates of the time, he had asked for the interview
with the intention of settling the whole question of his continued
tenure in office; but on arriving at Key West he decided to
change his tactics and confined himself to reporting on his European trip, leaving it to the President to raise the matter of
tenure. Apparently the President did not avail himself of the opportunity. He sat for a while with Forrestal and Gruenther in a
palm grove; to the reporters, who were allowed to witness the
session from beyond earshot, the conversation seemed animated,
but Charles G. Ross, the President's press secretary, told them
that it had involved only Forrestal's European report. To a blunt
question as to whether Forrestal would continue in the Cabinet,
Mr. Ross replied, "I don't know what is in Mr. Forrestal's mind,"
and Forrestal himself, on leaving from the airport, denied that
the question of resignation had come up. [24]

[23] *The New York Times,* 18 November 1948.
[24] *New York Herald Tribune,* 19 November 1948.

[The inference is that Forrestal had hoped to get from the President a firm request that he remain in office, together with the assurances of appreciation, understanding and support which he would certainly require if he was to fulfill its extremely difficult responsibilities—and to which, it will seem to many, he was entitled. Whatever was said, it is clear that this he did not get. Nevertheless Forrestal decided to "stay on" for the time being, at best a precarious course. He may well have decided against his better judgment; it was certainly against the judgment of many of his closest friends.

CHAPTER XIV

The Diaries End

I

[With Forrestal's return to Washington the diary undergoes a rather marked change and soon dwindles away to little more than the daily appointment calendars. Reports of Cabinet meetings and lunches continue to appear, but they seem the reports of a spectator rather than of a participant and there are few even of these after the turn of the year. Notes of more informal conversations occur at increasingly long intervals. The diary itself makes almost no further mention of important issues, such as the military budget or departmental reorganization, on which Forrestal continued to be actively engaged. The appointment calendar, on the other hand, grows only heavier; the correspondence files more fluent, more exigent, covering a wider range of interests. Some who knew him in that winter feel that already signs of overwork and overstrain had appeared.

The day after the luncheon in Key West Forrestal answered a correspondent who had urged him to stay in office: "It goes without saying, of course, that I will not walk out unless I am satisfied that the continuity of the defense program is assured and that the organization is in good shape." [1] To another he spoke, perhaps for the first time in his correspondence, of the "strain" under which he was laboring: "You know from personal experience what an unceasing strain this job is, but you can multiply the problems of war, which were heavy enough, by a multiple of about ten to get the picture now. In war, of course,

---

[1] To Senator A. W. Robertson, 19 November 1948.

[it was production. Now it is trying to fit the tremendous demands of our military potential into the whole economy. However, the country is more important than I am, and if my continued presence for a while longer will contribute to cementing the foundations which are fairly well along now, I will probably have to yield." [2] Some ten days later he was writing to Fleet Admiral Nimitz that "I have no definite plans except the general one that I do not propose to stay on indefinitely—it will be nine years next June, which is quite an extension over my original plans of not becoming a bureaucrat";[3] but a few days later he could write flatly to another, "I am going to stay on." [4]

Forrestal went down to the airfield on Sunday, November 21, to welcome the President back from his Florida vacation, and attended the Cabinet lunch next day. (It was held in Blair House, thus marking the transfer from the White House, which had been abandoned to the rebuilders after one of the ceilings had given way under Miss Margaret Truman's piano, revealing the dangerous decrepitude of the old structure.) There was trouble in the U. N.; and the great debacle in China was already under way.

22 November 1948   *Lunch—the President*

Lunch with the President today. Cabinet plus Mr. Harriman.
Marshall reported on the activities at U. N., from which it would appear that our situation vis-à-vis Berlin, and the Russian situation in general, is rapidly deteriorating. Evatt, who is president of the General Assembly, is an active source of both irritation and uncertainty. The result of his activities and, to a lesser extent, Bramuglia's [Juan A. Bramuglia, Foreign Minister of the Argentine], who is chairman of the Security Council, has been greatly to undermine the American position among the neutral nations. He has succeeded in giving the impression that, after all, the Russian demands are not so extreme and unmeetable.

China: Situation there is going through a rapid process of deterioration. Thirty-three of the Nationalist government divisions surrendered, with equipment, and these included a num-

---

[2] To Ralph A. Bard, 20 November 1948.
[3] To Chester A. Nimitz, 2 December 1948.
[4] To Lou E. Holland, 7 December 1948.

ber of American-trained divisions. . . . The net result is the loss of a vast amount of American-bought equipment to the Communists.

26 November 1948   *Cabinet—China—Germany—*
                                                       Situation in Berlin

General Marshall discussed Germany and China.

1. *Germany*: Situation has been recently confused by a statement from too numerous "spokesmen" in the American Zone to the effect that the forthcoming elections of December 5 would make impossible the implementation of any currency system. . . . He had, as of today, stated the American position to Dr. [Philip C.] Jessup at the United Nations, repeating:

(a) That the United States proposes to remain in Berlin.

(b) That it is not willing to negotiate until the blockade is lifted by the Russians. . . .

(c) That once the blockade is lifted, the U. S. is willing to discuss economic matters and, specifically, the control of currency with any group that the United Nations designates.

2. *China*: Madame Chiang Kai-shek proposes to come to the United States and has asked for transportation by Navy plane. Marshall raised the question whether she should be permitted to come. The President said yes. In view of that decision Marshall proposes to give her every possible facility as the wife of a head of a friendly state. . . .

The military position in China has suffered vast deterioration. Equipment for 33 divisions, including 297,000 rifles, a large amount of automatic weapons, 105 and 155 millimeter guns and antiaircraft weapons, have been captured by the Soviets. There is in process a movement for the formation of a new Nationalist government headed by Dr. Hu Shih, formerly Chinese Ambassador to Washington. This would be accompanied by the retirement of Chiang Kai-shek and his withdrawal to the middle part of the country, possibly retaining a ceremonial title as head of the state.

Marshall referred to the suggestion that I made to Lovett on Thursday evening that we explore the reactivation of the AVG [American Volunteer Group, the "Flying Tigers," who provided air support for the Chinese armies prior to Pearl Harbor], and that we get a formal invitation from the Chinese government to remain at Tsingtao. Marshall said the latter would be easy to get, but he was fearful of the conditions that might accompany such an invitation.

He referred to the program of supply which was being handled by the Army with particular reference to the question of price, which, he said, had been raised by the Chinese. They want to buy the weapons out of surplus stocks at the 1945 price, whereas such weapons cannot be replaced except at a substantially higher price. . . .

Marshall read a paper from some office people in the State Department, who advocated going to the American public now to explain the inadequacies of the Chiang Kai-shek government. This paper stated that we had two alternatives: (1) to follow this .course, or (2) to continue to do all we can to support Chiang and accept the embarrassments that will accompany the disintegration of China.

With the President's approval, Marshall said he felt that he would reject his Department's paper advocating criticism of Chiang. He felt that this would administer the final *coup de grâce* to Chiang's government, and this, he felt, we could not do.

[The policy of the "office people in the State Department," which Marshall here rejected, was to be revived after his departure from office in the following year; in August 1949 the State Department released its celebrated and controversial White Paper on China. By that time, however, Chiang had been driven to Formosa. The White Paper certainly did not help him, but in a sense the *coup de grâce* had already been given by the Communists.

The diary contains two post-mortem notes on the presidential election, both of interest.

26 November 1948   *Conversation—the President*

The President recited tonight a most interesting analogy of the 1948 election. He recalled that in 1940, when he was up for renomination as Senator from Missouri, he attended a meeting in St. Louis at which a number of Democratic Party leaders tried to dissuade him from entering the primary contest on the ground that he could not possibly be elected. He said he listened to them until three o'clock in the morning, at which time he announced he would go into the primary and wage the best campaign he knew how, even if the result was only a single vote, which would be his own, cast for him.

He said he financed this campaign with a loan of eight thousand dollars from the Brotherhood of Railroad Trainmen, and he went out to speak in practically every county in the state with the result that he won a substantial majority.

[Rather more piquant is a note Forrestal entered as an "addendum" in the diary in the following month.

20 December 1948   *Conversation with the President*

The President . . . mentioned the fact that he had a letter from Senator Taft congratulating him on his election and saying that while the Senator might disagree on certain matters with the President, he would do everything possible to cooperate.

Taft in his letter also mentioned the fact that "as the President might gather neither he nor his wife were particularly disappointed in the result of the election."

[The major issue in these weeks, however, was still the 1949-50 budget. In a telegram of November 19, declining an invitation, Forrestal said tersely, "I am up to my ears here. Budget trouble." [5] The Joint Chiefs, with the aid of the McNarney Board, had seen the light, at least to the extent of reaching agreement on the "intermediate" program which Forrestal had so urgently and persuasively asked from them. They had even cut it below the $17.5 billion total which he had suggested; Forrestal's budget officers estimated that the program they now presented—looking to an aggregate establishment of 1,980,000 men

[5] To Jesse H. Jones, 19 November 1948.

[on June 30, 1950—could be handled on a budget of $16.9 billion. The President was still standing on the $14.4 billion "ceiling." On December 1—with the situation in China rapidly going from debacle to disaster, with the situation in Berlin still grave, with the world situation as a whole even "grayer" than Forrestal had thought it in October—he sent the "intermediate" proposal to the President. The final paragraph of his letter recorded at least one success; it said that he was authorized by the Secretary of State to say that the forces contemplated in this $16.9 billion proposal would be most helpful in the period of difficult international negotiations ahead. Marshall had come round at last.

A meeting with the President was arranged for December 9. Forrestal brought the subordinate Secretaries, the Joint Chiefs, McNeil and Gruenther; Webb and Souers were also present. The Defense officials had a map-and-chart presentation ready; the President listened politely, thanked them and said it was all very interesting. He then passed it off in a few minutes of cordial conviviality. The meeting lasted less than an hour; the Defense Department had got nothing and the President's $14.4 billion ceiling stood.

Forrestal, standing between the military and the civilian authority, had done his best to get a defense program both adequate from the military point of view and reasonable from the budgetary standpoint. He had not had too much help from either side, and the result was failure. But it was symptomatic of his own divided state of mind that he could still see all sides of the question. To his friend "Ham" Andrews, about to relinquish the chairmanship of the House Armed Services Committee, he wrote on December 13:

To Walter G. Andrews, 13 December 1948

. . . Our biggest headache at the moment, of course, is the budget. The President has set the ceiling at 14 billion 4 against the pared down requirements that we put in of 16 billion 9. I am frank to say, however, I have the greatest sympathy with him because he is determined not to spend more than we take in in taxes. He is a hard-money man if ever I saw one, and believing as I do that we can't afford to wreck our economy in the process of trying to fight the "cold war," there is much to be said for his thesis of holding down spending to the absolute minimum of necessity. . . .

The four years ahead look extremely complex and difficult to me. There are some problems that almost seem insoluble: China, the Middle East and France, but I won't bore you by going into any dissertations on them. . . .

[Forrestal had two other ideas which he laid before the President on December 20. He made no record of the meeting, but what he had in mind appears from an extensive memorandum he prepared in advance. He suggested that the appropriation of some $525 million for stockpiling raw materials should properly be regarded as a capital item and so removed from the expense budget; he also observed that out of the proposed increases in Service pay for which they were providing, the Treasury would recapture up to $200 million in income taxes. Applying both sums to the relief of the military budget would give an extra $700 million or so for military appropriations without breaking through the ceiling.

For Forrestal these were somewhat novel fiscal principles, and the fact that he should have advanced them suggests the sense of pressure under which he was laboring. He had also shifted his strategic concepts; he now proposed to put the bulk of these additional funds into six more long-range bomber groups. Obviously there was logic in this; for since the ceiling limit had emasculated the "balanced" force and left the country with virtually nothing but the atomic bomb on which to rely, it was all the more necessary to see that the strategic bomber force was adequate. His European trip, moreover, had given him a greater confidence in the heavy bombers. On his way home in mid-November he had dictated a series of "Points for the President." The first one was "the atomic bomb—its potency as a weapon should not be deprecated. Both Clay and Huebner believe the Russians do not want their people to know what it can do. Churchill has the same feeling. Clay says the Russians are constantly putting

[fear into Western Europe by talking about the tremendous power of the Red Army, and we have a weapon far more terrifying which we are apt to underestimate." He now expanded on this theme:

"Throughout my recent trip in Europe I was increasingly impressed by the fact that the only balance that we have against the overwhelming manpower of the Russians, and therefore the chief deterrent to war, is the threat of the immediate retaliation with the atomic bomb. I have substantial misgivings that reduction in the potential of the Air Force in the long-range bombing field might be misunderstood both by the world at large and particularly by our only enemy. The Air Force will have the heavy bombers necessary for carrying the atomic bomb, but these atomic carriers will need support by conventional bomb groups. . . ." After reviewing the general plans for an air offensive, Forrestal reverted to his previous doubts on the subject. "The central question, of course, is whether or not our bombers can get in to deliver this attack. A year ago I had substantial misgivings, and while nobody can say anything with certainty about war, I now believe the Air Force can get in with enough to deliver a powerful blow at the Russian capacity to make war." [6]

But this plea, like its predecessors, was unavailing. When the President sent in his budget (it went to Congress on January 10) it provided only $14.2 billion, exclusive of stockpiling, for the Armed Forces. Forrestal's "intermediate" program had asked for 1,980,000 men by the end of fiscal 1950 and fifty-nine air groups; the six groups for which he asked on December 20 would have given a total of fifty-four. The President's budget contemplated an aggregate strength of 1,617,830 and forty-eight groups. Actually, when war came in Korea as fiscal 1950 was ending, the Military Establishment was down to an aggregate strength of only 1,465,000. Only then did it become apparent how desperately the missing men and formations were needed; only then did the nation at last heave itself into that real effort of "balanced" rearmament which Forrestal had so clearly known to be required.

---

[6] See p. 355.

II

[His failure with the budget did not lessen the energy with
    which Forrestal pressed on the reorganization of his Department,
    in accordance with his own experience and the findings of the
    Eberstadt task force, which was now completing its report to
    the Hoover Commission. On December 3 he had proposed to ex-
    pedite the revamping of the Defense Department structure.

Memorandum for the President, 3 December 1948

I would like to suggest that you consider sending in a bill
immediately on the opening of Congress for the creation of
the post of Under Secretary of Defense in the National Military Establishment.

I don't want this action to prejudice our chances of getting
additional changes in the unification act, but I believe this particular change would go through immediately because the need
is so obvious.

It might be that you would want me to discuss this with the
Director of the Budget, the Speaker of the House, and the Vice
President as to advisability, and I would be glad to do that if
you should decide to approve the idea.

[He developed his own conclusions as to modifications of the
    Security Act in a letter of the same day to a friend and frequent
    collaborator.

To John McCone, 3 December 1948

The shape of the future, so far as the National Military
Establishment is concerned, is now beginning to emerge quite
clearly in my mind. It involves certain changes in the act, and
a strengthening of central control of budget procedures, legislation and public relations—both at the top and within the departments. Changes indicated in the organic act are, I think,
obvious to you: an Under Secretary of Defense, the removal of
the word "general" with a resultant strengthening of authority
in this office,[7] power of decision to the chairman of the Muni-

---

[7] See p. 497.

tions Board, a chairman of the Joint Chiefs of Staff and, in my
opinion, separation of the Joint Chiefs from their Services. On
this latter point I know you do not fully agree, but my experience in the last six months has convinced me that problems in
the area of politics, strategy, and money are so diverse and continuous that they will require the full time of these men.

[In his letter to Representative Andrews of December 13 he
explained that he had been taking counsel with General Eisenhower, who had been down from New York for three days, and
had asked him for more extensive help. "Beginning with January 20, Ike will be down here for about sixty days to advise
and consult with me." The letter continued to outline his reorganization plans, as he had done to McCone, adding that "the
only point where I am not entirely clear" was whether or not to
downgrade the Service Secretaries. If they were reduced to Under Secretaries he doubted whether it would be possible to get
the right men for the jobs, and whether the result would not be to
concentrate too much work on the Secretary of Defense. "The
only other point on which we may have difficulty would be on
the old point of the Chief of Staff." Forrestal was now clear that
the Joint Chiefs "ought to have a chairman," but "Uncle Carl
[Representative Vinson, about to succeed Andrews as chairman of the House Armed Services Committee] is still violent on
the question of the single Chief, and I would be inclined to accept the concept of a chairman with power to make specific recommendations to the Secretary of Defense." [8] Again writing to
the same correspondent ten days later, he suggested that Andrews "could be a great help" in getting through the proposed
changes, "particularly with Uncle Carl. The big hurdle in his
mind will be the words 'Chief of Staff,' but that's largely a matter of semantics. . . . With Ike here for sixty days I think we
can get the pattern set and prove its workability by pragmatic
experience—that 'pragmatic' is Harvard stuff. . . ."
    One definite achievement in unification was noted in a letter
to Roscoe Drummond of the *Christian Science Monitor*, express-

---

[8] To Walter G. Andrews, 13 December 1948.

[ing appreciation for an article by the latter on the new Weapons System Evaluation Group.

To Roscoe Drummond, 23 December 1948

. . . This has been cooking ever since last summer. The difficulty has been the removal of those human frictions that are inevitable in government, or, for that matter, in the military world, that are not removable either by law or directive (in both cases the solutions are apt to come unstuck by Thursday).

The real credit is due to Van Bush. The idea began germinating in his mind a year ago. All I had to do was back it.

[Meanwhile the larger issues of national policy did not disappear entirely from the diary. Forrestal recorded a Cabinet luncheon on the 20th.

20 December 1948   Cabinet—Indonesia—Australia

. . . Lovett discussed Indonesia and the action of the Dutch in seizing the capital and taking into custody the governmental leaders. He expressed annoyance at the gratuitous interference of Dr. Evatt, the Foreign Minister of Australia, who had, although not a member of the Security Council (they are a member of the Good Offices Commission), addressed a communication to the Security Council expressing the view that if the U. S. had taken firm and preventive action with respect to the intent of the Dutch government to intervene in the affairs of the Republic, the present situation might have been avoided. He [Lovett] reported that in an interview with Ambassador [Norman J. O.] Makin of the Australian Embassy, he had expressed himself in the strongest terms as to our government's dissatisfaction with this unilateral action on the part of Evatt. Makin was deeply apologetic and expressed the hope that he might be able to say to his government that we would like them to withdraw their suggestions. Lovett said he would not make such a request—that was up to the Australians themselves.

[The problem of China, as insoluble as ever, was growing more acute.

31 December 1948   *Cabinet—China—Palestine*

Subject this morning at Cabinet was China.

Lovett gave a summation of the recent dispatches from China. The program, in general, was for Li Tsung-jen to succeed Chiang after the latter's withdrawal (Lovett said that inclusion of Chiang's name on the list of war criminals prepared by the Communists had changed him back to an attitude of intransigence, and that he was now disposed to take command of the Army in the field).

The President said that Wellington Koo and other Chinese in Washington were now busily undercutting Madame Chiang and the Generalissimo. He hazarded the guess that back of the story in this morning's paper, which Lovett referred to, to the effect that a high official in the American government had said there would be a cutting off of ECA aid to China unless Chiang quit, was the hope that such a story would create further pressure on Chiang to withdraw.

Palestine: Lovett said the Israeli troops had apparently invaded Egypt. Specifically, they were reported to have attacked an airfield within the Egyptian border; that it was reported the British would notify us that the failure of the Israelis to withdraw promptly would automatically bring into operation the Anglo-Egyptian Mutual Defense Pact.

[It was the last day of the old year. Forrestal found himself answering that day a request from the president of Princeton, Harold W. Dodds, that he deliver the 1949 Stafford Little Lectures. "The subject," he wrote, "which interests me is the character of our government and the difficulty of policy formation and execution under the handicap of lack of a real parliamentary system." [9] And a few days later he wrote another correspondent, who had congratulated him on his first annual report as Secretary of Defense (published December 29): "My own principal impression at the moment is the tremendous amount of work that remains to be done—and also the tremendous job that faces us in the world and which therefore necessitates, we both agree, the

---

[9] To Harold W. Dodds, 31 December 1948.

[closest relationship between the economic and military aspects of our strength." [10]

Bedell Smith had flown in, and one of the now rare diary notes records a breakfast conversation with him on January 2.

2 January 1949   *Breakfast with Ambassador Smith*

. . . He said he had come to a somewhat different conclusion in recent months about the attitude of the Russians toward war. He thinks their long-term objective has not changed but, because of the risks of dissidence which they are running in undertaking to perfect the Communist control of their satellites, he is inclined to think that they have decided to go through on this line before taking any risk of war. . . .

In general he looks forward to an interval of apparent and possibly deceptive quiet.

As to Berlin he saw no chance of solution to this problem except through some face-saving action by the General Assembly next spring. When Smith left Moscow this time he called on Vishinsky, Gromyko and Molotov, and gave them every opportunity to raise the question of Berlin but none of them did so.

III

[Early in December the President had told his press conference that there would be no immediate changes in the Cabinet. Asked specifically about Marshall (who was in indifferent health) and Forrestal, he had replied that both had been requested to stay and had agreed to do so. Then on January 7 the resignation of both Marshall and his Under Secretary, Lovett, was announced. (Their letters were dated January 3.) Dean Acheson would become Secretary of State with the beginning of the new presidential term on January 20, and James E. Webb, Forrestal's antagonist in the Budget Bureau, would succeed Lovett. These changes would patently undermine Forrestal's own position. In Marshall he would lose a colleague whom, despite occasional differences of viewpoint, he greatly admired and respected; in Lovett he would lose one of his closest friends and most valuable collaborators.

---

[10] To Arthur A. Ballantine, 5 January 1949.

[On January 8 Symington released his first annual report as
Secretary of the Air Force. It bluntly renewed the demand for a
full seventy groups by 1952, thus reopening the controversy of
the previous year and further undercutting Forrestal's position. At
the same time the commentators, with Marshall now out of the
Cabinet, turned their attention to the Secretary of Defense. On
Sunday, January 9, Walter Winchell, a hostile critic since the days
of the Palestine controversy, broadcast a prediction that the President would accept Forrestal's resignation within the ensuing
week.[11] Winchell coupled this prediction with a bitter allegation
that Forrestal had formed a Canadian corporation in 1929 to reduce his federal income tax in that year, and with a fevered denunciation of the legislative proposals concerning the National
Security Council as being designed to "throw the country into war
without even notifying Congress."

Next day the White House correspondents asked Charles G.
Ross, the President's press secretary, about the Winchell prediction that Forrestal would be out of office within the week. Ross
said flatly that it was untrue. To avoid misunderstanding, he added
that all Cabinet members customarily submitted their resignations
on the advent of a new administration, but that he did not know
whether Forrestal's had been received. Forrestal was a luncheon
guest at the White House that day.

When he returned on Tuesday (January 11) for a private conference with the President, the correspondents questioned him
about this routine resignation. He told them that it had not yet
been submitted, but would be in the President's hands before the
inauguration on January 20. There was a brief interchange:

"Do you anticipate its acceptance?"

"No."

"Do you want to and expect to continue as Secretary of Defense?"

"Yes, I am a victim of the Washington scene."

This remark dampened the rumors of Forrestal's imminent departure from the Cabinet, especially after the President himself
gave it a lukewarm endorsement two days later. Asked at his
press conference if Forrestal's remarks meant that he would stay

[1] *The New York Times,* 11 January 1949.

[in the Cabinet, Mr. Truman replied that they meant just what they said.[12]

Forrestal himself began writing friends as though the die was cast in favor of remaining in public office a while longer: "To be perfectly frank, I had looked forward to leaving the service of the government this month, but my conscience, as well as a number of my associates, persuaded me that I should not leave an unfinished job." [13] "As you have probably noted from the newspapers since the date of writing . . . I have indicated I will stay on for an additional period." [14]

As soon as he returned to his Pentagon office from his White House visit of January 11, Forrestal dispatched to the President his *pro forma* resignation. Its casual tone implied, as Forrestal had told the reporters, that he did not anticipate its acceptance: "I send you at this time my formal resignation as Secretary of Defense. I believe there is such a document now in your files, but in order to be sure that there is one in your possession I am forwarding this so that you may have it available in the consideration of plans for your Cabinet at inauguration time."

There is nothing to show that Forrestal discussed his own tenure with the President at this time; but he may have spoken of the tenure of the Service Secretaries, especially Symington's. On the afternoon of the 11th Forrestal's Military Aide sent a long document to White House Secretary Mathew Connelly with this covering memorandum: "The President is expecting the attached draft of suggested remarks, as Secretary Forrestal has informed the President that they would be sent over today."

The "attached draft" was dated January 8. Cast in the first person, as if the President himself were speaking, it was an exhortation to the heads of the military Departments and Services, calling upon them to keep their differences within the military family or to resign, now that the new presidential term gave them a graceful opportunity to do so. A few sentences suffice to indicate the tenor of what Forrestal and those around him (the paper was drafted by a staff member) wanted the

---

[12] *The New York Times*, 12 and 14 January 1949.
[13] To William Ritchie, 12 January 1949.
[14] To Edwin Meissner, 13 January 1949.

[President to say to the heads of the Army, Navy and Air Force:
"If there is any doubt in the mind of any man present that he
can give to the decisions of his Commander-in-Chief and of the
Secretary of Defense, who, for these purposes, is the alter ego of
his Commander-in-Chief, the kind of loyalty I have been describing . . . now is the time for any such individual to speak his
mind. . . . I repeat that my duty to the country requires that I
demand and receive the utmost in loyal assistance, freely spoken
advice and proper subordination. At this moment of opening
the new administration, it is practicable for any man of distinguished record to leave a post in government without any adverse implications against him or his service. . . . So this is the
moment of decision. . . ."

President Truman never called the meeting for which these
"suggested remarks" could have been intended, but he did deflate
the Air Force again at his press conference on January 13 by
saying that he considered forty-eight air groups adequate. Although Air Force spokesmen pitched their advocacy of seventy
air groups several keys lower than in 1948, it still helped to defeat again the administration's plans for universal military service in 1949. And it was one more vexation for Forrestal to
bear; he spoke to colleagues during this period of "another end
run" by the Air Force around the military unity that he was trying to build.

On the evening of January 16 Drew Pearson renewed the radio
attack on Forrestal. Recalling Winchell's assertion that the President was about to accept Forrestal's resignation, Pearson insisted
that the President would have done so if Winchell's forecasting
of the action had not angered him. Pearson also repeated Winchell's attack on the old Canadian corporation and added to it a
trumped-up version of an old robbery of Mrs. Forrestal's jewels
that reflected on Forrestal's personal courage.

This personal attack so stung Forrestal that he had his attorneys draw up a libel complaint against Pearson. In obvious
distress, Forrestal turned to his friends and associates, receiving
from them the almost unanimous advice that he should sue and
that a suit would be successful. Yet he never authorized the complaint to be filed in court, shrinking from the notoriety such an

[action would bring. A week after the Pearson broadcast, when a guest on another radio program erroneously accused Forrestal of having a major financial interest in a cartel controlling the old pro-Nazi firm of I. G. Farben, friends of Forrestal secured a retraction and apology for him.[15] These and other attacks so hurt Forrestal that he confessed to a friend that he could no longer listen to the popular Sunday night news-commentator broadcasts.

There is no doubt that Forrestal was tired. Early in January, while he and others were working at the White House on the President's state of the Union message, one of the President's closest advisers noticed how weary and nervous Forrestal appeared; this man and a colleague remarked to each other that Forrestal's long-standing, unconscious habit of scratching the crown of his head had become so continuous that a raw spot was beginning to appear.

As Forrestal's fatigue increased, some associates in both the White House and Defense Establishment felt that he became less and less willing to reach decisions. Even after decisions were made, he frequently wanted to reopen them. Amendments to the National Security Act held more interest for Forrestal at this time than almost any other subject, yet it seemed difficult for him to fix his ideas about the final form of the amendments. Indecisiveness increased the always heavy load of unfinished business in the Secretary's office, an accumulation that worried both Forrestal and his staff, driving him to adopt a still more exhausting work schedule. At least one intimate of both the President and Forrestal recalls discussing this situation with the President and finding him aware of it.

On January 21, the second day of Truman's new administration, General Eisenhower came back to full-time duty as Forrestal's principal military adviser. The Secretary asked the general to help formulate amendments to the National Security Act on which the Services would agree. Principally, however, he wanted Eisenhower to work with the Joint Chiefs of Staff to produce an agreed-upon war plan that could be made the basis of future military budgets—and he stated that the budgets should be within some reasonable limit. The problem was the familiar

---

[15] *The New York Times,* 24 January 1949.

[one of trying to resolve strategy, inter-Service rivalries and fiscal limitations.

Despite the heavy reliance at once placed on Eisenhower, as Forrestal's schedule of conferences shows, the pressure on the Secretary's office continued. Forrestal was not a person who could reach decisions lightly, with or without assistance. General Eisenhower recalls, "One of the reasons he felt such an acute need for some help was his inborn honesty and his very great desire to serve the country well. He would listen carefully to presentations, even where he was certain that these were partisan and even prejudiced; his ability to see truth on both sides of bitter questions led him to a turmoil, out of which it was difficult to form a clear-cut decision in which he could personally have real confidence."

Very probably, when Forrestal had written on January 13 that he would stay on for "an additional period," he and the President already had discussed some definite limit on that period, for within a little more than two weeks Forrestal apparently was helping the President arrange for his successor. Forrestal's calendar for January 28 shows that he went to the White House for a Cabinet meeting at ten o'clock in the morning and that he had a conference with the President at eleven; he had no other appointments before lunching alone with one of his assistants, Marx Leva. Neither Forrestal's diary notes nor his letters disclose anything more about the occurrences of this day.

However, Louis Johnson, who succeeded Forrestal as Secretary of Defense, has given a more detailed account of that morning's events: ". . . In the latter days of January . . . the President sent for me and told me that Mr. Forrestal wanted to talk to me. He said that Mr. Forrestal was my friend and that he wanted me to listen to him accordingly. Mr. Forrestal was then at the White House for a Cabinet meeting, to which, after talking with me, the President went. I crossed through the White House, through Mr. Connelly's office, and Mr. Forrestal, coming down the corridor from the Cabinet room, called to me. The press might have gotten wise then but they missed the bet.

"I waved Mr. Forrestal back, went through Mr. Connelly's office and met him there. Then it was that Mr. Forrestal asked

[me, with the approval of the President, to take over his job as Secretary of Defense. Mr. Forrestal did not return to the Cabinet meeting. He and I spent that time in discussions and later visited with the President.

"I told Mr. Forrestal that a story had been printed saying I had been undercutting him—seeking his job. Mr. Forrestal replied that he had double-checked the story and was satisfied that there was not, and had not been, a word of truth in it. . . .

"After the Cabinet meeting Mr. Forrestal and I visited with the President, who insisted I accept his offer of the Secretaryship of Defense. . . ." [16]

According to Johnson, the date agreed upon at this meeting for Forrestal to leave was May 1, three months in the future. The interim period was to be used to brief Johnson on the duties that he would take over. In fact that briefing began at once, Johnson asserts; two months later, and in Forrestal's presence, Johnson told the House Armed Services Committee, " . . . during these last sixty days . . . the only well kept secret . . . is the fact that Jim and I have been working together. . . ." [17] Johnson also told a press conference at this same time, "Since late in January, Jim Forrestal and I did confer, did work together when I went to Key West . . . with a lot of secret papers of the Department with the approval of the President. We were working all through that period and since." [18]

Forrestal's records offer only scraps of information bearing on this January 28 episode and its aftermath. His daily calendar and the log kept by his office orderly both show that at 2:30 on the afternoon of February 4 Forrestal paid a two-hour visit to the Shoreham Building, the office building where Johnson's law firm has its Washington office and an unusual port of call for Forrestal; neither the calendar nor the log says whom he saw there. Later, after Johnson had left on February 7 for Key West, members of Forrestal's staff were sent occasionally to Johnson's

[16] Remarks to Post Mortem Club, 17 May 1949; in Hearings before the House Armed Services Committee, August 1949 (p. 490), Johnson fixed the date of these discussions as "the latter days of January, about the 28th or 29th."
[17] House Armed Services Committee Hearings, pp. 486, 553.
[18] Press conference transcript, 29 March 1949.

[Washington office with more data for forwarding to Johnson in Florida.

Yet there is some evidence that Forrestal considered his own departure and Johnson's accession less firmly set than Johnson evidently did. On February 4, the same day that he paid his two-hour visit to the Shoreham Building, Forrestal revived and urged an idea that he had first broached in December, the creation of the post of Under Secretary of Defense. Now he wanted the job established quickly. Telephoning Senator Tydings, chairman of the Senate Armed Services Committee, Forrestal asked, "Millard, how promptly do you think we could, as an interim measure, get through a bill for an Under Secretary? . . . Vinson has put a bill in on the Under Secretary, or rather he is going to, and he thinks it will go through the House very quickly."

Senator Tydings replied that he believed such a bill could pass quickly, but he warned that it might become jammed behind the backlog of defense legislation that was piling up, especially in the House. Forrestal promised to arrange a meeting with Tydings and Vinson at which the three of them could assign priorities to the various defense bills then pending before Congress.[19]

Forrestal had talked with at least one of his assistants about the possibility of bringing Johnson into the Military Establishment as Under Secretary, if such a position was created, with the further possibility that Johnson later might "fleet up," as the Navy would express it, to the Secretaryship. But Forrestal also talked as late as mid-February of the possibility that, whenever he left office, someone other than Johnson would succeed him, though Johnson was regarded universally as the active candidate for the job. Johnson himself has denied emphatically that he sought the Secretaryship of Defense.

When an old friend and wartime associate[20] called on February 9, Forrestal asked him abruptly, "Should I quit this job?" When the friend expressed the hope that he would stay in public service, Forrestal replied almost irritably that he hated it, everything about it, and particularly the publicity that went with it. He ended by disclosing that he had told the President that he was

---

[19] Transcript of conversation with Tydings, 4 February 1949.
[20] Charles S. Thomas.

[getting out by the first of June. Three days later, on February 12, this same friend learned from a member of the President's personal staff that Forrestal was resigning of his own volition, effective May 1.

Forrestal attended a Cabinet meeting on February 11 at which Secretary of Commerce Charles Sawyer discussed the availability of pipe for the Saudi Arabian pipeline. Forrestal, reversing a long-standing position, felt that from a military standpoint the matter was no longer critical because of revisions in the estimates of oil requirements. The figures, he noted, now indicated "that we could, by the application of strict rationing in the United States, fight a war for a considerable period of time without access to the Middle East." He instructed John Kenney, Under Secretary of the Navy, so to inform Secretary Sawyer.[21]

At lunch on February 15 Forrestal listened patiently while a friend[22] to whom he had already disclosed his determination to leave office explained why the action should be deferred for about ninety days. Forrestal discussed some of his reasons for wanting to resign but took occasion to remark that he felt the President had always been very fair with him and that there was nothing in their relations that he could criticize. This feeling of fair treatment at the President's hands continued, according to most of Forrestal's associates, throughout his life, although Forrestal did come to feel that he had lost the President's confidence. It was at about this time that Forrestal received the offer, or the intimation of the offer, of one of the more important ambassadorships, but he declined.

Johnson, who had been a director of the company manufacturing B-36s, had asked Forrestal to make any decisions about that airplane before leaving office, and Forrestal had promised to do so. On February 28 Forrestal apparently decided the one pending question about the Air Force's controversial intercontinental bomber. The Air Force had been asking for money and authority to add auxiliary jet engines to the big bomber, and Forrestal finally authorized the modification.

The following day, March 1, saw the beginning of a swift

---

[21] Diary, 11 February 1949.
[22] Charles S. Thomas.

[climax in Forrestal's secretly discussed resignation. His calendar and the log kept by his orderly show that, after a morning of only two appointments and few telephone calls, none after 10:30, Forrestal went to the White House. The entry on his calendar reads, "12:30: the President (White House) off-the-record." He did not return to his office until 2:20. He then had only four visitors, the last at 4:15, but he remained in his office alone until 6:35, when he went home. He left no record of any of this day's events, but at least one friend came to understand later that the President at the midday meeting had asked Forrestal to send his letter of resignation over at once and that this request had been a "shattering experience."

Until this interview Forrestal evidently had felt that submission of his resignation letter was not an urgent matter. Now he began to work on it at a fever pitch. During the evening he phoned Marx Leva, one of his assistants, asking him to come to the Forrestal home, but when Leva explained that he was not free to do so, Forrestal asked to see him promptly in the morning. Through the night Forrestal twice called one of his closest friends and advisers in New York, to discuss the draft of the letter. The next morning at his office, as the letter went through various revisions, Forrestal kept advancing its effective date until he fixed it for March 31. Leva finally asked whether the President wanted him out of office by March 31, arguing that the timing was bad. Forrestal replied that the President wished him to stay until June 1 but that he wanted to get out sooner.

The letter was dispatched to the White House in the late forenoon of March 2, some hours after it was expected. It began, "It has been my privilege to have served our country for over eight and one half years. . . ." It cited the "substantial progress" achieved under the National Security Act of 1947 and the still greater progress to be expected under the proposed changes in it. "These circumstances," Forrestal continued, "enable me for the first time to take into account those urgent personal considerations about which I have spoken to you and submit my resignation in the hope that you may accept it, effective on or about March 31. . . . I am mindful of the wish that this will not mark the end of our association, and repeat that if at any time

[in the future you desire to call upon me for service, I shall be at your command. . . ."

The President replied that "your letter received this day confirms our many previous conversations and discussions. I am therefore fully cognizant of the considerations which prompt your desire to relinquish your duties as Secretary of Defense. At my personal urging you have agreed to remain in Washington far beyond the time when you had expressed a hope of leaving government service. . . . For all that you have done in your country's behalf and for the service which you will continue to give out of your abundant experience, I tender you heartfelt assurance of my gratitude and appreciation."

Although both letters were dated March 2, they were not released until March 3 along with an announcement of Johnson's appointment.

On this interchange the diary ends. To Forrestal, it apparently came with the force of a dismissal under fire. He had wished for retirement. He had been half prepared to relinquish his post to an ambitious claimant. He was not prepared for the events of March 1, when he apparently was asked abruptly to send in a resignation letter. The experience seems to have undermined his self-confidence and unduly exaggerated that sense of inadequacy and failure from which, like most thoughtful, sensitive and high-minded men, he was never wholly immune. Through the next three and a half weeks he was to discharge the duties of his office with his usual competence. But privately he began to reveal a state of emotional depression which for the first time raised in his friends a sense of alarm. It was increasingly apparent that he was cracking under internal stresses which imperatively demanded relief and attention.

IV

[Mr. Johnson was duly appointed and confirmed, and on March 28, at a brief ceremony in the central court of the Pentagon Building, Forrestal saw his successor sworn in as Secretary of Defense. The ex-Secretary drove to the White House to pay his final respects to the President. There, to his complete surprise, he found that a second ceremony had been arranged. The Cabi-

[net, the military chiefs and other high officers of government were waiting for him; in their presence the President himself read a citation for "meritorious and distinguished service" and pinned the Distinguished Service Medal on his civilian coat. Forrestal could not find words to respond.

"It's beyond me—beyond my—" he began.

"There you are," said the President, "you deserve it, Jim."

At a formal dinner honoring Johnson that evening, Forrestal's impromptu and brief speech struck guests as particularly gracious. The next morning, before taking off by plane for Florida, Forrestal attended a special meeting of the House Armed Services Committee, called to honor him—a rare occurrence in Washington. Both Chairman Carl Vinson and Representative Dewey Short, ranking minority member, eulogized him, and again Forrestal replied briefly and gracefully.

Directly after the meeting Forrestal left by air for Hobe Sound, Florida, as a guest of Robert Lovett, his old friend and colleague in so many crises of state. The effect, unfortunately, was not what had been hoped. With his final departure from office Forrestal was precipitated into a depression so severe that within a day or two psychiatric help seemed imperative. A Navy psychiatrist, Captain George N. Raines, arrived on the evening of March 31, but did not interview the patient, as he learned that Ferdinand Eberstadt was due next day, bringing the eminent specialist Dr. William C. Menninger. It was determined that hospitalization was necessary. On April 2 Forrestal was flown back to Washington and admitted that evening to the Naval Hospital at Bethesda, Maryland.

By the end of April he was responding well to treatment. He seemed his old self to numbers of his friends and associates, including the President, who visited him. The moods of depression recurred, but with decreasing frequency and severity. By the middle of May his physicians were looking forward to his discharge in another month or so, and as a necessary part of the treatment they risked a relaxation of the restraints that had been set around him. It was a tragic miscalculation. On the night of May 21-22 he was reading late in his room on the sixteenth floor; the book was Mark Van Doren's *Anthology of World Poetry,* and

[he was copying from it William Mackworth Praed's translation of
Sophocles' dark and solemn "Chorus from Ajax."

> Fair Salamis, the billows' roar
>   Wanders around thee yet,
> And sailors gaze upon thy shore
>   Firm in the Ocean set.
> Thy son is in a foreign clime
>   Where Ida feeds her countless flocks,
>   Far from thy dear, remembered rocks,
> Worn by the waste of time—
> Comfortless, nameless, hopeless save
> In the dark prospect of the yawning grave. . . .
>
> Woe to the mother in her close of day,
> Woe to her desolate heart and temples gray,
>   When she shall hear
> Her loved one's story whispered in her ear!
>   "Woe, woe!" will be the cry—
> No quiet murmur like the tremulous wail
> Of the lone bird, the querulous nightingale—

The copying ceased on this word; the sheets were laid in the
back of the book and the book itself set down open at the page.
It was three o'clock in the morning. Forrestal went into a small
diet kitchen on the same floor, which he had been encouraged to
use, and fell to his death from its unguarded window.

Thus a great and singularly selfless public career reached its
tragic end. A memorial bronze now stands at the Mall entrance
of the Pentagon; but the real memorial is within, in the teeming
offices of the vast establishment for defense, which owed so much
to his patient architecture, and beyond, across the river over
which the bronze turns its gaze, in the capital to which he contributed the courage, insight and firmness of his counsel, in the
great nation which he served to the limit of his high abilities and
with unswerving integrity of purpose.

PRINCIPAL OFFICERS

INDEX

Principal Officers

STATE DEPARTMENT
  SECRETARY OF STATE
    Cordell Hull, March 1933–Nov. 1944
    Edward R. Stettinius, Nov. 1944–June 1945
    James F. Byrnes, July 1945–Jan. 1947
    George C. Marshall, Jan. 1947–Jan. 1949
    Dean G. Acheson, Jan. 1949——

  UNDER SECRETARY OF STATE
    Joseph C. Grew, Dec. 1944–Aug. 1945
    Dean G. Acheson, Aug. 1945–June 1947
    Robert A. Lovett, July 1947–Jan. 1949
    James E. Webb, Jan. 1949——

  COUNSELOR OF THE DEPARTMENT
    Benjamin V. Cohen, Sept. 1945–July 1947
    Charles E. Bohlen, Aug. 1947–June 1949
    George F. Kennan, June 1949——

WAR DEPARTMENT
  SECRETARY OF WAR
    Henry L. Stimson, Jan. 1940–Sept. 1945
    Robert P. Patterson, Sept. 1945–July 1947

  UNDER SECRETARY OF WAR
    Robert P. Patterson, Dec. 1940–Sept. 1945
    Kenneth C. Royall, Nov. 1945–July 1947

  ASSISTANT SECRETARY OF WAR
    John J. McCloy, April 1941–Nov. 1945
    Howard C. Petersen, Dec. 1945–July 1947

559

CHIEF OF STAFF
Gen. George C. Marshall, Sept. 1939–Nov. 1945
Gen. Dwight D. Eisenhower, Nov. 1945–Feb. 1948

NAVY DEPARTMENT

SECRETARY OF THE NAVY
Frank Knox, June 1940–April 1944
James Forrestal, May 1944–July 1947

UNDER SECRETARY OF THE NAVY
James Forrestal, June 1940–April 1944
Ralph A. Bard, June 1944–July 1945
Artemus L. Gates, July 1945–Dec. 1945
John L. Sullivan, June 1946–July 1947

ASSISTANT SECRETARY OF THE NAVY
Ralph A. Bard, Feb. 1941–June 1944
H. Struve Hensel, Jan. 1945–March 1946
W. John Kenney, March 1946–July 1947

ASSISTANT SECRETARY OF THE NAVY FOR AIR
Artemus L. Gates, Sept. 1941–July 1945
John L. Sullivan, July 1945–June 1946

CHIEF OF NAVAL OPERATIONS
Adm. Ernest J. King, March 1942–Dec. 1945
Adm. Chester W. Nimitz, Dec. 1945–Dec. 1947

DEPARTMENT OF DEFENSE (set up in July 1947)

SECRETARY OF DEFENSE
James Forrestal, Sept. 1947–March 1949
Louis A. Johnson, March 1949–Sept. 1950
George C. Marshall, Sept. 1950——

DEPUTY SECRETARY OF DEFENSE
Robert A. Lovett, Sept. 1950——

DEPARTMENT OF THE ARMY
SECRETARY OF THE ARMY
Kenneth C. Royall, Sept. 1947–April 1950

UNDER SECRETARY OF THE ARMY
William H. Draper, Sept. 1947–Feb. 1949
Archibald S. Alexander, Feb. 1949——

DEPARTMENT OF THE NAVY

SECRETARY OF THE NAVY

John L. Sullivan, Sept. 1947–May 1949

Francis P. Matthews, May 1949——

UNDER SECRETARY OF THE NAVY

W. John Kenney, Sept. 1947–May 1949

Dan A. Kimball, May 1949——

DEPARTMENT OF THE AIR FORCE

SECRETARY OF THE AIR FORCE

W. Stuart Symington, Sept. 1947–April 1950

UNDER SECRETARY OF THE AIR FORCE

Arthur S. Barrows, Sept. 1947–April 1950

CHIEFS OF STAFF

CHIEF OF STAFF TO THE COMMANDER-IN-CHIEF

Adm. William D. Leahy, 1942–March 1949

CHAIRMAN OF THE JOINT CHIEFS

Gen. Omar N. Bradley, Aug. 1949——

CHIEF OF STAFF OF THE ARMY

Gen. Dwight D. Eisenhower, Nov. 1945–Feb. 1948

Gen. Omar N. Bradley, Feb. 1948–Aug. 1949

Gen. J. Lawton Collins, Aug. 1949——

CHIEF OF NAVAL OPERATIONS

Adm. Chester W. Nimitz, Dec. 1945–Dec. 1947

Adm. Louis E. Denfeld, Dec. 1947–Oct. 1949

Adm. Forrest P. Sherman, Nov. 1949——

CHIEF OF STAFF OF THE AIR FORCE

Gen. Carl Spaatz, Sept. 1947–April 1948

Gen. Hoyt S. Vandenberg, April 1948——

MUNITIONS BOARD CHAIRMAN

Thomas J. Hargrave, Sept. 1947–Sept. 1948

Donald F. Carpenter, Sept. 1948–June 1949

RESEARCH AND DEVELOPMENT BOARD CHAIRMAN [1]

Vannevar Bush, Sept. 1947–Oct. 1948

Karl T. Compton, Oct. 1948–Nov. 1949

---

[1] Before the Department of Defense was set up this was known first as the Office of Scientific Research and Development, then as the Joint Research and Development Board. Through the various changes it was headed by Vannevar Bush, 1941–1948.

NATIONAL SECURITY RESOURCES BOARD CHAIRMAN
  Arthur M. Hill, Sept. 1947–Dec. 1948
  John R. Steelman, temporary appointment until April 1950

CENTRAL INTELLIGENCE AGENCY DIRECTOR
  Gen. Hoyt S. Vandenberg, June 1946–April 1947
  Rear Adm. Roscoe H. Hillenkoetter, May 1947–Aug. 1950

NATIONAL SECURITY COUNCIL [2] EXECUTIVE SECRETARY
  Sidney W. Souers, Sept. 1947–Jan. 1949
  James S. Lay, Jr., Jan. 1949——

Other Cabinet Members (*including those held over from the Roosevelt administration*)

SECRETARY OF THE TREASURY
  Henry Morgenthau, Jr., Jan. 1934
  Fred M. Vinson, July 1945
  John W. Snyder, June 1946

ATTORNEY GENERAL
  Francis Biddle, Sept. 1941
  Tom C. Clark, July 1945
  J. Howard McGrath, Aug. 1949

POSTMASTER GENERAL
  Frank C. Walker, Sept. 1940
  Robert E. Hannegan, May 1945
  Jesse M. Donaldson, Dec. 1947

SECRETARY OF THE INTERIOR
  Harold L. Ickes, March 1933
  Julius A. Krug, March 1946
  Oscar L. Chapman, Jan. 1950

SECRETARY OF AGRICULTURE
  Claude R. Wickard, Sept. 1940
  Clinton P. Anderson, June 1945
  Charles F. Brannan, June 1948

---

[2] Composed of the President, the Secretary of State, the Secretary of Defense, the Secretaries of the three Armed Services Departments, and the NSRB chairman.

SECRETARY OF COMMERCE
Henry A. Wallace, March 1945
W. Averell Harriman, Oct. 1946
Charles Sawyer, May 1948

SECRETARY OF LABOR
Frances Perkins, March 1933
Louis B. Schwellenbach, July 1945
Maurice J. Tobin, Aug. 1948

BUREAU OF THE BUDGET

DIRECTORS
Harold D. Smith, April 1939–June 1946
James E. Webb, July 1946–Jan. 1949
Frank Pace, Jan. 1949–March 1950

AMBASSADORS

To Great Britain
John G. Winant, 1941–March 1946
W. Averell Harriman, April 1946–Oct. 1946
O. Max Gardner, Dec. 1946–Feb. 1947
Lewis W. Douglas, March 1947–Sept. 1950

To the U.S.S.R.
W. Averell Harriman, Oct. 1943–Feb. 1946
Gen. Walter Bedell Smith, March 1946–March 1949

To China
Patrick J. Hurley, Dec. 1944–Nov. 1945
Gen. George C. Marshall, Nov. 1945–June 1946
J. Leighton Stuart, July 1946——

To France
Jefferson Caffery, Dec. 1944–April 1949

To Italy
James C. Dunn, Nov. 1946——

Index